CONTEMPORARY SOCIOLOG AND THEORIES

Contemporary Sociological Thinkers and Theories

SANDRO SEGRE
University of Genoa, Italy

Routledge
Taylor & Francis Group

LONDON AND NEW YORK

First published 2014 by Ashgate Publishing

2 Park Square, Milton Park, Abingdon, Oxfordshire OX14 4RN
711 Third Avenue, New York, NY 10017

Routledge is an imprint of the Taylor & Francis Group, an informa business

First issued in paperback 2018

British Library Cataloguing in Publication Data
A catalogue record for this book is available from the British Library

Library of Congress Cataloging-in-Publication Data
Segre, Sandro.
  Contemporary sociological thinkers and theories / by Sandro Segre.
    pages cm
  Includes bibliographical references and index.
  ISBN 978-0-7546-7181-7 (hardback) 1. Sociology--History. 2. Sociology. 3. Sociologists. I. Title.
  HM447.S44 2015
  301--dc23

                                                                    2014015622

ISBN 978-0-7546-7181-7 (hbk)
ISBN 978-1-138-32294-3 (pbk)

MIX
Paper from
responsible sources
FSC   FSC™ C013985
www.fsc.org

Printed in the United Kingdom
by Henry Ling Limited

Contents

Foreword

This work aims to introduce to a public of scholars and doctoral students some authors and theoretical perspectives, which are apparently among the most influential on contemporary social theory. The definition of the concept of theory and social theory in particular is debatable, possibly because of its "enormous diverse and multifaceted" aspects (Calhoun et al. 2002: 19). Students of social theory have often stressed both similarities and differences between the conceptions of theory in the natural and the social sciences. The conception of theory and of social theory in particular, as will be here abided by, will accord with a conventional one. Theories, both in the social and the natural sciences, if conventionally defined aim to formulate systematic, abstract and general statements that are induced from empirical reality. All theoretical statements "transcend the particular and the time bound" and attempt to explain empirical events for the present times in abstract, non-evaluative and formal terms (Turner 1998: 2).

Theory, in this sense, purposes to be scientific in that statements aim at prediction and explanation of phenomena, and generating new research hypotheses (Ritzer 2000: 4). Emphasis has also been given here, as other authors have done, to the conflicting and incompatible views on its nature and presuppositions, which characterize social theory and sociology in particular (cf. Alexander 1982: 1–5; 1987: 1–21; Joas and Knöbl 2009: 5–12; Baert and Carreira da Silva 2010: 1; Seidman 2013: 2–5). Social theory should have a wide range of applications to important social issues. This work, like other works on contemporary social theory, aims to convey essential information on prominent authors and theories, with an emphasis on general theories which may be applied, at least in principle, to several fields of inquiry. It differs from other works on the same subject in many ways, however.

The work, first of all, focuses on contemporary theory only, in keeping to its title. In this respect, it is unlike works on social theory that provide information also on the classical sociological tradition, as especially represented by Marx, Durkheim and Weber (see for example Baert and Carreira da Silva 2010; Seidman 2013). As a further difference, this work gives a conventional definition of social theory in this very foreword, but does not devote a chapter to this theme, as other authors have done (cf. Joas and Knöbl 2009). It does not seek, moreover, to derive from theoretical principles, such as they may be found in past or contemporary sociological theorists, an abstract structure of sociological theory (see Turner 1982, 1998). It also makes no attempt to distinguish between micro and macro theoretical approaches, as this distinction has been variously interpreted, and has been found controversial (Collins 1988: ch. 11).

Given the present limitations of space and time, finally, this work does not deal with some directions, both old and new, of contemporary sociological theory. It does not deal, in particular, with Critical Theory, Cultural Studies, Expectations States Theory, Feminist Social Theory, Globalization, Theories of Consumption, and World System Analysis. Also, major contemporary authors such as Bauman and Elias have not been considered here, while the presentation of actor-network theory has been confined to a brief note at the end of the chapter on network theory. It is hoped that these lacunae will be remedied in the future. The work has been given a modular structure, to the effect that readers may choose those chapters and perspectives they find most proximate to their interests. Each chapter contains a rather detailed introduction to a perspective or author. The chapters are of different lengths, but there are no book-length chapters. All of them are divided in several sub-chapters according to the particular themes, in which a particular perspective or the thought of a given author are articulated.

Each chapter, furthermore, contains in its final part information on the current reception of that perspective or author. Any selection of the relevant contributions to social theory is inevitably affected by the author's orientations and preferences; still, an effort has been made keep to a presentation unbiased by pre-conceived ideological orientations. Several selection criteria of the secondary literature have been used, such as the reviewers' scholarly reputation; the notoriety of their evaluation, whether positive or negative; and the extent to which they cover different aspects of a perspective or of the constitutive elements of an author's thought.

References

Alexander, J.C. 1982. *Positivism, Presuppositions, and Current Controversies*. Berkeley, CA: University of California Press.

Alexander, J.C. 1987. *Twenty Lectures: Sociological Theory since World War II*. New York: Columbia University Press.

Baert, P. and Carreira da Silva, F. 2010. *Social Theory in the Twentieth Century and Beyond*. Cambridge: Cambridge University Press.

Calhoun, C., Gerteis, J., Moody, J., Pfaff, S. and Virk, I. (eds) 2002. *Contemporary Sociological Theory*. Oxford: Blackwell.

Collins, R. 1988. *Theoretical Sociology*. New York: Harcourt Brace Jovanovich.

Joas, H. and Knöbl, W. 2009. *Social Theory: Twenty Introductory Lectures*. Cambridge: Cambridge University Press.

Ritzer, G. 2000. *Modern Sociological Theory*. Boston, MA: McGraw-Hill.

Seidman, S. 2013. *Contested Knowledge*. Chichester: Wiley-Blackwell.

Turner, J. 1982. *The Structure of Sociological Theory*. Homewood, IL: The Dorsey Press.

Turner, J. 1998. *The Structure of Sociological Theory*. Belmont, CA: Wadsworth Publishing Company.

Chapter 1
The Neofunctionalism of Jeffrey Alexander

Preliminary Remarks

Jeffrey Alexander's (1947–) reputation as a sociology theoretician is considerable both in the United States and in Europe. Alexander received his university education in the United States, first at Harvard, where, during the 1960s, he had the opportunity to study Marx, Weber, Durkheim, and Parsons in depth. Then he continued his studies at the University of California, Berkeley, where he graduated with a thesis on Parsons. After a first teaching period spent in Los Angeles at the University of California, he is currently teaching at Yale University (Alexander 1998a: 8–10). Alexander is an outstanding representative of the neofunctionalist perspective he personally contributed to formulate, and is well known among sociology theoreticians for his epistemological orientation, which he calls "strong program."[1]

The Neofunctionalist Perspective and the "Strong Program"

The neofunctionalist perspective ensues from the discredit of the functionalist approach, especially in Parsons' formulation, which the neofunctionalist perspective intends to reformulate. This perspective draws on several elements of Parsons' theory: the distinction among personality, culture and society; a systematic analysis of the relations existing between culture and society; and differentiation as an essential characteristic of social change (see Joas and Knöbl 2008: 336). Alexander and other representatives of this perspective have charged functionalism with several criticisms, as follows: it contains conservatively oriented and unverifiable ideological assumptions; it presents the social actors as culturally determined, and consequently, not introducing the element of contingency in their theory of social order; it underestimates the relevance of social conflict and change; and it does not sufficiently distinguish between an abstract notion of equilibrium, which may prove useful as an analytical concept, and equilibrium as a condition of really existing societies.

The neofunctionalist program, in the formulation given by Alexander (who mentions in this regard also some other authors, especially Luhmann), has tried to make up for these deficiencies in different ways. The voluntaristic, symbolic and contingent aspects of action, as enunciated by Parsons but not sufficiently considered in his theory, have been taken into greater account. Greater importance has been attached to elements of strain and conflict, considered inherent in society, rather than to equilibrium and social integration factors. Different interpretations of Weber and Durkheim from those formulated by Parsons have been proposed. Greater attention has been paid to Marx's epistemological teachings and to the micro-sociological theoretical schools of thought. The neofunctionalist program of studies and research includes, in Alexander's opinion, a new definition and conceptualization of the relations between culture and society, in which no integration is assumed (as Parsons does). Instead, the elements of tension existing both among subcultures, and between the social and the cultural system, are carefully considered.

Furthermore, the neofunctionalist program involves a critical reinterpretation of Parsons' contributions which does not intend to reiterate Parsons' fundamental error. According to Parsons (in Alexander's opinion), the normative elements of social reality have ultimately greater importance than instrumental elements (Alexander 1983b: 272). This critical reinterpretation is focused on social change (the contingent aspects and the possible dysfunctional consequences of which are particularly stressed), political sociology (Parsons' arguments about the stability of the democratic system are questioned) and profession sociology (the conflicting relations existing within single professions and among different professions, and the importance of

---

1 Alexander has also authored, with Kenneth Thompson, *A Contemporary Introduction to Sociology* (see Alexander and Thompson 2008).

particular interests in professionals' behaviors are highlighted) (Alexander 1984: 21–3; 1985a, 1998a: 216–28; Alexander and Colomy 1990: 44–55; 1998: 65–76; 2004: 207–208). This neofunctionalist program of studies is "multidimensional," in the sense that it intends to provide non-reductionist descriptions, explanations and interpretations of social life in relation to the problems of action and social order.

Conversely a reductionist program explains these problems, whether referring to conditions that are external to the actors and cannot be changed by them, or only to internal conditions, such as interiorized social norms, but not to both kinds of conditions at the same time. The "strong program" claims the autonomy of culture from any social determination, and involves consequently a new way to carry out sociological investigations. It conceives action as the product of actors' voluntary commitment to achieve goals or put moral norms into effect; but at the same time, action is constrained or affected by an external environment. This epistemological program concerns social sciences as a whole, without making distinctions among different disciplines, and demands to be systematically referred to the subjective meanings, which the actors, whether individually or collectively, give to reality, and to pay attention to the constraints the actors meet with in their social life.

Cultural products, which originate from the scientific community a scholar belongs to, are included in this program of studies. Investigations conforming to the "strong program" move from the epistemological assumption that knowledge produced within the sphere of social sciences – in the sense of understanding and explaining social reality – requires a particular interpretation of cultural phenomena. This interpretation should highlight that cultural phenomena are socially produced; they are, however, not determined by the social structure and, in general, by the contents and the meanings of social life. Cultural phenomena have therefore their own autonomy toward such meanings and contents. It is assumed that culture itself shapes social life, and forms an environment that is internal to the actor, and analytically distinguished from it.

The "strong program" attaches great relevance to meanings, symbols, narratives, beliefs and ideologies, collective representations, and in general, to the cultural aspects of social life. The "strong program" seeks to interpret and reconstruct the details of the constitutive elements of culture by identifying its individual and collective actors, and taking into account the hierarchies and the social institutions that mediate the relation between actors and culture. A methodology conforming to the "strong" program involves a set of procedural practices. There is, in the first place, an identification of the relevant social actors. A careful and thick description, a reconstruction and interpretation of the meanings to be attributed to a particular set of relations, and an investigation of the social consequences that directly come from those meanings, are also necessary.

In other words, a causal investigation seeks to highlight the immediate cultural causes of events that occur in the social world, based on a careful and detailed reconstruction of the culturally mediated meanings the actors give to their actions and experiences in those particular circumstances. Social causes, or causes relating to the social structure, which are emphasized by weak programs, have only an indirect relevance for the "strong program," in the sense of subjecting the symbolic-cultural structures to continuous pressures and changes with particular and historically contingent results (Alexander 1982a: 65–7; 1987: 11–15; 1988b: 36; 1990: 25–6; 1998a: 214–18; 2005; Alexander and Smith 2003: 12–14; Cordero et al. 2008). We shall focus in this chapter on this multidimensional orientation, and on the theoretical and empirical research which Alexander has conducted in keeping with this approach. The theme of collective representations, on which the author has dwelt in his latest works, will be also considered (Alexander 2004, 2009). Finally, we shall provide some information on the reception of his work.[2]

"Strong Program," Cultural Sociology, and Post-Positivism

If by culture is meant a system of significant symbols, its sociological study, called "Cultural Sociology" has been pursued by Alexander keeping to the "strong" program. An effort is made to keep explicit the distinction between analyses placed at different levels of generality or abstraction. Alexander makes a distinction between these different levels. Presuppositions are placed at the highest generality level. They

---

2   Introductions to Alexander's sociological thought can be found in Camarda 1992; Cisneros and Pérez Fernández del Castello 2000; Colomy 2005; Colomy and Turner 1998; Donati 1990.

are assumptions concerning the nature and the meanings of social reality as regards the nature of action and social order, and consequently the opportunities and the constraints actors (whether individuals or communities) meet with by relating with others. Presuppositions are of a metaphysical nature, and therefore cannot be empirically validated, but they contribute to produce theories by inspiring and guiding the notions drawn from the empirical world. They are useful in sociology and in social sciences in general, because they establish their epistemological foundations, in the sense that they point out the general standards of validity for these sciences, and provide them with general principles able to subsume principles deriving from lower analytical levels.

In addition, presuppositions produce in the sphere of social sciences the traditions and the research programs that connote each discipline. To this end, they avail themselves of discourses, or arguments, which establish the standards of truth and validity for each discipline, suggest specific research programs, and aim at persuasion. Presuppositions are relevant for dealing with matters of sociological interest placed at all the different analytical levels. The debate on metaphysical presuppositions is recurring in the social sciences, and distinguishes them from natural sciences. The usefulness of debate consists in pointing out these presuppositions, and in showing the opportunity of changing them, if necessary. Progress in social sciences consists in this, according to Alexander. Social changes involve a theoretical change only if they contribute to produce a reformulation of the metaphysical presuppositions. If shared, metaphysical presuppositions also imply sharing the positions that are situated at a lower analytical level, and therefore close to the empirical world. In contrast to the positivist or empiricist conception, according to which theories are based on objectively verifiable facts (and scientific progress is of a cumulative nature, as it involves the elimination of theories not conforming to empirical results), Alexander recalls the results of the post-positivist reflection on the foundations of knowledge.

Theories are generalized discourses which establish the typical validity standards of a social science. Sociological traditions, ideologies, arguments, explanations and debates, which refer back to disciplinary presuppositions, converge in theories. Therefore, theories have unavoidably a non-empirical origin and nature, though they refer to the empirical world, and claim an objective validity for their propositions. "Facts" – or empirical results – are interpreted according to existing theoretical orientations; theories are often preserved, though there are empirical results incompatible with them, through ancillary hypotheses and the formulation of additional analytical categories. Finally, theoretical changes take place not because of new empirical evidences, but because of the scientists' new epistemological and theoretical orientations.

Differently from positivist epistemology, the post-positivist epistemological approach states the impossibility of any knowledge of the natural or social reality that is not oriented by non-empirical presuppositions. Therefore, it is not sufficient to observe the empirical reality, but it is also necessary to interpret it making use of theoretical knowledge, and to reformulate it taking not only these remarks, but also alternative theories and traditions of thought into account. In the social sciences, the members of the same scientific community must make a "hermeneutic" interpretation, and an effort in mutual understanding, in order to conduct a theoretical investigation. Indeed, only in this way is it possible to make a comparison and establish a dialogue between different research programs and alternative presuppositions. Furthermore, only so does it become possible to explain structures of meaning which escape the control of particular actors (individuals and communities), though they are at the core of power structures. According to Alexander, who adopts a post-positivist epistemological approach, the empirical material highlighted by investigations carried out within the sphere of social sciences not only requires to be understood – it also requires to be interpreted for the public of the members of the same scientific community.

What is empirical takes therefore a symbolic nature, which is essential for its creation, presentation and persuasive capacity before a public of fellow scholars. In general, a symbolic communication made by any actor (whether an individual or a community) in front of any kind of public demands an effective performance and a representation capable of seeming convincing for the public that from time to time is relevant, considering that in modern societies there are a variety of publics for each actor. The success of a collective presentation/performance depends on actors' (i.e. journalists, leaders of social movements, experts) ability to "merge" – so to say – with the texts they perform and with the public with which they communicate. The successful outcome of a presentation/performance, which is proved by the way this public receives and evaluates it, has political consequences because it strengthens or changes actors' power and legitimacy

(Alexander 1982a: 30–33; 1987a: 1–21, 291–301; 1995: 110–23; 2004b; Reed and Alexander 2009: 38, note 8; Cordero et al. 2008: 532–3).

Ideological orientations are situated at a lower and more specific analytical level than presuppositions. Ideological orientations are, in turn, more generalized (in a decreasing order of abstraction and distance from the empirical world) than models, concepts, definitions, classifications, laws, complex and simple theoretical propositions, methodological assumptions, and finally empirical observational statements, which are therefore influenced in their contents by research programs and scientific traditions. The intention is manifold: firstly, to avoid both their conflation, from which overlapping and confusion would result; secondly, to avoid the reductionism, which would derive from using only a single analytical level; and finally to formulate theories, the presuppositions of which are different and incompatible. This incompatibility is illustrated by the theories that adopt individualistic presuppositions, according to which social order is the result of interactions among individuals.

Collectivistic presuppositions, which state that social order pre-exists to individuals, provide a further illustration. In the first case, it is assumed that action involves a double element of interpretation, through which we aim at understanding the world, and strategization, through which we seek to transform it. Meanwhile, we neglect the constraints the actor encounters in the social and cultural system, which build the environments external to action. In the second case, a material or normative coercive character is imputed to this external environment. Individual action would therefore have no autonomy. In either case, theoretical analysis would not be able to include a different analytical level, and consequently, to formulate a general theory of society. Briefly stated, the result is a reduced explanatory capacity. The deficiencies resulting from the influence of the positivist and empiricist epistemology are recurring in natural and social sciences, and have been a hindrance to their progress.

To this epistemological orientation which he considers wrong and misleading, Alexander counters with his approach called "theoretical logic." "Theoretical logic" is connoted not only by an explicit reference to the key presuppositions for carrying out an empirical research but also by the persuasion that scientific progress develops in virtue of changes occurring in the empirical and the non-empirical world. The latter is connoted by metaphysical and dogmatic presuppositions – which therefore are not subject to assessment – characterizing any scientific thought. "Theoretical logic" deals with the key sociological themes of action and social order considering all the aforementioned levels of abstraction, and keeping to the "multi-dimensional" approach and to the "strong program" of Alexander's neofunctionalist perspective. The distinction between sociological theories placed at micro and macro analytical levels becomes therefore irrelevant.

Action is conceived at the same time as a micro-action, in the sense of resulting from the contingent meanings the actors attribute to their experiences, and as a macro-action, in the sense that there are structures which emerge from micro social processes and influence them. A distinction between micro and macro investigation levels is only made for study purposes (which are called "analytical" by Alexander). This theoretical approach is called "multi-dimensional," as it considers action both normative (i.e. guided by norms) and instrumental (i.e. aimed at pursuing objectives), and ordered by means of structures internal and external to the actor. In virtue of its multidimensional nature, this approach does not involve the inconveniences of one-dimensional approaches, which conceive action as merely instrumental or merely normative. In the first case, action is determined or limited by external economic and political control sources, and the individuals' possibility of controlling their own actions is not recognized.

In the second case, action is considered only normative, and therefore it is determined or limited by interiorized moral structures, which are an actor's inner sources. This second point of view is unacceptable, as the first one, but for different reasons. In fact, in this case, the possibility that social order depends on external structures is ignored, regardless of individuals' participation and consensus. In this connection, Alexander proposes a distinction between "action" and "agency," which are both analytical categories, and consequently do not concretely exist. Action is defined by Alexander as the movement of persons, intended as actors, in time and space. Agency means actors' freedom to move among the three structured environments of the social, the cultural, and the personality system. Action means, therefore, the exercise of this freedom – freedom of "agency," in this case – by persons who act insofar as they are actors (Alexander 1998; 214–18).

Alexander argues that it is unacceptable to make use of an exclusively micro- or macro-sociological point of view. Both points of view do not sufficiently consider, in his opinion, the relevance of culture for a theory of action. Like personality, culture should be intended, in this case, as an internal structure of action itself and as an actor's inner environment. On the contrary, society – intended as a system of roles, and hence, of norms and sanctions – forms the external environment to action (Alexander 1982, 1987a: 1–21, 281–5, 330–32; 1987b, 1988a, 1988b: 11–45, 304, 316–26; 1990b: 25–6; 1995: 119–23; 2003: 13–14; 1998a, 2009: 34–5; Alexander and Giesen 1987; Alexander and Colomy 1990; see also Turner and Colomy 1998).

A "thick" – that is to say, detailed and careful – description of contents and meanings, considered as unitary texts, which form an environment internal to action, and are socially shared and placed in their historical perspective characterizes the strong program of "cultural sociology." A historical perspective has an interpretative or hermeneutic nature. This sociological research program assumes the autonomy of culture from any different determination (as classes or social structure). The strong program assumes, in addition, the capacity symbolic structures, which form the internal environment of action, have to provide non-cultural structures with meanings capable of giving individual and collective actors' actions a sense. Alexander aims at clearly distinguishing "cultural sociology" from the "weak" program, which belongs instead to the sphere of the sociology of culture. The weak program understands culture, and in particular the production of symbolic apparatuses, as a result, or an effect, of social structures or forces. These social structures and forces become therefore decisive, instead of being merely binding, for the social actors (Alexander 1984: 23; 1998: 216–17; 2005).

The Weak Program

Differently from the "strong" program, the "weak" program does not seek to make a sociological study of culture. Therefore it neither dwells on the environment internal to action (using Alexander's words), that is to say on the meanings actors attribute to their social life, nor does it explain which are the specific actors and the causal mechanisms, from which an alleged effect on culture results. It rather seeks to study culture as an environment external to action and as a dependent variable devoid of autonomy, and of an influence of its own. The social and institutional structure, social classes, and capitalism in general, can become the independent variable (Cordero et al. 2008: 529, 535). For those who pursue the "weak" program – like Parsons and the neo-institutionalist school – culture represents an external environment to action, rather than a context of meanings experienced and interpreted by the actors. In contrast with the "strong" program of cultural sociology, neither the independence of culture from social life, nor the dependence of its meanings on the local contexts in which it is produced are recognized (Alexander 1998: 216–21; 2003: 23).

Different sources have inspired the "weak" program, and each of them identifies a specific version of the "weak" program. Among these sources, Alexander points to some classic authors as Marx, Durkheim in his early works; Weber for some aspects of his thought; and Parsons. Classic are, in Alexander's opinion, those non-contemporary authors – especially the aforementioned ones – whose works receive particular consideration because contemporary sociologists – without any need of evidence – consider them as useful and illuminating as some more recent works, and even fundamental in particular social disciplines. Their importance for social sciences results from this general positive evaluation. Classic authors are able to make discussions easier as they focus them on questions considered relevant, provide the same standards of relevance, give legitimacy to new theoretical orientations, and formulate generalized theoretical discourses (Alexander 1987b).

This kind of discourse, in Alexander's terminology, involves a discussion made for interpretative or expository, rather than for explanatory, purposes. In this meaning of the word, discourse concerns the foundations of a discipline, that is to say, the epistemological presuppositions, the ideological and metaphysical implications, the conceptions of the world and the historical grounds of sociological argumentations, for the purpose of shedding light on the origins and the theoretical consequences of their disagreement. These discussions highlight cognitive and evaluative disagreements, which are recurring and unavoidable in the major perspectives of social sciences. In contrast with natural sciences, social sciences are interpretative disciplines. Each of them is oriented by different and competing fundamental presuppositions. Therefore, empirical validations do not put an end to these discussions (Alexander 1987b: 25–9; 1995: 122–3). Concerning in particular neofunctionalism, a "general discourse" highlights the problematic aspects of the functionalism of Parsons and other theoreticians, whether individually considered or compared to each other. In the case of Parsons, in particular, the purpose consists in reconstructing, reviewing and reprocessing the conceptual apparatus and the theoretical nucleus of functionalist formulations, taking also the critical literature on Parsons, and functionalism in general, into account.

An Appraisal of Classic and Contemporary Authors According to the "Strong" Program

Alexander has devoted several monographic research works to an examination of the epistemological presuppositions, which have been adopted implicitly or explicitly by some outstanding authors. These authors are both classic (as Marx, Durkheim, Weber and Parsons) (Alexander 1982b, 1983a, 1983b, 2013), and contemporary (as Giddens and Habermas). For each of them, Alexander keeps to his personal epistemological approach, stressing on a number of occasions the overlapping and conflation of different analytical levels, and the theoretical reductionism resulting from them. Concerning Marx, Alexander remarks that this author proposed a merely instrumental solution to the problem of social order, as he made it depend on the power of the ruling classes, which rationally act for this purpose; but at the same time formulated a voluntaristic theory of change, according to which the revolution and the socialist society were the consequence of individual and non-instrumental actions.

However – Alexander argues – Marx has put the stress on external conditions as those determining individuals' action and therefore not subject to their control. In this case too – as in the case of capitalism – individual action is subject to a coercive social order. Durkheim, as Marx, would have wavered in his work between an instrumental, determinist and individualistic vision of social order, and an opposite idealistic vision, according to which social order results from a general commitment to collective morality. The latter conception of order is produced by circumstances that are external to individuals, as it can be found in individual consciences. Both Marx and Durkheim have not made a sufficiently clear distinction between normative and instrumental actions, and between separate levels of analysis (Alexander 1982b: 61–77, 154–7, 203–10, 212–14, 292–6, 301–306, 461 note 202).

Weber is – according to Alexander – ambivalent in his evaluation of the consequences of modernity. For, on the one hand, his sociology is pervaded by "disillusionment and existential despair that psychological maturity and cultural integrity cannot be sustained"; but on the other, it points to the "increasing autonomy and strength of the individual," which modernity has made possible (Alexander 2013: 31). These individual qualities are subservient to the person's goal of self-control, but also to the mastery of a disenchanted and rational world. This mastering spirit, a consequence of this-worldly asceticism, is embodied in modern bureaucracy and politics. In turn, they have concurred to producing individuation, but also "the desire for voluntary subjection" and "a constant tendency for cynical adaptation to the demands of the day," of which the "soullessness of modern politics" is a manifestation. Yielding to modernity's "destructive, depersonalizing forces," or confronting this tendency which represents modernity's dark side, is a person's "existential choice."

Weber, however, does not explain how modernity's "destructive moments can be overcome" (Alexander 2013: 43, 46, 50, 52). As to Parsons, his functionalism had the merit of reformulating Weber's, Durkheim's and Freud's contribution in virtue of a merely analytical distinction among the personality, the society and the culture systems, but it neither shed light on the nature of values, nor did it aim at interpreting them. Furthermore, by identifying culture with consensus, and by viewing order as culturally guided, Parsons showed a normative reductionism. He also disregarded the "endemic strain" (Alexander 2013: 65) that follows from disregarding the value of justice. This hindered a broader conception of order (concerning the "reductionism" Alexander attributes to Parsons, see Camarda 1992: 403–406). Alexander's neofunctionalist program of studies involves reconstructing and revising Parsons' functionalism from different points of view.

First of all, any variance from a tendency to institutional differentiation has been considered. In addition, it has been avoided explaining change only in terms of strict systemic explanation, giving instead theoretical room to accidental factors, conflicts and social movements. Then, different effects of differentiation from those pointed out by Parsons have been considered, and it has not been maintained that such effects are necessarily beneficial to the single actors and to the social systems. Finally, Alexander has not followed

Parsons in the latter's conception that conceptual patterns reflect an objective reality, and values are the expression of institutionalized functional needs in particular roles that exist in the social world. Values have been understood, instead, as the result of an interpretation and analysis process of the meanings and the discourses produced by the social actors. Likewise, Alexander has not understood culture as a simple institutional regulating and control mechanism, as – according to Alexander – Parsons and other followers of the weak program have understood in the sociology of culture.

Based on the strong program, culture is instead considered as consisting of interconnected symbolic meanings resulting from typifications. During this process, the actors bring back the contingent aspects to structured forms of meanings, making use of the experiences they have achieved. Therefore, the actors do not limit themselves to passively responding to a pre-existing social order, but they define it symbolically, and acting in this way, they produce and reproduce it throughout their social life; they turn it into actions, and stabilize it. A sociological explanation implies a preliminary investigation on the interpretation of the meanings the actors give to what they do, to their collective representations, narrations and conceptual categories, and to the social consequences of those interpretations. Alexander also dwells on Parsons' evolutionary theory of modernity and societal community. He calls this theory Parsons' utopia, which is in keeping with Parsons' "ambivalence about order and normativity" (Alexander 2013: 66), according to Alexander.

By societal community, Parsons designates a society that has succeeded in connecting integration and justice, while refraining from following a non-normative orientation. A theory of social order, able to interpret and explain such a society, cannot include rationalistic utilitarianism or radical positivism. Alexander objects that there is a tension between integration and justice, as Parsons sees them. The evolutionary process of the social systems – "Parsons' major strategy for maintaining evolutionary optimism" (Alexander 2013: 72) – provides no solution to this tension. His notion of societal community is therefore ambiguous and unsatisfactory insofar as it sheds no light on contemporary major fears and dangers, such as the possibility of total destruction following a thermonuclear war. A more satisfactory theory of societal community would involve understanding and inquiring into the factors conducive to the dark side of modernity, and into the possibilities of civil repair (see Alexander 1983b: 51–4, 211, 272–6; 1984: 17–23; 1988b: 194–5, 281; 1990b: 4–6, 25–6; 1995: 120; 1998a: 61–73, 157–8, 165–74, 219–21; 2013: 62–77; Alexander and Colomy 1990: 44–55; 1994: 207; Alexander and Smith 2003. See also Reed 2009: 3).

Alexander affirms that, among these authors, only Max Weber has come close to a "multidimensional" conception of action and social order, making use in his historical sociological works, of causal explanations along with a sympathetic understanding of empirical phenomena, such as historical change and conflicts between social classes. A full acceptance of this conception has been hindered – in Alexander's opinion – by the lack in Weber of an explicit framework – at an analytical level of general presuppositions – that a "multidimensional" conception could be based on. Furthermore, Alexander thinks he sees ambivalence in this conception, as Weber supports from time to time either a materialist and instrumental epistemological position, or an idealist and normative stance in his works. Some passages in Weber's works seem to show discontinuity between his analysis of pre-modern societies, in which normative and instrumental elements are considered, and that of contemporary society, in which instead an instrumental and reductionist epistemological position prevails. This position would be illustrated by a number of examples in Weber's works.

If we consider, in particular, Weber's democratic theory, democracy is only a way – more effective than others – to assert the power of a nation state in a Darwinian struggle for ruling the world, rather than universal values and ideals. Similarly, a democratic competition among political leaders is simply a more effective instrument – compared to bureaucratic selection – for the task of leading a nation, because a leader's interest consists in meeting the needs of the electorate. According to Alexander, Weber's analysis of democracy suffers from reductionism. Alexander thinks he can identify the same kind of reductionism in other works of Weber, such as the essays on modern bureaucratic and judicial administrations, which Weber considers oppressive and effective instruments of power and regimentation, or in the treatment of inequality in status, which rests on the interest of the privileged social strata in preserving their privilege (Alexander 1983a: 16–19, 55–7, 98–127, 175–6; 1987).

Alexander makes an appraisal of contemporary authors as Blumer, Bourdieu, Coleman, Collins, Foucault, Garfinkel, Giddens, Goffman, Habermas and Mead, and of classic authors as Marx, Durkheim, Weber and Parsons, based on his epistemological presuppositions. He includes among the representatives of the "weak" program, as well as Parsons and the contemporary authors we shall mention, also the ethnographic school of Birmingham, some institutionalist economy scientists as Commons and Veblen, some contemporary sociologists who focus on the cultural meanings contained in social networks, as Granovetter and other representatives of the new economic sociology, and finally, some non-Marxist structuralist authors, as Foucault in France, and Blau in the United States. All these authors, who can be considered representatives of the "weak" program, have not provided – in Alexander's opinion – a satisfactory theoretical contribution.

We shall briefly mention in the following pages Alexander's critical remarks in this regard. Focusing first our attention on Alexander's reception of authors considered close to structuralism, the extremely critical nature of his essay on Bourdieu's work is well known. In Alexander's treatment, symbolic order (particularly referred to the concept of "habitus," the vagueness of which is stressed), social order, and consequently actors' practices are not placed by Bourdieu at the same level of theoretical importance, despite the author's statement of intent. According to Bourdieu (in Alexander's interpretation), social and cultural formations are external and pre-existing to social actors, but capable of determining their internal dispositions, and hence their habitus, regardless of the symbolic processes through which their identities are formed.

As illustrated by Bourdieu's empirical studies on the French educational system or those on consumer choices and aesthetic preferences, the field of social forces the competition of which the habitus derives from, reflects, reproduces and is homologous to the capitalist social and economic environment in which it is situated, though not coinciding with it. Therefore these studies do not shed light on the specificities of the actors, the institutions and the social environments in general in which the actors act. In other words, they do not fully explain how decisions are made and the reproduction of society is kept in real social environments described in detail. Notwithstanding Alexander's appreciation for the thick descriptions of some social and cultural environments provided by Bourdieu, these gaps turn into theoretical deficiencies. For example, Bourdieu does not consider it relevant whether political institutions are authoritative or democratic, as they all concur to the reproduction of power and inequality (Alexander 1995: 128–217; 2003: 18–19).

Alexander identifies the same epistemological and theoretical reductionism in Foucault's work. He appreciates Foucault's analyses of the ways in which discourses (as the author means this term) act to form knowledge and become power instruments, since knowledge and power, in his opinion, are closely connected to one another and to the social structure. However, Foucault does not consider culture according to Alexander's strong program, that is to say, as an independent symbolic apparatus subject to actors' interpretations and connected in different and contingent ways to the institutional apparatus. Foucault, on the contrary, considers culture, according to the weak program, as depending on the power structure. Alexander objects that the "discursive fields" do not have the internal homogeneity Foucault attributes to them, and they cannot be used to legitimize power to the extent affirmed by this author (Alexander 1995: 103; 1998a: 169; 2003: 19). Alexander formulates similar objections also to Giddens' and Habermas' work. In Giddens' structuration theory, as in other works, this author neglects mentioning the cultural conditions through which the meaning structures actors learn and keep in their interaction are formed (Alexander 1987a: 378–9; 1988b: 311–12; 1998a: 213, 222; Reed and Alexander 2009: 37–8, note 8).

As to Habermas, communicative rationality, which is the key concept of his work, is, in Alexander's opinion, culturally and institutionally connoted, since in modern societies, rationality requires a cultural mediation to become a relevant guide to action in any particular concrete case. The external moral and cultural order, according to Habermas, destroys interpersonal relations, which can no longer be informal and based on trust, due to the predominance of instrumental action over communicative action. Still, as Alexander remarks, the distinction between these two kinds of action can only be made for analysis purposes, because they concretely compenetrate each other. However, Alexander shares Habermas' thesis that communicative rationality (overestimated by Habermas, according to Alexander) can and must be exerted by actors who mean to rationally control their communication, which is subject to being systematically twisted by the strains embedded in capitalism. In that case, the actors, insofar as they share the same life world, can consciously commit themselves to reducing the probability that communication is distorted without their fully realizing it (Habermas 1985, 1987a: 372; 1995: 118–19; 1998a: 169, 222).

The major representatives of symbolic interactionism have been closely examined, too. Mead, in particular, who is considered one of the founders of this perspective, has focused his analysis on the creation and interpretation of the meanings that take shape during or through interactive processes. These meanings are contingent and are not predetermined, since they depend on a variety of actors' interpretations and answers to other actors' attitudes and significant gestures. All actors are bound by institutional constraints, which are both external and internal at the same time. Alexander argues that Mead presents sometimes the genesis of meanings as the joint result of the attitudes of some actors, and of the answers given by others, showing an empirical difference as if it were relevant to a theory of social order. This is not possible, because in that case meanings would depend on contingent and specific interactions. Therefore, in general, nothing could be said about the meanings, the cultural and material constraints, and the institutional and macro-sociological sources of social order (Alexander 1987a: 205–14; 1988b: 245–50; Alexander and Giesen 1987: 9–10).

Blumer's symbolic interactionism overemphasizes – according to Alexander – the position of a single social actor as an interpreter and creator of contingent meanings and attitudes, which are experienced and tested in the social world. In this case, though the existence of an order and of social structures, and consequently, of structured meanings is recognized, its origin and its revealing itself are not explained, as in general happens in the case of the individualistic theories of action. Blumer neither has, nor is consequently able to propose, a theory of society (Alexander 1987a: 215–27; 1988b: 250–53). As a further example of individualistic theory, and the problems resulting from it, Alexander mentions Homans' exchange theory (Alexander 1987a: 172–91, 216). Partly similar critical remarks are also formulated in the case of Goffman, who is considered the most outstanding representative of symbolic interactionism after Blumer (Alexander 1987a: 230). Goffman – Alexander argues – resumes Blumer's individualistic approach, and changes it by stressing its dramaturgical aspect. An insincere and manipulative actor, alienated from the social system and from cultural life, is placed at the center of the action. Alexander wonders whether social order is possible in such conditions, which seem instead to lead to disintegration.

Together with an individualistic conception of social order, Goffman introduces a completely opposite theory inspired by Durkheim and Parsons. According to this conception, the actors strive to keep a "front," that is to say, a collective image and representation socially and culturally prescribed according to standards of propriety, dignity, opportunity, and so on. Goffman shows therefore a dualism and ambivalence between these two different conceptions of order. Empirical and theoretical strains result from them in all his works. In Alexander's opinion, this problem is entirely shared with the perspective of symbolic interactionism and results from its individualistic assumptions. Collins' work is an example of this approach. Collins, who is one of the most well-known contemporary representatives of symbolic interactionism, shows in his work an unresolved strain between a conception of the actor as a subject who willingly adopts a non-rational behavior, and a conception, in which, on the contrary, the actor rationally acts within predetermined situations to obtain unequally distributed material resources (Alexander 1988b: 35).

Though more favorable, his appraisal of Garfinkel's ethnomethodology is also critical. Alexander identifies a first and second period in Garfinkel's production. In the first period, Garfinkel conceives social order as the product of mutual adjustment processes between actors who have interiorized the rules that make it possible. Rules are the ways in which a system of activities is organized, and in this regard, Alexander quotes a passage of Garfinkel (Alexander 1988b: 237). However, already in this period, there is a basic ambivalence, since the products issuing from individual interactions cannot result at the same time from rules or other structural elements external to the actors. In the second period, this ambivalence is solved by a theoretical renunciation. Order is a consequence of actors' practices situated in specific organizational contexts. Actors' practices themselves form the rules, without making reference to rules or meanings external to these contexts any longer (Alexander 1987a: 259–61; 1988b: 233–45).

Finally, we would like to briefly mention the reception on Alexander's part of Coleman's work *Foundations of Social Theory* (1990). As Alexander notes, Coleman – and in general the Rational Choice Theory, which is fully enunciated in this work – shows a utilitarian – and consequently, reductive and reified – conception of the human beings and the social world, as if individual and collective action could be exhaustively explained by the single individuals' hedonistic calculation. An attempt to explain the meanings individuals give to their actions is deliberately lacking. This lack involves consequences of considerable theoretical relevance since, in Coleman's opinion, social order, and the mutual trust supporting it, result from rational calculations based on one's advantage, considering that only thus could actors meet their interests. Alexander objects that this individualistic solution to the problem of order is unacceptable, because collective interests are long-term interests, while the rationality of each actor is limited in time. As a consequence, it is not plausible postulating that actors find some advantage in transferring their rights to collective structures in exchange for future benefits, and the existence of social norms and democratic institutions cannot be explained in this way (Alexander 1992b).

The Theory of Civil Society and Related Empirical Research

The empirical research carried out by Alexander, whether on his own or with collaborators, has conformed to his "strong" program. Therefore it has kept the distinction between different analytical levels, has identified the relevant actors, and has dwelt on the meanings and the social consequences of their actions, focusing in particular on civil society. This is a peculiar social sphere, limited in space and time, which in democratic societies penetrates and is interpenetrated by non-social spheres (or worlds), such as market, politics (as for example, democratic institutions like political parties, lobbies and associations), family, and cultural institutions as religion and science. Civil society is, at the same time, a utopian project and promise of integration and participation, as well as a normative idea of society. In the last two centuries, a large variety of interests and rights have made reference to the stock of meanings and practices that form civil society. This variety may be prejudicial to the compactness of civil society when the production of partial solidarities affects its overall solidarity.

This happens, in particular, when a tragic event of any origin permanently marks the collective conscience and memory of the group that has experienced it, because it creates or emphasizes the internal solidarity of the group, but prevents it from sympathetically participating in the sufferings experienced by other groups. While the common notion of trauma makes it directly result from particular tragic events experienced by individuals or collectivities, the sociological notion proposed by Alexander insists on assuming there is a cultural mediation among an event, the carrier group of those who have been affected by it, and a plurality of other subjects. In order to talk about a strictly "cultural trauma" not only must the group be persuaded that it has been traumatized by that event, but also others must be able to identify themselves with the group and symbolically and emotionally participate in the event in virtue of common linguistic, religious, legal codes, or codes of any other kind, to such an extent that the event loses a part of its emotional and identity call and finally becomes institutionalized (Alexander 2004a).

In civil society – thanks to the support provided by the public opinion and some institutions like press, associations, and legal institutions – as well as individual autonomy, cooperation and egalitarian spirit, trust and solidarity can assert and keep themselves. Solidarity is understood in a universalistic sense – without excluding particular individuals or collectivities – as widespread commitment in support of public interest. Public interest is defined so that it may have sense in the world of everyday life and among common persons. Nonetheless, a well-established civil society in its spirit and in its institutions is not sufficient to make the project of civil society be not merely utopian, as it must ensure, on the contrary, that democratic social life takes roots in individual consciences. A plurality of powers, separate and independent from each other, none of which should dominate the others, and a plurality of discourse communities and society projects, none of which should unconditionally prevail, are required for this purpose. In addition, free interactions among actors, who commit themselves to make up for conditions and circumstances incompatible with this utopian civil repair project, are also necessary (Alexander 2001: 587–9; 2006: 3–9, 31–6, 43–50, 194–5, 551; Cordero et al. 2008: 532).

Alexander argues there will always be exclusion towards some unwelcome social categories, such as particular ethnic and racial groups, religious minorities, criminals or psychopathic persons. Their exclusion, which may be institutionalized, is justified by the negative characteristics attributed to those who belong to these social categories. These characteristics, considered unbecoming or "polluting," counter the favorable characteristics many members of a society attribute to themselves and to the group they belong to. Excluded social categories are considered socially impure, not deserving solidarity, and therefore unfit to participate in civil society and democratic life. The persons who belong to these categories deserve exclusion since they have one or more negative connotations resulting from their belonging: they are irrational, passionate, non-autonomous, deceitful, greedy, without any sense of honor, and inclined to pursue only their own interests.

The institutions polluted by these social categories are arbitrary, sectarian and prepared to favor only a few people rather than public interest.

In virtue of these binary categorizations, through which some categories of persons or collectivities are positively, and other ones negatively connoted, it is maintained in the discourses concerning society that some members incorporate the evil, that their participation in public life would therefore be detrimental to civil and political society, and that, consequently, keeping their exclusion is a matter of public interest. If these binary categorizations are institutionalized, civil society becomes internally fragmented and contradictory, and strength and violence are used against negatively connoted social and ethnic categories. This happened, for example, in the case of Germany's working class before World War I, and more recently, in South Africa, during apartheid, in the case of the black ethnic community (Alexander 2006: 265–8). A part of the public opinion supports and contributes to spread these representations of groups different from its own. In fact, public opinion mediates between the discourses made in civil society, and the institutionally regulated spheres of social life.

This happens in different ways: through the mass media as social solidarity creators or destroyers; through the creation of symbolic representations of collective feelings and the interpretation or construction of events; through opinion polls, which give the public a voice, even though manipulated, on matters of general interest; and finally, through civil associations, which formulate the matters to be submitted to the attention of the public opinion (Alexander 2006: 53–104). Alexander argues that democracy involves the existence of a fully developed democracy, independent of the state, and capable of exerting social power over it through its communication and regulatory institutions. The discourses that take place in civil society can legitimize and support, through appropriate ideological arguments, the inclusion or, vice versa, the exclusion of others in political society, based on their alleged suitability or "purity." Parties, which politically aggregate and represent different and contrasting arguments, or their leaders, make use of these discourses and ideological arguments to depict them as primitive persons because of their assumed inborn primeval characteristics. Their ideas and actions are therefore incompatible with the moral uprightness duty, and in general, with the moral and legal obligations deriving from one's belonging to civil society (Alexander 2006: 107–50, 193–5).

These obligations connect and, at the same time, divide the sphere of civil society from other social spheres. In the last 150 years, the boundaries among these spheres have become less sharp and more permeable, due to the growing differentiation and independence of civil society (Alexander 2006: 107–50). "Purity" or "contamination," as discriminating standards for one's belonging or non-belonging to civil and political society in which democratic institutions exist, became effective during the procedure that in 1972–74 led to President Nixon's resignation. Nixon had aroused public contempt for having committed or ordered (according to the public prosecutor) serious violations of the law. On several occasions Alexander dealt with the so-called "Watergate" scandal, which followed this indictment, and with Nixon's attempts to tamper in different ways with the evidences, pointing out the steps that drive a complex society as the American one to reconstruct its violated moral foundations (Alexander 2003: 141–5, 155–17; 2006: 142–3, 147–50).

The cultural aspect of the democratic systems is stressed by the legal and judicial institutions in the United States, with particular reference to the Civil Rights Act and its implementation, but it has neither been recognized by the sociological theory nor by the legal theory. Nonetheless, this is just the aspect that connects with the reasons, the relations, and the institutions that make civil society possible. Civil society cannot be considered focusing merely on the logical-formal and procedural aspects of laws, on the pragmatic aspects of negotiations and the coercive aspects of power. Laws, and especially constitutional laws, are of paramount importance as institutions regulating civil society and institutionalizing its democratic law systems and solidarity. In every differentiated and plural society, there is an unavoidable strain between behaviors characterized by solidarity, which assert themselves in civil society, and instrumental behaviors aimed at attaining economic efficiency in view of monetary advantages, which connote economic society.

Legal capacity to regulate civil society has been undermined by the exclusion of some categories of persons – especially women and non-white persons – from fully enjoying their civil and political rights. However, to make amends for the damage resulting from it, several civil repair procedures have been introduced. These procedures make use of the institutions in charge of communication and social regulation to spread and preserve a different and better image of the excluded categories, to provide them with a respectable, non-discrediting identity, thereby promoting their inclusion in civil society. Social movements aim at achieving the purpose of those in whose name they act, succeed in turning from their isolation and public-discrediting identity to become members by full right of that society. Civil society would then lose its fragmentary nature, which is increased by the presence of several collective identities within it, and would gain in terms of solidarity (Alexander 2006: 193–234).

Examples of social movements are the feminist movements and the movement for the civil and political rights of the blacks in the United States. Alexander has examined in depth both social movements. The female gender was excluded from the civil sphere until the twentieth century, in the name of a binary code that confined it to the family sphere emphasizing its alleged moral inferiority compared to the male gender. A feminist point of view began to counter this binary code in the nineteenth century. Women would not have benefited from entering a civil sphere dominated by men in the name of their natural, moral and civil superiority, Throughout the 1970s and 1980s, a different feminist ideology began to spread, which claimed the complete equality of the two genders and made use, for this purpose, of universalistic arguments, which denied the existence of any inborn difference between them. Cultural differences resulted instead from the two genders' social construction processes. This issue ideologically paved the way for the full entry of the female gender in the sphere of social society (Alexander 2006: 235–63).

The movement for the rights of the American blacks is another example of institutionalized exclusion from civil society, followed by a civil repair and institutionalized inclusion process. This process could be accomplished thanks to the success of a social movement which had already set this goal in the 1960s. During the 1930s, a cautious change in this direction had already begun to emerge, though it was thwarted not only by a deeply rooted prejudice in the American society – which especially in the states of the South was dominated by the white population – about the blacks' moral, civil and intellectual inferiority; but also by the presence of a very united black civil society, separated from that of the whites. Black civil society was characterized by a strong ethical-religious imprint and by a complex network of communication and regulatory institutions, churches in particular. It professed values that were not different from those of the white civil society.

The success of the movement for the civil rights of the blacks can be explained, according to Alexander, as well as by the strong power of these churches to aggregate the black minority, by its universalistic and non-violent ideological message, which gained consensus and support also in the white public opinion and in the institutions that contributed to form and support it, for example the press in the north of the United States. Consensus and support can be also explained thanks to the political gifts of the preacher Martin Luther King, the charismatic leader of the movement, a personality with great appeal for the media. In his speeches, King stressed universalistic values of justice and non-violence referring to the Old and the New Testament, and claimed also for the blacks the enjoyment of civil and constitutional rights. He therefore succeeded in winning also quite a few whites to the cause of the movement (Alexander 2006: 264–316).

His appeal to inter-racial solidarity stirred the interest of many outstanding members of civil society, who urged a political reform and civil repair action for the black minority. This action was hindered in the south of the United States by the strong opposition of the white majority, the southern press, and the local political and legal authorities. The institutional support granted by the federal authorities and by the Supreme Court was, however, not enough to reach this goal. A direct action by King himself, by his sympathizers and followers, was therefore considered necessary. Some of them openly refused to obey the rules of apartheid, avoiding at the same time any violent action against the police or other authorities. This behavior was interpreted by hostile persons and institutions of the south as an arrogant challenge incompatible with the rules of civil society, and by others who lived in the north and were favorably disposed towards the blacks' cause – including the great press and the future President Kennedy – as worthy of admiration and identification.

Their support and the violent acts of the police against the blacks paved politically the way to the changes that took place in the following year, 1964, when the Congress passed the Civil Rights Act. The pursuit of this goal was hampered by some riots organized by the black minority, which the leaders of the movement were not able to control, which temporarily put the movement in a bad light to the eyes of the public opinion of the north. However, new acts of violence committed by the police, this time against children who were peacefully marching in the town of Birmingham, in the south of the country, not only led to the economic de-segregation of that town, but deeply and lastingly impressed the entire white public opinion in the United States, and urged President Kennedy to openly stand up for de-segregation in the name of the fundamental values of the American democracy. Thanks to this intertwining of political communication, inter-racial solidarity and regulatory repair measures aimed at making up for the deficiencies of civil society, Martin Luther King had become a hero for both the blacks and the whites of the north.

The Civil Rights Act did not put an end to the politically disadvantaged condition of the blacks, because there was still no legal protection of their political rights. The volunteers from the north who did their outmost to guarantee these rights in the south ran serious dangers and in some cases were even killed. More effective proved the action of some black activists who for a long time had been fighting for their ethnic group, and already had a wide experience and a network of contacts. Their activism led to an extremely severe police repression in Alabama, which deeply shook the public opinion of the north and paved the way to the enactment, in 1965, of the Voting Rights Act, to the formulation of which the leaders of the movement gave their contribution as advisers. The Civil Rights Act and the Voting Rights Act, ratified by the Supreme Court, ensured effective protection against legal, political and economic discriminations to the black minority. Through the institutionalization of the civil and political rights of the black minority, and the subsequent legal measures for putting these rights into effect in social and economic life through the so-called Affirmative Action, the movement began to decline.

The radicalization of the movement in its political message, in the ethnic composition of its followers, and in the activities it carried out, which were successfully pursued by its leader Carmichael, also contributed to this outcome. The solidarity it sought did not include the white population. Therefore it became increasingly difficult to keep a large favorable audience and the support of the great press, though Martin Luther King was opposing this radicalization process. The inclusion of the blacks in the American civil society continued to be pursued also in the following decades. Nevertheless, the project of peaceful coexistence among different ethnic groups – called "multiculturalism" – has always been rejected by some militant intellectuals belonging to the black minority, because it would de facto ratify the whites' domination, as well as by some conservative intellectuals, since this project would weaken the compactness of the American society. Alexander notices, paradoxically, a convergence between these critical positions, which move from opposite fronts, in their disownment of an American civil society that, though fragmented, does, however, exist in the United States and in other democratic countries as England and France.

Alexander declares his agreement in this regard, but points out the non-fulfillment of the utopian promise implied in the civil society project, and consequently, its fragmentations and limitations (Alexander 2006: 317–407). The concept of "common identity" is defined in different ways according to standards depending on specific historical, cultural and territorial conditions. These standards set some limits to a universal extension of civil society. In other words, there are always some categories which remain excluded from it, in actual and in moral terms. In democratic societies, legal instruments ensuring protection for these categories – as, for example, the prohibition of institutionalized discriminations in the United States and in India – and social movements, which act for the cause of the outcast and promote their assimilation, do not guarantee that their inclusion in civil society is actually achieved. There may be resistances on the part of opposite movements, in the name of a claimed primeval identity of those who are included in it. Their successful outcome might lead to symbolic and actual conflicts between those who are included and those who are excluded, and ultimately, to a deterioration of civil society.

Alexander dwells upon assimilation, hyphenation (or dual belonging) and multiculturalism, as typical inclusion forms of an ethnic group. Assimilation involves a declared abandonment of group identity. On any occasion in which a group must publicly show a collective identity, the identity of the leading group is favored, even if a subordinate group keeps its original identity. A significant example of assimilation in the United States concerns the black ethnic group after the enactment of the Civil Rights Act and the progresses in education and in the labor market that have followed it. Assimilation is unsteady and does not wipe out the stigma of the identity of a previously discriminated group, but confines it to the sphere of private life. Hyphenation may lead to greater tolerance towards a different ethnic group, which is therefore perceived as more acceptable and less "polluted" by primeval aspects incompatible with the dominant group.

However, this condition may also stir up hostile feelings against a particular group, and against immigrants in general, especially if diversity rests on racial standards. As a consequence, in this case the civil sphere is fragmented according to those standards. Finally, multiculturalism distinguishes itself from other inclusion methods for an attempt to purify, rather than remove, the unwelcome characteristics attributed to the different group. Its diversity is interpreted as a particular kind of the constitutive qualities of civil society, which is fully acceptable and can be openly shown, and is proved by the actual possibility of marriage exchanges with the dominant group. Multiculturalism conflicts with the subordinate group's assimilation requests. These inclusions are mutually incompatible in civil society, in which the case of the Jewish religious group represents a significant example.

Alexander attentively examines this group, and consequently, anti-Semitism as a set of discrediting beliefs and exclusion practices against it. Alexander argues that Jews' assimilation and inclusion processes have never been completely accomplished. The Christian tradition has always refused to acknowledge to this religious minority – on grounds of the negative characteristics attributed to it – an ability and willingness to socially, culturally and institutionally participate in the Christians' society. The subsequent inclusion attempts made during the age of Enlightenment were hampered by a persistent anti-Semitism. According to a widespread opinion, Jews had to earn their integration by giving up their religious and cultural diversity, and by devoting themselves to some activities – such as agriculture – that would have withdrawn them from going in search of money profits, in order to start the process of their full participation in civil life.

Jews' emancipation from previous restrictions, whether legal or of another kind, was warmly supported not only by some intellectuals of the Age of Enlightenment but also by some spokesmen of the Jewish communities. The latter did not recommend giving up the Jewish religion, but instead Jews' full inclusion in the civil and political society. Those who followed Judaism in a traditional way and isolated themselves from public life did not enjoy their appreciation. However, this coveted emancipation could be only partly achieved. As a matter of fact, Jews, even those who converted, remained a religious group scorned and stigmatized as anti-social, which therefore did not deserve full participation in civil society. The so-called "Dreyfus Affair" – the judicial vicissitude of a Jewish captain of the French army unjustly charged with espionage in favor of Germany – pointed out how precarious Jews' emancipation was, not only in France. In other countries too, as for example in the Austro-Hungarian Empire and in the United States, we can find a number of evidences in literature, essays and biographies that bear witness of a strong presence of anti-Semitic prejudice.

Herzl's Zionist project represented a reaction to this ancestral, primeval antagonism against the Jews, as Alexander calls it. If inclusion is not possible, and on the contrary, it exacerbates anti-Semitism, then a withdrawal from the European civil society for the purpose of emigrating, or going back, to the Promised Land is advisable. The tragic experience of the Holocaust made the full inclusion of the Jewish people in the civil society of the Western world finally possible. In turn, the Holocaust was the result of an incomplete inclusion of the Jews in the civil societies of the Western world. Even in the United States, where the mythical image – supported by Hollywood films – of a free country, open to any religious creed and ethnic group, inclusion implied renouncing all Jewish peculiarities in the name of national solidarity. Many Jews were prepared to pay this symbolic price to legitimately participate in the public sphere, but new restrictions against immigrants in general, enforced immediately after the outbreak of World War I, stopped this project.

In the United States, during the period between World Wars I and II, the previous limitations on Jewish participation in universities, corporations, free professions and other institutions, went on. Alleged dangers that would have affected the civil society, due to the negative and indelible characteristics attributed to the Jews, were put forward as a justification, especially their tendency to act in concert in order to control the organizations in which they took part or worked. However, this justification became hardly tenable as soon as the foreign powers with which the United States were in conflict began to appeal to it, and the atrocities produced in those countries by anti-Semitism came to light after the war. In this new favorable cultural atmosphere, thanks also to the contribution of several essays and musical productions (in this connection, Alexander reminds us of the successful musical *Fiddler on the Roof*), the Jewish associations succeeded in mobilizing the American civil society in a joint effort aimed at fighting anti-Semitism.

Nonetheless, this effort did not prove fully successful, as a latent anti-Semitism, or in any case, an ambivalent attitude towards the Jews, who in turn are often ambivalent towards their Jewish identity, continued to persist in the American cultural and institutional reality. An analysis of some literary texts connoted by a Jewish background, as *Portnoy's Complaint* and other novels by Philip Roth, or movies like Woody Allen's *Annie Hall*, evidences the wish of these authors to depict the protagonists as persons who are clearly connoted as Jews and at the same time absolutely normal people from both a sociological and human viewpoint. A multicultural way is therefore proposed, though implicitly – as distinguished from assimilation – to incorporate Jews into American civil society as persons worthy of respect and affection. The tendency, which is widespread among observant Jews and sometimes also among those Jews who are assimilated, to cultivate and publicly display the differences between Jews and Gentiles, conforms to multiculturalism.

Power and money – generally speaking, the accumulation of goods in non-civil spheres – may be instrumental in obtaining civil repair and recognition in the civil sphere. The boundary relations between these two spheres "can be conceived in terms of facilitating inputs, destructive intrusions, and civil repairs" (Alexander 2013: 135). To the extent that there is such a boundary, problems having quite a different nature are considered as either problems of the individuals, for whom institutionalized psychotherapy – "a central feature of modern life," according to Alexander (2013: 140) – could provide the solution; or problems of society, which is therefore in need of civil repair. Alexander, in his most recent book concerning what he calls "the dark side of modernity" (2013), sets out not only to conceptualize this dark side, but also to suggest possible repairs. A number of undesirable features, or "strains," connote this dark side.

They are as follows: impersonal and bureaucratic organizations, connoted by secrecy and elitism; commodification, at the expense of other social concerns; the uniformity created by the culture industry; lack of social ties and ensuing isolation; the demise of traditional communities; stigmatized identities; predatory nationalism and war; techno-scientific destruction of nature; finally, threats to the emotional coherence and stability of the modern self. Alexander puts forward specific suggestions to repair each of these social strains; for example, as to the social strain caused by isolation, technological devices such as Internet and Skype are mentioned as appropriate instruments to sustain long-distance communication. Modernity, the author concludes, can cause dangerous social strains, but can also repair them. Its effects are therefore ambivalent (Alexander 2013: 147–57).

The Reception of Alexander's Work

Alexander's reception has been critical in most cases. However, there have also been several favorable evaluations, and the critical remarks have often concerned different aspects of his work. Commentators have focused their attention both on Alexander's body of work, and on individual works, from the early essays on classic authors, as Marx, Durkheim and Weber, to Alexander's most recent work, *The Dark Side of Modernity* (2013). We shall therefore mention in this section the appraisals concerning his work in general, as well as those focusing on specific works and themes, leaving aside the reception of this last work by Alexander, on which evaluations have so far not yet come out. As regards general evaluations, the presence of positive and negative appraisals does not question in any case Alexander's relevance in contemporary sociological theory. It has been argued, on the one hand, that this author has contributed, more than Parsons or others, to an in-depth study of culture, of its elements of strain and the conditions that make a well-functioning society possible. Furthermore, Alexander's analysis of Parsons' theory of action, the distinction among the different levels of abstraction and the theorizations – from the metaphysical to the empirical environment – which have been used in social sciences, have been particularly appreciated. According to Alexander, these levels form a *continuum*, and consequently, any investigation in the sphere of social sciences must critically dwell upon each of them (Joas and Knöbl 2008: 9–10, 17–18).

There are, however, several critical remarks. The emphasis put on "discourses," in the sense Alexander attributes to this term, does not contribute to Parsons' attempt to develop a conceptual pattern to be used for a functional analysis of the empirical world. The concept of neofunctionalism itself is generic and badly defined. Indeed, there is no agreement on what forms a system, though it is a key concept for this perspective (Joas and Knöbl 2008: 337–8; Turner and Colomy 1998: 57). The "strong program," too, proposed by Alexander as a distinguishing element of his cultural sociology, has been subject to critical comments. It has been observed, in this connection, that Alexander is not always consistent in his distinction between the "strong" and the "weak" program; that the description of the latter is unsatisfactory and grotesque; and finally, that the distinction between welcomed social components of civil society and those rejected because considered polluting disregards the possibility that a group, or a cultural aspect, can meet with an ambivalent reaction escaping dichotomous contrapositions (Kurasawa 2004).

Emirbayer (2004, 2007) shows his appreciation for the "strong" program and Alexander's cultural sociology, especially as regards the thesis of its autonomy, and the investigation on the constitutive elements of culture, as well as its relation with the social structure. However, this author remarks that quite often the "strong" program does not provide any indication on how precisely culture interacts with the socio-structural environment of action changing and being changed by it. In other words, whatever the causal direction, Alexander does not explain (his research on Watergate being an exception) which causal mechanisms intervene in the particular circumstances the study is focused on. Mouzelis, in his appraisal of Alexander's work (Mouzelis 1999), advances some criticism, though, like Emirbayer, he seems to appreciate Alexander's reformulation of Parsons' conceptual apparatus. This reformulation keeps – Mouzelis argues – the distinction among the three systems (society, culture and personality), introduces a useful distinction between action and agency, and allows bypassing Parsons' impoverished vision of the social actor as passively manipulated by his/her social and cultural environment. Nonetheless, Alexander does not explain which are the elements of the cultural environment, and how do they relate in general (not only in particular cases) to non-cultural environments. As to his conceptualization of civil society, Mouzelis remarks that, as in the past, there are still some particularistic forms of solidarity, which do not contribute to the solidarity connoting civil society, as defined by Alexander, and on the contrary, clash with it.

McLennan's comments (2004, 2005) differ from the previous ones because of their strongly critical nature. The author observes, in the first place, that the "strong" program developed by the new sociology of science has insisted on sociological (non-cultural) explanations of scientific knowledge, differently from Alexander's homonymous program. Secondly, Alexander has not made a clear distinction between cultural sociology and culture, because cultural sociology, too, does not mean to ignore the wider social context. In addition, the search for causal explanations of cultural phenomena does not relate to Alexander's "strong" program but rather to the program of the new sociology of science. McLennan notes, in this regard, that it is not justifiable to consider the sphere of cultural phenomena separately from the sphere of social phenomena, as the autonomy of the former cannot be understood in that sense. Furthermore, the importance of sentiments and symbolic world in guiding conducts, which at first sight may seem considerable, should be evaluated from a historical-social perspective rather than being limited to appearances.

"Purity" or "contamination" standards to include or exclude some social categories would require a precise indication of what the author understands as pure or impure, since these designations are produced by a social construction. Alexander limits himself to a non-exhaustive discussion of these analytical categories. On the other hand, Alexander's analytical category of "cultural trauma" represents a development compared to the historically undetermined use previously made of other categories. Moreover, McLellan wonders whether the study of cultural traumas is the only, or the main, field of activity of cultural sociology, whether that field does not actually refer to psychology rather than to sociology, and whether such a "trauma" could not be better investigated taking non-cultural factors into account, and particularly those of a political, social and economic nature. A critical evaluation of this analytical category leads McLellan to question the other conceptually connected category of "civil society." According to Alexander, the category of civil society, if strong enough, would ensure protection against cultural traumas.

McLellan objects that the thesis expounded in the "strong program" is not sufficiently argued, because Alexander's insistence on the relevance of values, rather than on other constitutive elements of civil society, is neither historically nor theoretically justified. Civil society, in Alexander's opinion, is a utopian construction of thought, but the solution he provides to approach it – a multicultural society – is unsatisfactory, because in that case, a number of groups would be competing. Each group, in fact, tries to enforce its culture and identity, and to claim its rights in order to enjoy a part of material and social benefits. McLellan concludes that Alexander, by overemphasizing culture in his social analysis, has hampered his aspiration to formulate a multidimensional social theory. As mentioned, Alexander objects that McLellan has misunderstood him. In Alexander's theoretical conception, culture as an environment internal to action has indeed only a relative autonomy from the social system, which constitutes its external environment. The interpretation of culture as an array of practices and beliefs requires placing an investigated cultural phenomenon – for example, the political crisis called "Watergate," which led to President Nixon's resignation – in its historical perspective, in order to come to a reconstruction of the meanings socially conferred to this object (Alexander 2005b).

We wish to mention here also some critical comments, published in the form of reviews, which concern specific works (books or chapters) written by Alexander. We shall begin from those comments, which were published first, notably the four books forming the *Theoretical Logic in Sociology*. Poggi (1983), dwelling upon the first of them, notes that – despite some analogies with Parsons' *Structure of Social Action*, especially the attempt to provide social sciences with conceptual and theoretical foundations – Alexander does not resume Parsons' thesis of Marx's, Durkheim's and Weber's convergence in outlining a theory of action; rather, he merely focuses on the two terms "action" and "order." In Poggi's opinion, these terms are not only key words in Parsons' arguing, but also, in Alexander's language, non-demonstrable presuppositions of the scientific process. Alexander's discussion of these two terms, however, is unsatisfactory – according to Poggi – because the problem of action, but not that of order, is relevant both from an epistemological and a sociological point of view. Furthermore, the need to write other volumes can hardly be understood, since the problems of action and order are already exhaustively dealt with in the third chapter of this first volume. This third chapter – which is focused on the problems of action and social order – does not pave the way to subsequent books, as it seems to put an end to Alexander's epistemological discussion.

The presentation and review of Alexander's second volume (1982b) made by Wallace (1984) is oriented to criticism. Wallace extensively examines the first volume, and remarks, as Poggi does, the obscurity of the expression "theoretical logic." This expression recurs in Alexander's work and has great importance for the author, but – as the other key term "multi-dimensionality" – it is not clearly, consistently, or explicitly defined. Likewise, "presuppositions" is a polysemous term, since it can mean either "conceptual definition" or "empirical generalization." Alexander does not seem to know this semantic difference. In addition, he does not explain the connection existing between the existential (presuppositions) and ethical (ideological orientations) statements that can be found in his work. The same ambiguity connotes also the conceptions of sociology and theory, which in Wallace's opinion are expressed in an inconsistent and obscure way.

The interpretations of Marx and Durkheim, which take up the second volume, are questioned as follows: concerning Marx, an examination of his texts does not confirm at all Alexander's thesis, according to which Marx, in the works of his maturity, would have removed any consideration for intentions and human creativity. As to Durkheim, Alexander affirms – in this case, too, clashing with Durkheim's explicit statements – there has been no continuity in the thought of this thinker; as he thinks, on the contrary, to see some "antinomies" in them, which have no textual ground. A survey of Durkheim's texts would instead reveal a strong thematic and conceptual continuity, in particular as regards some presuppositions of Durkheim's thought. According to this author, beliefs and practices, together with the physical environment, contribute to form and preserve moral integration and social solidarity.

Collins considers the critical remarks addressed by Wallace and other commentators to *Theoretical Logic in Sociology* (the four volumes that jointly form Alexander's first work) unjustified, though he has some reservations in this regard, too. In his review, he expresses a comprehensive evaluation of Alexander's third and fourth volumes, which deal respectively with Weber and Parsons (Collins 1985). Collins gives a favorable opinion about the fourth volume, which he considers the most important work on Parsons ever published, and he appreciates the lucid style of Alexander's formulation. In Collins' opinion, the theme of multidimensionality and its nature and presence, or absence, in the classic authors he considers, are Alexander's main concerns in all the four volumes.

Dwelling upon Weber, Collins considers him a multidimensional thinker, in the sense that materialistic (economic and political conditions) and idealistic elements (religious beliefs and normative prescriptions) combine in his works. If instead the term "multi-dimensional" means the simultaneous presence of a micro-sociological and a macro-sociological point of view, the former prevails in Weber's methodological writings, whereas a macro-sociological point of view prevails, instead, in his historical works. Concerning Parsons, Collins reports and seems to share Alexander's criticism of other commentators who would have mistaken Parsons' analytical distinctions for empirical descriptions of the social reality. Collins raises instead some objections towards Parsons' theory of social change in the presentation Alexander makes of it. Parsons proved to be a multidimensional thinker in formulating his conceptual pattern, Collins remarks, but his theory of change in terms of social differentiation is far less satisfactory than Alexander thinks. Multidimensionality does not constitute an epistemological principle, but rather a heuristic strategy aimed at investigating the empirical world in its different aspects – ideal, cultural, economic, political, etc. – and at obtaining theoretical teachings from it.

We consider now the appraisals of some individual essays or contributions written by Alexander, instead of his monographic works. The harsh criticism addressed by Alexander to Bourdieu's work, as previously mentioned, did not go unnoticed, considering the reputation of Bourdieu and Alexander himself. Lamont (1998) remarks that though Bourdieu actually exposes himself to Alexander's theoretical and normative criticism, the French author cannot be labeled as a neo-Marxist thinker at all, considering the influence Weber and Durkheim had on his thought. Alexander should have had to specify the elements of originality – if any – in Bourdieu's contribution and take other available appraisals into account. Concerning the "cultural trauma" thesis, Joas (2005) argues that a tragic event that has remained engraved in the collective memory of a group and, according to Alexander, has been socially constructed by it, is objective, and therefore it objectively exists from a sociological point of view.

Therefore, that event exists regardless of its social interpretation and construction, and its construction can be also made by persons or groups that did not directly experience it. Alexander would have conflated the investigation – surely useful – on the rise and spreading of the claim of having been submitted to a trauma with the presuppositions or the consequences of a psychological trauma on the single individuals. Finally, we wish to mention here an appraisal recently written by Emirbayer (2007) concerning Alexander's monographic work, *The Civil Sphere*, which we previously mentioned discussing its contribution to a theory of civil society. Emirbayer notes that this book reveals not only the ideas expressed by Alexander, but also those of the sociologists of his generation educated in the 1960s, and reflects similar discussions produced by the changes occurred in Eastern Europe after the fall of the Soviet Union.

In *The Civil Sphere*, Alexander's rejection of the cynic position, according to which rights result from power, leads him to study the institutional sources of mutual respect, civil solidarity and participative democracy. These sources are recognized in the existence of a vital civil society independent of political society. Emirbayer remarks, in this regard, that – notwithstanding Alexander's contribution to the literature on this theme – his theory of cultural codes neither considers the importance of emotions as a reason for solidarity, nor how relationships based on solidarity produce feelings of solidarity, the origin of which is not explained, nor what the boundaries of this "sphere" are; nor finally, why the symbolic aspects in the construction of civil society receive in his treatment greater importance than material aspects, for example money, organizational networks, and power. Further weaknesses identified in this work consist, among other things, in the attention paid to the history of incorporations in the civil sphere of American groups, rather than European ones, as well as the lack of an in-depth examination of the ways in which groups, whose identity is not consolidated, incorporate, and of the weaknesses of the multiculturalist idea.

References

Alexander, J.C. 1978. "Formal and Substantial Rationality in the Work of Talcott Parsons." *American Sociological Review* 43: 177–98.

Alexander, J.C. 1982a. *Positivism, Presuppositions, and Current Controversies*. Berkeley, CA: University of California Press.

Alexander, J.C. 1982b. *The Antinomies of Classical Thought: Marx and Durkheim*. Berkeley, CA: University of California Press.

Alexander, J.C. 1983a. *The Classical Attempt at Theoretical Synthesis: Max Weber*. London: Routledge & Kegan Paul.

Alexander, J.C. 1983b. *The Modern Reconstruction of Classical Thought: Talcott Parsons*. Berkeley, CA: University of California Press.

Alexander, J.C. 1984. "Social-Structural Analysis: Some Notes on Its History and Prospects." *The Sociological Quarterly* 25: 5–26.

Alexander, J.C. 1985a. Introduction, in Alexander, J.C. (ed.), *Neofunctionalism*. London: Sage.

Alexander, J.C. 1985b. "Habermas' New Critical Theory: Its Promise and Its Problems." *American Journal of Sociology* 91: 400–12.

Alexander, J.C. 1987. The Dialectic of Individuation and Domination: Weber's Rationalization Theory and Beyond, in Scott Lash and Sam Whimster (eds), *Max Weber: Rationality and Modernity*. London: Allen & Unwin, 185–206.

Alexander, J.C. 1987a. *Twenty Lectures: Sociological Theory since World War II*. New York: Columbia University Press.

Alexander, J.C. 1987b. The Centrality of the Classics, in A. Giddens and J.H. Turner (eds), *Social Theory Today*. Cambridge: Polity Press, 11–57.

Alexander, J.C. 1988a. The New Theoretical Movement, in N.J. Smelser (ed.), *Handbook of Sociology*. Newbury Park, CA: Sage, 77–101.

Alexander, J.C. 1988b. *Action and Its Environments*. New York: Columbia University Press.

Alexander, J.C. 1990a. "Commentary: Structure, Value, Action." *American Sociological Review*, 55: 339–45.

Alexander, J.C. 1990b. Analytic Debates: Understanding the Relative Autonomy of Culture, in J.C. Alexander and S. Seidman (eds), *Culture and Society: Contemporary Debates*. Cambridge: Cambridge University Press, 1–27.

Alexander, J.C. 1990c. Il nuovo movimento teorico: un'articolazione, in J.C. Alexander (ed.), *Teoria sociologica e mutamento sociale*. Milan: FrancoAngeli, 49–58.

Alexander, J.C. 1992a. Durkheim's Problem and Differentiation Theory Today, in H. Haferkamp and N.J. Smelser (eds), *Social Change and Modernity*. Berkeley, CA: University of California Press, 179–204.

Alexander, J.C. 1992b. "Shaky Foundations: The Presuppositions and Internal Contradictions of James Coleman's Foundations of Social Theory." *Theory and Society* 21: 203–17.

Alexander, J.C. 1995. *Fin de Siècle Social Theory*. London: Verso.

Alexander, J.C. 1998a. *Neofunctionalism and After*. Oxford: Blackwell.

Alexander, J.C. 1998b. Introduction: Durkheimian Sociology and Cultural Studies Today, in J.C. Alexander (ed.), *Durkheimian Sociology: Cultural Studies*. Cambridge: Cambridge University Press, 1–21.

Alexander, J.C. 2000. *Sociología cultural*. Barcelona: Anthropos.

Alexander, J.C. 2001. "Robust Utopias and Civil Repairs." *International Sociology* 16: 579–91.

Alexander, J.C. 2003. *The Meanings of (Social) Life: A Cultural Sociology*. Oxford: Oxford University Press.

Alexander, J.C. 2004a. Toward a Theory of Cultural Trauma, in J.C. Alexander et al., *Cultural Trauma and Collective Identity*. Berkeley, CA: University of California Press, 1–30.

Alexander, J.C. 2004b. "Cultural Pragmatics: Social Performance between Ritual and Strategy." *Sociological Theory* 22: 527–73.

Alexander, J.C. 2005a. Contradictions in the Societal Community: The Promise and Disappointment of Parsons's Concept, in R.C. Fox, V.M. Lidz and H.J. Bershady (eds), *After Parsons*. New York: Russell Sage Foundation, 93–110.

Alexander, J.C. 2005b. "Why Cultural Sociology is not 'Idealist.' A Reply to McLennan." *Theory, Culture and Society* 22: 19–29.

Alexander, J.C. 2006. *The Civil Sphere*. Oxford: Oxford University Press.

Alexander, J.C. 2013. *The Dark Side of Modernity*. Cambridge: Polity Press.

Alexander, J.C. and Colomy, P. 1990. Neofunctionalism Today: Reconstructing a Theoretical Tradition, in G. Ritzer (ed.), *Frontiers of Social Theory*. New York: Columbia University Press, 33–67.

Alexander, J.C. and Colomy, P. 1994. Funzionalismo e neofunzionalismo, in *Enciclopedia della Scienze Sociali*, Volume 4. Roma: Istituto della Enciclopedia Italiana, 199–214.

Alexander, J.C. and Colomy, P. 1998. Neofunctionalism Today: Reconstructing a Theoretical Tradition, in J.C. Alexander, *Neofunctionalism and After*. Oxford: Blackwell, 53–91.

Alexander, J.C. and Giesen, B. 1987. From Reduction to Linkage: The Long View of the Micro-Macro Link, in J.C. Alexander et al. (eds), *The Micro and Macro Link*. Berkeley, CA: University of California Press, 1–42.

Alexander, J.C., and Thompson, K. 2008. *A Contemporary Introduction to Sociology: Culture and Society in Transition*. Boulder, CO: Paradigm Publishers.

Alexander, J.C., Marx, G.T. and Williams, C.L. 2004. Mastering Ambivalence: Neil, J. Smelser as a Sociologist of Synthesis, in J.C. Alexander, G.T. Marx and C.L. Williams (eds), *Self, Social Structure, and Beliefs*. Berkeley, CA: University of California Press, 1–13.

Alexander, J.C. and Reed, J. 2009. "Social Science as Reading and Performance: A Cultural Sociological Understanding of Epistemology." *European Journal of Social Theory* 12: 21–41.

Alexander, J.C. and Sciortino, G. 1998. On Choosing One's Intellectual Predecessors: The Reductionism of Camic's Treatment of Parsons and the Institutionalists, in J.C. Alexander, *Neofunctionalism and After*. Oxford: Blackwell, 117–46.

Alexander, J.C. and Smith, P. 2003. The Strong Program in Cultural Sociology: Elements of a Structural Hermeneutics, in J.C. Alexander (ed.), *The Meanings of Social Life: A Cultural Sociology*. Oxford: Oxford University Press, 11–26.

Camarda, M.E. 1992. "Jeffrey Alexander: la ricostruzione neofunzionalista della teoria della differenziazione." *Rassegna Italiana di Sociologia* 33: 391–423.

Cisneros, I.H. and Pérez Fernández del Castillo, G. 2000. Introducción, in J.C. Alexander (ed.), *Sociología cultural*. Barcelona: Anthropos, 9–14.

Coleman, J.S. 1990. *Foundations of Social Theory*. Cambridge, MA: Harvard University Press.

Collins, R. 1985. "Jeffrey Alexander and the Search for Multi-Dimensional Theory." *Theory and Society* 14: 877–92.

Colomy, P. 2005. Jeffrey Alexander, in G. Ritzer (ed.), *Encyclopedia of Social Theory*, Volume 1. London: Sage, 8–9.

Colomy, P. and Turner, J.H. 1998. The Neofunctionalism of Jeffrey C. Alexander, in J.H. Turner, *The Structure of Sociological Theory*. Belmont, CA: Wadsworth, 43–59.

Cordero, R., Carballo, F. and Ossandónet, J. 2008. "Performing Cultural Sociology: A Conversation with Jeffrey Alexander." *European Journal of Social Theory* 11: 523–42.

Donati, P. 1990. La sociologia multidimensionale, plurale e connettiva, di Jeffrey, C. Alexander, in J.C. Alexander (ed.), *Teoria sociologica e mutamento sociale*. Milan: FrancoAngeli, 7–47.

Emirbayer, M. 2004. "The Alexander, School of Cultural Sociology." *Thesis Eleven* 79: 5–15.

Emirbayer, M. 2007. "Review of *The Civil Sphere*, by Jeffrey Alexander." *American Journal of Sociology* 113: 1464–8.

Habermas, J. 1985. Questions and Counterquestions, in R.J. Bernstein (ed.), *Habermas and Modernity*. Cambridge, MA: MIT Press, 192–216,

Habermas, J. 1986. *The Theory of Communicative Action. Vol. 1: Reason and the Rationalization of Society*. Cambridge: Polity Press, 397–9.

Habermas, J. 1989. *The Theory of Communicative Action. Vol. 2: The Critique of Functionalist Reason*. Cambridge: Polity Press, 280–1.

Joas, H. and Knöbl, W. 2008. *Social Theory*. Cambridge: Cambridge University Press.

Joas, H. 2005. "Cultural Trauma? On the Most Recent Turn in Jeffrey Alexander's Cultural Sociology." *European Journal of Social Theory* 8: 365–74.

Kurasawa, F. 2004. "Alexander, and the Cultural Refunding of American Sociology." *Thesis Eleven* 79: 53–64.

Lamont, M. 1998. "Review of *Fin de Siècle Social Theory: Relativism, Reduction, and the Problem of Reason* by Jeffrey C. Alexander." *American Sociological Review* 103: 1068–9.

McLennan, G. 2004. "Rationalizing Musicality: A Critique of Alexander's 'Strong Program' in Cultural Sociology." *Thesis Eleven* 79: 75–86.

McLennan, G. 2005. "The 'New American Cultural Sociology': An Appraisal." *Theory, Culture and Society* 22: 1–18.

Mouzelis, N. 1999. "Post-Parsonian Theory." *Sociological Forum* 14: 721–35.

Poggi, G. 1983. "The Alexander, Quartet: Early Impressions." *American Journal of Sociology* 89: 197–200.

Reed, I. 2009. "Culture as Object and Approach in Sociology." in I. Reed and J. Alexander (eds), *Meaning and Method: The Cultural Approach to Sociology*. London: Paradigm Publishers, 1–14.

Reed, I. and Alexander, J.C. 2009. "Social Science as Reading and Performance: A Cultural-Sociological Understanding of Epistemology." *European Journal of Social Theory* 12: 21–41.

Thompson, K. 2001. "Cultural Studies, Critical Theory and Cultural Governance." *International Sociology* 16: 593–605.

Thompson, K. 2004. "Durkheimian Cultural Sociology and Cultural Studies." *Thesis Eleven* 79: 16–24.

Turner, J.H. and Colomy, P. 1998. The Neofunctionalism of Jeffrey Alexander, in J.H. Turner, *The Structure of Sociological Theory*. Belmont, CA: Wadsworth, 42–59.

Wallace, W. 1984. "Alexandrian Sociology." *American Journal of Sociology* 90: 640–53.

Chapter 2
Pierre Bourdieu (1930–2002)

Preliminary Remarks

The French sociologist Pierre Bourdieu is one of the most widely read and studied authors in France and all over the world (Lahire 2001a: 13; Wacquant 2002a: 549). His works have been translated into many languages and are very influential. Because of their ambition and complexity, his works have been interpreted and evaluated in different ways. In this chapter, we shall briefly mention first his key concepts, such as habitus, practices, representations, field (particularly, the field of power), capital and reflexivity. We shall provide a comment about each one of these concepts, based on texts written by Bourdieu himself and by his close collaborator Wacquant, and bearing in mind that Bourdieu prefers operational definitions of these concepts, that is, mostly addressed to research purposes. After a short description of his methodology, we shall then dwell upon epistemology, which aims at overcoming the alternative between an "objective," or structuralist, point of view external to social actors, and a "subjective," or constructivist and phenomenological point of view, which moves from the interpretation actors give to their social world. We shall then try to show the interrelations among concepts, in the use Bourdieu made of them not only for theoretical purposes, but also for research ones. We therefore provide, for explanatory purposes, some examples of his empirical research. Finally, we shall briefly mention a part of the reception of his works both in France and abroad, and particularly in Anglo-Saxon countries.

Key Concepts

We dwell upon the above-mentioned key concepts, in order to draw their sense from a variety of works written by Bourdieu. *Habitus* is understood as a set, or a system, of individual actors' dispositions. Actors are connoted by socially acquired dispositions (that is, cognitive abilities, perceptions, attitudes, inclinations, preferences, tastes, conceptions, appreciations, actions). The dispositions that constitute the habitus are of a different nature:

- a physical-corporal nature, such as posture and gestures;
- a moral nature, when they concern the system of values;
- a cognitive nature, if they refer to all individual representations of reality.

In any case, the dispositions constituting the habitus are lasting and transferable to others, and result from incorporation in individual actors of the social reality they collectively contribute to construct. In this way, the learned social reality – external to actors, and in this sense, objective – affects their *practices* (that is, what actors do and how they do it, according to their knowledge and beliefs). This social reality also affects their *representations* (that is, the ways in which they subjectively represent reality). Actors are usually not aware of this conditioning, given them since their childhood, which is therefore unconscious. Actors' dispositions induce each actor to contribute in constructing organizing and reproducing, in its personal style, social reality as a known world, a world taken for granted, provided with meaning, interest, and value. Actors' dispositions distinguish them according to the specific communities to which they belong, which in turn result from the homogeneity of individual members' life conditions, particularly referred to their social class; but at the same time lead them to carry out and organize distinctive practices – about which they are mostly unaware – towards other actors and communities. Specific universes of meanings correspond to different universes of practices. This correspondence, which is generally almost perfect, generates taken-for-granted frameworks of thought and perception, and beliefs of unquestioned validity Bourdieu defines by the term *doxa*. These universes of meaning endow with legitimacy the corresponding universes of practices. In case there is a perfect correspondence, the subject incorporates without reservations the outer world in its own system of thought and practices, that is, its system of action (Bourdieu 1977: 76–88, 164–71; 1983: 119, 456–7; 1984: 81–2; 1986: 255; 1990a: 52–65, 86–8, 135–41; 1993: 273–4; 1998: 6–8, 55–6; Bourdieu and Wacquant 1992: 128–40; Wacquant 1992a: 20–23).

Field

In the use Bourdieu makes of this term, field designates a social space formed by a network of relations – in the first place, power relations – objectively existing among social positions. This social space structures the relations between the elements (objects and actors) that constitute it, and is continuously changed by the power struggles occurring among the actors who operate within it. Examples of social positions are domination, subordination, and homology. Examples of fields, in this sense, are economic, artistic, scientific, educational (that is, concerning learning) fields. The relations among positions have their own specificity, which makes them unique, and determine for those who hold those positions (actors or institutions) access to, or exclusion from, the benefits – in terms of power – that are an object of struggles and monopolistic appropriation attempts. The outer world determines actors' practices and beliefs through the mediation exerted by one or more fields, and within these fields, actors' distribution among the social positions. Objective power relations structure and determine the relations among the subjects who hold them because they establish the possibilities of access to social positions. This determination takes place only in the last resort, as subjects engage themselves to preserve or change power distribution. Consequently, power relations, both within individual fields, and among different fields, are changing and cannot be defined in the abstract. Subjects who for some time operate in a field – or a network of power relations – acquire a practical sense; that is, they know how to move (both to the letter and in a symbolic sense) in order to achieve their contingent objectives (Bourdieu 1984: 295–6; 1990a: 66–8; 1998: 31–4; Bourdieu and Wacquant 1992: 94–115; Wacquant 1992a: 15–19).[1]

Capital

Bourdieu makes use of this term in the broad sense, as a synonym of power. Capital indicates a set of stable constraints, objectively present in social reality, and advantageous for some classes of actors, but not for other classes. These objective constraints, which are of an economic or a symbolic nature, determine the possibilities of success for the practices actors have symbolically learned and use to carry out in actual terms in social life according to their inclinations and abilities. Within capitalist societies, it is possible to make a distinction among economic, cultural and social capital (whereas in soviet or sociodemocratic societies, the political capital is instead relevant). All these kinds of capital can be converted one into another. The ruling class ensures the perpetuation of its power and privileges by exerting its control on capital transfer. The state – holding the monopoly of legitimate violence, which is not only physical but also moral – grants legitimacy to the power it exerts, which appears as being exerted as a public service. This is true not only as regards the transfer of economic capital, which consists of goods and services offered on the market, through hereditary channels. It is also true for the other kinds of cultural and social capital which cannot be immediately converted into money, which do not have a market price – hence, cannot be conveyed through legacies and cannot be purchased on the market. Non-economic capital exchange is, in fact, of a merely social nature.

  Cultural capital consists of cultural goods that have been inculcated, acquired, incorporated by actors at different levels. Cultural capital presents itself in the institutionalized form of acknowledged educational or academic qualifications formally accessible to anybody, and therefore, formally independent of those who are in possession of them, but in fact achievable at the highest levels only by the ruling class. However, cultural

---

1 For an in-depth analysis of Bourdieu's notions of field, capital and habitus, see Gorski 2013b. In particular, as regards the scientific field, cf. Bourdieu 1990b; 2001: 67–165. About the concept of field in Bourdieu, cf. also Lahire 2001b: 24–6.

capital is available largely in a non-institutional form, handed over from generation to generation, such as economic capital, but not through hereditary channels. Its acquisition takes place from childhood through the teaching – which is not made at school and is often carried out unconsciously – of notions, language skills, and behaviors convenient for the social class of origin. Besides being incorporated in social actors, or institutionalized in educational qualifications acknowledged by the state, cultural capital is expressed ("objectified") through particular material objects and means; e.g., written texts, monuments, paintings, machinery, which may be appropriate not only in economic, but also symbolic terms. The cultural capital builds up a consistent universe – or system – of objective relations, which is not reducible to what individual actors or communities may appropriate, since it is independent of the actors with which it combines every time. However, actors make use of it as though it were a resource and a stake during the quarrels that occur in the field (artistic, scientific field, etc.) and in the social classes in which they act. An explanation of it is the competition among actors who aim, being in possession of high educational degrees, at achieving the maximum economic benefit from them. This competition produces an inflation of educational qualifications, and therefore lowers their economic benefit.

Social capital designates a range of real or potential resources connected with the existence of a stable network of relations, which is based on mutual acquaintance and acknowledgement. Each member obtains, in virtue of its belonging to the network, a credit – both in an economic and/or in a symbolic sense – which entitles it to make exchanges of different kinds with the other members. The wider the volume of relations an actor has at its disposal both directly and indirectly, thanks to the networks to which belong the actors with whom it relates, the greater the social capital volume the actor has available. A relation network is constructed and maintained through the continuative efforts of individual actors or groups (for example, family groups), with the purpose – pursued not necessarily consciously – to transform accidental relations (for example, with neighbors, or for business reasons) into relations involving mutual moral and/or juridical obligations. If an actor inherits membership in a group (such as a family or nobility group), it also inherits the group's social capital, insofar as the actor represents it (in the double sense of a theatre representation, or performance, and a legal representation).

Both cultural and social capital may be transformed into economic capital, which is the ultimate cause of the effects produced by the other types of capital. Consequently, the ruling class portion controlling cultural capital (such as intellectuals and academicians) is subordinate to the ruling class portion controlling economic capital (that is, non-economic forms of capital are subordinate to economic capital). However, the transformation of a kind of capital into another is imperfect and costly, in the sense that in some cases it may not even take place at all, or only partly take place, and in any case requires time and efforts. For example, cultural capital may not completely transform itself into economic capital, and vice versa. Again, transforming economic capital into social capital assumes a personal and family commitment that turns into a waste of economic capital. The risks produced by converting one type of capital into another become greater – particularly in the case of conveyance of a property – when the economic component of capital is concealed; for actors may not identify this component, which is the ultimate cause of its existence and permanence. On the other hand, concealing it makes the possession of a social and cultural capital more profitable. A more profitable and less risky conversion is at the base of the strategies that aim at preserving the capital and the social standing by minimizing the costs and losses deriving from conversion itself. By reproducing the capital, we legitimate not only the right to take possession of it in an exclusive way, but also the right to reproduce it. Successful reproduction sanctions its legitimacy (Bourdieu 1986. See also Bourdieu 1977: 171–83; 1990a: 63–4, 108–10, 112–25, 131–4; 1998: 34–60; Bourdieu and Wacquant 1992: 98–9; 118–19).

Reflectivity

By this term, Bourdieu points out the sociologists' moral, methodological and epistemological need to bring knowledge, and collectively watch over all that remains implicit and is taken for granted in the field of sociology; since this is part of the common sense and the professional ideology of this discipline. It may concern theories, problems, judgment standards, evaluations used by the researcher's scientific community.

Through reflectivity, a sociologist intends to shed light on the conditions – and particularly, the field of forces acting inside and outside his activity of study and research – in which sociological knowledge is actually produced. Through reflectivity, a sociologist aims at making clear to himself the intellectual and moral relation with his matter of study; further, at safeguarding his intellectual independence, and at identifying which are, in sociology, the actual, objectively existing, possibilities to act in view of ethical goals. The reflectivity principle and method are used to control the distortions that may derive from the researcher's social origin (such as social class, ethnic group, gender), from his belonging to the academic field and his or her position in the social world. Researchers, as intellectuals, tend to think rather than acting in the social world.

Reflectivity is then a methodological instrument and pursues a cognitive-scientific goal. Habits, power positions, consolidated interests in the scientific field of sociology, and dominant opinions deeply hamper reflexivity. Furthermore, the ethnocentric prejudice leading a sociologist to share the assumptions of his class and his intellectual sphere, or professional group, also represents an obstacle. An obstacle, too, are the intrusions of sociology in the scientific field made by governmental organizations and driven by economic interests, especially in mass communication management. In particular, the public or private subjects controlling research funds do exert their power on the way in which research is formulated and developed. A sociologist must consider this power in order not to be influenced by it, thus jeopardizing the objectivity of the knowledge thereby obtained (Bourdieu 1984: 292–3; Bourdieu and Wacquant 1992: 71–2; 88–9, 182–4, 199, 214–15; Bourdieu, Chamboredon and Passeron 1983: 100–106; Wacquant 1992a: 36–59).

Epistemology

Bourdieu pays great attention to the conditions in which those who work in the area of social sciences, particularly sociologists, use to think and act. The sociologist's profession demands that a researcher consider at close quarters actors' practices in the very moment in which they take place. His purpose, which conforms to the reflexivity principle, is twofold: firstly, to know the conditions that make possible the different experiences, perceptions, knowledge, evaluations and representations of the social world actors use to make; and secondly, to shed light on the whole set of actors' different and contrasting points of view, without adopting anyone of them. In accordance to pragmatism, especially Dewey's, Bourdieu rejects received and taken for granted notions on the social world, and emphasizes knowledge acquired through practical experience; namely, experience that is oriented to achieve solutions to problems. Still in keeping with Dewey, Bourdieu's scholarly pursuits aimed to promote democratic politics (see Emirbayer and Schneiderhan 2013: 144–8).[2] In order to be at the same time correct, from an epistemological point of view, and useful in practice, sociological knowledge must not be only abstract and bookish. Only by keeping to the reflexivity principle, a sociologist is then in the position to understand how individual attitudes and behaviors are socially conditioned; and as regards himself, to keep a sufficient freedom of thought and action towards the very strong conditioning exerted by the action fields in which he thinks and acts.

To structuralist epistemology, Bourdieu objects that it fails to study how this structure actually forms, as it prefers to consider actors' (persons or groups) activities and preferences as though they were their own specific attributes, devoid of any sociological interest. In other words, it neglects how actors – building up the social structure through their practices – put relations into action. Though objectively existing, these relations assume a symbolic form, and have therefore their own logics and effectiveness, which is independent of both the objective conditions of power relations and the actors' distribution within the social space. Bourdieu objects to constructivist and phenomenological sociology that individual practices and action strategies are not contingent and ephemeral. Practices and strategies produce, on the contrary, supra-individual emerging effects, which do not coincide with the sum of individual actions. The social space in which actors act is historically formed by the experiences they have stored up all together during their social life.

---

2   As Emirbayer and Schneiderhan observe (2013: 138–56), Bourdieu's work differs from Dewey's in other respects. Cases in point are Bourdieu's field-theoretic approach, his conceptualization of different forms of power, and his theories of the modern state and of habitus.

However, actors' representations and practices symbolize positions objectively held by the actors in this social space, and result from them. Actors' objective distribution in the space of the relations among their positions is dialectically related with the ways in which this distribution is learned and represented by the actors. Within each one of those relation spaces, or areas – such as the economic, political, cultural areas – reciprocally homogeneous practices are produced. Areas are objective structures binding actors' practices. The "habitus" – that is, the set of individual dispositions – by incorporating the social structure, makes the internal practices of each area homologous, and mediates among different areas (Bourdieu 1977: 3–4; 1984: 292–3; 1990a: 25–41, 104–11, 121–41; 1998: 3–4; 2001: 222–3; Bourdieu and Wacquant 1992: 88–9, 120–21, 136–7, 198–200; Nash 2003; Wacquant 1992a: 7–11).

Methodology

Bourdieu does not share an uncritical use of the research methods conventionally used in the social sciences, such as questionnaires and structured interviews. Their inadequacy derives in the first place from their inability to shed light – except by using different research methods – on the fields and the conflict of interests that are (in his opinion) central themes in any sociological inquiry. In the second place, Bourdieu considers it necessary not to exclude the stock of information in possession of a sociologist both by his profession and by his being a social actor, because this information – on condition it is controlled through a comparison with the information obtained by means of observation – is scientifically relevant. Hence, his recommendation that sociologists should attempt to achieve detailed, in depth, and possibly direct information and knowledge about the subjects' lifestyle. Consequently, research should be addressed to the habitus and the practices through which the subjects actually put into practice their attitudes and behaviors. This should be so, even when those practices (such as etiquette rules, dresses, furniture, habits, aesthetical and gastronomic tastes, etc.) are not directly related to the object of inquiry. Therefore, a sociologist should not refuse to "get his hands dirty in the kitchen of empirics" (Bourdieu 1983: 514). In the third place, some peculiar methods, such as structured interviews, force the subjects to give answers to questions and matters about which they are not informed, and which are extraneous to their life experience. The subsequent working out process the sociologist carries out on the collected answers makes them even more abstract, and consequently, less useful to sociological knowledge. Drawing up conclusions does further worsen this inconvenience when it is aimed – in the name of an alleged "scientificity" – at being neutral, detached, and therefore distant from the subjects' lived experience.

Bourdieu does not deny utility to traditional research methods. On the contrary, he avails himself in his empirical inquiries (as we shall soon see) of structured interviews, deliberately non-representative samples of the investigated populations, and variable indicators, such as demographic characteristics, social origin, capital in its different forms. However, he recommends researchers to carefully consider the limits of the information collected in this way, and make efforts for integrating them in the way we previously mentioned, remaining the "habitus" and the social relation space (or field) the major inquiry subjects. As a privileged method, Bourdieu suggests analyzing the correspondences among different power positions (and hence, among the subjective dispositions of those who hold them). Correspondence analysis may reveal a homology among different fields or sub-fields. In this way, for example, was highlighted a correspondence between production of goods and production of tastes in the French population by changing the relation between demand and offer according to the different social classes. Again, in the French university context, the distribution of economic and social power indicators among teachers is the same in the different discipline sub-fields and closely follows the oppositions that usually may be found between the fields of economic power and cultural power (Bourdieu 1983: 235–9, 267–77, 505–22; 1984: 60–73, 147–51, 287–8).

A Unitary Conceptual and Theoretical Framework

Within this framework, some key concepts are put in relation, thus showing which theoretical use Bourdieu intends to make of their relation. According to Bourdieu, fields form the object of study of social sciences.

These fields, consisting of objectively existing power relations, are unrelated with the individuals moving inside them. Individuals are relevant insofar as they have the necessary properties (determined in terms of power) for effectively acting in one or more fields. The different fields in which practices are produced are reciprocally independent. However, different fields of relations may be reciprocally connected. In that case, if they synchronize, they are able to produce a historical event expressing at the same time both the intrinsic potentialities of the individual fields and those deriving from their connection. Though actors have a habitus resulting from their specific relation field, and consequently each field is marked by its own habitus, it is possible, however, that there exists a homology of positions among actors placed in different fields.

The habitus is a socially acquired way to establish actors in dispositions, which turn into actors' stable and reciprocally connected practices. Actors' practices are therefore structured and determined to a great degree by their habitus, and ultimately, by the power relations existing among the positions held by the actors. A sociologist must take into account the interconnection between habitus and practices, though the fields in which they are conducted are independent. The habitus relates with a relation field in two ways. In the first place, the field, or the intersection among different fields provides the habitus with a structure. In turn, the habitus derives from a mostly unconscious incorporation of categories of thought existing in the social world. Furthermore, different kinds of habitus correspond to different kinds of field. The social world and consequently the field system encompass the habitus. On the other hand, the acquired habitus works in such a way as to make subjects understand their social world, and act in relation to it.

Actors do experience the social world, which means both the notions and the practices that are provided with meaning, including those taken for granted (for example, walking). Social world experience is a primary experience subjects acquire and incorporate since their childhood. Capital, in all its aspects, operates – that is, it exists and is effective – through the power relations forming the fields, as well as through the practices identifying them. Therefore, a field is determined by the distribution of the different kinds of capital acting within it. Their relative weight, and hence, their distribution, are subject to historical changes, because and by means of actors' competition and the conflicts deriving from them. Strategies and action courses do not only depend on actors' perception of how they are placed in a relation system, or field, but also on the objective power distribution within that field.

Subjects intend to preserve or change this distribution, but their attempts encounter objective constraints in the more or less rigidly structured social reality in which they act. The habitus may be defined as an incorporated capital. A reflexive analysis – that is, an analysis making use of the reflexivity principle and method – aims at shedding light on the relation between the actors' habitus and their position in one or more social fields, and consequently, on the social origins of their practices. This is also valid particularly for sociologists insofar as social actors. Sociologists, and in general thinkers and scientists, have to conduct a reflexive analysis concerning the scientific field, in which they operate. They should do so in order not to accept supinely and inadvertently the professional ideologies, which dominate in that particular field (Bourdieu 1977: 72–95; 1983: 14–18; 1984: 295–6; 1986: 76; 1990a: 66–98; 2001: 221–3; Bourdieu and Wacquant 1992: 88–90, 101, 105–108, 121, 127–30, 136, 214–15; Wacquant 1992a: 16–19, 27).

Two Examples of Empirical Studies

We shall now briefly mention these empirical studies (Bourdieu 1983, 1984) to comply with Bourdieu's request to note that he is not limited to the formulation of concepts, but also makes use of them in empirical investigations. In fact, Bourdieu always set himself against abstract sociological theory, which is distant from actors' actual practices, and is therefore useless (in Bourdieu's judgment) to those who wish to conduct empirical research. For this purpose, both studies can illustrate the usefulness of key concepts, such as habitus, field, and capital.

Distinction

In his essay *La distinction* [On Distinction], Bourdieu sheds light on the distribution of aesthetic tastes in social classes. Accordingly, the same work of art – for example, a piece of music – is differently appreciated in conformity with the educational level, or with the social class of the audience. Class is determined by the relations existing between attributes, such as occupation or educational level, and the size of the different kinds of capital; for these relations exert, at any moment and over time, effects on practices, on the value attributed to them, and on the actors' habitus. The lower-middle class and the ruling class have in fact their peculiar ways to distinguish themselves from the working class. Cultural works provide an advantage, or a symbolic profit, not only in terms of cultural distinction, but also in terms of legitimacy of their existence. In the field of cultural good production, classes and class segments compete to adopt goods, objects, and practices to be used as distinction marks. For this purpose, they make use of peculiar distinction strategies, which are carried out within a space of objectively existing relations. These relations determine in each class or class segment a complete range of possibilities and impossibilities. If the ruling class establishes legitimate culture, the different segments within it contend to establish a legitimate domination principle, and make thus symbolically prevail the particular kind of capital (whether economic, educational, or social) they hold in comparison with others.

However, correspondence analysis does not help understanding why particular classes or class segments show an elective affinity with specific cultural practices, such as the possession of artistic objects, and particular aesthetical attitudes through which they are able to bear witness of their peculiar personality. In this regard, Bourdieu remarks that aesthetical choices, such as ethic choices in general, determine a lifestyle, and consequently, a set of practices distinctive of both a person and the class or class segment to which it belongs (such as the old and new middle classes). Therefore, in this way the hierarchical position of a class, or class segment, in the ever-changing field of power relations is established. The lower-middle class, which is relatively devoid of culture, does not question the legitimacy of official culture and the distinction its possession involves. Rather, it explicitly acknowledges official culture by displaying good will and cultural docility. The members of the lower-middle class are insecure of the cultural legitimacy of their preferences, because of their insufficient education. They are also timorous of revealing their ignorance, thus exposing themselves to derision. They are accordingly consumers of popularization works, as produced by reliable representatives of the legitimate culture. Moreover, they show particular attachment to the most traditional or conservative ethical or aesthetical attitudes (Bourdieu 1983: 343).

We can distinguish, among the different fractions of the lower-middle class:

- a fraction in economic decline (this is often the case of small artisans and traders);
- a fraction in upward movement (middle managers, technicians, office employees, primary school teachers); and
- a new fraction (relatively well educated persons who belong to area of new professions involving presentation, representation, sale of symbolic goods and facilities, such as adpersons, dieticians, secretaries, and nurses; or also belonging to consolidated but expanding professions, such as jewelers, frame-makers, and upholsterers).

Each fraction of the lower-middle class shows its own specificity in attitudes and aesthetical preferences. The fraction in decline does emphasize austere and traditional tastes. The rising fraction – which draws its privilege from educational capital – shows an ascetic rigor. Finally, the new segment – whose privilege derives from social capital, rather than from educational capital – is inclined to adopt marginal forms of culture, which are not fully acknowledged by educational institutions and claim to become a culture alternative to the official one (such as psychoanalysis in a popularized form, jazz music, cinema, science fiction).

The position of members of the working class is characterized by an urgency to satisfy their primary needs, due to their scarce income. Consequently, they have developed a "taste for the necessary" (Bourdieu 1983: 378), which reveals itself in the choice of practical clothes and furnishing objects, without decorations they consider useless. Necessary, too, are considered the objects, such as knick-knacks, arranged in the living rooms and entrances of the workers' houses for furnishing purposes. The lack of economic and cultural capital makes it so that their choice – from the point of view of bourgeoisie members – is considered very bad taste. In women, but also in men, the taste for the necessary involves a refusal of this class to invest time and energies, besides money, in health and beauty cares. In men, instead, their sexual identity makes insistent reference to virility and physical force values. For the members of the working class, in general, an acceptance of being dominated, and hence low self-esteem levels, correspond to an objectively dominated social position. Their inferiority in job positions, educational capital and wages bear witness to this. Their lifestyle is characterized by low-cost substitutes of valuable goods and by the awareness of not being in possession of socially appreciated theoretical (and therefore useless, from a practical point of view) knowledge. Therefore, the domination to which they are submitted is economic and cultural at the same time.

For those who belong to the working class, self-esteem is related to political awareness, even though this does not involve their disowning any of the cultural domination to which they are subject. Bourdieu maintains that political competence designates a technical or socially acknowledged ability. This expression may therefore have both the specific sense of recognizing and dealing with political issues, and the more general sense of being socially qualified for dealing with those issues. The lack of answers to questionnaires may be an evidence of political incompetence in both senses, and becomes more frequent the most questions depart in contents and form from the interviewees' experience. Questions concerning everyday or private life, or family morals, obtain a higher percentage of answers, while this percentage drops when answers require political competence, in the sense of technical ability to provide appropriate answers. This ability derives from political ability in the broad sense, and is positively related with educational level and social class, besides gender (in favor of the male gender). The lack of answers is therefore evidence of the social expropriation of less cultured and more needy persons, in contrast with the claims of bourgeois and petty-bourgeois persons to have a personal opinion, and consequently their tendency to answer political questions (however, "not all answers are opinions") (Bourdieu 1983: 419).

Therefore, the probability of not giving answers to a political questionnaire depends, though not mechanically, on the class status; on the habitus it generates; and ultimately, on the unconscious political attitude resulting from them. The autonomous production of answers to questions formulated by others has the effect of imposing a range of problems and possible answers that are extraneous to the interviewees. What interviewees intend to express through their answers results the more twisted the less these subjects are in the position to identify the implicit political and ideological position of the question. In that case, subjects interpret the question according to their moral perception of the social world, as there is no continuity between the political language used by politics professionals, close to the ruling class, and their personal life experience. The lower-middle class, in particular, identifies itself with the ruling class and wishes to be socially recognized by it, but politically tends to express indignation because of its social non-acknowledgement and fear of being declassed. It contaminates politics and morals in its answers to questions, which are expressed in a political language, which is poorly understood, and extraneous to its own experience.

In order to practically (instead of conceptually) know the social world, subjects put into action some cognitive structures – such as high/low, strong/weak, fine/rough –, which incorporate the social structures they have experienced. In this way, they contribute to preserve the social world. On the other hand, by virtue of this incorporation, they know how to move in the world, both socially and physically, with their bodies. Categories and classification systems are the stake in disputes among groups, where each group tries hard to use them at its own advantage. Classifications, once institutionalized, become official sources of power, competences, and privileges. Words therefore reflect, though imperfectly, actual inequalities. Official classifications determine social identity and are used as either distinction or infamy marks.

Homo Academicus

This work aims at bringing out and formalizing the standards, or criteria, that regulate practices in the academic or university fields. These standards, which are codified, and consequently, institutionalized and made homogeneous, are used as acknowledged principles of division and hierarchy within this field. There is a plurality of such principles, or standards. Examples of them are teachers' age ("senior," "junior") and the novelty of the knowledge or analysis produced ("old," "new"). Standards are used for polemic purposes, as an instrument in power conflicts. From them result real, actual distinctions inside the field, and corresponding to the intuition and experience university professors have of them. As regards this field, such as any other field, social sciences must be reflexive. That is, if they intend to shed light on the stakes in the power conflicts that occur inside the university, social sciences should have as an object the distinction and classification standards commonly used in the academic field, and should avoid actually introducing them in a non-declared manner, and being therefore involved in those conflicts. The purpose of inquiries is collecting information on the field – a multidimension space formed by objectively existing relations – in which interactions evidence the actors' specific properties and mutual differences. The actors in question are not individuals in the flesh, but rather communities, which occupy a particular area ("region") in the space of relations. In the academic-university field of science, expressive styles do strictly correspond to the social representations and norms required for producing the effect of scientificity, or scientific truth. This is particularly true in the field of human sciences, where the search for this effect goes along with the use of a philosophical language, which is incompatible with the search itself.

This text first tackles the question of power foundations and forms in the French university faculties of letters and human sciences on the eve of 1968. Then, Bourdieu dwells upon the deep changes that were taking place in that period, which produced changes in the power relations between the university faculties of letters and social sciences, despite many attempts to preserve the previous power structure and hierarchy. If cultural capital is dominated by economic capital, represented by those who control industry and trade, in the field of cultural production those who hold this kind of capital in an institutionalized form, such as university professors, dominate in turn. They dominate, in virtue of their career opportunities and regular income, those who, such as writers and intellectuals, do not have these advantages. This condition is witnessed by some particular indicators of social integration (as being married and having children), and by indicators of adhesion to the ruling order (for example, receiving decorations and honorific titles). Considering the respective position of some faculties (sciences, letters, law, medicine) in a power hierarchy, these indicators show a decreasing advantage in terms of cultural prestige, but an increasing advantage in terms of economic and political power.

Using the method of correspondence analysis, Bourdieu shows that this double hierarchy tends to reproduce. In fact, law and medicine professors often come from economically privileged families; they increase their inherited privilege with earnings from professional activities, have a large social capital at their disposal, and hold leading positions in organizations exerting economic and political power. As a result, promoting the importance of scientific research in the medical field, or teaching in famous research centers such as the Pasteur Institute, is not as respectable, or a comparable source of power; as compared to the achievements by those who prefer cultivating social relations and winning competitions, which enable them to climb to a higher hierarchical level. One makes a career for oneself through co-optation, and the habitus homogeneity between a candidate and the group, in which it wants to take part, is rewarded. Those who teach, instead, scientific and literary disciplines, frequently come from culturally, rather than economically, privileged families, and do not show any particular appreciation for practices and symbols (such as ceremonies, awarding of honors, traditions) related to social order. They prefer to establish an internal prestige hierarchy based on their own peculiar standards (educational curriculum, university career, place in which they teach). According to those standards, decisive importance is attributed to the professors' habitus, shaped by the families of origin.

Critical Reception of Bourdieu's Work

On Bourdieu's works, there is nowadays a great deal of literature, which is quite heterogeneous as regards his evaluation. We shall give in this section some selective indications, by reporting first the most favorable evaluations, then the intermediate ones, and finally, the mostly or completely negative comments. Among Bourdieu's admirers and commentators, particular attention deserves, for many reasons, Loïc Wacquant. As an interviewer and commentator, Wacquant took part in the publication of a work, which he co-authored with Bourdieu, and in which he explained the theoretical and epistemological content and assumptions of Bourdieu's works (Bourdieu and Wacquant 1992). As a Bourdieu expert, Wacquant is the author of an introduction to Bourdieu's works, which proposes to shed light on what, in his opinion, is their basic aim. Bourdieu's aim, according to Wacquant, has been to pursue a kind of sociology that may become a "total science," which is able to "preserve the fundamental unity of human practice across the mutilating scissures of disciplines, empiric domains, and techniques of observation and analysis" (Wacquant 1992a: 26–27).

Again in his role as an expert, Wacquant published a short essay, in which he criticizes Bourdieu's reception in the United States, which is considered "confused and contradictory" (Wacquant 1992b: 237) as regards the perception of his sociology. In fact, Wacquant contends, Bourdieu's theoretical references do not appear clear, sometimes his style is scarcely appreciated, and the concept of habitus seems obscure. In keeping with Wacquant, this perception flows from inadequate and fragmentary knowledge of Bourdieu' works, and of contemporary French sociology in general (Wacquant 1992b). Finally, as a researcher on the social condition of poverty and marginality, Wacquant appreciates Bourdieu's sociology for its ability not to consider that condition as a separate issue, and those who experience it as active subjects rather than passive bearers of pre-established cultural models (Wacquant 1996: 133, note 13; 2002: 1493). Wacquant therefore considers perspicuous, scientifically fruitful, and completely acceptable the concepts, explanations and epistemological guidelines formulated by Bourdieu. Some other commentators of Bourdieu share Wacquant's entirely positive evaluation.

The French introduction written by Louis Pinto is an example in this sense (Pinto 2002). Pinto attentively considers Bourdieu's conceptual and theoretical framework, as well as his epistemological position, and concludes that the most significant contribution of his sociology does not only consist in his conceptual apparatus, through the notions of capital, field, and reflexivity. It also consists in Bourdieu's ability to change, through these notions, the boundaries between science and philosophy, and provide a more convincing anthropological conception than the "neo-liberal vision of a rational and calculating individual" (Pinto 2002: 243). Positive evaluations have also concerned some particular areas of Bourdieu's production. His notions of cultural capital, symbolic production and habitus would allow investigating the ways and dispositions that form the habitus, and encourage individual reception of particular symbolic goods made collectively available by cultural capital (Lash 1993: 208–10). Camic (2013) in his investigation of Bourdieu's work has focused on a problem of sociology of knowledge; namely, on the relationship between social, and in general, external factors in the production of knowledge on the one hand, and internal factors such as culture, broadly defined, on the other.

According to Camic, and to other authors as well (Camic mentions Collins in this connection), Bourdieu has laid greater stress on internal factors, for he has viewed "knowledge production mainly in terms of the social dynamics operating inside particular intellectual fields" (Camic 2013: 188). This is so, Camic observes, only if the analysis concerns relatively autonomous fields of knowledge production. In keeping with his "internalist" viewpoint, Bourdieu makes use of two arguments. Firstly, a relation is stated to exist between the position of knowledge producers in a field and their intellectual stance. Secondly, Bourdieu has laid stress on the struggle between the established representatives of cultural production and those who wish to enter this cultural field. Nonetheless, external factors are also deemed important in that they constitute the social conditions, which internal factors reflect and mediate. Bourdieu's empirical work on knowledge production overcomes, according to Camic, the contraposition between the internal factors of knowledge production. Bourdieu hints at the overlapping and multileveled position of fields in the social space. Only this conception of fields, Camic maintains, would include "the full ensemble of additional fields that Bourdieu's empirical work mentions in passing" (Camic 2013: 195).

In a peculiar area of study, such as linguistics, appreciation has been conferred to a thesis formulated by Bourdieu; namely, that there are no rules shared by actors (communication codes, in this case), apart from the actual practices carried out in the (communication) relation among them (Hanks 1993: 139–41). Moreover, in a recent article Emirbayer and Johnson (2008) provide an exhaustive presentation, as well as a positive evaluation, of Bourdieu's contribution to the study of organizations. Some of Bourdieu's notions such as field and capital, they argue, have entered the scholarly literature on organizations. However, most authors in this area of studies have failed, according to Emirbayer and Johnson, to distinguish between relations of interaction and of structural force, as implied by Bourdieu's notion of field. This notion and the related one of organizational field refer to structures of power as exerted in any of its forms by occupants of distinct positions, who are therefore bearers of different amounts and combinations of resources. Organizational fields constitute, in the authors' words, "a space of struggle for organizational power." Thus the holders of capital in any form – whether they are leaders of social movements or of religious organizations or major representatives of the fashion industry – compete for dominant organizational positions in their own field of power.

The current literature on organization theory has failed, according to these authors, to pay due attention to Bourdieu's notions, jointly considered, of field, capital and habitus. They have therefore perpetuated distinctions, which are theoretically sterile. Instances thereof are those between micro and macro analytical levels; between determinist and voluntaristic theories of action; and between social psychology and sociology. Other merits of Bourdieu's social theory are, firstly, his emphasis on the symbolic aspects of organizations, as evidenced by his concepts of cultural and symbolic capital, and position taking in the struggle between organizations that compete in the field of power, in which they are embedded. Another merit has been his method of correspondence analysis. The associations and relations between different conceptual elements such as positions and position taking are thereby mapped into an organizational field (see Emirbayer and Johnson 2008). Dobbin (2008) and Swartz (2008), like Emirbayer and Johnson, also explore and emphasize the theoretical relevance of Bourdieu's notions of habitus, capital and organizational field. Swartz, in particular, in a recent contribution has formulated some "metaprinciples" in Bourdieu's sociology. In his judgment, they "characterize Bourdieu's work and can be usefully employed for approaching new areas of sociological investigation" (Swartz 2013: 21). These "metaprinciples" are as follows.

Firstly, there is Bourdieu's objective to focus on power and domination. Bourdieu's sociology rejects sociological determinism in order to bring into light how, in addition to power, violence and capital, cultural forms of differentiation constitute and maintain social inequality. Secondly, the methodological principle of breaking with received notions and categories concerning the social world as a necessary step to reconstruct the broader social and historical world, which has produced both the actors and the way they interpret their world. Thirdly, there is the principle of reflexivity. In keeping with this principle, all concepts should be employed reflexively; namely, the researcher's own stance and social location should be critically examined to prevent from projecting them into the research object. Finally, sociological analysis – its intended meaning and empirical content – should be understood as instruments of which sociologists avail themselves to help create a more open and egalitarian social world. Bourdieu's notions of field, capital, stance and position, and habitus should be interpreted and used accordingly (Swartz 2013). We shall dwell now upon some authors who – much as Wacquant – positively evaluate the works of Bourdieu, and refer to a plurality of his writings, thus evidencing their good, non-fragmentary knowledge of these works. However, their evaluations include some reservations as well.

Craig Calhoun, whose theoretical production has been deeply influenced by Bourdieu (Calhoun 1995), is the author of introductions and evaluations concerning Bourdieu's works, and is one of his few interpreters Wacquant seems to appreciate (Wacquant 1992a: 47, note 84). Bourdieu – Calhoun remarks – has contributed with his concepts of habitus and field to make us understand how knowledge incorporated in social relations, and not explicitly formulated, is able to influence even social relations. According to Calhoun, however, Bourdieu – with his notion of capital as a power relation – did not sufficiently consider how capital mediates among different fields. In other words, Bourdieu did not examine in depth how capital is able to coordinate among social relations, which belong – in the complex contemporary societies – to different systems. Information technologies, large administrations and organizations, and impersonal markets, are cases in point. The relations among those systems produce changes both in fields and in the habitus, thus disclosing opportunities for critical analyses and innovative political actions. Consequently, innovation and social/cultural changes are not sufficiently investigated (Calhoun 1993: 82–4; 1995: 154–6; 2000: 726). In a recent contribution, Calhoun (2013a) has pointed to four social and political transformations that in his judgment have shaped Bourdieu's theory and empirical research.

These are as follows:

a. How state power and the expansion and intensification of market relations have uprooted traditional ways of life, as instantiated in colonial Algeria and the Pyrenees region in France. As for Algeria, in particular, Bourdieu merged ethnography and statistics to show how the attraction of urban life deeply affected the peasants' traditional habitus.

b. How the differentiation between state and market power, and in general the creation of relatively autonomous fields, have given rise to modern society in the course of the nineteenth century and thereafter.
c. How the expansion of the welfare system and the economy in the first three decades after the Second World War held an unfulfilled promise of greater equality and opportunities for social participation.
d. How neoliberalism subsequently launched a successful attack on social welfare.
e. Calhoun then considers Bourdieu's research on:
f. The French educational system, and observes that Bourdieu's goal was to demonstrate that culture, its pretension of neutrality notwithstanding, actually was "a politically salient engagement with continuing transformation in French society" (Calhoun 2013: 47).
g. Social inequality and the pursuit of distinction. Calhoun focuses on Bourdieu's thesis that social hierarchies belong to the struggles to change the world.
h. Fields result from struggles between actors competing for domination by using their specific capital, and providing distinctive goods.
i. Neoliberalism. Bourdieu, according to Calhoun, argued that neoliberal reforms not only wreak pernicious economic and social psychological consequences on individuals, but also destroy the social institutions that provide meaning to people's lives.

Wacquant expresses favorable opinion also as regards another interpreter of Bourdieu, Rogers Brubaker, with whom Wacquant had some extensive conversations focused on the works by this French scholar (Wacquant 1992b: 229 note 1, 261). On a par with Calhoun, Brubaker too has contributed to introduce Bourdieu to Anglo-Saxon scholars through detailed and well-informed introductions (Brubaker 1985, 1993), in which Brubaker refers to Bourdieu's general conceptual and theoretical pattern calling it "metatheory" (Brubaker 1985: 749–50). Furthermore, the author points out the basic end, which he attributes to Bourdieu's sociology, of overcoming the opposition between the "objective" and the "subjective" aspects of social life (in the various senses of these terms). Brubaker also points to two "problem-clusters" Bourdieu would seek to solve through his conceptual framework. In the first place, there is a problem-cluster concerning the different symbolic, cultural and cognitive tools through which class power is exerted and reproduced. Bourdieu's solution consists in the thesis, according to which power takes different and separate forms (economic, cultural and social capital).

In the second place, there is another problem-cluster regarding the relation between aspects of social life that depend on actors, and other ones that, instead, do not depend on them. The interconnected concepts of structure, habitus and practices are formulated in such a way as to give an answer to these problems. Brubaker – and similarly other interpreters, such as Mounier (2001: 39–53) – dwells upon the concept of habitus and on the interpretations that have been given of it. The habitus – he reminds us – is incorporated in institutions that generate the most varied range of non-intentional practices, from sport to symbolic practices, and is imperfectly shared by social actors. Therefore, this concept may be used to describe the material, symbolic, objective and subjective aspects of social life (cf. also Bronckart and Schurmans 2001: 173). Bourdieu's attempt to provide the social world with a conceptual and theoretical framework, without neglecting, however, the diversity of actors' practices, is considered by Brubaker – though he is a great admirer of Bourdieu – contradictory and unsuccessful. In fact, Bourdieu provides a description and an explanation of the social world, which give an excessively systematic and structured image of it, while neglecting both the aspects of fluidity and the differences between a society and another (Brubaker 1985, 1993).

The objections of other interpreters are not basically different, but their evaluations are less positive than those expressed by Calhoun and Brubaker. It is, however, useful to remember that some reservations have been expressed in conjunction with appreciations for the theoretical relevance – at least potential – of his conceptual apparatus and his theoretical production.[3] It has been remarked that Bourdieu neglects considering both the internal differentiations among the structures, or fields, in which power is distributed (Parker 2000: 48), and

---

3   We do not mention here the interpretations of Bourdieu's works, whose contents and tones, considered excessively critical, have not been shared even by researchers who have expressed objections towards him (Inglis 2003: 255–6; Lahire 2001a: 8–9).

"the emerging properties of particular situations," which do neither derive from social structure properties, nor from single individuals' creative abilities (Layder 1994: 156). In addition, actors are connoted by peculiar elements such as experienced situations; the language they use in rationally evaluating the opportunities to pursue their interests; their aesthetical and moral values; the variety of practices put in service of those values. These specific elements neither identify themselves with the actors' interests, nor are limited to the result of the conflict between the interests of particular actors and those of others (Parker 2000: 48–51). Likewise, Patrick Baert appreciates the explanation Bourdieu provides about structure stability, meant as the result of the clever and unconscious reproduction actors make of it in virtue of their habitus, that is, in virtue of incorporated dispositions. However, he objects that Bourdieu explains neither the causes of the stability of those individual dispositions, nor the individuals' ability to employ their tacit knowledge for the deliberate purpose of changing or preserving their practices, and thereby, the social structure; rather than limiting themselves to reproduce it unconsciously (Baert 1998: 33; cf. also Garnham 1993; Lemieux 2001: 223–7).

Further objections concern Bourdieu's key concepts. The plurality and indeterminateness of their meanings, and their alleged theoretical inadequacy, have been found objectionable. Some commentators have focused on the concepts of habitus, practices, and field. The concept of habitus, in particular, has been often considered too undetermined to become scientifically useful (DiMaggio 1979: 1468; Lahire 2001c: 126–30). Though this concept implies "the assumptions of a person's unity and permanence," it is, however, "a black box identified essentially through its effects" (Corcuff 2001: 110; cf. also Nash 2003: 53–6). As a source of behaviors, writes Jenkins, who is a particularly critical interpreter, the habitus – as Bourdieu described it – is "at best not clear, and at worst, mysterious" (Jenkins 2005: 70). In another work, Jenkins remarks that Bourdieu's indications on the relation between habitus and objective conditions of reality external to actors may be interpreted in the most different ways. These conditions produce the habitus; or, rather, the habitus conforms to these conditions; or again, there is a dialectic relation between conditions and habitus. Since all these interpretations are possible, it is difficult to understand how the habitus may produce practices (Jenkins 1992: 79; cf. also Collins 1993: 126–8).

As to the concept of practices, it has been remarked that Bourdieu's position – according to which actors delude themselves to consciously set targets and orient their actions to their achievement; while, as a matter of fact, they conform to the socially imprinted habitus – contradicts common experience. For, in keeping with it, actors knowingly act, at least sometimes, rationally. They do not therefore delude themselves (Jenkins 1992: 73–4). This position is also contradictory, since the actions that conform to the habitus of individuals and social classes are explained both because of actors' strategies (whether consciously pursued or not), and as actors' adaptation to external needs, as produced by the social world with which they relate (Bronckart and Schurmans 2001: 158). In other words, the mechanisms through which opportunities and structural constraints change into individual behaviors are not clear, because there is no mention of the reasons a researcher might plausibly attribute to actors in order to explain their behavior (Elster 1983: 69–71, 106–108; cf. also Nash 2003: 56–9).[4] The use of explanatory mechanisms is unnecessary if the explanation does not consider deliberately what individuals do, or intend to do (Martin 2003: 10–11, 14–15). However, Bourdieu – as we have seen – does not intend neglecting at all the individual experience of the social world. In addition, Bourdieu does not use a theory of socialization explaining how individuals learn their habitus as a part of their own identity, and through it, actively contribute to such learning. Finally, he does not explain how, at the same time, it is possible that interiorized habits are not changed into practices, or are mutually dissonant, or again, how individuals take their distance from their social roles (Alexander 1995: 144–5, 158; Cicourel 1993: 111; Lahire 2001c: 131–4; Nash 2003: 49–53).

The concept of field, such as apparently Bourdieu means it, has been deemed to be not clearly established. Is it perhaps a field perhaps determined by the practices professionally carried out by some actors struggling with one another or with other actors? Or, in a more restrictive way, by the practices carried out by prestigious

---

4   To this objection raised by Elster, one of the most outstanding representatives of the Rational Choice Theory, and in general, to the supporters of this perspective, Bourdieu answers that the restrictive conception of practices, which connotes this perspective, does simplify them arbitrarily; furthermore, it does not consider at all the complexity of the ways in which they have established themselves over the history in their relation of mutual influence with the objective structures (Bourdieu and Wacquant 1992: 123; cf. also Jenkins 1992: 73).

actors, and aimed at bringing a symbolic capital to the field? (Lahire 2001b: 34–5). Finally, the fields Bourdieu considers are "disembodied," in the sense that attention exclusively focused on more or less dominant positions, the struggles and strategies of actors who act in a particular field, divert the his investigation from what characterizes the field in its practice and conception specificity, and in its independence from other fields. Bourdieu's theory does not permit to show what literature actually is, in the case of the literary field; what law or science actually are, if those are, instead, the investigated fields. In addition, it does not permit to know what do those acting within one of these fields say (Lahire 2001b: 40–48).

Not only the precision but also the theoretical usefulness of the concept of field have been considered unsatisfactory by some commentators. Considering these objections jointly, in Bourdieu's argumentation, firstly, each field does not seem to be independent of the socially existing power relations. Furthermore, it is not clear whether the actors' habitus pre-exists to the social space of the relations inside and outside fields, or instead, the making of the habitus results from actors' position in this social space. Finally, the conceptual and theoretical relation between field and institution is not clear enough (Alexander 1995: 157–64; DiMaggio 1979: 1468; Jenkins 1992: 89–90; Martin 2003: 25–8). In addition, Bourdieu does not provide sufficient details on the relation among the different factors he points out as constituting elements of a field, such as, for example, the intellectual field. A number of questions have been raised in this connection, such as: is it an intrinsic tendency of this field to make itself independent of power? Or does it derive from the progress of school education? Or, again, does it derive from the founding act of an individual, such as Baudelaire did in the literary field? (Fabiani 2001: 89–90).

Again, Bourdieu seems to attribute more importance to what is produced in a field than to the way in which production takes place. In the case of intellectual production, the result is a lack of attention to the users' public (Fabiani 2001: 84–6; Lahire 2001b: 48–51). Finally, Bourdieu neglects to consider the specificity of the ways in which, in each particular field, practices connoting power struggles are carried out (Friedland 2001: 143–4). Eyal's detailed and rather critical examination of Bourdieu's notion of field deserves attention here (see Eyal 2013). Eyal acknowledges as one of Bourdieu's merits that this notion directs attention to bundles of relations, rather than to single individuals or other individual entities. He objects, however, that fields are merely "distinct spheres whose contents are clearly bounded and well distinguished from another" (Eyal 2013: 158); what occurs in the space between them is not an object of inquiry. Eyal has further objections. If it is granted that, according to Bourdieu, "the total set of relations between fields as well as … the struggles in the field of power over the value of the various forms of capital" determine the relations between fields themselves (Eyal 2013: 160), Eyal wonders in what sense fields are autonomous.

He wonders, in other words, how fields relate to each other, and what the criteria of membership are. Fields boundaries are, Eyal maintains, important in defining a field; for what actors who are outside these boundaries do impinge on the conducts of those who are inside. Marginal actors exist only in a social and symbolic space between fields, and at the frontier of any given field. The concept of field can be therefore hardly useful to studying the activities of external or marginal actors. Rather, boundaries are relevant insofar as they constitute "thick boundary zones." These zones are "functioning as fuzzy zones" – that is, disputed and ill-defined zones – of separation and connection" (Eyal 2013: 175) between spaces. They provide opportunities for actors in a field to raid and exploit resources in other fields, but also to take advantage of their condition of marginality, and operate as bridges between them.

One of Bourdieu's alleged theoretical insufficiencies concerns his concept of culture. This key concept of Bourdieu's sociology, which has been vivaciously debated, is connected with the previously mentioned reservations regarding the concepts of habitus, practices, and fields. Fields may be not only overlapping according to Bourdieu, Camic has observed, but also hierarchically nested in a structure of mutual relations. This structure influences or determines the production of knowledge, as Bourdieu has argued; but it is not clear, Camic objects, whether or not this structure of relations – an internal factor – has greater influence on the production of knowledge than external factors. In other words, these two different sources of influence, external and internal, on knowledge production are not clearly related to each other. It would be then preferable to "liberate Bourdieu's sociology of knowledge from the dualistic model" (Camic 2013: 195). Camic points to further theoretical flaws in Bourdieu's theoretical framework, as Bourdieu fails to indicate, firstly, how the high-level struggles relate to the lower levels ones; secondly, "what one knowledge production field draws from other fields" (Camic 2013: 197); and finally, what are the effects on cultural production of the variable strength of the connections between different fields.

According to Jeffrey Alexander and other interpreters, Bourdieu would have intended the relation between social structure and cultural production in a deterministic way. Actors incorporate the habitus, and carry it out through their practices in the different fields, in which they are placed and act. If the habitus in individual actors and social classes is a manifestation of the objective power relations, it is not then necessary "to analyze the cultural concepts pertaining to culture production separately from their relation with the social structure" (LiPuma 1993: 18). The symbolic and cultural context, in Bourdieu's sociology, would therefore derive – according to these critical remarks – from the structural context of power relations expressed, reproduced and legitimated by culture, to which it is, however, subordinate. In other words, objective structures would exist independently of the subjects' consciousness (Cicourel 1993: 102). There would be a circular relation between structure and habitus. Objective power structures produce the habitus, which in turn reproduces those structures. Bourdieu's references to actors' creativeness are necessarily abstract and indefinite, because he neglects considering interactions among actors as a subject of analysis provided with its own theoretical relevance (Alexander 1995: 128–217; Collins 2004: 379, note 23; Lash 1993: 198–9; LiPuma 1993; Staubmann 2005: 175–7).[5]

As Alexander remarks, despite the fact that Bourdieu claimed to reject rational choice theory,[6] his conceptualization of the habitus leads him actually to approach it. Bourdieu's actor unconsciously pursues a careful strategy of adaptation to the conditions resulting from its own position, and from the position of its social class, within objectively existing power relations. Therefore, the actor is unconsciously rational. However, the notion of "unconscious strategy" is considered a theoretical oxymoron by Alexander (Alexander 1995: 152–7). Reflectivity itself – or, the need for a social science researcher to control distortions coming from its position in a power relation field – has no room in Bourdieu's deterministic approach. For the set of relations inside and outside the power field, which in this particular case is the university field, determines the scholar's self, like the self of any other social actor. Bourdieu's actor cannot then make an independent choice (Alexander 1995: 162–73, 179–86). As another critical interpreter remarks, the ability of social sciences to exert reflexivity, and thus produce scientific truths instead of reproducing the beliefs taken for granted in one's relation network, is granted by Bourdieu only to those who share his political ideas (Monod 2001: 243–4).

However, these negative evaluations should not make us forget that Bourdieu – as we remarked at the beginning – is one of the most read, quoted and influential contemporary sociologists, as we can infer from the worldwide circulation of his works and from the number of foreign languages in which his works have been translated. Some interpreters of the sociological theory who do not share Wacquant's unconditional acceptance, nor Alexander's drastic rejection of it, have called attention to Bourdieu's project. They have remarked that its aim is to overcome the antinomy between micro- and macro-sociological perspectives. Attention has also been called to the conceptual apparatus put in service of this project (Camic and Gross 1998: 456–7). The category of social capital, introduced by Bourdieu, has inspired several empirical and theoretical studies on this subject (Portes 1998: 3–4). His works concerning social privilege preservation through the educational process have been quoted as influential sources even by non-French commentators (Bidwell and Friedkin 1988: 453, 458). Bourdieu's essay on distinction, in particular, has stimulated several socio-psychological inquiries on identification processes and identity construction, particularly through lifestyles and consumer preferences (Cerulo 1997: 394–5; Zukin and Maguire 2004: 181–2). Therefore, despite some quite often-negative evaluations, the evidences of the lasting influence of Bourdieu's theoretical production and empirical research, even in the Anglo-Saxon countries, are not lacking (cf. Gorski 2013a: 2–6).

---

5 Bourdieu defends himself from the accusation of determinism by arguing that social actors determine their own habitus and campus through their perception and evaluation categories, which are socially and historically established. Consequently, they are determined inasmuch as they determine themselves (Bourdieu and Wacquant 1992: 135–6).

6 Other interpreters of Bourdieu have preferred to emphasize the complementary, rather than the contraposition, between rational choice theory and Bourdieu's theory of practice. See Ermakoff 2013.

References

Alexander, J.C. 1995. *Fin de Siècle Social Theory*. London: Verso.

Baert, P. 1998. *Social Theory in the Twentieth Century*. Cambridge: Polity Press.

Bidwell, C.E. and Friedkin, N.E. 1988. The Sociology of Education, in N.J. Smelser (ed.), *Handbook of the Sociology of Education*. London: Sage, 449–71.

Bourdieu, P. 1977. *Outline of a Theory of Practice*. Cambridge: Cambridge University Press.

Bourdieu, P. 1983. *La distinzione*. Bologna: Il Mulino.

Bourdieu, P. 1984. *Homo Academicus*. Parigi: Minuit.

Bourdieu, P. 1986. The Forms of Capital, in J.G. Richardson (ed.), *Handbook of Theory and Research for the Sociology of Education*. New York: Greenwood Press, 241–58,

Bourdieu, P. 1990a. *The Logic of Practice*. Stanford, CA: Stanford University Press.

Bourdieu, P. 1990b. Animadversiones in Mertonem, in J. Clark, C. Modgil and S. Modgil (eds), *Robert, K. Merton: Consensus and Controversy*. London: The Falmer Press, 297–301.

Bourdieu, P. 1992. The Practice of Reflective Sociology (The Paris Workshop), in P. Bourdieu and L.J.D. Wacquant (eds), *An Invitation to Reflexive Sociology*. Chicago, IL: The University of Chicago Press, 217–60.

Bourdieu, P. 1993. Concluding Remarks: For a Sociogenic Understanding of Intellectual Works, in C. Calhoun, E. LiPuma and M. Postone (eds), *Bourdieu: Critical Perspectives*. Chicago, IL: The University of Chicago Press, 263–75.

Bourdieu, P. 1998. *Practical Reason*. Stanford, CA: Stanford University Press.

Bourdieu, P. 2001. *Science de la science et réflexivité*. Parigi: Raisons D'agir.

Bourdieu, P., Chamboredon, J.-C. and Passeron, J.-C. 1983. *Le métier de sociologue*. Berlin: Mouton.

Bourdieu, P. and Wacquant, L.J.D. 1992. The Purpose of Reflexive Sociology (The Chicago Workshop), in P. Bourdieu and L.J.D. Wacquant (eds), *An Invitation to Reflexive Sociology*. Chicago, IL: The University of Chicago Press, 61–215

Bronckart, J.P. and Schurmans, M.-N. 2001. Pierre Bourdieu – Jean Piaget: habitus, schème et construction psychologique, in B. Lahire (ed.), *Le travail sociologique de Pierre Bourdieu*. Parigi: La Découverte, 153–75.

Brubaker, R. 1985. "Rethinking Classical Sociology: The Sociological Vision of Pierre Bourdieu." *Theory and Society* 14(6): 745–75.

Brubaker, R. 1993. Social Theory as Habitus, in C. Calhoun, E. LiPuma and M. Postone (eds), *Bourdieu: Critical Perspectives*. Chicago, IL: The University of Chicago Press, 212–34.

Calhoun, C. 1993. Habitus, Field, and Capital: The Question of Historical Specificity, in C. Calhoun, E. LiPuma and M. Postone (eds), *Bourdieu: Critical Perspectives*. Chicago, IL: The University of Chicago Press, 61–88.

Calhoun, C. 1995. *Critical Social Theory*. Oxford: Blackwell.

Calhoun, C. 2000. Pierre Bourdieu, in G. Ritzer (ed.), *The Blackwell Companion to Major Social Theorists*. Oxford: Blackwell, 696–730.

Calhoun, C. 2013a, For the Social History of the Present: Bourdieu as Historical Sociology, in P.S. Gorski (ed.), *Bourdieu and Historical Analysis*. Durham, NC: Duke University Press, 36–66.

Camic, C. 2013b. Bourdieu's Two Sociologies of Knowledge, in P.S. Gorski (ed.), *Bourdieu and Historical Analysis*. Durham, NC: Duke University Press, 183–211.

Camic, C. and Gross, N. 1998. "Contemporary Developments in Sociological Theory: Current Projects and Conditions of Possibility." *Annual Review of Sociology* 24: 453–76

Cerulo, K.A. 1997. "Identity Construction: New Issues, New Directions." *Annual Review of Sociology* 23: 385–409.

Cicourel, A.V. 1993. Aspects of Structural and Processual Theories of Knowledge, in C. Calhoun, E. LiPuma and M. Postone (eds), *Bourdieu: Critical Perspectives*. Chicago, IL: The University of Chicago Press, 89–115.

Collins, J. 1993. Determination and Contradiction: An Appreciation and Critique of the Work of Pierre Bourdieu on Language and Education, in C. Calhoun, E. LiPuma and M. Postone (eds), *Bourdieu: Critical Perspectives*. Chicago, IL: The University of Chicago Press, 116–38.

Collins, R. 2004. *Interaction Ritual Chains*. Princeton, NJ: Princeton University Press.

Corcuff, P. 2001. Le collectif au singulier: en partant de l'habitus, in B. Lahire (ed.), *Le travail sociologique de Pierre Bourdieu*. Parigi: La Découverte, 95–120.

DiMaggio, P. 1979. "Review Essay on Pierre Bourdieu." *American Journal of Sociology* 84(6): 1460–74.

Dobbin, F. 2008. "The Poverty of Organizational Theory." *Theory and Society* 37: 53–63.

Dreyfus, H. and Rabinow, P. 1993. Can There be a Science of Existential Structure and Social Meaning?, in C. Calhoun, E. LiPuma and M. Postone (eds), *Bourdieu: Critical Perspectives*. Chicago, IL: The University of Chicago Press, 35–44.

Elster, J. 1983. *Sour Grapes*. Cambridge: Cambridge University Press.

Emirbayer, M. and Johnson, V. 2008. "Bourdieu and Organizational Analysis." *Theory and Society* 37: 1–44.

Emirbayer, M. and Schneiderhan, E. 2013. Dewey and Bourdieu on Democracy, in P.S. Gorski (ed.), *Bourdieu and Historical Analysis*. Durham, NC: Duke University Press, 131–57.

Ermakoff, E. 2013. Rational Choice May Take Over, in P.S. Gorski (ed.), *Bourdieu and Historical Analysis*. Durham, NC: Duke University Press, 89–107.

Eyal, G. 2013. Spaces between Fields, in P.S. Gorski (ed.), *Bourdieu and Historical Analysis*. Durham, NC: Duke University Press, 158–82.

Fabiani, J.-L. 2001. Les règles du champ, in B. Lahire (ed.), *Le travail sociologique de Pierre Bourdieu*. Parigi: La Découverte, 75–91.

Favereau, O. 2001. L'économie du sociologue ou: penser (l'orthodoxie) a partir de Pierre Bourdieu, in B. Lahire (ed.), *Le travail sociologique de Pierre Bourdieu*. Parigi: La Découverte, 255–314.

Friedland, R. 2001. "Religious Nationalism and the Problem of Collective Representation." *Annual Review of Sociology* 27: 125–52.

Garnham, N. 1993. Bourdieu, the Cultural Arbitrary, and Television, in C. Calhoun, E. LiPuma and M. Postone (eds), *Bourdieu: Critical Perspectives*. Chicago, IL: The University of Chicago Press, 178–92.

Gorski, P.S. 2013a. Introduction. Bourdieu as a Theorist of Change, in P.S. Gorski (ed.), *Bourdieu and Historical Analysis*. Durham, NC: Duke University Press, 3–15.

Gorski, P.S. 2013b. Bourdieusian Theory and Historical Analysis, in P.S. Gorski (ed.), *Bourdieu and Historical Analysis*. Durham, NC: Duke University Press, 327–66.

Hanks, W.F. 1993. Notes on Semantics in Linguistic Practice, in C. Calhoun, E. LiPuma and M. Postone (eds), *Bourdieu: Critical Perspectives*. Chicago, IL: The University of Chicago Press, 139–55.

Inglis, D. 2003. "Review of J. Verdès-Leroux, Deconstructing Pierre Bourdieu: Against Sociological Terrorism from the Left." *European Journal of Social Theory* 6(2): 253–68.

Jenkins, R. 1992. *Pierre Bourdieu*. London: Routledge.

Jenkins, R. 2005. Bourdieu, Pierre, in G. Ritzer (ed.), *Encyclopedia of Social Theory*, I. London: Sage. 66–71.

Lahire, B. 2001a. Pour une sociologie a l'état vif, in B. Lahire (ed.), *Le travail sociologique de Pierre Bourdieu*. Parigi: La Découverte, 5–20.

Lahire, B. 2001b. Champ, hors-champ, contrechamp, in B. Lahire (ed.), *Le travail sociologique de Pierre Bourdieu*. Parigi: La Découverte, 23–57.

Lahire, B. 2001c De la théorie de l'habitus à une sociologie psychologique, in B. Lahire (ed.), *Le travail sociologique de Pierre Bourdieu*. Parigi: La Découverte, 121–52.

Lash, S. 1993. Pierre Bourdieu: Cultural Economy and Social Change, in C. Calhoun, E. LiPuma and M. Postone (eds), *Bourdieu: Critical Perspectives*. Chicago, IL: The University of Chicago Press, 193–211.

Layder, D. 1994. *Understanding Social Theory*. London: Sage.

Lemieux, C. 2001. Une critique sans raison? L'approche bourdieusenne des médias et ses limites, in B. Lahire (ed.), *Le travail sociologique de Pierre Bourdieu*. Parigi: La Découverte, 205–29.

LiPuma, E. 1993. Culture and the Concept of Culture in a Theory of Practice, in C. Calhoun, E. LiPuma and M. Postone (eds), *Bourdieu: Critical Perspectives*. Chicago: The University of Chicago Press, 14–34.

Martin, J.L. 2003. "What Is Field Theory?" *American Journal of Sociology* 109(1): 1–49.

Monod, J.-C. 2001. Une politique du symbolique?, in Lahire, B. (ed.), *Le travail sociologique de Pierre Bourdieu*. Parigi: La Découverte, 231–53.

Mounier, P. 2001. *Pierre Bourdieu: Une introduction*. Parigi: La Découverte.

Nash, R. 2003. "Social Explanation and Socialization: On Bourdieu and the Structure, Disposition, Practice Scheme." *The Sociological Review* 51(1): 43–62.

Parker, J. 2000. Bourdieu: Structuration through Power, in *Structuration*. Philadelphia, PA: Open University Press, 39–51.

Pedler, E. and Ethis, E. 2001. La légitimité culturelle en questions, in B. Lahire (ed.), *Le travail sociologique de Pierre Bourdieu*. Parigi: La Découverte, 179–203.

Pinto, L. 2002. *Pierre Bourdieu et la théorie du monde sociale*. Parigi: Albin Michel.

Portes, A. 1998. "Social Capital: Its Origins and Applications in Modern Sociology." *Annual Review of Sociology* 24: 1–24.

Saint-Jacques, D. and Viala, A. 2001. À propos du champ littéraire: histoire, géographie, histoire littéraire, in B. Lahire (ed.), *Le travail sociologique de Pierre Bourdieu*. Parigi: La Découverte, 59–74.

Staubmann, H. 2005. Culture as a Subsystem of Action: Autonomous and Heteronomous Functions, in R.C. Fox, V.M. Lidz and H.J. Bershady (eds), *After Parsons*. New York: Russell Sage Foundation, 169–78.

Swartz, D.L. 2008. "Bringing Bourdieu's Master Concepts into Organizational Analysis." *Theory and Society* 37: 45–52.

Swartz, D.L. 2013. Metaprinciples for Sociological Research in a Bourdieusian Perspective, in P.S. Gorski (ed.), *Bourdieu and Historical Analysis*. Durham, NC: Duke University Press, 19–35.

Wacquant, L.J.D. 1992a. *Toward a Social Praxeology: The Structure and Logic of Bourdieu's Sociology*, in P. Bourdieu and L.J.D. Wacquant (eds), *An Invitation to Reflexive Sociology*. Chicago, IL: The University of Chicago Press, 1–59.

Wacquant, L.J.D. 1992b. How to Read Bourdieu, in P. Bourdieu and L.J.D. Wacquant (eds), *An Invitation to Reflexive Sociology*. Chicago, IL: The University of Chicago Press, 261–4.

Wacquant, L.J.D. 1993. Bourdieu in America: Notes on Transatlantic Importation of Social Theory, in C. Calhoun, E. LiPuma and M. Postone (eds), *Bourdieu: Critical Perspectives*. Chicago, IL: The University of Chicago Press, 235–62

Wacquant, L.J.D. 1996. "The Rise of Advanced Marginality: Notes on Its Nature and Implications." *Acta Sociologica* 39(2): 121–39.

Wacquant, L.J.D. 2002a. "The Sociological Life of Pierre Bourdieu." *International Sociology* 17(4): 549–56.

Wacquant, L.J.D. 2002b. "Scrutinizing the Street: Poverty, Morality, and the Pitfalls of Urban Ethnography." *American Journal of Sociology* 107(6): 1468–1532.

Zukin, S. and Smith Maguire, J. 2004. "Consumers and Consumption." *Annual Review of Sociology* 30: 173–97.

Chapter 3
Ethnomethodology

Preliminary Remarks

We shall first consider the object of study, the purpose, and the basic concepts of this perspective, connecting conversation analysis and cognitive sociology to it. Special attention will be paid to the contribution of Harold Garfinkel (1917–), who is the founder and the most outstanding representative of ethnomethodology (see Garfinkel 1984, 1988, 1996; Garfinkel and Sachs 1970. For an introduction to ethnomethodology, see Dal Lago and Giglioli 1983; Fele 1992, 2002; Giglioli 1993; Heritage 1984, 1987; Rawls 2000; Ritzer 2000: 245–70; Sharrock 1989, 2001; Zimmerman and Pollner 1971: 80–103). Though the followers of the ethnomethodological perspective have preferred to carry out research instead of indicating the theoretical sources that are relevant for it (Lynch 1999: 212–17), we shall dwell upon its relations with: (a) the phenomenological, interactionist and functionalist perspectives; (b) classical authors, such as Durkheim and Weber; (c) contemporary theoreticians, such as Alexander, Giddens, Collins, Goffman and others. Finally, we shall mention some fields of application, such as conversation analysis and the study of institutions and work environments.

Object of Study, Purpose, Premises and Basic Concepts

The methods (that is, the practices, or procedures) by which subjects (or "members") collaborate in providing their everyday activities – while they are performing (or "producing") them within specific local contexts – with order, meaning, description, explanations, and hence, rationality, are the object of study of ethnomethodology. Therefore, the context is a continuously renewed contingent creation produced by the members. The subjects, or "members," may be either persons involved in a particular interaction ("practical activity"), or an external observer of that context. In any case, members provide descriptions, interpretations and explanations (accounts) of that context, which are "ways in which persons organize views of themselves, of others, and of their social world" (Orbuch 1997: 455). Some examples of local contexts are a trial in a court; a university lecture; a series of recordings and conversations of scientists jointly engaged in a research activity in an astronomical observatory; intervention coordination activities carried out by call-center operators assigned to receive and sort out requests for aid and assistance.

The purpose of ethnomethodology is to shed light on the stable characteristics (the "invariant properties," or "formal structures") of everyday activities, for they are characterized by their uniformity, reproducibility and typicality, apart from the local context in which they are produced. They form the methods by which the members identify and reproduce in any contingent circumstance (a casual conversation, a business meeting, a written report, the drawing up of a company balance sheet, etc.) what they consider as common sense. The ethnomethodological perspective assumes that:

- Everyday-life phenomena – such as activities and reasoning – have a meaning, which the members generally understand and take for granted or evident.
- The members know and are able to recognize the invariant properties.
- These properties – like these phenomena – are produced by the members in local contexts.
- The members are competent, that is, able to know what they have to produce and the way in which they have to produce it in their verbal and non-verbal interactions, and consequently know the social order they create in any circumstance and place in which they are interacting. This order is contingent, as it changes depending on circumstances and places.
- A local context is formed by the methods through which the members provide it with sense and order.

- The agreement on the sense of phenomena – that is, its consistency and compatibility with the context – derives from the joint action (from the "work") of all the members.
- Descriptions, interpretations and explanations (accounts) of the social order, including those provided by the social scientists, are an integral part of the social order the members cooperate in locally producing. Therefore, the social order does not exist apart from the accounts members produce in particular local contexts. Consequently, the social order is an order of sense, recognized and newly formed in any particular circumstance.
- Descriptions and explanations provided by social scientists are based, in principle, on the same competence of the other members of that order.

This last assumption (called "unique adequacy") needs some explanation. Ethnomethodological research demands that a researcher have the same competencies as the members, whose practices (such as activities and reasonings) are his/her object of study. Therefore ethnomethodologists should have a first-hand knowledge of what is kept for granted within a particular milieu, and namely, be completely familiar with the stock of knowledge and practices that count for common understanding and social order. According to ethnomethodologists, the method called "documentary interpretation" is uniquely adequate to understanding what the members do and say in a particular environment, since those members make use of it in giving a sense to their interactions with the others. This method involves a systematic observation of the procedures through which members – in general, tacitly – jointly provide usual phenomena with a sense.

Only in this way is it possible to point out the modalities with which those who take part in a particular social context provide it with a common understanding, and consequently, an order or social structure. The meaning a subject attributes to a particular phenomenon is consistent with the knowledge it already has at its disposal. The subject considers this meaning evident and believes it is considered evident by the others (by other subjects in general, or by other particular ones) (Jedlowski 1994: 57–9). Depending on contingent circumstances, the social context may be considered as a job interview, a university exam, a request for alms, a scientific experiment, a medical examination, a meeting with some friends, etc. Researchers, like any other member, apply common-sense interpretations to the phenomena they observe in order to make them intelligible both to themselves and to others. The interpretations of those phenomena are necessarily selective, as they neglect some details the members consider insignificant because they are incompatible with their common-sense interpretation. Answers given by others to the questions put by the subject, operating instructions of an appliance or a computer, behaviors observed by the police and legal authorities entrusted with the production of criminal statistics, may become the object of a selective interpretation. In all those cases, the members provide a plausible interpretation of a phenomenon, which they draw from a repertoire of commonly understood interpretations, while neglecting the elements of the phenomenon that do not comply with that kind of interpretation.

The purpose of documentary interpretation is to point out and explain ("to document"), in the light of the examined phenomena, the background of common sense. What is documented by activities and reasoning forms the meaning context, or model, that is, the stock of knowledge considered relevant in a particular circumstance, which is the object of understanding. In other words, the background context is used as a reference by social scientists and ordinary people alike when they provide an observed phenomenon with a meaning. Not only the model is documented by the observation of a phenomenon, but also the description, interpretation or explanation (account) of that phenomenon form the model itself. The meaning context changes depending on the interpretation (or description, or explanation) given to it in every circumstance. The accounting of a phenomenon and its meaning context are therefore reciprocally related (reflexive property of accounts). The documentary interpretation method is used not only in ethnomethodology but also in everyday life. For example, the explanation of a death as a suicide involves a particular interpretation, in terms of common sense, of the meaning context that has characterized the last period, or the whole life, of the deceased person (this person might have committed suicide because he/she was depressed, socially isolated, seriously ill, jobless, etc.).

Therefore, that account becomes constitutive of a consistent meaning context attributed to that person at the moment of its death, and also prior to it. Consequently, the ethnomethodologists' interest is addressed to the way in which a meaning context is formed rather than to the reason why it has been formed in that way, considering the external, social and cultural constraints, as well as the expectations and identities of the actors (Silverman and Gubrium 1994: 180). A common-sense explanation can be formulated either by researchers, or by medical or judicial authorities, or by ordinary persons. They are, in any case, members of the social order, socially competent and able to understand one another. Therefore, they are in the position to account for, and by their account, to change a locally produced phenomenon (that is, within a particular meaning context), in the very moment they attribute a meaning to it, and – by doing so – form it. Members assert their competence when they use their stock of common sense in everyday life. This stock consists of a relatively stable corpus of knowledge, skills, beliefs, which is "socially warranted" in its validity (Garfinkel 1963: 215).

This stable stock of knowledge pre-exists the local context, which is contingent and changing. Members apply that stable stock of knowledge to any relevant context in that moment (that is, to the local environment of meaning, so that it appears in any particular circumstance to them). By doing so, these members prove there is a connection between the world of common sense and that particular context. Therefore, the contingent context they create and explain through their practices has the same properties of order, regularity and rationality characterizing the stable stock of knowledge they have available, and hence, the world of common sense in which they take part.

However, this connection does not exist in itself, since it is a consequence of what the members do, of the practices (activities and accounts) of which they avail themselves. These practices are stable ways, or "methods," by which members unavoidably provide the local context in which they are produced with the characters of uniformity, reproducibility, typicality, rationality. Though these methods are stable ("invariant"), the local contexts to which they can be applied are changing: the set of those methods, which each time are applied to different contexts, is called the "contingent corpus." The application of general knowledge to a particular context occurs by using the so-called "indexical" language expressions, which take their sense just from the context in which they are formulated. These indexical expressions refer to the relation between the particular circumstance of the moment and the underlying context of meaning in which, according to those who use that expression, that circumstance must be placed in order to be correctly understood.

Therefore, depending on the person who is speaking or acting, these indexical expressions specify the relation between the particular circumstance to which that utterance or behavior refers and the wider context of common sense that is recalled in that way. Examples of indexical expressions include these: in this case, here, now, bearing in mind the actual circumstances, in the light of these circumstances, for any practical purpose. Every time the members recall that context, they create it. In fact, a context of meaning does not exist in the abstract, that is, apart from member practices. Their "work" (in the ethnomethodological sense of active, continuous and collaborative commitment) produces that particular meaning context, and consequently the order or the social structure; the structure being socially created as soon as it is understood. In fact, through the indexical expressions, the members not only recall the context but also create the order (the uniformity, habit, consistency and rationality) they attribute to the underlying meaning context, that is, to their world of common sense (Garfinkel 1996: 6; Heritage 1984: 142–59).

In this way, that particular interaction occasion, too, receives the same character of uniformity, habit, consistency and rationality as any other similar occasion. The members consider all these occasions similar and, at the same time, make them similar through their practices. For example, the evening meeting of the members of a family, who have already met in the morning and use to meet every morning and evening, is a habit just because those persons consider it a habit and make it so by using suitable indexical expressions. In other words, through those expressions, the members create and re-create in any circumstance the sense, order and rationality of the social structure, showing themselves socially competent and, therefore, trustworthy. Accordingly, the use of indexical expressions is unavoidable in order to give a sense to the accounts (descriptions, interpretations and explanations) formulated either verbally or in writing, the members – including observers and experts in any field – provide in a particular circumstance. For example, when the actions or the intentions of a member have been misunderstood by the others and, in order to re-establish trust, it is necessary to give an account of the circumstances in which that misunderstanding occurred (Young 1995: 260–61).

The method of documentary interpretation, by which the members recall the underlying context of sense, allows understanding what different ways of carrying out investigations cannot reveal. Ethnomethodology aims at radically setting itself against the typical investigation ways, or methods (called by ethnomethodologists "constructive analysis"), that belong to traditional sociology (which is called "formal analysis, with particular reference to Parsons). Ethnomethodology does not question the methods (such as the statistical-quantitative methods) used, and the results achieved, by traditional sociology in describing and explaining the social order. Ethnomethodologists do not give their opinion on whether these descriptions and explanations (or accounts) are correct, suitable, important, consistent (ethnomethodological indifference) or not (Garfinkel and Sachs 1970, pp. : 345–346). Consequently, they do not appropriate any "social science model, method, or scheme of rationality for observing, analyzing and evaluating what members already can see and describe as a matter of course" (Lynch 1999: 221). From an ethnomethodological point of view, it should be remembered that traditional methods in sociology do not consider the need for the members, sociologists included, to use indexical expressions in order to give a sense to what they do and say. These expressions are considered by traditional sociology as an inconvenience, an obstacle to the achievement of an objectivity ideal in ordinary and scientific communication.

In fact, according to this ideal, communication should not dwell upon the local contexts of meaning in which it takes place, and be rational, consistent and complete in describing, interpreting and explaining the peculiar circumstances to which it refers. The remedies, which are suggested usually, and also by traditional sociology, in order to eliminate references to those circumstances, and consequently, indexical expressions, are to be clear in using words and utterances, and therefore always bear in mind the particular context in which they have been produced. These remedies are ineffective, because any formulation is included in a contingent context of meaning of which it is necessarily an integral part. Therefore intending to be clear and bear in mind the contingent context is not a remedy. Any communication must necessarily refer to it and, consequently, the use of indexical expressions becomes unavoidable.

In addition, the objects of traditional sociology are recognized phenomena described in terms of common sense, which in turn represents an actually used, though not recognized, resource. Ethnomethodology considers, instead, common sense as a recognized resource, and sets the formal properties of the everyday life world as its specific object of investigation. In other words, it investigates how – that is, through which procedures, standards or rules – common sense categories (such as, for example, the distinctions between male and female or between different jobs) are, at the same time, built and used through a collaborative work of the members. They are ordinary persons, as well as demographers and sociologists. In fact, these members create those categories every time they apply them, in the way they consider appropriate, to a particular circumstance or investigation. The creation of categories should therefore conform to what the members consider as common sense in that particular context of meaning. Categories indicate the activities and the other attributes (such as obligations, rights, knowledge) pertaining to the persons to which those categories make reference (for example, all the activities, knowledge, etc., pertaining to a waiter or to a lawyer).

The application of categories is governed by the consistency and economy rules. The consistency rule states that using a category involves using other ones belonging to the same group of categories (for example, the categories of lawyers, physicians and architects belong to the category group of professions). The economy rule prescribes that, within a group of categories, in any particular circumstance only a single category can be correctly applied to a particular member (for example, a person we meet in the street may be described either as "a passer-by" or as "my lawyer," but not simultaneously by both categories) (Fele 2002: 106–14; Psathas 1999: 142–6; Wieder 1971; Zimmerman and Wieder 1971: 290–95).

Among common sense categories, some of them – such as status, role and rule – are also commonly used in social sciences, though several attempts have been made to define these terms rigorously and objectively. In fact, social sciences, too, make use of interpretative procedures and common sense typifications every time analytic categories are applied to particular events or experiences in order to understand them. The interest of ethnomethodology is focused on the interpretative procedures by which social actors and observers (social scientists included) provide interactions with a meaning. Ethnomethodology dwells particularly upon the process by which the notion of social structure or organization is acquired and upon the use of language. The socialization process is not conventionally meant as a passive acquisition of norms and rules by a subject (such as a child or a stranger), but rather as an active acquisition of interpretative procedures through a continuous interaction of this subject with other ones (children and adults).

Once these procedures are learned, they provide interpretative patterns, which are used to give a sense to those interactions. If socialization has been successful, the interpretative patterns deriving from it are generally shared. Consequently, they conform to what is considered common sense in any contingent interaction produced within a particular social organization. In this way, the subject becomes socially competent. Interpretation patterns and procedures cannot exist outside the contingent interactions through which they have been formed, in which they can be applied, and which they constitute at the same time. The ethnomethodological analysis of language learning and use is aimed at highlighting the use actors make of these interpretative procedures in order to provide their interactions with meaning and existence (Cicourel 1974).

Conversation Analysis

This branch of study, which was started by Sachs, Schlegloff and Jefferson between the 1960s and the 1970s, is focused on the properties of conversations considered as a particular form of interaction (for an introduction, see Fele 2000: 121–42; Heritage 1984: 233–92). The sequences of continuous or successive turns of talk among participants form the analysis units. "Sequence organization, adjacency pairs, repair, turn-taking," are consequently the object of study (Fele 2002: 139). Participants collaborate in maintaining an order in their verbal interactions, and use to this end the cognitive resources they have at their disposal, considering themselves morally obliged to do so. Accordingly, this order is cognitive and moral at the same time (Heritage 1984: 292). It is interactively kept in any conversation, thus making conversation possible, and is characterized as follows:

1. It is achieved through conversation, and therefore cannot exist outside it.
2. It reveals itself through reciprocal (generally, not expressed) expectations, which change depending on the situation. For example, if participants define a situation by the same standard as an exam, a question is not interpreted as a request for information, but as a way for allowing the investigating person to check whether the person questioned knows the answer.
3. This order regulates turn-taking allocation, though not strictly, and possibly also the maximum number of these turns, establishing the repair mechanisms in case of errors or rule infringement.
4. As particularly regards turn-taking allocation, the order in verbal interactions establishes the circumstances determining who has the right to take the turn of talk (for example whether the current speaker is entitled and obliged to select the following speaker, or whether self-selection or another kind of standard may be applied to the following turn of talk, etc.).
5. It also regulates coordination problems among participants, such as talk overlapping and silences, or conversation fragments concerning events of different specificity (from background events in comparison with the object of a conversation, to immediately relevant events).
6. It reveals itself in several ways; for example, when, with regard to the conversation flow, there are negative elements (such as refusals, disagreement, and incomprehension) with hesitations, apologies, unnecessary explanations, and verbal mitigations. The maintenance of this order, as a result of the joint member "work," allows achieving mutual comprehension and communication (intersubjectivity) throughout the conversation. Otherwise, order and intersubjectivity would become impossible, because no single participant is in the position to fully control by him/herself the result of that verbal meeting (Fele 2002: 121–42; Heritage 1984: 233–92; Sachs, Schegloff and Jefferson 2000; Schegloff 2000).

Conversation analysis is generally considered as belonging to the ethnomethodological perspective, though some researchers have expressed their reservations (Ritzer 2000: 250) and some representatives of symbolic interactionism have shown their interest in this object of study (Fine 1990: 128–9). In fact, some of the themes of this perspective (such as the attention paid to the accounts provided by the members), as well as some investigation objects (such as the study of work settings) have been continued and further developed. In addition, some of its assumptions, or premises, are also shared by ethnomethodology. In particular:

1. Interactions (conversations) have an order, which is known, understood, by participants. While they are talking, these participants – who, until proved otherwise, are assumed to be socially competent members – discover, and at the same time create and keep, the social order (organization, structure).
2. The action of participants forms and renews, at the same time, its context, or environment: interaction is placed within a context of which it is an integral part.
3. All the interactive elements, including the apparently less significant and minor ones (such as gestures, grunts and other non-verbal elements), are relevant in showing its organized character.
4. The *ethnomethodologists'* task is to discover and describe the methods and procedures through which members carry out and contextually place their activities. The ethnomethodological approach concerning those methods and procedures (investigation on how) precedes any causal investigation concerning the properties of wider contexts (for example regulatory or organizational contexts) that bind or guide the interaction in that particular context (investigation on why, a peculiarity of traditional sociology) (Heritage 1984: 241–4; 1987: 258–60; Hilbert 1992: 197–203; Silverman and Gubrium 1994; Turner 1971: 187).

Like any other object of study in ethnomethodology, conversations are relevant in carrying out a micro- and, at the same time, macro-sociological analysis (Hilbert 1990). This may be illustrated by the following examples. First of all, some pieces of conversations occurring in particular contexts may underline the same recurring organization (for example, in the ways in which participants make efforts to find a remedy for problems and obstacles). In the second place, the turn of talk sequence within a conversation may emphasize stable differences of power among participants. Finally, the contexts in which those conversations are placed, and which those conversations create (for example, a conversation on medical issues in a hospital environment) bind, or guide, or direct those conversations (Schegloff 1987).

The conversations' object of study may occur in any informal or institutional context. At the beginning, the researcher's attention was focused on the object of informal everyday contexts (Heritage 1984: 237–40; 1987: 257): for example, the contexts provided by children's conversations (with other children or adults), in which communicative competences are produced and developed (Speier 1971). Later on, as from the 1980s, this analysis was extended also to institutional contexts, such as classrooms and courtrooms, and to institutional meeting places for doctors and patients. As from the 1990s, ethnomethodologists have mostly dwelt upon new institutional contexts. Among them, we mention:

1. Indirect interactions (mediated by computers) between computer designers and users, each category of subjects being characterized by specific assumptions that might create problems in the user–machine relations.
2. Relations between interviewers and interviewees, and the associated interpretation problems of their statements (questions and answers, respectively) and, as regards interviewers, in answer coding.
3. Finally, relations between subjects who have speech troubles and speech therapists, whose task is to help them to overcome the problems caused by their communication deficiencies (Arminen 1999: 255).

Ethnomethodology's Relation to Durkheim and Weber

Garfinkel's infrequent references to Durkheim and Weber include an appreciation of the potential contribution of these two classical authors to ethnomethodology. Garfinkel refers to Durkheim's statement concerning the objective reality of social action, and interprets it (in dispute with Parsons) as a described and explained reality, which members organize and reproduce at the same time (Garfinkel 1988: 103; 1996: 10–11). As regards Weber, Garfinkel refers to the relevance given by this author to social actor trust: in the case of market transactions, trust is the necessary condition for calculating the transaction results in advance (Garfinkel 1963: 208–209). He also refers to the potential contribution of this author to the study of the relation between individual experience structures and social order organization (Garfinkel 1952: 1, cited in Heritage 1984: 9). A different matter is the relation between ethnomethodology, on one hand, and Durkheim and Weber, on the other hand. An in-depth study (Hilbert 1992, particularly: 162–5) has pointed out a strong theoretical continuity between these authors.

In detail:

a. The notion of reflexivity (of a reciprocal relation between the description of a social order and the order itself) is compatible with the relevance Durkheim and Weber have attributed to the activities carried out by the actors and aimed at creating and maintaining the social order.

b. Ethnomethodology as well as Durkheim and Weber do not reify the social structure, in the sense of attributing to it an effect that may leave actor practices out of consideration. In addition, concerning the explanation of social action, they consider the constraints involved in this structure.

c. According to another shared thesis, these constraints, though deriving from actor practices, have a real, or objective, character.

d. Ideas, according to Weber, and psychic manifestations, according to Durkheim, are able to exert constraints on individuals only insofar as they are transformed into their individual activities or practices.

e. It is another shared thesis that, for individuals, social order and reality assume these activities or practices, and derive from them.

f. Ethnomethodological indifference is compatible with Weber's indifference to the truth content of ideas, as well as with Durkheim's indifference to the attribution of a moral character given to a particular community by its members.

g. Another thesis shared by ethnomethodology as well as by Weber and Durkheim, states that intersubjectivity – or the possibility different subjects have to understand and communicate with one another – is the result of the practices of actors who are jointly engaged in supporting an objective world.

h. Considering that (from Durkheim's point of view) social order coincides with social reality, the typical-ideal (in Weber's classification), rational, traditional and charismatic guidelines of action, and hence, social order, are formed (from an ethnomethodological point of view) by the practices of competent members.

i. These practices are indispensable for preventing an *anomie* condition, and, at the same time, supporting actor orientations toward realities *endowed* with an either bureaucratic-rational (Weber) or sacred (Durkheim) character, which are different from the everyday reality members encounter and constitute.

Ethnomethodology Relation with Parsons' Functionalism, Schutz's Phenomenology, and Symbolic Interactionism

The relations between ethnomethodology and other sociological approaches are an object of discussion, and hence, at least partly, controversial. Garfinkel and some other ethnomethodologists have mentioned on several occasions the existing contrast between ethnomethodology and Parsons' functionalism, and, instead, the continuity between ethnomethodology and Schutz's phenomenological sociology (without underlining their differences). The relation between ethnomethodology and symbolic interactionism has been discussed by several representatives of the former approach, such as Boden, Wieder and Zimmerman, and Denzin, who is close to the latter perspective.

Concerning the contrast between ethnomethodology and functionalism, we can see that "traditional sociology" (reference is made to Parsons, and in general, to the American functionalism) (Hilbert 1992: 169) does not consider the introduction of individual actions into a context of rules as a problem. When this introduction is imperfect, both the action and the actor are considered as socially deviant, and consequently, social control mechanisms are introduced, so that rules may determine the action. The ethnomethodological approach objects that:

a. The application fields of rules are not (and cannot be) sufficiently determined.

b. Rule application modalities to particular meaning contexts, that is, to particular situations, are not (and cannot be) sufficiently defined.

c. This conception does not consider the most relevant thing for the actors: a reciprocal possibility to understand each other and to morally answer for their actions. From an ethnomethodological point of view, rules are constitutive of a contingent meaning and activity context members create every time they interpret and transform them into practice.

d. There is a reciprocal, or reflexive, relation between rules and context: the contextual application of rules creates a contingent context and, at the same time, depends on it.

The ethnomethodological reconsideration of the relation between action and rules falls within an overall criticism to functionalist and neo-functionalist sociology. According to Garfinkel, Parsons' analytic-formal sociology has made a distinction between actual or "concrete" actions and actions interpreted by analytic categories. In this connection, it has maintained that order does not derive from the plenum of actual reality, which is considered as not empirically observable, but from the application of analytic categories (Rawls 2000: 570). Ethnomethodology acknowledges the merits of traditional sociology in observing and describing the social order. However, ethnomethodological studies have evidenced that this order (or structure, or meaning) is spontaneously created within local contexts, and reflexively described and accounted for by the members. Parsons and conventional sociology in general, necessarily miss what is the actual focus of the ethnomethodological approach, namely, how order ensues from what members do. It is not a question of pursuing a radically individualistic program of study focused on actors,' or members,' practices, leaving aside meanings, rules, and norms. Garfinkel responds in this way to Alexander's neo-functionalist criticism, upon which we shall later dwell (Alexander 1988: 236–45). Rules do not pre-exist to a given context of meaning. Instead, they are implemented as soon as they are found, described and explained.

In contrast, the relation of ethnomethodology with Schutz's phenomenology is based on a declared continuity, despite some significant differences. The object of both sociological approaches is the common-sense world considered as a flow of experiences subjects use to arrange according to their own relevance standards, which in turn differ from those that are relevant in scientific knowledge. Therefore, subjects interpret and account their world of meaning while they are socially building it. The epistemological principles of neutrality (phenomenology) and ethnomethodological indifference (ethnomethodology) are necessary for identifying the socially given premises, which conform to and support common-sense interpretations. These premises reflexively interact with the observation contents and the ways in which they have been carried out (Garfinkel 1963: 210–14; 1984: 76–9, 100–103, 272–7; Schutz 1962: 40–44. See also Cicourel 1974: 33–9; Heap and Roth 1973: 364; Muzzetto 1997: 289–90, 313–14; Sharrock 2001: 252).

Investigative methods that are consistent with these two perspectives (respectively, the formulation of ideal types and the documentary interpretation method) serve, however, different objectives. The typical-ideal method of phenomenological sociology has the purpose of achieving a relatively objective interpretation of the aspects of reality having an intersubjective character. Intersubjectivity is achieved through typifications formulated by social actors, and constitutes one of their a-priori assumptions. These social actors take for granted, until proved to the contrary, that their points of view are exchangeable, and that their relevance system is consistent with those of the other actors (Schutz 1962: 11–12). As we previously remarked, the documentary interpretation method pursues a different goal: to show how intersubjectivity is the result of the localized and contingent practices of the actors, or members, the method itself being one of those practices (Fele 2002: 42–7; Garfinkel 1984: 76–103; Heritage 1987: 237–9, 242; Heap and Roth 1973: 364; Muzzetto 1997: 289–91; Rawls 2000: 547–8).

The conception of social world is different here, too, since, according to ethnomethodology, it is formed by intentional acts of consciousness. According to ethnomethodology, it is formed instead by interpretative and explicative procedures, or practices, through which subjects provide the social world with a meaning in particular meaning contexts (Giglioli 1993: 666; Heap and Roth 1973: 363–4; Holstein and Gubrium 1998: 140–41). Finally, the potential theoretical contribution is also different. In phenomenological sociology, it is the identification of how social reality is stratified according to the actor relevance systems (Schutz 1964: 120–34). In ethnomethodology, this contribution is the identification of the stable or "invariant" properties that create and give order and meaning to localized social contexts.

Like symbolic interactionism, both Schutz's phenomenological sociology and ethnomethodology underline "how meanings are created by actors interacting in situations" (Turner 1998: 413; cf. also Denzin 1983: 133–5), and, more generally, the social construction process of common sense knowledge in everyday life (Douglas 1971; Psathas 1968: 510–20). In addition, symbolic interactionism shares with ethnomethodology an interest in the sociology of accounts (descriptions, explanations, interpretations). Furthermore, conversation analysis – an investigation field that may be considered as proximate to ethnomethodology – dwells, like symbolic interactionism – upon "the intertwining of meaning, shared symbols, joint action, and social order" (Boden 1990b: 265). However, the perspectives of phenomenological sociology and symbolic interactionism do not agree with the ethnomethodological conception of order as determined by a situation (Meltzer, Petras and Reynolds 1975: 79), or better, by a local meaning context.

Ethnomethodologists consider the structured, orderly character of the social world, such as it appears in everyday life and in sociological descriptions and explanations, as the result of a continuous collaborative activity of the social actors (Boden 1990b: 191; Garfinkel 1988: 103; Zimmermann and Wieder 1971: 290–91). This conception of social order has not been judged quite convincing on the symbolic interactionism approach. In fact, the objection has been raised that it is not clear "where and how does the meaning originate, how it is organized, under what conditions it is stabilized, and most centrally how one goes about studying such fabrics and conditions of human experience" (Denzin 1971b: 296; cf. also Fine 1990: 139). In the study of processes (such as socialization and the making of the self and identity) and structures (such as organizations and organization fields), the interactionist perspective underlines their symbolic character, whose sense is negotiated within the boundaries provided by consolidated meanings (Charon 2001: 168–9; Denzin 1983: 135–8; Fine 1993: 78–9; Sandstrom et al. 2001: 219–21, 224–5).

In contrast with this perspective, according to which situations and meanings are established and agreed by the selves of interacting actors, in ethnomethodology, "enacted local practices are not texts which symbolize 'meanings''meanings' or events" (Garfinkel 1996: 8). The activity, or "work," by which people give a meaning to their lives and worlds, contextually changes and therefore is not an automatic process (Holstein and Gubrium 1998: 142–3; Lemert 1979: 297–9; Silverman and Gubrium 1994: 194–5). Dwelling upon the way in which the actors define a situation (as the symbolic interactionism perspective suggests) is only a preliminary stage to ethnomethodological investigation. This investigation should be aimed at identifying the ways in which the actors give a sense to their environment while they are building it through their practices (Cicourel 1995: 111). The interest of ethnomethodology in contingent situations, which constitute these processes and structures, and are included in them, may point out the invariant practices through which common sense is formed and kept within interaction micro-contexts (such as, for example, in a conversation, and in general, in the use of language in any circumstance).

These observations suit Goffman in particular, an author who is often considered close to the symbolic interactionism perspective, and they also suit other outstanding representatives of that perspective. As regards Goffman, his work has been considered by some representatives of ethnomethodology as "an extraordinary starting point and an almost inexhaustible source of inspiration for those who have begun to take the study of communicative situations and conversation forms seriously" (Fele and Giglioli 2000: 13. Cf. also Cicourel 1964: 65). Furthermore, Goffman has been assigned the merit of having introduced a social actor model provided with common-sense rationality. This has allowed Goffman not only to specify and check hypotheses throughout his ethnographic research. Goffman's social actor model is, however, considered inadequate, since the author does not explain whether and how the social actor's perspective differs from the researcher-observer perspective. In addition, Goffman – like Mead and other representatives of symbolic interactionism, such as Tamotsu Shibutani and Ralph H. Turner – does not explain how these actors achieve the interpretative procedures (or general rules) by which they interpret their environment, thus providing it with a social and normative order. An order through which – like an external observer – the actors are able to recognize the correctness and suitability of the observed behaviors (Cicourel 1964: 59–60, 65; 1974: 23–33, 40–41).

The Relation of Ethnomethodology to Certain Contemporary Sociology Theoreticians

Garfinkel's works, and in general, those of the representatives of the ethnomethodological perspective, have encouraged a great deal of exegetic – and often critical – literature (Fele 2002: 65–6). Here, we shall only consider the evaluations made by some of the numerous scholars who have personally contributed to the sociological theory. This will allow us to better assess the reception of ethnomethodology by some influential sociologists who are differently oriented. Generally speaking, we leave here apart Garfinkel's influence on contemporary sociological theory, as in most cases it can be hardly assessed. However, we shall mention his influence on Giddens, which this author openly recognizes.

We previously briefly mentioned the evaluations made by the neo-functionalist researcher Alexander, but now, we wish to examine them more in detail. Alexander objects to Garfinkel and the other ethnomethodologists that focusing on the contingent practices of the members (the social actors) may provide a theoretical contribution on condition that the collective rules are considered. In fact, these rules form the social order, and organize and tie up individual activities. Disregarding this common normative foundation involves a radical individualism. If actors produce norms and meanings through their activities, they do not take into account the existence of a social order. Therefore, the notion itself of indexicality loses its sense. In fact, through indexical expressions, the subjects recall that order (Alexander 1988: 236–45).

Collins, too, has expressed partly similar evaluations. According to Collins (1992: 347–65), ethnomethodology has evidenced the weakness of cognitive theories that neglect the problem of indexicality in any communication or interpretative procedure. Another merit of ethnomethodology is its contribution, in micro-sociological terms, to the description and explanation of macro-sociologically relevant phenomena. Examples of it are the bureaucratization process; the use of political tactics exploiting the legitimization, which power draws from its stability; the social change deriving from a precarious coexistence of local micro-orders. However, Collins seems to share Alexander's criticism, according to which common cultural rules are taken for granted without explaining how persons acquire this culture (Collins 1992: 354). Collins adds some other critical remarks: in the first place, "the world is not always considered ordinary by any person on any occasion," and therefore, the validity of a common understanding for the members cannot be a-priori assumed. In the second place, Garfinkel has given two different answers to the question: what keeps society together? First of all, there is "a set of procedures through which persons avoid questioning reality." Secondly, any breach of the usual procedures by which the actors support and build their ordinary world produces strong emotional reactions that reaffirm the infringed procedures (Collins 1992: 350–51, 357–9).

Commenting on the ethnomethodological perspective from the point of view of symbolic interactionism, Denzin objects that this perspective does not explain how meanings and rules, and hence social order, are formed and strengthened. In addition, it does not indicate which is the most suitable investigative method, considering that the documentary analysis method is commonly used by the ordinary social actors (Denzin 1971b: 296–7). In his criticism (which is carried out from a point of view which grants a privilege to situation analysis, and therefore is close to the symbolic interactionism approach), Goffman connects Garfinkel's ethnomethodology to Schutz's phenomenological sociology. The object of both perspectives is, in fact, the common-sense world of everyday life articulated in different "finished provinces of meaning" or "multiple realities." Particularly Garfinkel maintains that the sense of the whole everyday reality is generated by a limited number of rules sociologists are asked to point out. However, he does not specify how many are these rules, which standards determine their number, which is the relation existing between everyday reality and the different imaginary "worlds," and whether the world of meaning of everyday life is produced by its own rules (Goffman 1974: 3–6, 8).

Finally, Giddens remarks that the observer's validity criteria cannot coincide with those used by the subjects: an observer – such as a social scientist, and particularly, an ethnomethodologist – provides descriptions and explanations of what the actors do. Their validity cannot be assessed through the common sense standards used by the actors themselves, because "otherwise, the result would be a hopeless relativism." Different standards, namely, those used by an observer or a researcher, become therefore relevant. In addition, Garfinkel does not seem to make any distinction between two different meanings of the word "context." Consequently, his thesis, according to which the meaning of an expression depends on the context, is not clear. In fact, in a first meaning of this term, the word context refers to the space-time position of statements. In a second meaning, it refers to the existence of tacit rules that make it possible to understand these statements (Giddens 1979: 48–55). Despite these objections, Giddens shares without reserve the interest of ethnomethodology in the analysis of the local contexts of interactions, declaring in this regard his intellectual debt to Garfinkel. Therefore, according to Giddens, too, socially competent members act within local contexts complying with rules, or procedures they create as soon as they apply them (Giddens 1984: xxv, 18, 71).

Some Applications of the Ethnomethodological Perspective

A great deal of empirical research has been carried out according to this perspective or to contiguous ones, such as conversation analysis and cognitive sociology. Several investigations concern institutional and particularly, work settings (Fele 2002: 143–203; Heritage 1987: 261–5; Ritzer 2000: 261–4). For illustrative purposes, reference will be made here to some investigations, which Garfinkel and other ethnomethodologists carried out not only in work environments. The documentary method has been used to shed light on the common-sense premises guiding subjects in their interpretation of particular events, and the reciprocal trust in member cooperation to observe and keep those premises. These premises include a set of beliefs on reality, the self, and the others, which by ethnomethodologists are called "mundane reason" and are based on the prejudice (as Pollner calls it) of a "real" or "objective" order of events (Pollner 1995: 22, 242).

The sociological community is familiar with the empirical investigations carried out by Garfinkel, sometimes also with the cooperation of some colleagues (Garfinkel 1963, 1984; Garfinkel et al. 1981). Some of these investigations had an experimental character. In one of them, for example, the researcher deliberately infringed, without giving any explanation, the rules prescribing the correct moves of a particular party game, and studied the reactions of the other participants (such as showing surprise, perplexity, irritation or amusement). In a second test, some students – further to the researcher's invitation – were asked to provide with a meaning and comment the answers a false "adviseor" gave to questions concerning their personal problems. As a matter of fact, these answers had been given at random and therefore had no sense. Nevertheless, these students expected that the answers were delivered by a real adviser and consequently, they created the sense of those answers by themselves. In some other tests, the subjects were assigned to simulate being guests in their own homes; or, to repeatedly ask for explanations on the (actually, absolutely clear) meaning of a particular statement made by one of their relatives or by an acquaintance; or, again, to ask the cashiers of a supermarket for a discount. In all these examples, the researcher had led the subjects to infringe the common-sense expectations of the other persons who were taking part in that particular situation: their reaction brought to light those expectations, which were usually tacit or taken for granted.

Garfinkel carried out also investigations of a non-experimental character, mostly concerning particular work settings. In one of these investigations, the author proved that there was an actual – though not declared – cooperation between the staff of a suicide-prevention center and the officer charged of investigating the causes of some suspicious deaths. In fact, all the cases – always of a different nature – submitted to their attention, were jointly interpreted according to common-sense categories used in their peculiar environment. This cooperation led to the issuing of a report, in which a particular explanation of a suspicious death was reported in such a way as to contrast in advance any criticism, according to which that explanation might be incomplete or wrong. This report was always open to any revision, despite the pretense of being exhaustive and exact. Similarly, during a judicial trial, the ambiguity of any concrete situation, emphasized by the different and incompatible interpretations maintained by the attorneys, made it impossible to literally apply the formal rules prescribing the behavior of a member of the jury in expressing verdicts (such as impartiality, observance of laws and judge's directives, attention to the arguments of the parties and to the probative material, without, however, making a judgment while a trial is still in course, etc.). The verdict was formulated in such a way as to validate the decision made, showing at a later stage its common sense, rationality and procedural correctness, though the members of the jury had not been aware of it until that moment.

In another study, Garfinkel pointed out that the patient records kept by a non-residential psychiatric clinic were so incomplete that they did not even allow reconstructing their course within the organization. Those records included biographical details, entry and exit dates, information on provided treatments, the way in which the first contact had taken place, the professional position of those who had addressed the patients to the clinic, etc. However, through those records it was not possible to determine which patient characteristics might prove relevant in predicting that course. The presumed predicting criteria were in fact coinciding with those used in selecting the patients, and therefore, instead of being general and impersonal, they would change depending on the need to plan the entry and exit flows of patients, or on the relation established between the staff of the clinic assigned to fill the records and the patients. As a matter of fact, each patient was a special case, with its own history and discharge perspective: the knowledge the staff had of that particular case would influence the contents of the records. In addition, these relations observed several non-declared rules. In virtue of those rules, the medical and nursing staff used to cooperate in keeping under psychiatric treatment patients they actually neglected, but whose discharge would have been considered inappropriate. Discharging those patients would have been considered an irresponsible action from a medical point of view, in the light of possible future events and the medical practices in force in that clinic. The incompleteness of records was, therefore, an integral part of the social organization of that clinic. That organization was known by the staff and its knowledge was taken for granted.

In a different work environment – an astronomical observatory – Garfinkel and his colleagues pointed out how the activities jointly carried out by a team of astrophysicists during a night of work were essential for the purpose of defining an object, which had been recorded by the optical observation instruments, and up to then was unknown, as a "pulsar" (that is, according to the astronomical terms generally used in that particular environment). The discovery of this pulsar, the shape and definition an initially undefined object had taken, were not a simple consequence of those recordings. They were a consequence of their intertwining with the concomitant practices of the scientists: their observations on a register book, written in different moments of that night, and their associated dialogues and comments. Those practices were entirely contextual to that particular physical (the astronomical observatory) and time (that night of work) setting. The difference of those observations, collected in different moments of that night, did not prevent them from being used for the production of a unitary report that might be acceptably argued and justified by other colleagues-scientists at a later stage. Therefore, conforming to an assumption of ethnomethodology, those practices did not only produce the discovery of a pulsar, but also the pulsar itself, as that object could not exist independently of them.

Garfinkel's investigations are not exclusively focused on particular work or organizational environments. In one of his first publications, the author dwells upon the necessary conditions for the success of a degradation, or loss of status, ceremony. The accuser places him/herself as the visible representative of the moral order of a group, and considers the accused subject as though it had always belonged to a category of persons deserving indignation, ritual destruction and symbolic removal from the lawful order (Garfinkel 1956). In another well-known study, the author aims at pointing out all the activities (the "work") necessary to understand and, at the same time, form what is generally considered common sense (consequently, not in a particular environment, such as for example a work environment). The different anatomical, cultural and social distinctions between male and female have the value of generally shared common sense. The study is focused on a transsexual teenager (Agnes), originally belonging to the male sexual gender.

The examined stages are three. During the first stage – until the age of 17 years – this person was considered by the others (but not by herself) a male. During the second stage, Agnes developed a feminine aspect, though she anatomically had male characteristics (however, with an undeveloped and not functioning sexual apparatus) and, on her request, was operated by the removal of her male organs. Agnes had to overcome a difficult physical, social and cultural adaptation to her new condition. Finally, during the third stage, as from the age of 19 years, her adaptation was successfully completed. In an appendix, the reader is informed that, as from the age of 12 years, Agnes had secretly taken estrogenic substances with the effect of inhibiting a normal sexual transformation during the puberty. The sexual belonging of Agnes – this is the thesis Garfinkel seeks to demonstrate – is not a natural event, which leaves aside her position within common sense contexts. On the contrary, this belonging derives from a number of consistent and ongoing activities, which subjects carry out in order to keep, both for themselves and for the others, a stable and non-equivocal sexual position.

Several other authors have carried out ethnomethodological research activities. In this regard, Garfinkel himself (1988: 106–107) and other researchers (Fele 2002: 143–203; Heritage 1984: 293–304; 1987: 251–6; Ritzer 2000: 261–4) have provided some examples of investigations carried out in a similar way. Many of these investigations concern work, or in general, organizational environments – or contexts – such as laboratories, factories, offices, places in which music is played or art works are exhibited, call centers for emergency calls, control towers. An environment may be simultaneously located in different places, such as in the case of transactions among currency market operators (Knorr Cetina and Bruegger 2001). These studies, which usually include an analysis of member conversations, are aimed at pointing out how members make these environments relevant, how these environments influence the way in which members interact, and how conversation analysis and social structure study mutually integrate themselves. In other words, these investigations emphasize the practices through which members – by means of categories – set and create a particular organizational context (Psathas 1999).

The methodological and epistemological studies, which formulate critical evaluations on the reliability and validity of the usual investigation methods and official statistics, are kept apart from those empirical investigations. In the first case, these methods consist of interviews, questionnaires, demographic, historical and experimental surveys. These methods assume that the social actors are able to perceive and interpret in a stable and uniform way their action in everyday life, and that everyday life is sufficiently determined in all its aspects. In fact, only on those non-realistic conditions a researcher would be able to classify and measure social phenomena considered relevant (Cicourel 1964). In the second case, as particularly regards suicide and crime statistics, they cast no light on the arbitrary character with which they are formulated. Considering an event as either a suicide or a crime depends on stereotype interpretations and, consequently, on decisions made by particular social actors (police officers, coroners, magistrates). These social actors are influenced by regulations, knowledge and assumptions they generally take for granted and apply in different manners to a contingent case (Cicourel 1995; Eglin 1987).

References

Alexander, J.C. 1988. *Actions and Its Environments: Toward A New Synthesis*. New York: Columbia University Press.

Arminen, I. 1999. "Conversation Analysis: A Quest for Order in Social Interaction and Language Use." *Acta Sociologica* 42: 251–7.

Baert, P. 1998. *Social Theory in the Twentieth Century*. Cambridge: Polity Press.

Best, J. 1995. Debates about Constructionism, in E. Rubington and M.S. Weinberg (eds), *The Study of Social Problems*. New York: Oxford University Press, 341–51.

Boden, D. 1990a. People Are Talking: Conversation Analysis and Symbolic Interaction, in H.S. Becker and M.M. McCall (eds), *Symbolic Interaction and Cultural Studies*. Chicago, IL: The University of Chicago Press, 244–74.

Boden, D. 1990b. The World as It Happens: Ethnomethodology and Conversation Analysis, in G. Ritzer (ed.), *Frontiers of Social Theory: The New Syntheses*. New York: Columbia University Press, 185–205.

Charon, J. 2001. *Symbolic Interactionism: An Introduction, an Interpretation, an Integration*. Upper Saddle River, NJ: Prentice Hall.

Cicourel, A. 1964. *Method and Measurement in Sociology*. New York: The Free Press.

Cicourel, A. 1974. *Cognitive Sociology*. New York: The Free Press.

Cicourel, A. 1995. *The Social Organization of the Juvenile Justice*. New Brunswick, NJ: Transaction Publishers.

Collins, R. 1992. *Teorie sociologiche*. Bologna: Il Mulino.

Dal Lago, A. and Giglioli, P.P. 1983. *Etnometodologia*. Bologna: Il Mulino, 9–51.

Denzin, N.K. 1971a. Symbolic Interactionism and Ethnomethodology, in Jack D. Douglas (ed.), *Understanding Everyday Life*. London: Routledge & Kegan Paul, 259–84.

Denzin, N.K. 1971b. Symbolic Interactionism and Ethnomethodology: A Comment on Zimmerman and Wieder, in Jack D. Douglas (ed.), *Understanding Everyday Life*. London: Routledge & Kegan Paul, 295–8.

Denzin, N.K. 1983. Interpretive Interactionism, in G. Morgan (ed.), *Beyond Method*. Newbury Park, CA: Sage, 129–46.

Douglas, J.D. 1970. *Understanding Everyday Life: Toward the Reconstruction of Sociological Knowledge*. New Brunswick. NJ: Transaction.

Eglin, P. 1987. The Meaning and Use of Official Statistics in the Explanation of Deviance, in R.J. Anderson, J.A. Hughes and W.W. Sharrock (eds), *Classic Disputes in Sociology*. London: Allen & Unwin, 184–212.

Fele, G. 1992. "La comprensione nell'interazione." *Rassegna Italiana di Sociologia* 33: 422–38.

Fele, G. 2002. *Etnometodologia*. Bologna: Il Mulino.

Fele, G. and Giglioli, P.P. 2000. Introduzione, in P.P. Giglioli and G. Fele (eds), *Linguaggio e contesto sociale*. Bologna: Il Mulino, 7–34.

Fine, G.A. 1990. Symbolic Interactionism in the Post-Blumerian Age, in G. Ritzer (ed.), *Frontiers of Social Theory: The New Synthesis*. New York: Columbia University Press, 117–57.

Fine, G.A. 1991. "On the Macrofoundations of Microsociology." *The Sociological Quarterly* 32: 161–77.

Fisher, B. and Strauss, A.L. 1978. Interactionism, in T. Bottomore and R. Nisbet (eds), *A History of Sociological Analysis*. New York: Basic Books, 457–98.

Garfinkel, H. 1952. The Perception of the Other: A Study on Social Order. Unpublished dissertation, Department of Social Relations, Harvard University.

Garfinkel, H. 1956. "Conditions of Successful Degradation Ceremonies." *American Journal of Sociology* 61: 420–24.

Garfinkel, H. 1963. A Conception of, and Experiment with, "Trust" as a Condition of Stabled Concerted Actions, in O.J. Harvey (ed.), *Motivation and Social Interaction*. New York: The Ronald Press, 187–238.

Garfinkel, H. 1984. *Studies in Ethnomethodology*. Cambridge: Polity Press.

Garfinkel, H. 1988. "Evidence for Locally Produced, Naturally Accountable Phenomena of Order, Logic, Reason, Meaning, Method, Etc. in and as of the Essential Quiddity of Immortal Ordinary Society (I of V): An Announcement of Studies." *Sociological Theory* 6: 103–109.

Garfinkel, H. 1996. "Ethnomethodology's Program." *Social Psychology Quarterly* 59: 5–21.

Garfinkel, H. and Sachs, H. 1970. On Formal Structures of Practical Actions, in J.C. McKinney and E.A. Tiryakian (eds), *Theoretical Sociology*. New York: Appleton-Century-Crofts.

Garfinkel, H., Lynch, M. and Livingstone, E. 1981. "The Work of a Discovering Science Construed with Material from the Optically Discovered Pulsar." *Philosophy of the Social Sciences* 11: 131–58.

Giddens, A. 1979. *Nuove regole del metodo sociologico*. Bologna: Il Mulino.

Giddens, A. 1984. *The Constitution of Society*. Oxford: Basil Blackwell.

Giglioli, P.P. 1993. Etnometodologia, in *Enciclopedia della Scienze Sociali*, Volume 3. Rome: Istituto della Enciclopedia Italiana, 664–72.

Goffman, E. 1974. *Frame Analysis*. New York: Harper & Row.

Heap, J. L. and Roth, P.A. 1973. "On Phenomenological Sociology." *American Sociological Review* 38: 354–67.

Heritage, J.C. 1984. *Garfinkel and Ethnomethodology*. Cambridge: Polity Press.

Heritage, J.C. 1987. Ethnomethodology, in A. Giddens and J. Turner (eds), *Social Theory Today*. Oxford: Polity Press, 224–72.

Hilbert, R.A. 1990. "Ethnomethodology and the Micro-Macro Order." *American Sociological Review* 55: 794–808.

Hilbert, R.A. 1992. *The Classical Roots of Ethnomethodology: Durkheim, Weber and Garfinkel*. Chapel Hill, NC, and London: University of North Carolina Press.

Holstein, J.A. and Gubrium, J.F. 1998. Phenomenology, Ethnomethodology, and Interpretive Practice, in N.K. Denzin and Y.S. Lincoln (eds), *Strategies of Qualitative Inquiry*. London: Sage, 137–57.

Jedlowski, P. 1994. "'Quello che tutti sanno.' Per una discussione sul concetto di senso comune." *Rassegna Italiana di Sociologia* 35: 49–77.

Knorr Cetina, K. and Bruegger, U., 2001. "Transparency Regimes and Management by Content in Global Organizations: The Case of Institutional Currency Trading." *American Sociological Association 96th Annual Meeting, Regular Session on Social Theory*. Chicago, IL: August 18–21.

Lemert, C. 1979. "De-Centered Analysis." *Theory and Society* 7: 289–306.

Lynch, M. 1999. "Silence in Context: Ethnomethodology and Social Theory." *Human Studies* 22: 211–33.

Meltzer, B.N., Petras, J.W. and Reynolds, L.T. 1975. *Symbolic Interactionism: Genesis, Varieties and Criticism*. London: Routledge & Kegan Paul.

Muzzetto L. 1997. *Fenomenologia ed etnometodologia. Percorsi della teoria dell'azione*. Milan: FrancoAngeli.

Orbuch, T.L. 1997. "People Accounts Count: The Sociology of Accounts." *Annual Review of Sociology* 23: 455–78.

Pollner, M. 1995. *La ragione mondana*. Bologna: Il Mulino.

Psathas, G. 1968. "Ethnomethods and Phenomenology." *Social Research* 35: 500–20.

Psathas, G. 1999. "Studying the Organization in Action: Membership Categorization and Interaction Analysis." *Human Studies* 22: 139–62.

Rawls, A. 2000. Harold Garfinkel, in G. Ritzer (ed.), *The Blackwell Companion to Major Social Theorists*. Oxford: Blackwell, 545–76.

Ritzer, G. 2000. *Modern Sociological Theory*. Boston, MA: McGraw-Hill.

Sachs, H., Schegloff, E.A. and Jefferson, G. 2000. L'organizzazione nella presa del turno nella conversazione, in P.P. Giglioli and G. Fele (eds), *Linguaggio e contesto sociale*. Bologna: Il Mulino, 97–135.

Schegloff, E.A. 1987. Between Micro and Macro: Contexts and Other Connections, in J.C. Alexander, B. Giesen, R. Muench and N.J. Smelser (eds), *The Micro-Macro Link*. Berkeley, CA: University of California Press, 207–34.

Schegloff, E.A. 2000. "On Granularity." *Annual Review of Sociology* 26: 715–20.

Schutz, A. 1962. *Collected Papers, I. The Problem of Social Reality*, ed. M. Natanson. The Hague: Martinus Nijhoff.

Schutz, A. 1964. *Collected Papers II. Studies in Social Theory*, ed. A. Brodersen. The Hague: Martinus Nijhoff.

Segre, S. 2002. "Phenomenology and Symbolic Interactionism." *American Sociological Association 97th Annual Meeting, Regular Session on Social Theory*. Chicago, IL: August 16–19.

Sharrock, W. 1989. "Ethnomethodology." *British Journal of Sociology* 40: 657–77.

Sharrock, W. 2001. Fundamentals of Ethnomethodology, in G. Ritzer and B. Smart (eds), *Handbook of Social Theory*. London: Sage, 232–48.

Silverman, D. and Gubrium, J.F. 1994. "Competing Strategies for Analyzing the Contexts of Social Interaction." *Sociological Inquiry* 64: 179–98.

Speier, M. 1971. The Everyday World of the Child, in Jack D. Douglas (ed.), *Understanding Everyday Life*. London: Routledge & Kegan Paul, 188–217.

Turner, J.H. 1998. *The Structure of Sociological Theory*. Homewood, IL: The Dorsey Press.

Turner, R. 1971. Words, Utterances, and Activities, in Jack D. Douglas (ed.), *Understanding Everyday Life*. London: Routledge & Kegan Paul, 169–87.

Young, R.L. 1995. "Misunderstanding as Accounts." *Sociological Inquiry* 65: 251–64.

Wieder, D.L. 1971. On Meaning by Rule, in Jack D. Douglas (ed.), *Understanding Everyday Life*. London: Routledge & Kegan Paul, 107–35.

Wilson, T.P. 1971. Normative and Interpretive Paradigms in Sociology, in Jack D. Douglas (ed.), *Understanding Everyday Life*. London: Routledge & Kegan Paul, 57–79.

Zimmerman, D.H. and Pollner, M. 1971. The Everyday World as a Phenomenon, in Jack D. Douglas (ed.), *Understanding Everyday Life*. London: Routledge & Kegan Paul, 80–103.

Zimmerman, D.H. and Wieder, D.L. 1971. Ethnomethodology and the Problem of Order: Comment on Denzin, in Jack D. Douglas (ed.), *Understanding Everyday Life*. London: Routledge & Kegan Paul, 285–95.

Chapter 4
Exchange Theory

Preliminary Remarks

Exchange Theory consists of a set of concepts, propositions and assumptions formulated for the purpose of describing and explaining the presuppositions, procedures and outcomes of social exchange. The focus of attention will be the reciprocal obligations created by social actors when exchanging resources. The network of relations among the actors (people, or groups and organizations) constitutes the unit of analysis (Emerson 1976: 359; Gergen 1980: 270–71). The concepts and fundamental assumptions will be precisely defined, along with the theories that have been used and relevant traditional theories with reference firstly to Homans, Blau and Coleman, and secondly to the writings of Richard M. Emerson (1925–82), Karen S. Cook, and other authors who have stated their main theories with reference to the aforementioned writers. As for contemporary works, particular attention will be paid to Network Exchange Theory.

Outline of Introductory Literature

Brief introductions on Network Exchange Theory are found in Cook (1977, 1982); Cook, O'Brien and Kollock (1990); Emerson (1976); Molm (2001); Molm and Cook 1995; Ritzer (2000: 271–93); Timasheff and Theodorson (1976: 340–50). More detailed introductions are found in Bredemeier (1978); Chadwick-Jones (1976); Ekeh (1974); Heath (1976); Turner (1998: chs. 20, 22, 25). For a brief introduction in Italian, see Crespi (2002: 256–60). The introductions in Emerson, Ritzer and Turner give an overall view of those authors and formulations which most concern exchange theory. The introduction by Cook and Whitmeyer (2000) dwells only on Emerson. The contributions of Cook and Molm concern Emerson and his collaborators, and focus specifically on production theory and empirical research which explicitly recall Emerson, while Homans and Blau are only briefly examined. On the other hand, these last two mentioned authors are either the main subject of interest or even the exclusive one in the remaining introductions, which have been quoted. Coleman – as we shall see – is generally dealt with in the field of Rational Choice Theory.

Concepts, Assumptions and Theories

Actors, resources, social exchange – with reference to the structures and processes that describe them – contribute to constitute the conceptual apparatus of this theory together with other concepts like power, dependence and position in a network of relations. The *social actors* are examined (a) for their specific characteristics (for example, friends or relatives of the subject, or organizations having well-established relations with others); or (b) as exchangeable occupants of social position, like qualified workers or top managers in an organization. *Resources* include not only commodities but generally anything material or symbolic that is given a positive value by the actors. Therefore, *resources* represent not only income, capital and goods that can be bought and sold on the market but also fame, power, norms and values.

    Exchange Relations are those repeated transactions between actors who interact according to a *reciprocity principle* in order to obtain a benefit or result, that has a valued outcome, and to avoid a negative one. The reciprocity principle does not imply either equality or balance between what the parties have obtained or hoped to obtain (though under equal conditions, the exchange tends towards a balance over time), or that this principle is always sustained by norms or put into practice by the social actors (though this often happens). Finally, neither does it imply that a balanced exchange requires a balance of power. In addition, exchange relations are not negotiated. In this regard, they differ from negotiated exchanges, in which the amount and exchange conditions are subject to negotiation (Emerson 1969: 391; Gouldner 1960; Molm and Cook 1995: 218–19).

Profit is equal to *rewards* less *costs*. Rewards and costs refer to behavioral stimuli. Given that an individual receives an initial stimulus, like a situation or certain behavior (*discriminative stimulus*), and another stimulus (positive or negative) from the environment, called *reinforcement*, it is the latter which conditions further behavior. In other words, the desire to obtain positive reinforcement (a prize or a reward, or another desirable event) thereby avoiding a negative one (a cost, a punishment, or another undesirable event) conditions further behavior. The concept of *operant behavior* is central to exchange theory. Operant behavior of a particular subject (animal, person or group) can, in turn, be a stimulus for others, starting off and maintaining an exchange relation among other subjects whose behavior is a reinforcement to others. Rewards and, in general, positive reinforcement consist of anything that the individual considers to have value. In other words, everything that he/she wants but is not sure to obtain is valued positively, and therefore acts as positive reinforcement increasing the chances that his/her behavior will occur again. Costs are considered both as (a) negative reinforcement incurred in a transaction, like an unfavorable activity carried out by others; (b) opportunity to act, that is, benefits or potential rewards which have been given up to allow the transaction to occur (Emerson 1969: 388; 1976: 349; Homans 1961: 57–61). Costs are therefore not only of an economic nature. The distinguishing characteristic in an exchange relation is the aim to reach a positive outcome which, in the field of behavioral psychology, is called positive reinforcement. Discriminative stimulus, reinforcement and operant behavior are concepts containing mutual references, and therefore form one conceptual unit (Blau 1964: 88–91; Emerson 1969; Heath 1976: 2; Homans 1958: 603; 1961: 13).

Exchange theory and economic theory share the assumption that social actors involved in an exchange, act rationally so as to maximize their advantage. They also share the concept of opportunity cost, to the effect that an implicit cost is involved when foregoing the chance to make a profit. However, exchange theory diverges from economic theory in several respects (Blau 1964: 93–7; Ekeh 1974: 200–03; Emerson 1969: 388; 1987: 11–2; Molm 2001: 270–71). It considers a chain of exchanges rather than a single one; long-term relations between social actors that know each other, rather than short-term relations between social actors and the market. It also examines the existence of a moral obligation of reciprocity, which cannot be exactly defined or quantified, rather than stipulated contractual obligations and their assigned economic value. The presence of feelings such as gratitude and moral debt, and ethical values, which are not found in economical exchange are also allowed for. Therefore a reward can be not only economical, but also psychological (Ekeh 1974: 116). The source of value can be varied, coming from behavior, specific characteristics or relations which concern the individual (Homans 1961: 54–6; Levinger and Huesmann 1980: 174–6; Thibaut and Kelleychs: chapters 1 and 2).

The terms benefits and rewards are synonymous, but the latter is used by authors close to the school of behavioral psychology. According to this field of study, in the formulation given by Skinner, animal and human behavior can be understood and described as the effect of subsequent stimulus or reinforcement – positive or negative –received by an organism after having responded to an initial stimulus coming from its environment. Different responses, followed by the same reinforcement are considered analogous. The tester has prepared the environment in advance so as to isolate the organism (generally pigeons or other animals) from unwanted stimuli (the Skinner box), so that only the reinforcement is presumed to produce and define the behavioral response (Skinner 1971: 15–6). If we are dealing with people, rather than animals, then the environment could be a school, a hospital or any institution that isolates the social actors from the external world. In contrast to behavioral psychology, exchange theory concerns sociology. From a sociological point of view, also the tester is involved in an exchange of reciprocal stimuli, just as the other participants in the experiment. Indeed, the animal in the *Skinner box* conditions the tester, as well as being conditioned by him/her (Emerson 1976: 338–40; 1987: 40–5; Homans 1961: ch. 1; Schwartz 1980: 241–5).

Different things, evaluated positively by an individual, belong to the same value domain or exchange domain if the acquisition of one reduces the unitary value of all the others. The acquisition of things belonging to different domains, such as the family and work, does not have this same effect. Deliberate and well-pondered choices, therefore rational, are made only within the same value domain. Actors choose among things that belong to different domains, according to several criteria: the value assigned to them, the probability (in their opinion) of obtaining them and according to the competence they believe to have in those domains.

An exchange relation that concerns more than one domain (for example, one that is, at the same, both business and friendship) has primacy on the others. A social exchange assumes that the actors, when choosing, have an idea of the others' preferences, that they take them into consideration and that they compare them with their own choices (Cook and Emerson 1978: 726; Emerson 1987; Molm 1987; Molm and Cook 1995: 216).

The frequent use of concepts, such as benefit, reward and cost, follows the assumption that the actors act rationally. Therefore they choose a particular course of action, rather than another, in order to achieve a maximum result, or advantage, or profit, for themselves or for their group. Exchange theory shares this assumption with the *Theory of Rational Choice*, which is one of the traditional theories of reference (particularly for the theoretical current which considers negotiated exchanges as cooperative games). Rationality, which we assume the actors involved in the exchange use, is examined from the actor's point of view, taking into consideration their knowledge, beliefs and their actual ability to act in view of an objective and to evaluate the consequences of their actions. In contrast to other versions of the Rational Choice Theory, Exchange Theory explains not only behavior, but also rules, outcomes and institutions (Heath 1976: 76, 101, 172; Homans 1961: 79–82).

Close to the Rational Choice Theory and Exchange Theory is the social psychological theory of groups formulated by Thibaut and Kelly (1959). The authors have introduced the concepts of *comparison level* and *comparison level for alternatives*. The first concept indicates a standard or frequent term of reference, which the subject considers when evaluating the level of satisfaction that he/she gets from a relationship. The second concept (comparison level for alternatives) examines the alternatives available (indeed, a unsatisfactory relationship can be maintained due to a lack of alternatives). This concept is similar to that of cost, as intended in the theory of exchange (Emerson 1969: 388), and indicates the minimum level of satisfaction necessary for a relationship to continue, given the existing alternatives. Within a couple, each partner evaluates costs and rewards inherent to the relationship (these come from elements within and outside the couple), by comparing them to what could be obtained in other relationships. As the two partners in a couple interact, they can influence each other forcing the other to change his/her behavior. In the most extreme case, a relationship will cease to be interactive when partner A takes full control of the costs and rewards which partner B obtains from every exchange with Partner A. Norms and roles allow the members to control each other's behavior, without the costs and uncertainties inherent to the exercise of influence.

There is a greater number of possible coalitions within larger groups than within a couple, and this potentially increases each partner's costs and rewards.

Furthermore, larger groups are characterized by a status structure, norms and group objectives, and new social roles to satisfy group needs (For an introduction to Thibaut and Kelley's theory 1959, which highlights the connections between game theory and behavioral psychology, see Chadwick-Jones 1976: ch. 3. For the relationship between this work of Thibaut and Kelly and further developments in the theory of exchange see Griffin 1991: ch.16.)

In transactions, resources are exchanged. As mentioned, resources in the wider sense of the word may be economic or non-economic, tangible or intangible. One classification of resources, appropriate to contemporary American culture and proven empirically, distinguishes between six classes of resources: love, status, information, money, goods and services (Foa and Foa 1980; Gergen 1980: 262–3). Exchange relations are *restricted* if they occur between a couple of actors (dual relations); *generalized*, if they occur between many actors. In the latter case, the benefit which the actors try to obtain, does not come from the actors with whom they interact directly, but from others, and is therefore indirect. It follows that the total number of actors involved in an exchange receive a benefit, both individually and as part of the group (Ekeh 1974: 51–5).

Homans, Blau and Coleman's Contributions to Exchange Theory and Their Reception

Exchange Theory, in the version presented here, is largely taken from the formulations of Emerson, Cook and their collaborators. These formulations were inspired by the earlier works of Homans and Blau, which therefore will be taken into account, though only briefly. Then, some of Coleman's theses will be presented, once again only in summary form, without dwelling on their reception. Indeed, these theories are ascribable to a different theoretical field, Rational Choice Theory, and contain little reference to the aforementioned authors. Nonetheless, their relevance to the theory of exchange is worth noting.

Homans

George C. Homans (1910–1989) is best known for his book concerning the elementary forms of social behavior (*Social Behavior: Its Elementary Forms*), published in 1961 and republished in a new edition in 1974. Therefore, reference will be made primarily to this text, giving preference to the original 1961 edition. In addition, other texts by Homans which treat the theme of social exchange (Homans 1958, 1969) will be considered. Initially, an earlier work of Homans, *The Human Group*, will be mentioned, in which the author argues a theory of behavior of social groups. This work examines group behavior, considered as a system composed of interdependent elements whose reciprocal relations concur in generating, over time, a change within the group itself. Considered as a whole, the group also changes due to exposure to an external environment, both social and normative, in which it has to survive. Through a detailed presentation of empirical studies, concerning the social life of distinct groups, differentiated according to numerous characteristics (roles, relations and internal processes of control and integration, composition in terms of age and sex, ability to cope with changes in surrounding environments, level of stability, variety of these environments), the author presents his basic thesis. The relations between feelings, activities, interactions, norms, that is, between the elements, or variables, which constitute the hypotheses, remain constant in any group. The thesis is divided into several interconnected hypotheses. Proving these hypotheses enabled Homans to verify that these variables (feelings, activities, interactions and norms) are constantly related. However, the values of these variables change, due to changes in the relations between the group and the environment, and specific factors for each group: for example, the ability to exercise authority or social control can vary, or cultural traditions or technology can change (Homans 1950).

Homans's next and important book, *Social Behavior: Its Elementary Forms*, differs from his former work, *The Human Group*, in that the author does not only set out to arrive inductively at generalizations taken from literature which relies on the results of empirical research. There is a further objective in his later work: to explain the causes for which the generalizations are valid (Homans 1961: 8–14). In other words, it is a question of formulating sociological theories and deducting the validity in specific cases of social behavior.

The subject matter is the elementary forms of social behavior. The *forms* are *elementary*, meaning that they are easily explainable; manifested during direct contact and observable between individuals, as usually occurs in limited circles; those not institutionalized or universal (according to the author). Behavior is actual, not that prescribed by norms, and it is *social*, in the sense that it is directed intentionally towards at least one other person who, in turn, responds by behaving in a particular way. This response constitutes for the first person a reward or a punishment and, usually, a cost (not necessarily economic).

Two disciplines – economics and behavioral psychology – study social behavior as a variable which depends on the rewards and punishments that result from interacting with others. Furthermore, Exchange Theory shares with the marginal utility theory of economics the principle of, the exchange of goods, and the proposition that the value of a commodity (economic theory) or activity (Exchange Theory) is determined by its abundance or scarcity. However, Marginal Utility and Social Exchange theories differ regarding some basic principles. Unlike economic theory, that of social exchange foresees the exchange of only one good (only one activity) at a time, and the value of that good cannot be precisely measured. Instead of examining a single exchange, what is studied is a number of exchanges over time and how the participants involved in the exchange influence each other's behavior from one transaction to the next.

The terms "operant behavior" and "reinforcers" have been borrowed from behavioral psychology, for which, as Homans says, "there is a vast body of evidence, both clinical and experimental" (Homans 1969: 13). Referring, not only to human behavior, but also animal, the author describes *operant behavior* as that carried out by a subject, human or animal, to obtain a reward or avoid a punishment, having previously experienced that such behavior brings about particular outcomes. How much or low less is available of something that the subject desires (for example, food) and his/her frame of mind intensity of the subject's desire) help determine the subject's behavior. There is also another factor which contributes to determine the subject's behavior.

Positive or negative effects – called *reinforcers* – which come from environmental situations. After the subject has behaved in a certain way, he/she/it expects to receive a reward or punishment (receive or not receive food), which therefore modifies the experience and also the subject's future behavior. If an expected reward is refused this causes anger (also in animals, it seems); while receiving it, not only stimulates the rewarded behavior but also creates positive feelings. An example of a positive reinforcer for human beings could be if the others in the subject/s' group change their opinion, and the subject/s reach agreement by conforming to the change, or the subject/s could decide not to change opinion and therefore not conform.

Therefore a reinforcer has an effect on a subject's behavior. The effect depends on the *frequency* of interactions between a subject (person or animal) and others, and on the *value* of the reinforcer, that is, on the degree of reward or punishment that is associated with the last unit received. The higher the reinforcer (reward or punishment) is, in terms of frequency or value, the more behavior will change. If the subjects who receive and give the reinforcer are people, then this last proposition is valid only if other conditions are equal. In fact, an individual's behavior is modified by the frequency and by the value of the reinforcer received not only during an interaction, but also in previous similar ones. How similar these situations are increases the probability of behavior changing. Furthermore, the value of the reinforcer decreases as its frequency increases (principle of satiation). Reinforcers received indirectly, from third parties, modify an individual's behavior by means of those with whom he/she is interacting now, or by means of those with whom the individual has related in the past.

Conferring social status, or approval, or showing liking, constitutes a positive reinforcer, or reward. Even an expected punishment not received, that is, a cost not sustained – is considered a reward. The difference between a reward and a cost is the profit. More precisely, the difference between a positive reinforcer and a negative reinforcer is the profit (in a psychological not economic sense). A cost can be a punishment, or refusal of a reward, or taking something back, or refraining from enjoyment. Cost varies according to the level of deprivation, or unavailability of a reward and its value. As physical costs (like, fatigue) and psychological costs (like, confessing inferiority) increase, the reward decreases more than proportionally. In an exchange, units of non-economic goods available (for example, the ability to offer help) are exchanged for units of goods that are desired (for example, social approval). An exchange undergone for the purpose of receiving a psychological profit continues until a balance is reached, for each participant, between costs and rewards. Considerations on distributive justice determine the definition of equal costs and rewards, and hence the point of equilibrium in the social exchange. What is "fair" depends on how much was given or received in previous, similar situations and on how much the others, involved in the exchange, gave or received. In other words, what is "fair" depends on what one invests compared to the others. In an exchange the person harmed will probably react by showing anger, which will probably increase according to how much he/she is harmed. Exchange theory assumes, like Rational Choice Theory, that the subjects involved in an activity are rational, which means that they choose between the alternatives available (and based on their previous experiences), those that in the short term are the most suitable for reaching their objectives. However, unlike Rational Choice Theory, Exchange Theory does not take as given perceptions and values but rather seeks to explain them.

Experimental studies have proven that the intensity and occurrence of a subject exercising influence, that is, attempting to modify another person's behavior; and showing feelings and expressing approval and satisfaction, all conditions being equal, depend on the costs and benefits that result. Therefore, rewards and costs modify not only animal behavior, but also human behavior. Social approval is a positive reinforcer that is given, particularly to those who conform to shared norms. A norm is a declaration about what behavior should be followed in certain circumstances. One conforms for various reasons, due to the actual norm itself, or to obtain advantages or approval. In any case, approval of those who conform to a norm is greater in proportion to the number of people conforming and according to how valuable the norm is. The probability of nonconformity occurring depends on the value given to incompatible activities with the norm and the value given to approval received from others not conforming to the norm. Opposing sentiments, of hostility and aggression, ensue from individual or group competition. These sentiments will be more intense, the greater the injustice, or relevant deprivation, according to a criterion of distributive justice. On the one hand, mutual satisfaction tends to increase among individuals jointly involved, like allies, in competition. On the other hand, mutual deprivation and solidarity towards the members of your own group promotes cohesion within the group.

Mutual satisfaction doesn't result from forced interactions, even if they are frequent. In addition, the most esteemed people receive and provide a greater number of interactions. One also interacts frequently with people who are esteemed equally, but also, even if less often, with those of whom we have little esteem. How can these facts be explained? People held in low esteem have little to offer and, therefore, are therefore not sought and they probably tend to interact with others similar to themselves. Furthermore, choosing the people with whom we interact does not only depend on mutual satisfaction or whether we esteem them or not. The choice also depends on – as experimental studies have proven – the application of abstract criteria of distributive justice that aim to ensure equity in social exchange. The result is a comparison and evaluation of congruence between what the subject obtained from the interactions (one's profit) and what the others obtained. The evaluation takes into account reciprocal characteristics, such as age, sex, social position, ability. Following this comparative evaluation, it is not reciprocal satisfaction, but equity in the exchange which is relevant to obtaining a profit from interaction. The greater the profit a subject receives from an interaction, the greater is his or her satisfaction. The amount of profit depends not only on an evaluation of benefits and costs, but also on the frequency with which an activity is rewarded.

A person who provides valuable services is able to make others obey him, is esteemed and exercises authority over them. Obedience is a cost, both for those who obey because they cannot act freely and they could be punished, and also for the holder of authority who by acknowledging and enforcing his authority naturally limits his interaction with those obeying him. While an exchange of equivalent services produces equality in terms of social status, awarding esteem and obeying create inequality. In this case, it is not possible to exchange an equivalent service for what has been received. Research has shown that nonconformity to norms is more frequent among people of high or low status than among those of medium status. Indeed, people of high status have little to gain by conforming and those of low status have little to lose by violating a norm. This conclusion, which comes from research carried out in small groups, seems to be valid, at least in part, for whole societies. Every time a person accepts services from others without being able to repay them, he/she acknowledges his/her inferior status compared to them and therefore pays a social cost. An equal exchange does not have this cost, but neither does it provide the benefits that come from interacting with a subject of high status. Those that exercise influence increase the probability of maintaining their superior status, as long as their status is not questioned by people at the bottom of the status hierarchy, who have nothing to lose from a change. Emitting an activity depends on a situation that acts as a stimulus, and on how convenient it is to emit the activity. This is valid both in small groups and for society as a whole. However, in the latter case, the relations between basic processes, like stimulus-situations and evaluations of convenience which modify behavior, are more complex. Institutions are the result of social exchange processes. During these processes, deferred rewards and punishments, that is, those not given immediately, have acted as reinforcer activities, creating persistent forms of behavior and, therefore, a social organization with special roles. Over time, elementary behavior can conflict with *institutionalized behavior*. Tension results which cannot always be resolved within the existing situation.

Homans's theses, according to which frequency and the value of rewards and punishments determine behavior, and in particular social exchange, have received a lot of attention from scholars, but also criticisms. The main area of interest has been the theory of distributive justice, in particular (a) the exact meaning of the concepts: equity, distributive justice and reciprocity, and the possible overlapping of their meanings; (b) compatibility between the principle of distributive justice on the one hand and, on the other, behavioral psychology (given the importance of the actors' motives and emotions) and, therefore, all arguments preceding Homans; (c) the relationship between social exchange and altruism. The various and numerous attempts to verify this theory have been seriously affected by vague definitions and logical and theoretical uncertainties (Chadwick-Jones 1976: 242–53).

Only a few of the criticisms concerning Homans's theses will be pointed out here. Firstly, the author has only given psychological explanations for behavior, rather than sociological. It is then difficult to understand why some things have value in particular groups and societies, and not in others (Razak 1966). Homans has replied that sociological propositions are almost never general enough and they derive from other propositions of a psychological nature, like those he himself has formulated (Homans 1966). Secondly, if we do not accept that behavior is conditioned by stimuli and reinforcers, then we cannot associate animal and human behavior, as the latter has a symbolic character.

Indeed unconditioned human behavior derives from its symbolic character different aspects that distinguish it from conditioned behavior: (a) past activities are neither a necessary nor sufficient condition for present activities; (b) it is creative, not static; (c) it is regulated by shared norms, rather than being individual and indifferent to norms; (d) finally it allows generalizations in time and in space. Furthermore, Homans's conception of social exchange has several and serious shortcomings: (a) it does not adequately apply the economic model of exchange; (b) it ignores forms of behavior that cannot be made similar to the exchange, or behavior other than that emitted to gain approval, esteem or liking; (c) it uses forced analogies between behavioral psychology and economic theory, in particular between economic and psychological rewards; (d) it does not allow predictions about probable behavior when there are new situations; (e) it arbitrarily reduces relations among several actors to relations between couples, even if the empirical research adopted to sustain his theories generally refers to large groups; (f) the relation between an exchange carried out for a profit or for a consideration of equity and justice is not explained; (g) such considerations do not explain clearly the relation between distributive justice and punishment, abiding by both these forms of justice by conforming to the general criteria of merit (rather than to that of acquired rights or needs) (Boulding 1962; Chadwick-Jones 1976: 168, 187, 196; Ekeh 1974: 87–165; Heath 1976: 136–7, 141).

Other objections regard his argumentation. Firstly, the author's statements do not always derive from his fundamental theses, but from assumptions or principles that are introduced according to the arguments in discussion at that moment. The conceptual framework– costs, investments, profits, distributive justice, etc. – is too imprecise to allow strict, empirical testing. The concept of value, in particular, is considered both in terms of behavior and cognition. In the first case, the object of analysis is constituted by what determines the amount of the benefit connected to a particular behavior (such as its frequency, the activity performed and its cost). In the second case, what are relevant are the motives such as the perception and evaluation of the benefit and costs) that connect behavior to the reinforcers. Therefore, it is impossible to come to conclusions that can be strictly applied to a variety of cases. What is more, the author does not specify under which conditions, conforming to norms, or competing, or similar values, or other events bring about a reward or positive reinforcement, rather than an opposite result. The concept of "reward" itself does not help much in understanding social phenomena, and is of no help in explaining them, as it is not defined clearly. Neither is it possible to seek to measure with indicators, that are considered objectives, how much a reinforcer is subjectively perceived as a reward. Thirdly, the principle of satiation, which has proved useful in physiological fields, is difficult to apply when values are involved.

Finally, the conclusions reached inductively by the author are derived from sources that have questionable scientific value, and what constitutes a reward is indicated in a contradictory way (Abrahamsson 1970; Chadwick-Jones 1976: 164, 169–72; Davis 1962; Turner 1998: 266–8).

Blau

Peter M. Blau's (1918–2003) important text for exchange theory is: *Exchange and Power in Social Life* (1964). In this work Blau proposes to elaborate a theory of interpersonal association that, despite frequent reference to Thibaut and Kelly, and to Homans, is supposed to be an original contribution. Indeed, Blau not only rejects the behavioral psychology theories, but also presents a different opinion. He considers the theory of exchange a necessary premise to a theory of social structure, which is defined as a complex of heterogeneous substructures, interdependent and placed on several analytical levels. He aims to deduce what the macro-sociological processes are that govern social structure, starting from the study of micro-sociological processes that characterize interpersonal relations.

Among the macro-sociological processes, like the processes of legitimization of social objectives and authority, and processes of interdependence and differentiation between the substructures that comprise social structure, social exchange is particularly important. This is defined as by Homans as any behavior carried out in pursuit of an end employing the appropriate means. Therefore, exchange is, by definition, rational behavior, according to the goal or value. The importance of exchange to the theory of social processes is that it derives from relatively simple processes and leads to relatively complex ones. Exchange is a social relation, regulated by norms, that ensues from relations between individuals and interdependent groups. It cannot be traced back to the psychological motives of each actor: in this sense, the properties of social exchange can be called "emergent properties" of the interactions among elements (like individuals or groups). Such properties connote the interactions, rather than the elements themselves, and they are therefore structural properties.

Social exchange processes derive from interpersonal associations and, ultimately, from psychological dispositions. Interpersonal relations tend towards reciprocity and therefore towards a balance between benefits offered and received according to social criteria, keeping in mind, though, that non-economic exchanges have no market price. Even relations inside the social structure tend towards a balance. The same forces that bring balance from one point of view bring imbalance from another. For example, if the under-privileged manage to better their conditions through political parties or trade unions, a condition of deprivation follows for the petit bourgeoisie, whose members will be forced to turn to the opposite, right-wing parties. Social integration results from bonds of reciprocal attraction. These bonds, in turn, result from the desire to obtain social approval from within a particular group and, therefore, from the desire to attract the other members. To maintain group cohesion, reciprocal attraction must be accompanied by the approval of others and therefore, there must be restrictions on competition for social approval.

Blau dwells, in contrast to Homans, not only on the interpersonal processes in a group, but also on the elements, such as norms, values, power, organizations, social classes and other complex structures, that are present in large groups and which have macro-sociological relevance. Those involved in the exchange are not isolated individuals, but groups and organizations. An exchange is equitable, according to Blau, when it conforms to social norms. Therefore, Blau does not uphold Homans's individualistic approach, according to which the notion of equity comes from expected benefits and costs. Social exchange is an intermediate case between the mere calculation of advantages, extrinsic to the actors, and the mere expression of intrinsic affection. It differs from economic exchange because there are no precise obligations, that is, they are not defined in a contract, and because trust is required and induced. Sentiments of gratitude, personal obligation and trust come from social, rather than economic exchange. According to Blau's sociological theory, it is a social fact (in the sense of Durkheim) that social exchanges are mediated by norms, values, organizations (cf. on this matter Ekeh 1974: 178–9, 185–6).

Exchanges that are not reciprocal imply a differentiation in power, for power is established through the allocation of unnecessary benefits. Rather than considering the benefits inherent to an exchange, like Homans, Blau dwells on the power to supply benefits. Faced with power, the possible reactions, aside from subordination, are the following: exchange benefits, if there are the necessary resources available, otherwise look for other sources for supply, if there are any, or extort the benefits if the subjects (individuals or groups) have coercive power, or decide to give up the benefits for some ideal. In class-stratified communities, social exchanges among members of different classes supplement and sustain competition for social approval. Group cohesion depends on whether expectations have been met concerning the members' objectives or the group's objectives. These expectations, in turn, depend on social norms that establish evaluation criteria and on the presence of reference groups. The principle whereby marginal utility decreases as benefits increase can be applied to exchange – inside a group – where there is, on the one hand respect and obedience, and on the other hand, advice and help.

Exercising power allows collective efforts to be organized. This is only possible if the power is legitimate, that is, if the subordinates consider obeying the holder of power to be bound by norms. Opposition to power comes from the following combination of factors: the subordinated group has been treated unjustly, has a large internal communication network, and wants to take revenge for the injustice and the exploitation it has suffered. In large groups, shared values promote relations in space and time, even beyond direct contact, and legitimate social order. However, the persistence of the social order, and of the values that support it, require a process of institutionalization, that is, formal procedures that uphold organizational principles of social life.

While a macro-social structure is made up of components, or substructures, which are interdependent, a substructure (like a social circle, or an ethnic group, or an organization) is made up of interactions among individuals. Some substructures include other substructures, while others intersect with each other. A systematic theory of social structure must therefore take into consideration integrated relations, differentiation and organization of the substructure, as well as changes in the boundaries among the substructures due to individual and organizational mobility from within. In conclusion, interdependence and, at the same time, incompatibility among various substructures that intersect means that there are continuous encounters and reshuffling among forces that balance and those that unbalance social structures. Consequently, social structures are continuously subjected to forces that both narrow their boundaries and change them.

Blau's theory, herewith outlined, has stimulated empirical research which aims to prove specific theses, particularly those regarding the relations among social exchange, power and conflict. Furthermore, his theory has been accredited merit for studying conflict, different status and political behavior, as well as the variety of structural conditions that bring about social exchange (Chadwick-Jones 1976: 333–59). However, the theory has also received various objections, some of which follow. Firstly, it has been noted that the analogy between economic and social exchange, and, more generally, the use of concepts related to processes of individual psychology adopted in the study of group processes and social structure, entail the use of analogies that could be plausible, but the author has not sufficiently substantiated these with his empirical research or that of others. The same concepts, particularly those of exchange and reciprocity, take on different meanings depending on whether they are used to explain phenomena at a micro or macro-sociological level of analysis. Thirdly, the concept of benefit could be confused with that of stimulus: as both of them actually increase or keep up the frequency of response. Fourthly, it has been pointed out that power, in Blau's theory, not only ensues from social exchange, but also helps to determine the conditions by using coercion, and it can originate from the ability to make others dependent on future benefits, or from the norm of reciprocity that rules when one receives benefits. In addition, an unbalanced relation does not necessarily imply an imbalance of power, as it could be a temporary imbalance, or actually an unstable relation, or finally it could concern a particular circle of relations, and be balanced by an opposite imbalance in another circle. Fifthly, another unacceptable assumption has been noted whereby individual behavior is summed according to shared values, with the aim of constructing, like the economists, a supply and demand curve for social goods. Finally, it has been pointed out that, following the generic definition that Blau gives for social exchange, every interaction can thereby be defined, and furthermore, that in an institutionalized society, in which impersonal norms and fixed criteria of status prevail, the environment in which individuals can seek maximum utility in their interpersonal relations is limited. (Bierstedt 1965; Chadwick-Jones 1976: 313–14, 338, 356–9, 389–90; Cohen 1968: 123; Emerson 1976: 342; Heath 1968, 1976: 60, 65–7; Turner 1998: 281; Wrong 1967: 673–4).

Coleman

James S. Coleman (1926–95), as previously mentioned, is generally placed in the field of Rational Choice Theory. Coleman's work is relevant to the theory of exchange because he formulated and elaborated a conception of the social actor who is involved in exchanges with others with the aim of fulfilling his own interests (Molm 2001: 269). A brief summary of Coleman's treatment of exchange from his work which especially deals with this theme, *Foundations of Social Theory*, will be presented here. A detailed presentation will not be given here. Coleman begins with the assumption that rational actors relate with each other, exchanging resources over which they have control and in which they are interested. Therefore, their actions are interdependent. In other words, their interdependence follows from the control that the actors have (in varying degrees) over resources and events, and from what they hope to gain from such events. An actor's interest in a particular resource depends on his or her interest in all the other resources of the social system. The interdependence of actions can come about in several ways: as a consequence of an actor's action on others; as a bilateral exchange between actors, which occurs in a negotiation or a contract; as an interaction among actors who act in a competitive market; as a collective decision undertaken through pre-established procedures (for example, through voting); and finally, as a result of formal organization or obedience to procedural norms. Anyway, the aggregation of behavior, preference and individual decision does not determine collective behavior.

Since it is assumed that the actors are rational, the exchange, which is not necessarily a market exchange, is carried out until equilibrium is reached if it is reached at all. Equilibrium is reached when the actors can no longer obtain, through further exchanges, a better satisfaction of their interests. The resulting maximum utility is defined exclusively by the actors' values (and not, therefore, by external criteria). The actors interact both directly, and also through other actors or organizations. The latter case, which occurs frequently, renders social transactions which are not market-oriented (like those which occur due to different status or prestige of the actors), similar to market transactions. Only market transactions, however, require the use of money as the means of exchange having legal tender, the writing up of balance sheets and a clearing house between debits and credits.

Social transactions also have debits and credits, and even the presence of mediators: however, what is missing in this case is a unit of account which is universally recognized. Moreover, in this case goods are generally indivisible (as are, for example, trust and appreciation). Within a social system, there can be subsystems in which exchanges are interdependent as it occurs, for example, in a scientific community. In a subsystem, given an initial distribution of resources controlled by the actors, each of them has (in varying degrees) resources which have a value, since they are desired by the others. Each actor has, therefore, power to control the relevant events. If there is balance of power among the actors, each person controls an amount of each resource that is determined by his or her interest in it, by the value of that resource and by the value of all the resources that that person controls.

The actors' interests in particular resources and the control they have over them are micro-sociological concepts, while the value of the resources and the power that the actors exercise over them are macro-sociological concepts. In the latter case, the actors are no longer considered individually, but as a part of a system of action. It is assumed that the actors carry out social exchanges to reach utility maximization in a market of social goods (for example, the job or marriage market) that is considered approximately similar to a competitive market of commodity goods. The actors, who are considered similar to economic operators, have therefore all the information about their interests and their initial control of the social goods, or events, in which they are interested. Consequently, it is assumed that social goods, such as jobs and potential marriage partners, are perfectly divisible (every job and every potential marriage partner can be considered individually) and transferable (that is, able to be bought and sold freely). It is also assumed that their exchange does not affect the social system, and their supply and demand always meet at a point of equilibrium.

If this approximate analysis is not pursued, and we consider indivisible goods, and, in particular, social goods (for example, an event that some actors want, but which would be damaging for others), then their enjoyment has external effects, as regards the actors involved in exchange of goods. These external effects mean that the exchange can benefit some actors at the expense of others. The pursuit of individual interests is therefore no longer a guide to rational behavior, and actor interdependence is not limited to the exchange, but extends to the whole set of relations. The result is conflict, negotiations, collective decisions and the use of coercion to ensure their respect. The exchange of non-market goods involves, as a consequence, the social need to establish rational norms that indicate the rights and duties of the actors. It becomes socially necessary, in other words, to enact norms that prescribe behavior maximizing utility for each actor as well as for the social system. Consideration should also be given to obligations which are inherent in the social structure, and can therefore impede the exchange between two particular goods or actors, while promoting it for other couples of goods or actors. The results are barriers between the actors, and ultimately a different rate of exchange of resources and a different distribution of them among the same actors. In such a case, no point of equilibrium may be reached in the exchange of social goods (Coleman 1990. See also Cook, O'Brien and Kollock 1990: 170–73; Lindenberg 2000: 535–6).

Coleman's theory, only briefly outlined here, is relevant to exchange theory insofar as – assuming that each actor has a given system of preferences –the aim is to maximize utility obtained in the exchange, and that the actor has control over some of the goods or events – this theory permits us to predict the value of every event (that is, the level of importance or desirability) according to the actors; the resources which each actor has (for example, in terms of power); and finally, the control over events or social goods that every actor exercises after all exchanges have come about. Coleman's theory has generated much interest, it has influenced fields of study and even trends in social policy (especially in the field of sociology of education), it has been highly appraised, and it has stimulated empirical research and a much lively debate (Ritzer 2000: 303–4).

While it is important to consider the presentation of the theory of rational choice, it would be pertinent here to consider the reception of Coleman's theory as regards social exchange, for this is the subject of study here. Paying attention, first of all, to theoretical objections, it has been pointed out that the analogy between social exchange carried out in corporations and market exchange cannot be maintained, even though money is used in both cases. Indeed, corporations compensate their employees not only with money, but also with esteem, which is the specific means of social exchange. Both money and esteem imply trust and it is on this basis that social relations are established (La Valle 2002). It is appropriate to mention here an empirical research that aimed to verify by way of experiment Coleman's theory of social exchange. The tester made realistic the theory's deliberately unrealistic assumptions (actors are looking to satisfy their own interests, they are perfectly informed, goods are divisible). On the planned research agenda, the experimenter involved a small sample of subjects in a series of exchanges of non-economic goods (tokens of different colors), to which the subjects had given different values after negotiating for them in pairs. The results of the research confirmed Coleman's theory, in that they verified the reliability of its predictions (Michener, Cohen and Soerensen 1977).

Network Exchange Theory, which will be discussed now, aims to describe the conditions and indicate the mechanisms that produce power differences among the positions occupied by social actors in a network relation of exchange. It is assumed that the actors try to maximize their power, namely their control over others, which is meant as a benefit, and they try to avoid subordinate relations, which are meant as costs (for an introduction to Network Exchange Theory, see Molm 2001; Molm and Cook 1995: 217–28; Willer et al. 2002). An exchange network is defined as a set of two or more interconnected exchange relations (Cook 1982: 180; see also Emerson 1976: 358; Cook and Emerson 1978: 725). In an exchange network, for every couple of relations, the frequency or size of exchanges within a couple varies to favor exchanges in other couples. In order for a network to be set up, the flow of resources needs to be reciprocally dependent. This means that the flow of resources exchanged between a couple changes those exchanged within other relations. Therefore, an exchange network is not established if social actors are only connected two by two. This occurs, for example, between separate couples of friends, that is, couples who have no relations between them, even if one or more individuals can belong to more than one couple. Therefore, an exchange network is made up of at least two couples of social actors and there must be at least one relation between an actor in one couple and that in another, such that each couple is connected with one or more couples.

If the actors cooperate to receive benefits from an exchange, such cooperation makes the same exchange more likely in other relations. In such a case, the actors are said to be positively connected. Instead, they are negatively connected when, within an exchange network, they compete to obtain benefits, thereby reducing the probability of the exchange continuing in other relations. Relations, which are initially cooperative, can later become competitive, and vice versa. Furthermore, exchanges can be either of a competitive or cooperative nature, as occurs in a negotiation. In an exchange network, cooperative relations between couples of actors can become competitive relations with other actors: an actor who takes a central position can reap advantages by cooperating with all the others, who, however, are competing amongst themselves.

If the others come to an agreement, the imbalance of power in the central actor's favor is reduced or cancelled. This happens if the others form a coalition, where the actors guide their behavior in order to present themselves to the opposition as if they were only one actor. A coalition's success implies that the members respect the norm of not competing among themselves. A representative of the coalition can be entrusted to assure that the norm be respected, and he or she, therefore, has authority over its members and access to the group's resources. The imbalance of power can be reduced if each actor makes an effort to satisfy one of the central actor's needs, thereby becoming irreplaceable. The power of a member in a group results not only from the group being dependent on that member, but also from the value he or she assigns to rewards (like social recognition) that are received from the group. A member's power is greater, all other conditions being equal, the lower this value; the lower, for example, is the member's interest in social recognition (Cook and Emerson 1978: 724–25; Emerson 1969: 396–99). The theory of exchange, as elaborated by Emerson and Cook and their collaborators and followers, has a peculiar quality: it can be applied to both micro- and macro-social contexts. This is possible due to two elements. Firstly, the actors can be either individuals or groups, and their individual characteristics (feelings, norms) are important only if they influence the exchange relation. Secondly, exchange relations can be, as already shown, restricted or generalized. The attributes and outcomes of these relations, and not their micro or macro context, are the subject matters of exchange theory (Cook 1987: 219; Turner 1987: 224). The concepts of *power* and *dependence*, and generally the joint consideration of the conceptual apparatus of exchange and network exchange theories, have allowed the formulation of a considerable number of theoretical studies that adopt concepts and propositions both from

Network Exchange Theory and from behavioral psychology. In an influential article that appeared in 1962, and in subsequent works, Emerson – referring to the thesis of Thibaut and Kelley (1959), according to which an unsatisfactory relation is maintained when there are no alternatives – stated that power results, within an exchange network, not only from the availability of resources which are valued by the parties, but also from the dependence of some actors on others. In such a case, the latter control the rewards and the costs inherent to the social exchange, which is therefore unbalanced in their favor. On the other hand, in the case of reciprocal dependence, an exchange will continue even if there is a balance of power amongst the actors.

Power, according to the students of exchange theory, is not a feature of the actors (as Homans holds), but of the structure of their relations (*structural power*). Indeed, power, which is manifested through the network relations, comes from the particular structure of the network and from the position of the actors in it. For example, there can be – all other conditions being equal – a relation of economic dependence, and therefore subordination, when actor C depends upon B; for example, a wife C is economically dependent upon husband B who has a job, and B depends upon A (the husband B is economically dependent upon company A). Therefore, there is a flow of money from A to C through B (from the company to the wife through the husband). Consequently, the bond between B and C (marriage) has increased the power of A (the power of the company), increasing the number of actors over whom economic power is exercised. However, in exchange, A receives from B a different resource (work). B also receives a different resource from C (affection). Moreover, power does not generically imply control over other actors, as Homans, Blau and even Emerson would hold. Instead, a person holds power if he is able to give benefits and thereby making those who receive them dependent on him/her (cf. Willer 1999: 19–29).

The dependence of some actors upon others, and the resulting power, are always in some measure reciprocal, as has been pointed out by behavioral psychology and the theory of network exchange. When two or more actors depend equally, one upon the other, there is a balanced exchange relation. In other cases, it is unbalanced. Dependence can often diverge in some fundamental aspects: for example, in the quantity or type of reward obtained, or in a different control in a relation. In an exchange network, if there is an imbalance of power, and therefore a not perfectly reciprocal dependence of some actors upon others, those who occupy more powerful positions can use their power to influence the actions of the other participants, but this does not necessarily happen. The actors can negotiate on the conditions of exchange and on the agreements that ensue (*negotiated exchange*), or they can contribute individually to the exchange, without negotiating (*reciprocal exchange*). In the case of negotiated exchange, the bilateral relation excludes third parties from exchange rewards and the actors are better off exchanging with partners who are less powerful than themselves, and therefore forced to offer better conditions. In this type of exchange, the risk is of being excluded from the exchange. As a protective measure against this risk, it is rational to increase one's offer, which results in an increase in the inequality of power and rewards among the participants.

In the case of reciprocal exchange, rewards (like a service or favor) are provided unilaterally, therefore, the participants do not expect either a return, or the reciprocal dependence that could follow in the future. Both parties can only establish the conditions of the exchange over time, when they will have finally realized the nature of their reciprocal relationship. Reciprocity can mean equivalence in what the parties do, or equivalence in terms of value or frequency. If actors try to obtain maximum advantage in a reciprocal exchange (as they do in a negotiated exchange, if they act rationally), then the exchange will be the more advantageous for them, the greater the number of other partners and the more frequent the exchanges with each one of them. However, in reciprocal exchange, the actors do not try primarily to maximize their rewards, rather to decrease their risk of loss. Note that the risk in this type of exchange is not that of being excluded, rather it is that of not being reciprocated, thus actors can take protective measures, like reducing the frequency and the amount of that which is given.

The dependence of some actors upon others assumes not only a more unfavorable relation between costs and benefits inherent in the exchange but also the lack or high cost of alternative relations and the high value that they give to the desired resource. In particular, there is a relation of dependence and imbalance of power if some actors – starting negotiations with third parties – actually exclude, or could exclude, certain others from this negotiation, thereby weakening the latter. This weakening effect results also from the lack of an alternative partner, with whom otherwise it would have been possible to form a coalition. If there is an imbalance of power, through the processes that ensue, the disadvantaged actors try to reduce their dependence and thereby decrease their disadvantage. Social exchange can return to a position of balance in several ways: by increasing the value of one's behavior for the other party, or by increasing the number of alternative relations available, or by decreasing for oneself the value of the others' behavior, or finally by reducing the number of alternative relations that are available for the other party.

In a series of transactions exchange relations tend towards (all other conditions being equal) a state of balance, where, for every couple of actors, one actor's potential profits are equal to the other's potential losses. Activities of resistance or new evaluations, in a reductive sense, of mental costs are examples of such processes. Some actors can make, even unintentionally, not only other actors dependent on them, but also an entire network of relations. This happens when an actor stops participating in a network, and the benefits that all the other actors received from his participation diminish. Actors often make use of structural power that is available to them by setting up relations of exploitation, whereby damaging those in a position of dependence. However, this can also not happen, even in the case of a negotiated exchange. Indeed, actors may not be aware of their superior power over a partner (as happens when exchange relations occur as a matter of fact and neither partner knows about them), or they may be held back by considerations of equity, or they may still be unable to stimulate the desired behavior in their partner.

The case of power exercised by actors who are inferior to that may come about in certain situations, which have been studied by Network Exchange Theory. These situations have in common that actors seek to maximize their advantage. In the first situation, the most powerful actors opt for an exchange strategy that minimizes risks and uncertainties, exchanging with less powerful actors over a short period of time. Exchanges with other powerful actors result, in the long term, more advantageous, but also more risky in the absence of trust. In another situation, actors seek to obtain maximum advantage from every exchange, without attempting to influence the behavior of the other actors and bearing the costs that result from the extra effort and from greater uncertainty. In the long run, this use of one's power generally turns out to be advantageous to, and is characteristic of, those who have the most power in an exchange relation. Their wise use of power, which aims to obtain long-term benefits even if foregoing those in the short term, strengthens their superiority. Such superiority gives them the chance to award benefits also to others, but it does not encourage the use of coercion.

The use of coercion is risky as it can entail not only profits, but also losses. Losses are more likely if who is coerced experiences– in the absence of shared norms that legitimate the losses – a feeling of injustice, which causes resistance to the coercion. Therefore, those who have more incentive to use coercion are those who have little to lose. Due to scarcity of resources they cannot give enough benefits and, therefore, they are in a condition of inferior power in respect to the other party. Due to their inferiority, they can lose all their scarce resources, if the other party also decides to resort to coercion. Reciprocal exchange induces trust between the parties and affective commitment to a much greater extent than in a negotiated exchange, for, due to frequent and regular exchanges, the participants – aware of the uncertainty of the relation and of the risk of being damaged – can evaluate better their partners' trustworthiness. Therefore, the use of power against these partners, the search for alternative partners, and the uncertainty and the inherent risk in the exchange, are progressively reduced. In the case of a negotiated exchange, too, there may be feelings of cohesion among the participants, but they prevail with more difficulty, compared to a reciprocal exchange, due to a shorter time perspective.

Referring particularly to negotiated exchange, a fruitful development of the theory of exchange has examined as much the structure of network relations as feelings, affection and emotions of the participants, thereby moderating Emerson's strictly structuralist point of view. Indeed, Lawler and his colleagues have dwelled on the causes and consequences of feelings of cohesion among actors in an exchange network. Feelings of cohesion and commitment towards relationships with others are stimulated by relationships that are not only frequent and useful in reaching shared objectives, but also equal in power (frequency being equal), and, therefore, similarly placed in a hierarchical order. When actors are in a network exchange relation, power comes from the actors' position – other conditions being equal – but their feelings and emotions are important for cohesion and other features of the relations. As can been seen from carrying out a task together, shared responsibility tends to stimulate amongst the participants feelings and emotions (like pride or shame, emotional attachment or detachment) which affect not the individuals but the relations among them and possibly those of the whole group or whole network.

These feelings and emotions are more important in groups that create together and voluntarily one event or good, compared to groups whose members are committed by a contract, or to other cases where individual contributions can be distinguished. Furthermore, such feelings and emotions are stronger, the more stable, controllable and positive are perceived the relationships amongst the participants. In such a case, if there are repeated exchanges, the relationships take the form of a group that has dense ties. Particular configurations in a network or structure stimulate feelings and emotions, which are expressed according to specific norms (that concern for example jobs roles). Feelings and emotions have in turn an impact on how social actors perceive themselves in interactions, and therefore also have an effect on the single relationships and the entire structure of social relations. The results of the exchange – like its frequency and nature – also produce emotions that can modify social cohesion.

The central position in a network gives an advantage only if it causes the other actors to be dependent on the actor who occupies that position. Power can result, in particular, from a privileged position in a series of exchanges, as happens in favor of the one who has a superior place in a hierarchical organization. In such a case, power is the result of a few actors' ability – whether they be single actors or actors in a coalition – to occupy a central position in the exchange network and thereby monopolize to their advantage the entry of other actors, in order to obtain certain benefits. The value given by these other actors to the entry determines the amount of reward obtained by the central position actors. The monopolistic power of the mediators comes, in particular, from the fact, that those wishing to obtain certain benefits have to apply to them for entry. The advantage, held by a privileged position, decreases as the number of transfers increase when, at each transfer, there are other actors who are endowed with power, and therefore cannot be excluded from the exchange. If there is a hierarchy of authority, the advantage, in terms of power given to the actor who occupies a central position, can extend to the lower levels of the hierarchy, if the actor occupying a lower level position also has enough power to avoid being excluded by the central position actor. In feudal times, for example, the sovereign could not exclude his fief holders from having relations with him. On the contrary, nowadays, the fact that in a hierarchical company top managers can be fired limits their power.

In a positively connected network (characterized by non-competitive relationships, in particular cooperative), the actor who occupies a central position can act as a broker and use the power given by this position, to his or her own advantage as well as to others', who – as said before – are not in competition with each other. In a negatively connected network, however, there is competition between the actors in a non-central position, as they all want to exchange with the actor who occupies a central position. The former are in a weak position, and risk being exploited if they cannot turn to others to form a coalition. Realizing their dependent position and therefore, inferiority, they may react showing feelings of dissatisfaction and relative deprivation. These feelings are stronger if they know that other actors who are also in a dependent position have managed to form a coalition, thereby reducing their disadvantage. Therefore, coalitions amongst actors are easier either when they share a position of inequality within the whole group, or when they share a disadvantageous position compared to others and they perceive to have been treated incorrectly or unjustly by the other party in the exchange. An already existing group identity decreases the advantage, in terms of power, of the actors in a central position, but also the frequency of exchange amongst the disadvantaged actors, and therefore the opportunity to form a coalition amongst themselves (Cook and Emerson 1978: 723–4; Corra and Willer 2002; Emerson 1962, 1969: 389–94, 396–8; Lawler and Yoon 1996, 1998; Lawler and Thye 1999; Molm 1987, 2001: 265–6; 2003; Molm and Cook 1995: 220–26; Molm et al. 1999, 2000; Willer 2003; Yamagishi 1987).

Power is different from influence. As mentioned, power here is understood as potential power, indicated by the ability to obtain a favorable distribution of resources. This ability, in turn, is given by the position in an exchange network. On the other hand, some actors exert influence on others – according to the Status Characteristics Theory – if the latter modify their behavior, expecting to receive in exchange benefits for themselves or their group by virtue of the competence they impute to the former. Such expectations, which can be unfounded, create a hierarchy of status or social esteem, such that when there is a mutual task, the privileged actors have a greater chance to act, act more, they receive a better evaluation for what they do, and therefore have more influence on group decisions. Considering power and influence jointly, exercising influence, which results from social status, turns potential power into the actual ability to distribute resources, and transforms weak power into strong. Status, which turns into exercising influence, is an indirect source of power, while the ability to exclude is a direct source. Power and status influence each other and potentially consolidate an exchange network, making it legitimate. In particular, the social status of the actors involved in an exchange is transferred to that which is exchanged, and influences the negotiation (in the sense that it gives an advantage to high status actors).

A few network configurations, among others that are also possible, and the consequences for actors in terms of power, will now be referred to:

a. Actors who do not need to have exchange relations with others are connected in an exclusive way to others if these others do need to interact with them. This happens, for example, when one individual is desired by many as a possible partner in a business or marriage relationship, while he or she has no need to tie himself or herself to anyone, or when an employer does not have to employ any worker in particular, while every worker needs to work and he or she cannot go to another employer for work.

b. Actors who have to interact with many others in order to benefit are connected to the others in an inclusive way. An example is a company that depends on many suppliers, each of whom is irreplaceable and therefore exercises power over the company, whilst the latter is not able to create competition amongst the suppliers.

c. Actors who are privileged in a series of transactions derive power from the fact that the others have to interact with them first. This is the case of brokers. Their benefit in terms of money or status is greater, the greater the number of direct and indirect relations mediated by them, and is lower the greater the number of actors they need to ensure that their mediation work has a successful conclusion. Therefore, brokers make instrumental use of their positions in a network. When there are several mediators involved in a transaction, this instrumental use is more likely and advantageous if they cooperate together rather than compete.

If actors interact in a rational way and if they are in a situation of inferior power in exclusive relationships, they try to connect with others with whom they can share this inferior condition. Indeed, as we have seen, the total number of actors benefit, both individually and as a group, from relations of generalized exchange (Ekeh 1974: 51–5), which are found amongst unqualified workers. It is therefore rational for them, other conditions being equal, to link with others to form trade unions. As this does not often happen, many scholars have asked why not. In this regard, the theory of exchange adds support, also empirically, to a well-known Marxist theory. According to this theory, the creation of trade unions requires that the interested parties have group solidarity and, ultimately, a dense network of relations amongst the actors.

Olson has objected to such a theory and, in keeping with Rational Choice Theory, stated that it is convenient for the individual to pay the costs of association only in the presence of particular advantages ("selective benefits") for those who associate and/or disadvantages (like punishment) for those who do not (Olson 1965). However, one can reply that the selective incentives are not sufficient to stimulate – as the research demonstrated – those who do not have power to associate, whereas punishment weakens their cohesion. Therefore, in order to explain trade unionism, the marginal utility point of view, according to which actors seek maximum benefits in cases of restricted exchange relations (that is, relations between couples), has to be abandoned. It would be better to adopt the opposite point of view, according to which generalized exchange relations allow solidarity to be reached as a particular public good (Gillmore 1987).

Unlike unqualified workers, whose power depends only on having established reciprocal bonds, powerful actors do not need (other conditions being equal) other bonds. Therefore, every actor who exercises power has an interest in seeking his or her own maximum utility in limited exchange relations (that is, between couples). Nevertheless, this proposition does not hold if power is exercised over many subjects, with whom the holder of power has generalized exchange relations. Distinct resources are exchanged: the actor that holds power sets the objectives and how to achieve them, and defines the tasks and ensures group norms are adhered to, while the subordinate actors give the former status, influence and legitimacy (Hollander 1980). Thus, exchange theory is useful not only for the study of cultural structures which give a normative context to the exchange, but also for the study of individual behavior, where the individual (as is assumed) typically uses strategies that maximize the advantage obtained in an exchange. On these separate subject matters there are two different research directions in exchange theory, one using a macro-social unit of analysis, and the other a micro-social (Befu 1980).

If actors have reached equilibrium of power, each one of them is better off if they add links in order to modify, in their favor, the relations of power. This holds both for those actors who would be without power if they were not linked, and for actors who are powerful anyway, but the former are influenced above all by moral considerations of solidarity, and the latter by considerations of personal benefit. It can be generally stated that every exchange network is subjected to continual attempts by those participants in the transactions, who are in a position of inferiority or equilibrium with the others, to modify relations of power, (Cook 1977, 1982: 182–92, 195; Emerson 1962; Marsden 1987; Molm 2001: 264–8; Willer et al. 2002).

Reluctance to fully exploit known superiority of power, commitment towards actors with whom there have been transactions in the past, and binding norms in general, limits the attainment of benefits in exchange relations. Binding norms can be derived from several ethical principles of equity and justice (Cook and Emerson 1978: 727–8, 733–8). These terms can be explained as: (a) moral right (as opposed to moral duty and, in particular, reciprocal duty), (b) merit (or contribution), and (c) necessity. None of the terms are definite, nor are the aforementioned principles compatible with each other. Thus, their interpretation and application in specific cases are uncertain and contradictory (Bredemeier 1978: 434–8; Heath 1976: 134–44). Students of the theory of justice have favored the criterion of merit which may be understood by referring to procedural rules (according to various interpretations of the term), or to equal distribution (also open to interpretation) (Leventhal 1980).

Keeping in mind the maximization of utility assumption, the principle of equal distribution, in particular, can be interpreted according to social position, along with other criteria. A privileged position induces norms which sanction the benefits-to-merit ratio and, implicitly, the legitimacy of the inequality, whereas a working-class position favors egalitarian norms. In developing countries, the degree to which there is an open or closed attitude regarding social change and, therefore, the rural or urban context, is also relevant. In a rural context, a low social position seems to lead to norms that favor a redistribution of incomes according to a principle of necessity. Instead, in an urban context, popular norms tend to be those that allow, according to a principle of merit, material benefits to be obtained in order to benefit from modernization (Heath 1976: 144; Parkin 1971: ch. 3; Tallman and Tallman 1979).

As we have seen, the reciprocity principle is an ethical criterion that governs social exchange. Generally, social and market exchanges depend on observing trust norms that are of an institutional nature and whose purpose is to guarantee that the parties receive an equivalent amount for their services. What the actors are interested in is their evaluation or impression of equivalence in the exchange. The actual equivalence, or lack of it, has no consequences in the exchange when the actors are not aware of it (Pryor, Graburn 1980). An actor engaged in an exchange assumes that the other party shares his values, as well as his preferences and utility (Stinchcombe 1986). The reciprocity norm is widely, if not universally, shared. However, as it is generic, it is interpreted and applied differently according to the cultural contexts which single out particular rules that govern an exchange, and also according to the objectives the individuals want to pursue (Ekeh 1974: ch. 2).

Unequal exchanges, which give rise to exploitation, violate the reciprocity principle. In other words, the rights and duties of the actors engaged in the exchange must be complementary: if exploitation is to be avoided, the rights of one party must correspond to the duties of the other. This means, at least, observing the norm according to which those who have been given help have the right to be helped and not harmed by those who have received it, given that the receivers are morally in debt to the helpers (Gouldner 1960). A most wide interpretation of the reciprocity principle involves the norm by which benefits are given to one who is in need (thus, also to unknown people) in the hope of receiving from others, also unknown, a return if it should be necessary. Observing the altruistic norm, taken in its widest sense, maintains extremely generalized exchange relations (Titmuss 1971: 237–9).

According to the equity principle, being morally in debt constitutes a moral obligation to honor that debt. An actor who feels morally in debt maintains to have received more than he/she has given and therefore senses a discrepancy, or incongruence, in his or her behavior. This is a particular case of equity, where the debtor knows the reason for his/her debit, third parties are not taken into consideration, and the debit can only be decreased by a more favorable relationship between how much the creditor has given and how much he or she has received, and furthermore, a symbolic payment from a third party does not reduce the debit or moral obligation. The dimension of the obligation depends, above all, on the actor's perception of the benefit received. Nevertheless, the value the actor gives to the costs incurred by who gave the benefit is also important, although to a lesser degree. Sensing that one of his actions has given rise to the benefit received creates a further criterion that the receiver uses to estimate the size of his moral debit. How such a debit is perceived (its presence and its amount) leads the receiver to exchange in return, according to a reciprocity criterion, keeping in mind the importance of the debit and the opportunity to re-exchange. The receiver can also decide to reduce his debit by decreasing the importance of it or of the costs incurred by the giver, or by attributing selfish motives to the giver's action, or finally by denying responsibility for such an action (Greenberg 1980).

Therefore, general rules of equity guide the comparison between that which an actor holds to have given and received. This can be illustrated examining how actors apply the norms to exchanges, in which they are involved each time, and also by examining how considerations of legitimacy influence these exchanges. Regarding the first point, the widest normative context is relevant in the case, referred to by Thibaut and Kelley (1959), where specific actors establish a comparison with others during an interaction. The general norms are, in fact, stated, interpreted and applied in the course of the comparison. The norms emerge through the exchanges and while they are taking place. The norms change according to the type of actors involved and the type of exchange, which can be distributive (where the actors exchange resources) or productive (where the actors combine their resources in order to obtain a product).

Participants in an exchange evaluate it cognitively and morally, adapting to this particular case a general rule of justice, particularly equality or redistributive equity.

The equality norm would presumably come up amongst participants in a collective action, since each of them has the same power and can control how much the others receive. The rule of redistributive justice – meant in the sense that each actor must receive according to the value of his or her contribution – could easily come up in a productive exchange. In fact, such a rule may be considered by the participants as the most suitable for maximizing profit, whereby each participant may hope to gain more power over the others by increasing his or her contribution to the collective product. Exchange Theory, and particularly *Network Exchange Theory*, pays special attention to the subject of legitimacy in relations of power. Taking into account that each social exchange is included in a normative context, considerations regarding the legitimacy of an exchange will certainly influence its course and outcome. Generally, coalitions are formed with greater difficulty if there is no legitimacy in the exchange, and it is also less likely that an exchange will take place if it is retained illegitimate by one or more partners, even if they would have benefited. Furthermore, exchanges which are considered illegitimate may not be completed and, if they are, the conditions of exchange are influenced negatively for those that offer goods or follow procedures that the other side considers illegitimate.

The legitimacy of an action carried out by a hierarchical group depends on the legitimacy given to its leader by the other members. This legitimacy comes not only from the regular election procedures and nominations– in the eyes of the subordinates – but also from how they evaluate the leader's competence, efficiency and honesty. Legitimate power – as individual guidance or group validity – affects, in several ways, how power is exercised in a network exchange: exchanges regarded as legitimate are more frequent, involve less use of power, and compared to illegitimate exchanges are less likely to be opposed by those subjected to the power. It is therefore less likely that they will form a coalition even when they could benefit from it (Hollander 1980: 113–17; Stolte 1987; Walker and Willer 2003; Willer et al. 2002: 131–5).

David Willer and his collaborators have formulated a theory of network exchange, named by them "elementary" (see Corra and Willer 2002; Markowsky et al. 1993; Walker and Willer 2003; Willer 1999, 2003). This theory will be taken into consideration as relevant, not only for the subject of legitimate exchange (as we will see now), but also in general for the whole research field of *Network Exchange Theory* (Molm 2002: 266). The theory proposes to relate external and internal properties to the social actors. Properties considered external to the actors are those coming from the social structure and from relationships amongst actors (like exchange relations, coercion, joining together of resources or conflict). Properties regarded as internal to the actors are, in particular, their decisions, beliefs and preferences. The elementary theory formulates models for every level of analysis (actors, relationships, social structure) with which actors' activities can be predicted. Actors transfer and receive actions (called here "sanctions") which can modify, in a positive or negative way, the preferences or values of the same actors and others, and they can also modify indirectly the relationships amongst the actors.

According to the "elementary" theory, there are several principles which guide the actors' actions and decisions. The *first principle* states that actors choose from various possible courses of action, the action which in their opinion (which could be wrong) will maximize future satisfaction of their preferences, taking into consideration the behavior expected from the others. In this case, the actors adhere to strategic rationality. On the other hand, parametric rationality states that each actor considers only his or her preferences.

If coercion exists in a relationship between two actors, the preferences of one are also the preferences of the other, but what is a positive sanction for one is the opposite for the other. If instead the actors' orders of preference are reciprocally incompatible then there will be conflict. As conflict creates costs (not only economic) for the actors, they can decide to give up on reaching maximum satisfaction of their preferences, and rather try to come to an agreement with the other side. A rational and perfectly informed actor aims to reach a maximum of satisfaction and a minimum of the costs associated with conflict with the other side. The ratio between satisfying preferences and the costs of conflict indicate an actor's resistance in an exchange. The *second principle* states that an agreement is reached if the interests of the actor and the other party are in balance, and therefore their resistance to the exchange is the same. If this occurs, the actors exercise equal power in the relation.

Therefore, distribution of power in network exchanges differs according to the particular structure of the relationships. The interests of the actors change accordingly and, indirectly, so does their behavior. In a network exchange, there are five typical connections:

1. *Exclusion:* in every triad (that is, in every network with three positions, held by actors A, B and C), an actor A can exchange with an actor B or with an actor C to obtain a benefit, but not with both. In general, given Ni, the number of exchange relations linked to actor i; given Mi, the maximum number of exchange relations from which an actor can benefit; given Qi, the minimum number of exchange relations an actor must complete in order to benefit, an actor i is connected in an exclusive way if Ni is greater than Mi or equal to Qi (Qi is greater than 1).

2. *Null connection*: in every triad, an actor A may exchange with another B, with another C, or with both. Generally speaking, for each actor i, Ni is equal to Mi, and both are greater than Qi (Qi equals 1).

3. *Inclusion:* in every triad, an actor A must exchange with B and with C, in order to benefit. Generally speaking, for each actor i, Ni is equal to Mi and Qi (Qi is greater than 1).

4. *Inclusive-exclusive connection:* in every triad, an actor A, who is linked to B, C, and D, can exchange at most with two of the others, and in order to benefit actor A must exchange with both. In general, for each actor i, Ni is greater than Mi, which is greater than or equal to Qi (Qi is equal to 1).

5. *Inclusive-null connection:* in every triad, an actor A, connected to B, C, and D, has to exchange with at least two of the others in order to benefit. In general, for each actor i, Ni is equal to Mi and greater than Qi (Qi is greater than 1).

The typology, which may be applied to all network exchanges, has proven useful for establishing empirically the validity of some assumptions. *Firstly,* all positions whether central or peripheral have the same structural power in a network (power that comes from the network configuration) only if the connection is null. *Secondly*, an exclusive connection gives power to the actor or actors who are able to exclude others from obtaining a benefit, thereby occupying a central position in the network. In such a case, the peripheral actors are at a disadvantage, and indeed the competition that exists between them leads them to accepting more and more disadvantageous conditions while they continue to exchange. However, coercion that the peripheral actors have to bear decreases and is eventually annulled if they form a coalition. In this case, relational power counterbalances structural power. A network which is made up of connections between positions at different hierarchical levels (as in the case of bureaucratic organizations) is exclusive only if the power is centralized. *Thirdly,* in an inclusive connection (where each actor has to exchange with each of the others to benefit) central positions only give minor power while the peripheral ones give greater power, in comparison to exclusive connections. The effects of inclusion on the actors' power increases along with the increase in the number of exchanges. If the number of direct relations carried out by an actor i in a network increases, then power relations will only change if the networks are inclusive. The number of direct relations connected to a position is called degree.

Power here is intended as potential power, that is an actor's ability (determined by the structural relations that connect the positions in a network exchange) to obtain rewards when his or her interests conflict with those of others. This ability depends both on situations concerning the actors, who are assumed to use rational strategies to keep or increase their power, and on their positions, each position receiving and exchanging resources with the others. The use of power, which is shown during the actual distribution of the resources, depends on the actors' status as indicated by how much the actor dishonored and esteemed. The high status of an actor is reflected in the things available to him or her, and leads to favorable, shared expectations regarding the actor's contribution to the execution of a common task. In turn, power gives status by virtue of the benefits (like rewards and resources) it is able to obtain. However, it has been observed that in small groups the power that some actors have may produce negative feelings in others, thereby cancelling the positive effects of power accruing from status.

A particular index of power – *Graph-theoretic Power Index* (*GPI*) – examines connections which have only one position in common, which are alternatives amongst themselves and which link each position to each of the others. This index sets, for each position, the number of advantageous connections (in terms of power) net the number of disadvantageous ones. Thereby not only can power be measured but axioms can also be formulated from which theorems can be derived to predict the conditions under which two or more rational actors will exchange resources. In the case, which will be now illustrated, of multiple exchanges, the notion of domain is useful to simply the calculation of the power index. A domain is made up of *subnetworks*. Changes within subnetworks do not bring about changes in the others. In particular domains there may be some unique exchanges (one exchange per round and per relation), called a *unique exchange network*. A particular position can have more than one unique exchange in each round, up to a maximum number, only if it has many relations, each one with a different partner.

If there are multiple exchanges (*multi-exchange network*) in each round the actors exchange with many partners, possibly in many domains. Generally, it is more convenient for an actor to have a large number of different relations to choose from, in order to increase his or her power. Indeed, having many possible alternative relations to choose from creates a source of power for the actor, because he or she can exclude some partners from the relation (even if they would be available), and choose others who have to follow the conditions laid down by the actor. Therefore, an actor *i* is dependent on another actor *j* if a missed exchange between *i* and *j* excludes *i* from the exchange. Actors with little power can be excluded from the exchange by actors with strong power; however, the former can effectively compensate their inferiority by establishing more relations. Also actors with little or medium power, which have equal power in a network of exchange, can become stronger by forming a coalition, whereas if they remain passive and in reciprocal competition they remain in a relatively weak situation.

However, this is not valid necessarily for actors with strong power. These actors have an advantage in the distribution of resources as they can exclude others from a relation without excluding themselves. They are interested in increasing the number of relations with the weaker actors, but not with the other stronger ones. Therefore, position in a network exchange is a source of power for the actors who owing to their position have alternatives in the exchange and therefore can exclude some partners and favor others. In other words, an actor is weaker, the lower his chances are of being included in an exchange. If the outcome of an exchange is uncertain, strong differences in power amongst the actors tend to reduce both involvement of the weaker actors in the exchange, and also the inequality between weak and strong actors.

Weak actors prefer to try to exchange with others less powerful than themselves. If they manage to, then these actors acquire power, while those that were previously strong become weaker. If there are no strong actors, the actors try to exchange with others who have equal power, as they have the same probability of being included in the exchange. Finally, an exchange with more powerful actors only occurs when there is no alternative, that is, if weak actors are forced to. The result is that weak actors prefer to exchange amongst themselves, rather than with actors stronger than themselves. Therefore, a relationship is suboptimal (namely, without maximum advantage), when its presence reduces the possible number of exchanges amongst rational actors within the whole network, since they are not interested in exchanging in suboptimal. Suboptimal relations can occur not only amongst strong actors (who are better off exchanging with weaker actors), but also amongst weak ones when one or more actors are never excluded, and the remaining have an equal chance of being so. In the case of suboptimal relations a hole in the network is formed which divides forming new networks with denser relations: these networks are constituted by connections, often informal, amongst weak actors, with little difference in power amongst them, as it is generally the case of a group of friends.

Conclusion

After having specified the field of research of Exchange Theory and touched upon the introductory literature, this presentation has dwelled on the concepts – actor, resource, social relation, profit and cost, stimulus and reinforcement – and on the relationships between the theory of exchange on the one hand, and economic and behavioral psychology on the other. Then Homans's and Blau's contributions (well noted and discussed) to the theory of exchange have been examined in conjunction with the more recent contribution by Coleman. Concise information on their reception has also been provided. Much space has been taken by Exchange Network Theory, with reference both to the formulations of Emerson, Cook and their collaborators and followers, and also to Willer, Markowsky and other exponents of the so-called elementary theory of exchange networks. In this connection, the theoretical importance, for *Network Exchange Theory*, of some concepts have been discussed such as: exchange network, power, dependence and influence, negotiated and reciprocal exchange, coercion, reciprocity and redistributive equity, exclusive, inclusive and null connection.

References

Abrahamsson, B. 1970. "Homans on Exchange: Hedonism Revisited." *American Journal of Sociology* 76: 273–85.

Alexander, J.C. and Reed, J. 2009. "Social Science as Reading and Performance: A Cultural Sociological Understanding of Epistemology." *European Journal of Social Theory* 12: 21–41.

Befu, H. 1980. Structural and Motivational Approaches to Social Exchange, in K.J. Gergen, M.S. Greenberg and R.H. Willis (eds), *Social Exchange: Advances in Theory and Research*. New York: Plenum Press, 197–214.

Bierstedt, R. 1965. "Review of *Exchange and Power in Social Life* by Peter M. Blau." *American Sociological Review* 30: 789–90.

Blau, P.M. 1964. *Exchange and Power in Social Life*. New York: Wiley.

Blau, P.M. 2002. Reflections on a Career as a Sociologist, in J. Berger and M. Zelditch (eds), *New Directions in Contemporary Sociological Theory*. Lanham, MD: Rowman & Littlefield, 345–57.

Boulding, K.E. 1962. "Two Critiques of Homans's *Social Behavior: Its Elementary Forms. An Economist's View*." *American Journal of Sociology* 67: 458–61.

Bredemeier, H.C. 1978. Exchange Theory, in T. Bottomore and R. Nisbet (eds), *A History of Sociological Analysis*. New York: Basic Books, 418–56.

Chadwick-Jones, J.K. 1976. *Social Exchange Theory: Its Structure and Influence in Social Psychology*. London: Academic Press.

Cohen, P.S. 1968. *Modern Social Theory*. London: Heinemann. Italian translation: *La teoria sociologica contemporanea*, 1971, Bologna: Il Mulino.

Coleman, J.S. 1990. *Foundations of Social Theory*. Cambridge, MA: Belknap Press.

Cook, K.S. 1977. "Exchange and Power in Networks of Interorganizational Relations." *The Sociological Quarterly* 18: 62–82.

Cook, K.S. 1982. *Network Structures from an Exchange Perspective*, in P.V. Marsden and N. Lin (eds), *Social Structure and Network Analysis*. London: Sage, 177–99.

Cook, K.S. 1987. Emerson's Contributions to Social Exchange Theory, in K.S. Cook (ed.), *Social Exchange Theory*. London: Sage, 209–22.

Cook, K.S. and Emerson, R.M. 1978. "Power, Equity and Commitment in Exchange Networks." *American Sociological Review* 43: 721–39.

Cook, K.S., O'Brien, J. and Kollock, P. 1990. Exchange Theory: A Blueprint for Structure and Process, in G. Ritzer (ed.), *Frontiers of Social Theory*. New York: Columbia University Press, 158–81.

Cook, K.S. and Whitmeyer, J. 2000. Richard M. Emerson, in G. Ritzer (ed.), *The Blackwell Companion to Major Social Theorists*. Oxford: Blackwell, 486–511.

Corra, M. and Willer, D. 2002. "The Gatekeeper." *Sociological Theory* 20: 180–207.

Coser, L. 1971. *Masters of Sociological Thought*. New York: HBJ.

Crespi, F. 2002. *Il pensiero sociologico*. Bologna: Il Mulino.

Davis, J.A. 1962. "Two Critiques of Homans's *Social Behavior: Its Elementary Forms. A Sociologist's View.*" *American Journal of Sociology* 67: 454–8.

Ekeh, P. 1974. *Social Exchange Theory: The Two Traditions*. London: Heinemann.

Emerson, R.M. 1962. "Power-Dependence Relations." *American Sociological Review* 27: 31–41.

Emerson, R.M. 1969. Operant Psychology and Exchange Theory, in R.L. Burgess and D. Bushell (eds), *Behavioral Sociology*. New York: Columbia University Press, 379–405.

Emerson, R.M. 1976. "Social Exchange Theory." *Annual Review of Sociology* 2: 335–62.

Emerson, R.M. 1987. Toward a Theory of Value in Social Exchange, in K.S. Cook (ed.), *Social Exchange Theory*. London: Sage, 11–45.

Foa, E.B. and Foa, U.G. 1980. Resource Theory: Interpersonal Behavior as Exchange, in K.J. Gergen, M.S. Greenberg and R.H. Willis (eds), *Social Exchange: Advances in Theory and Research*. New York: Plenum Press, 77–94.

Friedman, D. 1987. Notes on "Toward a Theory of Value in Social Exchange," in Cook, K.S. (ed.), *Social Exchange Theory*. London: Sage, 47–58.

Gergen, K.J. 1980. Exchange Theory: The Transient and the Enduring, in K.J. Gergen, M.S. Greenberg and R.H. Willis (eds), *Social Exchange: Advances in Theory and Research*. New York: Plenum Press, 261–80.

Gillmore, M.R. 1987. Implications of Generalized Versus Restricted Exchange, in K.S. Cook (ed.), *Social Exchange Theory*. London: Sage, 170–89.

Gouldner, A.W. 1960. "The Norm of Reciprocity: A Preliminary Statement." *American Sociological Review* 25: 161–78.

Greenberg, M.S. 1980. A Theory of Indebtedness, in K.J. Gergen, M.S. Greenberg and R.H. Willis (eds), *Social Exchange: Advances in Theory and Research*. New York: Plenum Press, 3–26.

Griffin, E. 1991. Social Exchange Theory of John Thibaut and Harold Kelley, in *A First Look at Communication Theory*. New York: McGraw-Hill, 196–205.

Heath, A. 1968. "Economic Theory and Sociology: A Critique of P.M. Blau's *Exchange and Power in Social Life.*" *Sociology* 2: 273–92.

Heath, A. 1976. *Rational Choice and Social Exchange*. Cambridge: Cambridge University Press.

Hollander, E.P. 1980. Leadership and Social Exchange Processes, in K.J. Gergen, M.S. Greenberg and R.H. Willis (eds), *Social Exchange: Advances in Theory and Research*. New York: Plenum Press, 103–18.

Homans, G.C. 1950. *The Human Group*. New York: Harcourt, Brace & World.

Homans, G.C. 1958. "Social Behavior as Exchange." *American Journal of Sociology* 63: 597–606.

Homans, G.C. 1961. *Social Behavior: Its Elementary Forms*. New York: Harcourt, Brace & World.

Homans, G.C. 1966. "Reply to Razak." *American Sociological Review* 31: 543–4.

Homans, G.C. 1969. The Sociological Relevance of Behaviorism, in R.L. Burgess and D. Bushell (eds), *Behavioral Sociology*. New York: Columbia University Press, 1–24.

La Valle, D. 2002. "Il capitale sociale nella teoria dello scambio." *Stato and Mercato* 65: 305–34.

Lawler, E.J. 2001. "An Affect Theory of Social Exchange." *American Journal of Sociology* 107: 321–52.

Lawler, E.J. and Thye, S.R. 1999. "Bringing Emotions into Social Exchange Theory." *Annual Review of Sociology* 25: 217–44.

Lawler, E.J. and Yoon, J. 1996. "Commitment in Exchange Relations: Test of a Theory of Relational Cohesion." *American Sociological Review* 61: 89–108.

Lawler, E.J. and Yoon, J. 1998. "Network Structure and Emotion in Exchange Relations." *American Sociological Review* 63: 871–94.

Leventhal, G.S. 1980. What Should be done with Equity Theory? New Approaches to the Study of Fairness in Social Relationship, in K.J. Gergen, M.S. Greenberg and R.H. Willis (eds), *Social Exchange: Advances in Theory and Research*. New York: Plenum Press, 27–55.

Levinger, G. and Huesmann, L.R. 1980. An "Incremental Exchange" Perspective on the Pair Relationship, in K.J. Gergen, M.S. Greenberg and R.H. Willis (eds), *Social Exchange: Advances in Theory and Research*. New York: Plenum Press, 165–88.

Lindenberg, S. 2000. James Coleman, in G. Ritzer (ed.), *The Blackwell Companion to Major Social Theorists*. Oxford: Blackwell, 512–44.

Lovaglia, M.J., Skvoretz, J. and Willer, D. 1999a. Negotiated Exchange in Social Networks, in D. Willer (ed.), *Network Exchange Theory*. London: Praeger, 157–84.

Lovaglia, M.J., Skvoretz, J. and Willer, D. 1999b. Recent Problems and Solutions in Network Exchange Theory. Part 1: An Automated Approach to the Theoretical Analysis of Difficult Problems, in D. Willer (ed.), *Network Exchange Theory*. London: Praeger, 259–69.

Lovaglia, M.J. and Willer, D. 1999. An Alternative for Predicting Weak Power, in D. Willer (ed.), *Network Exchange Theory*. London: Praeger, 184–92.

Markowsky B. et al. 1993. "The Seeds of Weak Power: An Extension of Network Exchange Theory." *American Sociological Review* 58: 197–209.

Markowsky, B., Willer, D. and Patton, T. 1999. Power Relations in Exchange Networks, in D. Willer (ed.), *Network Exchange Theory*. London: Praeger, 87–108.

Marsden, P.V. 1987. Elements of Interactor Dependence, in Cook, K.S. (ed.), *Social Exchange Theory*. London: Sage, 137–48.

Marsden, P.V. 1988. Brokerage Behavior in Restricted Exchange Networks, in P.V. Marsden and N. Lin (eds), *Social Structure and Network Analysis*. London: Sage, 201–18.

Michener, H.A., Cohen, E.D. and Soerensen, A.B. 1977. "Social Exchange: Predicting Transactional Outcomes in Five-Event, Four-Person Systems." *American Sociological Review* 42: 522–35.

Molm, L.D. 1987. Linking Power Structure and Power Use, in K.S. Cook (ed.), *Social Exchange Theory*. London: Sage, 101–29.

Molm, L.D. 2001. Theories of Social Exchange and Exchange Networks, in G. Ritzer and B. Smart (eds), *Handbook of Social Theory*. London: Sage, 260–72.

Molm, L.D. 2003. "Theoretical Comparisons of Forms of Exchange." *Sociological Theory* 21: 1–17.

Molm, L.D. and Cook, K.S. 1995. Social Exchange and Exchange Networks, in K.S. Cook, G.A. Fine and J.S. House (eds), *Sociological Perspectives on Social Psychology*. Needham Heights, MA: Allyn and Bacon, 209–35.

Molm, L.D., Peterson, G. and Takashashi, N. 1999. "Power in Negotiated and Reciprocal Exchange." *American Sociological Review* 64: 876–90.

Molm, L.D., Takashashi, N. and Peterson, G. 2000. "Risk and Trust in Social Exchange: An Experimental Test of a Classical Proposition." *American Journal of Sociology* 105: 1396–427.

Olson, M. 1965. *The Logic of Collective Action*. Cambridge, MA: Harvard University Press.

Parkin, F. 1971. *Class Inequality and Political Order*. London: MacGibbon and Gee. Italian translation: *Disuguaglianza di Classe and ordinamento politico*, 1976, Turin: Einaudi.

Pryor, F.L. and Graburn, N.H.H. 1980. The Myth of Reciprocity, in K.J. Gergen, M.S. Greenberg and R.H. Willis (eds), *Social Exchange: Advances in Theory and Research*. New York: Plenum Press, 215–37.

Razak, W.N. 1966. "Razak on Homans." *American Sociological Review* 31: 542–3.

Rice, E. 2003. "The Effect of Social Uncertainty in Networks of Social Exchange." Paper presented at the Annual Meeting of the American Sociological Association, Atlanta, Georgia, August 16–20.

Ritzer, G. 2000. *Modern Sociological Theory*. Boston, MA: McGraw-Hill.

Schwartz, B. 1980. New Developments in Operant Conditioning and Their Implications, in K.J. Gergen, M.S. Greenberg and R.H. Willis (eds), *Social Exchange: Advances in Theory and Research*. New York: Plenum Press, 239–59.

Simpson, B. and Willer, D. 1999. Recent Problems and Solutions in Network Exchange Theory. Part 1: A New Method for Finding Power Structures, in D. Willer (ed.), *Network Exchange Theory*. London: Praeger, 270–84.

Skinner, B.F. 1971. *Beyond Freedom and Dignity*. London: Bantam Books.

Skvoretz, J. and Willer, D. 1999. Negotiated Exchange in Social Networks, in D. Willer (ed.), *Network Exchange Theory*. London: Praeger, 129–54.

Stinchcombe, A.L. 1986. Norms of exchange, in A.L. Stinchcombe (ed.), *Stratification and Organization: Selected Papers*. Cambridge, England: Cambridge University Press. Italian translation: Norme dello scambio, 1991, in M. Magatti (ed.), *Azione economica come azione sociale*. Milan: FrancoAngeli, 81–118.

Stolte, J.F. 1987. Legitimacy, Justice, and Productive Exchange, in Cook, K.S. (ed.), *Social Exchange Theory*. London: Sage, 190–208.

Tallman, I. and Tallman, M.I. 1979. "Values, Distributive Justice and Social Change." *American Sociological Review* 44: 216–35.

Thibaut, J.W. and Kelley, H.H. 1959. The *Social Psychology of Groups*. New York: Wiley. Italian translation: *Psicologia sociale dei gruppi*, 1974, Bologna: Il Mulino.

Timasheff, N.S. and Theodorson, G.A. 1976. *Sociological Theory: Its Nature and Growth*. New York: Random House.

Titmuss, R.M. 1970. *The Gift Relationship*. London: Allen & Unwin.

Turner, J. 1987. Social Exchange Theory: Future Directions, in K.S. Cook (ed.), *Social Exchange Theory*. London: Sage, 223–38.

Turner, J. 1998. *The Structure of Sociological Theory*. Belmont, CA: Wadsworth.

Walker, H.A. and Willer, D. 2003. "Legitimacy and Power in Exchange Structures." Paper presented at the Annual Meeting of the American Sociological Association, Atlanta, Georgia, August 16–20.

Willer, D. (ed.) 1999. *Network Exchange Theory*. London: Praeger.

Willer, D. 2003. "Power-at-a-Distance." *Social Forces* 81: 1295–1334.

Willer, D. et al. 2002. Network Exchange Theory, in J. Berger and M. Zelditch (eds), *New Directions in Contemporary Sociological Theory*. Lanham, MD: Rowman & Littlefield, 109–44.

Wrong, D.H. 1967. "Some Problems in Defining Social Power." *American Journal of Sociology* 73: 673–81.

Yamagishi, T. 1987. An Exchange Theoretical Approach to Network Positions, in K.S. Cook (ed.), *Social Exchange Theory*. London: Sage, 149–69.

Chapter 5
Michel Foucault (1926–1984)

Preliminary Remarks

Foucault's work, which can be classified with difficulty amongst the academic disciplines, continues to influence social sciences in general, and sociology in particular. Its influence is felt not only in the author's native country, France, as Foucault is in fact very read and discussed also in other European countries and in the English-speaking world. In this chapter, we shall first provide a short introduction to some of the most important concepts and themes dealt with by Foucault's work, namely those of archaeology, archive, discourse, statement, episteme, genealogy, power, knowledge, sexuality and historicity. We shall then expound its contents, grouped by themes, which resume, develop and arrange these themes within a setting that is historical, linguistic and social at the same time. Finally, we shall give some concise information about the reception and interpretation (both very wide and heterogeneous) of Foucault's work, and in that context, we shall briefly report some divergences in its evaluation. In addition to books, which Foucault himself published, reference will be made to his lectures at the Collège de France in the 1970s, which came out posthumously (see Foucault 2003a; 2003b; 2006).

Relevant Concepts and Themes in Foucault's Work

Foucault makes us of a language of his own, which is not easily understandable.[1] In this language, the concepts of "statement" (énoncé, enouncement) and "discourse" (*discours*) seem to be preliminary to the whole work. Discourse is not a set of signs, but rather "a set of statements," or "practices that form systematically the objects they talk about." "Discourse," more precisely, may indicate a general ambit of statements, or a particular group of them, or also the orderly practices through which a given number of statements can be explained. Discourses make use of signs – and particularly, words – to designate things. Statements are sets of utterances, which form the constitutive unity of discourses. They are formed by propositions and are characterized by their performing a peculiar function, called "enunciative function." Performing this function implies formulating the rules through which a sentence obtains a meaning and a proposition takes the value of truth, and specifying the author of the statement; its subject within a range of statements that specify its position and relation with others; its identity, considering its material support (papers or other), its information content and the possibility of being used and reused. The analysis of statements requires determining and analyzing the operating conditions of the enunciative function. In virtue of these conditions, a set of signs takes a specific existence and visibility. A "discursive practice" is the set of rules (historically and socially determined and effective in a particular economic, geographical or linguistic area) that define such conditions.

The analysis of discourse points out the range of statements in which a discourse is placed and by which it is conditioned, because it is this field that determines the meaning and the boundaries of a discourse. The analysis of discourse, in its critical part, aims at establishing a set of principles in it. A first part of this analysis concerns the principles (or forms) of discourse exclusion, limitation, appropriation and rareness. These principles help constituting or organizing a discourse that otherwise would be a continuous, confused and disorderly murmur. In particular, Foucault makes a distinction among a principle of discourse break (to be made effective where discourse becomes less full, more rarefied); a principle of discontinuity and randomness

---

1   An English dictionary of the terms used by Foucault is available on the website: foucault.info/Foucault-L/archive. In Italian it is possible to consult the website: www.Ilgiardinodeipensieri.eu, the lexicon of Foucault's *Archaeology of Knowledge*, edited by Elena Maggio. There are several introductions to Foucault's work. See in particular Danaher, Schirato and Webb 2000; Dean 1994; Gutting 2005; Todd 2006.

(according to which discourses are considered discontinuous practices that may cross, approach, but also ignore or exclude each other); and finally, a principle of specificity (according to which discourse is a practice imposed to things rather than a set of pre-established meanings that have only to be deciphered).

In a second part – called "genealogical" – this analysis seeks to shed light on how the statement power of discourse has imposed, developed and changed itself, that is to say, its power to constitute an ambit of propositions about which one can express a judgment of truth or falseness. Foucault calls this area "positivity" (*positivité*), by which he means that analysis refers in this case to the actual formation of discourse, that is to say, to the a priori reality conditions of statements. In other words, the notion of positivity refers to the conditions, through which a discursive practice is exercised and transformed. The subject matter of the author's analysis is the origin of these principles, or forms, of discourse, and the way in which discourse is produced; namely, by answering what needs or by exercising what constraints. Starting from the manifestation and regularity of a discourse, one inquires not only into its origin, but also its boundaries, and the outcome of the causal series of events. The genealogical analysis of discourse keeps to a principle of outward appearance in relation to discourse itself. By means of this principle it is possible to determine the outer conditions of discourse possibility; and in addition, how statements are characterized, exist, transform themselves and disappear, and hence, their history, with its aspects of regularity, or on the contrary, of contingency.

Statements have an inner consistency, mutual compatibilities; but they also have some discontinuities in terms of breaks and change, which require an appropriate concept formulation in order to interpret and study them. The material support of a statement (the words and sentences it makes use of) does not ensure at all the possibility repeating it out of the particular time and place in which it is stated. Its repetition depends rather on the identity of its use possibilities and on its information content. A statement is, in other words, a set of signs, which has always the same existence modality even in different times and places and with a different material support. Investigation must reprocess the documents of the past, point out the discontinuities (that is to say, scansions, interruptions, internal consistencies, overlapping, and incompatibilities) that can be found in what documents keep a trace of. A discursive event (événement discursif) has its own unity and individuality compared to others that are contiguous to it. The question is to establish the conditions of its existence, and let therefore emerge the internal relations of a set of statements that form the discursive event, as well as the relations among groups of statements, and also between them and events of a different nature.

Though statements present themselves in a scattered way, it is, however, possible to see some regularity in their manifestations as, for example, a compatibility of themes, a time order, or a mutual dependence. If the inherent regularities of a discourse are pointed out, they allow describing the whole set of concepts that characterize a discursive practice. A discourse, or a set of statements is then characterized by the regularity of a practice. If these regularities emerge, analysis can identify a "dispersion system" (*système de dispersion*), through which these regularities have constituted a "discursive formation" (formation discursive). A discursive formation assumes there are rules by means of which it is possible to group a set of scattered statements and relations, such as the rules to be enforced for their grammatical analysis. These rules apply to all those who speak within a discursive field. The object of any discourse – for example, the psychiatric discourse on madness, or the medical discourse on illness – presents itself as a set of relations among institutions, socioeconomic processes, regulatory systems, classification types, etc.

Discursive relations refer to discourse itself, and define its specificity compared to others, the regularities to be established among scattered statements, the practices forming the subject of a discourse, and therefore bound the field of discursive practices in respect to non-discursive ones. This occurred, for instance, in the case of seventeenth- and eighteenth-century economic theories, as considered in their relationship to the practices and interests of rising capitalism. Different "strategies" – that is to say, different ways to treat, bound, group or link together the discourse objects – can derive from a single set of relations existing in a discursive relation. For example, economic discourse defined itself in seventeenth century and partly also in eighteenth century, because of a peculiar choice of concepts and statements that can be related to practices and interests of the rising capitalist bourgeoisie. The theme of statements can differently relate with their authors, as they may be interchangeable in each particular discourse (for example, in the mathematic discourse) and, according to the particular discursive practices, may hold different positions and play different roles.

An "archive" (archive) is, in Foucault's words, "the general system of the formation and transformation of statements." To this archive, which can never be completed, belong the rules – or "laws" – that prescribe both what can be thought and said, as well as what cannot be thought and said because is placed out of a discursive practice. To this archive belong also the rules that build up, group and order the statements which otherwise would be an "amorphous multitude" of utterances. An archive establishes, in other words, an "enunciative field" (*champ énonciatif*), which – besides the descriptions of the archive itself – also includes an analysis of the discursive formations. To the archive belong also the conditions that establish, in the case of statements – that is to say, the discursive practices – their reality and identity, as well as the more or less extended application field of the rules that establish – for any field of statements – its object, concepts, procedures and use strategies. Therefore, different authors who may have lived in different times and written different works are able to produce the same discursive formation even in the absence of mutual influences.

The analysis of "positivities" (the conditions through which a discursive practice is exercised and transformed) is designated by the term "archaeology" (*archéologie*). An "archaeological" investigation seeks to define the formation rules that characterize a set of statements. This implies a description of the discourses, meant as practices constituting an archive, and of the rules that preside over the discursive formations. This investigation should not be mistaken for the history of ideas. As opposed to the history of ideas, "archaeology" does not consider what appears or is concealed in discourses considered as documents that show the existence of something related with something else, and does not linger over the sequence of the events of thought. Therefore, neither is "archaeology" interested in individually defined works, nor in those included in their overall context or in a network of causal connections. Neither is it interested in the authors of those discourses.

"Archaeology" deals instead with discourses in themselves, considered as unique entities, that is to say, using Foucault's language, "monuments." As Foucault stated in his lectures, by analyzing discourses archaeology of knowledge sets out to show "that the discovery of truth is really a certain modality of the production of truth" (Foucault 2006: 238). Accordingly, by investigating discourses and their truth claims, archaeology of knowledge "takes the relationship of knowledge and power into account." This relationship, which is evidenced in discursive practices, constitutes a main object of interest and research on the part of Foucault (Foucault 2006: 256 note 13). Power, in Foucault's own definition, is "essentially that which represses. Power is that which represses nature, instincts, a class, or individuals"; power relations in our society "are essentially anchored in a certain relationship of force," which was historically established by means of war (Foucault 2003a: 15).

As a method of inquiry, the "archaeological" investigation of knowledge involves the analysis of the discontinuities, or interruptions, that can be identified in the discursive practices and formations, and consequently, in the statement fields. If an archive is subject to "archaeological" research, its analysis aims at inquiring into discourses as single events with their differences and peculiarities. Discourses have already taken place. They, therefore, cannot take place again and do not belong to us any longer; but by virtue of this investigation, their operating system can be determined. Its purpose is to describe the discursive practices that connote it and make it possible; the statement function that is exercised within it; and the broader discursive formation to which the archive belongs. Thanks to this "archaeological" investigation, the archive appears as a practice that makes a variety of statements appear like as many regular events, and consequently, the rules of a practice that allows statements to exist and regularly change themselves are emphasized. "Archaeology" considers the types and the rules of specific discursive practices which provide discourses with their own identity.

Analysis focuses on the homogeneous fields of regularity in the statement practices, which characterize and make a discursive formation – but also statement heterogeneities – possible. These heterogeneities are the intrinsic oppositions – that is to say, the insurmountable differences, or "contradictions" – between the particular discourses on which "archaeological" analysis dwells, and any other discourse. The intrinsic oppositions between a particular discourse and any other establish and set the boundaries of what can be said within that particular discourse. They may concern the object, the statement modalities, the concepts, the theoretical options through which a particular discourse differs from others. "Archaeological" analysis does not claim to be a science, but instead a method for analyzing statements. This analysis pursues several aims:

- to point out a set of discursive formations that have interrelations subject to descriptions, thereby excluding any other discursive form;

- to show how each one of them has formed at the level of the statements, of the strategic choices, of the rules that have presided over their formation or over the replacement of a formation with another, which relates with the previous one in terms of breaks and discontinuity;
- to stress, in a discursive formation, any analogy and difference in some of their aspects (as the application field or the historical genesis);
- to highlight complementarity and subordination relations, or interrelations between separate discursive formations referred even to different ages, or between a particular discursive formation and a non-discursive system (such as institutions, economic practices and processes, political events). In the second case, the purpose of "archaeological" analysis may be, for instance, to point out how political practices have determined the sense and the form of a medical discourse by setting its object, application field and social functions.

A discursive formation reveals itself in a plurality of fields, for example the scientific, literary, juridical, philosophical, political field, and so on. Therefore, scientific discursive formations do not constitute a privileged "archaeological" investigation field. If this is the case, all the constitutive elements of a discourse that claims to be scientific become relevant, including its contradictions and gaps, as well as its acting as an ideology. The analysis of scientific discursive formations (of their "positivities" – which is the ambit of their constitutive propositions – of their knowledge, of the regularity relations existing among discursive practices) is indicated, using Foucault's words, by the term "episteme" (épistémè). The moment in which a discursive practice becomes autonomous (for example, that concerning madness), it constitutes the "threshold of positivity" (*seuil de positivité*) that precedes or accompanies a transformation into another discursive formation, with its own assessment and consistency norms on which its claim to be a scientific discourse rests. This transformation involves passing the "threshold of epistemologization" (*seuil d'*épistémolog*isation*). The last threshold, concerning formalization (*seuil de la formalisation*), requires establishing the necessary axioms, the elements used, the structures of propositions considered legitimate.

Mathematics is a discursive formation that has passed all these three thresholds (positivity, epistemologization, formalization). Not all scientific discursive formations have followed one another in this way, as though they were evolution stages. The particular history of a science, like biology and economics, shows on the contrary that the discursive practices that characterize it have transformed themselves (as in general happens in all discursive practices and formations) through breaks, discontinuities and separations. In other words, they have their own "historicity" (*historicité*), which must be investigated. "Historicity," in the use of this term made by Foucault, means a history of man, in the sense that human beings are active subjects of their own history, and indirectly, also of psychology, sociology, language, and in general human sciences, as these disciplines take object and methods from history. Whatever the human science investigation is focused on, the use of "historicity" implies not considering the chronological sequence of events science deals with; but rather carrying out an "archaeological" analysis to stress the internal organization of its discursive formations.

"Archaeological" analysis differs from epistemic analysis in that it considers the historicity of a particular science, and consequently, the internal discontinuities that make it different from another science. For instance, through a comparative investigation that has disregarded the historicity inherent in any language, some basic discontinuities from early nineteenth-century philology have been noticed between the linguistic family of the Indo-European languages and the one of the Semitic languages. Similarly, the historicity inherent in each individual species has been disregarded in biology, too, but it has been necessary to consider also the external environment because of its ability to affect living beings. Analysis has then focused on the life conditions of living beings. However, "archaeological" analyses do not limit themselves to examine exclusively scientific discursive formations, since they can also refer to other discourses and practices. For example, it is possible to make an "archaeological" analysis of sexuality, painting or political knowledge.

Epistemic analysis considers instead discursive formations and their constitutive propositions, and dwells, unlike "archaeological" analysis. If necessary, the scope of epistemic analysis extends beyond the thresholds of positivity; for it also comprehends the thresholds of epistemologization and – in the case of some particular discursive formations – also formalization. In the classical age (in the seventeenth century and partly in the eighteenth century), grammar and natural history were part of the episteme, and knowledge concerning life, work and language was considered inadequate in principle compared to absolute knowledge. In the modern age, instead, the episteme also includes, along with natural sciences, human sciences such as psychology and sociology. In addition, scholars think that the limits of knowledge do not come from the outside (as the classical age used to believe), but are instead inherent in knowledge itself. These limits inherent in knowledge, connected in the modern age to the nature of human knowledge, are a presupposition for the pursuit – endless, in principle – of knowledge itself (Foucault 1966: 229–30, 305–307, 375–85; 1969: 11–20, 25–5, 37–43, 66–7, 106–107, 116–204, 243–55, 272; 1971: 47–72; 1984: 12, 19–20).

Investigation concerning the knowledge produced as regards mental alienation is an example of both "archaeological" and epistemic analyses. This investigation implies the history of the constitution process of a homogeneous field of statements, through which – as we shall later see – some persons were designated as unsocial in "classical" age, but as alienated in the modern age. The constitution of this field of enunciative practices made it possible and promoted first, in the classical age, their confinement together with other persons considered unsocial as well; then, in the modern age, their segregation and medical-psychiatric treatment. In the modern age, indeed, medicine and psychiatry constituted themselves as sciences claiming objectivity and a positive field of knowledge of their own. The "positive science of mental diseases" is a manifestation of that claim to objectivity, and assumes as an a priori condition a synthesis between social and juridical evaluation. An "archaeological" investigation seeks to stress the epistemological configuration that has made this knowledge possible. In other words, this investigation aims at showing the conditions of "positivity" (of reality and identity) of its statements, and the presuppositions and the language of medical-psychiatric knowledge. The "archaeological" investigation also concerns the knowledge produced by social sciences in general (the épistémè of this knowledge), which distinguish it from the knowledge produced by proper sciences.

Positive knowledge within the domain of human sciences, in the study of sociology or psychology, results from epistemological assumptions that ensure it a specific investigation field and an internal consistency. However, human sciences are not proper sciences. In fact, compared to the latter, their configuration and presuppositions are radically different, and they lack in the formal criteria of scientific knowledge; that is to say, they do neither show the typical characteristics of objectivity nor the systematic nature through which a particular kind of knowledge can be called "scientific." Nevertheless, they "belong to the positive field of knowledge" because of their consistency and relation to their field of study. Social science knowledge shares with the knowledge produced by natural science the assumption of knowledge objectivity, which is a peculiarity of modern age. "Archaeology" has the task of investigating the "positivities" of these sciences (that is to say, the conditions by which social sciences claim the truth of their discourses), and the differences between social and natural sciences.

History, psychoanalysis and ethnology are preliminary to any other social science, as all of them exercise a preliminary and critical function over the knowledge they produce. History, by pointing out man's historicity, his historically determined nature, allows social sciences – psychology, sociology and linguistics – investigating the historical contents of human activity. Psychoanalysis, by studying the unconscious, finds the limits of what we can scientifically experiment. Finally, ethnology, by investigating cultures other than ours, shows alternative positivities situated outside a historical time. If by structure we mean a stable relation among the elements of a whole, the structure of individual experience can be made possible by pre-existing social structures, and they can find in turn a certain number of individuals for any option they present. However, the possibility of carrying out a structural analysis of a scientific discourse – whose legitimacy is not denied by Foucault – does not allow pointing out the "historicity" of discourse, first of all in the sense of its breaks and discontinuities, formation of regularities, its own exclusion, accumulation, transformation and connection rules with different discursive practices, but also in the sense of its origin and temporality.

A structural analysis (of a discourse, but also of a language, a myth, a literary text, or something else) is not, in other words, conducive to focusing on the "archaeological" and "genealogical" characteristics of a discourse and the consequent practices; nor to investigating their peculiarities and changes, which is instead a privileged object of study for Foucault. This object of study is also incompatible with the assumption of a transcendental cognitive subject (such as in Kant's theoretical and in Husserl's phenomenological philosophy). Its investigation focuses instead on the empirical subject, which is determined in a historical and anthropological sense, and thinks and acts in the world; as well as on the discursive formations that condition and supports such practices and thought, their limits and their interruptions and changes. Foucault's analysis of the "positivities" of the discursive formations has therefore an empirical character, since it is based exclusively on statements and on their forming and transforming systems (the "archives") (Foucault 1966: 366–93, 397–8; 1969: 191–3, 259–74; 1972: 112–13, 176).

Knowledge – i.e. all that is produced through and within scientific discursive formations – is a modality of power (*pouvoir/savoir*). Power is meant, in its more general sense, as an actually exercised ability to change other people's actions. In other words, power can be considered as a set of consequent actions, through which some individuals or groups (which must be formally free, that is to say, not be slaves) are driven to follow others. Therefore, power is not exercised over persons, but instead over their actions, and involves an ability to limit or differently order the activity field of other people. Even though those who are subjected to power may, whether temporarily or permanently, allow its exercise, power is not a manifestation of consent understood as general agreement. On the contrary, searching for an agreement or resorting to violence are available instruments for exercising power. The objects of investigation may be in particular: social differentiation systems produced by social, economic and cultural differences through which power can be exercised in a variety of contexts and conditions; pursued aims, which may be economic, political, or of a different nature; used means, which may range from physical to economic coercion, and to the construction of control and surveillance systems; and finally, institutionalization forms, as well as the rationalization degrees of their exercise.

In the past, from the Middle Ages until eighteenth century, power resulted only from law and from the rights it provided for, which were enforced through bans and sanctions by a unitary and absolute power. In the modern age, power mechanisms have changed. Control techniques of the dominated have been used instead of law and rights, and powers have not been confined within the area of the state apparatuses. Furthermore, power and knowledge have been combined in discourse, so that a variety of discursive elements can be found today in power strategies. The combination of power and knowledge in discursive formations has resulted – according to Foucault – from the need, in the modern age, to make of any individual, classified as a case, the object of impersonal control procedures. Hence, the rise, by the end of eighteenth century, of human sciences, or social sciences, as discursive formations with scientific claims through which it was possible to ground, legitimate and produce those procedures, intended as "rituals of truth."

Indeed, since early nineteenth-century power has no longer revealed itself directly as a punishment power over the subjects' bodies, and as a power personified by the sovereign and exercised by means of a legal and juridical apparatus. Power has instead addressed itself to the control and domination of the subjects' souls as a discipline instrument over their bodies. This power is built and validated through impersonal and objective administrative procedures, as well as through techniques applied by experts specialized in different areas: educationists, psychologists and psychiatrists. These procedures and techniques allow the continuous exercise of power over society, which is the object of administrative and economic control techniques, but also over the souls of single individuals (in Foucault's language, respectively, macro- and micro-physics of power) (*macro et microphysique du pouvoir*).

Control exercise and domination practices take place in a unitary, continuous, and comprehensive temporal dimension produced by domination itself. Since the moment in which the control of time became an instrument of power, history has become a history of the present. The history of punishment power directly exercised over the bodies, as in the past before modern age, involves in fact a reference to the present, a "genealogy" of the modern soul over which power is currently exercised. This "genealogy" goes along, but does not identify itself, with another kind of historical analysis, "archaeological history," through which the discursive practices that form scientific knowledge reveal themselves. The manifestation and the exercise of knowledge/power involve the continuous and repeated procedure of examination. Through examination, an individual becomes the object of a formal procedure, registered by documents, that helps classify him/her as a case within description, judgment, measurement and comparison procedures.

Examination is therefore an impersonal technique for exercising a power that refers to an objective knowledge. The individual in general, and some categories of individuals in particular, such as children, sick persons, prisoners, mental patients, are in the modern age the object, and at the same time the effect of, power, which has a procedural and impersonal character, and is based on a knowledge that claims to be objective and scientific. Power/knowledge, control exercise and domination practices might lead to a subjection of the dominated without any space and time limits, which, however, encounters an obstacle in the subjects' resistance. Scientific discourse, like any other discourse, can actually be an instrument and an effect of power, as well as an obstacle to it and a starting point for resistance and opposition strategies. In the modern age, power reveals itself in unequal and mobile relations. Its exercise assumes a strategy, that is to say, purposes, intention, calculation, but this does not imply choices or decisions made by individual or collective subjects, such as governors, or in general, a political or economic power group.

Power can be exercised in a variety of areas (families, small groups, institutions) on condition that the various power centers and the ways in which it unceasingly reveals and transforms itself may converge into a unitary strategy. In fact, are there no places in which power is concentrated, or subjects that preside over its rationality and can be thus identified as power-holders. On the contrary, the variety of power areas, and the opposition ingrained in its exercise allow power being anonymous, and allows the continuous presence of redistributions, convergences and realignments in power relations. These relations form a dense network that goes across apparatuses and institutions, social strata and individuals, producing resistance wherever power is exercised. Power analysis must therefore consider the ways, or mechanisms, through which it is exerted, regardless of legal systems, juridical apparatuses and natural persons that hold it, as the sovereign, and must try instead to point out the strategies immanent to power mechanisms.

From the nineteenth century, power relations have increasingly coordinated themselves with production activities and communication resources, thus achieving greater effectiveness and efficiency in exercising control and surveillance over the subjects. The strategies of power share with its relations and ambits the characteristics of anonymity, invisibility and non-verifiability. As power is placed in a strategic field of relations, the outcome of the processes and struggles that concern it is not, and cannot be, pre-established. In fact a variety of forces acts in this field. These forces establish their own organizations and strategies, unceasingly meet themselves and conflict locally, and define power itself. These processes and struggles that cross the field of power/knowledge do not only determine which are the subjects who hold knowledge but also how and based on what knowledge constitutes itself. Power/knowledge is locally exercised over bodies and souls – the latter in the form of soul-care or "pastoral" power, a form of growing importance and extent – and is subject to continuous variations, which concern not only those who exercise or suffer it, but also the knowledge by means of which power is exercised and reveals itself.

The relations of power/knowledge and of resistance to it, which are intrinsically unequal and dynamic, make use of strategies, in the sense of a set of means used for effectively exercising or keeping power. However, to attain their purposes, these strategies in turn necessarily make use of local micro-relations, which are therefore in the service of a comprehensive strategy. Foucault suggests studying power relations by considering the different and antagonistic strategies through which these relations reveal themselves. The study of forms of resistance to power is therefore an integral part of the analysis of power. Consequently, there is no power if there is no resistance to it; and resistance is increased by intensifying power relations. As power, with its mechanisms and strategies, does not know limited ambits, resistance to it can be found everywhere, and therefore neither it has a specific place in the network of power relations, nor must be considered external to power. Any form of resistance – whether necessary, possible or improbable, spontaneous or organized, individual or collective, peaceful or violent – can exist only in a strategic field of power relations in which this kind of resistance is a constitutive element.

Therefore, power does not only proceed from the top to the bottom, that is to say, from those who hold an institutional power to subjects who cannot oppose it, but also from the bottom, from the dominated. Considering that power and knowledge are linked by discursive formations, which in the modern age constitute social sciences and the other sciences, each power strategy comprises a variety of discursive elements, including the constitutive discourses of resistance to power that originate from the dominated and characterize them. Sciences are investigation methods through which human beings are transformed into subjects, in the dual sense of individuals submitted to other people's control and dependence, and provided with self-consciousness and identity. Subjects are an object of investigation in philology and linguistics, insofar as they are speaking beings, living beings in biology, and productive beings in economics. There are, in addition, other power strategies.

For example, the practices through which the subject is separated from others, or is internally divided. Therefore, some subjects are set against others for different reasons (for example, persons who are sound of mind and body against those who are ill, honest and respectable persons against criminals). Another example of power strategy Foucault dwelt upon since the second half of the 1970s are the practices through which human beings learn to recognize themselves as subjects who have a sexuality over which it is considered socially necessary to exercise control power (as we shall see in the following pages). The variety of pursued strategies and discursive elements that can be found in each strategy may make its exercise fragile and changeable. In addition, the dominated are prepared to accept power only as a partial limit to their freedom. Furthermore, power has some mechanisms at its disposal for asserting and consolidating itself, which can prove effective on condition they are rationally used.

This implies that these mechanisms of power exercise must not be disclosed to the dominated, and moreover, that appropriate strategies must be used to ensure their effectiveness. Appropriate are the strategies that consider not only the plurality of the discursive elements at stake, but also the existing power relations, their continuous change, their distribution in a variety of groups and institutions, and the complex distribution of oppositions, and consequently, of the points of resistance. Most of these points of resistance are usually mobile and transitory, but occasionally able to produce splits and groupings in society. Resistance techniques are highlighted – as power techniques – by a genealogic analysis that takes into account their historical formation in its elements of continuity, but also of change and break (Foucault 1963: 82–3, 89–102, 119; 1969: 248–9; 1975: 36–40, 188–90, 217–27, 234–5; 1982, 1998: 81–102).

Power relations and the discursive formations that constitute them have in sexuality a point of support of paramount importance. All over the modern age, that is to say since the late eighteenth century, special power and knowledge mechanisms have formed, which had sex and sexuality as an object, and hence bodies and their possible use in the service of comprehensive pseudo-scientific knowledge and power strategies. These mechanisms have let sexuality become not a biological and natural event, but instead a historical construction that can be subject, like any other one, to genealogical analysis. The modern conception of sexuality has involved conceiving women's bodies filled with sexuality; a systematic effort to control children's sexuality and adults' procreative behavior from an economic, political and medical point of view; finally, a bestowal to psychiatry of the task of intervening and treating (in the sense of "making become normal") as soon as an anomaly in sexuality is identified.

Psychiatric discourse, like the other "scientific" discourses of modern age, makes therefore use of particular notions put in the service of bio-political strategies exercised in a plurality of institutional places (schools of any educational level, barracks, workshops, prisons). By the term "bio-power" (*biopouvoir*), Foucault understands using power/knowledge and the interventions and controls based on it, to manage, govern and transform human life – and the body, in particular – by conforming it to the power strategies pursued from time to time. The constitution of sexuality as a specialized scientific discourse has been made possible by an alliance between marriage and kinship relation, on the one hand, and institutional apparatuses of a legal and economic nature, on the other. These apparatuses have been used to regulate sexuality by establishing what is allowed and what is forbidden because perverted, and in addition, to determine what institutional intervention is required for a form of sexuality identified in this way, and through which particular institution. Furthermore, the same apparatuses have connected sexuality with the economic areas of production and consumption. Psychoanalysis has introduced itself in the discursive formation concerning sexuality, and has cemented an alliance between family and outer institutional environment, which is represented not only by the doctor, the judge, and the teacher, but also by the psychoanalyst.

The purpose has been to control children's sexuality, as well as their family members', by means of procedures aiming to guide and orient consciences. Psychoanalysis has been at the same time a technique for relieving, whenever excessive, the effects of the taboo of incest; and a theory that sets out to explain the pathologic consequences of sexual repression by focusing psychoanalytic investigation on the connection between sexual desire and norms regulating sexuality, and particularly the prohibition of incest. If sexuality has become, with psychoanalysis, the object of a discourse that claims to be scientific, this has not implied the end of psychological and historical-political repression. On the contrary, psychoanalysis has strengthened the alliance between family and other institutions, because the patient who has successfully completed a therapeutic treatment has to go back to them by permeating them with sublimated sexuality. Nonetheless, psychoanalysis has addressed its search for truth to the institutional sources of psychological repression: the family and the system of alliances supporting it. In Wilhelm Reich's version, the purpose of psychoanalytic investigation is to get rid not only of repression, but also of the historical-political institutions on which it is grounded, which produce domination and exploitation (Foucault 1963: 47–9, 104–14, 129–31).

Foucault's Research

The concepts and themes we have examined are respectively used and illustrated in some historical-epistemological investigations, which have made their author well known since the 1960s. These investigations are focused on the conceptions and manifestations of power/knowledge from Greek and Roman times to nowadays. There are, however, some other themes that have been dealt with in separate periods. In the 1960s, Foucault's investigation was of an "archaeological" nature, and therefore focused on discontinuities or interruptions in discursive practices and formations, and aimed at pointing out "two great discontinuities in the episteme of the culture of the western world," situated respectively at the beginning and at the end of classical age (from the second half of the seventeenth century to the end of the eighteenth century) (Foucault 1966: 13). Therefore, it concerned scientific discursive formations, that is to say, knowledge as an instrument and a manifestation of power. In the 1970s, the author's investigation had instead a "genealogical" nature, and dwelt on the succession – before, during, and after the classical age – of the ways (or "technologies," using Foucault's words) in which power has been exercised over bodies and souls (Foucault 1975: 39). The purpose of this research was therefore to create "a genealogy of the current scientific-judicial apparatus" (Foucault 1975: 30), by investigating its procedures, objectives and transformations in the classical age and afterwards.

From the publication in 1976 of *The Will to Knowledge* to his death in 1984, the author's interest turned to a history of sexual behaviors considered as an object of concern and moral problematization. This problematization concerns the practices, through which persons have committed themselves to regulate their own conduct; they have done so by making their existence the result of intentional practices that have been an object of reflection. The history of how existence has resulted from these practices and their history are called "history of truth." Neither behaviors nor ideas, neither societies nor ideologies are relevant for it; but instead the problematizations, through which existences have become an object of moral reflection, and the practices that have constituted them. "Archaeological" analysis lingers over problematization forms, which are quite different in the Greco-Roman and in the Christian culture; while "genealogical" analysis studies instead the origin of problematizations, and therefore, the practices that have constituted them, as well as their changes (Foucault 1984: 17–21). Notwithstanding the differences of the themes tackled, the investigations made by Foucault are of an "archaeological" and/or "genealogical" nature, that is to say, aimed at identifying the discursive practices, and their statements and transformations. We shall dwell now upon each one of these periods, and provide a summary of the works that characterize them.

Three works among Foucault's most known ones belong to the 1960s, the *History of Madness* (*Madness and Civilization: A History of Insanity in the Age of Reason* 1961), *The Birth of the Clinic*, published in 1963, and *The Order of Things*, published three years later. The last work, which deals with the wider theme of classical and modern discursive formations (episteme), will be considered first and in more depth. Classical seventeenth century episteme – as Foucault argues in *The Order of Things* – differs from the sixteenth century one. In that century, the elements of knowledge (language, animals, plants, stars) were juxtaposed one another. Scholars thought they were connoted by analogies among signs that have to be deciphered, and that, by analogy, affinity or other forms of similarity, they reflect the things of the world. On the other hand, in the sixteenth century, a set of independent signs (language, for example) reflects the things of the world, or represents them. Signs (signifiers) therefore coincide with the representations of things (with meanings). In the seventeenth century it is no longer a question of discovering similarities among things by deciphering signs with obscure meanings, but instead of discerning among things and, on this base, formulating an order that may establish how they relate with one another.

Classical episteme presents itself as a science of calculable order, its differences and identities, and its genesis. The empirical representations of this order, when its constitutive elements are simple (not complex), can be studied by means of a mathematical science (Mathesis), which takes algebra as a universal method. On the contrary, in the event of complex elements, such as experience perceives them, the empirical representations of this order present themselves as signs. In classical age, science had the duty to analyze these signs, through which it has access to the order that rules (as it was thought) over the world of things. In classical thought, signs provide things with an identity of their own and a possibility to combine, and can be analyzed – with a method different from algebra – through exhaustive classifications, or taxonomies, represented by tables. The meaning of things, and hence, their image, can be drawn (so it was thought) from a complete table of signs, which establishes relations, measures and identities among things, and therefore their order, and through which the ideal of knowledge in the classical age, and its discursive form, or episteme, are summarized. Scholars came to the formulation of these tables of identities and differences through a form of analysis, called genetic, by which they used to proceed from the discovery of the simple constitutive elements of this empirical order of things (in life world, in production, in language) to their progressive composition and combination.

In classical episteme, natural history, the theory of money and value, and general grammar are sciences which investigate on the signs provided by our empirical representations, and actually make use of tables to order, classify and represent them. According to classical episteme, the study of language involves analyzing a grammar order, considered as a system of identities and differences among the elements of language (such as words, verbs and propositions). Each language has a particular grammar, which can be studied by comparing it to the grammars of other languages, but language in general assumes the existence of the verb "to be." In fact, without this verb (as it was argued), there would be no possibility of speaking, since if there are no verbs, it is impossible to represent a variety of things through a single word. According to classical seventeenth- and eighteenth-century episteme, language plays a representative role of the things that have been named. According to classical thought, to assign a name to things would mean to name their being. Though, depending on the various languages, names are different, it is possible to find some constant elements in them, and consequently in languages. Analyzing roots, isolating verb endings and prefixes, allows us coming to monosyllabic elements provided with a constant meaning even though placed in different words, which can be found in a large variety of languages belonging to populations that may be even very distant.

Through natural history scientists believed it was possible to represent things, and have consequently access to them even before naming them. Things and language both belong to the domain of representation. This belief led to the publication of catalogues, treatises and inventories, which in the classical age connoted, along with the general comparative grammar of different languages, also anatomy, botany and zoology. Things and language, indeed, can be better observed and known by showing the order or the coordination of their representations, and the structure or composition of their constitutive elements. Classical age knowledge is therefore based on classifications, or instead taxonomical. Given an object of study – for example, botany – it is necessary to designate all its constitutive elements (plants), and each of them receives a name that characterizes it and, at the same time, puts it in relation with other elements, assuming that all those elements together constitute a single system of identities and differences. These identities and differences are pertaining, as they concern the distinctive character of a studied object (a particular plant), while other identities and differences are intentionally disregarded. Through this method, it is possible to denominate and classify any element or group of elements, and the purpose of knowledge is thereby achieved. However, this goal can be achieved also in another way: first, a complete description of an element chosen at random (of a particular plant, for instance) is provided, secondly only its differences in relation to another element are specified, then those of the first two elements in relation to a third one, and so on. At the end of this process, which firstly investigates the general characteristics and then the peculiar ones, the distinctive features of a particular species or a particular kind are highlighted by choosing at will the specification level, and hence the generality level, of the element identified in this way.

Both proceedings define identities by placing them in a broader context of differences, and aim at formulating classifications without gaps, according to the scientific ideal of classical age. However, these classification tables did not allow understanding the chronological sequence of events, which (as the scholars of that age knew very well) limits the temporal validity of any classification by introducing discontinuity and incompatible forms. Both requirements – to classify kinds and species and to describe the temporal sequence of events – coexisted, and jointly formed the body of natural science knowledge in the classical age. On the other hand, this knowledge makes use of names to designate the distinctive features of the things that belong to nature and the differences among them, starting from their classification among mineral, plant and animal kingdom. Natural history and general grammar (that is to say, the theory of language) were therefore intertwined in the classical age, and jointly constituted its episteme, and hence, the conditions that made any knowledge possible.

The same episteme was at the origin of the analysis of wealth carried out all over the seventeenth century and for a good part of the eighteenth century. Prior to the classical age, during the Renaissance, it was a common belief that coins could exactly measure the value of the metal – for example, silver – contained in them, their intrinsic value. Classical age replaced this configuration of thought with a quite different one, according to which the capability of precious metals to measure the value, and the capability of objects to receive a price, depend on their capability to be exchanged, and therefore to be used for currency. Metals and other objects do not have an intrinsic value, and therefore, they cannot have a right price in the sense of corresponding to such a value. On the contrary, the same monetary unit, passing from hand to hand, can be used to represent identities and differences among things by grouping and distinguishing them. In other words, the monetary sign represents wealth, as in natural history the characteristics of a species represents a particular species according to its similarities and differences with other species, and exchange is what transforms goods into values.

Based on this assumption, some classical-age economists, here called "utilitarians" – among whom are Condillac and Galiani – have wondered on what conditions an exchange system of useful things confers value to a good, and other economists – the "physiocrats" – on what conditions to appraise a good as a useful thing can confer it value, given an exchange system. These two theoretical domains are not only internally consistent and chronologically simultaneous, but also similar and complementary to one another, as archaeological analysis has pointed out. Moreover, their theoretical configuration is the same, compared to the natural history and general grammar one. The orders of nature, language and wealth have a consistent and observable structure. Classical thought had raised the issue of the relation between the names of things and their order, and had solved it by formulating taxonomies through which all things received their specific name within a system of identities and differences, the name representing therefore things themselves.

In this way, classical episteme ignored all that could not be represented as order in a discourse, in nature, and in needs. The break with that episteme was not only vast, as it embraced the whole knowledge in its visible manifestations, but also profound and radical, like the break that in the seventeenth century had put an end to Renaissance episteme. This discontinuity can be not explained, but can be "archaeologically" analyzed by highlighting the positive characteristics of classical knowledge, that is to say, the conditions through which discursive practices have formed and transformed, and the taxonomies formulated within the domain of that episteme. In the modern age, in the nineteenth century, but already in the last decades of the previous century, scholars had instead formulated the existence of empirically observable analogies between different organizations that follow one another over time. This is the case – making use of designations formulated as from that century – of political economy, biology and philology.

In economics, with Adam Smith the time of economy is no longer a cyclic time of enrichment and impoverishment, or of continuous production growth thanks to economic policies in the position to increase production more than prices, but instead the internal time of an organization, which measures the necessary work for satisfying workers' needs and wishes. In biology, there is no longer a parallelism between the classification of a kind or a species and its designation with a particular name. Consequently, a name no longer represents a kind or a species. There are instead invisible and deep functions of the organs, which are indicated, but not stressed, by their name. Names correspond, in fact, to their evident and superficial characteristics, but not to those functions. Taxonomies lose therefore their scientific relevance. Finally, in philology, scholars do not consider any longer the question, which is fundamental in general grammar, of whether there was a primitive language, changed because of historical events external to it, whose words have common roots with known languages. They go instead in search of elements that link languages, and the similarities and differences in the way to change words depending on their mutual relation.

The dissolution, in the late eighteenth century, of a homogeneous field of representations and classifications of things led to a reflection, carried out by Kant's theoretical philosophy on the transcendental conditions of each experience. This reflection corresponded, in the scientific field, to epistemological investigations on the a priori reality conditions of the statements – on "positivities" – of sciences (biology, philology and economy). The unification of classical knowledge dissolved again on grounds of the analysis of identities and differences. In the modern age, each kind of knowledge is related to its transcendental foundation, and therefore, to the subject that experiences and builds his/her own empirical world and knowledge. The knowledge of life (biology), language (philology), and production (economics) involves investigating the fundamental modes of knowledge, the concealed forces considered to be at the temporal and causal origin of empirically observable phenomena. The works of the economist Ricardo, the biologist Cuvier, and the philologist Bopp show how the fundamental modes of knowledge have formed.

Ricardo introduced history and anthropology in economic analysis, showing that production – the quantity of which depends on the work time necessary to produce victuals by which a population can be fed – does not sufficiently increase over time as this population grows. Therefore, lacking new lands to be destined to cultivation, the balance between production and consumption can be achieved only in consequence of famines producing massive reductions in the population (apart from other unpredictable catastrophic events). With Cuvier, the classical project of a general taxonomy fails, and consequently, the assumption of the existence of a great natural order of all living beings. What approaches the animal species, or the bodily organs, are the functions they reciprocally perform. These functions, which are not directly accessible through observation, provide not only an organization, or structure, but also a temporal continuity, until an external event puts an end to the life possibilities of a particular species or living form.

With Bopp and the other early nineteenth-century linguists, like Schlegel and Grimm, language is no longer a representation system of things (as in the classical age), and languages do not distinguish themselves any longer by the way in which the elements of these representations combine (for example, whether vowels or consonants prevail). In contrast to the classical age, in the modern age language is considered an activity of those who speak, and a way to manifest and do their will. A language identifies and distinguishes itself from others through the particular ways in which sounds, syllables, verbs and words mutually relate according to a not immediately visible regularity the linguist aims at bringing out. In general, language is considered a set of phonetic elements, or sounds, regardless of the letters with which they can be transcribed. Based on this assumption, a comparative and systematic study of the grammatical structures within languages becomes possible, and in particular, the study of the Indo-European and Semitic language systems, their analogies, differences and evolution.

In biology, as in linguistics, though in a partly different way, the study of the internal variations of the elements of a system (a single species, or a language), the study – in Foucault's words – of their inner historicity, has been put aside in order to carry out a diachronic investigation of their outer historicity. This investigation is focused on the outer world in which these elements are included, and sheds light, through a comparative method, on the functions and conditions of existence. However, this outer world is not directly represented, as in the classical age. The philological analysis of language, in particular, shows it as a historical reality whose structure is not immediately evident. From here the subsequent developments in the direction of structuralism (the study of the pure forms of the unconscious or of the essence of literature, regardless of literary genres) and phenomenology (the study of the pure forms of lived experience) would originate.

Episteme has therefore changed. In the classical age, there was no possibility of existence for human sciences, because man, or the human nature, was not the object of a specific knowledge, and did not find a place in classical episteme. On the contrary, in the modern age, human finiteness becomes the center of thought. Man's finiteness (finitude) explains the finiteness of his body, the fact that he has needs, produces, has a language, and the limited notions we have in this regard. Modern age thought focuses on a concrete man, who has a bodily existence but also works and speaks, and who is set as a subject of knowledge by modern thought. Two different aspects ("duplex man" or *homme doublet*) are attributed to man, and therefore knowledge concerning man takes two different ways. On the one hand, it is shown that man's knowledge depends on his bodily, anatomic and physiological conditions, and on the other, that knowledge depends on historical, social or economic conditions.

In the second case, knowledge forms within the domain of interpersonal relations and is influenced by them. There may be a history of human knowledge as empirical knowledge, but also as prescriptive and transcendental (using a Kantian term) knowledge, which indicates the forms empirical knowledge must take, and wonders about man's ways of being, about his lived experience (as phenomenology aims to do), about the horizons of his thought and about what cannot be thought (*l'impensé*). What is not thought, because it cannot be thought, is the shadow that accompanies modern thought, because it is external and stranger to man, who through reflection constitutes his own knowledge and his own essence as an active subject, and in this way transforms it. Among the possible examples of this process, we can mention Marx's alienated man and Freud's unconscious. Hence, the constant attempt of modern episteme to bring what cannot be thought into knowledge, and particularly the empirical knowledge about man, whose full identity must be found again or discovered.

Then, language does no longer represent things (as in the classical age). Through language the contents of human experience are revealed. These contents cannot be directly analyzed, but only after having considered the distance between what reveals itself as a representation or a sign, and what actually is (exists), that is to say, the essence of man and language. The analytics of finiteness (*analytique de la finitude*) seeks to show the limits of the contents of experience produced by what is not thought and cannot be thought, and remains therefore extraneous to knowledge. By showing these limits, we show how the essence of man is determined and limited. The analytics of finiteness has therefore as an object all what can be given in general to human experience, and all what cannot instead be given. The field of modern episteme loses the homogeneity of classical episteme and breaks, taking three different approaches: mathematic and physical sciences; sciences, such as linguistics, biology and economy, which establish causal relations among similar elements, or consider these elements as constant components of a structure; finally, philosophical reflection on concepts and problems formulated within the domain of empirical disciplines.

As we mentioned in the previous pages, Foucault maintained that human sciences are not proper sciences. If their object – man – is determined and limited in its essence, human sciences do not hold a clear place in the space of knowledge. They participate in all the three aforementioned modern episteme orientations, but do not completely belong to any one of them. Therefore, they have no objectivity and no systematic nature, although they have a homogeneous field of statements at their disposal and have their own "positivity." They take a place, in particular, at the boundaries of biology, economy and philology, but not within them. This makes them unstable, precarious and uncertain in their epistemological foundations. An "archaeological" analysis of human sciences points out their particular episteme, as well as the diversity of that episteme in comparison with the one of sciences in the narrow sense. The object of these pseudo-sciences – man – assumes the end of discourse, meant as a set of statements by which things are objectively designated. If language – and consequently, discourse – forms again as an objective structure, then there is no longer an epistemological space for human sciences, and therefore no possibility of existence for them.

As we previously briefly mentioned, the *History of Madness in the Classical Age*(*Histoire de la Folie à l'Age Classique*), and *The Birth of the Clinic* (*Naissance de la Clinique: Une Archéologie du Regard Médical*) preceded by a few years the investigation on the forms of knowledge in general, contained in *The Order of Things* (*Les Mots et les Choses*). The two former works were published in the 1960s, as the last one, and focus on the discursive formations that concern, respectively, madness and illness. In his *History of Madness*, Foucault lingers on the treatment reserved by the administrative and/or medical authorities in the Western world, and especially in France, from the Middle Ages up to nowadays, to persons considered insane. Treatment has accorded to the episteme that has prevailed in a given historical age: the Renaissance, the classical age, and the modern age. In the fifteenth century, in several European countries, a "ship of fools" frequently appears in many paintings of some outstanding artists, and progressively takes the place of the depiction of the end of the world, a theme recurring in the Middle Ages, which remains also in the collective imagination of the subsequent "classical age." In the Renaissance, madness expresses not only the threats and temptations, but also the secrets and weaknesses of the world. It is at the same time a negative image symbolizing disorder and destruction, but also a positive one, an image of man's critical consciousness, and virtually, of justice and truth.

In the sixteenth century, madness and reason are placed in mutual relation, in the sense that they refuse and presuppose each other. Madness is no longer considered a denial of reason and a symbol of evil, but instead a part of reason itself. At the end of that century and in the first decades of the following one, the theme of madness appears in different forms: a literary image, symbolized by the character of Don Quixote; vain presumption deserving moral condemnation; right punishment for the misdeeds of the mind or of the heart; desperate passion; and, in early the seventeenth century, a stage of a journey that brings man back to reason at the end. Just in this last form, during the second half of the seventeenth century the classical experience of madness developed all over Europe. It involved the separation of those who were considered insane by the others, and their confinement not in a ship but instead in a building called "hospital." The hospital was not a treatment or a nursing home, but instead a police and judicial administrative structure, largely independent of the sovereign's and the courts' authority. Partly backed by public finances, this institution was assigned to perform welfare tasks, and to act at the same time as a prison, since poverty would stress (as it was believed) behaviors deserving repression and punishment, such as being idle, lazy and dissolute.

The poor and the mad, with which these behaviors were related, were in fact considered an obstacle to public order and an effect of disorder, and they had not only to be helped but also punished for their moral faults, even when judicial penalties were lacking. The right to welfare went along with one's obligation to be subject to the physical and moral constraint of confinement and forced labor. Through this coercive measure, the authorities believed they were not only in the position to cope with unemployment, or at least, with its more visible social effects, but also (during the following century) to re-educate poor, idle, ill and perverted persons (such as those who were suffering from venereal diseases, the libertines and the sodomites), and in general, the individuals considered unsocial. The non-attainment of these goals (in the seventeenth and eighteenth centuries a non-negligible percentage of the population was confined) proved over time that the institution of confinement and forced labor was at most a transitory remedy, in the long run ineffective in contrasting idleness and poverty. On the other hand, in this way it was possible to pave, from an institutional and organizational point of view, the way to the subsequent experience of mental patients' confinement.

The archaeology of mental alienation implies writing the history of the process of social removal and outcasting, which was put into practice on a large scale all over the classical age. This process joined in a single category, morally connoted in a negative way, those guilty of insanity with those guilty of prodigality, blasphemy and licentiousness, since they were all expressions of senselessness. Internment had therefore the purpose of reforming the person in a moral and religious sense. In the eighteenth century, the age of Enlightenment, libertinage cohabited with Reason forming a world apart from it and marked by irrationality. Internment took then the meaning of separation of the world of irrationality from the world of rationality, which is imitated by insanity and to which is opposed. The irrational remained, however, negatively connoted. The mad received medical care, like the other confined persons, for fear that in the detention places infectious diseases such as a "prisons fever" might occur and spread; but in general also for fear of the inmates' senselessness or madness.

Over time these places took on more the character of houses of correction rather than that of hospitals, so that confinement was usually decided without consulting the doctors, but instead by considering the peculiar and outrageous behaviors kept by individuals deemed to be devoid of any truth and moral and legally not responsible. Psychological judgment on the inmate's personality was added in that case to moral judgment. Throughout the classical age – and therefore still in the eighteenth century – Reason was considered as belonging to the domain of ethics, and consequently insanity was seen as something shameful, animal-like and threatening that deserves being punished with confinement, but also controlled through it for fear that it may further spread. Later on, in the modern age, the moral judgment of madness did not disappear, but the consideration of insanity changed, as from the late eighteenth century it took a medical character claiming scientific objectivity. The consciousness of madness, at the end of classical age and at the beginning of modern age, means one's consciousness of not being mad.

This consciousness rested on the existence and on the norms – considered reasonable by definition – of the group to which one belongs, giving the possibility of indicating others as mad. A mad person would be therefore immediately and evidently recognizable. Madness, or non-reasonableness, on the other hand, would have an almost unperceivable profile because it escapes – so it was believed – discursive Reason, since it sets itself against it without being extraneous to it, such as non-being counters being. Insanity imitates Reason in the form of delirium, which in its bodily and spiritual manifestations (as dream or error of the soul, night or blinding of Reason) would be its constitutive element, and necessary and sufficient condition. Eighteenth-century medicine sought the immediate cause of madness in a bad functioning or alteration of the nervous system and of the brain, but could not succeed in finding it empirically at an anatomical or physiological level. As to its remote causes, the list continued to grow and scholars were unable to find an agreement neither on what and how many such causes were, nor on the prevalence of causes concerning the body or the soul. In the classical age, madness was represented through some figures situated within the experience of non-reasonableness, each one provided with its own coherence.

These figures were designated by the names of dementia and frenzy, mania and melancholy, hysteria and hypochondria. Dementia was a generic and abstract word used to indicate every alteration of the spirit, or of the rational soul, for any cause, remaining indefinite what it actually was. Dementia was countered by frenzy, which was precisely described in its manifestations and causes. Mania and melancholy both obeyed a principle of coherence, but were, however, opposed in that mania would focus on a single object, while melancholy would distort concepts and notions. Therefore their causes would be different and specific. These figures of madness – not a conceptual system or a set of symptoms – structured the perception of non-reasonableness in the classical age. As for hysteria and hypochondria, their peculiar characteristics were not determined in a consistent way, despite many attempts in this sense, and they remained undefined for a large part of the classical age. *Vis-à-vis* the care classical age medicine devoted to the description and classification of diseases and their presumed causes, its cognitive commitment to find the remedies was much smaller.

As in the past, in the eighteenth century, too, people continued to believe in the possibility of finding a universal remedy, or a panacea, and in a specific remedy considered effective against particular diseases, disregarding whether this belief was actually resting on empirical grounds. As regards the treatment of madness, the therapeutic ideas of that time privileged iron to strengthen the body, which was considered weakened; its purification through various methods and based on different beliefs; immersion for ablution purposes and to rebalance the liquids and the solids of the body (since particular therapeutic powers were in fact attributed to water); and in addition, regular movements of the body and journeys in order to counter both the excessive immobility and the agitation that may result from insanity. In any case, the suggested and applied therapies were never merely psychological, as the soul was not considered separate from the body. To fight the passions and deliriums of insanity, scientists suggested patients' sudden awakening from sleep, meant as the sleep of Reason; participation in theatre performances where the deliriums troubling mad persons are put on the stage; work, in order to bring them back to the immediacy of real life, and in this way, to Reason.

Under the constraint of confinement, the figures of non-reasonableness, or senselessness, lost their distinctive nature over time, and converged in the general category of libertinage. Madness instead (distinct from non-reasonableness) increasingly became an object of attention all over the eighteenth century. Its previous classifications – mental alienation, imbecility and fury – were considered insufficient, on grounds of the new sensitivity to this theme that characterized the eighteenth century. Throughout that century, the moral meaning of nervous diseases deeply changed, in the sense of investigating their causes in the lifestyle, in the excess of passions and imaginations that would have irritated the nerves in the modern age, where man is left to his passions and anxieties. In late eighteenth century, at the end of the classical age, it was recommended to take nature as a model for fighting madness. Where animality had been a symbol and an expression of uncontrolled passion, now the calm of animal life was taken as a model, since an animal cannot be mad. Hysteria and hypochondria were fully assimilated to mental diseases, thus combining also moral judgment with medical diagnosis. Already in late eighteenth century, madness was considered a sign of moral degeneration produced by human causes (heredity and social environment). The way to nineteenth- and twentieth-century psychiatry, which has shown to share these assumptions, began then to be paved.

From the nineteenth century, a form of consciousness of madness has become prevailing and has let madness become the object of a medical-objective knowledge which has made it defenseless and powerless. Using Foucault's words, this is the analytical consciousness of madness. After having abandoned the fruitless classification attempts of the previous century, with their clear and distinct concepts, which were however inapplicable since madness has no internal order, modern age classifications start from the assumption that knowledge of madness, with its passions, imaginations and deliriums, is possible. It became then an object of medical-scientific study of madness as mental disease, while non-reasonableness no longer received doctors' attention. The positivist approach to the study of madness – which Foucault designates as an analytical consciousness of madness – did not immediately assert itself after the end of classical age. For a few decades – during the first half of the nineteenth century – a historical consciousness of madness prevailed, since its origins and forms were considered historically determined. This peculiar and transitory consciousness of madness paved the way to analytical consciousness, thus putting definitely an end to the classical assumption according to which man holds the truth, while mad are those who have lost it. In fact, if madness is historically determined, so is truth.

In the nineteenth and the twentieth centuries, two different fields of madness experience have developed: a theoretical and abstract field, in which concepts belonging to medical theory find a formulation and an application, and a concrete field, characterized by the psychiatric asylum experience; since with the French Revolution mad persons were confined in distinct environments divided from other patients and common prisoners. The separation between patients submitted to medical treatment and prisoners submitted to guardianship and control dates back to the late eighteenth century as well. For persons suffering from mental diseases and alienation, confinement gradually took on an exclusively therapeutic meaning; but it was a doctor's task to give his opinion – on demand of the courts – on limiting mad persons' freedom. If that was the case, medical opinion overlapped moral judgment. Though the psychiatric asylum kept its patients apart from the others and had no other purpose but providing them with medical treatment, the asylum convicts had, however, become subject to an authority that could decide – in the name of psychiatry, a science that claims to be objective – whether they were mad and had to be confined in the psychiatric asylum for their own good.

Chains, used before the institution of the psychiatric asylum, were replaced with the assessment – which sought and purported to be objective and scientific – of the status of madness. Along with this new assessment was the convict's prospect to be treated and cured of that disease, in order to be in the position to recover, together with Reason, also all that connotes a man; namely, his human nature, and with it, truth and morals. Recovery from madness then involved a moral process aimed at patient's reconstruction as free, reasonable and responsible subjects. The psychiatric asylum sought to set itself as an educational instrument and a surrogate of the family. The mad persons who lived in it were not considered completely adult individuals, and therefore were subject to continuous judgment, and prisoners of a moral and social world that had the doctor as its representative, and whose authority the doctor was entrusted of towards them. Mad persons could be studied and classified, but no form of dialogue was possible with them, since they were mere objects of examinations and of medical-psychiatric interventions.

Their condition has remained the same until nowadays, and the resort to psychoanalysis has not changed it. All over modern age, this conception was contrasted by another historical-sociological and humanitarian conception about madness and its therapy. According to this alternative conception, represented by Freud and other scientists, madness is an alteration of the relation of the spirit with itself, and therefore therapy involves knowing the psychologicalal mechanisms that have produced it. There is, however, a consistency between these two approaches, though they are conflicting: the binary structure of non-reasonableness of the classical age – truth opposed to error, being to not being – has been replaced with a ternary structure, accessible to scientific investigation. Its elements being the alienated man, madness and the truth it holds, which, although concealed, can reveal itself through an objective analysis of the psychiatric symptoms. However, madness must not measure itself and be subdued to science, and hence, to Reason. Where, in the classical age, the work of an artist, a philosopher, a man of letters was all the same with the author, so that, if he was insane, he could be active through his madness (Goya's work is an example of it), in the modern age, madness puts an end to creativity and therefore destroys the work (as evidenced, for example, by Nietzsche and Van Gogh). Therefore, madness celebrates its triumph over Reason, which believes to rule over it.

In *The Birth of the Clinic*, published in 1963, two years after the *History of Madness*, the author's investigation focused on medical knowledge in "classical" and modern age. We shall provide a brief account of this work, as well as of Foucault's coeval essay on the surrealist author Raymond Roussel. Until the end of the eighteenth century, Foucault argues, medicine was interested in a condition of health, and therefore in a condition of body functioning considered regular. The purpose was to ascertain where and why this functioning had been troubled, and to re-establish its regularity. Throughout the eighteenth century, the medical experience was intended as an empirical experience of a particular knowledge that had to be confirmed or disproved by a sort of jury formed by a public of students of medicine. At the end of that period, however, doctors' attention moved from what happens on the outer surface of the body, and is therefore immediately visible, to the interior of a sick body. A disease – as it was thought – reveals itself through particular symptoms. After the discovery of pathological anatomy, at the beginning of the following century, physiological processes were put in relation with anatomic alterations.

Along with a new way of interpreting the symptoms of a disease, which attributes less importance to clinical symptoms, through pathological anatomy it was necessary to discover a new investigative method, in virtue of which an anatomic lesion was considered as the revealing sign of a disease, which must be considered in conjunction with physiologic phenomena. Disease was considered a reaction of the body to a pathogenic agent, and therefore there are no essential characteristics of a disease (as it was formerly maintained). This new conception of disease has involved an objectively well-grounded relation between what is visible and what can constitute a medical-scientific discourse. The individual is at the same time the subject and the object of a positive knowledge. In contrast with classical thought, according to which finiteness meant only denial of infiniteness, the consideration of death, and consequently of man's finiteness, is an assumption for a scientific investigation of diseases. Medicine has had therefore a methodological and epistemological importance for the constitution of human sciences.[2]

Raymond Roussel (1877–1933), a French author close to the current of surrealism, who committed suicide because his literary and theatre works did not meet the approval of the public and the critics, was a peculiar and solitary person known for the oddness of his life and works. Foucault's essay is attentively focused on his production. Roussel – as Foucault remarks – aimed at removing from language, and hence, from discourse, any reference to a human or non-human subject. The existence of subjects implies, in fact, creativity and unpredictability, which usually give life to a literary creation. By eliminating subjects, language makes only reference to itself, and therefore, Roussel's texts lack any casualty, inspiration, and randomness in narration. The origin of language is, however, an external element with respect to language itself, which though being accidental, cannot be eliminated. In the use Roussel makes of it, language is destroyed by its being fragmented into separate narrative blocks. Each block is formed by strange images of men and animals, and includes stories of metamorphoses and other extraordinary events. According to Foucault, in Roussel's narration, events follow one another in two different ways. Words and events are linked by Roussel's explicit indication of their common and visible existence (because, for example, they have appeared together) despite their illusory nature; or by oppositions and analogies, similarities and dissimilarities, identities and differences.

So, a world of unique, impossible and new unknown things takes shape, a magic circle placed out of time, as they derive only from language their possibility to exist and recur even after their disappearance, to find themselves again and find their past time, and to infinity, to relate with one another. The narration order is obscure, non-visible. It is an order that is waiting to be deciphered. What is told and visible – the narration – cannot be used for deciphering it, despite an abundance of descriptive details, but instead refers back to another narration which, like the previous one, has an obscure order of its own, which in turn is placed out of time as well. Each narration refers back to another one, without getting through it. In fact, the narrative blocks can be connected in different visible and invisible ways, and language itself becomes a puzzle and a labyrinth.

At the center of the labyrinth – invisible and placed beneath visible things, inaccessible and devoid of anything that may be seen – there is the birth or origin of discourse, which is external and accidental in relation to language. Narrated things become visible if words, and hence, language, are connected to them. Its ability to connect identities and differences, and its ambiguity of meanings would have upset Roussel (Foucault 1963b).The reasons of Foucault's interest in the figure and writings of Roussel are not immediately evident, and at a first sight; for it is not clear how this interest may relate with the themes Foucault dealt with during the 1960s and early 1970s. In this regard, the literature concerning this author has provided some indications, as we shall later see.

The works I, *Pierre Rivière, Having Slaughtered my Mother, my Sister and my Brother … A Case of Parricide in 19th Century*, and *Discipline and Punish*, published towards the mid-1970s (respectively, Foucault 1973, 1975), are focused, like *The Birth of the Clinic*, on the techniques of power exercise in periods characterized by different episteme. However, these works differ from those that had preceded them in some regards. In the first place, for their intention to present a genealogy of power, that is to say, a history of the current scientific and legal body through which the power to judge and punish reveals itself. In the second place, they dwell upon two ages, the classical and the modern age, in order to show how this power made use of different methods (or "technologies") and rules. Punishments and controls were in fact addressed to bodies in the classical age and to souls in the modern age, in this case with the necessary support of sciences,

---

2 Foucault's *History of Madness in the Classical Age* was originally published in 1962 and is an extremely well-known work by this author. In addition, the reader may also be referred to Foucault's lectures at the Collège de France on psychiatric power (1973–1974) (Foucault 2006).

or pseudo-sciences, dealing with man and with new professional roles, such as educators, psychologists and psychiatrists. In the third place, these works contain a "micro-physics of power," because they turn their attention to the effects of power exercise over individuals' souls and bodies.

We shall give now a brief account of the work on Pierre Rivière, of which Foucault was the editor and co-author, while we shall dwell a little longer on *Discipline and Punish*. In *I, Pierre Rivière, Having Slaughtered my Mother, my Sister and my Brother ... A Case of Parricide in 19th Century*, Foucault (1973) deals once again with the theme of insanity, but widens it by treating it jointly with the theme – later extended and studied in depth – of judicial discourse. The author lingers on a multiple murder which occurred in France during the 1830s. This murder was peculiar not only for the number of victims and their close family ties with the murderer, a young countryman whose name was Pierre Rivière, but also because he left a memorial in which he claimed, with religious arguments, the ethical necessity of his act. This memorial was interpreted by judges and psychiatrists as evidence of his mental disease. In fact, on the one hand, the murderer maintained that his gesture was an act of absolute justice, even wanted by God himself, because it would have rescued his father from the tyranny of his wife and other family members. As this homicide would have been punished with death (which actually was not inflicted by reason of Rivière's incapacity), the murderer, perfectly informed of that possibility, which instead he wished, intended his death on the scaffold as an extreme sacrifice in the name of the divine justice, which would have brought him a posthumous glory.

To Rivière's religious discourse, Foucault countered the discourses with scientific claims of the psychiatrists, who diagnosed a case of monomania, and therefore of complete incapacity, which won Rivière the commutation of the death sentence to life imprisonment. A comparison between different discourses including totally incompatible truths was one of the reasons of Foucault's interest in this psychiatric-judicial case: the contraposition of incompatible discourses and the complete victory of the psychiatric-judicial discourse over the religious one, which judges and psychiatrists did not even consider, shows which discursive formation is suitable for power. Another reason was the large quantity of documentary materials, consisting of psychiatric reports and legal records resulting from the homicide, which shed light on the use made of the memorial left by Rivière. Modern episteme cannot, in fact, attribute truth to the memorial, but only to the psychiatrists' actual or alleged scientific knowledge.

Discipline and Punish is a work divided into sections dedicated to the themes of capital punishment and penalties, discipline and prison. Capital punishment, which Foucault examines at the beginning of the work with horrifying details, belongs to classical age. The acts of extreme violence exercised on the bodies of the condemned, sometimes even after their death, are – as the author argues – an integral part of power technology in that age. In fact, in the classical age, in which power is absolute, exclusive and secret, torture is a judicial deed in the strict sense of the word, both in terms of a pretrial investigation act and in terms of punishment. If the judicial authority suspected guilt, an accused person could not be innocent (as it was argued), but at most guilty of a minor crime. The confession, wrought out through torture, was considered as evidence that the crime an accused person was charged with had been actually committed. Whereas, according to the authority, the lack of a confession proved only that not that particular crime had been committed, but another one considered less serious, and therefore the punishment could no longer be death inflicted in the most painful way as to length and duration of the pangs of death, but instead a less painful kind of death, or imprisonment.

Punishment was not aimed at re-establishing justice, but instead at stating publicly and visibly the superiority of political power over those who, by committing a crime, would have challenged it by disobeying the authority. The more this challenge was serious, the greater the punishment had therefore to be. Therefore, in the execution of a punishment, there was a proportional standard but also a ritual element. The sovereign, as the symbol and representative of this power, decided about the death sentence according to the procedures established by the judges, or to modify or stop it at his will. However, the people were asked to participate as public witnesses and guarantors of the punishment. Hence, the rituality of punishment in the classical age, whose effects were not always those the authority expected and desired. Sometimes, people's participation – as Foucault remarks – was not limited to attending and witnessing the pain of the condemned person and encouraging the executioner. The bystanders were often actively involved in practices the authority did not welcome, such as providing moral support to the condemned, swearing against religion, cursing the judges, or physically attacking the executioner. In doing so, they could assume the attitudes and behaviors of the condemned person, who had nothing left to lose. Likewise, the announcement of the condemned person's crime after the execution had ambivalent effects, since it might justify the execution or redound to the condemned person's glory or of his or her crime itself.

For all these reasons, in the last decades of the classical age it began to seem increasingly clear that punishment by death could no longer be accepted, and that therefore it was necessary to find different forms of punishment. Cesare Beccaria and other reformers of the penal law gave rise to a literature that recommended moderation in punishment for the sake of humanity. Humanity, such as it was then considered, remained, however, an instrument at the disposal of power, which in turn sought to make use of more rational mechanisms to better control and punish its subjects. At the eve of the transition to modern age, the new orientation of punishment techniques was based on tolerance of the crimes made by the bourgeoisie, such as tax evasion or unlawful business operations, but instead on repression of the crimes committed by the lower classes, such as theft. Along with the new merchant economy, also a new technology of punishment power was created, which aimed at rationally and precisely calculating the punishment so that it could be severe enough to prevent and avert the reiteration of a crime. Consequently, there was no humanitarian spirit in punishment mitigation, but instead a new dissuasive, rational and calculating orientation in power.

Therefore, power became ideological, in the sense that it aimed at controlling in the most profitable and effective ways the ideas of the subjects, and through this control, also their bodies. New codes were formulated and new tactics toward criminals were developed in order to meet that orientation. At the same time, the new pseudo-science of criminology attributed a non-human nature to criminals. These were alternative ways for de-humanizing criminals and making the punishment of a crime impersonal and objective. Punishment lost the arbitrary nature it had in the classical age and prior to it, and through the establishment of a strict relation between crime seriousness and punishment duration, the dissuasion from committing or reiterating crimes was proposed. Dissuasion efforts would have been made by promoting in criminals an evaluation, easily understandable by them and by any other subject, of the costs and benefits resulting from one's choice of whether committing crimes or not. Therefore, punishment was not aimed at restoring the authority of the sovereign, as in the classical age, but instead the authority of law. The culprit – as it was argued – must learn to keep to the law in order to reintegrate himself or herself in social life.

Consequently, the way to enforce the punishment changed. Detention in closed areas, instead of torture and execution in a public space, involved for power a new way to treat the condemned person's body and soul (a new "physics of power"), with the purpose to obtain complete control and domination. Compulsory hard labor was introduced, but also a wage to improve the prisoners' fate during and after their imprisonment. Likewise (first in Philadelphia under the Quakers' influence, and then in other places) the principle of continuous control of life, times and bodies of the condemned persons was introduced, as they were removed by their imprisonment from outer social life. Prison was intended not only as a punishment, but also as a rehabilitation instrument through which the condemned persons' mood was put to a test and improved. Acting on their moods, manipulating their souls and, with them also their bodies, had the purpose to prevent them from committing new crimes. The body had already been an object and target of power in the classical age, when paramount care was devoted to making soldiers a docile and well-disciplined instrument of combat. However, a new attitude toward the body began to gain ground in the last decades of that age, and along with it, a micro-physics of power.

The human body became then an integral part of the mechanisms of power. The discipline of the bodies did not remain circumscribed in the military environment, but involved instead a subject's militarization also in other environments, such as the school, the workshop, and the hospital. For this purpose, these persons were submitted to meticulous controls conforming to regulations and under the authority of inspectors. The rationality that inspired these controls aimed at pursuing the discipline of bodies and souls, and was both technical and economic at the same time; because through its economic effectiveness it intensified the power apparatus by using it as an instrument for the purposes it pursued from time to time: reforming morals, preserving health, spreading education, and so on. A precise place was assigned to each individual, in order to classify him/her and therefore, to better control and continuously watch over his/her activities and use of time. Since all the time units were exactly and completely identical in terms of length and contents, time became serial and inclusive. Surveillance was therefore both individual and generalized (micro- and macro-physics of power), and was endless.

The ultimate purpose was to produce an automatic docility in individuals, and collectively, a perfectly organized and orderly society. Discipline, to be obtained and kept both individually and collectively, is the peculiar characteristic of modern age. It involves not only an intense and continuous hierarchical control, but also the existence of architectural systems in the position to make it possible in institutional environments, such as barracks, schools, prisons, factories, and so on. A perfectly rational architectural device – whose prototype and model is the system called "panopticon," planned by Bentham toward the end of the eighteenth century – allows controlling all subjects with one sight, in any moment and detail of their life. The panopticon is the symbol and the laboratory of power in the modern age. Differently from the dark prisons of classical age, the panopticon sheds full light on each prisoner in order to better control him/her, thereby conforming to the widespread and capillary character of power. In contrast with the sovereign's invisibility, the central tower of the panopticon is perfectly visible to each prisoner. Although the prisoners cannot see the guard placed in the tower, from his place the guard can and must see all the prisoners.

It does not matter who the guard is, because he/she is completely irrelevant – like the prisoners – in his or her individual characteristics. In fact, power is impersonal in the modern age. Disciplinary punishments are intended to correct the faults one has made rather than avenge an offended law, and go along with rewards for the behaviors that conform to the authority's will, with a continuously updated penal accounting that relates to the norms in force all the behaviors of all subjects, taking into account individual differences. The examination procedure, as an impersonal and objective technique used by power to classify, control, punish and record the dominated persons, is functional to the goal of discipline, of which it constitutes, like the panopticon, one of the mechanisms. The examination produces rituals of truth and domains of objective knowledge: modern age power has therefore a creative capability of its own. Discipline, thanks to all the techniques it makes use of, minimizes the economic and political costs of power exercise, maximizes its extension and intensity. Finally discipline conforms to the requirements of the different apparatuses of power by improving and enhancing the mechanisms of subjection. Formal and juridical freedoms involve using these mechanisms, and making sure that there is not, and there cannot be, any parity and reciprocity between those who exercise discipline and coercion, give punishments, establish and implement examination procedures, and those who instead suffer them.

In the modern age, detention raises the procedures included in the other means of discipline to a maximum level of intensity by limiting freedom and aiming at making prisoners docile and sociable. Seclusion is functional to the process of a prisoner's forced individualization, and his or her work is used for submitting and conforming him or her to the production apparatus. The gradualness of the punishment accords to the prisoner's behavior allows quantifying and modulating it, by giving it more or less explicitly the contractual form of a relation based on wages. In the twentieth century, the establishment of a new role in penal justice, i.e. the judge assigned to apply a punishment, is functional to the purpose of increasing the moral standards of prisoners, that is to say, submitting them to the requirements of power. In view of this purpose, as from the nineteenth century, scientists set themselves the objective to know the criminal's biography, to "scientifically" identify a dangerous criminal, and therefore combine the penal discourse with the psychiatric one, provide a justification to the pseudo-science of criminology, and on these grounds legitimize the double objective of punishment and correction. The criminal is therefore a creation of the detention methods of punishment supported by the pseudo-science of criminology.

Criticism to detention in prisons had already appeared during the first half of the nineteenth century, and since then, it has been repeated without any important change. Prisons do not decrease criminality rates and, on the contrary, imprisonment gives rise to relapsing and to new criminality, both because it encourages solidarity and criminal organizations, and because when a former convict comes out of the prison, he does not succeed in finding a proper job, while his family falls into poverty. Finally, prisons are expensive, both directly and indirectly, because they are not able to repress criminality. On the other hand, neither the positive effects of imprisonment – although praised since the nineteenth century – have been noticed so far, nor the recommendations and proposals of reform of the prison system, which find their origin in the nineteenth century too and since then have followed one another, have succeeded in changing anything. This is not surprising, because its role has not changed of class domination instrument; for, by means of punishment, the dominated class is kept in a condition of subjection, while the crimes committed by the bourgeoisie are not punished. Furthermore, imprisonment concerns criminals who are less danger to power because they do not change it. On the contrary, criminals can be even used by power, particularly through the ambiguous relations the police has always kept with crime.

Along with prison, the alternative and illegal principle of out-of-prison detention has never disappeared; thereby extending the prison system – which with its control and observation system is an instrument of power – far beyond what juridical rules provide for, and lowering the threshold beyond which punishment becomes natural and accepted. Insofar as it is a device and an instrument of power, the prison system can counter a great force of inertia to those who want to transform it. This explains its solidity, all the more so because it connects itself with other institutional devices with which it contributes to exercise a normalizing power over subjects; that is to say, an education or re-education in the soul and in the behaviors to conformity imposed by power.

From the mid-1970s until 1984, the year in which Foucault died, his production was characterized – except from some texts published in the form of short contributions or interviews, which resumed and examined in depth the theme of power and other related themes that had already been dealt with in his previous works (see in particular Foucault 1982) – by a new research direction the author could not complete, which focused on the theme of sexuality in the modern age and in the Greco-Roman past. In these works, sexuality is understood as a particular, and therefore changing, historical experience which is characterized by a correlation, in a particular culture, among knowledge domains, norm types, and subjectivity forms. Sexuality is therefore studied from a genealogical point of view, which in a particular age becomes archaeological. The author's interest is focused on the discursive formations that constitute knowledge/power and it makes use of; the ways validated by knowledge (games of truth, as Foucault calls them) in which the subjects consider themselves and the others as subjects and objects of sexual desire; the different ways and intensities in which activities and pleasures linked to sexual behavior have become the object of moral attention. This attention has never been lacking in this ambit of life and must be understood as a set of values and action rules institutionally imposed to individuals and groups (Foucault 1984: 10–14, 17–21, 36).

In Foucault's opinion, the history of sexuality is a history of how, over different historical ages and in a deliberate and meditated manner, human beings have constituted themselves as moral subjects with practices pertaining to their sexual life, or have imposed themselves to others according to a conception of sexuality judged ethically correct. In ancient times, these practices and conceptions used to define the aesthetical values of a person, his or her art of existing, and ultimately, the person as such, and were later radically changed first by the Christian faith with its pastoral power on bodies and souls, and in the modern age, by doctors, educators or psychologists. Despite his focusing on the theme of sexuality, the author's conceptual apparatus and basic interests continue to remain unchanged, and consequently, also the attention he pays to the archaeological and genealogical elements of power, to its macro- and micro-physical strategies and manifestations, and finally, to the episteme that connotes human sciences – or pseudo-sciences, according to Foucault – and their particular discursive formations supporting, besides being an integral part of them, power systems. The experience of sexuality in the modern age is the main theme, particularly in The *Will to Knowledge. The History of Sexuality* (1976) and *Herculine Barbin dite Alexina*(1978), while in *The Use of Pleasure* (1984) reference is made instead to the Greek classical age (fourth century B.C.), and in The *Care of the Self* (1986) to the first two centuries A.D.

The Will to Knowledge is a thesis work (as usually all Foucault's research works), in which the author argues that, from the nineteenth century onward, power has taken control of bodies and the pleasures they can give and receive. Through this control, the whole conduct of the subjects has been submitted to domination with the help of doctors, psychiatrists and other professional roles who gain economic and power benefits from the control of bodily pleasures. As a consequence, sexuality has pervaded and penetrated modern society, involving conducts (defined perverse), ages (the infant age), relations (like those between teachers and pupils), and spaces (like schools and prisons). Power extends its control over them in the name of discursive formations that claim to have an objective and scientific value. Confession is an integral part of these pseudo-scientific discursive formations. By combining with the doctors' or psychiatrists' examinations or interrogations, confession, as a technique aimed at producing truth, confession has become an element of a sexual pseudo-science, which has established a system of legitimate knowledge power makes use of in order to control and subjugate – whether directly or through the families – the individuals' souls and behaviors by means of interdictions and sanctions exercised also outside the state apparatuses.

The conception of sexuality is historically determined. The control of the domains and forms in which sexuality reveals itself has continuously grown since the seventeenth century, resting on a system of increasingly detailed rules and knowledge in the service of an ever-increasing invasive power. Psychoanalysis belongs to modern age in its attempt to fully exercising its control in the name of a therapy of sexuality that claims to be scientific. This therapy draws its legitimacy from the assumption that the souls and behaviors of the patients (of both sexual genders) are permeated with sexuality, from which problems would result for the patients themselves, their families, and society in general. Sexuality-control techniques, considered in their genealogy (in the sense Foucault attributes to this term) do not attest at all progressive repression of sexuality, followed by a slow decline in the twentieth century; but instead an uninterrupted growth of repressive methods and processes since the classical age, as well as the use of medical techniques since the nineteenth century.

Psychoanalysis, as a theory, has maintained that repression is socially necessary and therefore we must submit ourselves to social and judicial rules. However, as a therapeutic technique, it is meant to mitigate the effects of repression by encouraging the patients to express their incestuous desires within the domain of a psychoanalytic discourse. In opposition with power techniques, which have tried to make the bodies become efficient instruments in the service of the state, those that have regulated the biological and demographic processes have been put in the service of production. If, in the first case, we can talk about bio-politics, in the second case we shall talk about bio-power; that is to say, the use of power and knowledge to transform human life. In the nineteenth century, bio-power became socially prevailing and required new techniques or procedures for its exercise.

The control of sexuality with the help of notions claiming to be scientific has involved full control of the bodies, of their energies and sensations, and of their pleasures. Freud's psychoanalysis, far from releasing subjects from repression, has been used for putting into practice this new strategy of power. To illustrate this thesis, Foucault dwells on the early history of psychoanalysis, and especially on successful construction of hysteria as a mental disease on the part of Charcot, a neurologist who had been Freud's teacher (Foucault 2006: 308–32). As Foucault argues, this construction was made necessary by the absence of organic evidence of any pathological condition. The construction was conducted according to the following steps.

Firstly, a symptomatological scenario was organized to the effect that Charcot himself, with his authority, power and status as a hospital doctor, elicited the production of symptoms in the form of hysterical attacks on the part of the patients, who were under hypnosis. Secondly, the symptoms were manifested as Charcot expected. This conformity was taken by Charcot as evidence of the patient's morbid condition. But – as Foucault argues – it was rather evidence that Charcot was a captive of his patient, who by producing some symptoms rather than others could confirm or disconfirm the doctor's authority; the more so, if the patient produced the symptoms of hysteria – such as pretending so suffer from sexual spasms – so frequently, that it was impossible for Charcot to verify whether these symptoms were genuine or feigned. The patient's was in fact, according to Foucault, a "neurological body fabricated by the doctors" (Foucault 2006: 323).

Herculine Barbin dite Alexina, a work that saw Foucault both as editor and commentator, concerns – like the journal of Pierre Rivière – nineteenth-century discursive formations having some events told by the protagonists themselves as subjects, which had called the attention of the press and of different institutional roles of that period. Foucault's attention focused on the memoirs of Herculine Barbin, a French hermaphrodite who lived in the mid-nineteenth century. After having been considered at the beginning a female by the registry office, as soon as in puberty some sexual characters of the opposite gender began to reveal themselves, along with an attraction for the female sex. Herculine Barbin became for judges, doctors and psychiatrists, religious exponents and the press an object of examinations – imposed rather than required - which continued also after her/his death. After having obtained from a court the change in the registry of her/his sexual identity, the protagonist also in this new condition went through different and painful events accompanied by a more or less complete social isolation, up to the decision to commit suicide when she/he was still very young (Foucault 1978). The case of Herculine Barbin was used by Foucault as an example and a proof of how sexual identities result from a social construction process. This process is carried out by institutionally authorized subjects, such as doctors and judges, who are able to impose the discursive formation considered correct, regardless of the subjects themselves (see Sassatelli 2005: 272–3).

In *The Use of Pleasure*, the author focuses on sexuality in Greece during the classical age. As in other ages and cultures, in Greece too, sexuality was subject to moral rules. However, the aim was specific – to achieve wisdom through appropriate spiritual conditions – as well as the sphere of admitted and regulated sexual relations, which in Ancient Greece conformed to few and simple principles, and included also homosexual relations, though adult men were not allowed to take a passive role. Although the actions and the contacts that give pleasure were objects of literary and philosophical treatment, there was however no attempt to seek the manifestations of desire in the soul, such as the father confessors or the conscience directors did instead in the subsequent Christian age. According to the ethical code of classical Greece, for a man in the full sense of the word – that is to say, free, adult, and in possession of political rights – sexual activity is not immoral (as wisdom does not involve, in fact, suppressing one's desire), but instead its excess (as wisdom involves, in fact, controlling one's desire).

Pleasure, which could be pursued but had to be satisfied at the right moment and with moderation, and asceticism – to be sought, like pleasure, with moderation – allow a man to constitute himself as a moral subject, because he is not a slave to desire. The virtue of temperance – as it was argued – had to be practiced by those who want to come to truth, while the pursuit of pleasure would have turned into an obstacle. The art of living was an aesthetic value, but had also a moral value and a value of truth. The pursuit of health through the practice of dietetics, like the pursuit of pleasure through sexual activity, belonged to the art of living and therefore received a moral connotation. Temperance prevents the pathological effects of sexual excesses, but also the dangers resulting from sexual acts performed in inappropriate moments. In fact, sexual intercourse, which is not an evil in itself, is dangerous for the body and the soul because it leads persons to lose their self-control, involves energy waste, and is associated – with the production of new individuals – with the future death of the man who has copulated.

Marriage forces only the wife to fidelity – as it was argued – as indeed, her virtue consists in it, since she is submitted to her husband's power and authority. However, by displaying his fidelity, the husband seeks to be the master of himself. This was a value of paramount importance, according to the ancient Greeks. Only those who are the masters of themselves can look after their house and their goods in the best way, and can properly accomplish their social duties. Moderation in sex expresses the ethics of male power inside and outside the home boundaries, and reflects in this way a form of justice. The most honorable sexual activity is performed by man within marriage. Extramarital relations – no matter whether with men or women – were an object of moral concern, not because they were blameworthy and condemned in themselves, but because they revealed a violation of the principle of temperance. Homosexual relations, in particular, were accepted – though never recommended – on condition they occurred between men (never between women), and the adult male kept an active role, remaining the passive role exclusively played by adolescents. The mere suspicion that it might not be so was particularly unbecoming. As regards the other subject, he was submitted to constraints, but also had some prerogatives.

If he was not a slave, he could accept or reject intercourse at choice, but could neither continue his homosexual relations after his adolescence – as soon as he came to his full manly age – nor prostitute himself and in general accept indiscriminately any contact. He could not even identify himself with the passive role he had in any case to play, because this identification would have been incompatible with his future manly roles. Therefore, the adolescent, too, had to be as moderate and alert in his sexual life as his adult partner. Homosexual relations between adults and adolescents were morally necessary and socially useful provided they were based on friendship and teaching, or respectively, learning of truth and wisdom, but never on love. On the contrary, an approved conjugal relation was never erotic, but could be amorous. Sexuality, and in particular homosexuality, were an object of a moral reflection, which had in temperance its basic principle. By insisting on the existence of superiority and inferiority positions in the sexual sphere, moral reflection established an analogy between sexual intercourse and social relation. Over time, philosophers' and moralists' attention shifted from homosexual to heterosexual affairs, and women's sexual behavior became the center of attention in Greece after the classical age.

The "archaeological" and "genealogical" analysis of sexuality continued in *The Care of the Self*, the last book Foucault was able to complete before his untimely death. The objects of study are, like in *The Use of Pleasure*, ethics and sexual practices in ancient times. This work focuses particularly on the subsequent period ranging from the Hellenistic age to the first centuries after Christ. In that period, sexual ethics became stricter and more rigorous, considering that sexual activity – like other activities, such as meditation or reading – should be devoted to the improvement and the care of the person, and addressed not only to the soul but also to the body. Therefore, in that period medicine began to gain importance as a way of thinking and a practice concerning both the soul and the body. The practices concerning the self were placed in the service of a self-control ethics. Pleasure, which results from the lack of soul and body troubles, acceptance of only what results from the subject's free, rational choice and self-improvement were in fact the ethic goals of this age.

The relations with other subjects were regulated as regards conjugal and political life. During the Hellenistic age, marriage was increasingly considered a voluntary union between peers, guaranteed by the public authority, rather than a relation in which power was entrusted to the husband (as in classical Greece), but inequality did never completely disappear. As to political life, the ethic formation of the person as a citizen was no longer possible. Political activities confirmed instead people's prestige and position resulting from their birth and social class, since these signs are external to a person and therefore do not characterize his/her essence. The ethical nucleus classical Greece had given to political life began therefore to disappear. The relation with one's body was intended in a broad sense as a relation with one's self and with the outer world. Medicine was assigned to define this relation, as it prescribed – with the best possible diet – also the best possible life conduct, including sexual life. There were, however, quite a few ambiguities in this regard. On the one hand, the seed and the sexual intercourse were favorably considered; but on the other hand, people were afraid of the dangers concerning the intercourse, the diseases that might result from it, the violent tension and the waste of energy. The value of abstinence for men and women was praised, and cautiousness in sexual activity was recommended, however, without mentioning the acts that were not recommended.

In the Hellenistic age, married life conduct had to be – as previously – marked by an ethics of self-control and self-improvement, but a form of reciprocity began to impose itself at the same time, according to which the wife had to become a preferential partner with the same dignity as the husband, and both spouses were bound to mutual attachment, affection and respect. Differently from past customs, the husband's adultery was condemned (the wife's adultery having always been condemned), and the literature of that age, on which Foucault widely dwells, was lavish with advice for the good sexual life of the spouses. A married woman, in particular, had to avoid both any excessive availability or, on the contrary, rejection. For both spouses, physical pleasure was not a purpose, but instead a means for obtaining the partner's love and friendship, and a sign they had been achieved. A harmonious conjugal union – as the Stoics argued – would promote a person's harmonious relation with him- or herself. In this prescribed lifestyle, which was focused on the conjugal union, homosexual affairs with adolescents, although not condemned, began to lose their importance.

However, this occurred not because of homosexuality in itself, which was still admitted in that age and had even its supporters, but for another reason: namely, because of the usually ephemeral nature of this kind of love in contrast with the stable and lasting relation based on love of a married couple. In the following centuries, until the fourth century A.D., less attention began to be paid to homosexual unions, and within heterosexual and conjugal unions, the values referring to the purity of the spirit – and until the wedding – also of the bodies, imposed themselves for both sexes. This new ethics had been prepared to some extent by the more austere sexual ethics of the Hellenistic age compared to that of classical Greece. The new moral was focused on the value of renunciation and self-control, while the only accepted kind of sexuality was the one existing between spouses. However, there was not in it the principle, which found instead its full expression in the Christian religion, according to which sexual activity in itself represents an evil, whose signs can be caught only through a continuous and careful interpretation of thoughts and conducts.

The Reception of Foucault's Work

Foucault's works have enjoyed a very wide reception also among sociologists, even though the author did not consider himself a sociologist, and his place in the field of sociology is questionable. Therefore, the presentation of his works is of necessity selective. We shall first mention some general introductions, and provide a comparison of these essays. We shall then consider some interpretations of this work made by scholars considered particularly qualified not only for their familiarity with Foucault's work, but also for the personal relations they kept with him. We shall then expound some interpretations and critical evaluations released by historians (but also the replies of some authors who do not share them) and sociologists, such as

Habermas and Giddens. Finally, we shall examine a few exegetic contributions that concern some particular aspects of Foucault's work. As usual, in this case too, we avoid taking directly side on the work.

1

The introductions to Foucault are numerous and addressed to different publics. We shall not linger on introductions likely addressed to a students' public, and in any case of a clearly popular nature, however without any intention to call into question the competence of their authors (see, for instance, Danaher, Schirato and Webb 2000; Horrocks and Jetvic 2000). Furthermore, we shall not consider the chapters dedicated to this author included in introductions to the sociological theory, even though well informed and, within the limits of a chapter, also relatively complete (see in particular, Baert 1998). We shall instead mention some introductions (presented in their chronological order of publication) written by some authors who are very familiar with Foucault's works and have an in-depth knowledge of them. Their comparison will not concern the themes these introductions deal with, considered that they are always exhaustive; but instead the relevance each introduction gives respectively to these themes, and therefore the likely weight the authors have wanted to give to some particular works by Foucault or to some of his production periods, as well as some comprehensive evaluations of them.

The essay by Alan Sheridan, who translated into English a good part of Foucault's production, divides these works into two components considered clearly distinguished. The first part, called *Archaeology of Knowledge*, includes the works written in the 1960s and 1970s, before the introduction of the concept of genealogy, and in particular: *History of Madness*, *The Birth of the Clinic*, *The Order of Things*, *Archaeology of Knowledge* and *The Discourse on Language*. The second part, called *Genealogy of Power*, includes the entire subsequent production until 1980, and excludes therefore the books dedicated to the history of sexuality in the Greco-Roman age. The organization of this book suggests that Sheridan thinks Foucault made use of "archaeological" analysis only in his early works, while over time his analysis would have become "genealogical." According to Sheridan, who mentions some interviews given by Foucault, the reason of this change would consist in the fact that in the early works, the implicit presence of power relations in discursive formations would have been ignored (Sheridan 1980: 116). This remark was taken up also by other commentators (Baert 1998). In his long conclusion, Sheridan dwells upon Foucault's biographic events, the intellectual context, and the author's reception in France and in the English-speaking countries, particularly the United States.

Barry Smart provides his introduction with a completely different organization, lingering first on the various themes treated by Foucault, subsequently on the concepts of archaeology and genealogy, then on power/knowledge and the related themes of body and sexuality, and finally on the political manifestations of power (state and government) and on resistance to them. Despite the different character of his introduction, Smart, too, remarks a change in Foucault's tone, after the *Archaeology of Knowledge*, in the direction of "genealogical" investigation. However, Smart notices that there is continuity of themes and interests in the two periods, particularly as regards Foucault's interest in the ways in which discursive practices transform themselves. Archaeological analysis continues to remain also in the second period, with the purpose of providing a method for isolating and analyzing particular discursive formations. Archaeology is therefore considered complementary to genealogy: this applies also to Foucault's research on sexuality. However, only genealogical analysis contains an explicit criticism to power, as it reveals itself in unequal relations, and to the techniques it makes use of (Smart 2002: 42, 54–5, 62).

Mitchell Dean, the author of another well-known introduction to Foucault (Dean 1994), shares with Smart the interpretative thesis of a complementarity between archaeological and genealogical analysis. Archaeological analysis – he argues – provides the necessary methodological condition for genealogical analysis, in the sense that it is a method for obtaining the necessary separation from validity norms and standards of particular disciplines, thereby preparing the genealogical analysis of their historical change and of the struggles that have produced this separation: a history of truth and present, in Foucault's words. Through genealogical analysis it is possible to point out how power – with its techniques, practices (government practices, in particular), discursive formations (concerning, for example, madness or sexuality), ethics and rationality – reveals itself and articulates in different forms, historical times, and spaces, for example a school or a hospital (Dean 1994: 33–6, 141, 172–3, 215). In addition, Dean (1994) formulates some well-constructed thematic comparisons between Foucault and other important twentieth-century authors, such as Braudel, Weber, Adorno and Horkheimer, Habermas and Elias. Though all these authors share in particular the theme of rationalization, Dean aims, however, to illustrate the specific nature and the interest of Foucault's contribution.

Finally, it is worth briefly mentioning the introductions to Foucault's work written by Gary Gutting (2003a; 2005). These introductions can be understood not only as guides to Foucault's reading, but also as reviews – although partial – of his international reception. As guides to Foucault's reading, they stand out because they examine the conceptual relations between archaeology and genealogy (the method used by genealogical investigation is the archaeological one, but it has a critical purpose that is not implicit in archaeological analysis). But also because they focus on the relations between Foucault's thought and some contemporary currents of thought, such as structuralism and existentialist philosophy (Gutting 2003a: 45–6, 49–50, and 61–2). The evaluations provided by Gutting on Foucault's reception indirectly lead to the themes and issues Foucault himself had dealt with. Gutting is not neutral at all in his evaluations.

His objections concern the criticism, which he considers groundless, addressed to the *History of Madness* (Gutting 2003a: 15, 39–41; 2003b; 2005: 39–41) and to Foucault's theory of power (Gutting 2003a: 20). They also concern some comprehensive interpretations of his work. According to Gutting, some of them attach too much importance to the particular course Foucault wanted to give to his life in some periods, and omit indicating that this course later changed in favor of an active political commitment, thereby misinterpreting his works (Gutting 2003a: 23–4). Other critics unduly privilege (according again to Gutting) only a single aspect of these works, his historical investigation method, overlooking that Foucault formulated the theories and the methods he used for his individual inquiries, but did not aim at formulating generally valid theories and methods (Gutting 2003a: 2–6). Gutting's introductions stand out also because they pay attention to a usually neglected aspect of Foucault, his interest in avant-garde authors and in the extreme character of their literary experiments, and his relations with some of the most outstanding representatives of the French twentieth-century intellectual milieu, such as Bataille and Bachelard (Gutting 2003a: 14–19, 62–3).

2

Foucault was acquainted and even made friends and established an intellectual exchange relationship with the French philosophers Canguilhem (of whom he had been a follower) and Deleuze. In the United States, where he lived and taught in the last years of his life, he entered in a relationship based on cooperation and mutual esteem with two teachers of the Berkeley University of California, Dreyfus and Rabinow. These personal relationships led all these authors not only to express their keen and deep interest in Foucault's work, but also to write several interpretative essays on Foucault's thought in general, or on some of its elements. We shall briefly examine these essays, beginning with an essay written by Canguilhem (2003) on the notion of episteme, which he considers not immediately intelligible. According to Canguilhem, this notion indicates a configuration of stable discursive formations through which the cultural productions of different sciences are perceived. The different kinds of episteme cannot be evaluated through value ratings, but can be analyzed in their "archaeology." In Canguilhem's opinion, Foucault was urged to formulate, rather than a general archaeology of knowledge, an archaeology of human sciences through which it were possible to show when and how the human being has become an object of scientific and philosophical knowledge.

We shall consider now the dense essay written by Deleuze. The author carries out an in-depth exegetic and interpretative work on some of Foucault's key concepts. A group of statements complies with the same rules of formation, which are not shared with other groups, with which it relates instead through rules of variation. Furthermore, a statement relates with its constitutive elements (arguments, objects and concepts), and is complementary to the institutional and non-discursive environment (for example, the political or the economic environment), from which these elements originate. Each statement refers back to something else, and defines itself in relation to it. This "something else" can either concern or not concern it at all, be external (*dehors*: outside, Deleuze quotes literally Foucault). Archaeological analysis aims at shedding light on the concealed, invisible sense of a statement (what is said), starting from the historically determined discursive multiplicities (sentences and words) that form it. This concealed sense is not the structure of a statement, because it goes across different structures (for example, different visions of the world) placed in different ways in time and space. Each discursive formation, for example a scientific or juridical one, includes discontinuity elements (*coupure*) with respect to already existing or future formations.

The changeable power relations that constitute power and take place between groups make sure that the combination, or diagram, of these forces may constantly change over time and space, within a particular social field (such as the school or the army) and between a social field and another. The connection between forces makes room for points – for instance, discursive formations – that are not well connected, in which there may be resistance, change and innovation, and over which external forces, such as institutions, can act. What is visible and can be stated can constitute knowledge, and become consequently the object of epistemological investigation. This investigation aims at revealing what is considered as truth in a particular historical age, how people must see and speak according to that age (whereas "archaeological" investigation seeks to point out statement regularities). What is visible and can be stated can also become the object of external (institutional) rules. Power is a pure function, that is to say, it acts independently of the forms in which it incorporates itself and of the means it makes use of. In modern societies, it acts as a disciplinary function on bodies, and as a pastoral function on souls, and always meets with resistance. The practice of power is different and irreducible in comparison with that of knowledge. There is indeed a micro-physics of power, in which power strategies privilege movable and non-locatable relations over which the knowledge of human sciences cannot be exercised.

There is a relation with ourselves, as bodies but also as beings who have an identity, who seek truth and want to be free, who resist to power and have a memory of themselves. Over this subjectivity, which connotes modern age, the strategies of power/knowledge cannot be fully exercised; for, depending on the changeable power relations, subjectivity remains to some extent and for some aspects external to power. Foucault's core interest, according to Deleuze, is the history of the conditions in which knowledge, power and self-reveal or do not reveal themselves. In other words, the conditions of existence of what can be seen and said, which is therefore subject to different and changeable power relations, and of what remains instead external, differ from these conditions insofar as it is a thought and one's relation with his/her own inner life. Finitude – or, the impossibility to be fully human in relating with the external forces of power and be conscious of this limit – can be overcome only if a man builds an active relation between his inner life and the external forces that tend now to dominate him, thus achieving the height of his existence.

Among the contributions of authors who kept personal relations with Foucault, it is worth mentioning the famous and often-quoted essay by Dreyfus and Rabinow (1983; see also 1986). Their basic thesis states that in general, Foucault's work can neither be considered structuralist nor hermeneutic, because none of these approaches would comply with Foucault's wish to understand social practices and their effects. Foucault is not a structuralist, because in the works that followed the *Archaeology of Knowledge* Foucault showed he did not share the elimination made by structuralism of the meaning of action. He is a critic of hermeneutics (as an interpretation of human experience), because it is no use pointing out concealed meanings to obtain an understanding in the position to make actors better prepared to withstand power practices and strategies. The *Archaeology of Power* can be considered a structuralist work, because the author focuses on the regularity of the relations among the statements of a discursive formation, regardless of their sense.

In this work, Foucault explores the limits of the possibilities of knowledge in the modern age, and argues the thesis according to which these limits paradoxically give us the possibility of knowing ("analytics of finitude"). The dual character of man in the modern age – dual for several aspects: insofar as he is a subject, but also an object of knowledge; and surrounded by what cannot be understood, but also the origin of any understanding; a historical product, but also a source of history – puts a problem to the knowledge human sciences have tried to overcome in vain, as Foucault argues. Dreyfus and Rabinow recognize in the *Archaeology of Knowledge* two basic weak points: first, it is not possible to understand what influence institutions have on the discursive systems; secondly, the "archaeological" method does not allow investigating the relation between truth and knowledge, on the one hand, and between institutions and practices from which they derive, on the other.

The subsequent works put the "archaeological" investigation in the service of the "genealogical" one, in an attempt – according to the authors – to overcome these weak points. By combining the two kinds of analysis, Foucault puts into practice a method the two authors call "interpretative analytics," which would help him overcoming these difficulties. A scholar who keeps to this method is aware he is just a product of what he studies, and therefore cannot place himself outside his object of investigation (Dreyfus and Rabinow 1986: 114–15). "Genealogical" analysis shows that there is no theory can afford to leave the culture and the history of the society on which it focuses out of consideration. "Archaeological" analysis sheds light on the fact that shared practices are significant only in a particular cultural situation, and therefore they are historically determined. However, in these works there are some questions that remain still open, which the authors want to stressing (Dreyfus and Rabinow 1983: 206–207). They concern truth (in particular, to what extent the discursive formations of natural sciences are independent of power relations? Should historical research be guided only by today's concerns, or are there other validity standards?); resistance (Why one must resist to power? What resources have to be used to resist?); power (What is power? Is it a productive reality of practices or a heuristic principle? How does it concretely exercise its effects?).

3

We report now a brief summary of critical comments to Foucault's work. In this case, we prefer not to consider the reservations expressed within a comprehensive appraisal of Foucault's work, but instead some contributions in which a critical approach prevails. We shall make a distinction between the contributions of some historians, who in general have negatively judged the *History of Madness* but sometimes have also written in defense of it, and the contributions of some sociologists who have shown they did not share Foucault's "archaeological" method and theory of power. Beginning from the *History of Madness*, this work has given rise to a great deal of controversy, especially among English historians (see Gutting 2003b). We shall report hereafter some of the major critical evaluations and the answers resulting from them.

Talking about confinement in mental hospitals, Scull (1990) remarks that in the nineteenth century this practice, on which Foucault insists so much, was much more widespread in France than in England. As regards the latter country, the author would not have gathered sufficient evidence. The reforms started by Pinel and Tuke were considered an attack to medical treatment rather than the opposite. Finally, in no country did the Madmen's Ship ever have the spread Foucault attributes to it. Porter (1990), instead, focuses on the previous period, on classical age, and argues – referring again to England – that is does not correspond to truth that mad persons were always indiscriminately confined with criminals, idlers, ill persons and prostitutes, and that already in that age the mad were considered able to be re-educated and reintegrated into society. In defense of Foucault's research and of the author himself, several critical remarks have been formulated, which can be summarized as follows:

a.   Some of his English critics may have known only the translation of the abridged French edition of the *History of Madness*, and therefore a good part of the text and documents supporting it would have escaped them.

b.   Critics may have not noticed that Foucault would have identified as the crucial innovation brought by Pinel and Tuke not merely the creation of institutions for mental alienated persons, but instead the creation of special institutions delegated for this purpose, where the therapeutic effectiveness depended on what the specialized personnel working in them did.

c.   The contents of the *History of Madness*, which is a vast work and the most extensive one among Foucault's writings, do not lend themselves to be reduced to a systematic transition from a particular repressive system in the classical age to another one in the modern age. On the contrary, the book shows that the repressive and productive aspects of some forms of power cannot be easily separated.

d.   Confinement, as an institutional practice belonging to classical age, may have been more widespread in France than elsewhere, but Foucault was only interested in the fact that in that age it was possible to intern some categories of persons, thereby isolating them from the social world.

e.   Foucault makes use of historical facts to illustrate his own interpretative pattern, while Porter and the other conventional historians use them to support it. Foucault's interpretative pattern makes reference to the different experiences of madness in the classical age, as well as in the modern age, and the reported documentation is actually used to illustrate these different experiences (Gordon 1990; Gutting 2003b).

As regards the sociological reception of Foucault's work, it is perhaps advisable to make a distinction between sociologists who give an evaluation without having a sociological theory of their own as reference, on the one hand; and, on the other, outstanding representatives of contemporary theory, who have dwelt upon Foucault from their personal theoretical point of view. Here, we limit ourselves to mention, amongst the former, the article written by Fox, which is very critical towards Foucault, though we need to remember that he has a large number of admirers – as Fox himself states – in the sociological community. Fox's criticism concerns the following points. In the first place, Foucault does not establish in what the relation between discursive and non-discursive formations consists; but he seems to stress a one-way causal relation, since discursive formations would be external manifestations of power/knowledge. If this is the case, he does not even explain the reason why only some particular practices, but not other ones, become discursive. Secondly, also the relation between power/knowledge and body is not clearly explained, because the latter does not seem to have, in Foucault's writings, any positive feature as an entity in the position to resist power. Under what circumstances does it then become possible to resist? How much this resistance can be successful? Finally, the theme of sexuality discussed in Foucault's last period, introduces the actors' self as a non-discursive remnant in the position to resist power/knowledge, in contrast with the previous theses, however without dwelling upon the constraints that condition the formation of subjectivity.

Among the representatives of contemporary sociological theory who have confronted themselves with Foucault's work, we wish to mention in particular Habermas and Giddens. Habermas remarks that Foucault's criticism of power, and to the pseudo-truths it generates, leaves him without a normative standard to be used for evaluating the truth contents of discourse. This seems paradoxical in an author who gives ethical importance to the search for truth in the modern conditions of institutionalized power. As far as he is concerned, Habermas puts himself as a defender of the tradition of Enlightenment, to which we are indebted for the modern guarantees of freedom and legality. Furthermore, a stress is placed on a public sphere in which speaking and listening without constraints, except for the respect for the other participants, have relevance, and human rights are safeguarded. Habermas is aware of the possibility that instrumental reason (power, for Foucault) may spread to the detriment of communicative reason. However, this would not have to do with Enlightenment, but instead with the negative effects of capitalism.

Foucault, on the contrary, considers an ethic approach relevant when people's resistance to power is privileged and a critical spirit (which is not a heritage of Enlightenment) prevails in an age in which power insists on subjects' visibility and establishes the institutions assigned to their surveillance and the practices resulting from them. The pretensions to validity of any discourse – Foucault argues – do not evade the historically determined limitations produced by power relations. Despite these important differences, both authors share an Enlightenment-related ethical commitment in favor of the use of rationality. However, their commitment to this ethic is within its proper limits; to the effect that it rejects any pretension to truth concerning the transcendent reality, and submits to a critical examination also one's deepest beliefs (Habermas 1986: 107–108; see also Dreyfus and Rabinow 1986: 110–15; Hoy 1986: 8–9; Ingram 2003: 254–62; Jay 1986: 192).

Like Habermas, Giddens too dwells critically upon the way in which Foucault has conceived and treated power, but his criticism is based on different assumptions. Giddens considers power as "the capacity to achieve outcomes" (Giddens 1984: 257). It is not an impersonal and collective attribute, as for Foucault, because an explanation of the effects of power must imply the existence of actors who are conscious of what they do. Nevertheless, Giddens agrees with Foucault in not considering power an ability of single individuals. For both authors, power is incorporated in stable properties of the social systems. Furthermore, Giddens adds that these properties (or "resources") are consciously used by actors during their interactions, and therefore they are power instruments whose exercise meets with resistance. It is true that Foucault, too, underlines the resistance to power offered by the dominated persons, but Giddens remarks that he does not provide a conception of social actors, but only of meekly subject bodies. This conception is not realistic even in those institutions, for example prisons, in which any subjects' activity should be strictly controlled and regulated (Giddens 1984: 14–16, 153–8, 257–8).

4

We shall briefly mention now some contributions, which refer to the relations between Foucault's thought and particular philosophical investigation fields, such as ethics, epistemology and phenomenology, or focus on particular themes, such as archaeology, genealogy and power/knowledge. Foucault's core ethical theme has been understood as a need to escape the forced boundaries, thoughts and actions that limit political action, ethics and people's relation with themselves. According to Foucault, ethics concerns the forms in which subjectivity is established and experienced, and in which one's thoughts and conducts are governed. For Foucault, ethics would have different aspects: a substantive aspect, which specifies which parts of an individual are relevant for an ethical code; an aspect concerning subjection ways to an ethical code; an instrumental aspect, which indicates the means developed for becoming ethical subjects; an aspect concerning the aims of behavior, that is to say, what kind of persons we wish to become by behaving morally (Bernauer and Mahon 2003: 160; Davidson 1986: 228–9; 2003: 126–7).

The ethical theme connects itself with the epistemological one, because one of Foucault's primary cognitive objectives corresponds to them jointly considered, namely, to ascertaining through what forms of government (in a broad, not only political, sense) people have been driven to submission; in other words, through what kind of techniques and power strategies, forms of political rationality, knowledge with pretensions to truth (Smart 1986: 160–63). According to Foucault, truth and power are actually connected, in the sense that each power system produces its own truths (Hacking 1986: 38–40, Rouse 2003: 115). The denunciation of the disciplinary system, however, assumes an ethical code, and the implemental principles of that code, to be used as reference: in this connection, Foucault would have been reticent, as some commentators have remarked (Walzer 1986). In addition, Foucault would not have noticed the ambivalence inherent in the control techniques employed in the modern age.

The discipline that can be obtained through them is based either on the subjects' egalitarian participation, or on a chain of command of an authoritative nature. The political and social consequences resulting from the prevalence of either system are considerable, but Foucault would not have lingered on them, as he would have instead addressed his work to the purpose of underlining the subtlety of the repressive mechanisms created by the ruling classes (for example, the "pastoral power" over consciences). Therefore, Foucault would have addressed his ethical task as a student to the purpose of resisting domination and exploitation, and resisting the "pastoral power" and the power exercised over the subjects' bodies. Consequently, he would have aimed at and done his utmost for urging them to constitute themselves as ethical subjects able to understand the mechanisms of power, and therefore in a position to better oppose them (Bernauer and Mahon 2003: 154–7; Rorty 1986: 46–8; Taylor 1986: 81–3).

The presence of the phenomenological theme in Foucault's thought has been a subject for discussion as well. As it has been remarked, there are references, particularly in *The Order of Things*, to the author's departure from Husserl's phenomenology, which would remain empirical despite its aim to be purely transcendental. This confusion between the two analysis methods of lived experience, that is to say, the empirical and the transcendental one, would continue to remain, in Foucault's opinion (or better, according to some of his interpreters) also in Husserl's latest work. The "archaeological" and "genealogical" investigation methods involve, like the phenomenological method, keeping aloof from the immediacy of lived experience. However, this experience, on which phenomenological research is focused, makes use of historically determined categories of thought. In contrast, the methods used by Foucault seek to highlight, but not to assume as data, these historically determined categories (Han 2003: 185–7).

Several in-depth exegetic contributions concerning the "archaeological" and "genealogical" methods and the theme of power/knowledge, which is central in Foucault's thought, have been published. We shall briefly mention some of them. The difference between these two methods has been argued in the following terms: "genealogy" is not as neutral and detached as "archaeology," which investigates the practices through which some particular discursive and non-discursive formations attribute and keep a value of truth or falseness to their statements. "Genealogical" analysis distinguishes itself from "archaeological" analysis because of its polemic interest in the historically determined emersion of these practices; and along with them, its interest in the subjectivity and the modern forms of power; for these forms seek to shape it by means of appropriate strategies in the position to control its manifestations, and in particular, sexuality. Therefore, "genealogy" is ultimately a historical investigation on the constitution of subjectivity and sexuality within a context of power relations that tend to coerce them. If this investigation is successful, the irrationality for the subject of some particular practices and beliefs imposed by power is highlighted (Bernauer and Mahon 2003: 154–7; Flynn 2003: 36–9; Hoy 1986: 6–7, 20–21; Smart 1986: 166–7).

Modern power relations have been described by Foucault – as it has been authoritatively maintained – as non-monolithic (considering the subjects' possibility to resist them); and yet, they are in any case effective in their use of control and subjugation techniques and strategies. The discipline, first of the bodies and secondly of the souls, by escaping at the end of classical age the control exerted by law and codes, in the modern age has colonized the world. It has done so by making use of new power techniques; of new discursive formations (those, in particular, of human pseudo-sciences);, and finally, of new conceptions of truth institutionally sanctioned as scientific and objective discourse, but in fact subsidiary to the maintenance of a cultural, social and ideological power. Responses to this power can result not from some kind of comprehensive alternative, since there are no general alternative principles to which one can appeal; but rather from practices and discourses that take into account, in their ethical and political choices, the ever-changing configurations of power relations (Bernauer and Mahon 2003: 157; Rouse 2003: 114–19; Smart 1986: 159–66).

Finally, a note is in order about the reasons of Foucault's interest in the person and the works of Roussel, as testified by the book on which we have dwelt in the previous pages. The most exhaustive in-depth research is included in the introduction to Foucault's book written by the philosopher Macherey (1992). The author presents and discards other proposed explanations, and particularly the one according to which Foucault's interest in Roussel's work would be a consequence of the mental alienation of this author. Keeping to Foucault's text and integrating it with some of his other writings, particularly a passage situated towards the end of *The Order of Things* (1966: 394), Macherey suggests instead that Foucault would have tried to make madness fall into Roussel's work itself, in the sense that for Roussel work and insanity cannot be divided, but on the contrary, penetrate each other, as they both reveal the experience of finiteness in life (the experience of death), and in language (through its dissolution in Roussel's works).

Roussel's suicide would be consistent with this experience. In his aforementioned introduction to Foucault, Gary Gutting gives an explanation compatible with the one provided by Macherey, though he seems not to know it. In Gutting's opinion, Foucault would have been initially attracted by Roussel's social and intellectual marginalization, as well as by his being defined a mental patient. The loss of subjectivity in language and its destruction would be related with the loss of subjectivity in his physical person, with his death. Language ambiguity in Roussel's treatment would correspond to the ambiguity of his death by suicide, as it remains unclear whether he ultimately wanted to die, or save himself, or be saved. The removal of subjectivity from language would find in Roussel an analogy with Foucault's intention, expressed in *The Order of Things*, to subordinate the subject to the constraints existing in language and in other structures (Gutting 2005: 4–9).

It has been remarked (Sheridan 1980: 86–8) that the statement that there is a subject's subordination to the structure conforms to Foucault's thesis, according to which modern episteme would involve the end of discourse as a unitary formation, and its fragmentation in a variety of discourses, each one with its own pretension to objectivity. The ambiguity of the meanings expressed through language and perception, and the introduction of several discourses into one another by means of a series of digressions, such as they are expressed in Roussel's work, find a complete formulation in some of Foucault's coeval works; as in them he decrees the decline of subjectivity in modern episteme (Bruns 2003: 377–8; Jay 1986: 183–6).

References

Baert, P. 1998. *Social Theory in the Twentieth Century*. Cambridge: Polity Press. Italian translation: *La teoria sociale contemporanea*, 2002, Bologna: Il Mulino.

Bernauer, J.W. and Mahon, M. 2003. Michel Foucault's Ethical Imagination, in G. Gutting (ed.), *The Cambridge Companion to Foucault*. Cambridge: Cambridge University Press, 149–75.

Bruns, G.L. 2003. Foucault's Modernism, in G. Gutting (ed.), *The Cambridge Companion to Foucault*. Cambridge: Cambridge University Press, 348–78.

Canguilhem, G. 2003. The Death of Man, or the Exhaustion of the Cogito?, in G. Gutting (ed.), *The Cambridge Companion to Foucault*. Cambridge: Cambridge University Press, 74–94.

Danaher, G., Schirato, T. and Webb, J. 2000. *Understanding Foucault*. London: Sage.

Davidson, A.I. 1986. Archaeology, Genealogy, Ethics, in D.C. Hoy (ed.), *Foucault: A Critical Reader*. Oxford: Blackwell, 221–33.

Dean, M. 1994. *Critical and Effective Histories: Foucault's Methods and Historical Sociology*. London: Routledge.

Deleuze, G. 1986. *Foucault*. Paris: Les Éditions de Minuit.

Dreyfus, H. and Rabinow, P. 1983. *Michel Foucault: Beyond Structuralism and Hermeneutics*. Chicago, IL: The University of Chicago Press.

Dreyfus, H. and Rabinow, P. 1986. What is Maturity? Habermas and Foucault on "What is Enlightenment?" in D.C. Hoy (ed.), *Foucault: A Critical Reader*. Oxford: Blackwell, 109–21.

Flynn, T. 2003. Foucault's Mapping of History, in G. Gutting (ed.), *The Cambridge Companion to Foucault*. Cambridge: Cambridge University Press, 29–48.

Foucault, M. 1963a. *Naissance de la clinique*. Paris: Presses Universitaires de France. Italian translation: *Nascita della clinica*, 1969, Turin: Einaudi.

Foucault, M. 1963b. *Raymond Roussel*. Paris: Gallimard. Italian translation: *Raymond Roussel*, 2001, Verona: Ombre Corte.

Foucault, M. 1966. *Les mots et les choses. Une Archéologie des sciences humaines*. Paris: Gallimard. Italian translation: *Le parole e le cose*, 1967, Milan: Rizzoli. English translation: *The Order of Things*.

Foucault, M. 1969. *L'archéologie du savoir*. Paris: Gallimard. Italian translation: *L'archeologia del sapere*, 1971, Milan: Rizzoli.

Foucault, M. 1971. *L'ordre du discours*. Paris: Gallimard. Italian translation: *L'ordine del discorso*, 1972, Turin: Einaudi.

Foucault, M. 1972 (1961). *Histoire de la folie à l'âge classique*. Paris: Gallimard. Italian translation: *Storia della follia nell'età classica*, 1963, Milan: Rizzoli.

Foucault, M. 1973. *Moi, Pierre Rivière, ayant égorgé ma mère, ma soeur et mon frère ...* Paris: Gallimard (text edited by the author, with an introduction and a chapter by the author himself). Italian translation: *Io, Pierre Rivière, avendo sgozzato mia madre, mia sorella e mio fratello ... un caso di parricidio nel 19. Secolo*, ed. Michel Foucault, 1976, Turin: Einaudi.

Foucault, M. 1975. *Surveiller et punir*. Paris: Gallimard. Italian translation: *Sorvegliare e punire*, 1976, Turin: Einaudi.

Foucault, M. 1978. *Herculine Barbin dite Alexina*. Paris: Gallimard. Italian translation: *Herculine Barbin, detta Alexina B.; Memorie di un ermafrodito presentate da Michel Foucault*, 1979, Turin: Einaudi.

Foucault, M. 1982. Afterword. The Subject and Power, in H. Dreyfus and P. Rabinow (eds), *Michel Foucault: Beyond Structuralism and Hermeneutics*. Chicago, IL: The University of Chicago Press, 208–26.

Foucault, M. 1984. *L'usage des plaisirs*. Volume 2 de l'*Histoire de la sexualité*. Paris: Gallimard. Italian translation: *L'uso dei piaceri. Storia della sessualità*, 2, 1984, Milan: Feltrinelli.

Foucault, M. 1986. *The Care of the Self*. Volume 3 of *The History of Sexuality*. New York: Pantheon Books. Italian translation: *La cura di sé. Storia della sessualità*, 3, 1985, Milan: Feltrinelli.

Foucault, M. 1998. *The Will to Knowledge*. Volume 1 of *The History of Sexuality*. London: Penguin Books. Italian translation: *La volontà di sapere. Storia della sessualità*, 1, 1978, Milan: Feltrinelli.

Foucault, M. 1998b. Sessualità e potere, in *Archivio Foucault. Interventi, colloqui, interviste. 3. 1978–1985. Estetica dell'esistenza, etica, politica*. Milan: Feltrinelli, 114–31.

Foucault, M. 1998c. Prefazione alla storia della sessualità 1984, in *Archivio Foucault. Interventi, colloqui, interviste. 3. 1978–1985. Estetica dell'esistenza, etica, politica*. Milan: Feltrinelli, 233–9.

Foucault, M. 1998d. Che cos'è l'Illuminismo? 1984, in *Archivio Foucault. Interventi, colloqui, interviste. 3. 1978–1985. Estetica dell'esistenza, etica, politica*. Milan: Feltrinelli, 217–32.

Foucault, M. 1998e. Che cos'è l'Illuminismo? 1984, in *Archivio Foucault. Interventi, colloqui, interviste. 3. 1978–1985. Estetica dell'esistenza, etica, politica*. Milan: Feltrinelli, 253–61.

Foucault, M. 1998f. Le maglie del potere 1981, in *Archivio Foucault. Interventi, colloqui, interviste. 3. 1978–1985. Estetica dell'esistenza, etica, politica*. Milan: Feltrinelli, 155–71.

Foucault, M. 2003a. *Society Must Be Defended: Lectures at the Collège de France 1975–1976.* New York: Picador.

Foucault, M. 2003b. *Abnormal: Lectures at the Collège de France 1974–1975.* New York: Picador.

Foucault, M. 2006. *Psychiatric Power: Lectures at the Collège de France 1973–1974.* New York: Picador.

Fox, N.J. 1998. "Foucault, Foucauldians and Sociology." *British Journal of Sociology* 49 (3): 415–33.

Giddens, A. 1984. *The Constitution of Society.* Cambridge: Polity Press.

Goldstein, J. 1979. "Review of *Discipline and Punish.*" *Journal of Modern History* 51: 116–18.

Gordon, C. 1990. "*Histoire de la folie*: An Unknown Book by Michel Foucault." *History of the Human Sciences* 3: 3–26.

Gutting, G. 2003a. Introduction. Michel Foucault: A User's Manual, in G. Gutting (ed.), *The Cambridge Companion to Foucault.* Cambridge: Cambridge University Press, 1–28.

Gutting, G. 2003b. Foucault and the History of Madness, in G. Gutting (ed.), *The Cambridge Companion to Foucault.* Cambridge: Cambridge University Press, 49–73.

Gutting, G. 2005. *Foucault: A Very Short Introduction.* Oxford: Oxford University Press.

Habermas, J. 1986. Taking Aim at the Heart of the Present, in D.C. Hoy (ed.), *Foucault: A Critical Reader.* Oxford: Blackwell, 103–108.

Hacking, I. 1986. The Archeology of Foucault, in D.C. Hoy (ed.), *Foucault: A Critical Reader.* Oxford: Blackwell, 27–40.

Han, B. 2003. The Analytic of Finitude and the History of Subjectivity, in G. Gutting (ed.), *The Cambridge Companion to Foucault.* Cambridge: Cambridge University Press, 176–209.

Horrocks, C. and Jetvic, Z. 2000. *Introducing Foucault.* Cambridge: Icon Books.

Hoy, D.C. 1986. Introduction, in D.C. Hoy (ed.), *Foucault: A Critical Reader.* Oxford: Blackwell, 1–25.

Ingram, D. 2003. Foucault and Habermas, in G. Gutting (ed.), *The Cambridge Companion to Foucault.* Cambridge: Cambridge University Press, 240–83.

Jay, M. 1986. In the Empire of the Gaze: Foucault and the Denigration of Vision in Twentieth-Century French Thought, in D.C. Hoy (ed.), *Foucault: A Critical Reader.* Oxford: Blackwell, 174–204.

Macherey, P. 1963. Présentation. Foucault – Roussel – Foucault, in M. Foucault, *Raymond Roussel.* Paris: Gallimard, i–xxx.

May, T. 2003. Foucault's Relation to Phenomenology, in G. Gutting (ed.), *The Cambridge Companion to Foucault.* Cambridge: Cambridge University Press, 284–311.

Megill, A. 1987. "The Reception of Foucault by Historians." *Journal of the History of Ideas* 48: 117–41.

Porter, R. 1990. "Foucault's Great Confinement." *History of the Human Sciences* 3: 47–54.

Rorty, R. 1986. Foucault and Epistemology, in D.C. Hoy (ed.), *Foucault: A Critical Reader.* Oxford: Blackwell, 41–9.

Rouse, J. 2003. Power/Knowledge, in G. Gutting (ed.), *The Cambridge Companion to Foucault.* Cambridge: Cambridge University Press, 95–122.

Sassatelli, R. 2005. Esperienze, racconti, identità. Riflessioni sul cross-genderismo, in G. Muzzetto and S. Segre (eds), *Prospettive sul mondo della vita.* Milan: FrancoAngeli, 261–82.

Scull, A. 1990. "Michel Foucault's History of Madness." *History of the Human Sciences* 3: 57–67.

Sheridan, A. 1980. *Michel Foucault: The Will to Truth.* London: Tavistock.

Smart, B. 1986. The Politics of Truth and the Problem of Hegemony, in D.C. Hoy (ed.), *Foucault: A Critical Reader.* Oxford: Blackwell, 157–73.

Smart, B. 2002. *Michel Foucault.* London: Routledge.

Taylor, C. 1986. Foucault on Freedom and Truth, in D.C. Hoy (ed.), *Foucault: A Critical Reader.* Oxford: Blackwell, 69–102.

Todd, May. 2006. *The Philosophy of Foucault.* London: Acumen.

Walzer, M. 1986. The Politics of Michel Foucault, in D.C. Hoy (ed.), *Foucault: A Critical Reader.* Oxford: Blackwell, 51–68.

Chapter 6
Anthony Giddens

Preliminary Remarks

Anthony Giddens (b. 1938), one of the most famous contemporary sociologists, taught at Cambridge University and was at the head of the London School of Economics before retiring from academic teaching.[1] During the 1970s, his works dealt with some of the most important classical authors in social science, such as Marx, Weber and Durkheim, claiming their relevance in contemporary sociology and sociological theory (Giddens 1973). We shall, however, not dwell here on these works, considering their introductory nature, in the first case; and in the second case, because they are preparatory to his theory of structuration, for which Giddens is best known. We prefer instead to focus on other coeval and subsequent works. In the 1970s, and afterwards, Giddens's investigations addressed also to several formulations of this theory and to issues referring to the epistemology of social science. In the 1980s, 1990s, and in the first decade of this century, Giddens explored the themes of modernity and globalization, and their consequences on individuals' identity and social relations. Our exposition follows this line of studies and theoretical considerations, and completes it with some additional information on the reception of his works.

The Field of Study and the Tasks of Sociology

As Giddens argues in the first chapter of his *Sociology* (1983), this branch of knowledge mainly deals with institutions and the conditions of their change in advanced societies. He adds that the study of sociology should make use of sociological imagination, that is to say, it should focus on history, anthropology, and critical theory, the latter in the sense of asking ourselves what social changes are desirable and how is it possible to achieve them. Nonetheless, as Giddens remarks in other works, what we call "social theory" is marked by "disagreement on absolutely essential matters: i.e. what should its field of study be and what procedures should it consider correct" (Giddens and Turner 1987: 10).

This disagreement, which has created a lot of confusion and is produced by conflicting theoretical statements[2] and incompatible epistemological positions,[3] results, as from the late 1970s, from the end of "orthodox consensus." This consensus concerned our opportunity, from an epistemological point of view, to follow in sociology, too, the model of natural science, and from a theoretical point of view, to orient ourselves to the perspective of functionalism (Giddens 1979: 235–40). Giddens intends therefore to give his contribution to an epistemological debate, of which he is conscious and on which he is informed, taking in this regard a precise epistemological stand.

Theory of Structuration: Introduction

As we shall see in the next pages, in which we mention the reception of this author, the theoretical contribution concerning the theory of structuration, to which Giddens reverted in several works (1976a, 1977, 1979, 1981c;1984), is generally considered of great importance for understanding his thought.

---

1   Details and information on Giddens's life and intellectual career, provided by the author himself, can be found in Giddens and Pierson 1998: 28–51. Several and mostly critical introductions to his thought are available. See, in English, Craib 1992; Kaspersen 2000; in Italian, see Di Meglio 2002.

2   Using Giddens's own words (1979: 238): "The Babel of theoretical voices that currently clamor for attention."

3   See Giddens 1981b.

By the term "structuration," Giddens intends the set of conditions on which depend not only the continuity or change of the rules and the constitutive resources of a social structure but also the reproduction of the social systems. The theory of structuration is included in a larger conceptual and theoretical apparatus. We shall first focus on this conceptual and theoretical apparatus.

Theory of Structuration: Conceptual and Theoretical Apparatus

Giddens fully formulated his conceptual apparatus concerning the theory of structuration in some of the works he wrote in the 1970s and 1980s: *New Rules of Sociological Method* (1976) (Italian translation: *Nuove regole del metodo sociologico*. Bologna: Il Mulino, 1979); *Studies in Social and Political Theory* (1977)[4]; *Central Problems in Social Theory* (1979); in addition, the article "Comments on the Theory of Structuration" (1981) and *The Constitution of Society* (1984) (Italian translation: *La costituzione della società*, 1990), which is often considered the most complete exposition of this theory. The concept of identity is formulated and discussed in later works, in particular in: *Modernity and Social Identity* (1991) (Italian translation: *Identità e società moderna*, 2001) and *The Consequences of Modernity* (1990) (Italian translation: *Le conseguenze della modernità*, 1990).

We shall now formulate the definitions of the concepts Giddens makes use of, in the hope that no unexplained elements remain. As well as the previously defined concept of structuration, the following concepts are relevant in his sociology:

Agency: All that the actors – intended as bodily entities – usually do, not necessarily in an intentional way, giving it a sense, expecting that also the others with whom they interact do the same, and taking usually into account – in a reflexive way – the course of their actions and their expected and unexpected consequences.

Rules: Prescriptions, which specify how to behave in pre-established circumstances, and how to sanction other people's behaviors considered incompatible with these prescribed behavioral manners.

Resources: All that, whether of a material (allocative resources) or an organizational (authoritative resources) nature, allows the actors achieving their aims during their social interactions.

Institutions: Constitutive practices of the social systems. To take an institutional nature, these practices should be lasting, stable, and spatially and socially widespread.

Institutional Analysis: Analysis of the recurrent ways in which the social systems reproduce themselves.

Structural Analysis: Analysis of the structuration processes in social systems.

Power: All the means the actors (whether individuals or communities) have available to attain their goals. Power is exerted through the ability of some groups or kinds of actors to influence the circumstances, in which others act, by exerting their control over the means the others have at their disposal.

Domination: Ability to deploy resources, which may be allocative, or of a material nature; or also authoritative, that is to say, exerting control over persons.

Ideology: Ways in which domination and exploitation are legitimized.

Social Systems: Institutionalized sets of social relations. These relations are recurring over time and space, but in general, they are neither internally well-integrated nor provided with clear boundaries. As a consequence, they are not easily recognizable and observable.

Social Structure: A set of rules and resources, which are exercised as properties of the social systems. These rules and resources are present as social actors' memories concerning the way in which they have to act in social life. They have a real existence only when and whereas they reveal themselves as practices, the sense of which is usually not made explicit because it is taken for granted. When these practices are jointly put into effect, they form and recursively reproduce particular social systems. Their implementation is carried out by socially competent actors, through structural principles, in specific historical circumstances, and in any contingent situation.

---

4 In this work, consisting of a collection of previously published essays, particularly relevant is the essay *Functionalism après la lutte* (1977: 96–134).

Duality of Structure: By this term, Giddens denominates a characteristic peculiar to the structural properties of the social systems, due to which these properties are continuously created and re-created by the actors in each interaction, and do not have an existence independent of interactions themselves. Therefore, interactions are the means that makes the existence of rules and resources forming the social structure possible; but they are also, at the same time, the result of those rules and resources.

Social Integration: A set of behaviors or conducts occurring during encounters in which several actors participate and mutually consider their own behaviors or conducts.

System Integration: A set of mutual relations, which establish and keep themselves not when all social actors are present at the same time, but rather among communities – not necessarily institutional ones – which are interdependent and mutually take into account their own activities, but are differently located in space and time.

Structural Principles: Organizational principles, which are structural properties of the social systems; they preside over the institutional system and the social integration of a society; and are effective in different times and places. It is possible to distinguish and classify different kinds of societies according to their specific structural principles.

Societies: Associations between – on the one hand – social systems, which are defined by particular structural principles and institution sets; on the other, specific places or territories, the occupation of which is considered legitimate by those who belong to them. Among those people, the feeling of a common collective identity prevails.

Double Hermeneutics: This term defines a double interpretative process, through which sociologists, and in general social scientists, interpret a reality which is already endowed in itself with significance, and becomes therefore a subject to be interpreted by the social actors. The interpretations made by social scientists are reflexively included in the common sense stock the actors resort to for their interpretations.

Routinization: A process through which some specific activities – such as actions and talks – are usually performed, and therefore are taken for granted in social life, since they give it continuity, stability and ability to reproduce itself.

Historicity: A conception of history as if it were connoted by the predominance of change, and by progress, rather than by repetition and tradition. This conception goes along with interventions in society, considered heralds of progress, to produce the desired changes.

Trust: A feeling of calm expectation, resulting from the experiences of the actors in their childhood, that their everyday life may keep for them continuity and predictability, and therefore can be taken for granted by the actors themselves. Trust may be placed either in known persons, or in the functioning of abstract and institutionalized relation systems, such as, for instance, the monetary system.

Ontological Security: A feeling of trust, preserved through routinization processes, that the social and natural world is actually the same that appears to the actors during their everyday activities, even if they have not formed it.

Locale: The physical place – i.e. houses, streets and towns – in which interactions among simultaneously present actors usually take place. These places are delimited by boundaries, which are symbolic, temporal and, often, material. Locales are typically divided into areas or regions, characterized by specific activities – namely, work, entertainment, or rest – which are often temporally divided (as happens in the case of the rooms of a house, or the neighborhoods of a town or a city).

Practical Consciousness: This term designates a set of abilities, skills and information, whether real or assumed, the actors have at their disposal. We make the most of these abilities in interactive life, in locally determined and different contexts. To participate in them, each actor has to show the others he properly knows and is able to correctly apply the rules that control social conduct. Thanks to this knowledge, the actors concur in a routinized way to preserve the reproduction mechanisms of the social system.

Strategic Conduct: Any conduct put into effect within the sphere of control strategies the actors carry out within contextually defined boundaries.

Analysis of Strategic Conduct: Analysis of actors' practical consciousness and their control strategies;

Societies: Social systems characterized by associations with specific territories, the occupation of which is considered legitimate by their members. The feelings of a common collective identity, which reveals itself in their practical consciousness, prevail among members.

Self-identity: A socially acquired feeling of biographical continuity and self-specificity the actor reflexively perceives, and to some extent communicates to others through regular and frequent interactions.

Reflexive Self-regulation and *Reflexive Monitoring of Action and Social Conduct*: This concept designates the continuous process through which a socially competent actor actively controls his own and other peoples' conduct in presence of others, making use of his practical consciousness for this purpose. The social process of regulation and reproduction of the social systems occurs as a consequence – not necessarily pursued or expected – of usual actions made by actors who act with intent, competence, and awareness – not necessarily accurate and complete – of the conditions in which their action takes place, and of the effects of that action. Actors contribute in this way to preserve the duality of the structure of the social systems, and social integration.

Time-space Distanciation: This term defines the ways in which social systems (and hence, societies) structure themselves in virtue of specific structural principles, and permanently embed themselves in a time–space dimension.

Modernity: A set of institutions and conducts marked by general detachment and disembedding of relations based on personal trust from local space–time contexts, called by the author "regions." Impersonal surveillance and control mechanisms put into effect by administrative institutions, make the recurrent reproduction of the social systems possible.

Tradition: A set of beliefs that gives continuity and shape to the lives of those who follow them, and draws its strength and substance from those lives. Tradition and modernity are not necessarily incompatible, though the age of Enlightenment called the authority of tradition into question.

Theory of Structuration: Theoretical Apparatus and Epistemological Premises

Giddens fully formulated and made use of his conceptual apparatus in some of his works published in the 1970s and 1980s, and in particular: *New Rules of Sociological Method* (1976) (Italian translation: *Nuove regole del metodo sociologico*. Bologna: Il Mulino, 1979); *Studies in Social and Political Theory* (1977): concerning this work, which collects some previously published essays, the essay *Functionalism après la lutte* (1977: 96–129) is particularly important in this case; *Central Problems in Social Theory* (1979); *A Contemporary Critique of Historical Materialism* (1981); *The Constitution of Society* (1984) (Italian translation: *La costituzione della società*, 1990). We shall focus on these works, as well as on other ones written by Giddens dealing with the same theme, to reconstruct this theory, bearing in mind, however, the number of subsequent and sometimes clarifying contributions published until nowadays (see in particular Giddens and Pierson 1998: 75–93).

The theory of structuration originates from different traditions of thought, as the author explains (Giddens 1984: xxii–xxvi). As well as the classical authors of sociology, i.e. Marx, Weber, and Durkheim Giddens frequently refers to in these works, and who are the subjects of one of his most famous exegetic writings (Giddens 1971, 2009), Giddens declares he is intellectually indebted to some philosophical and sociological schools of thought he selectively refers to for this theoretical formulation. We remember, in this connection, Wittgenstein's philosophy of language, Schutz's phenomenological and hermeneutical sociology, Goffman's symbolic interaction, and Garfinkel's ethnomethodology. Giddens moves from the assumption that, being social actors, the persons have – or think to have – appropriate abilities to understand what they are doing within the flow of their everyday life. This applies also when the actors are not able to account to others or to themselves for the reasons of their actions ("reflexive monitoring of conduct"), as instead happens, according to Giddens, in almost all cases. Knowledge and ability to apply these rules are taken for granted, until proved otherwise.

Structures – in the sense of practices the actors reproduce as a consequence of rules of conduct and available resources – make their enablement possible, but submit it to limits and constraints. The last term ("constraints") should be intended not only as material obstacles or social sanctions, but also as limits for an actor or a community (here, Giddens refers to Durkheim) to the possibility of choosing a course of action, in some circumstances. These limits result from the fact that every course of action takes place within a social structure and is bound by it, though nobody is obliged to follow a particular course of action. By observing and putting into practice rules of conduct, actors regularly produce and reproduce every day, along with these rules and through them, the institutional structures in which the social systems are organized. At the same time, structures are the means through which the actors can organize their conduct.

As we previously mentioned, structures are both the means and the result of actors' conducts; in this consists the duality of structure Giddens considers a principal aspect of his theoretical formulation. His theory of structuration aims at illustrating – by avoiding the use of functionalist concepts and theories – how human conducts continuously produce and reproduce themselves over time and space, through interactions provided with sense for the actors. The formulation of this theory involves a systematic use of the aforementioned concepts, with particular reference to the reflexive and competent control the actors exert on their own and other people's conduct. Actors act in a pre-formed sphere of objects and relations, but they reconstruct it during their everyday life and in local situations of relationships they jointly create during and through their interactive life, and constantly take into account in their conducts.

These relationships depend on the space–time contexts, and are provided with a significance the actors jointly create, by borrowing it also from social science itself. While they act and interpret the sense of other people's action, the actors contribute – unconsciously, in most cases, but competently – to form society, intended as a structure or a set of coordinated practices collectively reproduced, which generate the generally orderly flow of social life. As a result, sociology has the double opportunity to carry out an investigation on the aspects of social relations, which are contextual and delimited in time and space; but also to go beyond, through this investigation, the dualism in social science between the subjectivism of interpretative or hermeneutic perspectives, on the one hand, and the functionalist and structuralist perspective, on the other. In sociology, subjectivism is represented by Schutz's and Garfinkel's formulations, while functionalism characterizes Durkeim's and Parsons' sociology, and structuralism is present in linguistics with Saussure, and in anthropology with Lévi-Strauss.

Giddens dwells on the institutional elements that are present in any society and can be of a symbolic, political, economic or legal nature. These institutions make interactions possible, by transferring significations, orders and sanctions, thereby reproducing the structural properties of the social systems. Institutional analysis studies the connections between the structural properties of the social systems, and includes the formulation of structural principles. Placed at a high level of space–time abstraction, these structural, or organizational, principles, show how societies are integrated and how social institutions are organized and differentiate themselves. A classification of structural principles, and hence, institutions, makes a distinction among the following structural aspects of the social systems: signification transfer, along with the institutional correspondents of the symbolic systems and the linguistic structures; domination, the political and economic structures correspond to; legitimation, along with the corresponding legal institutions (Giddens 1984: 28–34).

With reference to the structural principle of the space–time distancing of interactions, Giddens makes a distinction between different forms or kinds of societies, i.e. tribal societies, societies divided into classes, and class societies. This distinction does not imply the use of an evolutionist theoretical pattern, as different kinds of societies can be found in the same historical period. In tribal societies, which are characterized by the lack of a state, there is no distinction between social and system integration. This distinction, instead, can be found in the other two kinds of societies, which differentiate themselves due to their different structural principles. In the case of societies divided into classes, which were well-represented by the imperial societies of the past, classes – though existing – were not necessary for identifying a structural (or organizational) principle of a particular society, and the spatial differentiation between city and countryside corresponds to the separations between social and system integration.

System integration is produced by a number of interdependent nation states, which form a single global system, and exert their authoritative power through military, administrative and political élites. On the contrary, in the case of class societies, such as the capitalistic one, social integration has lost any territorial anchoring. Structural, or institutional, analysis can highlight contradictions, in the sense that the structural principles, which give organization to a social system, may be reciprocally incompatible. In particular, the main contradiction of the organizational principle of a capitalist nation state occurs between the civil and the political society. A derivative – and hence, secondary – contradiction occurs between the capital internationalization process, and the strengthening of the nation states.

To a lower level of abstraction compared to structural, or institutional, analysis, some particular sets of rules and resources can be investigated, as they make social reproduction and change possible. An example in this sense is the monetary system, which makes the reproduction of the capital cycle possible. Finally, at an even lower level of abstraction, the study of institutionalized practices – for instance, through work division and the consequent structuration of classes[5] – highlights the structural characteristics of some particular social system. The theme of power, previously dealt with by mentioning commands and sanctions meant as products of institutional systems, is now further developed in conceptual and theoretical terms through the treatment of the contemporary world-system. Power – intended as the stock of available means to achieve pre-set objectives – is considered a constraint and an enablement at the same time, as both result from the use of sanctions. Sanctions may be positive, negative, or a combination of both characteristics.

First, Giddens argues, power (or domination, or exploitation) should be jointly studied with its symbolic legitimation, if we want to understand its ability to penetrate social life. The fact that actors are generally competent in living their social life does not mean that they accept their possible inferiority in terms of power as legitimate. Secondly, it is advisable to consider the limits of power, since the actors – though the power towards others they have at their disposal has a narrower and less effective scope – are not completely lacking some levels of control over their own and other people's actions. Time and space influence interactions, by binding and circumscribing them into pre-established areas (locales or regions, in Giddens's terminology); or, on the contrary, as happens in capitalist modernity, by disembedding them through distanciation processes of the social systems (and, hence, of the institutions and relations) from particular time–space settings.

In this case, the conditions that make both social integration (among individual actors, for instance, among friends), and systemic integration (among institutional communities, with variable distinction and connection degrees among them) possible, are changed. Though these two analytical levels are conventionally defined micro- and macro-sociological ones, Giddens – consistently with his definition of these terms – considers this designation scarcely useful, and even prejudicial. As a matter of fact, it reproduces the separation and irreconcilability between micro- and macro-sociological studies Giddens's notion of duality intends, instead, to overcome. In fact, structures are intended by him as the result of encounters situated in time and space, and therefore contingent, but these encounters are established and re-established by the actors over time and space. Social systems produce and reproduce their systemic nature – that is to say, the interdependence among institutional elements – in a variety of ways.

These ways consist in spontaneous "homeostatic" self-regulation processes, as feedback to events occurring outside the social system; or, in response to external events, in processes in which the influence of these events is controlled in order to achieve the goal of changing the social system in wanted ways; or, when a response is produced or influenced by actors' knowledge of the mechanisms through which the social system can self-reproduce itself: in this case, the system is able to reflexively self-adjust itself. The institutional systems (the set of practices that form the social systems) can analytically divide themselves into symbolic, political, economic and legal systems. Their classification concerns how the communication of symbolic significations relates to domination, in terms of control on allocation resources over material goods; or in terms of authority resources, with the consequent ability to exert power over persons and communities; or through legitimation, in the sense of normative regulation.

In particular, symbolic institutions concern the production of ideologies, and they put in relation the symbolic orders with the legitimation of domination. Political institutions imply a connection among domination (in terms of authority resources), meaning communication and legitimation. Economic institutions relate domination (in the sense of allocation of resources) with the communication of meanings and legitimation. Finally, legal institutions establish a relation between legal institutions, on the one hand, and on the other, the institutions through which domination and legitimation are exerted. Ontological trust – the trust that the world is really what it seems – depends on the continuity of everyday life, which makes it possible to carry out our usual, continuous and predictable, that is to say routinized, activities. This trust – that

---

5 Giddens refers, in this connection, to his previous book focused on class structuration in advanced societies (Giddens 1973).

events such as, for instance, one's internment in a concentration camp, are able to upset, driving the persons to try to reconstruct it as much as possible in those extreme circumstances – originates, according to Giddens, in the experiences made in one's childhood.

Giddens refers here the psychoanalytic theories developed by Freud, Erikson and other scientists. These experiences are divided into several stages, which progressively produce in the persons an ability to reflexively monitor and control conducts and body movements in presence of others. Stability, which characterizes the institutional forms of the social systems, establishes itself – Giddens argues – in virtue of routinized encounters. These encounters continuously produce and reproduce themselves over our everyday life, and are limited in space and time (or "regionalized," in Giddens's terms). Actors know the rules which govern their conducts, and apply them, thus contributing every time to their existence and continuity. The "regionalization" of the encounters involves a distinction Giddens has borrowed from Goffman, between *Front Regions*, that is to say, front space–time areas in which we are in presence of others, who act as an audience, and *Back Regions*, in which the interactions with others are limited to persons with whom we have established intimate relations, or do not exist at all.

Ontological trust forms and keeps itself in the *Back Regions*. Not only the frequency and the customary nature of these meetings contributes to this result, but also the giving out – at least partly – of the obligation to keep a physical image of ourselves and a conduct that are socially acceptable. Actors make use of their knowledge of their social and institutional world, and consequently, of their practical consciousness, if they intend to put a strategic conduct into effect, with a view to controlling other people's conducts. Giddens considers an example of strategic conduct a research made by the British sociologist Paul Willis concerning the activities of a group of kids belonging to the workers' class within a school. Willis' research, published in 1977 with the name *Learning to Labour*, had a considerable echo not only in Great Britain. Giddens considered it fully consistent with his theory of structuration, and focused on it for a long time.

The substantial and methodological reasons of Giddens's attention clearly emerge from the report he made of this research. In his opinion, the ethnographic study conducted by Willis properly highlights the "practical consciousness" of the youth whose behaviors were investigated; that is to say, their knowledge of the rules – even non-declared ones – that are effective both within and outside their school. They know very well that it is not convenient for them to openly challenge the teacher's authority, and that their future, once they have ended their studies, will be connoted by hand labor and subordination to the authority in the workplace. Among these subjects, many choose what they consider the best available course of action: that is to say, to outwardly adapt themselves to the school discipline, which anticipates the future discipline in the factory, but at the same time, to express – remaining within the limits of what is allowed or tolerated –their opposition to discipline and authority.

Moving from this research, Giddens discusses its implications for the theory of structuration and for the sociological theory in general. Actors have knowledge of their current social world (the school environment) and their likely future world (the factory, or the state of unemployed). It is actually their action – considered both as the effect of an exchange within the group, and between the group and the outer society – that should be subject to an investigation in order to obtain a convincing explanation of it. Giddens believes that their restrained but continuous daring behavior towards the authority should not be interpreted, in a functionalist way, as an adaptation to functional needs of the school or corporate organization. In fact, in this way, only a pseudo-explanation would be provided of it, lacking a consideration of how the members of this group consider and know the social order in force in their micro-environment and outside, and they unconsciously and reflexively reproduce it through their practices (structure duality).

Though the functionalist authors – as Giddens remarks – have offered an important service to sociological analysis by focusing on what the actors do, and on its consequences, these questions should not be necessarily expressed in a functionalist language, as no advantages would result. The fact that the British educational system perpetuates the existing class inequalities, though this result had not been predicted and pursued by the educational institutions, is a question that deserves to be explored; bearing in mind that an institutional action may have unexpected and unwanted effects, but also that those effects result from the intentional action of some particular actors. On this occasion and in other circumstances, Giddens formulated his objections to functionalism – in particular to the versions of it provided by Parsons and Merton – as a way to study the social system and its change, conceived in terms of evolution (Giddens 1984: 293–7;

see also 1979: 236–8; 1981: 15–19; 1990: 97–110; and above all 1996: 78–111). These objections can be summarized as follows:

a. Functionalism considers the effects – intended or unwanted – of an action carried out by actors, or institutionally, as if they were sufficient for explaining that action. However, it would be a completely unsuitable explanation, since it does neither show how and why the actors acted in this way, nor what consequences – either wanted or not – there would have been for them. The distinction formulated by Merton between evident and concealed functions does not make an exception, because this distinction does not make sufficiently clear – in the absence of a counter-factual investigation on what the likely effects of its lack would be – why an evident or concealed function involves particular consequences.

b. Functionalism provides only "synchronic" descriptions of the social system, in the sense that the internal relations in a social system are described by abstracting from the passage of time. Nonetheless, a social system can be conceived only in terms of its continuous self-reproduction over time, that is to say "diachronically".

c. Societies, or social systems, being neither persons nor bodies, do not have needs, and do not passively "adapt" themselves – as the functionalist sociologists use to say – to their social and natural environment. The biological origin of the functionalist metaphors impairs their explanatory ability, lacking an indication of the mechanism in virtue of which some aspects of the social organization are temporally followed by others. The concept of adaptation to the social or natural environment of some elements of the social system, cannot act as a mechanism in that sense, since it is too vague and generic a concept, unable to be used for explaining specific events that can be assessable in their empiric validity. Human beings, rather than passively adapting themselves to their environment, do actively relate with it, by reproducing and transforming it in view of the goals they have set.

d. The functionalist explanations of social change reveal other problems concerning the empiric reliability of some of its typical statements. Giddens believes that these problems are shared in general by the evolutionist patterns. These patterns are unilateral compression (the tendency to compress a number of different events into a unitary conceptual pattern), homological compression (the tendency to imagine the existence of homologies between the development stages of a society and individual personalities), normative illusion (the tendency to identify superiority, in terms of military, economic, or political power, with moral superiority), and temporal distortion (the confusion between history and historicity, that is to say, the persuasion that the passage of time does necessarily involve social change; this error connotes, in particular, historic materialism).

e. Finally, functionalism does not make a distinction between social and system integration. The former is a synonym of social cohesion, in the sense of an individual's integration in society; the latter points out the interdependence level between the parties of the social system. Giddens argues that integration, intended in the first sense, involves some theoretical difficulties in explaining dissent and divergence of interests.

To these critical remarks, Giddens adds further remarks towards structuralist sociology, both in Peter Blau's version, and in the quite different Althusser's one. To Blau, who maintains that it is not necessary to point out the single actors' motivations in the explanation of the social structure and the relations among its constituting elements, Giddens objects that without knowing the actors' motivations it is not possible to understand the mechanisms of social reproduction, that is to say, the ways and reasons through which actors carry out reflexively and contextually their activities. In other words, there is no place in sociology for a merely structural explanation. To Althusser, with particular reference to his concepts of "over determination" of the structure (in a Marxist sense) and "structural causality," Giddens objects that the structural factors of the production relations, and in a subordinate position the political and ideological factors, would determine individual conducts. According to Althusser, ideologies are, in particular, a constitutive element of social formations.

As a consequence, individuals would only act in support of social formations. Giddens remarks that this author wavers between metaphysical statements about causal priority – even though "in the last resort," a formulation Giddens considers obscure – of the economic factors and functionalist argumentations, the aforementioned reservations apply to. Althusser's conceptual pattern would be lacking in an analytical distinction between agency and structure, that is to say, a distinction between what the actors – intended as persons – do, and the rules and resources they continuously and reflexively reproduce through their action. Actors cannot be conceived as mere "bearers" of social relations, but they instead act with competence in their social relations, even if quite often, they are unable to foresee and control the consequences of their action.

This is the main objection Giddens addresses to the structuralist school of thought as a whole, but he also rejects the opposite epistemological position of methodological individualism. According to this school of thought, which is often traced back to Max Weber, the explanation of social phenomena can be only and fully formulated by bringing back the causal factors to the motivations of the individual actors. Giddens objects that social categories cannot be brought back at all to individual attributes. Collective decisions, for instance, can be made in an institutional environment, i.e. a government or another organization. Though these decisions result from those made by single individuals, they are imposed on all decision-makers, whether or not they were consenting. Concerning the explanation of social change, Giddens completes his rejection of the evolutionist thought with his own theorization, which is in line with his theory of structuration and makes use of concepts that fit it.

As a matter of fact, the ways in which social change occur can be conceptually formulated bearing in mind that in the modern world, there are time–space distanciation processes in the institutions and social systems that are at the origin of their change. These ways depend on the structural properties – and in particular, on the structural principles – of the social systems.[6] Accidental circumstances and events combine with the structural principles of the social systems, and consequently, with the main institutions, forming from time to time a different social totality. Therefore, social change results from an intertwining of causes, in the sense that some accidental factors influence the main institutions and their relations with one another. There are different degrees of change, and therefore change occurs in an unequal way. Actors' activities, or practices, reveal space–time boundaries, since they are physically or symbolically delimited, as happens in the different rooms of a house.

An important source of social change consists in the existence of mutual disputes (or "contradictions," in Giddens's language) between the structural principles that produce integration among institutions, and the reproduction of the social system. Giddens makes a distinction between primary contradictions (among structural principles) and secondary contradictions (which result from primary contradictions, as in the case of inner struggles within the capitalist system: for example, in the case of strains between capital internationalization and the strengthening of national states). Contradictions intended in this sense, highlight, as conflicts, the fault lines within the social systems. Differently from conflicts, contradictions do not involve real disputes among individual or collective actors depending on different interests. They point rather to the existence of obstacles to social integration depending on internal divisions within the social system. For example, there are different ways and possibilities of living in relation to what we consider possible and desirable.

The reproduction of the social system depends on unequal development processes and on organizations and social movements. These communities are formed by practices the social actors carry out in their everyday life by reflexively making the most of socially available knowledge. According to Giddens, this is possible only in modern age. Using Giddens's lexicon, historicity prevails in modernity, that is to say, a notion of history as progress, and a use of this notion to promote social and political change in the desired directions. Organizations and movements thus intend to help this purpose. However, as Giddens remarks, in contrast to Marx, and referring instead to Weber and Foucault, in modernity organizations have involved domination and exploitation rather than emancipation. These remarks lead Giddens to re-conceptualize social change, and in particular the institutional one, in a different way not only in relation to the functionalist and structuralist traditions, but also to the Marxist tradition.

Keeping to Giddens's conception, change occurs by transitions, each one involving a sequence of institutional forms of change called "episodes." "Episodes" concern institutional complexes or "societal

---

6 Concerning the meaning of these words, which are part of Giddens's lexicon, reference should be made to the definitions provided at the beginning of this chapter.

totalities," which include the main institutions, and take shape in particular space–time contexts.[7] Change is therefore conceived as a sequence of "episodes" having ascertainable beginning and end. Change is "conjunctural," since contingent circumstances and events locally and contextually meet and combine forming a sequence of "episodes" of varied intensity and extension. Examples of these "episodes," according to Giddens, are the formation of modern states, or the formation of cities in the agricultural societies of the past, considered as an accidental ("conjunctural") outcome of the relations between different social systems. The accidental events that give origin to these "episodes" are of a different nature, and include demographic or technological changes, wars, ideologies, influence of other states.

The temporal and spatial continuity of societies, and hence, the production of power, depend on the control of material (or allocative) and organizational (or authoritative) resources. While the evolutionary theories of social change have focused on this first kind of resources, it happened much less frequently – according to Giddens – regarding authority resources. Giddens thinks instead that gathering authoritative (rather than allocative) resources is of paramount importance for producing, preserving, or expanding the power of persons and institutions, and through it, the social system. Both kinds of resources imply the preservation and control of information and generate, as a consequence, the possibilities to reproduce – along with power and control structures – also the space–time relations that make the coordination of large quantities of people possible. In this way, the practices carried out by the social actors can be put into effect, since the institutions and the structural principles we owe the establishment of societies to can be preserved.

In modernity, the preservation of the social system depends on the institutionalized use of techniques and instruments of surveillance of the population established within the borders of a nation state, defined by the monopoly of instruments of violence (army and police) and administration within the area of a specific territory. Surveillance can be intended as attainment and store of information about individual conducts; or as direct supervision of those conducts. In modernity, the administration power of a state depends more on its surveillance ability – in both senses – than on the exclusive control a state exerts over the instruments of violence. Surveillance and monopolistic control of the instruments of violence, along with private property and the transformation of the natural environment, connote modern industrial capitalism. In modern capitalistic nation states, in which political power is divided and separated from economic power,[8] surveillance reaches an unequalled intensity compared to previous ages, this intensity being possible through the state control of information media and the progress in communications and transports.

The control of the population exerted through surveillance in some particular environments, such as prisons, psychiatric hospitals, but also workshops and offices, gives the modern capitalistic nation state a leading position compared to other political organizations. This form of control is not necessarily a totalitarian one, such as Foucault described it, and is the more effective, the more controlled persons accept it in their everyday life, even if their acceptance does not mean its convinced ideological legitimation. If, on the one hand, the ability to successfully exert surveillance over the population makes its government possible, on the other, it goes along with this participation, and as an effect of surveillance, with an opposite influence, since these influences and pressures are encouraged in favor of a democratic participation. Above all, social movements are active from this point of view, i.e. the modern ecological, pacifist, religious, ethnic and consumer movements, as well as the historical labor movement. These movements can be classified according to the nature of their objectives. Giddens makes a distinction between economic, political, moral, and civil right objectives. Whatever their objectives, social movements set themselves against the state policies and do not give legitimation to its institutional activities, especially to surveillance activities, which though existing in earlier ages, are an essential element for the exercise of power and social integration in modern capitalism.[9]

---

7 Concerning the notions of space and time in Giddens's sociology, and the use Giddens makes of them, see Gregory 1989; Saunders 1989.

8 Giddens (1981a: 213–20) criticizes the Marxist thesis—and namely the formulation Poulantzas gave of it—of a necessary subordination of the capitalist state to the interests of the bourgeoisie, intended as the ruling class. In fact, in that case, political power would depend on economic power.

9 A definition of nation state can be found in Giddens 1981a: 190–91;1985: 4–5. As to Giddens's theses concerning the institutional activities of surveillance of the population, the social movements, and the characteristics of modern capitalism and the capitalist state, see Giddens 1981a: 169–76; 1985. In this connection, Giddens refers to Weber and

The Theory of Structuration: Epistemological Premises

Giddens gives some epistemological indications about the aspects that should characterize social research and the reasons of his disagreement with the functionalist and structuralist schools of thought (see in particular, Giddens 1977: 28–129; 1979: 9–48; 1984: 207–27; 343–54). Differently from natural science, in social science it is not possible to formulate laws, that is to say, explanatory statements having universal validity, because these statements do not exist. It is only possible to formulate generalizations as regards the reasons that can be attributed to the social actors. These reasons can be considered the causes of their action. These actors actually provide generalizations that involve understanding the particular circumstances in which they acted. The space–time variability of those circumstances makes it impossible to reasonably generalize to other circumstances the causal mechanisms recalled from time to time. In addition, in social science, theories can become an integral part of a particular discipline, thereby keeping their relevance over time. Furthermore, although the cognitive contribution of this science is still limited, its practical consequences – if filtered in the world it studies – have been and still are considerable.

These indications are consistent with the theory of structuration, even if they do not explicitly refer to it. Therefore, Giddens's epistemology abstracts from distinctions between micro- and macro-sociological investigations, or from qualitative and quantitative investigations, which are incompatible with this theory. His epistemological indications can be summarized as follows. In the first place, it is necessary to investigate a reality that is already made up significant by others. In the second place, it is advisable to avail ourselves of patterns of significations, which are the same as those used in social life and literature, without providing, however, an in-depth description of them. Furthermore, we must attribute importance to the social abilities common individuals reveal in living their everyday life. Finally, research should consider how social life establishes and develops itself in limited spheres over space and time.

As a consequence, Giddens appeals to sociologists, and asks them to fully cooperate with historians and geographers in shedding light on the contextual aspects of interactions. The concept of "regionalization" of social relations formulated by Giddens, actually intends to serve this purpose. Investigations may focus on the ways in which the actors live their social life, usually within limited territorial areas (or "locales") and at institutionally pre-established time intervals, making thus possible both the coordination of their activities, and the constant (and reflexively carried out) reproduction of the social system. Research conforming to the theory of structuration implies the following stages:

a. A preliminary hermeneutic investigation of the patterns through which actors interpret the social reality;
b. Based on these premises, an investigation focused on the ways and forms in which actors' "practical consciousness" reveals itself, that is to say, the knowledge and the abilities actors make use of in any contingent situation (that is to say, locally delimited and variable over space and time);
c. Considering the previous points, a study of the unwanted effects of social actions and the conditions in which these actions have been carried out without actors' being aware of them;
d. Finally, an investigation focused on the institutional conditions that make social and system integration possible.

The stages (a) and (b) of this research are necessary to understand the stages (c) and (d), and vice versa. All these epistemological indications can be summarized in the recommendations to researchers – in line with the theory of structuration – to investigate the contexts of signification, circumscribed and delimited in space and time, in which social life is continuously produced and reproduced. This kind of investigation involves a scholar making an interpretative reconstruction of what the actors think they know (no matter whether right or wrong, or whether their knowledge is not declared, since it is taken for granted) about the ways to correctly behave in the contingent contexts they continuously encounter in their social life, and contribute through their interpretations. Usually these interpretations are not explicitly stated but are taken for granted by the actors

---

Foucault. However, towards the latter, he makes some objections concerning Foucault's contiguity to the structuralist perspective that Giddens considers unacceptable. See Giddens 1981a: 171–6; 1984: 157.

themselves and by those with whom they relate. Giddens makes a distinction between "common sense" and "mutual knowledge."

Common sense consists in beliefs applied to and included in all the activities through which society is produced and reproduced: in Giddens's lexicon, in practical consciousness. Mutual knowledge consists in competences, usually not explicitly recognized, the actors mutually take for granted, which may become the object of an investigation or, in case, of criticism (for example, as criticism of ideologies or other beliefs considered false) on the part of social science scholars, and in particular sociologists, ethnologists, and anthropologists. The criticism of beliefs and ideologies has an intrinsically political nature, since it is an intervention in society able to bring change. Nonetheless, this does not happen when (1) the described or analyzed circumstances occurred in the past; (2) they have not changed in the light of new information, since they do not change the relevant actors' motivations and reasoning, or are selectively used to preserve the existing order, or also when those who would make use of them are not in a position to do so; (3) the new information turns out to be false, or irrelevant, or is presented in such a way that it cannot have practical effects.

Tradition, Modernity and Post-Traditional Society

Giddens's attention has continued to focus on these themes which have characterized his publications as from the early 1990s, after he had elaborated his theory of structuration. In Giddens's sociology, the transition from the theoretical problem of the structuration of the social systems to the specific characteristics of modernity can be considered to have been achieved in the years 1990–91. In fact, both the latest versions of the theory of structuration, with clarifications and answers to critics (see Giddens 1990a; 1991b), and the first texts dealing with the theme of modernity (see Giddens 1990b; 1991a), date back to those years. Tradition (or habit) is the concept formulated both in opposition to modernity and as related to it. Traditions, intended as systems of pre-modern beliefs and practices, may have undergone some changes over time, and therefore are not necessarily ancient.

The thing that characterizes them is their calling out of question any definition of truth, which is considered conferred by tradition, and the existence of custodians of tradition itself (as for example, priests). The conservative school of thought affirms that there is wisdom in tradition. Modernity has not destroyed tradition, as the Enlightenment philosophers used to believe. On the contrary, it created it along with new ways to justify it. The word "modernity" defines, according to Giddens, a post-traditional system marked by various possibilities of behavior and ways of living institutionally offered to individuals, and also by events and actions, even distant in terms of time and space, which influence their lives. The consequences for them are situations of probability and uncertainty, but also of adventure and excitement, which involve a continuous effort to redefine, as well as their personal identity, also the organization of social relations, in a world that has escaped the control of single individuals or groups ("a runaway world").[10]

In modernity, meant as the general condition of a post-traditional society, trust is no longer of a personal nature, as in pre-modern societies (called "traditional" by Giddens); but is placed instead in abstract systems, which are impersonal and consequently devoid of specific and localized time–space references. Examples of abstract systems are the monetary system and modern technology. Giddens argues that to these abstract systems are entrusted the coordination of the relations and the time–space activities. As a consequence, the possibility is given for modern individuals to create a personal identity, or a self-identity for themselves. Modern individuals can thus preserve their own condition of ontological security together with their usual and institutionalized conducts, and thanks to them. This condition assumes the confidence that the social and natural world is actually as it appears to those who live in it, and therefore predictable, and can be taken for granted in everyday life activities (Giddens 1990a: 17–36; 1991a: 36–42; 1998: 94–117).

The institutional forms characterizing modernity – and in particular, capitalistic modernity – are a distanciation between time and space, and consequently, disembedding mechanisms of social relations from particular space–time positions. Due to the institutionalized and abstract nature, and hence devoid of particular

---

10 This is the title of a well-known book written by Giddens. The introductory nature of this book can be explained by its origin in some radio conferences the author held at BBC in 1999. See Giddens 2002b: xxxi.

connotations, of capitalistic modernity, the time of activities detached itself more than ever from space – that is to say, from the physical place in which they take place, up to the creation of a global space–time system.[11] Power or domination structures involve either allocative or authority resources. The second ones provide coordination and space–time organization to activities themselves. Uniform time measurement methods have been made possible by the organization and institutionalization of social life, which are typical characteristics of modernity. It has therefore become possible to combine activities carried out by different persons in different times without any need they directly met.

Trust rests both on the abstract systems of money and technology, which are symbolic means with which different relation spheres can relate in time and space, in a pre-established way; and also on expert systems. In virtue of the existence of expert systems, individuals usually think it is possible to rely on existing and socially available knowledge (not held by most individuals) in order to make decisions and live their lives in a predictable way. As well as by the separation between time and space, and the distanciation mechanisms of social relations from specific spatial and temporal inputs, modernity is also characterized by its regular use of institutionally obtained knowledge for the purpose of organizing, and in case transforming, the institutionally regulated social life we live. Modernity is therefore of a reflexive nature, in the sense that its institutional consequences retroact on modernity itself.

One of the consequences of it is that knowledge obtained through the institutions of capitalistic modernity – i.e. enterprises; the industrial organization of production; the institutions in charge of security, and consequently, a large use of surveillance devices, and the monopolistic control exerted by the state over the means of violence – is continuously subject to change, and in case, to denial, thereby diverging, due to this aspect, from the Enlightenment expectations of a continuous accumulation of knowledge. Modernity, intended as a set of economic and social processes, which promote a separation between time and space, involves the whole globe, and undermines traditional ways of living and practices everywhere. Giddens refers in this regard not only to economic globalization, which already partly occurred in the nineteenth century, but also to the globalization processes in knowledge and information exchanges, even of a scientific nature, which are considered constitutive of contemporary institutions.[12]

These exchanges were made possible before the invention of print, then of telephone and telegraph, subsequently of radio and television, and finally of electronic communication technologies, when the direct experience of events of traditional societies was backed up, and in most cases replaced, by experience mediated by communication means. Thanks to these means, events occurred in different times and places are presented to a public that combines them giving them a unitary sense (the so-called "collage" effect), and introjects them ("intrusion of distant events into everyday consciousness"). The consequences of modernity on people's individual consciousness are ambivalent. On the one hand, this variety of signs and images may involve, if it is not anchored to established times and spaces, a sense of disorientation and psychological uneasiness in general. On the other hand, modernity offers – thanks to its institutions – unprecedented and never-before-tested opportunities to establish relations with different kinds of culture and consciousness.

The effects of disaggregation, and on the contrary, of aggregation result for individuals from modernity. The current "high modernity" period is characterized by an awareness, which in the past was much smaller in terms of intensity and spread, that science and technology not only involve advantages but also risks and dangers the institutionally available technological and technical knowledge cannot avoid, and are often among its causal elements. In other words, there is growing awareness that knowledge provided by experts, even if necessary for producing trust in the modern abstract systems, can produce unexpected and unwanted consequences, thus marking our age with unpredictability and its erratic character. It is true that also the past ages experienced dangers and reasons for concern. Nonetheless, only the large and impersonal organizations that characterize modernity have produced cognitive and emotional uncertainties due to the possible malfunctioning of the abstract institutional systems. As a consequence, threats – which previously did not exist, since they were prevented by the presence of traditions – have been made to the time–space organization of the social order, and hence to the existential (or "ontological") security of persons, which

---

11   About the concept of "time–space distanciation," see Giddens 1981a: 4–5, 91–5; 1984: 258–9, 377.

12   Giddens reverted several times on the theme of globalization and the "reflexive" nature of modernity. See, in particular, Giddens 2000: 122–62; 2002b: 6–19; 2007: 49–59; Giddens and Pierson 1998: 218–19.

would no longer be able to rely on their living habits and their usual behaviors (or "routines"). Therefore, trust in a social and natural outer world – which is stable and predictable – is endangered, and along with it, the possibility of forming a stable experience of our neighbors and ourselves, and consequently, the possibility of forming our identity.

The self is reflexively formed by the person, which considers its past experiences and mentally discloses the future ones in advance. Consistency in the construction process of the self, results from the cognitive consistency with which we have experienced our course of life in the different transitions from a phase to the subsequent one. Each transition demands a redefinition of our self and new choices of our lifestyle which any definition of our person in this age of high modernity rests on. The different possibilities of choice as regards lifestyles, and consequently social relation networks – especially with persons with whom an individual is emotionally connected, such as friends, spouses and partners – create a variety of environments in which an individual can act in this period. However, this is true on condition that the circumstances of life, and in particular an individual's social position, allow it. The individual would lack stable guidelines for action, however, as this is the consequence of the number of influences individuals are subjected to by globalization processes.

Considering that an individual can in this period – if his life circumstances are favorable – choose those he can emotionally relate with, also in case of a conjugal relationship, which in the past was almost indissoluble, there is for the first time the possibility of creating (in Giddens's language) a "pure relationship." It is an intimate and long-lasting relationship, of a varied nature (sexual, friendly, parental), which is begun and kept only for what it is able to emotionally provide to the participants. Its premises consist in the trust and the power balance between the participants, in their mutual respect and commitment. A "pure relationship" is only possible in our post-traditional and high-modernity age. This age, indeed, offers the social actors an opportunity to plan and organize their lives and choose their lifestyle. Thus, high-modernity age offers an opportunity to consciously adopt particular behaviors, ways of socially presenting themselves and bodily aspects (as illustrated by the way of living of anorexic women).[13] In this way, an individual can create a self-identity, which takes reflexively his personal and institutional relations into account.

A consolidated self-identity is therefore necessary to reach in a relationship the emotional exchange of a "pure relationship" and the intimacy that connotes it. Nonetheless, men and women find it difficult to achieve this high degree of intimacy in their relations, and therefore they do not know each other well. A hindrance to it consists in the power differences existing between the two genders, which in most cases are in favor of the male gender, and the ambivalence of the female gender concerning male power. Transformations in intimacy involve, indeed, not only the communication possibilities between participants, but also equal power in the two genders. Since inequality, though often not openly recognized, continues to remain in the public and private spheres, it becomes impossible to have a "pure relationship" and the mutual trust resulting from it, while the two genders remain mutually unknown. This would explain, according to Giddens, the attempts to find intimacy, emotional exchange, and equal communication in homosexual, male and female relationships (see Giddens 1992; see also Giddens and Pierson 1998: 118–50).[14]

The current age has abandoned the normative guidance provided by tradition, and as a consequence, it has permanently exposed itself to a condition of risk, that is to say, to the possibility (considered as a probability estimated calculable) that abstract systems are not in a position to guarantee security. Although in modernity, the risks in connection with bad health- and work-related conditions have decreased, nonetheless, an institutionalized control of risk by the abstract institutional systems, and consequently, the possibility of control and plan the future ("to colonize the future," in Giddens's language) are called into question not only by new and more widespread diseases, but also by risks that did not exist before and are generated by the abstract systems themselves. An example is the disaster produced by the nuclear incident at Chernobyl. Another example is the risk connected with investments in the financial markets. On the other hand, the ways to reduce or limit risk are suggested by experts – scientists, doctors, economists, or other authorities, who

---

13   For an in-depth analysis of the concept of "pure relationship," see Giddens 1992: 94–6.
14   We shall focus in the next sections on the importance Giddens attaches to the achievement of "pure relationships" for the consolidation of democracy.

are often, even radically, in contrast with one another, and whose knowledge is brought into question at a later stage.[15]

As previously mentioned the colonization process of the future is a consequence of the existence and functioning of abstract systems. They are institutionalized systems of knowledge and power, which refer to themselves (and are therefore self-referential). These systems aim at controlling and monitoring the social and natural environment they contribute to create and shape, and involve ambivalent consequences. For single individuals, many risks, especially in the medical and health-related sphere, are no longer a threat, since they have been put under control through institutionalized interventions. On the other hand, for entire communities, the globalization process or other causes, which are also part of what Giddens calls the dark side of modernity, have produced or have enormously increased – along with our ability to control and change the material and social world – other kinds of risk, such as those coming from the financial markets and from the natural environment. Climate changes are important examples.

Paradoxically, abstract systems are those that actually provide our age with a generalized trust in their operation conforming to the individuals' usual expectations. In particular, their trust in the regular functioning of the monetary system and technology, which is a presupposition of "ontological security," as Giddens defines it. This functioning disregards, as it is typical in abstract systems, space–time restrictions. For the civil and political society, important consequences result from the existence and operation of abstract systems. Their traditional differences and contrasts have disappeared with the coming of modernity, due to the penetration of abstract systems in both of them. These systems have an area external to them, represented by crime, sexuality, death and diseases, both physical and mental. This area tends to escape their institutionalized control, which is exerted, as much as possible, through imprisonment and hospitalization, especially in psychiatric hospitals. The encounter and experience with typical events of this external area to the abstract systems, are institutionally kept "sequestered" from individuals' usual life.

This separation is a premise that their everyday life may proceed according to their usual treadmills, and therefore be predictable and routinized, and that individuals may benefit from the "ontological security" provided by the abstract systems. However, Giddens remarks that individuals do not passively conform to norms and rules coming from their social world they collectively create in every encounter, since in the current age of globalization and reflexive modernity, they are requested to particularly commit themselves in relating with the social world, in order not to be dominated by abstract systems, and hence to give up actively participating in the political society they institutionally belong to. The theme of democracy, which we have briefly mentioned, has had a particular importance in Giddens's world as from the 1990s. This is confirmed by the number of his publications which deal with and discuss not only how democracy can be defined and conceived, but also which opportunities and obstacles it encounters in the current age (see Giddens 1994a: 104–34; 1994b: 190–94; 1998: 70–78; 2002: 67–82; 2007: 185–2008; Giddens and Pierson 1998: 94–117, 204–17).

Democracy, Active Trust, Lifestyle and Generative Politics

The definition of democracy given by Giddens (in agreement with Weber and Bobbio, authors mentioned by him) is procedural, that is to say, some formal conditions are formulated, the fulfillment of which is considered necessary to the existence of democracy. These conditions are as follows: a real competition among political parties to gain power positions, regular and fair elections based on universal suffrage, and the existence of civil rights along with political rights. Giddens argues that, in the past decades, democracy has extended itself to several countries which previously, based on this definition, could not be considered democratic, though in most cases, they used to and continue to call themselves in this way. It could be argued that democracy, intended in this way, has been successful. However, Giddens remarks that just in those societies, in which democracy is more consolidated and deeply rooted, there is a widespread sense of disappointment and dissatisfaction, as regards the behavior of democratic governments and political party leaders.

---

15 Giddens has developed, on several occasions, a sociology of risk as a stable condition of modernity. See, in particular, Giddens 1990b: 124–57; 1991a: 133–7; 2002b: 20–35; 2009: 17–34; Giddens and Pierson 1998: 227–33.

As many people think, political leaders look after their own interests and those of their group, rather than looking after the interests of the community. Frequent scandals and corruption are deemed evidence of this. In particular, the opinion is widespread that these governments do not sufficiently take care of some important issues, as the protection of the natural environment and human rights, and do not make use of transparency in carrying out their activities. Giddens proposes, as a remedy to the distance between issues that concern politicians and those concerning citizens, to consolidate (or "democratize," using his language) democracy in a variety of ways. This is possible, in the first place, by encouraging people's participation in associations, and hence, civil society; by keeping a balance among civil society, market forces and government; in addition, by ensuring that external circumstances do not prevent people from showing their abilities and their qualities; finally, by countering the aspects inherent in the globalization process, which has contributed to producing citizens' disaffection towards the democratic institutions.[16]

For this purpose, it is necessary to strengthen these institutions there where they are patently weak. Giddens briefly mentions in this regard the political institutions of Russia, where a particular intertwining between representatives of the market and politicians has produced a sort of "gangster capitalism." The strengthening of the democratic institutions may ensue from transnational and international organizations, such as the United Nations and the European Union, the people support to which is judged "weak and uncertain" by Giddens (Giddens and Hutton 2001: 217). These organizations have juridical and real power to intervene – in particular, through their courts of justice – in the situations, in which the national states have abstained, or if their intervention has proved ineffective. Democracy tends to strengthen over time, because the democratic institutions get stronger if there are political traditions that support them. Giddens calls this process "institutional reflexivity." Giddens argues that there are two different conceptions of democracy which confront each other.

Democracy may be intended – in agreement with Habermas and other authors – as deliberative or dialogic democracy, that is to say, as public debate on matters of common interest. Or rather as liberal democracy, in the sense that the necessary and sufficient conditions for calling democratic a political system consisting in the presence of representative institutions, and a clear distinction between civil and political society. Giddens shares the dialogic conception of democracy, though in contrast to Habermas he maintains that dialogue in itself does not necessarily lead to the democratization of a society. Dialogic democracy seems to prevail in today's post-traditional societies, in a variety of spheres: the personal, the collective, and the organizational sphere.

In particular, a first sphere is represented by personal life, through the current pursuit of a relationship supported with no other end than the relationship itself (a pure relationship between peers, as Giddens calls it). Personal life democratization is a premise of democracy. As a matter of fact, a peer relationship in a couple, between friends, or between parents and children, paves the way to the forming and strengthening of independent persons who are respectful of other people's rights. A second sphere consists in the proliferation of social movements and self-aid groups. In both cases, a discussion of life aspects and spheres, which were previously subtracted to dialogue, is foreseen and encouraged. Examples of it are, respectively, the feminist movement and associations such as as Alcoholics Anonymous. Furthermore, a democratization process can take place between organizations providing for flexible and reflexive authority structures, in which the lower levels are encouraged to offer their contributions in terms of knowledge and experience. Finally, a dialogic democracy sphere can be found in supranational organizations, such as the United Nations, in which there are institutionalized spaces of dialogue between different nation states.

In addition to the previously mentioned institutional reflexivity, the globalization process is one of the elements in a position to promote dialogue between persons and institutions, and thanks to it, the democratization of today's post-traditional societies. For this purpose, it is however necessary to promote an "active trust," which is not achieved through weakened traditional relationships; rather, it is achieved in virtue of personal ties and social responsibilities, which the single individuals hold. It is also necessary to remove or lessen any obstacle to the possibilities of dialogue and to democracy. Among these obstacles, Giddens reminds us, there are inequality and poverty when they are so pronounced that they produce an underclass,

---

16　Concerning some short introductions to Giddens's idea of democracy in the current age of "high modernity" and globalization, see Giddens 1992: 184–204; 2000: 159–62; 2002: 67–82.

which is socially and culturally excluded from the rest of the population. The welfare state was established for the purpose of mitigating poverty and inequality through income redistribution policies and a variety of other interventions.

These interventions aim at providing compulsory insurances to be borne by the internal revenue service against risk produced by unwanted events that may undermine the well-being of single persons, i.e. old age, accidents and injuries, illness and unemployment. Giddens objects that the welfare state has not only produced dependence on its benefits and protests against its high fiscal weight, but has also proved scarcely successful in achieving its redistributive goals. This occurs also in the Scandinavian societies, where the abatement of poverty can be better explained by the domestic wealth increase. The welfare state has been instead successful, in Scandinavia and elsewhere, in the compulsory insurance policies against risk in connection with the above mentioned unwanted events. The kind of welfare state proposed by Giddens intends to preserve its advantages without producing perverse effects. Its basic purpose consists in constructing a "positive" welfare state. This welfare state would involve a policy that can emancipate from any dependence, including those resulting from the welfare states themselves in their usual formulations, which have redistributive ends.

A welfare state that intends to promote emancipation rather than dependence aims at encouraging "active trust" in the citizenry, by virtue of which the citizenry puts itself reflexively in relation with the constitutive institutions of the abstract systems, and with the globalization processes, by interacting with them. Whether this ideal objective is fully achieved or approximated, a dialogic democracy would result from it, in which cosmopolite citizens play an active role, and are in a position to independently and consciously live their lives. A widespread and consolidated "active trust" is connected with a new form of politics, called "generative politics,"[17] which intends to emancipate citizens from any dependence on experts, authorities, or institutions. Consistently with this end, it aims at encouraging active trust conditions in the citizenry.

This aim can be achieved by recognizing the autonomy of civil society, and in particular, the possibility of choose a personal lifestyle (or" Lifestyle Politics"). This aim can be also achieved by promoting an information flow from civil society to a decentralized political society; and by submitting any form of authority – whether experts, parents or others – to discussion and control. In fact, we live in an age characterized by a source of uncertainty and risk we did not know before – one, which comes from the institutions of modernity. According to Giddens, this risk and the related global possibilities of crisis cannot be removed in this age. They are not stably distributed – as it was previously the case – and are unpredictable. As a consequence, they cannot be controlled through either voluntary or compulsory insurances. They are instead the consequence of an unstable, reflexive and bi-directional relation between the action of single individuals and their natural or socio-institutional environment.

Concerning this last aspect, Giddens defines the uncertainty resulting from it as "manufactured" ("manufactured uncertainty") by the welfare institutions themselves. These institutions are not capable to offer protection against unforeseen risk by the social security systems, and especially, risk resulting from particular lifestyles. In the same way as the uncertainty they produce, these risks can be neither prevented nor controlled through measures and interventions coming from an authority whatsoever. Welfare institutions are not the only ones that produce uncertainty. In general, uncertainty is the consequence of a close integration in modern age between science and technology, on the one hand, and the abstract institutional systems' orientation to action control, on the other. In societies no longer guided by tradition, indications and prescriptions concerning the most appropriate action courses, coming from abstract systems, are presented as scientific truth. Nonetheless, they are continuously called into question also by non-scientists, due to the moral dilemmas they produce, as for example, the disputes concerning genetic engineering projects.

The traditional welfare state is ineffective, from this point of view. "Generative politics" aims at providing the material and organizational conditions capable to form an "active trust," in a position to enable individuals and collectivities to effectively face these global risks, rather than passively suffer its consequences. Therefore, "Generative politics" can reduce, or at least control, this new form of uncertainty. Lacking a guidance provided by tradition, individuals and collectivities widely and systematically resort to experts, who are considered qualified for facing or controlling the global risks and possibilities of crisis.

---

17   Concerning the concepts of generative politics, active trust, and positive welfare state, developed and discussed in the 1990s, see Giddens 1994, 1996b; 1998; Giddens and Pierson 1998: 162–7.

Experts, however, contradict each other and their knowledge becomes soon obsolete. Furthermore, in front of a variety of abstract institutional systems, they can show a kind of knowledge that can be only proved in specific and limited spheres of life.

Resorting to experts does not reduce the extent and the seriousness of the global risks of our age. These risks, which have always political implications, concern the following spheres of life: the environmental impact of social development; the considerable spread of absolute poverty; the potential violence, on a global scale, resulting from mass destruction weapons; and the widespread persistence of non-democratic and illiberal political regimes. Giddens argues that "generative" politics is the only effective way to keep these risks under control, thanks to the continuous political commitment of an active, emancipated, well-informed citizenry; for only a citizenry, which is thus characterized, is capable to produce within itself networks of solidarity and mutual aid. As previously mentioned, this is actually the kind of welfare compatible with "generative" politics, which is the only one – according to Giddens – capable to face the risks of our age by taking reflexively into account the social and natural environment in which it acts; the persons involved in it; and on this basis, to encourage a life style centered on the values of personal initiative and integrity.

To better illustrate how "generative" politics can face, through "positive" welfare, the risks and the consequent uncertainties of modernity, Giddens focuses on the issues of global poverty and climatic change (see, in particular, Giddens 1994a: 157–97, 202–12; 2009). Global poverty has been successfully limited, more than by the traditional welfare state, by promoting local development policies, a well-known example of which consists in the micro-credit granted to the poor peasants of the Third World. Another example consists in the health programs addresses to extremely poor populations or social classes, which have been encouraged to take care of their implementation. It appertains to public or private national and transnational organizations to formulate development programs that take local requests and interests into account, and to avoid creating inefficient bureaucratic structures aimed at pursuing different interests from those declared. The value and objective of work and capital productivity are not only kept, but in our post-traditional age of reflexive modernization, are even further extended up to involve our personal life.

In other words, they can be achieved if we refer to our living experience and identity. As a matter of fact, the mental development of a person can be strengthened by welfare policies in a position to create or preserve social interaction networks, in which each individual can be active, and receives – thanks to these policies – as well as a more flexible job market, also a second chance to act in case they are affected by some adversity, as for example, illness, unemployment or poverty (*politics of second chances*). New responsibilities towards ourselves and others can thus be found. Thereby, the abilities and skills, which we have at our disposal, can be converted into practice, and solidarity, self-confidence and respect, and ultimately a support to our identity may be obtained. At the same time, a welfare reformed in this way would reduce social exclusion. Consequently, it would also reduce the possibility of form and strengthen a dual job market and, therefore, an underclass of persons who are active in the secondary market, and who are accordingly marginal from a social and economic viewpoint.

Another example of "generative" politics concerns the impact of human action on the natural environment. Giddens remarks that this kind of politics has no clearly progressive or conservative connotation. An appropriate distinction concerns, instead, environmental policies, the risk of which is intended as referred to the external environment to human action, and ecological policies, in which the attention focuses on how it is possible to recover a harmonious balance with the natural environment, intended as non-human and pre-existing to our lives. The proposal to abandon large cities, considered incompatible with the environment, in order to live in small local communities, belongs to the debate on ecological policies. Giddens's position in this regard is negative: small communities are often oppressive, while large cities give often hospitality to local or district-based communities.

Furthermore, the tradition we intend to renew is a creation of modernity, and is a reaction to modernity itself, and in particular, to globalization (see in this connection, Giddens 2002b: 6–19, 36–50; Giddens, Pierson 1998: 127–34). The nature we intend to protect is a creation of modernity as well, and consequently it is not possible to define or protect it resting on tradition. Neither we can evaluate the greater environmental risks produced by modernity resting on scientific knowledge. These risks, indeed, differently from those of lesser seriousness, are unpredictable, and their occurrence can be neither determined in space nor in time. The environmental disaster of Chernobyl is an example. Other examples are the risks originated by climatic changes resulting from the global warming process. Giddens has dedicated a monographic study to this issue (Giddens 2009), which has been preceded by some more concise essays (see Giddens 1994: 188–90; 2000: 132–42).

This monographic study is prompted by a paradox: the non-immediate visibility of the environmental risk leads the population in general, and in particular the persons whose lifestyle has greater environmental impact, to do nothing to change their lifestyle, and reduce its impact, until the consequences on the environment are no longer controllable. On the other hand, environmental policies are expensive, and therefore, the companies and the states that want to implement them find themselves economically disadvantaged in comparison with others that do not follow them. As a consequence, there is no incentive for individuals, or private or public organizations, to put into effect behaviors respectful of the environment. Nonetheless, a policy that intends to counter climatic change can prove effective if it converges with other political or economic objectives, as for example, energy preservation. Furthermore, it is necessary to persuade both the public and the public administration, at all its different levels, to act in a responsible way from an environmental point of view.

Giddens dwells on the different positions existing in the environmental debate, from a skeptical position towards the foundations of the concern for the environment, to the catastrophic position, according to which global warming predicts quick, irreversible and disastrous changes. He also mentions an intermediate position, according to which the terrestrial ecosystem is frail and must be protected. Giddens refers also to a certain literature of non-negligible size, concerning possible environmental disasters not caused by human action, but by natural events as volcanic eruptions, seaquakes and tsunamis. Though Giddens's position is close to the intermediate one, nonetheless it differs from it by its optimism, not in the sense of underestimating the risk and danger that global heating, and in general human action on the environment, involve; but rather in the sense of showing the opportunities (which maybe will not be seized) of international cooperation and strengthening of transnational organizations, and in the first place, the United Nations.

These opportunities result from the global nature of the environmental problems, as global is the problem of climatic change. As previously mentioned, Giddens is extremely critical about the literature dealing with environmental matters. The study on climatic change sees him resuming and formulating with further details the reservations we mentioned in the previous pages: the intervention programs outlined in this literature are hardly feasible and inconsistent. The preservation of the natural environment is often mistaken by preservation of social and cultural traditions. The natural environment was often threatened or destroyed also in pre-modern societies, while its preservation is perfectly compatible with modernity. Furthermore, in modernity only, centralized resources required for facing environmental problems are available. Small communities do not necessarily involve democracy and harmony, as a large part of the ecological literature imagines, since they are often, instead, places of oppression.

Finally, the current scientific and technological civilization is an acquisition intended to survive. Indeed, it is not possible to restore a world we imagine closer to nature and distant from our civilization, as it is not possible to renew a lost tradition. Nature and tradition, as values deserving to be preserved, are indeed creations of modernity (see, in particular, Giddens 2002b: 34–5, 39), though "modernity destroys tradition." Therefore, to survive, tradition needs to be articulated and protected. This can happen if we start a dialogue with different traditions: fundamentalism directly results from lack of dialogue with other religious traditions. Today's post-traditional society is the first one we can call with good reason a global society. Globalization does not only imply that communications are confined within established spaces. They have become immediate thanks to technological progress. But it also means that financial markets have achieved paramount importance; that the deep political and ideological divisions existing until the 1980s between states and between societies have disappeared; and that personal relationships within couples and families have become more egalitarian (Giddens and Hutton 2001).

As a consequence of economic globalization, which has been generated under the impulse of capitalism (Giddens and Hutton 2001: 10), social ties are not inherited from the past, but must be created. In comparison with the past, there are now new forms of interdependence and dilemmas, but also new opportunities: a democracy based on public dialogue ("dialogic democracy"), through which conflicts – especially violent ones, whether of interest or of a different nature (such as, in general, ethnic and cultural conflicts) – can be resolved, are one of the opportunities that have been made possible by the globalization process occurred in post-traditional society (Giddens 1994a: 242–5; 1994c: 192–3). As from the late 1990s, Giddens took part in the British political debate, and put his sociological knowledge and his reformist and sociodemocratic political programs and orientations, in the service of the English Labour Party leaders Blair and Brown. It is worth mentioning in this connection the books originated by his active political participation *The Third Way* (Giddens 1998) and *The Third Way and Its Critics* (Giddens 2000, and the subsequent essays of similar political and ideological contents and nature) (Giddens 2002, 2003, 2007).

The Third Way, and the later works by Giddens on this subject, examine in depth the issues concerning "generative" politics we previously considered, and are consistent with it. These issues concern, in particular, the assiduous political commitment of the citizenry this policy assumes, along with the reformist values – equality, freedom (in the sense of citizens' independence from political power, and democracy – that characterize it. Giddens not only discusses each one of these values, but he also adds other values, which are not generally included in a left of center, i.e. sociodemocratic (in Giddens's opinion these two designations are equivalent) reformist program. These values refer to "cosmopolitan pluralism" and "philosophical conservatism." The first term denominates the cosmopolitan values able to offer continuity and social cohesion to a world subject to unpredictable changes. As regards philosophical conservatism, it means – using the author's words – "a pragmatic attitude towards coping with change" (Giddens 1998: 68).

This attitude is favorable to modernity, but also aware of its ambivalent consequences, and therefore it suggests caution in a variety of spheres of life, such as science and technology, ecology, or family policies. Giddens's support to the implementation of reforms is only partly in continuity with a sociodemocratic policy that aims at renewal by taking the historical experience and the recent political debate into account. Relevant in this sense were the end of the so-called Real Socialism in Eastern Europe, and the radical neoliberal program of Mrs. Thatcher's Conservative government in Great Britain. His "third way" is an attempt to go beyond both traditional social democracy and its objectives of equality and full employment, and its support to a broad and comprehensive welfare state; and neoliberalism, with its support to free trade, its opposition to the welfare state, and intentional neglect of its social consequences (Giddens 1998: 26; see also Giddens, Pierson 1998: 194–203).

The issues, which the "third way" sociodemocratic program intends to deal with, are consistent – Giddens argues – with the values of the left: solidarity, social justice, protection of the weak and the poor, trust in governments considered the most qualified organization for implementing these values (Giddens and Hutton 2001: 45; Giddens and Pierson 1998: 152). In his opinion, these matters are among the most important ones of our age: the consequences of globalization: individualism that should not be synonymous with egoism; political-ideological distinction between left and right; what organizations – whether only governmental or also private – are assigned to put a political program into practice; what policies have to be adopted against environmental risks. These programmatic points of the "third way" are supplemented with some of his prescriptions: i.e. every right should involve responsibility for those who claim it; norms should establish the legal liability of limited companies; any authority should be democratically ratified.

The program of Giddens's "third way" concerns both the political and the civil society, and is in line with the "generative politics" this program intends to turn into practice. According to this program, the main institution of the political society, the state, must keep an interactive relation with the civil society, availing itself of a variety of channels: direct democracy, referendums, and other deliberative procedures able to make democracy even more democratic. Civil society nourishes itself and flourishes thanks to small groups of citizens who meet to promote causes of general interest: from charitable to ecological causes, or those concerning the refurbishment of decayed neighborhood, or also by cooperating with government and local authorities and organizations in order to jointly face the problems related to crime occurring in a neighborhood community. The state keeps its functions also within a well-structured and active civil society. It must not englobe it because, in this way, the creation of a public sphere would be prevented, as happened in the past in the socialist countries of Eastern Europe.

Likewise, even within a family – an essential element of civil society – as well as in the other spheres of civil and political society, the "third way" program includes equal powers among all its members, mutual respects and autonomy, discussion, communication and lack of violence. According to Giddens, these are the same standards that make the achievement of democracy in society possible. Democratic education is, in Giddens's opinion, a practice that begins within families. A "third way" policy involves the pursuit of equality not only in the family and political sphere, but also in the economic sphere. Giddens's proposal, in this connection, is in favor of mixed economy, with synergies between the public and the private sector, and between equality and individual freedom. The author dwells with particular attention on how, according to this policy, equality has to be intended. It is neither a question of redistributive equality (differently from the traditional sociodemocratic program), nor a question of equal opportunities (differently from the neoliberal program). Equality should be instead intended in the sense of redistributing the possibilities of study, work, and access to information.

Thus intended, equality is incompatible with a strong concentration of income and assets, as in the United States; but it is also incompatible with a neoliberal policy aimed at dismantling the welfare state. Furthermore, a "positive" welfare, compatible with a "third way" policy, does not limit itself to protect, through social insurances, a population from risk, that is to say, from unwanted events, the occurrence of which is predictable and, hence, computable (unlike dangers, the occurrence of which is unpredictable). On the contrary, this kind of welfare intends to provide benefits in order to avoid dividing some categories of persons – such as the elderly and the unemployed – from the rest of society, and to encourage the spread of education among those who, due to their marginality in the labor market, would easily run into economic and social exclusion.

This condition does not only imply lesser living and working opportunities, but also a physical separation from the rest of society. The author's proposal consists in that the public welfare agencies cooperate with other private organizations, including those acting in the market, in social economy activities. Based on Giddens's proposal, the state remains an essential actor in a "positive" welfare. However, this kind of state, in which national identity is in general compatible with other ethnic and cultural identities, is cosmopolitan, multicultural and compatible with a civil society of a global nature. A cosmopolitan nation implies the existence of a global-scale democracy, such as the political and economic spheres institutionally represented by global organizations as the United Nations, the World Bank, the International Monetary Fund, and so on.

For the time being, the European Union has not yet taken these characteristics despite its progressive enlargement to an ever-growing number of nation states. In this super-national organization, there are still several complex problems of social and cultural identity, and legitimation to solve. These problems do considerably limit the possibility of establish a cosmopolitan democracy, and to consequently regulate the world economy, and in particular, the financial markets. The liberalist recommendations to leave the markets without rules, foreshadows serious and expensive environmental, social and economic crises, as well as deep economic gaps between the different countries and regions of the world. The basic objective the sociodemocratic program of the "third way" intends to pursue consists in reforming public and private institutions, whether national or super-national, so that they can meet the needs of the new global order.[18] The "third way" is neither favorable to state intervention, nor contrary in principle to the market, thereby distinguishing itself from some premises, or principles, of the traditional left-wing movements. Giddens does not sympathize with them, and calls them by the negative term of "myths."

These myths include the myth of inconsistency in programs and objectives the myth that there would be an orthodox version of social democracy and finally the myth that the sociodemocratic governments do necessarily increase taxation (Giddens 2002a: 14–23). A pervading state tends to produce bureaucracy, dependence on welfare services, tendency to create monopolies, and negative economic cycles, as well as other unwanted effects. Some specific characteristics of the market set themselves against these effects, such as its entrepreneurial dynamism, and consequently, its ability to create wealth. The "third way" is not even neoliberal, since the market rests on ethic and social premises that are necessary for its operation, but are incompatible with neoliberal policies, exactly as other policies aimed at monopolizing earning opportunities but devoid of these premises ("gangster capitalism").

Therefore, the "third way" intends to beat a new path in the sphere of economic and social policies, able to promote those changes in the market and in the civil and political society that make their consolidation and strengthening possible. This new path is left-leaning, Giddens argues, because it intends to reduce inequalities and pursue pluralism, equal opportunities, social justice, environmental protection, and improvement of public services, by resorting to the joint action ("partnership") of public and private organizations.[19] It is

---

18   See, in this connection and in particular, Giddens 2000: 159–62; 2003; Giddens and Pierson 1998: 170–84.

19   See, for instance, Giddens 2002a: 38–53. Giddens (2000: 38) refers to a well-known text by Norberto Bobbio, *Left and Right: The Significance of a Political Distinction*, University of Chicago Press, 1997; original Italian edition: *Destra e*

close to the orientations and the beliefs of many people, actually of most citizens. They are in general young persons, relatively well-educated and well-off, who do not share the statist programs of the old left, but are instead progressive in their claims of their personal freedom and of the free choice of their lifestyles. "Third way" policies aim at encouraging steady family ties, which involve taking on, even among children, active roles and responsibilities, and countering crime through actions able to bind local communities.

Though not being statist, the "third way" acknowledges to the state the functions of providing public goods, social protection, and civic order, and intends to oppose the mistrust of many people towards the institutions of representative democracy. A reform of the institutions intends therefore to strengthen democracy and civil society, in order to prepare them to better cope with the changes that have characterized the end of the twentieth century. These changes imply globalization (economic-financial, social, political and cultural globalization), changes in living everyday life, and the formation of a "reflexive" citizenry (Giddens 2000: 65). By this expression, Giddens designates a group of citizens who actively and consciously respond to the changes produced by modernity, and in particular, to the risks and uncertainties resulting from its coming (Giddens 2000: 65–8; Giddens and Pierson 1998: 214–18. See also, in this connection, Kaspersen 2000: 88–9).

Among the objectives of the proposed reforms, there is the need in the first place, to oppose, through appropriate reforms and institutional innovations, the unwanted effects of financial globalization; in the second place, to strengthen the human capital, and consequently, education; to strengthen the social capital, and hence, the relational networks with the so-called "third sector" of voluntary associations; to ensure equal opportunities, and consequently, a redistribution of income and patrimony. An indicator of the distance existing between life opportunities in the United States and those in the north European countries is that income distribution in the latter is much more egalitarian, and the share of relatively poor people is much lower, while the other European countries stay instead in an intermediate position. The reduction of inequality can be achieved through taxation and monetary transfers, as has happened, on a large scale, in some European countries. On the other hand, "third way" politics – by encouraging "active citizenry" – aim instead at listening at the proposals of persons who are entitled to receive welfare services, who are often much more active than one can imagine, and are able to formulate noteworthy proposals.

The victims of consolidated social and economic exclusion usually live in physically and socially segregated urban areas, and are particularly underprivileged both from an economic point of view, and if we consider the quantity and quality of the services they receive. Forms of cooperation with local authorities, firms, and voluntary associations, can improve their condition, provided they encourage the initiative of those who live in these areas. In that case, along with their own economic and social exclusion, the exclusion of the more privileged part of the population, which often lives, too, in segregated and socially homogeneous neighborhood, would decrease. A redistributive policy conforming to the "third way" intends to put an end to the self-perpetuating cycle of poverty and relative deprivation, since it does not only act in the economic field, but also redistributes public goods as health and education, and protects civil and political freedom. This applies both within the single states, and also between rich and poor states.

The Reception of Giddens' Works

In the secondary literature concerning Giddens, it is a recurring thing to link objections and criticism with appreciations, and therefore the reception of his work is varied and contradictory. Several scholars who have not skimped on criticism, have nonetheless appreciated some important aspects, as the richness and largeness of his theoretical formulations, the synthesis pursued in an age of theoretical fragmentation, and its interdisciplinary nature (see Baert 1998: 110; Craib 1992: 195–6; Jessop 1989: 119; Kaspersen 2000: 186). The reception of Giddens's works has been mainly focused, even if not exclusively, on the theory of structuration and on the conceptualization of social change.[20] Concerning the latter, Joas and Knöbl (2009: 306–307) have

---

sinistra. Ragioni e significati di una distinzione politica. Roma: Donzelli, 1994.
    20 Concerning some reviews of Giddens's work, see Baert and Da Silva 2010: 150–152; Kaspersen 2000: 157–8, 161–87; Outhwaite 1990: 68–72; Stones 2005. Stones reports also a summary of Giddens's replies to his critics.

been shown to appreciate Giddens's ability to catch the multidimensional and time-spatial nature of change and his refusal to explain it in a simplistic way.

However, these authors remark that, in this way, Giddens precludes himself any non-episodic explanation able to catch in a unitary and consistent way events that are complex and diverse. The perplexities of these commentators about the ability of Giddens's theory to persuasively explain historical and social change, particularly referred to his critique to historical materialism, are shared also by other authors (see, in particular, Bottomore 1990; Gregory 1989; McLennan 1990). The theory of structuration has produced an even greater debate. Bryant and Jary (2000: 688–90) have positively appraised it for its effort to connect within a unitary and synthetic pattern a variety of aspects of pre-modern, modern and late-modern societies. However, they object that Giddens has not answered in a persuasive way the objections raised by his critics, and that his later production, since the early 1990s, though innovative, has abandoned the in-depth theoretical analysis of his previous production, leaving these objections without an answer, so far.

On these objections, or at least on some of them, Bryant and Jary have dwelt in another work (1990: 22–30), resuming questions and criticism formulated by other commentators. The "structural principles," which are so important for the theory of structuration, are not sufficiently specified by Giddens. As a consequence, their use is arduous in empirical research and lends itself to different and conflicting interpretations. Are they epistemological indications that are not binding for research? Or, on the contrary, such as to exclude different choices? Or instead, can the tension between these two options be overcome by asserting the historically determined nature of actions and societies, so that reflexivity and contingency of what the actors do, would not allow us to formulate propositions which have general validity? Giddens, as well as his interpreters, seems to swing between the first, the second, and the third one of these possible interpretations.

The theory of structuration has engendered a great deal of criticism. Jary himself remarks that this theory, in the formulation provided by Giddens, does not overcome the dualism between structure and agency, since Giddens has not sufficiently and consistently explained the relations between these concepts. No alternative formulation of these relations is associated to his rejection of historical materialism or of evolutionist models of social change, since he limits himself to say that it is neither possible to empirically assess, nor theoretically state the existence of general explanatory models. In this way, Giddens precluded himself the possibility of formulating generalizations. Based on similar remarks made by other interpreters, Jary infers that Giddens has actually oriented himself, even if not explicitly, to the thesis of an independence of the political sphere from social and economic influences.

Therefore, the thesis of a duality of the structure has not been kept in his historical sociology, and the argument of this thesis is not sufficiently able to refute the opposite thesis formulated by authors close to historical materialism.[21] Jary's criticism to Giddens's distinction between "dualism" and "duality" is shared by other commentators (see, for example, Hekman 1990: 164). According to Jary, Giddens's knowledge of history, does not seem to allow him formulating more fruitful arguments and typologies than those already existing formulated by other authors. If the evolutionary model of historical and social change is rejected, and no other models are proposed, the object of analysis consists in single episodes devoid of a theoretical connection between them (Jary 1991: 142–58).

Mainly negative is also Richard Kilminster's (1991) contribution. This author seems to appreciate Giddens's theoretical synthesis, and his formulation of the concept of action he considers more persuasive than that provided by Parsons. However, Kilminster, who does not only dwell on the theory of structuration but also on other Giddens's theoretical contributions concerning historical and social change, formulates several objections. The first objection remembers Jary's one: if we reject a conception of change in terms of evolution and differentiation, which alternative conception does Giddens provide? How is it possible to conceptualize the connection between continuity and discontinuity? Furthermore, the references Giddens makes in his synthesis to a heterogeneous miscellany of twentieth century philosophers and sociologists leave the specific aspects of their works in the shade, and in particular, do not highlight Habermas's contribution to contemporary sociological theory.

---

21 Concerning the complex relation of Giddens's theory with Marxism – either of continuity or discontinuity, depending on considered elements – see Wright 1989.

Derek Layder is one of the most famous critics of Giddens's theory. Though appreciating Giddens's theoretical eclecticism and his intention to preserve, in his theoretical construction, actors' autonomy, Layder (1994: 140–49) calls attention to some weak points of this construction. In particular, he considers unsatisfactory both the insufficient clarity – in his opinion – of Giddens's non-conventional notion of structure, and the existence of a tension between the notion of structure and the notion of system in the way Giddens defines them. If "structure" and "system" are different aspects of the human activities sociologists' attention is focusing on from time to time, as it seems from the definitions provided by Giddens, the dualism between action and structure is not overcome, and therefore, an important theoretical objective of the theory of structuration is not reached. Furthermore, social actors, in Giddens's opinion, seen to have no other existence but for what they do and for the reasons they put forward. As a consequence, reality would have only a psychological existence, in contrast with Giddens's explicit position. Again, his emphasis on the lifetime of institutions, beyond individuals' life and contingent reasons, seems – according to Layder – referable to a conventional subjective conception of institutions.

As a matter of fact, this conception seems neither compatible with the intention to overcome the dualism between action and structure, nor with the characteristic of social systems to have their own features, which are partly independent from individuals' reasons and motivations. However, it is not clear how much autonomy Giddens grants to individuals: this autonomy seems appreciable when Giddens states that actors have freedom and ability to change the social world, but to a very limited extent if we assume- as Giddens seems to do – that actors reproduce usual and conventional ways of behaving in their everyday life. The notion of "ontological security," introduced by Giddens in the 1980s, which became particularly relevant in his subsequent production, provides a more complete, and psychologically more credible, vision of the social actor, at the price of unbalancing the theory of structuration in a subjective direction. Therefore, it remains unclear how action and structure reciprocally relate. Quite similar, and as well-known (see, for example, Elliott 2009: 140–41), though more detailed and structured, is John B. Thompson's appraisal (1989).

As Layder and other commentators, Thompson, too, critically examines Giddens's attempt to formulate a theoretical pattern through which the dualism between action and structure can be overcome. "Agency," intended as people's ability to act autonomously in the world, preserves this ability in Giddens's pattern due only to the particularly broad definition of this concept, able to include every individual in any situation. Concerning the notion of structure, intended by Giddens as a set of rules and resources, it is vague and ambiguous, and hence, unfit to explain how and why different persons and groups have resources that are not shared with others, and are subject to different constraints and limitations. It is a conceptual and not a methodological matter, Thompson adds. Indeed, it is not conceptually clear whether the reproduction or the change of rules and resources concerns only single institutions, or rather the whole social structure. Giddens replies (1989: 257–9) that the existence of constraints to actors' possible actions does not imply that the notion of agency may lose its relevance. Even if one course of action were possible, the presence in actors of wants or motivations subject to change will make it possible that several courses of action my open in the future.

The theory of structuration, the conceptual and theoretical relation between actors and structures, as well as the social order issue, as formulated in Giddens's treatment, have been analyzed also by other scholars. We remember here some of the most well-known contributions the secondary literature refers to, starting from the critical contributions provided by Mouzelis and Archer about Giddens's notion of structure as a set of rules and resources. Resuming Giddens's arguments, Mouzelis (1989) explains the lasting nature of institutions through the power exerted by collective actors placed at the head of hierarchical position, aimed at changing the structural rules the actors orient themselves to as a virtual order. The duality of a structure is a useful concept to indicate actors' orientation to rules and resources that form the structure, while the notion of dualism between subject and object can be used to highlight actors' strategic orientation towards observation activities of their own and other people's conducts, in order to preserve or change them.

More radical is Hekman's (1990) criticism, since this commentator considers epistemologically unfounded the distinction – derived from Enlightenment, in her opinion – between dualism and structure duality, and along with it Giddens's theory of structuration as a whole, which represents an attempt to overcome this distinction. Dualism and duality are synonyms, Hekman argues, and perpetuate the dichotomy between actor and structure, by placing it, instead, at the center of the theory of structuration. This author aims at giving up this kind of epistemology, considered deceptive and unproductive, in order to adopt a post-modernist one. In his concise answer (Giddens 1990: 300), Giddens declares he is not particularly interested in epistemological matters, and in any case, he does not think that a post-modernist epistemology may give a definite contribution to an investigation focused on the foundations of knowledge.

As to Margaret Archer's critical contribution (1990), this British scholar argues that the theory of structuration does not clarify in which circumstances actors, or rather structures have greater importance in the reproduction of social systems. If structures are facilitating, but at the same time, also constraining, Giddens is reticent about the way in which action and structure mutually relate over time. Anyway, he does not provide any indication on how this dualism can be transcended. In addition, this task is not easy, because these two elements – action and structure – act in different times, and the actors and the conditions promoting change or stability, remain unspecified.[22]

Kieran Healey (1998), in one of his articles, makes a critical appraisal of Mouszelis's and Archer's contributions. According to Healey, Mouzelis exposes himself to objections by accepting this notion, despite his disagreement with Giddens as regards his conception of structuration.

Healey argues that neither Giddens nor Mouzelis has clarified which is the origin of this hierarchy, and it is not possible to do so as long as the structure is not defined and conceptualized as a body of rules and resources. In his reply to Archer, Giddens (1990: 312–15) remarks that all social constraints are mediated by the actors, who attribute a reason to what they do. In other words, the rules and resources that form the structure, are embedded in actors' practices. As well as the listed objections, which concern the persuasive ability of the theory of structuration, there are further critical remarks about its empirical relevance. These objections do not involve the extreme thesis of its complete irrelevance, but rather the less radical thesis that theory does only a potential and indirect service to empirical research. Among these objections, we wish to mention Stinchcombe's and Gregson's contributions.

Stinchcombe (1990) notes that though the theory of structuration relates institutions to the specific space–time situations in which the interaction constituting them occurs, it does not provide any information about the historically produced larger space–time contexts in which they are placed. Referring, in this connection, to a classical contribution by Wright Mills (1940), who recommended placing investigations concerning actors' motivations within specific historical ages and situations to give them concreteness, Stinchcombe maintains that Giddens's conceptual apparatus is overly abstract, and consequently, scarcely useful to research. Giddens replies (1990: 299) that though his theory intends to place itself at a high level of abstraction, it is not devoid, for this reason, of useful implications to empirical research. Similarly, according to Gregson, the conceptual apparatus formulated by Giddens's theory is too abstract to directly produce empirical research. Nonetheless, as second-level theory, it can address research to issues of general interest, such as an analysis of modern capitalism. This can happen on condition that it is integrated by a conceptual apparatus apt to the conduction of more specific and less abstract research (Gregson 1989).

In this regard, Giddens (1989: 293–301) observes that his theory has not only inspired research in a number of sociological fields, but has raised also some criticism, for example from Gregson, which he does not intend to fully share. The conceptual apparatus he formulated, with particular reference to *The Constitution of Society* (1984), is important since it is able not only to orient research, especially concerning the relation between action and structure, and the constitution and reproduction of social practices; but it is also able to avoid some dangers inherent in research methods and in the interpretation of its results. Nonetheless, Mouzelis wonders what is precisely the connection between the possibilities and the opportunities produced by the social structure (intended as a set of rules and resources) and the structural properties of the social system, provided that – like the rules and resources of the structure – they offer action opportunities and impose constraints to individuals' actions. However, the amount and the relevance of opportunities and constraints remains unspecified in Giddens's theoretical pattern (Mouzelis 1989).

Ira Cohen, one of the most well-known scholars of Giddens, has dwelt a few times upon the theory of structuration (Cohen 1987, 1990). Though he expresses words of appreciation, he also adds several precise critical remarks. Cohen praises "the extraordinary breadth" of Giddens's work (Cohen 1987: 274), as well as his ability to give explanations of the social order – which are plausible and well-informed from a theoretical

---

22 Similar critical remarks can be found in Callinicos (1985: 135–44), who refers, in this connection, also to other authors.

point of view – and to formulate concepts without indulging – unlike Parsons – in their over-proliferation (Cohen 1990: 34, 44–5). Cohen's objections refer in particular to the theory of structuration. Giddens's theory, though considering actors' inclination to usually perpetuate social practices a central element, has not driven Giddens to focus (as Goffman did, and as it would have been instead advisable for the theory of structuration, according to Cohen) on the way the actors "anchor" these practices through mutual personal identifications and acknowledgements.

Cohen objects, in addition, that Giddens's distinction between roles and social positions the actors' practices correspond to, is problematic and a cause of ambiguousness. Rather than action alternatives, roles, on the one hand, and positions and practices, on the other, are for the actors – Gidden argues – extreme cases as to (a) determination of expected conducts, (b) their occurrence in circumstances of actors' simultaneous presence, and (c) closure of the relations among actors compared to the relations with others (Cohen 1987: 303–306). According to some critical commentators of Giddens, ambiguous and unsatisfactory, too, are his notions of institution, structure and social system, which cannot be simply brought back to a social order made of routinized behaviors. Giddens himself, in his work on the consequences of modernity (1990a), would have recognized that these behaviors, in the present – or post-traditional, in his words – age are called into question and have changed (Craib 1992: 158–9).

Subjects for critical attention, as regards the theory of structuration, have also been the use made by Giddens of language, and his notions of structure and structuration. As Callinicos (1985) remarks, language does not directly relate with practices, because, unlike them, it changes very slowly and, in addition, it is subject to its own constraints and limits. Furthermore, the concept of structure – if intended, according to Giddens, as a set of rules and resources – it absolutely unfit to overcome the dualism between "agency" (i.e. what actors do) and structure. Rules – which are essential to lay the foundations of actors' practices, according to Giddens's theory – are actually not necessary for this purpose, since their application depends, in turn (keeping to Wittgenstein, who is Giddens's reference philosopher in this regard), on the shared consensus of the members of a community.

However, according to Callinicos, Giddens does not seem aware of this difficulty. Concerning structure, it is conceived as the effect of competent actors' creative action. The result is an unbalanced conception of structure in favor of a consideration of the actor, to the detriment of the structure itself. Quite unsatisfactory, too, is the notion of power as one's ability to transform material things and social relations. This notion of power could be also intended in another sense, not as the ability to change persons and things, but rather as an intrinsic attribute of human nature. Nonetheless, Callinicos remarks, intended in this way, power cannot be studied any longer by keeping to an interpretative sociology of action Giddens himself intends to preserve, in any case, in his theory of structuration. As well as on social change, the theory of structuration, and the conception of power, the attention of Giddens's commentators has focused also on other themes tackled by him.

Giddens's attention focused on classes and social inequality, especially in his early work *The Class Structure in the Advanced Societies* (Giddens 1973). This theme has involved the formulation of critical remarks chiefly, but not only, by Marxist scholars. Among them, we want to briefly mention Wright's (1989) and Jessop's (1989) contributions. Wright upholds the Marxist thesis of historical materialism that the relations among social classes are of paramount importance in the analysis of structure and social changes, and recognizes a contiguity, in this regard, between Giddens's and the Marxist formulations. Jessop argues that Giddens, in his negative evaluation of the Marxist political theory, has neglected some important themes and authors, and especially, the theme of power a modern state exerts through the repression and the reproduction of the production capitalistic relations, rather than through the control of citizens and war, themes on which Giddens prefers, instead, to insist.

As a consequence, the relations among economy, civil society, and political authority, would have been left unexplored. According to some critics of Giddens, it would be an omission involving serious theoretical implications. Indeed, lacking this investigation, the reasons why public policies have had particular contents and directions, would not have been clarified. Giddens (1989: 259–75) replies to both commentators in the following terms. The thesis formulated on historical materialism is too restrictive, even if some Marxist authors, such as Poulantzas, and above all Gramsci and his notion of hegemony, have partly (but actually only partly, in Giddens's opinion) overcome those limitations. The attention of historical materialism is mainly focused on the relations among classes, as a primary explanatory factor, while it relatively neglects – Giddens maintains – the study of the institutional forms of the nation state, and its activities of surveillance and exercise of military power, and in general, its monopolistic control of the means of violence. This set of activities would allow modern capitalistic states to be independent from the economic order.

Dennis Wrong, a scholar whose political and ideological orientation is well away from Marxism, shows instead to appreciate Giddens's complex and structured concept of class, but he is not convinced by his criticism of the notion of industrial society – fashionable in the 1950s and 1960s (see Wrong 1990). John Urry (1990), who focuses, too, on Giddens's conception of class, not only criticizes his definition of middle class as if it were a sociologically well-established category, but he also considers the treatment provided by Giddens unfit and lacking, since it has not focused enough on the social and political consequences of its existence. In recent times, Atkinson (2007) has examined the theoretical relation between Giddens's notion of class, and the notion formulated by Bourdieu. Atkinson's remarks on the ambivalence of this notion, especially concerning the level in which a class conforms its lifestyle, and individuals' autonomy in determining it. Differently from Bourdieu, Giddens does not explain the reason why individuals differ from each other in the choice of their lifestyle.

Among the other themes tackled by Giddens and his critics, we wish to remember here the time–space notion in modernity, and the political-social project of the Third Way. Concerning the former, it has been remarked that Giddens's treatment, though producing discussions and research, shows nonetheless two important omissions. In the first place, Giddens fails to provide empirical indications about the constitution of society over time and space (Pred 1990); in the second place, he does not argue in a persuasive – that is to say, clear and consistent – way the thesis that space and time hold a central position in the structuration of social relations (McLennan 1990). Giddens replies only to some of these critical remarks (1990: 299), stating that his analysis of the notions of time and space has consistently highlighted their nature of social relations properties.

Concerning the second theme, i.e. Giddens's project of the Third Way, discussions have been even greater, up to suggesting his publication of a book focused on these discussions (Giddens 2000). Lars Bo Kaspersen, author of a valuable introduction to Giddens's thought, argues in this connection that Giddens drew his inspiration for his political theory from a number of different sources, such as the British progressive thought, Heidegger's and Wittgenstein's philosophy, and also from "Goffman, Garfinkel, and perhaps Weber" (Kaspersen 2000: 191; see also the contiguity of Giddens's program with Hobhouse's political philosophy, Di Meglio 2002: 130–31). By briefly referring to the number of critical remarks to his political project – that Di Meglio considers unfinished due to the inadequacy of its theoretical innovation – Giddens points out the following ones: (1) the lack of positively defined contents, rather than those opposing traditional social democracy and neoliberalism, (2) a de facto adhesion to a conservative program, (3) a de facto acceptance of globalization and market, and (4) an acquiescence and indifference to environmental issues (Giddens 2000: 22–6).

Giddens underlines the different nature of these critical remarks, and the different ideological positions of those who have been their spokespersons. He starts exclusivley from them in order to enunciate once again his program of the Third Way we previously examined. In summary, this program can be formulated as follows:

1. We should focus on the issues the traditional left-right debate has neglected.
2. The spheres of power, consisting of government, economy, and civil society, should be limited and bound in the interests of solidarity and social justice.
3. A new social contract should be based on the principle that there are no rights if there is no responsibility.
4. The program provides for investments in social and human capital.
5. The program pursues a redistribution of income and wealth, as well as the social inclusion of those who are particularly advantaged or disadvantaged from a social and economic point of view.
6. Finally, the program intends to respond to the challenge of globalization at a local, national and global level.

References

Archer, M. 1990. Human Agency and Social Structure: A Critique of Giddens, in J. Clark, C. Modgil and S. Modgil (eds), *Anthony Giddens: Consensus and Controversy*. London: The Falmer Press, 73–84.

Atkinson, W. 2007. "Anthony Giddens as Adversary of Class Analysis." *Sociology* 41(3): 533–49.

Baert, P. 1998. *Social Theory in the 20th Century*. Cambridge and New York: Polity Press & New York University Press.

Baert, B. and Carreira da Silva, F. 2010. Italian translation: *La teoria sociale contemporanea*. Bologna: Il Mulino.

Bauman, Z. 1989. Hermeneutics and Modern Social Theory, in A. Giddens and D. Held (eds), *Social Theories and Modern Societies*. Cambridge: Cambridge University Press, 34–55.

Bernstein, R.J., 1989. Social Theory as Critique, in A. Giddens and D. Held (eds), *Social Theories and Modern Societies*. Cambridge: Cambridge University Press, 19–33.

Bottomore, T. 1990. Giddens's View of Historical Materialism, in J. Clark, C. Modgil and S. Modgil (eds), *Anthony Giddens: Consensus and Controversy*. London: The Falmer Press, 205–10.

Boyne, R. 1991.Power-Knowledge and Social Theory: The Systematic Misrepresentation of Contemporary French Social Theory in the Work of Anthony Giddens, in C.G.A. Bryant and D. Jary (eds), *Giddens' Theory of Structuration: A Critical Appreciation*. New York: Routledge, 52–73.

Breuilly, J. 1990. The Nation State and Violence: A Critique of Giddens, in J. Clark, C. Modgil and S. Modgil (eds), *Anthony Giddens: Consensus and Controversy*. London: The Falmer Press, 271–87.

Bryant, C.G.A. 1991. The Dialogic Model of Applied Sociology, in C.G.A. Bryant and D. Jary (eds), *Giddens' Theory of Structuration: A Critical Appreciation*. New York: Routledge, 176–200.

Bryant, C.G.A. and Jary, D. 1991. Introduction: Coming to Terms with Anthony Giddens, 1–31, in C.G.A. Bryant and D. Jary (eds), *Giddens' Theory of Structuration: A Critical Appreciation*. New York: Routledge.

Bryant, C.G.A. and Jary, D. 2000. Anthony Giddens, in G. Ritzer (ed.), *The Blackwell Companion to Major Social Theorists*. Oxford: Blackwell, 670–95.

Calhoun, C., Gerteis, J., Moody, J., Pfaff, S. and Virk, I. (eds). 2002. *Contemporary Sociological Theory*. Oxford: Blackwell.

Callinicos, A. 1985. "Anthony Giddens: A Contemporary Critique." *Theory and Society* 14(2): 133–66.

Clark, J. 1990. Anthony Giddens, Sociology and Modern Social Theory, in J. Clark, C. Modgil and S. Modgil (eds), *Anthony Giddens: Consensus and Controversy*. London: The Falmer Press, 21–7.

Clark, J., Modgil, C. and Modgil, S. 1990. Editorial Introduction. Anthony Giddens: Consensus and Controversy, in J. Clark, C. Modgil and S. Modgil (eds), *Anthony Giddens: Consensus and Controversy*. London: The Falmer Press, 5–8.

Cohen, I. 1987. Structuration Theory and Social Praxis, in A. Giddens, J.H. Turner (eds), *Social Theory Today*. Cambridge: Polity Press, 279–308.

Cohen, I. 1990. Structuration Theory and Social Order: Five Issues in Brief, in J. Clark, C. Modgil and S. Modgil (eds), *Anthony Giddens: Consensus and Controversy*. London: The Falmer Press, 33–45.

Coser, L.A. 1990, in J. Clark, C. Modgil and S. Modgil (eds), *Anthony Giddens: Consensus and Controversy*. London: The Falmer Press, 195–204.

Craib, I. 1992. *Anthony Giddens*. London: Routledge.

Dandeker, C. 1990. The Nation State and the Modern World System, in J. Clark, C. Modgil and S. Modgil (eds), *Anthony Giddens: Consensus and Controversy*. London: The Falmer Press, 257–69.

Dickie-Clark, H. 1990. Hermeneutics and Giddens Theory of Structuration, in J. Clark, C. Modgil and S. Modgil (eds), *Anthony Giddens: Consensus and Controversy*. London: The Falmer Press, 145–54.

Di Meglio, M. 2002. *Teoria sociale e modernità. Il progetto incompiuto di Anthony Giddens*. Milan: FrancoAngeli.

Elliott, A. 2009. *Contemporary Social Theory: An Introduction*. London: Routledge.

Giddens, A. 1971a. *Capitalism and Modern Social Theory*. Cambridge: Cambridge University Press. Italian translation: *Capitalismo e teoria sociale*, 2009, Milan: Il Saggiatore.

Giddens, A. 1971b. "The 'Individual' in the Writings of Émile Durkheim." *European Journal of Sociology* 12(2): 210–28.

Giddens, A. 1972. "Elites in the British Class Structure." *Sociological Review* 20: 345–72.

Giddens, A. 1973. *The Class Structure of the Advanced Societies*. London: Hutchinson University Library.

Giddens, A. 1976a. New Rules of Sociological Method: A Positive Critique of Interpretive Sociology. London: Hutchinson. Italian translation: *Nuove regole del metodo sociologico*, 1979, Bologna: Il Mulino,

Giddens, A. 1976b. "Classical Social Theory and the Origins of Modern Sociology." *American Journal of Sociology* 81(4): 703–29.

Giddens, A. 1977. *Studies in Social and Political Theory*. London: Hutchinson.

Giddens, A. 1978. *Durkheim*. London: Fontana, 1985.

Giddens, A. 1979b. *Central Problems in Social Theory*. Berkeley, CA: University of California Press.

Giddens, A. 1981a. *A Contemporary Critique of Historical Materialism*. London: Macmillan.

Giddens, A. 1981b. "Classical Social Theory and the Origins of Modern Sociology." *American Journal of Sociology* 81(4): 703–29.

Giddens, A. 1981c. "Comments on the Theory of Structuration." *Journal for the Theory of Social Behaviour* 13(1): 75–80.

Giddens, A. 1982. *Sociology: A Brief but Critical Introduction*. London: Macmillan. Italian translation: *Sociologia*, 1994, Bologna: Il Mulino

Giddens, A. 1984. *The Constitution of Society*. Cambridge: Polity Press. Italian translation: *La costituzione della società: lineamenti della teoria della strutturazione*, 1990, Milan: Edizioni di Comunità.

Giddens, A. 1985. *The Nation State and Violence*. Cambridge: Polity Press.

Giddens, A. 1989. A Reply to my Critics, in A. Giddens and D. Held (eds), *Social Theories and Modern Societies*. Cambridge: Cambridge University Press, 249–301.

Giddens, A. 1990a. Structuration Theory and Sociological Analysis, in J. Clark, C. Modgil and S. Modgil (eds), *Anthony Giddens: Consensus and Controversy*. London: The Falmer Press, 297–315.

Giddens, A. 1990b. *The Consequences of Modernity*. Stanford, CA: Stanford University Press. Italian translation: *Le conseguenze della modernità*, 1994, Bologna: Il Mulino.

Giddens, A. 1990c. R.K. Merton on Structural Analysis, in J. Clark, C. Modgil and S. Modgil (eds), *Robert K. Merton: Consensus and Controversy*. London: The Falmer Press, 97–111.

Giddens, A. 1991a. *Modernity and Self-Identity*. Stanford, CA: Stanford University Press. Italian translation: *Identità e società moderna*. Naples: Ipermedium Libri.

Giddens, A. 1991b. Structuration Theory: Past, Present and Future, in C.G.A. Bryant and D. Jary (eds), *Giddens' Theory of Structuration: A Critical Appreciation*. New York: Routledge, 210–21.

Giddens, A. 1992. *The Transformation of Intimacy*. Cambridge: Polity Press. Italian translation: *Le trasformazioni dell'intimità*, 2008, Bologna: Il Mulino.

Giddens, A. 1994a. *Beyond Left and Right: The Future of Radical Politics*. Stanford, CA: Stanford University Press. Italian translation: *Oltre la destra e la sinistra*. Bologna: Il Mulino.

Giddens, A. 1994b. Living in a Post-Traditional Society, in U. Beck, A. Giddens and S. Lash (eds), *Reflexive Modernization*. Cambridge: Polity Press, 56–109.

Giddens, A. 1994c. Risk, Trust, Reflexivity, in U. Beck, A. Giddens and S. Lash (eds), *Reflexive Modernization*. Cambridge: Polity Press, 184–97.

Giddens, A. 1996a. *In Defence of Sociology*. Cambridge: The Polity Press.

Giddens, A. 1996b. "Affluence, Poverty and the Idea of a Post-Scarcity Society." *Development and Change* 27: 365–77.

Giddens, A. 1998. *The Third Way: The Renewal of Social Democracy*. Cambridge: The Polity Press. Italian translation: *La terza via*. Milan: Il Saggiatore.

Giddens, A. 2000. *The Third Way and Its Critics*. Cambridge: Polity Press.

Giddens, A. 2002a. *Where Now for New Labour?* Cambridge: Polity Press.

Giddens, A. 2002b. *Runaway World: How Globalization is Reshaping Our Lives*. London: Profile Books. Italian translation: *Il mondo che cambia: come la globalizzazione ridisegna la nostra vita*, 2000, Bologna: Il Mulino.

Giddens, A. 2003. Introduction. Neoprogressivism: A New Agenda for Social Democracy, in A. Giddens (ed.), *The Progressive Manifesto: New Ideas for Centre-Left*. Cambridge: Polity Press, 1–34.

Giddens, A. 2006. A Social Model for Europe?, in A. Giddens, P. Diamond and R. Liddle, (eds), *Global Europe, Social Europe*. Cambridge: Polity Press, 14–36.

Giddens, A. 2007a. *Over to You, Mr. Brown*. Cambridge: Polity Press.

Giddens, A. 2007b. *Europe in the Global Age*. Cambridge: Polity Press. Italian translation: *L'Europa nell'età globale*, 2007, Rome: Laterza.

Giddens, A. 2009. *The Politics of Climate Change*. Cambridge: Polity Press.

Giddens, A., Diamond, P. and Liddle, R. 2006. Introduction, in A. Giddens, P. Diamond and R. Liddle, (eds),*Global Europe, Social Europe*. Cambridge: Polity Press, 1–13.

Giddens, A. and Hutton, W., 2001. Anthony Giddens and Will Hutton in Conversation, in A. Giddens and W. Hutton (eds), *On the Edge: Living with Global Capitalism*. London: Vintage, 1–51.

Giddens, A. and Pierson, C. 1998. *Conversations with Anthony Giddens: Making Sense of Modernity.* Cambridge: Polity Press.

Giddens, A. and Turner, J.H. 1987. Introduction, in A. Giddens and J.H. Turner (eds), *Social Theory Today*. Cambridge: Polity Press, 1–10.

Gregory, D. 1989. Presences and Absences: Time-Space Relations and Structuration Theory, in A. Giddens and D. Held (eds), *Social Theories and Modern Societies*. Cambridge: Cambridge University Press, 185–214.

Gregory, D. 1990. "Grand Maps of History": Structuration Theory and Social Change, in J. Clark, C. Modgil and S. Modgil (eds), *Anthony Giddens: Consensus and Controversy*. London: The Falmer Press, 217–33.

Gregson, N. 1989. On the (Ir)relevance of Structuration Theory to Empirical Research, in A. Giddens and D. Held (eds), *Social Theories and Modern Societies*. Cambridge: Cambridge University Press, 235–48.

Healey, K. 1998. "Conceptualizing Constraint: Mouzelis, Archer and the Concept of Social Structure." *Sociology* 32(3): 509–22.

Hekman, S. 1990. Hermenutics and the Crisis of Social Theory, in J. Clark, C. Modgil and S. Modgil (eds), *Anthony Giddens: Consensus and Controversy*. London: The Falmer Press, 155–65.

Held, D. 1989. Citizenship and Autonomy, in A. Giddens and D. Held (eds), *Social Theories and Modern Societies*. Cambridge: Cambridge University Press, 162–84.

Hutton, W. and Giddens, A. 2001. Anthony Giddens and Will Hutton in Conversation, in *On the Edge: Living with Global Capitalism*. London: Vintage, 1–51.

Jary, D. 1991. "Society as Time Traveller": Giddens on Historical Change, Historical Materialism and the Nation State in World Society, in C.G.A. Bryant and D. Jary (eds), *Giddens' Theory of Structuration: A Critical Appreciation*. New York: Routledge, 116–59.

Jessop, B. 1989. Capitalism, Nation States and Surveillance, in A. Giddens and D. Held (eds), *Social Theories and Modern Societies*. Cambridge: Cambridge University Press, 103–28.

Joas, H. 1990. Giddens's Critique of Functionalism, in J. Clark, C. Modgil and S. Modgil (eds), *Anthony Giddens: Consensus and Controversy*. London: The Falmer Press, 91–102.

Joas, H. and Knöbl, W. 2009. *Social Theory: Twenty Introductory Lectures*. Cambridge: Cambridge University Press.

Kaspersen, L.B. 2000. *Anthony Giddens: An Introduction to a Social Theorist*. Oxford: Blackwell.

Kilminster, R. 1991. Structuration Theory as a World-View, in C.G.A. Bryant and D. Jary (eds), *Giddens' Theory of Structuration: A Critical Appreciation*. New York: Routledge, 74–115.

Layder, D. 1994. *Understanding Social Theory*. London: Sage.

McLennan, G. 1990. The Temporal and the Temporizing in Structuration Theory, in J. Clark, C. Modgil and S. Modgil (eds), *Anthony Giddens: Consensus and Controversy*. London: The Falmer Press, 131–9.

Mestrovic, S.G. 1998. *Anthony Giddens: The Last Modernist*. London: Routledge.

Mills, C.W. 1940. "Situated Action and the Vocabulary of Motives." *American Sociological Review* 5: 904–13.

Mouzelis, N. 1989. "Restructuring Structuration Theory." *Sociology* 37(3): 613–35.

O'Brien, M. 1998. The Sociology of Anthony Giddens: An Introduction, in Giddens, A. and Pierson, C. 1998. *Conversations with Anthony Giddens: Making Sense of Modernity*. Cambridge: Polity Press, 1–27.

Outhwaite, W. 1990. Agency and Structure, in J. Clark, C. Modgil and S. Modgil (eds), *Anthony Giddens: Consensus and Controversy*. London: The Falmer Press, 63–72.

Poggi, G. 1990. Anthony Giddens and "The Classics," in J. Clark, C. Modgil and S. Modgil (eds), *Anthony Giddens: Consensus and Controversy*. London: The Falmer Press, 11–19.

Pred, A. 1990. Context and Bodies in Flux: Some Comments on Space and Time in the Writings of Anthony Giddens, in J. Clark, C. Modgil and S. Modgil (eds), *Anthony Giddens: Consensus and Controversy*. London: The Falmer Press, 117–29.

Saunders, P. 1989. Space, Urbanism and the Created Environment, in A. Giddens and D. Held (eds), *Social Theories and Modern Societies*. Cambridge: Cambridge University Press, 215–34.

Sayer, D. 1990. Reinventing the Wheel: Anthony Giddens, Karl Marx and Social Change, in J. Clark, C. Modgil and S. Modgil (eds), *Anthony Giddens: Consensus and Controversy*. London: The Falmer Press, 235–50.

Sica, A. 1991. The California-Massachusetts Strain in Structuration Theory, in C.G.A. Bryant and D. Jary (eds), *Giddens' Theory of Structuration: A Critical Appreciation*. New York: Routledge, 32–51.

Shaw, M. 1989. War and the Nation State in Social Theory, in A. Giddens and D. Held (eds), *Social Theories and Modern Societies*. Cambridge: Cambridge University Press, 129–46.

Stinchcombe, A. 1990. Milieu and Structure Updated: A Critique of the Theory of Structuration, in J. Clark, C. Modgil and S. Modgil (eds), *Anthony Giddens: Consensus and Controversy*. London: The Falmer Press, 47–56.

Stones, R. 2005. *Structuration Theory*. New York: Palgrave Macmillan.

Thompson, J.B. 1989, The Theory of Structuration, in A. Giddens and D. Held (eds), *Social Theories and Modern Societies*. Cambridge: Cambridge University Press, 56–76.

Turner, J.H. 1986. "Review Essay: The Theory of Structuration." *American Journal of Sociology* 91(4): 969–77.

Turner, J.H. 1990. Giddens's Analysis of Functionalism: A Critique, in J. Clark, C. Modgil and S. Modgil (eds), *Anthony Giddens: Consensus and Controversy*. London: The Falmer Press, 103–10.

Urry, J. 1990. Giddens on Social Class: A Critique, in J. Clark, C. Modgil and S. Modgil (eds), *Anthony Giddens: Consensus and Controversy*. London: The Falmer Press, 179–89.

Urry, J. 1991. Time and Space in Giddens' Social Theory, in C.G.A. Bryant and D. Jary (eds), *Giddens' Theory of Structuration: A Critical Appreciation*. New York: Routledge, 160–75.

Wright, E.O. 1989. Models of Historical Trajectory: An Assessment of Giddens's Critique of Marxism, in A. Giddens and D. Held (eds), *Social Theories and Modern Societies*. Cambridge: Cambridge University Press, 77–102.

Wrong, D. 1990. Giddens on Classes and Class Structure, in J. Clark, C. Modgil and S. Modgil (eds), *Anthony Giddens: Consensus and Controversy*. London: The Falmer Press, 171–7.

Chapter 7
Erving Goffman (1922–1982)

Preliminary Remarks

Rather than consider the various and peculiar themes that characterize Goffman's investigation, we shall dwell on the themes that form his central idea:

a. the image certain persons get of individuals during direct interactions that take place in everyday life, and in the course of social situations;
b. the construction and maintenance of an image or an impression of themselves these individuals keep towards the persons they relate with;
c. the socially derived interpretative patterns with which the participants in interactions give them a sense;
d. the importance of this sense to create, keep or restore a cognitive order (i.e. shared cognitive presuppositions, whether linguistic or of a different nature, as for instance the rules on which a game is based) or a normative order (i.e. norms taken for granted and considered correct).

According to Goffman, a social organization results from a cognitive and normative order. These themes will be jointly dealt with in order to highlight their intertwining. We shall also briefly mention Goffman's elements of continuity and discontinuity with other authors who preceded him and with whom he confronted himself; and, finally, some recent interpretations of his sociology.

Social Situations, Interpretative Patterns, and Method

Interactions reveal themselves in social situations. Situations are environments in which two or more persons are physically present at the same time, so that their interaction becomes possible. Situations are defined according to organization principles that give a sense to events, at least to social events, and therefore cause individuals' involvement in these events throughout their everyday life. Associative life proceeds according to a cognitive and normative order in which individuals actively participate. By virtue of these organization principles of experience, individuals can actually use interpretative patterns that, once applied to the experienced reality, and in particular to the social reality, make it understandable to them. These interpretative patterns can be applied to specific events, that is to say, to segments of activity made, whether directly or indirectly, significant.

Direct patterns are called primary patterns, while indirect ones originate from them through transformations of the original sense of the experienced reality, and consequently, through different definitions of the situation. Indirect interpretative patterns can consist in changes of the initial sense of an event (therefore, for instance, a seller's demonstration test of the operation of an electric appliance can be used by a housewife for making him really do a particular housework job). If the change involves several persons, its successful outcome requires their agreement on a new definition of the situation (therefore, the transformation of reality in a theatrical fiction requires the cooperation of actors, audience, and other persons attending a performance). Indirect interpretative patterns may also consist of deceptive accounts, which require that some participants in a situation collude in suggesting a deceptive definition of the situation to the others (swindles, or also tricks that do not intend to harm the victim, are examples of deceptive accounts). If the definition of the situation allows it, the ability to deceive our neighbor is general.

Most activities carried out by individuals are carried out in the presence of others, and therefore are socially situated. As a consequence, an individual can be considered, at the same time, an actor who aims at projecting onto the audience an impression of him/herself and a definition of the situation, as well as the character performed by the actor on the stage, to which the audience attributes a self as a product of the performed scene. As happens in the case of a theater actor performing a character, in the case of social actors relating with others, the "self" they publicly exhibit, and the "self" attributed to them, both find their origin in the social representation and therefore are not personal characteristics. The theatrical metaphor shows nonetheless some explicative limits. Theater actors distinguish themselves from average social actors since they take a fictitious identity (the character's identity), which is distinct from that identity – that self – unrelated to their professional role they project – like any other social actor – onto others during their everyday life (Goffman 1969b: 288–91; 1974: 8–13, 43–7, 83–5, 127–31, 156–7, 247, 573; 1983a: 2–6; see also MacIntyre 2000).

The research method pursued by Goffman is of ethnographic origin, and is related to his anthropological education. This method involves a dual strategy. On the one hand there is a thick description of social reality as a theater performance, in which social actors play more or less pre-established roles. Social reality becomes a game, in which actors make rational moves in order to obtain advantages or avoid inconveniences. This strategy favors the point of view of external observers (i.e. scholars). On the other hand the matter of interest is the participants' point of view as regards the considered segment of social reality. Description concerns, in this case, how actors deal with situations they consider relevant, as demotion rituals, diversions from conventional rules, or information able to bring discredit on actors themselves. These two strategies are not mutually exclusive. Goffman's method has been influenced by some social science epistemologies – especially those followed by Parsons and Schutz – but cannot be identified with any of them (see R. Williams 2000).

Personal and Social Identity

The "self" an individual shows to others may diverge, even radically, from the "self" attributed to him/her; for two reasons.

First, intended as personal identity, the exhibited self is outlined in opposition to the social units (collectivities in general, groups or organizations in particular), in which individuals are situated, and with which they relate based on rules. Therefore, individuals have a personal identity that depends on how they show themselves to others as differentiated individuals and are, consequently, able to play differentiated roles and selves. Individuals' presentation of themselves is regulated by obligations and prohibitions, i.e. by norms. They try to cope with the changing and accidental circumstances of interaction at their best. Nonetheless, the previous official definition of situation is no longer tenable when events do not let themselves be incorporated within the activity, which individuals consider the most important, and which cannot be ignored. As a consequence, the individuals involved in such accidental events can no longer socially exhibit an identity; for example, when theater actors publicly show they have forgotten their cues, they make the dramatic illusion of the course of imaginary events performed by them and by their fellows untenable. In this way, the definition of situation as theater performance is compromised, since the actors have lost their identity in front of the audience.

Second, as regards the self socially attributed to individuals, they cast towards the bystanders an image (a self) that, though being a subject of ritual attention, is also exposed, in any moment of the interaction, to offense, humiliation and profanation. Whether institutionally or informally, they are submitted to a pressure that varies depending on the degree of social coercion, and which is aimed at driving them to redefine themselves as socially required. Therefore, individuals have a social identity, consisting of the roles and the selves that are socially attributed them, which are differentiated depending on the social status required from time to time.

Both identities, the personal and the social one, are mutually depending. They share the following defining elements:

a. They have to be distinct from the individuals' sense of continuity (from how individuals perceive themselves, that is to say, from their "ego").
b. They are always subject to the possibility of cognitive and social recognition.

c. They ensue from the individual's position in the social structure, and therefore vary as this position varies.
d. They are damaged by a stigma (i.e. an undesirable attribute that discredits a person).
e. They change insofar as an individual has a course of life marked by phases to which as many changes of the self (moral career) correspond, as happens in particular in the case of residents in jails, psychiatric hospitals, and other institutions.
f. Therefore they are not attributes of an individual. A biography may link a variety of an individual's social identities, which are mutually consistent, but the representation provided is insufficient because it is not possible to highlight all the identities individuals take by playing the number of roles their social life involves (Goffman 1961a: 14, 46–8, 127–8, 168, 314–20, 386; 1961b: 105–10; 1963b: 56–69, 105–106, 112; 1969b: 68; 1971: 223–7; 1974: 206; 1983a: 2–3; 1988b: 35–7, 57–8, 99).

The Representations of the Self in Encounters

By staging, in good or bad faith, a performance in front of an audience of bystanders, and by manipulating the impressions these persons can get of them, individuals aim at influencing the other participants, leading them to an encounter. The definition of encounter assumes the definition of direct "face-to-face interaction," which therefore implies the spatial and temporal presence of all participants, and consequently, their mutual awareness and the mutual orientation of their action.[1] This interaction, which occurs in everyday life, and is the main investigation subject in Goffman's sociology, is defined as a field provided with natural boundaries, and analytically consistent, in which one or more individuals who are present at the same time reciprocally influence their action (Goffman 1983a: 7). An encounter is intended by Goffman as a face-to-face interaction focused on a single center of visual and cognitive attention.

The participants in an encounter have the moral obligation to keep their attention to the commitment established by the encounter alert, without diverting it in favor of extraneous persons or events. In any focalized interaction, there are several attending persons at the same time, which reciprocally authorize themselves to communicate without showing particular curiosity or intention towards the others. This conduct would be in keeping with the norm of civil inattention. However, this norm applies only to those who behave correctly (Goffman 1961a: 8; 1969b: 26, 29–33; 1971: 26, 85–7, 179–81; 1974: 345–7). Goffman considers good manners, or civility, aimed at protecting the individuals' self, necessary not only for the social life of small circles, but also for the purpose of maintaining the more extensive social order (see Manning 2000). As social actors, individuals have pre-established action models at their disposal – i.e. "parts" or "routines" – they can perform on different occasions. During the encounter, each participant tries to protect his/her definition of the situation through defensive and protective actions, and with it, his/her social image, to the respect of which the participant has a moral right.

A dual obligation corresponds to this right: the other participants' obligation to be tactful, by accepting, until proven otherwise, the actor's definition of the situation; and the subject's obligation to be what he/she claims to be. On the other hand, the truth of the subject's representations is submitted to assessment, and if the falseness of any one of them is discovered – communicated, for instance, through inappropriate involuntary gestures, or other expressive inconsistencies – it destroys the representation, and threatens the whole relation in which the representation is included (Goffman 1969b: 24–6, 63–9; 1974: 84–5). Insofar as the representation acts in a fixed and generalized way to define the situation to the eyes of the other participants, the individual has and actively keeps a façade. This façade is connoted by a physical setting made of sceneries and furniture, and by a personal aspect consisting of physical, cultural, and social characteristics identifying the actor, who forces him/herself to keep it presentable if he/she is interested in the social life that surrounds him/her. Roles are characterized by pre-established façades: a façade becomes institutionalized if it is kept socially constant, even if it involves playing different roles (Goffman 1969b: 29–33, 39–40; 1971: 27–31).

---

1 Concerning the characteristics of face-to-face meetings in Goffman's view, see Manning 2000: Psathas and Waksler 2000.

Roles

Roles are typical responses from individuals who hold particular positions, and include obligations, expectations, and life conditions. Differently from actual responses, i.e. from the real behaviors of these individuals, roles do not depend on how they perceive and define their situation. As analytical categories, roles do not determine the fate of the persons who perform them, but nonetheless they influence it, since real activities and behaviors correspond (to some extent, but not completely) to the number of roles, and to as many personal and social identities. The position of an individual, and the related system of activities and roles can be better analyzed in their specific space–time situation: it is characterized by the simultaneous presence, at the same time and in the same place, of other subjects, with whom he/she visibly intertwines his/her activities. These direct, face-to-face interactions are social occasions when they are characterized by a particular event: meetings, when all participants are reciprocally and directly present; encounters or engagements, when there is a common center of visual or cognitive attention, towards which all of them show mutual availability.

The subject who performs a situated role has a variety of selves or personal identities, distinct from the official definition of the situation. The subject stresses these identities by means of a personal style in performing social roles, and distances him/herself from the role, or the roles, socially or officially attributed to him/her. Thus, a speaker involved in a lecture projects towards the audience a personal identity – by distancing himself, for instance, from the text with comments, or facing with performance problems (noise and other disturbances) – in the attempt to protect, as well as the situation (i.e. the lecture), his or her public image. Bearing in mind that roles do not refer to individuals, but rather to performed functions, we can also understand that single individuals can distance themselves from a role, and address to themselves, playing from time to time different roles. They reply to their own statements – that is to say, to what they had previously said – or stop a conversation in which they were taking part, to comment upon the meaning of these statements. The pronoun "I," when different roles are played by the same individual, shows different aspects, in the sense of personal identities, of his/her self.

On the other hand, the plurality of selves, or social identities, can reveal itself in the simultaneous performance of several normatively defined roles. So a surgeon can illustrate for didactic purposes an operation as soon as he performs it, playing at the same time two institutional roles which correspond to as many social identities. A speaker performs a variety of roles and social identities in front of an audience, since he enunciates a text and becomes an entertainer, trying in this role, with several devices, to give the audience the appearance of speaking in a spontaneous way, as if the text had been expressly prepared for that particular audience and for that occasion. The relation between an individual's personal and social identities corresponds to the prevailing interpretative pattern in a given social situation, and to the personal characteristics of the person who performs the role. The full undertaking of a particular social self – that is to say, embracing a role – is thwarted by the plurality of personal and social identities, which become relevant in performing situated roles (Goffman 1961b: 7–14, 87–8, 92–7, 134–5, 152; 1974: 288–90, 519–20, 573–4; 1983: 7; 1987: 80–82, 233–60; 1988b: 160–65).

Face

Different from the façade, through which individuals show themselves to others, is the face; i.e., the positive image individuals have of themselves, which can be shared also by others. Individuals are attached to their face, or image, and by showing tact they give evidence of their comprehension of the others' face. In order to preserve their face, in presenting themselves (and their personal identity), individuals have to reveal a consistent image as socially required when the contact is legitimate and institutionalized. When, instead, their image is unsuited to the situation, that is to say, when elements that are extraneous to the situation insert themselves in the interaction, and the rules of the encounter are no longer observed, individuals lose face. They compromise in this way their future image, unless the encounter is occasional or it is possible to give the others the impression of never having lost it (save face). Therefore, the face is not a person's attribute, but rather it is attributed and removed by the other participants in the interaction, by virtue of social norms. Society demands demeanor by rewarding composure, dignity and other character qualities; this is so especially in the presence of events, which involve uncertain and potentially serious consequence. Society, however, punishes with isolation and coercion those who do not behave in a socially correct way (as, for example, insane persons).

Society reserves deference to those who show demeanor. Preserving one's face is a presupposition of the social order, and therefore, it is normatively required through actions and behaviors able to make our actions consistent with the image we want to give of ourselves (face work). Losing face is the proof that we are not able to bear an encounter, and that we cannot exhibit an acceptable self. This would involve for all participants the impossibility to be confident in other people's similar pretensions, and ultimately to keep a social order. As a matter of fact, participants in an encounter have to conform to a ritual order, which demands to preserve their image, whether individual or collective, if any. Social order is resistant: interpersonal face-to-face relations resist in general to systematic violations, at least in the short run. Any violation of this order, and hence, any disorganization of interpersonal relations, especially face-to-face ones, and the consequent difficulty or impossibility for bystanders to give a sense to the situation, represents a negative experience. This kind of experience can be either involuntarily produced, for example by those who hold a visible stigma or by anybody else who is compelled to get out of all interactions because he/she is temporarily blocked by uncontrollable emotions; or voluntarily, as by Pirandello in his dramas, or by the actors of the *Living Theater*. It is pointed out by a growing continuum of agitation, progressively revealed by embarrassment, bewilderment and uneasiness for the bystanders. For the involuntary author of a negative experience, saving face – showing him/herself as an actor able to establish social relations again – means therefore saving the situation of the encounter, and with it, the social order in both its cognitive and normative aspects (in the previously mentioned senses) (Goffman 1961a: 305–308; 1963: 138; 1971: 234–5, 240–41; 1974: 378–438, 493–5; 1983a: 5; 1988b: 3–4, 7–18, 35–6, 49–50, 99–104, 151, 245–73).

Goffman's Sociology: Its Relations with Other Perspectives and Its Interpretations

Goffman explicitly relates to some contemporary or preceding sociological perspectives. We shall mention here those statements by Goffman, which concern the relations of continuity or discontinuity between Goffman, and other sociologists and theoretical perspectives. Reference will be made to the symbolic-interactionist perspective, as represented by Mead and Blumer, with the phenomenological perspective, as represented by Schutz and Garfinkel, and with Durkheim's functionalism. Based on these references, we shall also briefly examine some interpretations of Goffman's sociology.

Mead, Blumer and Symbolic Interactionism

The passages in which Goffman takes a stand on his intellectual debt to Mead and Blumer are not numerous, but since they are explicit statements they prove extremely interesting. These statements, whether of continuity or discontinuity, can be mainly drawn from his writings and also, in a subordinate position, from an interview issued in 1980 (see Verhoeven 1980). In the interview, Goffman declares he is "unsophisticated" in his epistemological knowledge and choices, but recalls his intellectual relationship, in the years of his higher education, with some representatives of Symbolic Interactionism, such as Cooley, Hughes, Strauss, Becker, Meltzer, Mead (and pragmatism in general), and Blumer, praising the last's wide-ranging perspective used in studying social action. He furthermore reminds us that he had not been a pupil of Blumer, adding that he does not consider appropriate the designation of Symbolic Interactionism coined by Blumer to indicate this theoretical current of thought. To Blumer, Goffman objects the too abstract nature of his research, underlined by the lack of both ethnographic studies, and attention to the organized – and hence, not freely fluctuating – character of social life.

At the same time, Goffman declares his continuity of interests, and even epistemology, with Durkheim and his anthropological school, and particularly with Radcliffe-Brown. His sharing Durkheim's positivism does not extend, however, to the language of quantitative sociological research, which recalls and imitates the language of natural science (he refers in this case to Lazarsfeld and his sociological school). Goffman reminds with approval Weber's epistemological principle of value freedom. Talking about Parsons, he shows to appreciate his well-known book on the structure of social action, and his having introduced Durkheim's and Weber's thought in the United States. In general, Goffman declares to be close to Parsons' and Merton's structural-functionalism as regards their continuity with the early functionalist anthropology. We shall dwell, in the next pages, on Goffman's intellectual relation with Parsons' functionalism. His statements of continuity with other authors can be summarized as follows:

1. The symbolic-interactionist perspective is adopted by Goffman with an explicit reference to James and Blumer. According to this perspective, which is here referred to in the version provided by Goffman, all that is real depends, within the overall organization of social life, on the consensual definition of a situation given by the individuals who participate in it, where each one of them adopts the other participants' point of view. Communications are of a symbolic nature, and the symbol must be understood by participants, though it has not to be necessarily visible. Social conditions outline, along with situations, also participants' personal characteristics, and with them, the required involvement and deference degree. These social conditions are subject to interpretation and negotiation, since the image of each individual among the other participants in the situation results from them. The interpretation of any situation is made through shared interpretative frames (Goffman 1961a: 47–8, 138–41; 1969b: 20, 291; 1971: 198–241; 1974: 1–2, 345–7, 506–11, 560–64; 1987: 111–12, 224; 1988a: 165; 1988b: 288).

2. To every individual who holds a position (in the sense in which, according to Goffman, Blumer uses this term) a "self" in socially attributed; a "me" corresponds to this self when the individual conforms to the social pressure (Goffman 1961b: 87–8, 93).

3. For any individual, the "me" cannot incorporate his/her "I." When we talk about ourselves speaking to others, there is in any case an "I," which is addressing to different persons (Goffman 1987: 205).

The statements in which Goffman, instead, distances himself from Symbolic Interactionism are the following:

1. Though it is possible to speak of a social definition of the situation, single individuals do not usually create this definition, and often continue to accept the terms in which the social conditions have been negotiated by them or by others. In addition, these definition and negotiation processes are not the only social organization principles, as the participants in a situation may not intend it in the same way, or may differently intend its temporal extent and, for each participant, the retrospective characterization of an event or of a social occasion may be quite different from his or her lived experience (Goffman 1974: 1–2, 7–10). Furthermore, Goffman does not stress, as instead Blumer does, the symbolic mediation in the definitions of situations; but rather the rules that govern interpersonal relations among actors who intend to rationally act (Fine and Manning 2000: 470).

2. Individuals do not passively take towards themselves the attitudes the others show towards them. If, by providing deference, the others contribute to form the "self" of an individual, he/she is not only obliged to show demeanor in exchange, but is also responsible for his/her image of demeanor, and for the others' image of deference (Goffman 1988b: 92).

3. When in an interaction participants pursue their interests in a calculated way, even to the detriment of those of the others (a strategic interaction, in Goffman's words), then each one takes the others' point of view, only insofar as it is useful to him/her (Goffman 1969b: 8, 122–3). Furthermore, considering participants' competition, it is not advisable ("whatever Mead may say") to simply put ourselves in the place of the others and attribute them our qualities of ability. We must, instead, imagine how much ability the other has, and act accordingly. In general, compared with Mead's social psychology and Blumer's Symbolic Interactionism, the strategic perspective – Goffman argues – distinguishes itself in that it is the only one that assumes a complete interdependence of results, players' reciprocal awareness of it, and their ability to use it, focusing on the conditions and awareness of this knowledge (Goffman 1988: 20, 91–2, 165–6).

4. A child's socialization takes place in a different way from what Mead maintains. Goffman argues that when a child learns to speak, it does not acquire a "generalized other," and consequently, Mead used

a wrong term; but rather the ability to speak in the name of other figures which, jointly considered, form a casual and heterogeneous gathering. At the beginning, these figures are toy-beings that are at hand (dolls, teddy bears, etc.), which are "particularized others." The child then learns, in the following years, to use language in this self-dissociate and imaginative way (Goffman 1987: 208). On the other hand, the concepts of play and game, which have great importance in Mead's theory of socialization, are not used by Goffman for this purpose or in this sense. Rather, they are used – in keeping with a strategic perspective – for the purpose of illustrating how a situation, which is defined as a game, obliges participants to act according to pre-established rules. These concepts are therefore used in the sense of those expressed by the game theory (Goffman 1961b: 34–7; see also, in general, Goffman 1969b).

Schutz, Garfinkel and the Phenomenological Perspective

Goffman considers the phenomenological tradition – the main representatives of which, in sociology, are Schutz and Garfinkel – from a very specific point of view. Goffman connects the ideas of these authors to the phenomenology of Husserl, who was the teacher of Schutz and his main point of intellectual reference, but he also underlines with greater insistence their continuity relation with the pragmatist philosopher William James. Continuity results, he argues, from a common interest in the study of the "worlds of meaning," or "finite provinces of meaning." In Goffman's opinion, James and Schutz intend to point out through these expressions the condition of reality that (a) is attributed to what is experienced, (b) what becomes, whether in fact or potentially, a subject of selective attention. It is therefore provided with symbolic boundaries, which distinguishes it from other spheres of experience; (c) what may belong to the world of nature or to the socio-cultural world, or to an imaginary world. Garfinkel's sociological contribution consists, according to Goffman, in extending the theme of multiple realities for the purpose of identifying the different "worlds" of meaning (Goffman 1974: 1–8, 347, 560–63).

Goffman declares to be James' continuer, but he shares, though not explicitly, the correction brought by Schutz, who argues that the different "worlds" have a socio-cultural, rather than objective, existence (Goffman 1974: 8–10). However, he distinguishes his own sociological contribution from the one derived from phenomenology (relating in this context Schutz and Husserl). The interpretative patterns, which give sense and organization to a lived experience, are in his opinion of social, and hence collective, origin. Therefore every beginning and every end of a particular activity, which is endowed with sense and organization (a theater performance, for instance), cannot be interpreted phenomenologically. It cannot, accordingly, be brought back to the phenomenological procedure of "putting in brackets" any common sense or scientific knowledge, in order to identify the mere lived experience as it presents itself to the consciousness of single persons, and in particular to phenomenologically oriented scholars.

Goffman does not discuss whether it is useful to use this procedure in the area of natural and social science, but limits himself to state that it useless for his research on the organization of social life (Goffman 1974: 250–52). To Schutz (and James), he objects that they have not specified the criteria for identifying the different "worlds" of meaning and their constitutive rules, and for distinguishing between primary and secondary interpretation patterns. In addition, they have not specified whether there is a single rule that distinguishes the world of dreams from the world of everyday life. Furthermore, Schutz has not sufficiently argued his thesis, according to which the transition from a "world" of experience to another is traumatic. (Goffman 1974: 5–6, 26, 347, 561–4).

Durkheim, Parsons and the Stuctural-Functionalist Perspective

Goffman usually makes, implicitly in most cases, a number of references to Durkheim's and Parsons' structural-functionalism. In particular, these references concern Durkheim's well-known theses on society as the origin and condition of morality. As a consequence, there would be equivalence between social and moral order, and rituals would be aimed at strengthening the connection between individuals and this order (Durkheim 1978: 169–73, 213–16; 1999: 389–91) As for Parsons' approach, he mentions the problem, which exists in any society, of how quite different elements in its population keep effective engagements compatible with social interest, and hence, with the existing normative order (Parsons 1964: 267–8). As it has been done with the other theoretical perspectives that have been previously considered, we shall refer here to the points in which Goffman approaches this perspective, as well as those in which he argues his dissent.

Among those belonging to the first group, we wish to point out the following propositions:

1. In a society there are widespread moral values which are reaffirmed at periodical intervals through ceremonies. The atmosphere of excitement resulting from them contributes to put even considerable differences in power among the participants in the background. Therefore ceremonies perform a function of social cohesion which combines with norms of respect and distance towards the single individuals, even if of a lower status. In this regard, Goffman explicitly refers to Durkheim (Goffman 1961a: 107–109; 1969b: 48, 81; 1987: 250).
2. In every interaction, from the most fleeting to the most lasting one, and especially in every talk, a "stabilized normative structure," or "normative order," is established (Goffman 1988b: 4. See also 1983a: 5; 1983b: 27–30), which is supported by expressive coherence required to individuals (Goffman 1969b: 63–9).
3. Any violation of the constitutive norms of this order, in particular through improper behaviors, such as they can be observed in psychotic subjects, has destructive effects on the social organization. Therefore psychiatrists do not act differently from policemen since they play the role of guardians of the moral and the social order (Goffman 1961a: 365–6; 1988b, pp. 151–65).

However, Goffman detaches himself for other aspects from the structural-functionalist perspective:

In general:

1. Goffman's sociology, focusing on direct interactions, keeps to a micro-sociological point of view which is opposed to the macro-sociological point of view of this perspective, even though it is useful to study the social structure.
2. Normative order is not necessarily consensual: what is considered desirable order from the point of view of a few, may be perceived as exclusion and repression from the point of view of others, and involve mortifications to the "self," which produce strains among those who suffer such mortifications (Goffman 1983a: 5–6; see also 1961a: 47–8, 83–92).
3. The maintenance of a normative order by means of cooperative attitudes and behaviors does not mean adhesion to it, but can rather result from a variety of different reasons (Goffman 1983a: 5).

In particular:

1. When there is a strong disparity in power among participants, the moral-normative order and the solidarity expressed through ceremonies are, in Goffman's opinion (and in contrast with Durkheim), a pretense which participants are aware of. Therefore, their participation depends on reasons that have nothing to do with sentiments of solidarity. These sentiments, which concern the links between individuals and social structure, are necessary for an individual commitment to the ceremony rather than for strengthening the set of social resources from which they originate (Goffman 1961a: 109–11; 1983a: 10).
2. The moral-normative order (Goffman argues, in contrast with Parsons) can find adhesion for reasons that differ from a firm belief in its legitimacy and justice. If desirable for a few, this order may involve exclusion and repression from the point of view of others (Goffman 1983a: 5–6).

Notes on the Reception of Goffman's Sociology

We shall point out and consider some interpretations to which Goffman's sociology has been subject to during the last quarter of the twentieth century. These interpretations have been selected either because they are particularly significant in themselves, or because they indicate particular interpretive tendencies. We shall first focus on some structuralist and functionalist interpretations of Goffman, then we shall briefly mention some other interpretative contributions, with particular reference to those by Collins and Giddens. However, we shall first mention an important exegetic contribution to the dramaturgic theme in Goffman's sociology. The authors of this contribution (Messinger, Sampson and Towne 2000) maintain that Goffman, through his metaphor of social life as theater, did not intend to say that social actors actually sense themselves as if they were professional actors engaged in a theater performance. The theater metaphor is instead an expedient used by Goffman to call attention to how social actors create, through their action, independently from their will, impressions of themselves in other actors. These impressions – no matter whether and how much grounded – change the behaviors of all participants in an interaction. On the contrary, professional actors do not primarily worry about the impressions they produce in others, but rather about how they succeed in making the characters they perform on the stage credible to the audience.

Concerning Goffman's late work *Frame Analysis* (1974), it aroused considerable interest and discussion. In a relevant exegetic contribution written soon after the publication of this book (1976), the modernist and postmodernist scholar Fredric Jameson remarks that Goffman seems uncertain between the aim to analyze the theme of "frame" – i.e. an interpretative pattern of events – as revelation of a reality that transcends individual experiences, and instead – in continuity with Goffman's previous production –aim to preserve, through the concept of actor, the metaphor of social life as theater. George Gonos, in an essay published in the following year, distinguishes himself for having oriented further and subsequent interpretations to a new direction as compared to Goffman's previous positioning among symbolic-interactionist sociologists. Gonos recognizes the foundations for a structuralist, rather than an interactionist, interpretation of Goffman in the analytical categories formulated in his *Frame Analysis*.

According to Gonos, through an analysis of the interpretative patterns of reality ("frames"), Goffman intends to highlight the rules that uniformly orient the definitions of individual situations and the conducts that prevail in them. These rules anchor any interaction focalized on the wider social organization. Thus, they provide social life with a structure, and hence, with stability. Social actors are unaware of these rules, and therefore, they do not contribute to interpreting and defining the situations through their subjectivity and their interaction. Situations do not result from a set of pre-existing norms and values. From the social structure instead – intended as a "framework of frames" made of microstructures, or "frames" – result both the definitions of the situations and the "selves" of those who take part in them (Gonos 1977; see also Trifiletti 1991: 378–81). Gonos's interpretation is as well-known as controversial (see Fine, Manning and Smith 2000: xxxi). We only mention here some objections that have been formulated. In the first place, it has been remarked that the attention paid by Goffman to rituals as constitutive elements of society is in close continuity not only with Durkheim's thought (Cahill 2000: 388–9), as Gonos argues, but also with Radcliffe-Brown's and Warner's. These authors were two Anglo-Saxon anthropologists influenced by Durkheim (Collins 2000: 314–24).

It has been objected that the whole conceptual apparatus used in *Frame Analysis* suits a dual conception of reality, as an objective reality that is stable and not precarious from the point of view of an external observer, in line with Gonos's and other commentators' "structuralist" interpretation (see Denzin and Keller 1981),[2] but also as a structure subjectively – and therefore differently –perceived by the participants in the collective construction of the "frame (Hazelrigg 1992). Furthermore, Goffman's continuity relation with Symbolic Interactionism is considered undeniable by some qualified scholars (Baert 1998: 76–77; Fine 1990: 124; Williams 1986: 349, 363). As a matter of fact, this relation is documented in Goffman's production by explicit connections with Mead and Blumer, and with Symbolic Interactionism as a choice sociological perspective. Quite often, in *Frame Analysis* too, we find, in particular references to the interactionist category of "definition of the situation." From a symbolic-interactionist point of view, nothing prevents each participant in the situation from putting him/herself in the other's place and from collectively providing this definition

---

2 As a matter of fact, Denzin's and Kaller's interpretative thesis, even if substantially in line with Gonos's thesis they explicitly refer to, differentiates from it due to its strongly critical nature towards Goffman, which prompted his reply. (2000). See, in this connection, Hazelrigg 1992.

(Goffman 1961a: 47–8, 137–41; 1961b: 19, 93; 1969b: 11, 16, 20, 291; 1971: 165; 1974: 255, 508–509, 572–3; 1987: 111–12, 222–30; 1988a: 20, 165–6).

In this connection, quite relevant are some statements made by Goffman in an interview dating back to 1980, shortly before his untimely death. Referring to Blumer, Goffman says he considers his methodological and epistemological writings very congenial. Still, his own sociology has not – Goffman avers – the psychological and social character of Blumer's approach (Goffman 2000: 215). Collins (2000: 73–4), too, has dwelt on Goffman's intellectual ties with Blumer, and with other representatives of Symbolic Interactionism as Thomas, Cooley, and Mead. He has stressed, however, Goffman's distance from these authors. This relation remains, in any case, controversial. Blumer, for his part, showed great appreciation towards Goffman, whom he defined an "innovative scholar of high order" (Blumer 2000: 3), but he objected that the scope of Goffman's investigation was too narrow, especially as regards face-to-face relations between social actors; this is the more so as they are not considered in a temporal perspective (Blumer 2000, 6–8).

The authors who inspired Goffman, as he himself declared – namely, James and Schutz – belong to different and incompatible traditions of thought, as compared to Durkheim and structural-functionalism in general (Goffman 1974: 2–8, 560). Gonos mentions Goffman's possible proximity to Durkheim, since they share a common structuralist sociological orientation (Gonos 1977: 855). For Goffman, social reality has not necessarily the stability and the binding nature, which Gonos's interpretation attributes to it; this was argued at least by a part of the secondary literature, as previously shown. Keeping to the writings by Goffman himself, even in total institutions, which are characterized by their coercive nature towards residents, social reality is precarious (Goffman 1961a: 111). As Goffman writes in *Frame Analysis* – it occurs in general when there is ambiguity in the interpretative pattern that has to be applied in particular circumstances, and also when it is not possible to rigidly determine the sequence of the turns of talk, as usually happens in everyday life (Goffman 1974: 303–308, 510–11). A Durkheimian interpretation of Goffman was proposed on several occasions by Pier Paolo Giglioli, and partly, also by Randall Collins.

According to Giglioli, Goffman's basic intuitions consist in formulating at a micro-sociological level two crucial statements made by Durkheim. The first one maintains that divinity is the product of collective rituals. The second one recalls Durkeim's thesis of the cult of the individual in modern society. It is, however, applied to Goffman's numerous statements about the importance of interaction rituals and frames in the local construction (i.e. in specific situations) of the selves or of individual identities. Giglioli conjectures that Goffman has drawn the instruments to analyze the selves from Durkheim and not from Symbolic Interactionism (Giglioli 1997: xiv–xxii, xxv, note 14; see also 1984, 1987: 21). Giglioli's reasoning can be opposed by means of the same objections previously addressed to Gonos and, in general, to the Durkheimian-structuralist interpretations. It has to be noted that the functionalist interpretation of rituals, as formulated by Durkheim, was accepted only with reservations by Goffman, who actually judged it not completely persuasive (Goffman 1961a: 109–10). What is more, Giglioli fails here to distinguish between personal and social identity. This distinction, which is very important in Goffman, is absent in Durkheim (Goffman 1963b: 2–3, 55–7).

Collins' interpretation (1992) coincides with Giglioli's in some aspects, but distances itself from it in other relevant aspects. Collins, like Giglioli, underlines Durkheim's influence on Goffman as regards the sacred character attributed to interaction rituals, and consequently, the sacredness of the individual self that forms through these rituals. However, Collins recognizes in Goffman's sociology a distinction among different degrees of sacredness in interactive rituals. In a maximum degree of sacredness, only the sacred object produced by the ritual asserts itself to the attention of the public, and the fact that it is a ritual is forgotten. In contrast, a minimum degree is characterized by informality and loss of sacredness in ritual performances. Furthermore, Collins tackles the theme of a multiplicity of the selves, as formed and revealed in a variety of interactive contexts.

This is a difficult and controversial issue (Fine 1990: 123). Collins remarks – in agreement with Giglioli – that Goffman considers the idea of a unitary self a myth. However, in his opinion, there is in Goffman a "self" underlying the different "selves" acting in the situation. This "self" reveals itself as a "motivational central unit," in the sense that individuals are not only allowed to orient themselves among alternative frames; but they also to use the other roles as a backstage, so that they are not completely absorbed by the obligations of the role, which must be performed immediately (Collins 1992: 257, 260–63, 315, 322–6, 371–3, 410–11). Collins does not completely agree on a Durkheimian interpretation of Goffman's thought, and deals in some detail with the theme of the unity of the personal identity in this author. Collins maintains that in Goffman there is a continuum in the abstraction degrees of the frames, from a micro-sociological to a macro-sociological analytical level. However, he does not examine this issue in depth (Collins 1992: 371–5) while it is at the center of the attention Giddens addressed to this author.

In Giddens' opinion, Goffman has provided – especially with his notion of focalized encounter or interaction, which involves the presence at the same time and in the same space of two or more persons, who are tactful and show to trust each other – some important analytical categories; for they are instrumental to highlight the ritualized conducts through which social systems establish and re-establish themselves in everyday life. In general, social actors know frames, and they put them into practice in their interactions, which take place in specific spatial and temporal contexts and in the co-presence of several persons. These frames give stability to social life. Consequently, social actors continuously establish and re-establish the institutions with competence, and root them in their everyday conducts, or practices. However, while the social actors exhibit their image of "face" to others, they engage their self-esteem, unlike theater actors who give life to a character. So, Giddens does not find fully appropriate Goffman's metaphor of social life as theater. In addition, he remarks that Goffman does not provide any indication about the limits and the ways in which social actors' competence reveals itself (Giddens 1984: 36–7, 66–83, 86–90, 124–5, 154–8).

In Giddens' opinion, ritualized conduct and frames allow considering Goffman's sociology relevant both to a micro-sociological and a macro-sociological analysis. Giddens does not aim at interpreting Goffman's texts as an objective, which is an end in itself, despite the interest and the textual accuracy of his reception of this author. He rather aims rather at incorporating their contributions to the formulation of his own sociological theory (Giddens 1984: 36–7). Another remarkable interpretation of Goffman, which also makes use of the notion of "frame" to formulate a personal sociological theory, is the one outlined by Travers (1992). This commentator reconsiders, as well as Goffman, also Garfinkel and the contribution of Durkheim's notion of anomy to the theories of both authors. Travers argues that this notion implies neither the destruction of the interpretative frame, as Goffman maintains, nor the unintelligibility of interactions performed in everyday life, as Garfinkel maintains. On the contrary, anomy – intended as uncertainty, confusion, non-determination, and incoherence – is in Travers' opinion, the foundation of social life. In its course, the participants in an interaction assiduously commit themselves to create an appearance of normality and stability, though this appearance is continuously called into question by the burst on the scene of unpredictable events, which are extraneous to the common definition of the situation.

Laura Bovone has dwelt on the theme of a connection between micro and macro, focusing in particular on Goffman. After having underlined the variety of sources that inspired Goffman (his dramaturgic approach would be "an expression of the eclecticism of contemporary sociology"), and having stated "his way of investigating … is absolutely at a micro level" (Bovone 1988: 25–6), she supports an interpretation of Goffman as a sociologist of the postmodern. In her opinion, Goffman makes use of a micro-sociological method to study both micro-phenomena, as encounters and interaction order, and macro-phenomena as social structures. In both cases, Goffman is "an interpreter of cultural trends that are progressively asserting themselves," namely those of postmodern sociology, characterized by their "emphasizing the communicative moment rather than the contents to be communicated." Individuals and society are no longer opposed, and "individuals can save themselves only by saving the situation" (Bovone 1992: 58–9).

Some objections can be expressed against this interpretation, in the light not only of Goffman's texts, but also of a part of the secondary literature. First, also in Goffman's late production, there are references to classical authors, as Durkheim and Mead, who are still significant for an analysis of the contents of communication (usually, for instance, in a lecture or in spontaneous talks) rather than for an analysis of the "communicative moment" (Goffman 1987: 205, 250). Secondly, Goffman paid attention to the connections between social structures and interaction order and to those prerequisites of a communication, which can make our behavior intelligible to others (Goffman 1983a: 9; 1983b: 50–51). Communication involves, therefore, trust in the existence of a relatively stable social structure and interactive order. These issues are exactly those critically discussed by the postmodern sociological school of thought (Kellner 1990: 266–7; Thomas and Walsh 1998: 383–4). Moreover, Goffman is eclectic, since he draws a part of his conceptual apparatus from several authors who preceded him. Nonetheless, his eclecticism does not mean that he gives up formulating explanations: for example, by investigating which are the basic comprehension patterns (or frames) available in our society to make events intelligible (Goffman 1974: 10). This contrasts with the tendency of a part of postmodern sociology to reject any attempt to formulate social theory (Kellner 1990: 277–8).

It is perhaps preferable to connect Goffman with some classical authors of the sociological thought as Weber; for Weber rejected deterministic explanations that simplify too much the different aspects and meanings of life experience (Dal Lago 1981: 509–11), but indicated what are the foundations of social order and the constitutive elements of the structure. The methods Goffman availed himself of, too, have been subject to commentators' attention and discussions. There is, however, a widespread consensus about Goffman's refusal to abide by the customary research methods, as used in sociology or social psychology for the collection and analysis of data and for the formulation of concepts. Goffman formulated a limited number of concepts, which are central in all his works (core concepts), in response to these critical observations. Examples of these core concepts are the words "occasion" and "move." By the first term, Goffman intends to designate the structuring context of action, while by the second, he refers to all that an actor conveys to others when it is his/her turn to act. In any case, as it has been argued, in Goffman's opinion, concepts are not means that aim at developing an ever-increasing sociological knowledge; they are rather provisional elaborations, which have been formulated for the purpose of analyzing specific research objects (R. Williams 2000).

The research method followed by Goffman and his epistemology have been subject to conflicting evaluations. The author's peculiar lack of attention – and apparently, lack of interest, too – to methodological and epistemological matters has disconcerted some of his commentators. This may be one of the reasons of their different interpretations, appraisals, and misunderstandings. The use of the dramaturgic model seem to have contributed to this result, since it has suggested a misleading image of the author as a cynical and detached interpreter to some of Goffman's scholars, and in particular to Gouldner (1970: 380–86). It has been maintained (but objected, at the same time) that this image has contributed to explain an alleged lack of recognition among academics and scholars (see Posner 2000a, 2000b), In this connection, Oromaner (2000) reminds us that Goffman's work has not only received very positive appraisal from some important reviews of the American and British sociological communities, and has been frequently quoted but also that even some of those scholars who have harshly criticized Goffman have shown their appreciation for Goffman's work.

References

Baert, P. 1998. *Social Theory in the Twentieth Century*. Cambridge: Polity Press.

Blumer, H. 2000. Action vs. Interaction: Relations in Public-Macrostudies of the Public Order by Erving Goffman, in G.A. Fine and G.W.H. Smith (eds), *Erving Goffman* Volume 4. London: Sage, 3–8.

Bourdieu, P. 2000. Erving Goffman: Discoverer of the Infinitely Small, in G.A. Fine and G.W.H. Smith (eds), *Erving Goffman*, Volume 1. London: Sage, 3–4.

Bovone, L. 1988. Micro–macro: Una dialettica congenita della sociologia, in L. Bovone and G. Rovati (eds), *Sociologie micro sociologie macro*. Milan: Vita e Pensiero, 7–37.

Bovone, L. 1992. Goffman: micro o macro?, in L. Bovone and G. Rovati (eds), *L'ordine dell'interazione. La sociologia di Erving Goffman*. Milan: Vita e Pensiero, 47–63.

Cahill, S.E. 2000. Following Durkheim into the Public Realm, in G.A. Fine and G.W.H. Smith (eds), *Erving Goffman*, Volume 4. London: Sage, 386–400.

Collins, R. 1992. *Teorie sociologiche*. Bologna: Il Mulino.

Collins, R. 2000. The Passing of Intellectual Generations, in G.A. Fine and G.W.H. Smith (eds), *Erving Goffman* Volume 1. London: Sage, 71–83.

Dal Lago, A. 1981. "Profondità e pericolo nella vita quotidiana. Note sul mondo sociale di Erving Goffman." *Il Mulino* 30: 500–12.

Denzin, N. and Keller, C.M. 1981. Frame Analysis Reconsidered, in G.A. Fine and G.W.H. Smith (eds), *Erving Goffman*, Volume 2. London: Sage, 65–78.

Durkheim, E. 1978. *Antologia di scritti sociologici*, ed. A. Izzo. Bologna: Il Mulino.

Durkheim, E. 1999. *La divisione del lavoro sociale*. Turin: Edizioni di Comunità.

Fine, G.A. 1990. Symbolic Interactionism in the Post-Blumerian Age, in G. Ritzer (ed.), *Frontiers of Social Theory: The New Synthesis*. New York: Columbia University Press, 117–57.

Fine, G.A. and Manning, P. 2000. Erving Goffman, in G. Ritzer (ed.), *The Blackwell Companion to Major Social Theorists*. Oxford: Blackwell, 457–85.

Fine, G.A., Manning, P. and Smith, G.W.H. 2000. Introduction, in G.A. Fine and G.W.H. Smith (eds), *Erving Goffman* Volume 1. London: Sage, ix–xliv.

Giddens, A. 1984. *The Constitution of Society*. Cambridge: Polity Press.

Giglioli, P.P. 1984. "Una lettura durkheimiana di Goffman." *Rassegna Italiana di Sociologia* 25: 401–27.

Giglioli, P.P. 1987. Introduzione all'edizione italiana, in E. Goffman (ed.), *Forme del parlare*. Bologna: Il Mulino, 7–21.

Giglioli, P.P. 1997. Introduzione all'edizione italiana, in E. Goffman (ed.), *La vita quotidiana come rappresentazione*. Bologna: Il Mulino, ix–xxvii.

Goffman, E. 1959. *The Presentation of Self in Everyday Life*. New York: Doubleday.

Goffman, E. 1961a. *Asylums*. New York: Doubleday.

Goffman, E. 1961b. *Encounters*. Indianapolis, IN: Bobbs-Merril.

Goffman, E. 1963a. *Behavior in Public Places*. New York: The Free Press.

Goffman, E. 1963b. *Stigma*. Englewood Cliffs, NJ: Prentice Hall.

Goffman, E. 1967. *Interaction Ritual*. New York: Doubleday.

Goffman, E. 1969a. *Strategic Interaction*. Philadelphia, PA: University of Philadelphia Press.

Goffman, E. 1969b. *La vita quotidiana come rappresentazione*. Bologna: Il Mulino.

Goffman, E. 1970. *Stigma*. Bari: Laterza.

Goffman, E. 1971. *Il comportamento in pubblico*. Turin: Einaudi.

Goffman, E. 1974. *Frame Analysis*. New York: Harper & Row.

Goffman, E. 1981. *Forms of Talk*. Philadelphia, PA: University of Pennsylvania Press.

Goffman, E. 1983a. "The Interaction Order." *American Sociological Review* 48: 1–17.

Goffman, E. 1983b. "Felicity's Condition." *American Journal of Sociology*, 89: 1–53.

Goffman, E. 1987. *Forme del parlare*. Bologna: Il Mulino.

Goffman, E. 1988a. *L'interazione strategica*. Bologna: Il Mulino.

Goffman, E. 1988b. *Il rituale dell'interazione*. Bologna: Il Mulino.

Goffman, E. 1992. L'ordine dell'interazione, in L. Bovone and G. Rovati (eds), *L'ordine dell'interazione. La sociologia di Erving Goffman*. Milan: Vita e Pensiero, 3–44.

Goffman, E. 2000. A Reply to Denzin and Keller, in G.A. Fine and G.W.H. Smith (eds), *Erving Goffman*, Volume 4. London: Sage, 79–90.

Gonos, G. 1977. "'Situation' Versus 'Frame': The 'Interactionist' and the 'Structuralist' Analyses of Everyday Life.'" *American Sociological Review* 42: 854–67.

Gouldner, A. 1970. *The Coming Crisis of Western Sociology*. New York: Basic Books.

Hazelrigg, L. 1992. "Reading Goffman's Framing as Provocation of a Discipline." *Human Studies* 15(2–3): 239–64.

Jameson, F. 1976. "On Goffman's *Frame Analysis*." *Theory and Society* 3: 119–33.

Kellner, D. 1990. The Postmodern Turn: Positions, Problems, and Prospects, in G. Ritzer (ed.), *Frontiers of Social Theory: The New Synthesis*. New York: Columbia University Press, 255–86.

MacIntyre, A. 2000. The Self as Work of Art, in G.A. Fine and G.W.H. Smith (eds), *Erving Goffman*, Volume 2. London: Sage, 333–6.

Manning, P.K. 2000. The Decline of Civility: A Comment on Erving Goffman's Sociology, in G.A. Fine and G.W.H. Smith (eds), *Erving Goffman*, Volume 2. London: Sage, 329–47.

Messinger, S.L., Sampson, H. and Towne, R.D. 2000. Life as Theater: Some Notes on the Dramaturgic Approach to Social Reality, in G.A. Fine and G.W.H. Smith (eds), *Erving Goffman*, Volume 2. London: Sage, 213–24.

Oromaner, M. 2000. Erving Goffman and the Academic Community, in G.A. Fine and G.W.H. Smith (eds), *Erving Goffman*, Volume 1. London: Sage, 213–36.

Parsons, T. 1964. *Social Structure and Personality*. New York: The Free Press.

Posner, J. 2000a. Erving Goffman: His Presentation of Self, in G.A. Fine and G.W.H. Smith (eds), *Erving Goffman*, Volume 1. London: Sage, 99–113.

Posner, J. 2000b. Rebuttal to Oromaner Paper, in G.A. Fine and G.W.H. Smith (eds), *Erving Goffman*, Volume 1. London: Sage, 120–21.

Psathas, G. and Waksler, F. 2000. Essential Features of Face-to-Face Interaction, in G.A. Fine and G.W.H. Smith (eds), *Erving Goffman*, Volume 4. London: Sage, 9–30.

Thomas, H. and Walsh, D. 1998. Modernity/Postmodernity, in C. Jencks (ed.), *Core Sociological Dichotomies*. London: Sage, 363–90.

Travers, A. 1992. "*Strangers to Themselves:* How Interactants Are Other than They Are." *The British Journal of Sociology* 43(4): 601–37.

Trifiletti, R. 1991. *L'identità controversa*. Padova: CEDAM.

Verhoeven, J.C. 2000. An Interview with Erving Goffman, 1980, in G.A. Fine and G.W.H. Smith (eds), *Erving Goffman*, Volume 1. London: Sage, 213–36.

Watson, R. 2000. Reading Goffman on Interaction, in G.A. Fine and G.W.H. Smith (eds), *Erving Goffman*, Volume 2. London: Sage, 191–207.

Williams, R. 2000. Understanding Goffman's Method, in G.A. Fine and G.W.H. Smith (eds), *Erving Goffman*, Volume 2. London: Sage, 75–96.

Williams, S.J. 1986. "Appraising Goffman." *British Journal of Sociology* 37(3): 348–69.

Chapter 8
Jürgen Habermas

Preliminary Remarks

Jürgen Habermas (b. 1929) is an influential and well-known author both as a philosopher and as a sociologist not only in his native country, Germany, but also in other European and English-speaking countries (Outhwaite 2000: 664–5). We shall examine in this chapter first his theory of communicative action, then his critical appraisal of some classic and contemporary authors in the light of his theoretical approach; his thesis on the rationalization and colonization of the life world, and the consequences of these processes on communicative action; the public sphere as a legitimation source; and finally we shall briefly deal with the reception of his works. We have chosen to stress in this chapter the elements of thematic continuity of his thought, rather than suggest the presence of different development stages. Our exposition concerns above all the sociological thought of this author, and only in a subordinate position his philosophical thought (see, in particular, Habermas 2009: 5–24), even if these two directions of thought cannot be clearly distinguished. The works by Habermas of chiefly sociological content are many. We shall focus in particular on the *Theory of Communicative Action* (1997a, 1997b). Originally published in 1981, the *Theory of Communicative Action* is often considered the work in which Habermas's thought has found its most exhaustive expression (see, for example, Petrucciani 2004: 101; Rusconi 1997: 32; White 1988: 1). The exposition of its contents will be constantly supplemented with references to other works by this author.

The *Theory of Communicative Action*: Communicative Rationality and Claims to Truth

The two volumes of the *Theory of Communicative Action* are focused on the relation existing between rationality and communicative action. The first book of this work includes an extensive introduction to the theme of rationality in sociology, and preliminarily dwells on the concept of rationality in social sciences (Habermas 1997a: 55–228). Rationality, in an instrumental sense, is an action oriented to success. Communicative rationality means instead an action oriented to the agreement of the participants in a linguistically mediated interaction ("communicative agreement"). Agreement is an action-coordinating mechanism among different participants who interact with one another, each of them adopting the other's perspective (Habermas 1991, 1997a: 84; 2007: 187–8; 2009: 143).

Agreement should be discursively motivated, that is, it should draw on arguments which are logically convincing to all parties and which address valid topics. I should be effective for "a universal audience", and not only for the participants. Agreement takes place among subjects in the first place among those who directly participate in a communicative process. This process takes place, however, within the sphere of the same linguistic community, thereby assuming their common belonging to a shared life world and a shared background of knowledge, and lays validity claims (*Geltungsansprüche*) – which in principle are always objectionable – for all those who belong to this community, and not only for direct participants. Agreement – or mutual understanding – is, in this sense, of an objective nature (Habermas 1991). There may be claims to truth, to normative justness, and subjective truthfulness or sincerity. Finally, conformity to evaluation standards, such as moral or aesthetical standards, may support a validity claim as well. Validity terms refer to a kind of background knowledge which is intersubjectively shared by the participants in communication. Insofar as these general validity terms are complied with, the participants belong to a moral community which in principle is open to all, that is to say, a universal community.

Each participant in this community is prepared to rightfully include others who differ from him, without any discrimination, and protect their diversity. As Habermas writes, justice has indeed "universalistic implications" (Habermas 2001: 297; see also White 1988: 48–55). Those who lay validity claims participate in communicative processes. They adopt their perspective and expect that their listeners take a stand as regards those validity claims, that is to say, that they evaluate them by a "yes" or a "no." Communications which do not lay any validity claim are cases of communicative pathology (Habermas 1985b: 203–204; see also Borradori 2003: 71–6).

Understanding the meaning of any text means understanding the reason why an author considers his statements true, expressed values right, and the lived experiences reported in them truthful. Only the interpretations which meet all these conditions are rational. Social sciences have an interpretative – or hermeneutic – nature because they are responsible for rationally reconstructing and critically appraising the validity claims laid throughout a communicative process (Habermas 1985b: 203–209; 2001: 280–84, 292–4; 2008b: 9–10, 55, 82; 2009: 30–38, 166–8). If validity claims are mutually recognized, the participants in an interaction belong to a moral community. Habermas carefully considers Kohlberg's theory concerning the shaping of moral conscience. According to Kohlberg, each stage of this evolutionary process points out a relative equilibrium in making value operations of moral matters and reveals, in comparison with the previous stages, an increase in one's cognitive and social capabilities, and a progress in learning normative justness standards and impartiality, and an increase for a participant or an observer in his ability to adopt the perspective of others.

Kohlberg has committed himself to prove empirically that all moral development stages can be found in a variety of cultures, and consequently they are of a universal nature. Habermas remarks that, for Kohlberg, compared to the previous stages, each non-initial moral development stage is more appropriate not only from a psychological point of view but also from a normative one. Concerning this last aspect, however, it is not easy for Kohlberg to prove the superiority of the sixth evolutionary stage (achievement of a morals based on formal justice standards) in comparison with the previous one (achievement of utilitarian morals) by making use of a universal validity standard; for normative statements – in contrast to descriptive ones – "can neither be assessed nor falsified" (Habermas 2009: 61). Habermas formulates other objections which refer to the empirical validity of this evolutionary pattern. It is impossible – he argues – to empirically assess without any twisting and distortion whether the transition to the sixth moral development stage has occurred everywhere even in quite different contexts.

This stage, which along with the previous one is called post-conventional, is connoted not only by a subject's releasing from compliance with norms and principles adopted by particular groups, as happens in the previous evolutionary stage, but also by one's adhesion to universal moral principles of justice any rational subject should know, adopt and apply in the everyday argumentative praxis. Every action oriented to agreement assumes that this last moral development stage has been reached. In many cases, it is, however, impossible to ascertain what stage has been reached, since only respondents who have reached this stage can understand the questions and answer them appropriately. The other respondents, keeping to a conventional way of thinking, are not able to pass to a post-conventional way, and therefore cannot intersubjectively share their perspective with the interviewer's point of view (Habermas 1982: 259–60; 2009: 199–201).

Kohlberg bases his empirical theory on ethic presuppositions of a philosophical nature, such as cognitivism (moral judgments have a cognitive content), universalism (moral judgments claim universal validity) and formalism (moral judgments are of a procedural nature and consequently disregard not only any normative content, but also participants' motivations and the situation given from time to time). Habermas maintains that his discourse ethics is fully compatible with Kohlberg's empirical theory and moral presuppositions (Habermas 1994: 49–54, 68–9, 83–7; 2009: 38–47, 126–41, 168–82). Norms and moral rules – even if not assessable – can be argued through topics supporting normative validity claims. To be valid, these norms and rules must be accepted by recipients, in order to establish a mutual dependence between language and the social world. In other words, to be valid, topics should not only be consistent (a formal requirement) but also based on experiences, needs and interests equally shared by all concerned subjects. Language does not exhaust the symbolic space of meaningful expressions, by means of which reasons are articulated (Habermas 2012).

Therefore, arguments have to conform to the moral requirement of the universalization principle. Ideally, all concerned persons take part in "a cooperative pursuit of truth, in which only the constraint of the best topic can assert itself" (Habermas 1994: 160). The truth of a statement involves for Habermas the firm belief that "it will stand all objections also in the future" (Habermas 1997c: 130). Moral universalism has an emancipative content because it is not bound to discourse areas and practices of limited extent. An impartial forming of a moral judgment involves that each concerned person adopts the perspective of all the others, as Meads theorized, is prepared to accept their critical remarks, gives freely his consent and does not follow only his own convenience. The norms which regulate an argument take in that case universal validity ("universalization principle") and comply with the condition that all concerned persons have to accept the consequences that presumably derive from their universal compliance, since norms are formulated to meet general interests.

A moral world conceived in this way conforms to the "universal communicative premises of argument, in general" (Habermas 2001: 294). It conforms, in particular, to the ethical-discursive principle that "only the moral rules which could find the consensus of all concerned persons as participants in a practical discourse can lay a validity claim" (Habermas 1994: 160. See, in this connection, Borradori 2003: 75–6). It is just the interchangeability of participants' perspectives which ensures "the impartiality of moral judgment" (Habermas 1994: 161). Also in our age, connoted by a pluralism of values, motivation and impartial application of norms is necessary to their legitimation, and corresponds to the idea itself of justice (Habermas 1994: 88–9, 91, 139; 2001: 303–309). The universalization principle used in this case, such as in general happens when the validity of universal commands has to be assessed, should not be mistaken for discourse ethics, which does not ground argument logics, but rather a theory of morals.

This theory not only assumes the universalization principle, but also a cooperative action guided by norms. In other words, it assumes in argument a normative content able to justify or, if necessary, criticize it. This normative content is put in support of participants' reciprocity, as long as they mutually recognize themselves as responsible and rational subjects, and as such are able to argumentatively reach an agreement. Thus, the rational foundation of knowledge, language and action are provided. Agreement, which originally is established between isolated subjects, changes into an intersubjective sharing of the life world, thanks to the universalistic nature of this ethics, which prescribes a rational creation of wills. Discourse ethics is either formal or procedural, that is to say, devoid of stable contents. Morality does not coincide with ethics, since the latter concerns practical issues, which may be decided through contingent norms, the application of which is bound by the possible consequences of action.

Morality concerns, instead, general evaluation matters referring to justice, solidarity – which is a corollary of it – and good life. These are abstract matters, distant from the life world, which in Kohlberg's opinion, are present only in the conscience of those who have reached the highest, post-conventional, stage of moral development, and are therefore able to adopt the perspective of all concerned persons. The validity conditions of a claim laid in an interaction are fully met in an ideal communicative (or linguistic) situation. This situation is open to anyone who can speak and act, and therefore is potentially unlimited, able to allow considering other people's interests on equal and impartial terms, without any distortion depending on power relations. On this basis, it is possible to put forward arguments, the validity of which is neither decided by dogmatic presuppositions nor by the imposition of stronger interests, but rather, from time to time, by good reasons, that is to say, by the free constraint of the best argumentation (Habermas 2007b: 27; see also 1991: 245–9; 1994: 72–3, 129, 143, 146–7; 1997a: 68, 98–104; 2001: 287–8; 2006: 224–9; 2007b: 26–33, 111–17; 2007c: 31–3; 2008d: 80–81; 2009: 49–85, 97–103; Borradori 2003a: 49).

The result consists in beliefs which are *ultimately* grounded on a discursively achieved consensus (Habermas 2009: 100. The underscoring has been made by Habermas himself). Consensus rests on shared normative beliefs, which make "the elementary functions of society" and "everyday practice" possible, and consequently, the interpenetration between different life worlds. Communicative action and argument do not coincide. Communicative action aims at establishing an agreement which is not limited to particular space-time contexts between subjects who mutually recognize themselves as peers. Argumentative action makes use of common language; it is used every day, and is an alternative to the use of power. If argumentative action becomes institutionalized, it aims at reaching an agreement as well, and involves renouncing power. However, it cannot be used every day, such as for example, juridical, scientific or arts critic arguments. Ideally, the parties involved in an argument are prepared to make use of linguistic communication to extend their social and normative world by mutual inclusion.

These ideal conditions can be approached only if unnecessary empirical limitations and unwelcome internal and external influences are neutralized through institutional regulations and procedures, and moral principles of universal validity are asserted (Habermas 1992a: 113–14; 2009: 97–141). Validity claims, which vary depending on the communicative contexts, may be whether accepted or rejected, since they are all criticizable in principle, and need to be justified, as they are supported by topics others can either accept or reject. Through their arguments, actors pursue, indeed, the common aim of coming to a mutual agreement on some issues in a natural social or subjective world, the sense of which is shared by the participants in an interaction (Habermas 2001: 286–8). The common goal of aiming at reaching an agreement, which is always questionable, and hence provisional, is called by Habermas "illocutionary," making use of a term coined by Austin, a representative of Anglo-Saxon analytical philosophy. "Illocution" is, in general, any action one carries out because he or she has said something (such as stating, suggesting, asking, commanding, promising, etc.) and its purpose can be inferred from what has been said.

An "illocutionary" act differs from a "perlocutionary" one, through which an agent aims at achieving an effect with the recipient (a listener, a reader) (see Habermas 1991: 340–42; see also Warnke 1995: 121). A communicative action is of an ethical and rational nature, and has the life world linguistically established and intersubjectively shared as a background. Communicative action is connoted as follows:

a. It engages several subjects in an attempt to obtain consensus in virtue of their shared interpretations of the situations;
b. It is not oriented to the single participants' success, but rather to agreement;
c. It is regulated by norms which coordinate the participants in a binding way because the participants themselves and others consider them valid, and are freely and collectively accepted, since they refer to common value orientations, and in particular the value of a collective pursuit of truth. These norms regulate the argumentative process, and are not valid out of this sphere;
d. It can be understood by all those concerned;
e. It allows each participant to assume other people's perspectives as a result of debates and arguments. Communicative agreement assumes the recognition of the other as a subject rightfully belonging to the moral community established by those who act responsibly.[1]

Theory of Communicative Action: The Conditions of a Perfect Communicative Rationality

In modern societies, the possibility of providing a justification to moral norms refers to their reasonableness, which should be valid for all the members of that society. The universalization principle and the acceptance of merely formal ethical principles, such as the obligatoriness of rules and the logical-argumentative rationality of discourses which take place in consultations and decisions, characterize modern thought. Habermas defines this kind of thought "post-metaphysical," due to the lack of generalized consensus on norms and values. Concepts as morals and justice are, however, universalistic in principle even if differently interpreted and applied (Habermas 1994: 39–43, 148–58, 210, 226–7; 1997: 48–51, 96–7; 2001: 105–30, 271–6, 294; 2008b: 39–60, 94–5, 104–105). There is perfect communicative rationality if there is intersubjective recognition, unlimited in its extent, of the mutual validity claims and the related consequences on action. This recognition assumes a plurality of conditions, such as (see Habermas 1973a: 91–4; 1994: 29, 162–3; 1997b: 59–60; 2001: 125–9, 288–94; 2008b: 15–17, 56–60):

1. Each participant should be prepared to rationally accept other people's reasons.
2. He or she should have equal possibilities in the choice and execution of discursive acts.
3. He or she should be prepared to understand other people's statements, by identifying him or herself in the perspective of all other participants. In other words, the universalization principle should be enforced.
4. He or she should be inclined to learn from his own errors and from other people's critical remarks about the validity claims he has laid.
5. He or she should be free of constraints or other hindrances to a cooperative pursuit of truth.
6. He or she should pursue this goal through argumentations supporting validity claims.

---

1 Habermas has reverted several times on these notions, as well as in the *Theory of Communicative Action*, also in other works. See, for example, Habermas 1991: 240–45.

7. He or she should cooperate so as to make the best argumentation, that is to say, the argumentation supported with the most convincing reasons, prevail.
8. He or she should be able to proffer valid statements, that is to say, true, correct, conforming to values, sincere, and intelligible statements. Their validity does not merely imply the possibility of accepting them, but rather the possibility of persuasion.
9. He or she should be able to plausibly argue, by means of procedural standards, the validity of his statements, thus achieving well-grounded consensus.

Habermas wonders whether a statement would be considered valid in a particular social and cultural circle, but invalid in another. Nonetheless, the author concludes that this thesis is not sufficiently argued as for the comprehension of modern Western societies. Habermas refers, in this connection, to the evolutionary model of cognitive learning formulated by Piaget, according to which there are stages in this process that can be understood by the subjects and can be intersubjectively assessed (Habermas 1997a: 117–53). In his *Theory of Communicative Action* Habermas (1997a; b) is particularly interested in Winch as regards the question whether the conception of rationality linguistically expressed through which a particular image of the world can be compared with others. In this regard, Habermas argues that different cultural references are incompatible only if they concern a single objective world which is not a subject of communication. In communication processes, indeed, in order to understand each other, the participants represent, express and appeal to a common-life world of which they share the knowledge and the basic presuppositions. A reciprocal attribution of rationality is essential in everyday life so that participants are able to reach an agreement with one another as well as mutual recognition. There is no rationality irrespective of the use of language (Habermas 1990: 314–15, 322–4; 2007b: 73, 97). This world is not only objective, but also social and subjective. Wishes and feelings belong to the subjective world. They do not correspond to actual conditions of the outer world, but rather to stances and needs toward it. If an actor expresses his wishes and his feelings, he implicitly raises a question of truthfulness (or sincerity) and authenticity (since wishes and feelings can be expressed in an imprecise way) (Habermas 1997a: 154–69).

Theory of Communicative Action: Action Oriented to Agreement and Success

In Habermas's philosophical and sociological thought there is a recurring and essential distinction between an action oriented to agreement, called communicative action, and an action oriented to success, called strategic action. In an ideal communicative situation, a cooperative action asserts itself for the purpose of reaching an agreement among participants, instead of a non-cooperative action oriented only to the success of some of them (Habermas 2006: 65). Actors' rationality "reveals itself in the conditions for an agreement reached in a communicative way" (Habermas 2006: 67). Force is a coordination mechanism of an action, which is alternative to agreement (Habermas 1982: 269).

In the case of strategic action, all or at least some of the participants try to influence the others. There is no common normative background, and consequently, no coordination mechanism able to be effective for all actors. Participants' coordination may therefore be lacking, and if there is coordination, it depends on the accidental intertwining of utilitarian calculations made by single participants who pursue the attainment of a benefit, for instance, money or power. In this case, language "shrinks to become an information medium" and "the conditions of normative validity are replaced by sanctioning conditions." Rational persuasion acts are of no importance in this case (Habermas 2006: 69–80, 126–33). In an ideal communicative situation, participants reciprocally connect their perspectives and simultaneously refer to a world, which is objective (all that about which it is possible to formulate true statements), social (interpersonal relations, jointly considered, legitimately regulated we address ourselves to with a normative attitude), and subjective (all the lived experiences a speaker has a privileged access to) world. Communicative action pursues agreement by definition, and therefore is not strategic.

An agreement achieved discursively guarantees the justness of moral opinions and the validity of the norms that justify them. In this case, communication has a binding power for all concerned persons. In modern societies, the life world, which is intersubjectively shared in all its elements (culture, society, and personality), is different from the world actors can directly accede in the form of objects and things (objective world), norms (social world) and personal life experiences (subjective world). The subjective world emerges from the life world and makes it possible. Both the actors who pursue agreement and those who pursue a strategic action address themselves to the life world, which is formed by a common background of knowledge (Habermas 1991: 250–63; 1994: 146–7; 1997c: 142; 2001: 289–90; 2006: 65–79, 89–99, 179, 126–33; 2007b: 30–31; 2009: 142–50; see also White 1988: 10–21).

Language is always relevant for an actor who relates with the world and can be used for different purposes, such as producing perlocutory effects (through which he induces other persons to do something); establishing interpersonal relations; expressing personal experiences (Habermas 1997a: 170, 176). In an action cooperatively oriented to agreement rather than to success, the validity claims laid by the actors, which are always criticizable in principle, find mutual recognition if an agreement is reached. For this purpose, the participants in an interaction must preliminarily share a comprehension or an interpretation of the world, which has to be taken for granted, and a common definition of the situation, and must coordinate their actions. Goal-rational action refer to the objective world; norm-rational actions refer to the social world (defined as "all legitimately regulated interpersonal relationships, jointly considered") (Habermas 2008b: 52), and finally, dramaturgical actions refer to the subjective world.

Differently from the participants in an interaction, a social scientist pursues the aim of interpreting its sense as an observer and does not intervene in the interaction itself. He is therefore a virtual participant who does not take part in the understanding and agreement processes, and to whom the possibility of discussing with others the validity claims laid by the actual participants in the life world is barred. However, the task of understanding the meaning of the participants' interactions is incumbent upon social scientists, and they have to reconstruct in an intuitive manner their semantic content. This is possible because social scientists share with each participant the structures of the mutual understanding processes, and hence, of the everyday communicative practice. Being an interpreter, a social scientist cannot help posing validity questions: if he did not do it, he would not be able to point out the meaning of an expression. The validity claims he lays are the same as those laid by the participants in an interaction. Nonetheless, unlike them, he studies them in depth and does not take the context of a communicative link for granted.

Habermas's Reception of the Classic Authors: Weber

Differently from other social scientists, Habermas aims at reconstructing the necessary rules and presuppositions of a communication oriented to agreement (Habermas 1997a: 222–4). These rules and presuppositions – he argues – are of a rational, and hence universal, nature. The Weberian theory of capitalistic rationalization as a process of historical-universal significance deserves, in this connection, particular attention, since this theory does not share the speculative, deterministic and evolutionary aspects of other typical nineteenth-century theories dealing with historical and social change, which find in Spencer an outstanding example. Weber's position is instead oriented to a cautious universalism (Habermas 1997a: 243). Rationalism is conceived in the Western world as a phenomenon of universal relevance. A methodical conduct of life, based on ethical principles, shows in fact its penetration in the sphere of personality of ethical rationalism.

This kind of rationalism is institutionalized in the sphere of culture, as it involves science, arts and law; it has penetrated the socialization agencies – especially the family – and is at the same time rooted in the structures of the individual consciences. It reveals itelf in culture, society, and personality (Habermas 1997a: 255–8). Rationality – Habermas argues – has several meanings for Weber. There is an instrumental, or formal, rationality, which is present in different areas of action (economy, science, law, administration, and so on). This form of rationality pursues effectiveness in the attainment of purposes by considering means, ends and consequences, and establishes a way of life guided by principles applied according to procedures. There is another kind of rationality in choosing between alternative actions, which aims at making consistent choices, and may be called strategic if the actor has to consider the choices made by other rational actors. If values offer some points of reference to a range of conducts of life, such as happens in the case of religious values, Weber talks about material rationality. Finally, there is a cultural kind of rationality, which express itself in symbolic (religious, juridical, and moral) systems, and consequently, in the images of the world. Cultural rationality, which reveals itself as disenchantement with the world, implies a differentiation of culture in the three cognitive, normative and expressive components (Habermas 1997a: 265–71).

Weber chiefly refers to the rationalism of the Western world, as it reveals itself in the cultural and institutional sphere. He investigates its consequences as regards the ideas and interests which assert themselves by acquiring normative validity and legitimacy. Weber wonders whether Western world rationalism has universal validity and significance, or instead is reserved only to those who belong to this particular cultural world. Calvinist Protestantism, due to the ethical, instrumental and cognitive cultural and to the resulting social rationalization of the conduct of life it involved, has allowed departure from any contemplative attitude and from forms of thought exempt from criticism. Capitalist rationalization, in turn, has been promoted by the Protestant professional ethics and by the consequent spreading of a methodic conduct of life, marked by worldly asceticism and by ethical rationalism. Ethical rationalism is incompatible with an ethics of brotherhood, and in general, with any ethics based on religion, as well as with the aesthetical and practical rationality of an artistic enterprise. It is, however, compatible with a capitalist economic ethics.

World disenchantment and its loss of transcendent meaning have been its consequences. Goal-rational action, by secularizing itself, has detached itself from its practical-moral foundations (Habermas 1997a: 334–45). In the same way, modern law, through the institutionalization of cognitive-moral rationality, has disconnected itself from values. Loss of sense and freedom for individual personalities, antagonism between values and the different spheres of life, which have become independent from each other, and life world fragmentation are then, according to Weber (as interpreted by Habermas), the ultimate consequences of the deployment of capitalist rationality (Habermas 1997a: 345–51). Habermas objects that in modern society, cognitive and instrumental rationality is institutionalized in the subsystems of state, economy and law.

Modern law, in particular, with its characteristics of positivity, legality and formality has detached itself from ethical traditions, and consequently, from a life world structured through communication. It is still an open question to determine the foundations of the legitimacy of law. These foundations must be sought – Habermas argues – in the tendency to a practical and moral re-foundation of law conforming to post-traditional conscience structures (Habermas 1997a: 351–78). Weber, however, explains sense not as a consequence of the interactions between subjects who understand each other from a linguistic point of view but rather as the consequence of the interactions between isolated subjects who intentionally pursue an agreement. As their action is goal-rational, these subjects are concerned with the consequences of their action rather than its value, and entrust the coordination of their actions to the complementarities of their mutual interests, and only secondly to claims of normative validity (only in the case in which the belief in the dutifulness of a particular attitude is asserted).

Further Remarks about the Distinction between Action Oriented to Success and Action Oriented to Agreement

Nonetheless, according to Habermas, Weber does not make a sufficiently clear distinction between relationships oriented by interests (orientation to success) and those oriented by normative consensus (orientation to agreement), and in addition, does not specify the practical and moral foundations of agreement. For these reasons, the fruitfulness of Weber's theory of action is limited. The theory of communicative action intends to remedy this inadequacy. In a normative agreement, a communicative intention prevails among the speakers. Both orientations – to success and to agreement – are relevant to the theory of communicative action. The comprehension of a linguistic act involves the speakers' mutual recognition of the validity claims they put forward through their statements. Those who obey, by accepting the command, show that they know what moral reasons the speaker has for putting forward a power claim. In this case, the power claim goes along with a normative validity claim, which is criticizable as well, such as in principle all the illocutions forming the communicative action (Habermas 2007b: 54–5; see also White 1988: 44–7). Both the power and the normative validity (or justness) claims are distinguished by a truthfulness claim. This claim justifies the listener's expectations that the speaker's behaviors are consistent with what he has said. By contrast to this, a truth claim implies instead that the content of the statements made are objective and factual.

The attainment of an agreement between at least two subjects able to speak and act involves that all these claims be met; namely, that the statements are mutually acknowledged as just in a normative sense, true and understandable, so that the subjects may be able to understand a linguistic expression in the same way (Habermas 1997a: 417–23). According to Habermas, linguistic actions may not comply with these ideal conditions. The distinction between communicative action (oriented to agreement) and strategic action (oriented to success) remains fruitful, however. Strategic action may be explicit or concealed, as it – whether consciously or unconsciously – makes use of deception. In the modern age, communicative action is changing as it has to catch the whole extent of social rationalization processes. Furthermore, there are some spheres of action which have partly evaded the institutionalization of goal-oriented rationality. To be better known, these spheres, which are no longer governed by tradition, demand an investigation on the life world of the subjects who are engaged in them in communicative action processes (Habermas 1997a: 446–56; see also Ingram 1987: 36–42). As Max Weber argued, a departure has taken place from the institutions based on tradition, which is a source of consensus on values, and hence, of integration. However, Weber did not recognize that not the goal-oriented rational action, but instead money, as regards the whole institutional body of the economic system, and power, as regards the administrative system, provide an institutional anchorage in the life world (Concerning Habermas's reception of Weber, see Giddens 1985: 97, 120–21; Joas and Knöbl 2009: 206, 236).

The theory of communicative action highlights the contradictory relation between the structure of everyday communication, the intersubjectivity of which involves the use of language, and the institutional bodies produced by modernity, which institutionalize action in relation to purpose and have money and power as coordination mechanisms. There is no competition between the different orientations of action towards agreement and success, but rather between the different principles of social integration which assert themselves in the differentiated life world and in the institutionalized and rationalized bodies of modernity Weber's sociology has dealt with. Weber's theory of modernization has been critically studied by some thinkers close to Marxism, such as Lukacs, Horkheimer and Adorno, as Habermas illustrates by dwelling on their reception and interpretation of Weber.

The Rationalization of the Life World and Its Consequences on the Social, Cultural and Personality Systems

The reproduction of the life world[2] concerns at the same time culture, thanks to shared interpretative patterns, society, in virtue of legitimate laws, and personality, through the ability to interact which makes the formation of personal identities possible. Each of the elements which compose the life world – culture, society and personality – is subject to troubles and disorders in the form of lack of sense, anomy, and psychic pathologies. In ideal conditions (with no troubles or disorders) an action oriented to agreement involves cultural reproduction and hence knowledge acquisition, social integration and hence action coordination through an intersubjective recognition of the validity claims laid by the participants, and socialization thanks to the forming of personal identities. The rationalization process of the life world has revealed itself in a variety of ways. In the first place, as a differentiation of culture, society, and personality, or even as the freeing of these three system from a rigid normative constraint. This process produced religious and cultural pluralism and a public use of reason, thus allowing communicative action to deploy its rationality potential. Further, as a trouble, a disorder, and a limitation to the life world to reproduce itself (Habermas 1990: 355–7; 1997b: 738–43; 2008b: 90–91).

The life world does not identify itself with society; for the actors neither fully control the actions themselves, nor the possibility of understanding them. Culture, through which the actors interpret, appraise and express the world, depends on extra-cultural factors, and in particular, on authorities whom the actors do not control. Finally, the process of understanding is limited by non-free and distorted communications, since

---

2   For an in-depth study of this concept, in the use made by Habermas, in addition to Habermas himself in the second book of his *Theory of Communicative Action* and in other works, see in particular 1990: 316–17, 349–51); see also Rosati 1994: 59–67.

there may be no connection between the life world – and especially the actors' intuitive knowledge – and the action system.

In other words, there is a disjunction between this system and the life world depending on the latter's exploitation made by the systemic imperatives. The social system, which evolution has made over-rational and over-complex, cannot be understood by the life world any longer. The integration between system and life world is lost when, by differentiating itself, power becomes an autonomous system in relation to parental legitimation. Legitimation – in the sense of "reciprocity and mutual respect" (White 1988: 154) – derives then from formal law, which institutionally sanctions, through binding decisions, the authority of the state.

State membership results from a juridical act, since one's birth is not enough for this purpose, though is sufficient for family membership. The state connects itself functionally with the spheres of culture and those of the political and economic systems. All these spheres distinguish themselves and make themselves independent from the life world. The state, moreover, confers legality on monetary exchanges. In modern societies, morals and law, through their differentiation and the establishment of law courts, allow the social and peaceful integration of the life world. In the last resort, this institutional and normative regulation of conflicts is available when there is no action coordination is in everyday life, which is subject to informal normative regulation. Legal ethic corresponds to the conventional stage of moral conscience. This stage is more advanced than the preceding stage, in which morals are still based on non-institutionalized traditional law; civil law does not distinguish itself from criminal law, and private law does not distinguish itself from public law.

The evolutionary stage, which follows the conventional one, is called the "post-conventional" stage. It is based on abstract ethical principles, such as the ethics of conviction and responsibility. Here, Habermas resumes the theses of the American psychologist Lawrence Kohlberg on the stages of a child's moral development. Only if these high evolutionary stages of moral development are reached is it possible to achieve the life world's rationalization. On this basis, new levels of social integration in modern societies may be attained, as well as an evolution of law and morals towards an abstract universalism, in the sense of value generalization (Habermas 1997b: 765–84).

Two different consequences result from value generalization, which is an aspect of life world's rationalization. In the first place, action oriented to agreement which acts in the life world, parts from action oriented to success, which instead acts in the social subsystems. Moreover, action oriented to agreement is affected by the pressure of rationality, which increases the need for comprehension and interpretation, and along with them, also the possibilities of dissent. This can make the linguistic formation of consensus, and consequently action coordination, more difficult. This occurs less and less through language and more and more through regulation and control means. Reputation and moral authority, which make use of language and act in the life world, lose their importance as instruments (or media) aimed at coordinating action in modern society, which is culturally differentiated.

Different, non-linguistic media are then required – such as money and power – which are more specialized, abstract from consensus established in a communicative way, and are therefore able to better coordinate over time and space complex networks of interactions. These interactions are put into effect by subjects who are no longer responsible for their actions. Once they have become juridically institutionalized media, money and power contribute to rationalize the life world, but at the same time, they also contribute to its destruction. In fact, these non-linguistic media promote goal-oriented rationality, and hence a strategic action oriented to success to the detriment of the world's religious and metaphysical legitimating. They exploit the life world and, as a consequence, they limit validity claims, they narrow down the possibilities of free communication, legitimating and social integration, and ultimately impair the links among the objective, social and subjective world. Thus, money and power, which are mechanisms of the social system, colonize the life world and produce a disjunction between it and the system, and consequently between social and systemic integration (Habermas 1997b: 785–809; see also Habermas 1990: 362–3 and Privitera 2010).

Life World Rationalization: Parsons's and Luhmann's Contributions

This is a systematically induced pathologic condition of the life world. The contributions of Talcott Parsons and other classical authors dealing with the theory of action and the systemic theory can shed light on this condition. Parsons considered both the connection between these two theories, and the strains between them. Habermas proposes to continue and improve on Parsons's contribution and interprets his own theory of action in the light of its systemic functionalism. As Habermas remarks, Parsons still faces the theoretical problem to link a concept of action referring to individual actors to a concept of an intersubjectively constructed order. Parsons's integration between these two concepts has not proved successful because Parsons has not considered how actors connect motivations and value orientations by using language as a coordination mechanism. This problem led Parsons in the 1950s to develop a new version of his theory of action. In this new version, the actors orient themselves to cultural objects, the meanings of which are intersubjectively known and shared.

The evaluation components of culture provide the connection between culture itself and action orientations, pointing out which are the abstract references of value and the validity standards. However, Parsons – as Habermas contends – has disregarded communication as a coordination mechanism of actions. As a consequence, the actors need to interpret consensually the cultural models they have learnt through the socialization process, and based on it, to find a common definition of their own situations. Likewise, Parsons's analytical scheme of the "pattern variables" and the concept of system do not provide a mechanism of mutual understanding. The concept of system, in particular, involves for Parsons both an integration of the action systems, and the consistency of meanings of the cultural systems. Cultural values and theory of action therefore remain separated; Parsons has, moreover, failed to clarify the relation between the cultural and social systems.

As a consequence, by means of his conceptual apparatus Parsons cannot explain the permanence of no longer functional cultural systems with respect to the requirements of the action systems. In other words, there is no link between life world and society. Habermas remarks elsewhere that Parsons's conceptual apparatus can serve at the most to provide orientations to research and empirical generalizations, but not general theories of social action (Habermas 1988: 53, 80, 188–9). Habermas intends to remedy Parsons's analytical insufficiencies through his concept of communicative action, which allows analyzing the connection among culture, society and personality considering them as elements of a symbolically structured life world (Habermas 1997b: 849–61; see also 1990: 342–3).

Habermas adds that Parsons has failed to distinguish between social and systemic integration even by means of these late conceptual formulations. Money and power, which Parsons denotes as regulation and control media between different systems, can neither represent the intersubjectivity of understanding through language nor indicate in which system linguistic communication can be situated. Parsons has not given a convincing explanation of the rationalization of the life world. Change is not assimilated into a rationalization process, as in Weber, but rather into institutionalization and systemic differentiation processes, the latter being schematized according to the well-known four-functional AGIL pattern.

Parsons infers from it the existence (in an analytical and not empirical sense) of a relation between modernization process, systemic complexity increase, and growing control capacity by the social system, on the one hand, and on the other hand greater inclusion and value generalization. Life world rationalization is assimilated to a process of systemic differentiation. Habermas remarks that these processes have to remain separate both conceptually and theoretically. Parsons seems to identify these two processes. However, a theory of modernity should identify and evaluate – as with Weber – the aspects of modernity which are susceptible to crisis and inner disaggregation.

Habermas's critical reflection on Luhmann's thought is focused on the same theme; namely, the connection between life world and society (or social system). We prefer here to dwell upon Habermas's objections in relation to his theory of communicative action. Habermas argues that Luhmann keeps nominalistic presuppositions in his investigation, even if they are not explicit. In other words, all that is universal is reduced to particular, to the "casual flow of events," thus renouncing an intersubjectively constructed hermeneutic investigation on the sense structure of the symbolic worlds (Habermas 1997c: 108–11). As Habermas remarks, Luhmann conceives meanings in functionalistic terms. The system, intended as a functionally differentiated society, takes in fact the place of the subjects, who would become subordinated constitutive parts. According to Luhmann, the system does neither have an identity of its own nor rationality. Habermas objects that in the first place, the social systems have symbolically established boundaries of sense, and secondly, that in a society with a developed public sphere produced by an aggregated public, there is the possibility of forming a conscience and an identity extending to the whole society without losing the connection with the life world. Nonetheless, this possibility has no place in Luhmann's systemic theory.

As a consequence, the function of linguistic structures as presuppositions for the development of individual consciences, systems and intersubjectivity is disregarded. Therefore, Luhmann is barred from an explanation of the way in which, thanks to language, subjects can understand and participate together in a life world constructed through a communicative process. In other words, Luhmann cannot explain how the individual consciences – or psychical systems – of the subjects relate to form a common perspective based on the intersubjective recognition of their respective validity claims. According to Luhmann's theory, culture, persons and society cannot be found in the life world, but form independent and separate environments from the social system, with which there are only contingent contacts, since there is no interpenetration between them. Living experience and action are considered functional equivalents and the only validity standard consists in the preservation of the system. Therefore Luhmann provides neither a standard of statements of provable truth nor justifications of moral justness based on discursive argumentations.

According to Habermas, furthermore, Luhmann fails to pay sufficient attention to language as an intersubjective foundation of the mutual comprehension processes. In contrast with Luhmann, Habermas argues that the category of sense is incompatible with the theory of systems, which evades all evaluations based on claims of truth. Rather than a contribution to sociology, Luhmann's theory is a biology-inspired metaphysical perspective. As a social theory, it is a form of ideology, which Luhmann himself intends as a functional ability to orientate and legitimize action. As Luhmann contends, according to Habermas, only a formal legitimating through procedures is valid. Habermas considers this kind of legitimating unfit to promote a cooperative pursuit of truth, and hence, communicative rationality (Habermas 1973b: 125–31, 146–55, 173–82; 1990: 375–83).

Life World Colonization and Communicative Action

Life world and social system are analytically distinguished but theoretically connected action spheres. Habermas affirms that Parsons and Luhmann have not succeeded in establishing this connection, which can be achieved through a critical theory of society. This theory is inspired to the Weberian rationalization theory but, differently from Weber, it proceeds from assumptions on the effects of capitalistic modernization. Weber left an analysis of systemic rationality implicit. This form of rationality is instead the focus of Habermas's theoretical interest. As organizational rationality, which is of a cognitive-instrumental nature, it connotes capitalistic modernization and penetrates though its media (money and power) into the institutional areas of economy and state, as Weber points out through his analysis of bureaucratization; but it also penetrates into other spheres of life that are communicatively structured, thereby creating hindrances in their symbolic reproduction.

The consequences of this penetration are as follows: on the one hand, better social integration in class-divided capitalistic societies; but, on the other, a colonization – or subjection – of the life world in order to avoid any imbalance in the material reproduction of the system, and consequently, hindrances to its control. Power, which is incorporated in bureaucratic mechanisms and has become similar to a machine, has made itself independent of subjects. Power has indeed trampled their freedom. It has done so by objectivizing and compressing relations within spheres of action, which are formally organized and legally regulated, but which are no longer integrated through the mechanism of mutual understanding. Consequently, solidarity links no longer connects them. All the symbolic structures which form the life world and therefore provide individuals with the sense and the reasons of their actions have been thus rationalized.

Through the colonization of the life world and the formal legalization and organization of the action links, the relevance and the use of these symbolic structures have been limited. The normative presuppositions of this action and the mechanism of linguistic understanding have also been eroded. An area of indifference and ethic neutrality has thus formed in the relations between organization and personality, as well as between culture and society. The communicative media are no longer necessary to reach consensus, as resorting to formal organizations which do not directly relate to the life world is sufficient for this purpose. Following Weber's directions, Habermas considers relevant, in this sense, the formal private organizations that are in charge to manage the private corporations, and the public, administrative, and legal organizations. The penetration of these institutional organizations into the life world has weakened the validity foundations of communicative action.

Habermas's thesis recalls but does not coincide with similar theses formulated by Marx and Weber. As regards Marx, capitalism would involve structural problems of systemic integration caused by capitalistic accumulation. Concerning Weber, problems would instead refer to social integration and would be caused by the predominance of goal-rational action in a variety of action spheres, and consequently, by an overburden of the institutional capabilities of abstract standardization, regulation and control. Therefore individuals' cognitive capabilities would be also overburdened. Weber's explanation of the rise of capitalism, and along with it, modernity, considers the key institutions of modern capitalism, that is to say, corporation and state, as causal factors.

Parsons's sociological theory follows Weber's theory in the analysis of these conditions, but departs from it in that it does not attribute a preponderant weight to the negative effects of modernity. Though being a careful observer of these effects, Weber does not take care about how power and money tend to expand their range of influence to other action spheres, and to produce, as well as an impoverishment of the communicative practice used in everyday life, also the departure of the life world from the subsystems in which rationality is institutionalized with respect to purpose. Habermas reminds us, in this connection, the contribution of some authors as Lukacs, Adorno and Horkheimer, who, though being close to Marxism, have felt Weber's influence. According to Lukacs' reification theory, the prevalence of rationality over purpose has led to a totally administered and reified world. As Adorno and Horkheimer, Lukacs follows Weber's teachings and focuses on the effects of rationality in relation to purpose, rather than use the systemic rationality concept.

An analysis of modernity compatible with the category of communicative rationality is therefore barred to these authors (see Joas and Knöbl 2009: 208–209; Wellmer 1985: 51–7). Marx, for his part, pays no attention to the differentiation process between state apparatus and economy, and hence to the political independence of the citizens. This process has implications that concern the differentiation between state and society (Habermas 2008b: 123). The differentiation process involves also new relations between social classes and new possibilities of control and guidance towards the life world. In addition, the concept of alienation is for Marx historically undetermined. Accordingly, Marx cannot relate alienation to the rationalization of the life world, or to capitalistic modernization. Finally, reification processes go beyond the sphere of work, which is only a channel and a manifestation of these processes. Regardless of this sphere, these processes can also result from the bureaucratization and monetization of the life world.

There are further limitations to Marx's conceptual apparatus, which refer instead to its epistemology. If the subjects relate with each other and with the natural world only through instrumental actions, then production makes itself independent of individuals' consciences. According to Marx, the task of social sciences would consist in highlighting, for the oppressed class, the institutionalized structure of the relations based on domination. Social sciences would therefore be assigned to perform a critical role toward the ideologies which legitimize domination. In contrast with Marx, Habermas remarks that in this way the actual nature of social sciences would not be brought into light. Social sciences have rather the task to obtain an interpretative knowledge of sets of communicative actions. Only in this way social scientists can highlight, regardless if their traditions of thought, how language, work and nomination – i.e. the objective context the interpretative work is applied to – can change the views of the world and the social actions (Habermas 1988: 161–70, 174, 182–9).

On the contrary, for Marx and for other modern age philosophers, the fallacious thesis holds true that the theory of knowledge is reduced to the methods aimed at achieving objective knowledge of the world. Social science, in this case, does not think over its presuppositions and can no longer be distinguished from natural science. In accordance with the positivist conception of knowledge and in the name of its objectivity, the relation between knowledge and contingent interests is not a reflection subject and is left unexplored. Non-contingent interest, of a moral nature, which concerns communicative and instrumental action, should instead become a reflection subject, because only in this way natural and human science can think over their own presuppositions, and this reflection activity may lead to the emancipation of knowledge from the influence of the objective world (Habermas 2002: 44–7, 61–3, 211–13, 299–300).

All these limitations (see Heller 1982; Joas and Knöbl 2009: 202–204) lead to the difficulty for Marxism to explain some relevant aspects of modern capitalism, such as state interventionism in economy (with the aim of stabilizing production), mass-democracy (involving the strain between capitalist investors' and voters' trust), and the welfare state (which has involved the institutionalization and the taming of class warfare). Due to the loss of importance of ideologies, the life world tends to build up as global knowledge intersubjectively shared by participants. The reification theory can now apply to the effects of modernity on the life world. In Habermas's language, these effects can be summarized as "cultural impoverishment" and "fragmentation of everyday conscience" (Habermas 1997b: 1022). The disjunction of the life world from the social system occurs by virtue of control media (money and power), which are independent of language and consequently not subject to the life world control. Money and power are not instruments of cultural reproduction, social integration or socialization, but rather instruments of monetization and bureaucratization (Habermas 1997b: 892–979). These media can neither allow nor replace the intersubjective condition of a life world" which is "subjectively produced, oriented in a moral sense, and inspired by conviction" (Habermas 1997b: 980).

Life World Colonization and Legitimacy Crisis

The processes through which agreement is achieved require a fully developed cultural tradition, which cannot be found in modernity. Under such conditions, according to Habermas, the life world is subject to institutional limitations. Media are then neither a source of orientation for the individuals nor a source of legitimating for the social and political system. Moreover, the social integration force of solidarity (Habermas 1998a: 47) is insufficient. This system finds itself, accordingly, in a chronic condition of legitimacy crisis. It is a sign, and at the same time, a cause of crisis that communication between individuals and groups is systematically blocked or distorted. Not only the social and political system is burdened with clash of interests between classes, which it is not able to solve; but also the communicative practice is channeled toward instrumental actions, action is differentiated and objectivized, and the life world is culturally impoverished by the destruction of the cognitive conditions.

The cultural system is unable to produce motivations in individuals. It is also unable to make norms that effectively bind them for a satisfactory commitment to their roles performance in a variety of institutional spheres. These spheres may be economic, political and administrative. At a systemic level, the cultural system cannot legitimize the authority and the social order, and preserve individuals' and groups' identities. Habermas identifies this condition of crisis, which he considers characteristic of advanced capitalism, as "pathologies of modernity" (Habermas 1997b: 1052. See in general 1997b: 807–809, 1051–52, 1069–88; 1997c: 123–4; 2007c: 26–8, 91–4, 118–20). Habermas explains how this condition, called "colonization of the life world," could be achieved with the tendency to juridical-formal institutionalization (or "juridification") of the relations between social system and life world. This tendency reveals itself in different phases.

First of all, a juridical system is established having characteristics of positivity, generality and formality, made binding by a bourgeois state which exerts a monopoly of the legal exercise of violence (a state based on the rule of law). Therefore, there is process of creation of constitutional guarantees aimed at protecting civil and political freedom. The subsequent democraticization process has extended political freedom to social classes other than the bourgeoisie. In particular, political freedom was extended to the working class and to minority ethnic groups based on the principle of popular sovereignty and democratic self-determination. However, this principle can hardly be put into effect if the solidarity link among citizens is called into question by internal ethnic, linguistic or religious minorities, which demand public ecognition of their collective identity. A constitutional guarantee of the rights of these minorities is the precondition for these rights to be included in the public sphere.

The liberal political conception includes the citizens' "negative" liberties from state interferences, and consequently, a division between civil society and politics. Citizens want an orientation based on their personal interests, and a willingness to make compromise. On the contrary, in the political conception Habermas calls "republican," citizens' liberties are of a positive nature, as they take the meaning of self-determination, freedom and mutual recognition of rights. The public sphere includes the political rights the citizens have available as subjective rights, towards each other and towards the state, within a community of free and equal citizens. In this case, the state stands as guarantor for one's freedom to fully take part in this community on equal terms as the other citizens. Therefore, the nature and the conception of the political process and the rights of citizenship are different, though both political conceptions bind power to the observance of norms considered legitimate, since they belong to a democratic state based on the rule of law.

In fact, the liberal conception favors individuals' strategic action, the "republican" rather than a communicative action oriented to agreement through a public debate within a variety of public spheres. These public spheres are independent, but nonetheless able to produce solidarity and social integration in civil society, which is assumed to be fully developed and not directly submitted to political control. Habermas examines civil society, as conceived by the "republican" conception, more in depth as compared to the liberal conception. Human rights and popular sovereignty can be effectively exercised without abusing one another only if, based on the "republican" political conception, the right and the practice of the exercise of communicative freedom are asserted.

The "republican" conception insists, as the liberal one, on the existence of fundamental rights as a presupposition for the exercise of communicative freedom. (Habermas 2004: 83–9; 2008b: 235–59). However, procedural rationality is, in this case, of a "moral kind," since in a democracy, institutionalized procedures "guarantee an impartial formation of judgment and will" (Habermas 2007d: 76). Popular sovereignty, which is a presupposition of democracy, reveals itself through forms that are at the same time procedural and compatible with the non-manipulated establishment of the public sphere. The public sphere is identified with the communication forms without a subject that regulates the flow of the discursive formation of different opinions and wills. In this case, morals penetrate the procedural legality through which the typical civil, political and social rights of modern constitutional democracies are made effective (Habermas 1997c: 35–7, 116–17; 2007c: 21; 2007d: 36–9; see also Baynes 1995: 209–13). Habermas, in this connection, refers to the "normative contents" of "democratic and constitutional practices" (Habermas 1997c: 116).

The formal procedures through which popular sovereignty is expressed rest not only, indeed, on parliamentary-democratic institutions, in which themes of general interest are discussed and decided. They rest also on a democratic and egalitarian democratic political culture, deeply rooted in the moral sentiments of a population accustomed to political freedom. This population forms, broadly speaking, the public opinion (Habermas 1992b: 449–52; see also Baynes 1995: 216–17). In Habermas's opinion, the rights of citizenship, guaranteed by these procedures, should not be circumscribed to particular political communities, but should instead have a cosmopolitan extension, and be therefore inspired by universalistic constitutional principles. This implies an immigration policy open to the introduction of collective identities, social opportunities and forms of cultural life different from ours. All this in the name of the liberal principle of the system of rights which are aimed at protecting individual and collective freedom, and in this case are put into effect through the principle of multiculturalism.

Equal rights for the foreign and the native populations submitted to the same state authority are in fact assumed, as well as an internal homogeneity in each ethnic and cultural minority. These minorities can be activated to claim equal rights as other minorities and the native population, or their recognition as autonomous legal communities, or even as independent states. Against these claims, which aim at the ethnic and ethical integration of groups and subcultures of different identities, Habermas objects that different cultural forms do not need collective protection, which is of questionable normative legitimacy. In a liberal society, the protection of individual rights is a sufficient requirement. In particular, the right of asylum should be granted for moral and legal reasons, which have to consider the different points of view of all the people concerned.

Through this protection, all citizens are given political integration as "citizens of the same nation" (Habermas 1997c: 37), which is grounded, within the framework of the rule of law, on mutual recognition and consensus as regards the legality and legitimacy of democratic procedures which conform to the ruling political culture of the country, and to the constitutional principles that are an expression of it, and take subcultural peculiarities into account. On the contrary, no opening exists towards fundamentalist subcultures and in general towards subcultures which are hostile to others and represent a hindrance to the ideological, normative, political and juridical integration of a number of groups having different beliefs (religious, political, and so on) within a single public sphere and political culture (Habermas 1997c: 37–8; 2007c: 23–4, 29–30; 2007d: 96–101, 135; 2008b: 155–8; 2008c: v–xi, 19–28; 2008d: 64–5, 73–90, 93–4, 99–110).

Habermas professes his adhesion to the project of Enlightenment, which he identifies with the project of modernity, and with the moral progress resulting from its achievement (Habermas 1996: 44–6; see also Borradori 2003b: 83–9). A complete integration among different subcultures – Habermas argues – assumes "the normative expectation of a public use of reason." For this purpose, the respective insights and reason have to be translated into "a universally accessible language" and result "morally convincing" for all involved parties. This implies avoiding any "ideological polarization" among them, and rendering recognition of equal dignity to each belief (Habermas 2008b: 43, 47, and 194–5). An appeal to reason does not admit exclusions, and therefore is universal (see Bernstein 1996: 255–6). In this connection, Habermas dwells upon the recognition and inclusion of the religious minorities.

These minorities have collective identities in which recognition becomes a cultural right referring to the liberal principles of state neutrality and pluralism concerning the views of the world. Dissent, like civil, political and religious freedom, receives in that case legal protection, and contributes to form an enlarged public sphere within which no component is excluded for the fact of being considered illegitimate. On condition that in the political and civil society there is integration, different forms of life (as religious creeds which clash with each other and also with lay positions) can coexist without involving social segmentation (Habermas 2008b: 157–8, 164–71, 204–13). A social state has been created within a democratic state based on the rule of law, by virtue of which the subjects entitled to receive services are able obtain them only at the cost of being submitted to an irruption of bureaucratic apparatuses in their life world, which becomes juridified by them.

Paradoxically, the consequences of this institutional intervention in the life world do not lead to greater social integration, but on the contrary, to disintegration. The links of life conform to power and money by detaching themselves from the mechanism of mutual understanding, and by combining with the juridical institutions. The social state – an expression of a utopian historical conscience focused on the no longer current value of work and on the no longer attainable goal of full employment – does not aim at protecting intersubjectively shared forms of life, unless it is driven to do so by a common political culture which now is absent, in Habermas's opinion.

The criticism coming from neoconservative intellectuals has contributed to this outcome, which he deplores. These intellectuals are hostile not only to the protections the state provides to work conditions, but in general to the obstacles put to the imperatives of technological progress, economic growth and administrative rationality. In Habermas's words, this is a new obscurity, which puts in the shadow, in the name of skepticism devoid of utopias, the Enlightenment project of a modernity which promotes progress in sciences, arts and morals (Habermas 1998; see also 1985a: 86–93; 1996: 53–4). The creation of a common political culture demands the support of a developed public sphere, divided into interdependent public spheres in communication with one another (Habermas 1998a: 24–7, 50–55).

By public sphere, Habermas means all the opinions, expressed either through institutional or informal channels, which jointly considered form the public opinion, since they are publicly expressed through political parties, mass media and associations. The formation of public opinion assumes that everyone can participate in free discussions within a public debate conducted without restrictions and manipulations. In fact, only in this way can opinions originally formulated through independently developed private reflections be fully formed. By public sphere, Habermas seems to mean a state-controlled or regulated sphere, which is accessible to all, relevant for all those who are subject to the state sovereignty, and concerns public interest. Private, on the contrary, is both the sphere of private property in market economies, and the intimate and personal life of each person (see Calhoun 1992: 10–14; Fraser 1992: 128–9).

In his study on the historical forming and subsequent crisis of public opinion in Germany, France and England (2008a), Habermas aims at formulating an evaluation of the bourgeois society within which public opinion was formed. Habermas shows its inner changes and its subsequent crisis and disintegration as soon as mass culture began to establish itself, but at the same time its political emancipation potential as a support to the democratic institutions (Calhoun 1992: 2–3). Different from the public opinion is the "quasi-public" opinion expressed by persons acting in parliamentary, governmental and private institutions (such as parliamentary committees, media, secretariats of parties and unions). Since this "quasi-public" opinion addresses the general public, it channels the informal opinions expressed by private persons, thereby contributing to form the public opinion. However, the "quasi-public" opinion cannot change into real public opinion; for it lacks the essential elements of a free debate among peers and in public controversy, and also in a bi-directional non-organized communication flow among private persons (Habermas 2008a: xxvi, 284).

This lack has concerned public opinion itself, and the developed public sphere which is its presupposition. Both have deeply changed over time, indeed – as Habermas argues – in consequence of the historical decline, in the nineteenth century, of the practice of holding public discussions. This practice was spread particularly in France, Germany and England within the private sphere of an incipient civil society. It was customary in the eighteenth century and the early nineteenth-century salons and cafes, and originally began to develop within the narrow and learned circles of the bourgeoisie. For a long time, public discussions had no political nature, since they constituted a neutral sphere in their relation to the powers. However, from the last decades of eighteenth century, this public extended as to include "the wide public of culture consumers" (Habermas 2008a: 193).

Discussions concerned political themes, and the modern communication mass media began to develop, first through the press. These mass media became institutionalized and legalized within the bourgeois constitutional state. Public opinion, intended in the aforementioned sense of free discussions within a public debate, is currently a pretense, for a public of readers of political questions and the electorate itself have disintegrated (Habermas 2008a: 247–53). Disintegration of public opinion has been a consequence of the direct or indirect influence exerted by mass media, the cultural industry in general, and the opinion leaders. There is not a public of politically autonomous citizens who decide on public affairs (as was assumed to be the case in a liberal-democratic state); but rather a disintegrated and manipulated collectivity of electors. These electors are unable to create public opinion through dialogue and exchange of ideas, that is to say, through "a discursive making of opinion and will" (Habermas 2008a: xxvii, 255–6; see also 2007c: 95–7). Nonetheless, it is possible to actually approximate the typical-ideal and normative concept of public opinion. For this purpose, discussions have to be made within the sphere of a free political communication. The public, moreover, must be differentiated, internally, socially and culturally. Also, it must participate in a variety of associations and organizations that, jointly considered, form the civil society. (Habermas 1992b: 438–41, 446–57).

The Public Sphere as a Legitimation Source and the Validity Claims of the Theory of Communicative Action

The communication flow forming the public sphere cannot be manipulated, since it is based on "the moral feelings of a population accustomed to political freedom" and therefore characterized by "a receptive political culture" (Habermas 2007d: 98; cf. also 1997c: 126–7). The constitutional liberal state was connoted by a separation of powers and by an abstract form of law, and was legitimated by a strict procedural rationality, as well as by moral and juridical norms. Its transformation into social state is compatible with the liberal state and even considers itself a continuity of it by granting political and social rights, and by providing a moral support to formal legal procedures (Habermas 2007d: 9, 74–6; 2008a: xxvii, 258–71; 2008c: viii–ix).

As regards the relations between states, Habermas focuses on Kant's project of perpetual peace two centuries after its formulation in order to test its topicality and feasibility. Modern states exert their power – one state towards the other – through the weak normative setting of their relations, provided first by the League of Nations, and then by the United Nations. The latter, however, are thwarted in their action by social strains and economic imbalances between member states, by social and political disintegration processes occurring in some countries of the so-called Third World, by the resurgence of nationalism, but even more by the weakness of juridical institutions in protecting human rights. Prosecuting the violation of these rights implies taking legal proceedings within the frame of a law system, which is no longer a state law, but instead, a cosmopolitan and universalistic law, as anticipated by Kant's project.

The institutionalization of human rights is insufficient both from a legal point of view, and from the point of view of their actual implementation by a national state, which would meet with excessive political responsibilities and with serious legality and legitimating problems. Supranational organizations, as the United Nations and NATO, along with the international courts, have proved unfit from this point of view, as evidenced by the number of massacres, in which they did not intervene at all, or in which their interventions proved absolutely ineffective. The unilateral interventions made by the only great power left, the United States, to protect fundamental rights or in the name of a hegemonic liberalism, raise, on the other hand, serious problems of legality, from the point of view of international law. These problems could be avoided by establishing an international criminal court, which would be an influential mouthpiece of a global public opinion within a society that has become globalized in economic and social terms (Habermas 1997b: 1022–46; 19997c: 133–5; 2004: 16–21; 2007: 107–91; 2008b: 125–73; 2008c: 224–53).

As Habermas argues, moral norms "have no right to be forcedly imposed as if they were legal norms" (Habermas 2004: 20). In addition, the moralization of law and politics involves a deplorable confusion between law and morals, "since a morally justifiable conduct is partly saved from legal regulations" (Habermas 2008b: 215). Insofar as they are subjective rights, human rights are subject to state protection. Their observance may result from a wish to avoid the predictable consequences of transgression, or to comply with law. In the second case, the norms which protect these rights are legitimate: Their legitimacy rests on popular sovereignty. This belief blends with the belief in human rights only if there are the communicative presuppositions that allow the creation of a political will in favor of their protection, which indeed cannot be imposed from the outside. Norms can become effective if they are accepted as legitimate by all those who, among those concerned, have given their assent by participating in a preliminary discursive process based on democratic procedures.

Conforming to its "discourse principle," which assumes ideal communication conditions in which all have equal opportunities to express themselves, this process allows – according to Habermas – the rational forming of one's will through a cooperative pursuit of rationality and truth not only by different individuals, but also by different and independent public spheres, none of which holds a predominant position. These ideal conditions lead to justify norms the validity of which, in the current "post-conventional" age, can be no longer accepted if they are not rationally argued. In conditions of institutionalized democratic procedures, social differentiation and ideological pluralism, the rational forming of will and opinions grants legitimacy and validity to the justification process of norms, and makes it possible to make a distinction in any political communication between truth and manipulation, and between emancipation and repression (Habermas 1987: 389–90; 1990: 338; 1992, 1996b: 107–11, 278–9, 296–305, 339–41, 356–8, 457–60, and 483–90).[3]

The discourse principle, democracy and morality are rooted in the "solidarity principle of equal respect and care for everyone." The validity of democratic principles rests on their acceptance on the part of all the members of any political community, for acceptance depends on the community's political culture and ethos (Habermas 2012: 52–3; see also Chambers 1996: 199). The political legitimating of norms is exposed to the accusation of covering the interests of the Western powers and protecting individuals to the detriment of the community. Habermas objects that the normative contents embedded in the discourse on human rights may have universal validity, and consequently conform to a "universalization principle" (Habermas 1982: 256–8).

This is so, however, as long as it is possible to participate in the debate on rights, all participants' conditions being equal. Equality is based on mutual acknowledgment and willingness to accept the perspective of all the other participants (Habermas 2008b: 216–32). The theory of communicative action is critical towards contemporary capitalism, since there is a growing systemic complexity which is neither put to use nor controlled. However, it is also critical towards some contemporary sociological approaches. For example, the theory of structural differentiation does not sufficiently distinguish the systemic aspects from those concerning the life world. The systemic theory of society, in the versions formulated by Parsons and Luhmann, investigates the structural differentiation brought by modernization, but does not pay attention to its pathologic effects and does not consider how the current social systems have historically formed.

Further kinds of approach to the theory of action – such as symbolic interactionism and phenomenological sociology – are focused on the study of everyday life in terms of a kind of sociology which includes, but does not dwell upon systemic processes, for the study of which they have an insufficient conceptual apparatus at their disposal. Finally, Habermas examines in depth the research themes of the first critical theory of society, developed since the early 1940s by Horkheimer and other scholars who belonged to the Institute for Social Research, and considers it insufficient, too, since it maintains that individuals' conscience limits itself to

---

3   For an in-depth examination of Habermas's democratic theory, see Chambers 1996.

introject without mediation the mechanisms of social integration. Habermas formulates his personal theory of communicative action bearing in mind the contributions and the limits of these alternative approaches. Differently from his theory, all these approaches do not anchor money and power to the life world, and consequently do not consider how these institutional spheres have interfered with the life world in capitalistic societies, as well as in those based on planned economy (Habermas 1997b: 1046–63).

However, only in capitalistic societies "the distortions of the life world take the form of a reification of communicative relations" in everyday practice (Habermas 1997b: 1063). In the bureaucratic and socialist societies of the second kind, there is simulation of the life world, which is absorbed, in practice, by the political system. The polarization between two spheres of action – one structured in a communicative way, the other one institutionalized – can be observed in the internal strains occurring in families, which do not succeed in preparing their younger members to be included in the organizations they will meet with in their adult life. Habermas interprets in this way the youth protest movements which have gained in political and social importance as from the late 1960s. The critical theory, with Adorno's and Horkheimer's studies on mass culture, is unsatisfactory, in Habermas's opinion. In fact, it is not only simplistic, non-historical, and burdened with the same errors as the Marxist functionalism, but also does not consider the changes in the bourgeois sphere and the national differences, and in general, the trends and countertrends, which connote the transformations of the communicative action.

On the one hand, mass media have an emancipation potential, since they disclose new communication opportunities detached from local and specific contexts of meaning, and, by doing so, encourage the creation of public spheres. On the other hand, mass media strengthen the effectiveness of social controls, and have therefore also an authoritarian potential, even if tempered by the independence of everyday practice of their manipulating possibilities. Their effects are ambivalent. The new conflicts have contents and goals which differ from each other, since it is possible to distinguish between participation and emancipation movements (as, for example, the feminist movement), on the one hand, and protest and rejection of today society (youth, ecology and peace movements) on the other. This rejection can extend as far as modernity as a whole, and re-echo in the youth movements even some recently expressed conservative themes (Habermas 1996a: 53–4).

These new movements concern different forms of living rather than distribution problems, and rise in the connections between social system and life world (Habermas 1997b: 1063–76). They can be explained, in Habermas's typical language, as the effect of "an overload in the communicative infrastructure" (Habermas 1997b: 1076). Protest heads therefore against the rationalization produced by the penetration of money and power into spheres of private life. The task of reconstructing the general and necessary presuppositions to action appertains to a philosophy that does not make any fundamentalist claim, since action is oriented to agreement and argumentative discourse. This kind of philosophy evaluates theories according to their consistency, and avoids giving opinions of truth or falsity as it is prepared to make self-criticism and to accept revisions.

Philosophical and sociological theories should conform to each other without laying universal validity claims. This is all the more true with reference to the theory of communicative action and to the society it creates, since they both refer to the life world, which is taken for granted and unproblematic. Therefore, in order to investigate it, we have to bring it to our conscience and change it into explicit knowledge under the stimulus of something able to make it problematic. The critical theory is aware of this; it knows, on the other hand, that it belongs to the objective contexts it investigates. The challenge which the theory of action has to face consists in the continuous threat made by the subsystems of power and money to enter the life world, thereby subtracting it from understanding and agreement (Habermas 1997b: 1076–88).

Reception of Habermas's Work

We shall examine in this chapter only a part of the positive appraisals and the critical remarks Habermas's work has received. This presentation is selective of necessity, because the secondary literature concerning this work is very extensive and variegated. We adopted a dual selection standard. We shall first limit ourselves to consider, with some exceptions, the secondary literature subsequent to the year (1981) in which the original edition of the *Theory of Communicative Action* was published. Since it is the most important work written by this author, the secondary literature succeeded in taking it into account. In the second place, we shall examine the secondary literature that pays particular attention to Habermas's sociological production, rather than his more philosophically oriented production, even if a clear distinction between them seems difficult and perhaps inappropriate.[4]

Secondary literature is exegetic and evaluational at the same time. Appraisals and criticism are often presented together in the same essay. Even the critics of Habermas's work recognize the importance of this author not only in the sociological field. Hans Joas (regardless of some of his objections we shall mention in the following pages) underlines the great intellectual influence exerted by Habermas's theory, especially in Germany and in the United States (Joas and Knöbl 2009: 200–201), as well as the thematic scope of his work (Joas 1991: 97). Alexander, who is very critical, too, towards Habermas's theory, shows great appreciation for his interpretation of Weber (Alexander 1985: 406–407; 1991: 55); for his communication theory, considered a valuable alternative to the Marxist reductive idea of the concept of action; and for his "rich and complex" description of social order (Alexander 1985: 423).

Among the favorable evaluations, we wish to mention a widespread acceptance of his fundamental thesis, according to which (as previously mentioned) communicative action in view of the achievement of rational agreement is a condition of legitimacy for the social and political systems of modernity, which is connoted by a procedural, rather than substantial, rationality. However, the fulfillment of this condition is hampered by the crisis of the public sphere in contemporary societies, and by the colonization process of the life world (Chambers 1996: 123–38; Outhwaite 2000: 666).

Habermas's contribution, through which he points out the different economic, cultural, psychological and social aspects of this crisis, has been considered extremely useful for specialized scholars (Calhoun 1992: 41). Furthermore, the systematic and innovative nature of Habermas's theory and his open theoretical approach, the topics produced in his defense of modernity, his large variety of themes and the competence with which the author has dealt them, have frequently found favorable appraisals.

This approach would be neither materialist nor idealist, and therefore not unilaterally derived from Marx or Parsons, two authors Habermas considers influential. His reference author would rather have been, for this and other reasons, Max Weber, from whom Parsons would have borrowed the thesis of the rationalization of modern culture and societies (see, for example, Alexander 1987: 371–3; Bernstein 1985: 3–4; Giddens 1982: 155; 1985: 97–8, 111, 120–21; Rosati 1994: 180–81). Habermas's notion and treatment of the public sphere has also aroused great interest and appreciation, as evidenced by the large number of references, especially in recent times, to Habermas's works focused on public opinion (see Civile 2010: 43). Secondary literature has dwelt, in particular, upon the cafes and the other meeting places in which the public sphere is formed (Jedlowski 2010), and upon the importance of mass media and electronic equipment for its development in the current age (Balbi and Isabella 2010; Tursi 2010; Veltri 2010).

Among the positive comments concerning other specific aspects of Habermas's work, Giddens (1982: 155) credits Habermas with the merit of having overcome through his theoretical contribution the division existing between the European tradition of philosophical and sociological thinking and the corresponding American tradition. Some commentators have also appreciated Habermas's democratic project, in which the principle of popular sovereignty conciliates the protection of individual rights (Baynes 1995: 221, 225). It has been argued that this project can be fully situated in Habermas's sociological theory. This project and this theory include, in fact, the normative principle, according to which every deliberation has to be discussed using rational topics, and be adopted if it is backed by the best topic (the most rationally convincing one), which is jointly sought by those who participate in a deliberative procedure.

Agreement does not exclude contrasts and disputes at all, but implies participants' equal rights, their shared moral commitment to be open to other people's topics, and their refraining from having coercive behaviors towards the others (Chambers 1996: 146–7, 158–60, 186–90, 206–207). Nonetheless, some critical remarks, often very detailed and made even by his admirers, are not lacking. We mention here only the reservations expressed by some commentators about some particular issues. Examples of these reservations are the extent

---

4   See Brunkhorst 2008: 99–104 for an exhaustive review of the existing secondary literature. Petrucciani's introduction (2004) includes a "History of Criticism" (2004: 165–91); readers should refer to if they want to have an idea also about the philosophically-oriented secondary literature.

of his main work, *The Theory of Communicative Action* (see, for instance, Giddens 1985: 111), which is judged excessive; the heterogeneity of his theoretical sources (Protti 1984: 113); and the incompatibility of the theory of systems, Habermas himself seems to adhere to, with his theory of democracy (McCarthy 1991: 132–3).

In addition, we wish to mention also the following critical remarks expressed by a plurality of scholars: the normative (rather than empirical) nature of the ideal linguistic situation Habermas's theory is based on (Antonio and Kellner 1992). Habermas's non-recognition of a variety of moral orientations which can be intersubjectively formed (Calhoun 1995: 74–5). The inadequacy of a merely procedural standard – the pursuit of communicative rationality as an ethical principle – as the ethical foundation for contemporary capitalism (Taylor 1991). The lack of any logical or empirical link among the validity claims (normative justness, sincerity, conformity to moral or aesthetical evaluation standards) which are laid to understand a linguistic act, on the one hand, and the different (theoretical, moral, and aesthetical) forms of arguing in support of these claims (Seel 1991). Finally, a too poor and schematic conception of the personality of those who participate in an ideal linguistic situation (Baert 1998: 148–9), and also of the life world and the instrumental action. As a matter of fact, both are interpenetrated – as it has been observed – by norms and meanings (Alexander 1991: 61–2).

We wish instead to mention in more detail some other critical remarks, starting from those formulated by some representatives of theoretical projects which are different from and alternative to Habermas's project, such as Joas, Alexander, Giddens, Luhmann, as well as some authors close to Marxism. Hans Joas (1991) examines Habermas's distinction among instrumental, strategic and communicative action, calling the semantic clarity of these categories into question and the theoretical fruitfulness of this distinction. As for the second aspect, Joas remarks that there are non-instrumental (or non-teleological) forms of action, which are not included in his classification even if they have relevance in non-social situations. In addition, this classification of different kinds of action establishes a relation between system and life world in a way Joas judges untenable. The theory of action, indeed, can be applicable also outside the life world, and consequently, outside the context provided by single individuals' action.

Therefore, at the level of systemic investigation, there is no need to resort – as Habermas does – to a functionalist perspective. The use of this perspective, which is suitable for an analysis of macro-social phenomena, meets – according to Joas – with insurmountable difficulties if joined with a theory, rooted in the life world, which aims at understanding, describing, and explaining the action of each participant in an interactive communication process. These difficulties call Habermas's basic thesis of a departure between system and life world into question, as well as the ability Habermas attributes to money and power to serve as communication media between the elements of the system. The critical remarks of Günter Dux (1991) are not basically different. This commentator argues that it is impossible to describe in terms of a communicative action model the institutional structures that have historically conformed and are still conforming social life.

Alexander (1991: 63–4) considers untenable the equivalence established by Habermas (according to Alexander) between communication and agreement, since communicating would not necessarily depend on cooperation among participants. Aspects of the two forms of action can be found – Alexander remarks – in any kind of action.

Giddens makes objections about the conceptualization of communicative action – which Habermas likens to interaction supported by consensual norms – and strategic action, which is intended as work. Communicative action is only a kind of action among others, Giddens argues. On the other hand, the concept of ideal linguistic situation has raised serious objections not only in Giddens. Though this concept, even as an abstract model, may prove useful for social analysis, it would unduly emphasize – as in the case of Parsons – the importance of social norms. Furthermore, Habermas does not provide any indication on how elements of power (for example, different access to resources or clash of interests) can hamper or in any case impair an ideal communicative situation.

As a matter of fact, power interpenetrates and changes social relations, and therefore it is not realistic to theorize based on the presupposition that there may be communications free of distortions. Furthermore, the validity claims laid by each participant in a discourse aimed at agreement – normative justness, truth and sincerity – can not only be unequal, due to differences in power existing among the participants themselves, but also be of a limited range, as they refer to a contingent discursive situation. In that case, these claims cannot be universal. Finally, Habermas does not clearly explain how functionalist concepts borrowed from

Parsons, such as the "steering mechanisms" of money and power, can account for how individuals and communities create their history in an active and conflictual way. Giddens also adds Habermas's plurality of meanings and lack of clarity with which he explains some concepts of the theory of communicative action, such as ideology, interest and distorted communication (Giddens 1979: 177–8; 1982: 158–61; 1985: 119; see also Calhoun 1995: 52–3, 206–207; Coole 1996: 240–42; Ingram 1996: 276–7). These critical remarks, which refer to some key concepts and propositions of Habermas's theory of communicative action, partly resume an in-depth evaluation of Habermas's theory previously made by Giddens. This evaluation is of a critical nature, too, although Giddens seems to appreciate the extent of Habermas's theoretical project, and in particular his ability to overcome the division existing between the philosophical orientations of the English-speaking countries and the European ones. Nonetheless, Giddens remarks that Habermas's work lends itself to several objections:

a. In the light of the investigations made by the so-called "new sociology of science," Habermas's position, according to which scientific knowledge does not need interpretations of the investigated reality but only causal explanations of the results of these investigations, cannot be accepted.
b. Work cannot be distinguished from interaction, which Habermas seems to identify with communicative action, and cannot be equalized to instrumental action. Work assumes, in fact, the existence of a linguistically mediated intersubjectivity which the subjects take into account in their communicative processes and in the actions resulting from them. However, Habermas does not explain how an awareness of the condition of their actions is produced in the subjects, and consequently, of their ability to transform the social and natural world, as becomes a theory that intends to be criticism of society.
c. Psychoanalysis, which represents a model of critical theory for Habermas due to its ability to remedy distorted communications through a dialogue between patient and therapist, cannot be – Giddens argues – a model in this sense. The result of psychoanalytic meetings may be attributed to the therapist's action rather than to a real Enlightenment process carried out by the patient with his help. Furthermore, a critical theory of society does not dwell upon voluntary dialogues between individuals, but rather on forced relations between communities. Indeed, these relations are marked by differenced in power, and therefore they lead to legitimating it rather than emancipating from it through communicative action.
d. Finally Habermas's thesis that an ideal discursive situation can lead us to truth through a justification of claims laid in this sense lends itself to the following objection. Habermas does not consider relevant the contingent and therefore changeable relation between – on the one hand – the world experienced by the participants in a discourse, and – on the other –the peculiar discursive justifications brought by the participants to support their claims of truth. These particular justifications cannot, in fact, abstract from jointly experienced meanings (Giddens 1977: 148–64).

Some theoretical remarks have been formulated also by Luhmann in a famous dispute with Habermas (Luhmann 1973; see in this connection, Bonanni 2009: 106–15). Luhmann observes that an action rationally aimed at achieving consensus, like any rational action, cannot account for the key problem of complexity. According to Luhmann, Habermas does not consider this problem, and it is useless – in that sense – to focus on the difference in complexity between system and environment. It is advisable – Luhmann argues – to consider the problem of complexity from a systemic point of view. It is actually what Habermas himself does, however, without clearly explaining the concept of system (Luhmann 1973: 253).[5] Furthermore, it is also advisable to examine the differences between action and system, without assuming – as Habermas does – that every subjectivity is intersubjectively formed. The intersubjective constitution of the world should instead be conceived according to the system theory, regardless of the motivations and the points of view of the acting subjects.

---

5 To make an appraisal of Luhmann's and Habermas's different reception of the system theory, see McCarthy 1991: 120–22, 134–5.

If the interactive contexts are contingently and intersubjectively formed, the possibility of communicating between subjects depends on those contexts and not on the subjects' own motivations. Discussion that Habermas judges necessary to rationally create agreement among participants can be better considered, in Luhmann's opinion, a system which is produced by the selective consideration participants show towards their past and towards the themes pertaining to the discussion itself. By rationality Luhmann means a morally prescribed condition for participating in it. Language cannot produce truth, "does not fulfil the function of motivating the acceptance of communications" – Luhmann objects to Habermas – but it is used "to increase choices of the possible truths." Likewise, discussion may not be used to clarify "highly complex themes" (Luhmann 1973: 229–31).

This does not apply in an ideal discursive situation, which outside small groups does not necessarily lead to real consensus. Therefore an ideal discursive situation is not relevant at a "global social level" (Luhmann 1973: 240). The question of validity "in the sense of a reduction to something 'just in this way and not otherwise' rationally regulated" (Luhmann 1973: 259), Luhmann continues, cannot be resolved by making reference to the consensus expressed by rational actors, as Habermas maintains, since this base of validity would exclude contingency and consequently would not face the problem of the reduction of the systemic complexity. Habermas's assumption that truth can be achieved within an idealized discourse seriously underestimates this problem, whereas it overestimates the relevance of power as an analytical category, and the ability of language to reduce the distance between life world and action (Luhmann 1973: 26–274).[6]

Finally, the insufficient references to power, such as exerted within the sphere of capitalistic production relations (see Cassano 1971), and Habermas's non-use of historical materialism in his theory (see Rosati 1994: 180–81), have become elements for criticism among some authors close to Marxism. Further critical remarks addressed to Habermas concern his imprecise formulation of the notions of communication free from dominance, of the crisis of legitimacy, and the degeneration of the public sphere, the existence of a variety of different publics, an insufficient arguing of his own theses along with their strong abstraction degree (Calhoun 1992: 34–9; Held 1982: 188–95; Protti 1984: 68–9).

Another well-known thesis argued by Habermas, the colonization of the life world, which Habermas considers extensive and wide enough to designate some fundamental processes in modern society, lends itself to several objections. Habermas is charged with dwelling almost exclusively upon the critical relations between system and life world, thus neglecting to consider possible problems arising within the system, such as, for instance, recurring economic crises. Furthermore, his treatment of social movements neither conceptually nor theoretically fits in with the dichotomy existing between system and life world. Finally, Habermas does not specify which is the relation between system and life world that does not produce the "colonization" of the latter, which are the indicators of this colonization process, and when, and based on what standards, the expansion of the system has pathological effects on the life world (Joas and Knöbl 2009: 243–6; See also Calhoun 1995: 205–12; Drexler 2000; McBride 2000: 435).

The objection concerning ethnocentrism deserves particular attention because of its moral and theoretical implications. As some critics have remarked, the author would show ethnocentrism not only by paying his exclusive attention to the forms modernity has taken in Western Europe rather than elsewhere (for example, in the countries which followed the soviet model in Eastern Europe) (Arnason 1991), but also through his model of communicative action. As a matter of fact, this model seems to emphasize "the influence of epistemological and ontological problems which are essential in the philosophical tradition of the Western World" (McCarthy 1982: 64). This objection of ethnocentrism, whether and to the extent it is right, calls into question the thesis, according to which the moral foundations of communicative rationality can be universally applied with particular reference to cognitive rationality. Its evolutionary development, in the terms formulated by Piaget, has been fully acknowledged by Habermas (McCarthy 1982: 65–78; Outhwaite 1994: 153–4; White 1988: 21). This thesis formulated by Habermas, though appraised by several commentators (see How 2001), has also been called into question with reference to the moral (rather than cognitive) development stages formulated by Kohlberg and included with a few changes in Habermas's theory.

It has been noted, in this connection, that the sequence of these stages in the moral development process of a person does not prove anything about the ethical preferability of a more advanced stage in comparison with

---

6   For a systematic comparison between Habermas and Luhmann, see Brunkhorst 2008: 64–75.

the previous stages. This question cannot be solved through empirical or rational issues, but only through a decision that cannot be objectively grounded (Lukas 1982: 145–8). Further objections have been made to the concept of communicative rationality. It has been remarked that Habermas does not say anything about the presuppositions which allow establishing a linguistic relation among the participants in a communication. A use of language characterized by formal and abstract standards of communicative rationality limits the area of discussion and the creativity of the public sphere and does not allow participants and scholars to catch the potentials of meanings (undertones, metaphoric, ironic, allusive expressions, etc.) through which the subjects can defend themselves from oppression. In addition, the subjects do not lay, in general, all the claims of truth analyzed by Habermas, but rather often combine, in their communication practices, a communicative action with a strategic action, and communicative practices are institutionally bound and regulated so that the subjects are not free to rationally pursue an agreement.

Habermas would not have made a conceptual and theoretical distinction between systematically distorted communication forms and dominance forms. Dominance, however, is a presupposition for a distorted communication, and the norms or rules which guide a non-distorted and effective communication are necessarily implicit. Indeed, explicit norms, as well as any consent obtained on procedural norms, are based on other norms, in an endless regression. Furthermore, Habermas's thesis, according to which the comprehension of subjects' motivations requires a scholar's and interpreter's normative commitment to rationality, is quite problematic. In addition, communicative rationality is an ambiguous category as it combines both social and cultural aspects of an action, and it is interpenetrated by ideological considerations. In fact, it implicitly involves the prerequisites of an ideal democracy. Without these ideological connotations, communication does not require – Alexander argues – cooperation, and a non-cooperative action does not necessarily involve lack of agreement between the parties, but rather lack of their mutual support in the communication process.

The intersubjective condition thus obtained is at the same time a presupposition and a consequence of communicative rationality. In addition, it can mean that actions either conform to norms, values or practices, or explicitly aim at establishing norms through consensus obtained by means of communication. The rationalization process is differently intended depending on whether one sense of communicative rationality prevails or the other. In the first case, rationality connotes an institutionalized world of rules which has to be reconstructed and submitted to criticism. In the second case, rationality involves, on the contrary, the need to avoid distortions in communication able to undermine the validity claims. Rationality, as a category can hardly fit to artistic and aesthetical expressions (Alexander 1985: 413–16; Bernstein 1985: 6, 192–6; 1996: 258–63; Bohman 1996: 203–204; 2000: 16–17; Calhoun 2002: 355; Giddens 1984: 31–2; Jay 1985; Langsdorf 2000: 30–32; Lavine 2000: 154–5; McCarthy 1985; Reich 2010: 49–50; Thompson 1982: 125–31; White 1988: 30–42).

As a consequence, according to these critical comments, the communicative model cannot accomplish the tasks Habermas assigns to it for a number of reasons: in the first place, the task to "explain intersubjectivity by keeping to the theory of communicative action" (Reich 2010: 49); in the second place, the task of keeping the contact and the balance between social-institutional system and life world. It would be first necessary to have communities able to stand political-institutional controls. As it has been previously remarked, this theme was developed by Foucault. Despite Habermas's critical objections to Foucault (Dallmayr 1996: 91–2, 96), which produced a heated debate (see Bohman 1996: 211–14), Habermas would have actually referred to this theme. In the third place, the task of protecting human rights by stating universal political ideals and by establishing the normative presuppositions for a social philosophy and a fair society. This task cannot be accomplished due to the lack of norms of a universal value, since consensus on procedures is not enough (Lavine 2000: 154–5).[7]

The evolutionist perspective of change adopted by Habermas has produced several objections, too. These objections are partly similar to Giddens' ones, in the sense that the concept of "steering mechanism" is considered scarcely useful to explain social change. Giddens himself has criticized the evolutionist perspective considering it empirically wrong and theoretically unfit and misleading (Giddens 1984: 227–43). Giddens has addressed also a part of his critical remarks against Habermas's evolutionism, which he not only considers ethnocentric but also empirically groundless like Piaget's and Kohlberg's evolutionist patterns, which are so

---

7 Habermas (1991: 252–6) replies that he divides the social-institutional system and the life analytically, and not empirically, as elements of social integration.

important for the *Theory of Communicative Action* (Giddens 1985: 117–19). Some of these critical remarks are included, with a more extensive and exhaustive treatment, in an essay by Michael Schmid (Schmid 1982).

This commentator examines in particular the dual evolutionary – individual and social – process considered by Habermas's theory, and argues – against Habermas and the evolutionist thinkers in general – that the transition from an evolutionary stage to the following one neither necessarily involves a moral of cognitive progress nor a progress in social integration. A different opinion – as in the case of Habermas – would have the consequence of formulating a positive judgment of the change we believe has occurred. This change does not objectively exist in an empirical sense, but would instead result from a reconstruction made by this author. Furthermore, a logic objection has been raised to Habermas's theory, since it would be contradictory. In fact, the two elements that characterize modernity according to Habermas – moral universalism (in the sense of the ability to apply moral norms to any topic, discourse, political community) and procedural rationality – do not seem compatible.

The typical universalistic claims of communicative rationality can neither be curbed by procedural limits nor presumably be effective for actors who have a different cultural and socialization levels, and hence different values, preferences and rules to follow. This pluralism nonetheless characterizes modern societies, which – when they are liberal – appeal to a principle of tolerance. In virtue of this principle, different cultures do not represent an obstacle to a communication free from power constraints, and on the contrary, all the different cultures relate to one another drawing mutual enrichment, although each one reserves the right to dissent (McCarthy 1992: 67–9; Moon 1995: 150–51; Warnke 1995: 138–40). Moral universalism, which involves the universal validity of norms regardless of ages and cultures, is divided by Habermas from ethical decisions, which apply and justify moral norms by appealing to principles that have only contextual, and consequently limited and contingent, effectiveness (Habermas 1985b: 215).

However, it has been remarked that the validity of norms may seem universal to some people due to their intellectual and cognitive limits, without being actually such for others or without the possibility of having certainties in this sense (Cameron 2000: 188–91). In general, Habermas's attempt to base the validity of moral norms on an assumed universal consensus has been considered questionable, despite the different conceptions in this regard, the scarce clarity of terms such as understanding and agreement in the use Habermas makes of them, and the ideological and subjective nature of social criticism (Chambers 1996: 139–44; Ingram 1996: 278–82; Protti 1984: 75–83. See also Passerin D'Entrèves 1996: 32–4). Furthermore, regardless of the difficulty of defining in a univocal way the concept of public sphere (Civile 2010: 42–4), Habermas would not have considered with sufficient attention some objections to his thesis regarding the establishment of a bourgeois public sphere in ages preceding the present age, as the following ones.

First, the scope of Habermas's research is limited by its historical placement in a by-now distant age when public opinion was not yet manipulated by non-democratic regimes. Secondly, the author seems to overlap a critical and normative evaluation of the public sphere to a historical and descriptive analysis. Since these investigations are of a different nature, they should remain divided. Finally, a public sphere regulated by norms does actually meet with obstacles in the presence of heavy social inequalities, lack of a variety of publics, access limitations depending on gender, social and economic category, and ethnic group standards, as well as on other restrictive standards (Civile 2010: 46–50). These obstacles or problems referring to the establishment of a public sphere do not seem to have the possibility of being overcome through arguments, since these arguments belong to the public sphere. The validity of the claims of truth is maintained through discursive arguments rather than through experience, and therefore escapes to scientific verification.

Furthermore, Habermas seems to define ambiguously the private sphere, since it may connote either the sphere of the moral and religious conscience of each person, or economic freedom protected from state interferences, or the sphere of intimate life. In addition, it is better to conceive a public discourse as if it took place within the public sphere which includes several publics, as their presence seems to promote a kind of public life which is a presupposition of democracy, and to hamper collective identities that limit its extension and its taking roots (Baert 1998: 149; Benhabib 1992: 89–92; Calhoun 1995: 240–48, 272–3; Fraser 1992; Hohendahl 1992: 105–108; Protti 1984: 82–3). Finally, the production of the public sphere is explained in a circular way, in the sense that, to provide a historical explanation of the forming of public opinion, place and individual propensity seem to influence each other. As a matter of fact, some places, as in particular cafes, have promoted a participant's propensity to discuss matters considered of collective relevance, but at the same time, this propensity "becomes active only when the persons have the interest, ability and willingness to do it" (Jedlowski 2010: 90–91).

Among Habermas's replies to his critics, we wish to mention the following ones. First, though communicative rationality is implicit in the communicative practices put into effect in everyday life and oriented to agreement (instead of success), it is achieved in non-probable circumstances. This is only a formal condition aimed at allowing the participants in linguistic interaction to coordinate their actions, achieve an agreement, and integrate their differentiated spheres of life. Second, moral norms are relevant for his theory insofar as they find expression and application in these rational communicative practices. Only in this way they can be brought back, at a later stage, to a conceptual unity and become a subject of theoretical consideration. Third, Habermas intends power in a different way compared to Giddens. As Habermas argues, it is not a power some people exert over others depending on their own strategic action, which is incompatible with an ideal communicative situation, but rather a mechanism aimed at reaching agreement, which is pursued as their common good (Habermas 1982: 225–6, 234–7, 268–9; 1985b: 210; 1992c: 462–4; 1991: see also Calhoun 2002: 355–6).

References

Alexander, J.C. 1985. "Review Essay: Habermas's New Critical Theory: Its Promise and Problems." *American Journal of Sociology* 91(2): 400–24.

Alexander, J.C. 1987. *Twenty Lectures: Sociological Theory since World War II*. New York: Columbia University Press.

Alexander, J.C. 1991. Habermas and Critical Theory: Beyond The Marxian Alternative?, in A. Honneth and J. Honneth (eds), *Communicative Action*. Cambridge: The MIT Press, 49–73.

Antonio, R.J. and Kellner, D. 1992. "Habermas, Pragmatism, and Critical Theory." *Symbolic Interaction* 15(3): 277–98.

Arnason, J.P. 1991. Modernity as a Project and Field of Tension, in A. Honneth and J. Honneth (eds), *Communicative Action*. Cambridge: The MIT Press, 181–213.

Baert, P. 1998. *Social Theory in the Twentieth Century*. Cambridge: Polity Press.

Balbi, G. and Isabella, S. 2010. I media e il privato in pubblico. Una storia, in P. Jedlowski and O. Affuso (eds), *Sfera pubblica. Il concetto e i suoi luoghi*. Cosenza: Luigi Pellegrini Editore, 107–28.

Baynes, K. 1995. Democracy and the *Rechtsstaat*. Habermas' *Faktizitaet und Geltung*, in S. White (ed.), *The Cambridge Companion to Habermas*. Cambridge: Cambridge University Press, 201–32.

Benhabib, S. 1992. Models of Public Sphere: Hannah Arendt, the Liberal Tradition, and Juergen Habermas, in C. Calhoun (ed.), *Habermas and the Public Sphere*. Cambridge: The MIT Press, 73–98.

Bernstein, R.J. 1985. Introduction, in Bernstein, R.J. (ed.), *Habermas and Modernity*. Cambridge, MA: The MIT Press, 1–32.

Bernstein, R.J. 1996. The Causality of Fate: Modernity and Modernism in Habermas, in M. Passerin d'Entrèves (ed.), *Habermas and the Unfinished Project of Modernity*. Cambridge: Polity Press, 245–68.

Bohman, J. 1996. Two Versions of the Linguistic Turn: Habermas and Poststructuralism, in M. Passerin d'Entrèves (ed.), *Habermas and the Unfinished Project of Modernity*. Cambridge: Polity Press, 197–220.

Bohman, J. 2000. Distorted Communication: Formal Pragmatics as a Critical Theory, in L. Hahn (ed.), *Perspectives on Habermas*. Chicago, IL: Open Court, 3–21.

Bonanni, M. 2009. *Discutere e decidere*. Milan: Guerini.

Borradori, G. 2003. Habermas. Ricostruire il terrorismo, in *La filosofia del terrore. Dialoghi con J. Habermas e J. Derrida*. Rome: Laterza, 51–89.

Brunkhorst, H. 2008. *Habermas*. Firenze: Firenze University Press.

Calhoun, C. 1992. Introduction, in C. Calhoun (ed.), 1992, *Habermas and the Public Sphere*. Cambridge, MA: The MIT Press, 1–48.

Calhoun, C. 1995. *Critical Social Theory*. Cambridge: Blackwell.

Calhoun, C. 2002. Introduction to Part VIII, in C. Calhoun et al. (eds), *Contemporary Sociological Theory*. Oxford: Blackwell, 351–7.

Cameron, W.S.K. 2000. Fallibilism, Rational Communication and the Distinction between Moral Theory and Ethical Life, in L.E. Hahn (ed.), *Perspectives on Habermas*. Chicago, IL: Open Court, 175–93.

Cassano, F. 1971. *Autocritica della società contemporanea*. Bari: De Donato.

Chambers, S. 1996. *Reasonable Democracy:* Jürgen Habermas and the Politics of Discourse. Ithaca, NY: Cornell University Press.

Civile, G. 2010. Sfera pubblica e opinione pubblica: gli storici discutono Habermas, in P. Jedlowski and O. Affuso (eds), *Sfera pubblica. Il concetto e i suoi luoghi*. Cosenza: Luigi Pellegrini Editore, 41–55.

Coole, D. 1996. Habermas and the Question of Alterity, in M. Passerin d'Entrèves (ed.), *Habermas and the Unfinished Project of Modernity*. Cambridge: Polity Press, 221–44.

Dallmayr, F. 1996. The Discourse of Modernity: Hegel, Nietsche, Heidegger and Habermas, in J.B. Thompson and D. Held (eds), *Habermas: Critical Debates*. London: Macmillan Press, 59–96.

Drexler, J. 2000. Response to William McBride's "Habermas and the Marxian Tradition," in L.E. Hahn (ed.), *Perspectives on Habermas*. Chicago, IL: Open Court, 439–44.

Dux, G. 1991. Communicative Reason and Interest: On the Reconstruction of the Normative Order in Societies Structured by Egalitarianism or Domination, in A. Honneth and J. Honneth (eds), *Communicative Action*. Cambridge: The MIT Press, 74–96.

Fraser, N. 1992. Rethinking the Public Sphere: A Contribution to the Critique of Actually Existing Democracy, in C. Calhoun (ed.), 1992, *Habermas and the Public Sphere*. Cambridge, MA: The MIT Press, 109–42.

Giddens, A. 1977. *Studies in Social and Political Theory*. London: Hutchinson.

Giddens, A. 1979. *Central Problems in Social Theory*. Berkeley, CA: University of California Press.

Giddens, A. 1982. Labor and Interaction, in J.B. Thompson and D. Held (eds), *Habermas: Critical Debates*. London: Macmillan Press, 149–61.

Giddens, A. 1984. *The Constitution of Society*. Cambridge: Polity Press.

Giddens, A. 1985. Reason without Revolution? Habermas' *Theorie des Kommunikativen Handelns*, in R.J. Bernstein (ed.), *Habermas and Modernity*. Cambridge, MA: MIT Press, 95–121.

Habermas, J. 1970. *Agire comunicativo e logica delle scienze sociali*. Bologna: Il Mulino.

Habermas, J. 1973a. Osservazioni propedeutiche per una teoria della competenza comunicativa, in J. Habermas and N. Luhmann (eds), *Teoria della società o tecnologia sociale*. Milan: Etas Kompass Libri, 67–94.

Habermas, J. 1973b. Teoria della società o tecnologia sociale, in J. Habermas and N. Luhmann (eds), *Teoria della società o tecnologia sociale*. Milan: Etas Kompass Libri, 95–195.

Habermas, J. 1981. *Jürgen Habermas Philosophisch-politische Profile*. Frankfurt: Suhrkamp.

Habermas, J. 1982. A Reply to My Critics, in J.B. Thompson and D. Held (eds), *Habermas: Critical Debates*. London: Macmillan Press, 219–83.

Habermas, 1985a. Neoconservative Culture Criticism in the United States and West Germany: An Intellectual Movement in Two Political Cultures, in R.J. Bernstein (ed.), *Habermas and Modernity*. Cambridge, MA: MIT Press, 78–94.

Habermas, J. 1985b. Questions and Counterquestions, in R.J. Bernstein (ed.), *Habermas and Modernity*. Cambridge, MA: MIT Press, 192–216.

Habermas, J. 1987. *The Theory of Communicative Action. Volume 2: The Critique of Functionalist Reason*. Cambridge: Polity Press.

Habermas, J. 1988. *On the Logic of the Social Sciences*. Cambridge, MA: The MIT Press.

Habermas, J. 1990. *The Philosophical Discourse of Modernity*. Cambridge, MA: The MIT Press.

Habermas, J. 1991. A Reply, in A. Honneth and J. Honneth (eds), *Communicative Action*. Cambridge: The MIT Press, 214–64.

Habermas, J. 1992a. *Dopo l'utopia*. Venezia: Marsilio.

Habermas, J. 1992b. Further Reflections on the Public Sphere, in C. Calhoun (ed.), *Habermas and the Public Sphere*. Cambridge: The MIT Press, 421–61.

Habermas, J. 1992c. Concluding Remarks, in C. Calhoun (ed.), *Habermas and the Public Sphere*. Cambridge: The MIT Press, 462–79.

Habermas, J. 1994. *Teoria della morale*. Rome: Laterza.

Habermas, J. 1996a. Modernity: An Unfinished Project, in M. Passerin D'Entrèves and S. Benhabib (eds), *Habermas and the Unfinished Project of Modernity*, 38–55.

Habermas, J. 1996b. *Between Facts and Norms*. Cambridge: Polity Press.

Habermas, J. 1997a. *Teoria dell'agire comunicativo. I. Razionalità nell'azione e razionalizzazione sociale.* Bologna: Il Mulino.

Habermas, J. 1997b. *Teoria dell'agire comunicativo. II. Critica della ragione funzionalistica.* Bologna: Il Mulino.

Habermas, J. 1997c. *Solidarietà fra estranei*. Milan: Guerini.

Habermas, J. 1998a. *La nuova oscurità*. Rome: Edizioni Lavoro.

Habermas, J. 1998b. *Between Facts and Norms: Contributions to a Discourse Theory of Law and Democracy.* Cambridge, MA: The MIT Press.

Habermas, J. 2000. *Profili politico-filosofici*. Naples: Guerini e Associati.

Habermas, J. 2001. *Verità e giustificazione*. Rome: Laterza.

Habermas, J. 2002. *Knowledge and Human Interest*. Boston, MA: Beacon Press.

Habermas, J. 2003. Ricostruire il terrorismo, in G. Borradori (ed.), *La filosofia del terrore. Dialoghi con J. Habermas e J. Derrida.* Rome: Laterza, 51–89.

Habermas, J. 2004. *Tempo di passaggi*. Milan: Feltrinelli.

Habermas, J. 2006. *Il pensiero post-metafisico*. Rome: Laterza.

Habermas, J. 2007a. *L'Occidente diviso*. Rome: Laterza.

Habermas, J. 2007b. *La condizione intersoggettiva*. Rome: Laterza.

Habermas, J. 2007c. *Legitimation Crisis*. Cambridge: Polity Press.

Habermas, J. 2007d. *Morale, Diritto, Politica*. Turin: Einaudi.

Habermas, J. 2008a. *Storia e critica dell'opinione pubblica*. Rome: Laterza.

Habermas, J. 2008b. *L'inclusione dell'altro. Studi di teoria politica.* Milan: Feltrinelli.

Habermas, J. 2008c. *Tra scienza e fede*. Rome: Laterza.

Habermas, J. 2008d. Lotta di riconoscimento nello Stato democratico di diritto, in J. Habermas and C. Taylor (eds), *Multiculturalismo. Lotte per il riconoscimento.* Milan: Feltrinelli, 63–110.

Habermas, J. 2009. *Etica del discorso*. Rome: Laterza.

Habermas, J. 2012. *Nachmetaphysisches Denken II: Philosophische Aufsätze*. Frankfurt am Main: Suhrkamp.

Habermas, J. and Taylor, C. 2008. *Multiculturalismo. Lotte per il riconoscimento.* Milan: Feltrinelli.

Held, D. 1982. Crisis Tendencies. Legitimation and the State, in J.B. Thompson and D. Held (eds), *Habermas: Critical Debates*. London: Macmillan Press, 181–95.

Heller, A. 1982. Habermas and Marxism, in J.B. Thompson and D. Held (eds), *Habermas: Critical Debates*. London: Macmillan Press, 21–41.

Hohendahl, P.U. 1992. The Public Sphere: Models and Boundaries, in C. Calhoun (ed.), *Habermas and the Public Sphere*. Cambridge: The MIT Press, 99–108.

How, A.R. 2001. "Habermas, History and Social Evolution: Moral Learning and the Trial of Louis XVI." *Sociology* 35: 177–94.

Ingram, D. 1987. *Habermas and the Dialectic of Reason*. New Haven, CT: Yale University Press.

Ingram, D. 1996. The Subject of Justice in Postmodern Discourse: Aesthetic Judgment and Political Rationality, in M. Passerin d'Entrèves (ed.), *Habermas and the Unfinished Project of Modernity*. Cambridge: Polity Press, 269–97.

Jedlowski, P. 2010. I Caffé e la sfera pubblica, in P. Jedlowski and O. Affuso (eds), *Sfera pubblica. Il concetto e i suoi luoghi.* Cosenza: Luigi Pellegrini Editore, 57–91.

Jay, M. 1985. Habermas and Modernism, in R.J. Bernstein (ed.), *Habermas and Modernity*. Cambridge: Polity Press, 289–307.

Joas, H. 1991. The Unhappy Marriage of Hermeneutics and Functionalism, in A. Honneth and H. Joas (eds), *Communicative Action*. Cambridge: Polity Press, 97–118.

Joas, H. and Knöbl, W. 2009. *Social Theory: Twenty Introductory Lectures*. Cambridge: Cambridge University Press.

Langsdorf, L. 2000. The Real Conditions for the Possibility of Communicative Action, in L.E. Hahn (ed.), *Perspectives on Habermas*. Chicago, IL: Open Court, 21–50.

Lavine, T.Z. 2000. Philosophy and the Dialectic of Modernity, in L.E. Hahn (ed.), *Perspectives on Habermas*. Chicago, IL: Open Court, 139–56.

Luhmann, N. 1973. Argomentazioni teoretico-sistematiche. Una replica a Juergen Habermas, in J. Habermas and N. Luhmann (eds), *Teoria della società o tecnologia sociale*. Milan: Etas Kompass Libri, 196–274.

Lukes, S. 1982. Of Gods and Demons: Habermas and Practical Reason, in J.B. Thompson and D. Held (eds), *Habermas: Critical Debates*. London: Macmillan Press, 134–48.

McBride, W.L. 2000. Habermas and the Marxian Tradition, in L.E. Hahn (ed.), *Perspectives on Habermas*. Chicago, IL: Open Court, 425–38.

McCarthy, T. 1982. Rationality and Relativism: Habermas's "Overcoming"of Hermeneutics, in J.B. Thompson and D. Held (eds), *Habermas: Critical Debates*. London: Macmillan Press, 57–78.

McCarthy, T. 1991. Complexity and Democracy: or the Seducement of Systems Theory, in A. Honneth and J. Honneth (eds), *Communicative Action*. Cambridge: The MIT Press, 119–39.

McCarthy, T. 1992. Pratical Discourse: On the Relation of Morality to Politics, in C. Calhoun (ed.), *Habermas and the Public Sphere*. Cambridge: The MIT Press, 51–72.

Moon, D. 1995. Practical Discourse and Communicative Ethics, in S.K. White (ed.), *The Cambridge Companion to Habermas*. Cambridge: Cambridge University Press, 143–64.

Outhwaite, W. 1994. *Habermas: A Critical Introduction*. Stanford, CA: Stanford University Press.

Outhwaite, W. 2000. Jürgen Habermas, in G. Ritzer (ed.), *The Blackwell Companion to Major Social Theorists*. Oxford: Blackwell, 650–69.

Passerin d'Entrèves, M. 1996. Introduction, in Passerin d'Entrèves (ed.), *Habermas and the Unfinished Project of Modernity*. Cambridge: Polity Press, 1–37.

Petrucciani, S. 2004. *Introduzione a Habermas*. Rome: Laterza.

Privitera, W. 2010. *La teoria di Jürgen Habermas*. Available at: www.formazione.unimib.it/DATA/personale/PRIVITERA/hotfolder/1/dispensa%20hHabermas.doc.

Protti, M. 1984. *L'itinerario critico. Tre studi su Jürgen Habermas*. Milan: FrancoAngeli.

Reich, W. 2010. "Three Problems of Intersubjectivity – and One Solution." *Sociological Theory* (28): 40–63.

Rosati, M. 1994. *Consenso e razionalità. Riflessioni sulla teoria dell'agire comunicativo*. Rome: Armando.

Rusconi, G. 1997. Presentazione, 31–42, in J. Habermas (ed.), *Teoria dell'agire comunicativo. I. Razionalità nell'azione e razionalizzazione sociale*. Bologna: Il Mulino.

Schmid, M. 1982. Habermas' Theory of Social Evolution, in J.B. Thompson and D. Held (eds), *Habermas: Critical Debates*. London: Macmillan Press, 162–80.

Schmidt, J. 1996. Habermas and Foucault, in M. Passerin D'Entrèves and S. Benhabib (eds), *Habermas and the Unfinished Project of Modernity*. Cambridge: Polity Press, 147–71.

Seel, M. 1991. The Two Meanings of Communicative Rationality, in A. Honneth and H. Joas (eds), *Communicative Action*. Cambridge: Polity Press, 36–48.

Taylor, C. 1991. The Two Meanings of "Communicative" Rationality: Remarks on Habermas's Critique of a Plural Concept of Reason, in A. Honneth and J. Honneth (eds), *Communicative Action*. Cambridge: The MIT Press, 36–48.

Thompson, J.B. 1982. Universal Pragmatics, in J.B. Thompson and D. Held (eds), *Habermas: Critical Debates*. London: Macmillan Press, 116–33.

Thompson, J.B. and Held, D. 1982. Editors' Introduction, in J.B. Thompson and D. Held (eds), *Habermas: Critical Debates*. London: Macmillan Press, 1–20.

Tursi, A. 2010. Dalla sfera pubblica letteraria alla blogosfera, in P. Jedlowski and O. Affuso (eds), *Sfera pubblica. Il concetto e i suoi luoghi*. Cosenza: Luigi Pellegrini Editore, 93–105.

Veltri, F. 2010. La sfera pubblica in rete?, in P. Jedlowski and O. Affuso (eds), *Sfera pubblica. Il concetto e i suoi luoghi*. Cosenza: Luigi Pellegrini Editore, 129–68.

Warnke, G. 1995. Communicative Rationality and Cultural Values, in S. White (ed.), *The Cambridge Companion to Habermas*. Cambridge: Cambridge University Press, 120–42.

Wellmer, A. 1985. Reason, Utopia, and the *Dialectic of Enlightenment*, in R.J. Bernstein (ed.), *Habermas and Modernity*. Cambridge, MA: MIT Press, 35–66.

White, S. 1988. *Jürgen Habermas. Reason, Justice & Modernity*. Cambridge: Cambridge University Press.

White, S. (ed.) 1995. *The Cambridge Companion to Habermas*. Cambridge: Cambridge University Press.

Chapter 9
Niklas Luhmann (1927–1998)

Preliminary Remarks

Niklas Luhmann formulated a sociological theory of social systems and dwelt on this notion possibly more extensively than any other social theorist has done so far. To this end, he made use of a number of Parsons' concepts such as social system, system differentiation, inclusion, pattern variables, double contingency, organization, and general theory of the action system. In this sense and to this extent, Luhmann followed Parsons' footsteps. He departed from Parsons in other respects, however, especially insofar as his notion of social system in concerned. This notion constitutes the unit of analysis of Luhmann's theory of society. Attention is paid, in this connection, first to Luhmann's conceptual apparatus, and then to his general theoretical framework. The last part of the chapter dwells on the reception of this framework.

The interpretive thesis is not disputed here that Luhmann's oeuvre could be divided in two parts, the first of the 1980s or before, impinging on the notion of social system; and the second of the following decade, and centered on the concept of autopoiesis or self-creation (see, for example, Febbrajo 1990; Stichweh 2000: 7–8). This oeuvre will be here considered unitary, however, for the sake of a convenient exposition. Some works by Luhmann, in which the author presents his sociological theory, will be here the main theoretical sources of information (see Luhmann 1970, 1984, 2009, 2012, 2013; Luhmann and De Giorgi 2003). In these works Luhmann formulates in similar terms his theory of society in conjunction with his conceptual apparatus. Other works by Luhmann, which deal with specific points of his theory, will be also discussed.

Luhmann's Notion of Social System

The social system has been Luhmann's main object of analysis (see especially Luhmann 1984, 2012, 2013; Luhmann and De Giorgi 2003). Its concept is preliminary to that of society, which Luhmann defines as the social system of mutually referring communications, which encompasses all the others. Communication is a self-reproducing mode of operation of the social system (on Luhmann's notion of communication, see especially Luhmann 2013: ch. 6). As with any other system, the social system distinguishes between itself and its environment, and reproduces this distinction. The system communicates with itself, or with the communicators and their partners. Conducting a preliminary selection of its component elements from its environment makes the existence of the subsystems possible. The subsystems have properties of their own. Each subsystem has its own self-references, environments and relations to the social system, and its own modes of complexity reduction. The analysis of society, and therefore of the social system, involves, according to Luhmann, the following abstraction levels. The general system theory is the most abstract level; the social system theory is at an intermediate abstraction level; finally, the theory of society is a particular case of social system theory.

The social system and its environment presuppose each other. By selecting from their environment some event (such as relevant information), systems mediate between the world's complexity (the sum total of the relations between its component elements), and the human ability to grasp and adapt to it. Society's functional differentiation implies the mutual determination of function, performance, and self-reflection; but it provides no indication either as to how differentiation occurs, or of the contingent effects of this mutual determination. It distinguishes modern society from all the previous ones, along with the full-fledged development of the communication media (on this notion, see especially Luhmann 1984: ch. 4; 2012: ch. 2; Luhmann and De Giorgi 2003: ch. 2). In modern times, the great expansion of society's communication network and possibilities has created a world society. Society has become one communicatively closed system, out of which cultures have no survival chances (Luhmann 1990b). At the same time, however, the opposite process of societal exclusion has accompanied societal inclusion. Large sections of several urban areas evidence societal exclusion and isolation: Luhmann refers to the Brazilian *favelas* in this connection (Luhmann 1997; see also Rasch 2000: 105–106). What is more, the world has reached an extremely high level of complexity, which exceeds this human ability by far.

The complexity of the social system can correspond, or be adequate at least, to its environment's complexity only by means of selection and reduction of the environments' complexity. The system's operations of selection and reduction of complexity occur in a temporal sequence. The system can realize different complexities – different selections, reductions and coupling of its component elements – at different times, and therefore in different ways. The social systems and subsystems are endowed with meaning. They also possess an identity, are the object of lived experiences and provide the reference points for actions. The social system uses communication as its specific process. Communication is the recursive outcome of the system's specific operations, which are a presupposition of its further operations; it is, furthermore, an instrument to observe, describe, create and reproduce itself only. Luhmann calls the process of self-creation "autopoiesis," a term borrowed from the biologist Maturana.

The social system is separated from all other systems, including the psychological system. This separation, which is communicative, and therefore operational, is no obstacle to their structural coupling. Structural coupling is a mechanism that both separates and unites different systems, each having its specificity. These systems are structurally coupled in the sense that short-living events, which originate from the environment, stimulate (or "irritate," as Luhmann writes) both the consciousness and the social system to confirm themselves. They can do so by continuing their own mode of operation or autopoiesis, thus each developing its own complexity and at its own pace. There is no guarantee of time-invariant coordination of different systems because of structural coupling. Moreover, systems can communicate within and about themselves by means of self-descriptions, in which they observe a self-produced difference between themselves and the environment; they can communicate about their environment; but never with themselves.

Systems can react to their environments only in keeping with their own structures, which are particular sequences of recursive (self-reproducing) operations that reduce the environment's complexity. There is therefore no communication between the systems and their environments. Luhmann designates as "resonance" this interconnection between system and environment, which – as he contends – occurs only exceptionally; namely, when systems are on different levels of reality, and environmental factors stimulate ("irritate") them. By form, Luhmann means the difference between the system and the environment. A form has two sides, which cannot be considered separately: the form itself (its inside), and the medium (its outside). Communication systems, which use language, can operate only by means of this difference; that is, the difference between meaning, which provides the medial substratum, and form.

The loose structural coupling of different systems, such as the psychological and social ones, involves the interruption of close temporal ties between the environment and the systems. The medial and invisible substratum (for example, meaning as actualized in every operation using a linguistic system) contains a great number of elements (for instance, words). A system medium such as language presupposes loose coupling, but implies making distinctions by means of words between loose and strict coupling. It confers unity to these distinctions, and involves the possibility of producing ever-new couplings. In contrast to loose coupling, strict coupling constitutes a form (for example, propositions in a linguistic system). Forms are not numerous, and are temporally unstable. Forms may be preserved by means of devices such as memory, writing, and printed books. Structural coupling concerns only forms, not systems mediums. The stability of the social system is premised on the loose (rather than tight) coupling of the social processes, as loosely coupled conflicts are less difficult to isolate, and their effects tend therefore not to be far reaching.

Medium and form presuppose each other, as forms are selected in the field of a medium. For example, a sentence is temporarily selected in the field of language; loosely coupled words become sentences and therefore forms, while language is the medium specific to the communication system. The selection of sentences, and therefore forms, implies the exclusion of all noises (in the case of spoken language) or signs (in the case of written language) that are not suitable to form sentences. This system can handle the difference between language and sentence, hence, medium and form. This difference is continuously maintained and reproduced at any time in which a sentence is spoken, thus concurring to the autopoiesis (self-creation) of the communication system. All communication implies and distinguishes between the following elements: information, utterance and understanding.

It presupposes a selection on the part of the system of the particular information, which is communicated to the system itself; it presupposes, moreover, a selection of all the actions that make understanding possible, and those actions, which are not communicated, but may be still relevant to the communication process. The social system is accordingly characterized (as systems are in general) by an identity of its own, and by an operative closure to the environment. Operative closure means that systems rely on their internal operations only. It results from the system's evolution, as produced by its complexity. The social system is coexistent and communicates with this environment, but differs from it cognitively and structurally. The system's autopoiesis entails that the environment does not directly contribute to its reproduction. As an ever-reproduced elementary operation, every single communication constitutes and implies society as a social system.

The world is the sum total of all communication, and as a social system comprehends all other social systems. Modern society has no center and no boundaries, and is more differentiated than any other has been so far. Societal communication does not presuppose operations on the part of individual consciousnesses; it rather presupposes a process of interpenetration between different systems, such as the psychological and the social systems (on the concept of interpenetration, see, in addition to Luhmann 1984, also Borch 2011: 38–40). Social communication mediates this interpenetration process with the medium of meaning (on the concept of meaning, see, in addition to Luhmann 2013, also Brunczel 2010: 55–7). Meaning is always shared. This medium cannot be negated, because it is a complexity-reducing mechanism, but also because it determines and reproduces the operations of the psychological and social systems. These two systems – the psychological and the social – are thereby coupled structurally. Other systems, such as the chemical, or biological, or physical, cannot influence social communication. There is not, nor there could ever be, a complete correspondence between the psychological or social systems and their environments.

Functional analysis dwells on the functions of the social system or of one of its subsystems. Subsystems constitute each other's environment and thus contribute indirectly to the environment of the social system. It dwells especially on their performance of equivalent functions and offers a number of functionally equivalent solutions to societal problems. Each solution is contingent, not necessary, for there are other options. Fundamental societal problems can be dealt with in such a way. Systems cannot directly contact their environments with their operations, since they are operatively closed. They distinguish themselves from their environments by means of differentiation. Consequently, they are less complex that the environment and have properties of their own. All distinctions presuppose a criterion, or code, containing a positive and negative value that applies to all the characteristics for which these distinctions are relevant. A code is a guiding distinction of a system, by which it identifies itself and its relation to the world, and receives an internal order.

It is established by means of second-order observations, that is, by observing the observers of a given system or subsystem, and must conform to the following requirements:

a. The code must translate a function into a difference between the social system and its environment.
b. It must completely cover the system's functional domain.
c. It must select relevant information from the external world.
d. It must provide this information to the system.
e. It must be open to new information concerning the criteria that determine the code values.
f. It must distinguish between a positive and a negative value of the code.
g. They are distinguished from one another, with no possible conceptual overlapping between any of them.

Systems can steer their operations by means of binary codes, which are contingency formulas that are not themselves contingent. Contingency is modernity's own value (Luhmann 2006). Contingency formulas are necessary to keep systems open to different alternatives. The social systems, in particular, differentiate themselves from society, which constitutes their environment. They do so by operating in the course of time this differentiation; that is, by making a distinction between two opposed elements that constitute a unity, if jointly considered. Instances of binary codes are as follows: true versus false connotes scientific subsystem; legal versus illegal communication, the law subsystem; owner versus non-owner connotes the economic subsystem; immanence versus transcendence, the religious system. The distinguishing criterion of a particular system or subsystem from its environment, which Luhmann calls code, completely corresponds to that system's particular function, and selects from its environment the essential information that define that particular system or subsystem.

The operation of coding considers no third elements, and the two operations constituting a binary code are mutually exclusive. The conditions which determine the circumstances when a given code is applied are called conditional programs. They link a system's operational method of self-reference with external reference as provided by its environment, supply the system with a set of possibilities that can assume various forms, and by doing so they complement codes. The social systems (like the psychological systems, but in contrast to the biological systems) are therefore able to observe and describe themselves. According to Luhmann and to system theory in general, environmental complexity results from the differentiated elements constitutive of a system. More specifically, it results from the number of their connections; from their qualitative differences; and from their temporal instability. These constitutive elements cannot be further decomposed. Complexity, thus conceived, is far too great for a system – any system – to be exposed to it, and still preserve its unity, stability, inner consistency, and ability to reproduce itself. There is, accordingly, an asymmetry between the complexity of the system and that of its environment, as the environment is more complex than the system.

A system relates to its environment by choosing a point of view, or reference, which distinguishes the system itself from the environment. Paradoxically, therefore, the system's unity presupposes a distinction, which cannot be derived from a previous unity. A system's self-preservation and reproduction entail the existence of "structures." Luhmann defines the concept of contingency as the outcome of second-order observations concerning the social system. Observing means for Luhmann (who refers to Spencer Brown in this connection) to make distinctions between what can be observed and what cannot be, and to make connections based on these distinctions. The operation of observing is itself unobservable on the part of the system: it is its "blind spot." In the light of this definition of contingency, a structure is a particular action system, in which the contingent elements of a system which are operative at any given time, may be also operative at other times and in other situations. These contingent elements are therefore confirmed and generalized as conditions for the self-reproduction, or autopoiesis, of the system.

The system is consequently provided with stability from the viewpoint of external observers. If there is a structure, stability connotes not the system's constitutive elements, but rather the conditions that govern their combination and existence. Luhmann considers structure the form of differentiation of modern society. A system must reduce by means of structures the excessive complexity of its environment in order to survive. It can do so in several ways: by temporally uncoupling from its environment, by using mechanisms (functional performances) that are reflexive (namely, that are applied to themselves in any given system or subsystem communicatively and selectively. For example, making decisions on decisions, teaching teachers, modifying norms by means of other norms); and by selecting its component elements from the environment itself. The individual consciousnesses are part of the environment of the social system, and are not therefore a condition necessary to its existence.

When the system reflects upon itself, it becomes aware of its contingency. Systemic reflection is accordingly conducive to an appreciation and evaluation of what the system should modify and preserve for the sake of its own continuity, and differentiation from its environment. Meaning is not the creation of the individual consciousnesses or psychological systems. Rather, meaning is a property and creation of the social system. Meaning is a medium of autopoietic systems; more specifically, it is the self-referential, momentary, and contingent consequence of social system's operational activities, such as selecting a given object of experience from the complex environment, connecting it with some other objects of experience, and neglecting all the remaining ones, which constitute the meaningless environment. No operation is free of meaning, whether for consciousness or communication (on meaning, see for instance Luhmann 2013: ch. 4).

As the contingent outcome of shared experiences, and as the object of mutual expectations, meaning presupposes intersubjectivity, hence communication. Whatever a system, and the social system in particular, endows with meaning at any given moment is thus distinguished from its environment, which has itself no meaning. Meaning, furthermore, reproduces this difference in all the contingent circumstances in which it reproduces itself, and refers to several distinct experiences, actual and possible. The psychological and the social systems are both necessary to constitute meaning. They distinguish, select and condense all meaningful experiences from the environment, according to the possibility of using them as valid and generalizable information; and typify them for further reference. Every form makes a distinction between itself on the one hand, and on the other, everything else, which constitutes the environment surrounding it.

Luhmann speaks of two sides of a unitary form, constituted by the system and its environment. A boundary divides these two sides. Not only individual consciousnesses but also social systems possess memory. Systems constitute meanings autopoietically, that is, by themselves. They do so by distinguishing with boundaries themselves from the environment. They actualize and retain meanings that are useful for communication purposes, and forget useless meanings. The selective retention of past events creates a social memory, and therefore a common culture, through repeated references to such events, and with the collaboration of the individual consciousnesses. As an indispensable communication medium, meaning is a potent form of reduction of the system's complexity; it therefore provides an important criterion of selection from the system's meaningless environment. Systems distinguish between an inside and an outside part; between, in other words, their own meaningful worlds, on the one hand, and on the other, what they have not distinguished, and have therefore not defined in any way.

The latter side of this distinction is meaningless from the systems' viewpoint. It constitutes an "unmarked space" in Luhmann's language, which is borrowed here from the British mathematician George Spencer Brown. The selection of the environment's component elements is contingent in the sense that other elements could have been selected as well to become part of the system. Consequently, a system's meaning is also contingent. It occurs as a short-lived symbolic event in the consciousness and in the social systems, which could be negated or differently determined, and which performs the function of reducing the system's complexity. Furthermore, systems have no contact with the environment from which they are distinguished. They refer only to their own distinction between what is inside and outside themselves; hence, they refer to themselves only, even when observing their environment. The environment has no meaning, for it makes no observations and therefore no distinctions. Observing the environment is, in other words, a system's internal cognitive activity.

Society can conduct observations on itself or its environment only through communication, which is a social operation. There is no direct relation, in other words, between society, or in general a social system, and the environment. In Luhmann's language, systems are closed operationally: in other words, there is no correspondence – whether temporal or of a different kind – between its own distinctions and the environment because of the systems' operational closure. The latter constitutes a different and external reality from the observer's viewpoint. System and environment are separated by means of a distinction, which the system itself has operated, between two different sides. Luhmann calls "form" this distinction. Meaning is the property of a system, not of the individual consciousnesses, and represents world's complexity as it can be actualized at any given moment. Actualized meaning connotes one side of the distinction; the other side has no connotation being devoid of meaning and order, and is accordingly an undefined situation.

It is therefore chaos, which is characteristic of an unmarked state. The two sides of a form presuppose each other, and their difference rests on a binary coding. For example, the legal system – which is a subsystem of society – presupposes the binary coding: legal versus non-legal. In keeping with Luhmann, observing always involves making a distinction. The differentiation between system and the environment makes the observer's knowledge of both possible. It is also necessary to this end, for there is no system without this particular differentiation. Systems, when sufficiently complex, can apply to themselves their own distinction between themselves and their environment. In other words, they observe themselves and their operations by making a distinction on the part of observers, who thus indicate something rather than something else.

Luhmann calls re-entry the operation which the systems (rather than external observers) perform, or are at least able to perform, by recursively applying to themselves their own distinctions; namely, systems observe themselves as systems, which differentiate themselves from their environment. A system makes a re-entry in two stages: first, by distinguishing itself from the world; and then by reintroducing this very distinction – which is different from any other – into the system. The form-constituting boundary between the system and the world is thus crossed with the operation of re-entry. Second-order observations (observing the observers) add to and complement first-order observations. One observer observes others who observe something. The operation of re-entry thus involves a further, second-order distinction, in addition to the first one between system and environment.

Observers produce knowledge by observing and describing something, and therefore distinguishing it from everything else (the unmarked space). In particular, observers may observe modern society. For instance, by observing prices in a market the second-order observer finds out how others (such as other participants in market transactions) buy or do not buy a given item at a certain price. Only in modern society observers are included in what they observe because they belong to this society, but at the same time they exclude themselves from it by the very operation of conducting observations, as observers cannot observe themselves (this is their blind spot, as Luhmann calls it). Modern society observes and describes itself by means of public opinion.

Public opinion, which depends on the mass media for its existence and inclusiveness, has taken the place of traditional lore (on Luhmann's sociology of the mass media, see Luhmann 1989, 1990b: 2000a). It is a self-referential, autopoietic system. As a second-order observer (observing the observers), the social system observes itself by means of self-descriptions as provided by the public opinion, which did not exist in pre-modern times. A second-order observer does not necessarily observe better than a first-order observer does. It is just a different one. Observing is not the only relevant operation a system performs while reproducing itself by means of a process of autopoiesis. Communicating is also important. Communication makes understanding, and therefore social systems, possible not only because it is meaningful (otherwise, it would not be communication) but also because it involves the use of language, and therefore the distinction between information and utterance.

Language connects the system of consciousness with the social system. Like all systems, they are operationally closed, but can be observed nevertheless. The coordination between these two different systems of consciousness is the contingent outcome of their mutual reference ("double contingency"; on this notion, see especially Luhmann 1984: ch. 3; 2013: 233–9). This outcome is contingent in the sense that it is not pursued deliberately. It is, however, the object of a shared experience, temporally defined, on the part of two subjects, ego and alter. They may reciprocally condition their conduct by referring to their expectations of each other's conduct. The social systems are the orders that emerge from this contingent complex of mutual expectations. Luhmann formulates a theory of social systems at different abstraction levels. At an intermediate level, the theory attempts to determine the operations of autopoiesis (the system's ongoing self-creation and preservation). A more abstract theory would investigate all self-referential and operationally closed systems (not only the social system, therefore).

A less abstract theory would deal with a particular self-referential social system, such as society. Its specificity can be to some extent brought into light by means of descriptions on the part of observers. There is not, however, one correct observation and description of any given social system, as several of them are equally possible. Society's unity cannot be discovered by unveiling its essence, for there is no essence. Luhmann's social systems theory makes no preferential use of causality for heuristic purposes. Causes and effects being intertwined, and for any effect there is an infinitude of causes. Therefore, it is impossible – as he contends – to impute a specific effect to a specific cause. In lieu of causal analysis, the functionalist method is recommended, as Luhmann argues; for only this method is conducive to the study of the ever-changing relations between the components of complex systems, and in particular of the social system. Functionalist analysis does not concern itself with ascertaining causal relations between systemic units. This analysis compares accordingly action systems, rather than single actions or functions.

The analysis of equivalent functions aims to ascertain the existence of alternatives, the systemic consequences of which are functionally equivalent. Luhmann's system theory concerns the relations between systems and their environments, as will be recalled, and considers action alternatives that are functionally equivalent in their systemic rationality (on Luhmann's notion of rationality, see Luhmann 2006). The comparison between different action alternatives may shed light on the rationality of an action system. Luhmann's concept of rationality bears on the distinction between the social system and its environment. Rationality, in this sense, involves considering and solving those problems which a system must solve in order to face the complexity of its environment.

From Luhmann's viewpoint, then, rationality concerns the social system rather than individual actions or the world. A system is rational to the extent that its structure enables it to account for and solve those problems which originate from environment's changes. Their solution involves the system's ability to re-introduce within itself the difference between itself and its environment, and still preserve its own identity. The rationality of single actions is therefore not theoretically relevant, as with Weber, Mannheim and Habermas, who have not solved the problem of how to aggregate individual preferences (cf. in this connection Marramao 1981), but rather that of the social system, which constitutes – as we recall – Luhmann's main object of analysis. The rationality of ecological policies rests, accordingly, on effective social communication of the problems that arise from environmental changes in modern, functionally differentiated societies. This amounts to explaining important negative aspects of modern society.

Communication and the Environment: Risks, Ecological Problems and Rational Communication

Luhmann's discussion of ecological problems is related to his concept of risk, conceived as potential loss caused by a decision. Risk, as implied in decisions bearing on the future, is a distinguishing trait of modern society. Risk is conceived in opposition to security (which is defined only negatively, as an oppositional concept) and is distinguished from danger, which is defined as loss caused by external, environmental factors. Luhmann's analysis bears on the social communication of risk rather than on risk as such. If it concerns environmental risks, ecological communication affects the public at large, legal experts, economists and politicians. First-order observers directly observe risk, which they view as pertaining to the objective, real world; second-order observers instead observe what and how the former observers see, and what they cannot see. Only second-order observers can therefore distinguish between risk and danger, according to their respective source. The reality of second-order observations draws its intrinsic value from the very operation of observing, and not from what is observed (risky behavior, in this case).

Ecological communication is rational from the viewpoint of system theory if and to the extent that it serves as a self-description of society and it does so by reintroducing into the social system both the difference between society and the environment, and the unity of them. System rationality is neither substantive, nor teleological (in contrast to Weber's goal rationality). Rather, it connotes a systemic condition in which the social system can process its own difference from the world, which is its environment. Rational ecological communication directs the system's information processing in such a way that the system can find solutions that are ever more satisfactory to the world's complexity. Finding rational solutions to this complexity problem becomes increasingly improbable with the world's evolutionary changes, and with the increasing differentiation of the social system.

In modern society, more than ever before, the future depends on decisions made in the past. It is impossible, however, to make predictions and calculations on their consequences because of the infinite number and concatenation of causes and effects in modern social systems. Risk analysis involves a temporal, legal, and social distinction between what occurs before and after a given event. It also involves a decision as whether or not to tolerate and absorb the risk or have other function systems take it. Technology provides no solution to this dilemma, and in any case does not eliminate or avert risk. Using technology to prevent risk is in and by itself a risky decision; as it may not be effective, and even trigger unanticipated and undesirable effects, such as ecological catastrophes. Observers – even second or third order observers, who are not directly affected by risky decisions – cannot avoid the dangers such decisions may cause; for in modern, differentiated society everyone could be affected.

Whether on the part of decision-makers or of the affected people, risk communication may be considered insincere and therefore not credible. Protest movements are constructs of the social system, which – being autopoietic – is open only to those forms of protest that it can reproduce within itself. Social movements address their protests against risky decisions in an attempt to elicit the attention of the public opinion and of the mass media to the social consequences of technological innovations. The mass media, in fact, provide their model of conduct. The media also make possible the self-perpetuation of the particular issues, which movements have raised. The political system, as a function of modern society, requires and enables the social system to make risky decisions; for example, interventions in the economy, or the approval or rejection of new drug, or changes in the educational or family policies (on Luhmann's political theory, see Luhmann 1975, 1981, 1987, 1990; see also Brunczel 2010, Part II; Rasch 2000: ch. 7).

The political system can also observe, describe, and explain risky behavior. Its decisions, however, are made under time constrains, which prevents it from selecting the proper time for reducing the risks involved in decision-making. Insufficient information and willingness to cooperate on the part of others – whether they are individuals and organizations – compound this problem. The political system is, as systems are in general, operatively closed and self-referential; it is open to environmental influences and sensitive to their perturbations only if it can handle them internally. Risks are accordingly relevant to the extent that this system deals with them.

More specifically, the political system attempts to eliminate or reduce risks by means of lawful action, legal regulations, and political interventions, according to the system's evaluations of time, opportunity, and the risks that are inherent in all interventions to control them. The economic, organizational and scientific systems make demands on the political system, which has the option to act or not to act in response to them. Participants in the economic system calculate risks, such as that of not been paid as agreed upon, and evaluate the risk posed by competition or by modifying the debt/equity ratio. Banks conduct their own risk evaluation by means of risk-management instruments and help the economy to observe itself from the viewpoint of the risks affecting them. Organizations, which are autopoietic systems, may seek to reduce uncertainty and risk by conducting second-order observations on their decisions and procedures.

However, their communication system tends to provide – rather than accurate risk analysis – ritualized reassurance, whether on its own initiative or following its leaders' directions. Moreover, the organizations' risk aversion creates dangers both to the organizations themselves and to others in the organizations' environment. Finally, science is a source of risks and dangers. This is also the case of the other subsystems of the social system; however, the stated goal of science – the pursuit of truth – may be conducive to undesirable side effects with which science as an autopoietic system does not concern itself. One risk for science is losing its reputation and authority when it gets involved in political or ideological disputes, for is then forced to use rhetorical means of persuasion, such as omitting information necessary to a correct evaluation of scientific statements. A way to avert this risk for science is to conduct on itself second-order observations; to the effect that it observes the uncertainty, which science itself generates, and that it accepts by adopting a constructivist perspective the insight that scientific truth depends – as truth does in general – on theory and method.

All the communication systems – those so far considered, and the others as well – are autopoietic, and therefore operate and resonate with their environment while keeping with their own code. They deal differently with their own environment, each in its own way. Religion can hardly contribute to the social resonance to exposure to environmental dangers as long as it depends on antecedent social awareness of them. The educational system may deal with environmental issues, as with any other theme, according to its code values; but also according to its ability to introduce awareness of environmental problems into the other subsystems of the social system. The differentiation between code (government and opposition) and programs (how it operates) concerns the political system, too, which resonates by means of public opinion. Environmental politics is restricted to measures requiring interventions on the part of the legal and economic systems. It is not necessarily open and willing to deal with environmental issues, especially if these are expensive or controversial. The resonance of the political system has therefore been limited.

Trust, Love, Power and Risk

Luhmann formulates a sociology of trust, power and risk in conformance to his social system theory, and connects these notions with the theme of complexity (on trust, see Luhmann 2000; on love, see Luhmann 1982; on power, see Luhmann 1975; on risk, see Luhmann 2008). The complexity of the environment exceeds human understanding, and therefore the very possibility to confer subjective meaning to the world. Reduction of complexity is accordingly necessary for the individual and social life. Trust, which is possible only in a familiar world, performs the function of reducing environmental complexity. A sociological theory of trust presupposes a theory of time, for trust giving involves present expectations concerning future events and, in particular, others' future behavior. Money, the truth and legitimate power are social mechanisms that may reduce complexity. Complexity reduction is advantageous to the individual personalities, to intersubjective communication and to the social system. Uncertainty cannot, however, be eliminated, as individuals cannot exert full control on their environments. Their expectations may therefore remain unfulfilled. Interpersonal trust is risky, as its betrayal may compromise the betrayed person's social reputation.

In very complex social systems, which are characteristic of modernity (on Luhmann's notion of modernity, see Luhmann 2006), interpersonal trust no longer suffices to face the world's complexity. The object of trust should rather be the social system; trust should then be generalized, and be systemic – that is, concerning the proper functioning of institutions such as the judiciary or the money system – rather than personal and private. Luhmann considers in some detail the money system, the truth, and legitimate power as complexity-reducing mechanisms. The money system makes personal trust superfluous, since it is more effective in performing the function of risk absorption. The truth makes personal trust possible, as it is conducive to the reduction of systemic complexity, and this in turn makes interpersonal trust possible. It makes possible, in other words, trusting that others (including unknown people) are telling the truth. Finally, legitimate power does not merely involve trust in the formal correctness on the part of the power holders, though formal (namely, moral and juridical) correctness is an important source of legitimacy. Legitimate power also involves trust in the political system as such.

Luhmann has dealt with the theme of power, whether legitimate or not, in some detail and in contraposition to what he calls the classical conception of power. Luhmann refers especially to Weber's notion that power rests on the ability on the part of the power holders to express their will even against resistance on the part of others. Power, Luhmann argues, is a means of communication the function of which is to enable the power holders to select the action alternatives available to themselves and others, and thereby to obtain that some events take place, no matter of what the will of the others – those who are subject to power – might be. Unlike other means of communication, power presupposes some deliberate action from all the involved partners, including the subjects. Deliberate action comprehends both doing something and not doing something else.

It is an asymmetric relationship, however. Those who are subject to power have an interest to avoid the undesired event, which is than greater than the interest the power holders have to produce it, while the power holders have a stake in making the message – that is, the readiness to produce the undesired event – consistent and credible as the object of their expectations. All the affected partners – including the subjects – are power holders, to the effect that they can restrict the action alternatives available to their counterparts. Luhmann accordingly rejects the hierarchical conception of power, which Weber and other classical authors have held. Their insistence on the central importance of physical coercion and the ability to inflict negative sanctions in a power relationship is retained, however; so is also the Weberian thesis that organizations provide a mechanism for the effective exercise of power in modern society.

Along with money and truth, legitimate power is then a mechanism for the reduction of the environment's complexity. For this mechanism to be effective, systemic trust must be available (if it is available at all) in the modern and complex social systems. Systemic trust, which for the individuals is equivalent to certainty, does not rest on individual motivations, which may be absent; but on these explicit mechanisms of complexity reduction. Individuals are thus enabled and committed to trust these impersonal mechanisms. They may thus realize that the world, which these mechanisms constitute, could also be differently constituted, and is in this sense contingent. Social life and the social order in the modern world depend on this impersonal and systemic trust. Ultimately, however, they depend on the reflexive character of trust. When applied to itself, trust implies that individuals incorporate each other's trust that their reciprocal social expectations are not disappointed; that, in other words, the individuals' social image as trustworthy is preserved, and they consider norms of conduct binding and therefore worthy of respect.

The social system relies on reflexive trust, which the complexity-reduction mechanisms make possible. Distrust is, like trust, a strategy to reduce the complexity of the social environment. These two strategies are functionally equivalent as they are both effective in this sense. They are, furthermore, connoted by the existence of thresholds, beyond which individuals start looking for reasons why they should, or should not, have a trustful attitude. Systemic distrust is socially destructive; accordingly, the social system requires strategies of individual behavior that have social acceptance, and mitigate whatever detrimental effect to the social system distrust may cause. Trust and distrust affect those expectations, on which the stability of the social system is premised. Disappointment and negative sentiments, such as anguish and hatred, may follow if such expectations are not satisfied.

However, alternative mechanisms – such as maintaining self-control and preserving a person's public image – may be activated to offset such undesirable consequences. Trust and distrust are attitudes subject to moral prescriptions. Moral norms must consider the great complexity of the modern social systems, however, and are rational if and to the extent that they increase their complexity. Goal rationality is not relevant here, as trust cannot be directed to the attainment of specific goals. For the individuals, trust and distrust may be both rational, according to the circumstances: either alternative may be rational if it is instrumental to preserve the social system by reducing its complexity. The sociology of society's moral constitution should focus on communication, and deal with the conditions under which esteem and disesteem (a binary code) can be communicated.

It accordingly has nothing to do with the individual consciousnesses, nor with moral values, which do not need explicit communication, and which cover conflicts that cannot be resolved. Rather, moral designates the contraposition between good and bad, or esteem and disesteem, and has a polemical origin. According to system theory, this contraposition keeps contingency within the system, separates the moral code from other codes, and preserves the distinction between the system and its environment. The sociology of moral is reflexive, that is, it is self-referential, and demands a moral quality for itself. Ethical theories are reflexive theories concerning moral that make a moral judgment about morality. Ethical theories may found moral insofar as ethical theories evaluate themselves according to their own standards, and uphold these evaluations even despite constant disappointments. Morality leads to conflict, as circumstances often put persons committed to morality in a contradictory and problematic situation.

Communication and system theory are also key concepts in other works by Luhmann, as we shall see starting with his well-known work on love as passion (see Luhmann 1998). Love, as Luhmann argues, is a medium of communication. Successful communication is quite unlikely as it must combine the selection of a communication content, which others accept, with the communicator's motivation to communicate something. Symbolically generalized communication media require a uniform code for a given media field (on Luhmann's notion of communication, see Luhmann 1989: 28–31; on his notion of symbolically generalized communication, see Moeller 2006: 26–8). They promote communication by adding opportunities for a subject to accept others' selection as premises of the subject's own selection. The motivation to communicate is thus encouraged, and the societal problem possibly overcome, which is caused by the improbability of this match. Like all the other communication media, whether linguistic or not – such as power, money, the mass media, truth, and art – love is a mechanism that reduces the world's complexity by selecting some possibilities and meanings from the environment, and thereby creating the social order. Love as a social system constrains communication to the effect that openness is expected and required from the partners, though this requirement exposes them to non-negligible risk.

As an institutionalized communication media, love encourages members to have positive feelings toward and expect them from each other. Though the ideal of companionship is similarly conceived, sexuality is – in contrast to the ideal of love – as not pertaining to it. This is so, in spite of its importance as a stabilizing factor in the relationship. The freedom of choosing the partner, which characterizes romantic love, has apparently not imperiled marriage and the family as institutions. However, society has so far failed to socialize people in learning to love. The isolation of lovers from society, and the grounding of love in sexuality, has prevented an institutional solution to the problem of how to learn sexuality, within the family or outside it. It has prevented, therefore, an adequate performance of the function of love as a symbolically generalized communication medium, though love is a strong communication medium for the couple. Other communication media, which are symbolically generalized, are truth, money, political power and art.

As a communication medium, truth presupposes that the content of a statement may be accepted by everyone, therefore not only by the participants. Money performs the function of mediating exchange by ensuring everyone's acceptance of all the others participants in the exchange of money with goods. Power implies the will to condition others' actions by limiting the selection of their possible options. The complexity of the social system is thereby reduced. In the case of legitimate political power, its legal coding has made politically organized coercive power available to private parties as long as they are in the right. As a precondition for the effective exercise of power, the communication between the partners must be successful. Power is rational to the extent that it preserves to all the affected partners the possibility of making decisions without reducing the complexity of the social system.

To this extent, power is democratic. Luhmann contrasts this non-normative conception of democracy with the traditional ones. The traditional conceptions, which abide by the principles of the domination of the people over the people and of everyone's participation in political decisions, are normative and ideological. They are also unusable, and the cause of undesirable effects, for they would restrict the scope of choices available to the citizenry, and would be in this sense irrational from the viewpoint of the social system. Choices are not necessarily functional from the point of view of the social system. They are risky when too many choices must be made in a given amount of time, or there are too many alternative decisions. In either case, power does not fulfill societal expectations, and fails to perform its function as a symbolically generalized communication medium. Democracy rather works with the code of government versus opposition. Only by means of this code is the highest authority made unstable and is therefore open to contingency; there is not forced consensus, moreover, and no overlapping of political and moral issues.

Finally, art is a closed and autopoietic system that uses perception rather than language as a communication medium. Consequently which art-specific medium is selected is irrelevant. Being autopoietic, moreover, art is based on second-order observations on the part of experts, who direct the audiences in distinguishing between what is art and what is not. Art has its own organization of space and time. In the works of arts, space and time form a unity for the sake of observations, and together they distinguish between the marked space, which they occupy, and the unmarked space, which is a reference to artistic possibilities not yet actualized.

Luhmann's Applied Sociology of the Social System

Luhmann has made a systematic attempt to apply his social system theory to a number of different areas of inquiry, such as the mass media, the welfare state, the organizations, and religious, the educational, and the legal systems. We shall provide here a presentation of his theoretical formulations in some of these research areas. Its length will vary roughly according to the space Luhmann has allotted to each research area.

The Sociology of the Mass Media

Luhmann has conducted a functionalist analysis of the mass media (see Luhmann 1989). As is the case with communication in general, a distinction is here in order between utterance and information as a necessary condition to communicate. Luhmann's analysis, however, impinges on the further distinction between system and environment, and in the particular case of the mass media, on the distinction between the social system and its cognitive environment. Referring to this distinction, the mass media perform the function to direct society's self-observation. By doing so, they derive from within themselves the stimulation to refer new communications to the old ones. There is therefore a recursive intertwining of the mass media with everyday interactions in the local social life (Luhmann 1990); and consequently, with the organizations of society as a whole.

The mass media communication involves their exercise of memory in that it must constantly recall and forget past events, in conformance to the cognitive environment's ever-changing conditions. The mass media communication system, nonetheless, is entirely self-referential. It decides which topics should be accepted and retained for public discussion, and – once having made public – which topic can be assumed to be known. Like all systems, the mass media system is operationally closed to the effect that it makes the internal distinction between self-reference and other-reference, constructs its own temporal horizons and information values, and decides how the world should be represented. The mass media communication is not, nor can be, limited to the individual's world of experience, though it is structurally coupled with the individual's psychological system. As an operationally closed system, the mass media do not pursue the objective truth, defined in keeping with external criteria, for their code is not (as is in the case of science) true versus untrue, but information versus non-information.

Their reality is the result not of direct observations but of second-order observations. The mass media observe what others observe; they do so and construct social reality accordingly by distinguishing information from non-information, in keeping with their own code. No one can escape in modern society from the mass media's second-order observations, since the mass media shape even direct observations as obtained, for example, by sightseeing. The term of culture provides a fitting designation of the reality, which the mass media as closed cognitive systems construct by means of their own operations ("operational constructivism"). There is nothing in the environment that corresponds to the operations by means of which the mass media construct their cognitive systems, for otherwise the system would dissolve into its cognitive environment, and could no longer learn from it. In turn, the resulting construction of reality presents this reality as unquestionably real, and the knowledge concerning it as a truth not subject to consensus.

The Sociology of the Welfare State

Luhmann's theoretical formulations on the welfare state, as is the case in general, are in keeping with his social system theory (see Luhmann 1990a). The welfare state has taken responsibility for its citizen's welfare, in line with traditional and modern tendencies to impute a global role to politics, not, however, with its limited possibilities of effective intervention. It has therefore proved illusionary. Traditional political theory is not only obsolete;, it has also contributed to produce the very reality which it cannot explain. As Luhmann argues, an alternative and more appropriate conceptual apparatus should include the concepts of system and self-reference. The political system should accordingly be conceived as an internally differentiated whose function is to make binding decisions, which in order to be effective must find acceptance on the part of the public opinion. Other conditions of their effectiveness are providing political leaders with opportunities of advancement, and their conformance to law.

The Sociology of Organizations

Luhmann has formulated his organization theory (see Luhmann 2005) in contrast to classical – especially Weber's – organization theories, and in particular, to their conception of organizations in ideal-typical terms as formal (that is, conforming to juridical norms), rational, goal-oriented and hierarchical, and using a written communication form. Luhmann objects that for a variety of reasons organizations do not necessarily use this particular form of communication, and prefer instead an oral form. As for goal-oriented rationality, Luhmann observes that this concept is hardly useful to organization theory, as which goal has been established depends on which temporal horizon has been selected. The symbolic use of rationality, in this sense, may serve the organization's own interests, rather than being useful for organizational studies.

The distinction between formal and informal organizations is also considered unacceptable; for all organizations work in keeping with informal rules. Luhmann has argued that a very different definition and conception of organization would be more useful. Organizations should be defined, according to Luhmann, as closed autopoietic systems that transform uncertainty into certainty by making decisions. They are based on the binary code that distinguishes members from non-members. Organizational actions are considered contingent decisions, which are made by people performing roles in the organization. Decisions are imputed to their motivations as components of their personality systems, and are made with reference to contingent events, which originate from their environment.

Absorbing uncertainty by means of decision-making distinguishes organizations from all the other autopoietic systems. Yet, rational, goal-oriented decision-making according to pre-established rules tends to foster the self-produced illusion that organizations can thus absorb the environment's ever-present uncertainty. The concept of rationality should be rather employed in keeping with the theoretical framework provided by system theory. The rational organization is one which as an autopoietic system makes operational decisions that effectively keep it distinct from its ever-changing environment. This conception of organizational rationality implies the ability on the part of the organization to observe itself in its relationship to its environment (second-order observations). This would imply a loose coupling of cognition and action.

The Sociology of Law

Luhmann has dealt extensively with the sociology of law from the viewpoint of system theory and functionalist analysis (Luhmann 2002, 2004). Luhmann prefers not to underline the law's functions of social control and integration, as these functions are questionable, and there are other more important. Rather, the law – as he writes – performs the functions of establishing, enforcing and stabilizing normative expectations. The law thereby puts a limit to temporal expectations and therefore performs risk control. The law, however, does not control its own risk, which follows from decision-making and is inevitable in a risky society such as ours. By performing the above-mentioned functions, it stabilizes the social system's relationship to its environment by classifying phenomena with its own code of legal versus illegal. The legal system is autopoietic and operatively closed, in the sense that it relies on its own operations, values, expectations and observations rather than on external information.

The legal system can fully differentiate itself from other systems only if it is itself internally differentiated. External factors such as considerations of justice and equity, of natural law and moral legitimacy are therefore relevant to it not directly and immediately, for there can be no criteria of legitimacy outside the law, but only as internally produced information, as "irritations" and resonance. Internal information must be consistent with the legal system's decisions, and are the product of second-order observations. Its functions of behavioral control and conflict resolution are political and juridical, and are realized by means of social operation, that is, by events which have no duration, and which differentiate it from the environment. The legal system's coding of legal versus non-legal requires that second-order observations in the system are possible. This may occur through legal argumentations, interpretations and comments based on legal texts, according to the legal system's internal theories of interpretation. Interpretations and argumentations do not change the law, however.

These second-order observations are necessary to produce legal notions through confirmation and condensation in the process of repeated use, and to differentiate the legal from other systems such as the political system. Moreover, second-order observations make the boundary between legal and non-legal blurred, and its crossing smooth and the coupling of legal with non-legal possible. The legal systems are linked through the formula "if – then" to conditional programs, which indicate the conditions that determine the circumstances when a given code is applied, if the expectations are stabilized. Unmet expectations acquire the form of norms in order to provide them with stability. Conditional programs, in the case of the legal system, specify the external (environmental) conditions on which it depends whether a system is legal or not, and fill this coding with content. Programs of the legal system are conditional programs. Courts make decisions as to whether s is valid or not in general, beyond a particular case. These decisions, which must be justified, and are indeed often justified with moral argumentations, are often contestable, especially when they decide on conflicts and political issues in general; they are nonetheless valid when made by courts.

Constitutional, or fundamental, rights perform the fundamental function of regulating communication in such a way, that the modern social order can be differentiated. They are therefore in a close relationship with all the communication media. They also perform the function of protecting individual freedom and dignity against state encroachments, and the political sphere from interference on the part of private interests. Additional functions of the fundamental rights are making the differentiated social order possible by generalizing reciprocal behavioral expectations; shaping the state's interest in politically relevant social phenomena, securing trust in the monetary and economic systems, and providing legitimacy to the state. This is possible, however, as long as political rights are effectively safeguarded. The political sphere has its own institutionalized criteria of relevance, autonomy and rationality. These criteria, which differ from those of public administration, are best instantiated by the institution of the universal and equal suffrage (Luhmann 2002).

The Sociology of Art

Luhmann investigated this field of studies in the last years of his life, in accordance – as is mostly the case with this author – with his system theory perspective (see Luhmann 2000). Art operates as an autopoietic system, which is based on communication with itself, and is decoupled from its social environment. The art system is accordingly autonomous from the artists themselves and from the audience. As is the case of any other system, the art system, too, has a boundary between a marked and an unmarked space. A peculiar trait of the art system is the problematic nature of the marked space; that is, the problematic definition of the essence of art. Luhmann dwells on the debate regarding the definition of art throughout history, namely, whether novelty, or beauty, creating illusion, or the ability to please and elicit admiration, connote art.

However art may be defined, external references, such as those having moral implications, are not accepted. The art system is autonomous in its self-reference, namely, it is autonomous in its self-description and in the self-reflection on its nature. In modern times, a radical break with the binding tradition of form has occurred, and the tempo of change has increased. The distinction between the art system and its environment is reintroduced into the art system itself in the form of the distinction between self-reference and hetero-reference. The system uses this operation of re-entry to determine its self, while the observer can use this distinction to conduct observations. What is considered art and non-art belongs to the art system. The art system depends in many ways on its social environment – in financial terms, for example – but the environment cannot determine what art is, or how artworks should be considered.

The Sociology of Religion

Luhmann has formulated his sociology of religion in conformance to his theory of the social system, and has dedicated two books to a detailed investigation of this theme (Luhmann 1991, 2013). Religion is viewed as an autopoietic component of the social system and a system in and by itself, which is based on self-observation and self-description, and is open to communication with others. Its code of immanence versus transcendence is operationally closed, but not in its meaning. Transcendence conceals the unfamiliar, is itself unfamiliar, and in monotheistic religions demands faith in one God. God's attributes, which are unobservable, are construed by means of second-order observations. The distinction between immanence and transcendence re-enters the definition of religion, for transcendence connotes religion, and religious explanations include both the values of immanence and transcendence. Its relation to morality in the modern world is precarious, even though religion makes use of morality; for religion and morality use different codes, respectively, good versus bad, and immanence versus transcendence. The possibility of attaining knowledge of God is therefore open, though only to a limited extent.

As a symbolically generalized communication medium, religion, and faith in particular, face the problem of finding acceptance even when this is not likely. This is often the case in modern, secularized times, in which individuals may be loosely integrated, if at all; complexity exerts pressure on all function systems, including religion; new religions are possible, based on different textual traditions, and the autonomy of the religious system has been fully realized. Morality supplies religion with programs that are essential to interpret the distinction between good and bad. In addition to providing individuals with identities based on their selves, religion inquires about the meaning of the subject-object distinction as its central concern. In the case of religion, meaning has three aspects. In the social aspect, the confirmation of faith is sought.

In the historical or temporal aspect, some points are considered privileged. In the factual aspect, a world creator is supposed to be omniscient, ever-present, all observing, and beyond all contingency, and therefore independent of distinctions. As a component of the social system, religion controls its identity by self-reflection, which is the operation that makes the system the object of its own consideration. The religious system controls its identity also by reference to itself, as religious communication based on rituals; for rituals distinguish religious communication from the non-religious one. The formulation of dogmas and the inquiries into theological problems, such as the problem of theodicy, point to the self-reference of religion as a system itself (besides being a component of the social system). Its ever-greater inner differentiation – i.e., in different dogmatic apparatuses – is accordingly relevant to system theory.

The function of religion in the social system – as Luhmann argues – is not to provide systemic integration, for it can be on the contrary quite disruptive of the social order, nor can the certainties or strength of faith measure religiosity. Society has become secularized and privatized to the effect that the individuals must decide their religious faith, and the modes and timing of their participation in religious organizations; and that they are aware of this obligation. Participation may occur according to different roles: as financial contributors, or as active members, or finally as employees of the religious organization. Religious organizations have adapted to the privatization and secularization processes. These processed have modified the functions of religion by making religious membership dependent on the members' individual decisions. In modern society, in fact, nearly all structures and operations can be attributed to decisions.

The functions of religion have also been modified by forcing the religious system to react to the secularization process, and to the secularized society that has followed consequently. The specific functions of religion in a secular society are to supply the world with meaning; to reduce the world's complexity and uncertainty, and therefore to master its contingency, and to provide it with a non-arbitrary, and hence determinable, relationship to its environment. This relationship varies, as religion cannot be tied to any particular form or faith. It cannot be affirmed with any certainty whether religion can still perform in today's world society these functions, especially the function of uncertainty reduction. Nevertheless, the differentiation of the religious system has now prompted the development of the religious organizations and dogmatic apparatuses. Religion is both an inner experience and a social institution like the Church, with a dogmatic apparatus of its own.

Faith could serve as a communication medium only if religions with their dogmatic apparatus are sufficiently complex and abstract to perform this function. This is not its only function, nor is its core function, which does not exist in the case of religion. Decisions concerning faith and the attendance of rituals are problems, the solution of which is entrusted to the religious organizations rather than to the individual members. Religion performs then important functions that have no functional equivalent, as no other component of the social system performs the same functions. The religious systems' functional differentiation increases the self-reference of their doctrines and organizations. Thus, the social system is enabled, on the one hand, to make use of this mechanism of complexity reduction; on the other hand, however, a secular society may find difficulty in relating to the religious subsystem.

The Educational System

This system does not possess a code of its own, as its central goals and values, such as education and socialization, may also be found in other systems. It exerts autopoietically the function of education with techniques of its own, and is responsible for the social selection effects of the educational process. Not only is the educational subsystem autonomous from other systems or subsystems but also each level in its organizational hierarchy is autonomous from the other levels. The self-reflection of the educational system has concerned pedagogic thought on the one hand, and the social structural development of this system on the other. This development has resulted from a differentiation process that began in the mid eighteenth century, and has brought about a multiplication of functions and didactic themes, in particular, the function and theme of political education. Moreover, the system's selection effects have been a privileged object of consideration and discussion, as these effects may came about with no one's accord. The educational establishment has not been so far prone to reflect on itself, its roles, programs, and reform projects.

What is more, the achievement of particular effects on the part of the educational system has proved quite uncertain when they have been deliberately pursued, and its two orientations – one to its function of providing education and socialization, the other to performance – have diverged. These divergences have not been the object of self-reflection on the part of the educational system. Self-reflection, as applied to the pedagogic function by means of a specific "contingency formula," lingers on the social system's reflexive operation of learning to learn. This implies that the educational process is oriented to the educational system itself, rather than to particular individuals such as the teacher or the pupils. Learning to learn does not merely require practical experience, but also considering the systemic consequences of the learning process; considering, therefore, how the educational system performs its functions in a functionally differentiated society.

The educational system is, as the social system in general, differentiated by means of pedagogic roles. If teaching promotes the process of functional differentiation, this process promotes in turn the expectations related to teaching. Learning to learn succeeds better if it considers environmental contingencies such as inadequate resources, whether of financial nature or otherwise; or the difficult and unpredictable relationships between the teacher and the pupils. This instance of "double contingency," as referred to the educational system, points to the complexity and to reflexive and temporal character of this system. Time-situated educational events are contingent, to the effect that both the experience of the past and the anticipation of the future are relevant to their present course. It is impossible to establish the effectiveness conditions of the educational process; for the character of the educational events is contingent, which makes these events unpredictable. The educational system has created its own complexity, the reduction of which has been taken care of by mechanisms such as organizational differentiation.

The educational system is a subsystemic component of the more inclusive social system, which is connoted by the ideal of equal educational opportunities for all the population. This ideal, however, though widespread, cannot be reconciled with the divisive consequences of functional differentiation, and in particular with the formation of social classes in modern society. There is therefore a lack of legitimacy for social inequality. Resorting to the selection of students according to impersonal and universalistic criteria, such as desert or merit, is in keeping with the ideal of equality of opportunity, but maintains or further produces social inequalities, and compensative education is not apt to overcome this problem. The state's intervention in educational matters, such as the selection of students by means of exams, seems to conform to these universalistic criteria and egalitarian ideals. Exams involve decisions, which the organizational differentiation of the educational system makes necessary. It has become apparent, however, that the selection of students actually follows social criteria. It therefore promotes inequality and social conflict.

These consequences are often considered incompatible with the ideal of the equality of opportunities, and therefore undesirable. Luhmann objects to the ideal of equal opportunities that in most cases there is no correspondence between educational titles and occupational achievement. This ideal performs, accordingly, an ideological function. Self-reflection on the part of the educational system should then abandon this ideal, and rather focus on the function of education for the social system. The teacher and the pupils mutually condition their conduct because of the double contingency character of their relationship. Still, the pupils' evaluations on the part of the teachers provide an important contribution to an effective selection of the pupils' careers. Binary codes are used in the evaluation process, such as praising versus blaming, passing versus failing, and good versus bad grades. These codes are important in that they supply linguistic rules guiding the evaluation and the selection, and therefore the pupils' careers.

Language is therefore the symbolic medium of the selection process. Functional equivalents in educational performances receive their evaluations and legitimacy through language. This medium, however, may produce a self-fulfilling prophecy, to the effect that teachers' current evaluations and definitions of performances, whether positive or negative, modify the future ones. They are accordingly conducive to the stable formation of marginal groups of underachieving pupils, most of whom are socially disadvantaged. This seems to be the unwelcome consequence of the evaluation procedures. These procedures, if and to the extent that they are rational, face validity problems, for they should pursue the incompatible goals of selecting good students, and not selecting bad students. The rationality of the selection procedures in the educational system is accordingly a goal, which is beyond reach. Using tests would be of no avail, for the problem would then be how to formulate valid tests. A possible though partial solution, as Luhmann suggests, would be combining an attempt to solve specific problems with providing general solutions to them.

Sociological Enlightenment and the Evolution of the Social System

The task, which Luhmann's functional analysis has set to itself, is to understand, investigate theoretically and reduce the complexity of the social system. This task connotes Luhmann's idea of sociological Enlightenment. This idea differs from the traditional and rationalistic conception of the Enlightenment (still present in Habermas, according to Luhmann), which failed to distinguish between communication and interaction, and maintained that the free public discussion can carry out the Enlightenment's. Sociological Enlightenment involves the preservation and increase of the social system's complexity. The chances of its survival would be thus enhanced and its dissolution into the system's more complex environment prevented. The theme of complexity paves the way to understanding Luhmann's evolutionary notion of social change (see especially Luhmann 2012: ch. 3; Luhmann and De Giorgi 2003: ch. 3). In keeping with Luhmann, external differentiation is the unlikely result of evolution, and concerns differences between the social system and its environment. Internal differentiation concerns the relations between subsystems.

In modern times, internal differentiation has brought a maximum of difference between the system and the environment. The consequences of the system's internal differentiation and its resulting complexity may be investigated by conceptualizing social change in modern times. Society's primary subsystems, insofar as based on functions rather than on social strata, as in previous times, have made increased complexity possible. In keeping with the theory of autopoiesis, evolution theory concerns operationally closed and autopoietic systems. Evolution presupposes an asymmetric relation between structure (the conditions that govern the stability of social systems) and the social systems. Luhmann's evolution theory concerns itself with changing structures, as Darwin and Spencer's theories do, and takes from these authors the notion that variation leads to selection, even though the facilities for variation and selection do not coincide, but rejects their notions of natural selection and adaptation. Rather, the central notions of Luhmann's theory are structural differentiation and coupling, autopoiesis, re-stabilization and chance.

In keeping with this theory, variations in operations, structures and systems are interdependent. Time is therefore a precondition of evolution. Accordingly, evolution concerns the changing conditions, in which systems operate their self-reproduction. They do so after that they have selected (therefore not rejected), and re-stabilized a particular random variation. A chance for greater complexity (and, therefore, a risk and an opportunity in the eyes of external observers of the system) follows from a tight connection between system and environment. This chance is a necessary condition to evolution, even though a system's complexity does not necessarily preserve it from destruction wrought by its environment. Randomness, or chance, become more likely because the complex structures of evolved systems offer greater possibilities both for deviations and for ways to cope with them, as compared to more simple structures. The stabilization of systemic change involves the re-stabilization of the system.

Evolution is not necessarily conducive to greater societal complexity, however, nor does it follow a pre-established universal path, as the history and sociology of religion show. The opposite consequence – less societal complexity – is also possible, as ecological problems and the consequent threat of collapse of social systems indicate. Inner societal differentiation has taken place in the following stages:

a. a first stage of segmentary differentiation, in which the system is not distinguished from the environment;
b. a second stage of different social layers, which constitute the principle of societal differentiation;
c. finally, a third stage, in which differentiation impinges on different social functions.

In keeping with Luhmann's notion of social systems as communication systems, evolution is a consequence of systemic variation. Systemic variation may be caused by the differentiation of societal system and the interaction system, but it may also be caused by deviant, unlikely or rejected communication between the social system and its environment, and by the structural contradiction and stabilization efforts on the part of the system by means of further selections.

Evolution theory makes no prediction as to the outcome of such efforts. Social systems, as action systems, achieve greater complexity to the extent that actions are related to other actions in such a way that collective actions take place. If there are institutions – especially, political institutions – that regulate collective actions, the social system extends its potential for meaningful communication within the system itself. By selecting specific functions for each subsystem, the system modifies to its advantage its relations to the environment. The subsystems are functionally related to each other in the environment; moreover, as the case of the religious system shows, they can control their own evolution by reflecting on themselves and their identity. Evolutionary change is compatible with mistakes and deviations, as considered from the social system's vantage point. It is conducive to making new distinctions between the system and the environment, to the assumption of new functions, and to enrichment of meaning (which is a property of the system, not of the individual consciousnesses). Evolutionary change, moreover, exploits random and unlikely variations in the social system and its subsystems in a great number of historically determined ways.

The symbolic structures of the social system have been relevant in that they have accelerated the pace of the system's evolutionary differentiation. World religions, in particular, have greatly contributed to further differentiating religion systems. The social system's differentiation and complexity, and possibly re-stabilization, follow consequently. Evolutionary upgrading – if and to the extent that it takes place – involves the system's greater complexity, and thereby greater chances of reducing the complexity of its environment. System integration and autopoiesis, but also their opposite, system disintegration, occur at all time. Evolutionary re-stabilization offers historically contingent solutions to problems of structural incompatibilities between the subsystems of a social system or between different systems. Selection switches its criteria in the process of evolutionary change. In modern societies, which are no longer based on the quality of what is selected, these criteria become unstable, and forms of evolutionary differentiation therefore vary unpredictably, thus making purposive social planning impossible.

Evolutionary advances – if and to the extent that they take place – involves the system's greater complexity, and thereby greater chances of reducing the complexity of its environment. Agriculture, writing, the press, the money system, and telecommunication are acquisitions of strategic relevance for the system, for they are conducive to its evolutionary upgrading. Evolutionary achievements, or advances, often originate in the need to cope with an environment that has changed. Technological development has been an important factor of societal evolution. Modern society is in fact dependent on it. Technology, however, involves great risk for the environment and the sources of energy supply, and quite possibly further technological progress will cause chaos rather than societal evolution. Ideas form an autopoietic semantic system that is subject, like all systems, to evolutionary change.

In modern times, the spread of writing, printing and the mass media has put an end to the primacy of oral tradition, and modified cognitive schemata and hitherto taken for granted, or deemed plausible, knowledge and interpretations of reality. Subsystem evolution has resulted from, but has also set into motion, both coding (that is, distinguishing by means of contrapositions) and programming (that is, establishing the conditions necessary to the operation of coding). Moreover, evolution is an autopoietic process, to the effect that it alters the conditions of further evolution, and subsystem evolution has increasingly contributed to the societal evolution. As the case of religion shows, the development of autopoietic systems may be an abrupt switch to a different principle of stability. Luhmann, however, declares he has no idea as to how and where evolution will get humankind any further.

The Reception of Luhmann's Work

Luhmann's work has received scholarly attention to an extent that few other sociologists have matched. He has been considered one of the contemporary authors in this field of studies who gained "a worldwide reputation for his theory of social systems" (Nollman 2005: 454–5). Other Luhmann scholars have formulated similar positive evaluations: "the most noteworthy contemporary social theorist" (Viskovatoff 1999: 481), "a great thinker" (Gumbrecht 2001: 49), and the author of "a rich theory of modern society" (Bechmann and Stehr 2002: 75). Luhmann's is a theory, according to Miller, that "explains positive and negative aspects of modern society in a comprehensive and theoretically profound way that seems to be quite unrivalled in present-day sociology" (Miller 1994: 109). Luhmann was a prolific writer, as he published a great number of books and articles during his relatively short life (he died of cancer at the age of 70). Even though Luhmann has had followers who have endeavored to clarify his thought and conceptual apparatus (see especially Corsi, Esposito and Baraldi 1996), the reception of his oeuvre has often been critical, with particular reference to some of his concepts borrowed from system theory; but criticism has been in many cases tempered by and mixed with praise.

In this connection, we shall selectively present this secondary literature, focusing on a fraction of this secondary literature, most of which has come out in the last 20 years. We shall, furthermore, distinguish appraisals that regard his work in general, and those concerning particular works by this author. Introductory works to Luhmann's thought have tended to variously combine and balance negative with positive evaluations. Hans Joas and Wolfgang Knöbl, who are the authors of a recent introduction to modern social theory, have deemed interesting Luhmann's analysis of the functions the social subsystems and the processes of exchange between them. However, they reject as unrealistic Luhmann's "radical supposition" – as they write – that the social system and its subsystems are fundamentally inaccessible to each other (Joas and Knöbl 2009: 277–8). Baert and Carreira da Silva, in another recent work on this subject, have found Luhmann's contribution to functionalist social theory innovative; but they object to his not sufficiently critical (in their view) attitude toward modernity (Baert and Carreira da Silva 2010: 81).

Harrington (2005: 285), in his appraisal of Luhmann's system theory, raises several critical observations, and prefers to dwell on them rather than on the positive aspects of this theory. Luhmann's work has been found objectionable on several grounds: it neglects social action; the notion of binary codes is simplistic; the capacity attributed to social systems to reproduce them is overstated; and issues of conflict and crisis, or concerning mixed cultural and organizational forms, receive little attention there. Such remarks on the part of all these authors do not seem to coincide in most cases. This may not be surprising as they have been formulated in the context of general introductory works on social theory. Their authors might therefore be not sufficiently cognizant of Luhmann's work, or participants in the debate concerning it.

It may be then worthwhile to focus – albeit selectively – on introductions on the part of scholars that deal exclusively with Luhmann, and should be therefore considered as Luhmann scholars. According to their evaluations, Luhmann's notions of autopoietic systems of communication and second-order observations are his most notable sociological accomplishments. More in general, they have viewed his theory of modern society as "audacious and stimulating" (Zolo 1985: 519; see also in this connection: Borch 2011: 134–7; Brunczel 2010: 262; Moeller 2006: ix) and have shown appreciation for his "theoretical imagination" (Schimank 1998: 181).

Many a commentator has dwelt on specific aspects of Luhmann's work. In this connection, we shall refer only to a couple of contributions that are noteworthy and relatively recent. Stichweh (2000) has focused on the rise of communication theory in Luhmann's thought as an alternative to action theory – a theoretical shift, in Stichweh's own words – and on the formulation of a conceptual apparatus to this end. According to Stichweh, the reasons for this theoretical shift are twofold. Firstly, the notion of communication is to be preferred to that of action or selection, because only the former notion distinguishes between social and biological systems. Secondly, communication is a more suitable category than other notions such as action to be a component of system theory and as a description of modern society, and of world society in particular.

Habermas' critical appraisals of Luhmann's system theory are rather well-known (see Habermas and Luhmann 1971; see also Borch 2011: 8–14; Moeller 2006: 187–91), but it may be worthwhile to recapitulate them. Habermas objects to Luhmann in the following terms. First, the world as the aggregate of all events and situations presupposes the existence of a system, which the world's complexity threatens. In keeping with Luhmann, the solution to this problem may involve either the reduction of the world's complexity or the increase in the system's complexity. Luhmann's solution is accordingly indeterminate. Second, system theory fails to distinguish between meaning and information, and is therefore incompatible with the category of meaning, even if this is broadly defined. Systems, if conceived of in keeping with Luhmann as communication networks, presuppose the intersubjective validity of meaning. This is necessary to obtain mutual understanding on the part of those participating in a discourse, if they wish to reach an agreement. Third, communicative action based on mutual understanding, rather than on instrumental action, constitutes society. Luhmann's system theory fails to distinguish between these two types of action. Fourth, Luhmann's system theory also fails to explain why systems should provide self-interpretations and self-reflections. Luhmann's systems are therefore not transparent to themselves.

The critical appraisals by authors different than Habermas are perhaps less well-known, but at least some of them should be mentioned here. Leydesdorff (1996) has taken issue with Luhmann's definition of information as "a difference that makes a difference." This is, as Leydesdorff argues, a definition of meaningful information, rather than of information in general. Information that is not directly meaningful – as in the case of second-order observations – is a source of uncertainty. Uncertainty can be reduced when second-order observers select information and endow it with meaning. Uncertainty reduction contributes to the local and provisional stabilization of the system, which can, however, be modified by any higher-order observation. The social system selects some events as meaningful rather than others, which are discarded as noise; the system therefore receives messages in distributed mode. Luhmann's focus on the actor's local and contingent understanding of communication is inadequate, for it does not clarify non-local and non-contingent communication, as performed by observing systems or subsystems by means of second-order operations. The interactions between functionally differentiated subsystems – that is, the operational coupling of interpenetrated subsystems – is conducive to the formation of a higher-order system of universalistic communication.

The concept of operation, which is of central importance to Luhmann's system's theory, also constitutes Clam's object of investigation. Clam (2000) contends that Luhmann has reformulated system theory in order to advance his thesis that society is a self-contained field where all social communication takes place. In keeping with Clam, Luhmann's theory has a central, not philosophically elaborated, "protological" conception of a system's self-sustaining operativity, whereby each operation of the system prepares and constrains, but does not determine, its successive operations. "A sort of temporally stable whirlpool," in Clam's own words (Clam 2000: 73), follows thence. Social communication, which is Luhmann's primary category, has the paradoxical character that it cannot communicate about itself and, in this sense, transcends itself.

Gumbrecht (2001) has broached the question of how Luhmann has seen "the Future from an angle of contingency" (Gumbrecht 2001: 56), to the effect that the present becomes broader, and contingency omnipresent. Dirk Baecker (2001), a former student of Luhmann and an expert on system theory, considers in some detail the very notion of system as it has been used in the sociological works by Parsons and, especially, by Luhmann himself, to the effect that Luhmann has used this notion as a methodological device in order to study not only what is included in a system, but also what is not included there. Baecker refers in this connection to the methodological preliminary remarks of Luhmann's *Theory of Society*, vol. 1 (2012: 13–18). Hauck (1999) has contended that Luhmann's work has not produced the radical break with the sociological tradition, as he has claimed. Rather, there is continuity with specific aspects of this tradition, such as the radical separation between the production of meaning and material production and between consciousness and society; wherein systems of consciousness and material structures are considered as society's environments, which are relevant to system theory only as perturbations of the social system.

However, all these concepts are derived according to Hauck from the sociological tradition. Also, the notion of evolution, as resulting from variation, selection and re-stabilization, has been borrowed from this tradition, and it is questionable, if for no other reason, because it gives pride of place to Western civilization. Hauck and the other commentators of Luhmann, who have been so far quoted, have been exegetical rather than critical. Several of these commentators, moreover, have acknowledged the relevance of at least some of his concepts and theoretical proposals (e.g. Febbrajo 1990: 9; Østerberg 2000: 23, 25). On the other hand, the authors of introductions to Luhmann's thought have oftentimes qualified their praises with fundamental reservations. Their evaluations have frequently included overviews of the secondary literature on Luhmann (see for example Brunczel 2010: 233–1).

In particular, with reference to these authors and the literature they cite:

a. There is no analysis of the spatial or material attributes of the environment;
b. The social system can perform other operations, in addition to autopoietically reproducing itself;
c. The notions of structural coupling and interpenetration are inadequate to account for the relations between system and environment;
d. Luhmann's binary logic, as instantiated by the contraposition between system and environment, ignores differences in the degree of intensity which connotes the presence of any given social phenomenon;
e. The social character of affects and emotions is ignored;
f. The implications of the autopoiesis theory for modern society cannot be easily reconciled with everyday experience;
g. Luhmann's theoretical decision to leave people and action out of consideration has undesirable theoretical consequences; such as making impossible any description or explanation of norms, conflicts, inequality and power;
h. The value of the pursuit of truth, to which Luhmann apparently subscribes, should receive particular relevance, as it is essential to scientific communication (Borch 2011: 139–40; Brunczel 2010: 234–5; Zolo 1985: 526–7).

In addition to these rather critical evaluations, which have been formulated in the context of introductions to Luhmann, there are several in-depth appraisals of specific theses that are found in Luhmann's work. There have been but few attempts to provide more balanced, or at least not exclusively critical, assessments. One of them is Schmidt's. Schmidt (2005) remarks that Luhmann's notion of function systems has two different meanings; for, on the one hand, the various function systems, such as the political, economic, and religious, are close, self-referential and autopoietic. This notion of function system provides no information on what takes place within and between the systems, but only on the distinguishing trait of each function system. On the other hand, this notion may serve a theoretical purpose in that it points to each function's actual performance, rather than to its autopoietic character. Most evaluations are critical, however.

They concern, generally speaking, Luhmann's notions of function and social system. With reference to Luhmann's theory of functional system differentiation, Miller holds that it "explains positive and negative aspects of modern society" (Miller 1994: 109). According to Luhmann, as Miller contends, in modern, center-less society different systems have their own rationality. There is, therefore, no overall system rationality.

Ecological communication would involve an intersystemic discourse, which would in turn imply second-order observations on the part of systems. Granted that different systems cannot have a collective rationality, they can, however, have a mutual knowledge regarding their different perspectives. There is consequently a possibility of coordinated dissent. Different systems, or their representatives, could then communicate with each other. Ecological communication is, however, hampered by the difficulty, on the part of modern democracies, to overcome the organized irresponsibility that follows from modern society's functional differentiation.

Also referring to Luhmann's differentiation theory and to the theory of social differentiation in general, Knorr Cetina (1992) has formulated several critical remarks. She has conceded that this theory is not trivial as it points to the extent and consequences of the division of labor. Still, she objects to this theory because it provides no information on the specific set of actions and functions characteristic of each subsystem; and also because Luhmann's thesis of social system's autopoiesis is untenable. Empirical evidence, drawn from studies that belong to the so-called new sociology of science, is not compatible with this thesis. It shows on the contrary that the production and the general acceptance or rejection of the findings, which are produced within the science subsystem, are influenced by a host of non-scientific criteria in addition to the criterion of the rational pursuit of scientific truth.

Trust in the capabilities and honesty of those who have produced them and the reputation of the institutions, where they are active, are instances of such criteria. Scientific rationality is therefore not immune to influences extraneous to the code, which Luhmann attributes to scientific findings, namely the alternative of true versus false. In contrast to what Luhmann claims, moreover, extraneous influences may be also detected in other subsystems, such as the political and the economic ones. Subsystems are accordingly neither homogeneous nor autonomous. Examples drawn from modern physics and astrophysics also illustrate the opposite process of functional dedifferentiation, while the science of molecular biology is not autopoietic. Thus, Luhmann's theory of functional differentiation is disconfirmed in several areas of scientific investigation. As a general conclusion, Knorr Cetina warns against attempts, such as Luhmann's, to include any given area of inquiry in a unitary theoretical framework.

More recently Nassehi (2004) has reconsidered differentiation theories, Luhmann's in particular, from the viewpoint of their semantic consistency and theoretical fruitfulness. Luhmann has offered, according to Nassehi, a realistic (rather than merely analytical) conception of social differentiation. This conception views society as the unitary horizon (in the phenomenological sense of this term) of all possible though unlikely communications. Society's problem is the coordination of these different societal components. Nassehi refers in this connection also to Knorr Cetina's exegetic contribution (1992), and objects both to Luhmann and Knorr Cetina that functional differentiation is a specific condition of a form of action, which is unable as such either to grasp the societal location of actions and organizations, or on this basis to consider a set of similar functional models. These theoretical limitations, which follow as a consequence of the focus on functional differentiation, hinder grasping and describing – theoretically and empirically – social inequality and exclusion. These are central sociological themes, however. Society should be accordingly conceived as the sum total, not of all communications, but of all possible communications.

Schwinn (1995) maintains that Luhmann has not succeeded in relating functions to society, considered as a unity; for society as a totality cannot be induced from its parts, and it is not analyzed as such. This flaw, as Schwinn contends, originates from Luhmann's rejection of the concept of action as an analytical tool. Luhmann's concept of autopoiesis is to be sure useful – Zolo (1985) maintains – to analyze societal complexity. Still, it presents a number of difficulties even disregarding its dubious consistency with Maturana and Varela's original meaning of this concept. First of all, it cannot contribute to evolutionary theory, to the extent that it points to the invariance of the autopoietic unit. The system's self-reference, furthermore, should bring into light its identity and autonomy, whose existence is conceived as being apart from observers, but this would imply the objective existence of what is observed. This epistemological position is therefore close, as Zolo maintains, to scientism and naive biologism. It is, accordingly, incompatible with the task of sociological enlightenment, which Luhmann assigns to his own sociology.

Østerberg (2000) has raised an objection to Luhmann, which he considers fundamental, namely that Luhmann has conflated two distinct processes in modern society, one of functional differentiation (in the sense of a process conducive to social integration) and the other of autonomization (in the sense of a process conducive to autonomous interest spheres). These two processes are opposite, however, for the former leads to integration, the latter to disintegration and conflict. Luhmann's autopoietic conception of modern society lays stress on the latter process; it is therefore misleading to connote the modern social system as functional (see also in this connection, but with a more positive appreciation of Luhmann, Marramao 1981). Hüttermann (1999), also focusing on Luhmann's notion of social system, remarks that this notion, that of autopoiesis, and system theory in general, are conducive to several theoretical difficulties.

They are as follows: circular argumentations; neglect of important sociological issues such as social inequality and scarcity of resources; neglect, furthermore, of important concepts derived from the sociological tradition, such as social integration and disintegration; banalization of culture, which is interpreted as mere contingency from the viewpoint of system theory; and finally, problems of empirical validity and logical consistency. Luhmann's discussion of functional system differentiation is situated, in a further exegetical contribution, in the theoretical context of ecological communication (Miller 1994). What this communication would need, but which is currently absent, is a functional coordination on the part of different systems by means of an intersystemic discourse. In turn, functional coordination requires a mutual knowledge, concerning the differences between their perspectives.

This has not occurred so far, however, since modern society's democratic institutions have failed to keep pace with society's process of evolutionary differentiation and with the possibility of dissent that flows from it. Kössler (1998), writing from a viewpoint which is close to Marxism, raises a number of objections against Luhmann. Some of them – such as his omission of a theoretical consideration of actor/action, inequality, and territory, and his giving pride of place to Western civilization – have already been mentioned. Kössler makes additional critical observations, such as the unsatisfactory analysis of the concept of a world society, and of the relation between binary codes and the forms of differentiation; further, he points to Luhmann's too abstract and simplistic model inherent to binary codes, which is hardly compatible with the complex historical reality.

Viskovatoff (1999) raises two fundamental objections to Luhmann's theory. First, it is not clear whether Luhmann means his theory is true from an empirical viewpoint. Second, it is also not clear how this theory relates to neighboring social sciences such as psychology, social psychology, and biology. Bußhof (1976), finally, remarks that Luhmann's category of political code – which involves the binary distinction between progressive and conservative in order to make collectively binding decisions – is too schematic, for it fails to provide information on differences between a lawful and an unlawful exercise of power; or to decide on fundamental political questions such as what are the political aspects of the public administration, or whether and how the latter should be distinguished from the political system; or on what use Luhmann's category of political code could be for politicians and students of politics.

References

Baecker, D. 2001. "Why Systems?" *Theory, Culture and Society* 18: 59–74.

Baert, P. and Carreira da Silva, F. 2010. *Social Theory in the Twentieth Century and Beyond*. Cambridge: Cambridge University Press.

Bechmann, G. and Stehr, N. 2002. "The Legacy of Niklas Luhmann" *Society* 39(2): 68–75.

Borch, C. 2011. *Niklas Luhmann*. London: Routledge.

Brunczel, B. 2010. *Disillusioning Modernity*. Frankfurt am Main: Peter Lang.

Bußhof, H. 1976. "Der politische Code: ein neuer Mythos in systemtheoretischer Sicht." *Kölner Zeitschrift für Soziologie und Sozialpsychologie* 28: 335–51.

Clam, J. 2000. "System's Sole Constituent, the Operation: Clarifying a Central Concept of Luhamnnian Theory." *Acta Sociologica* 43: 63–79.

Corsi, G., Esposito, E. and Baraldi, C. 1996, *Luhmann in glossario. I concetti fondamentali della teoria dei sistemi sociali*. Milan: FrancoAngeli.

Febbrajo, A. 1990. Introduzione all'edizione italiana, in N. Luhmann (ed.), *Sistemi sociali. Fondamenti di una teoria generale*. Bologna: Il Mulino, 9–49.

Gumbrecht, H.U. 2001. "How is Our Future Contingent?: Reading Luhmann against Luhmann." *Theory, Culture and Society* 18: 49–58.

Habermas, J. and Luhmann, N. 1971. *Theorie der Gesellschaft oder Sozialtechnologie*. Frankfurt am Main: Suhrkamp.

Harrington, A. 2005. *Modern Social Theory: An Introduction*. Oxford: Oxford University Press.

Hauck, G. 1999. "Radikaler Bruch?: Niklas Luhmann und die sozialwissenschaftliche Tradition." *Berliner Journal für Soziologie* 9: 253–68.

Hüttermann, J. 1999. "Kultur als Irritation? Über den Umgang der Luhmannschen Systemtheorie mit dem Problemfeld der Kulturbegegnung." *Berliner Journal für Soziologie* 9: 233–52.

Joas, H. and Knöbl, W. 2009. *Social Theory: Twenty Introductory Lectures*. Cambridge: Cambridge University Press.

Knorr Cetina, Karin, D. 1992. "Zur Unterkomplexitaet der Differenzierungstheorie." *Zeitschrift für Soziologie* 21(6): 406–19.

Kössler, R. 1998. "Weltgesellschaft? Oder Grenzen der Luhmannschen Gesellschaftstheorie." *Soziologische Revue* 21: 175–83.

Leydesdorff, L. 1996. "Luhmann's Sociological Theory: Its Operationalization and Future Perspectives." *Social Science Information* 35: 283–306.

Luhmann, N. 1970. *Soziologische Aufklärung 1*. Opladen: Westdeutscher Verlag.

Luhmann, N. 1975. *Politische Planung*. Opladen: Westdeutscher Verlag.

Luhmann, N. 1984. *Soziale Système. Grundrisse einer allgemeinen Theorie*. Frankfurt am Main: Suhrkamp.

Luhmann, N. 1989. *Ecological Communication*. Cambridge: Polity Press.

Luhmann, N. 1990a. *Political Theory in the Welfare State*. Berlin and New York: Walter de Gruyter.

Luhmann, N. 1990b. "Mass Media e culture locali." Available at: www.filosofia.3000.it.

Luhmann, N. 1991. *Funzione della religione*. Brescia: Morcelliana.

Luhmann, N. 1997. "Globalization or World Society? How to Conceive of Modern Society." *International Review of Sociology* 7: 67–79.

Luhmann, N. 1998. *Love as Passion: The Codification of Intimacy*. Stanford, CA: Stanford University Press.

Luhmann, N. 2000a. *The Reality of the Mass Media*. Stanford, CA: Stanford University Press.

Luhmann, N. 2000b. *Vertrauen. Ein Mechanismus der Reduktion sozialer Komplexitaet*. Stuttgart: Lucius and Lucius.

Luhmann, N. 2002. *I diritti fondamentali come istituzione*. Bari: Dedalo.

Luhmann, N. 2005. *Organizzazione e decisione*. Milan: Bruno Mondadori.

Luhmann, N. 2006. *Osservazioni sul moderno*. Rome: Armando.

Luhmann, N. 2008. *Risk: A Sociological* Theory. London: Aldine Transaction.

Luhmann, N. 2009. *Soziologische Aufklärung*, Volume 2. Wiesbaden: Verlag für Sozialwissenschafen.

Luhmann, N. 2012. *Theory of Society*, Volume 1. Stanford, CA: Stanford University Press.

Luhmann, N. 2013. *Introduction to Systems Theory*. Cambridge: Polity Press.

Luhmann, N. and De Giorgi, R. 2003. *Teoria della società*. Milan: FrancoAngeli.

Luhmann, N. and Schorr, K.E. 1999. *Il sistema educativo. Problemi di riflessività*. Rome: Armando.

Marramao, G. 1981. "Il 'possibile logico' come frontiera del sistema. Le dimensioni della razionalità da Weber a Luhmann." *Il Centauro* 1: 99–122.

Miller, M. 1994. "Intersystemic Discourse and Co-Ordinated Dissent: A Critique of Luhmann's Concept of Ecological Communication." *Theory, Culture and Society* 11: 101–21,

Moeller, H.G. 2006. *Luhmann Explained: From Souls to Systems*. La Salle, IL: Open Court.

Nassehi, A. 2004. "Die Theorie funktionaler Differenzierung im Horizont ihrer Kritik." *Zeitschrift für Soziologie* 33: 98–118.

Nollman, G. 2005. Niklas Luhmann, in *Encyclopedia of Social Theory*. London: Sage, 454–7.

Østerberg, D. 2000. "Luhmann's General Sociology." *Acta Sociologica* 43: 15.25.

Rasch, W. 2000. *Niklas Luhmann's Modernity*. Stanford, CA: Stanford University Press.

Schmidt, V. 2005. "Die Systeme der Systemtheorie. Stärken, Schwächen und ein Lösungsvorschlag." *Zeitschrift für Soziologie* 34: 406–24.

Schimank, U. 1998. "In Luhmann's Gesellschaft." *Kölner Zeitschrift für Soziologie und Sozialpsychologie* 50: 177–81.

Schwinn, T. 1995. "Funktion und Gesellschaft – Konstante Probleme trotz Paradigmenwechsel in der Systemtheorie Niklas Luhmanns." *Zeitschrift für Soziologie* 24: 196–214.

Stichweh, R. 2000. "Systems Theory as an Alternative to Action Theory?" *Acta Sociologica* 43: 5–13.

Viskovatoff, A. 1999. "Foundations of Niklas Luhmann's Theory of Social Systems." *Philosophy of the Social Sciences* 29: 481–516.

Zolo, D. 1985. "Reflexive Selbstbegruendung der Soziologie und Autopoiesis. Ueber die epistemologischen Voraussetzungen der 'allgemeinen Theorie sozialer Systeme' Niklas Luhmanns." *Soziale Welt* 36: 519–34.

Chapter 10
Robert K. Merton (1910–2003)

Preliminary Remarks

This presentation of Robert Merton's sociological work will roughly follow the order which this author has given to his subject matter in his celebrated work on social theory and social structure (1968). The first part will accordingly consider, first separately, then jointly, Merton's notions of social structure, sociological theory and middle-range theory. Merton's discussion of latent and manifest functions, the relationship between sociological theory and empirical research, and Merton's re-examination of functional analysis will be presented. Subsequently, Merton's well-known theory of social structure, as exposed in *Social Theory and Social Structure* and anomie, will be recapitulated. His studies on the relationship between bureaucratic structure and personality, on the role of the intellectual in public life, and on the self-fulfilling prophesy, will be then briefly illustrated. This text will subsequently dwell on Merton's contributions to the sociology of knowledge and of the mass media, and to his sociology of science. Other, possibly less well-known, works by Merton that also deal with social structure and related notions will be also touched upon here (see especially Merton 1976b). Finally, some information will be provided on the reception of Merton in an attempt to give a balanced consideration of appreciative and critical appraisals.

Sociological Theory, Middle-Range Theory, and Social Structure

As the author makes clear in the introduction (Merton 1968: 39), theory and sociological theory in particular are words that have been used so frequently that their meaning may have become unclear. Merton's sociological theory is middle-range, in the sense that it consists of a set of logically consistent conceptions which have a limited explanatory scope. They are accordingly neither simple working hypotheses, nor large-scale speculations having a conceptual apparatus of their own. These speculations should be instrumental in formulating empirically grounded generalizations on social conduct,[1] but they are hardly able to reach this goal.

Theoretical paradigms are instrumental to formulate middle-range sociological theories for a number of different reasons; for they have the function of defining with clarity and concision the fundamental concepts and their relations, and avoiding introducing new concepts that are not pertinent to the inquiry. Furthermore, they are conducive to interpretations that build on previous ones, thus serving the purpose of theory construction, and pave the way to the systematic comparison of the significant concepts. Theoretical and practical problems, which would be otherwise neglected, may thus receive attention. Finally, they are instrumental in conducting rigorous qualitative research. On the other hand, sociologists are well-advised not to consider sociological paradigms as having anything more than temporary validity as they are only starting points for the conduct of inquiry.

A precondition of functional analysis is clarifying the meaning of the concept of function. This term has been employed in a variety of ways, even disregarding meanings that are not relevant here, such as a public ceremony or an occupation. Function could then refer to the tasks which are incumbent to a social position, or to the reciprocal relationship between variables, or to those processes, whether biological or social, that contribute to the preservation of an organism, culture or society. Function, in any of these senses, refers to the objective and observable consequences of a given course of action, rather than to subjective motive or dispositions. Functional analysis rests upon the following premises or – as Merton calls them – "postulates."

---

1 The term "conduct," as distinguished from "behavior," refers, according to Merton, to purposive action, insofar as it "involves motives and consequently a choice between various alternatives" (Merton 1936: 895).

Firstly, there is the postulate of society's functional unity, according to which all the parts of a cultural or social system are mutually consistent. Merton observes that this is empirically unacceptable. Secondly, the postulate of universal functioning, namely, that all the cultural and social components of a system perform some sociologically relevant function. As Merton remarks, this is an empirical question, rather than a postulate. Finally, there is the postulate of functional indispensability. In keeping with this postulate, all the system's constitutive elements perform some indispensable function. Merton objects that this is a quite contentious assertion which should by impugned on theoretical grounds, for a societal component may exert a number of different functions, and different components may perform functionally equivalent functions.

The acceptance of any or all these postulates makes functionalist analysis vulnerable to the objection of being ideological, whether in a conservative or a progressive sense. Merton takes this imputation seriously, but refuses to accept it. He points to its inconsistent ideological evaluation, as some critics have maintained that functionalist analysis is progressive, while others think it as intrinsically conservative. Furthermore, Merton quotes and comments on a number of passages drawn from Marx's *Capital*, in which the ambivalent ideological orientation of dialectical materialism becomes apparent; for, according to Marx, this orientation is a potential source of social change, whether progressive or revolutionary; but it may also be conservative. There is not then any ideological tendency inherent to functionalist analysis, as the ambivalent ideological implications of religion evidence.

Merton sets out to formulate a paradigm – namely, a specific set of concepts, findings and problems – that connote functionalist analysis with the purpose of providing an answer to its basic questions. Functionalist analysis has a typical and recurrent object, which comprehends social roles, norms and institutions, organizations of groups, social control and social structure. Individual dispositions such as motives and goals also constitute an object of analysis, whether implicitly or explicitly. Individual dispositions are not functions, however. The concepts of function and dysfunction refer to the objective and multiple consequences of a purposive action for a social or cultural system in terms of the system's adaptation. The consequences that are irrelevant for the system are non-functional. Merton distinguishes, furthermore, between manifest and latent functions. The former set of functions is wanted and recognized on the part of the system's members, whereas the latter set is not. Shedding light on the manifest functions is instrumental to ascertaining consequences that have been neither pursued nor foreseen, to the advantage of sociological knowledge.

Functionalist analysis also investigates the social mechanisms – that is, how (as by means of roles, values, or institutions) functions operate; and the consequences for a social or cultural system, or for a system's component unit – such as individuals having a different status or subgroups – of transforming latent into manifest functions. The concept of functional prerequisite has so far served little heuristic purpose for sociological analysis, even though functionalist analysis makes use of it; for it is ill-defined, and has referred to biological (rather than sociological) requirements. Merton formulates the concept of functionally equivalent alternatives, which he considers of greater potential value for sociological analysis than functional prerequisite. In this case, a whole gamut of elements is focused as potentially satisfying a given functional prerequisite. The postulate of indispensability of a system's constitutive element is accordingly not maintained here.

Functional analysis, moreover, makes reference to the notion of structural context, or structural strain. This notion points to the limitations, which follow from the interdependence of the available alternatives. Social change as a theoretical problem can be investigated, within the framework of Merton's structural functionalism, by using his concept of social dysfunction. Merton defines this concept as "a designated set of consequences of a designated pattern of behavior, belief, or organization that interfere with a designated functional requirement of a designated social system" (Merton 1961: 732). A social dysfunction may cause the absence of social equilibrium, hence, social instability, the consequences and directions of which may be the object of functionalist inquiries. Functional analysis encounters the twofold difficulty of ascertaining which element should be analyzed, such as a group or culture, and how possible ideological implications should be detected. The choice of the object of analysis cannot be determined in advance.

However, the description of the social statuses and roles of those actors who display conduct deemed noteworthy and the meaning and significance of their conduct may shed light on its functions; alternative objects of inquiry are thus excluded. Merton formulates in this connection a set of basic concepts, problems and questions – a "paradigm," as he calls it – that may be of use for a theoretically fruitful functional analysis in sociology. To the extent that paradigms are developed "into more broader and more exacting theoretical constructions," they provide "both also serves other purposes, such as casting light on the postulates and presuppositions of functional analysis, and calling attention to its ideological and political implications" (Merton 1976a: 42). Paradigms are of use in order to conduct a structural analysis (Merton 1976a).

A paradigm is characterized in the following terms: it draws from several authors (especially Marx and Durkheim) and disciplines; deals with phenomena, such as the distribution of power and influence, at both the micro and macro levels; emphasizes the social strains, conflicts and dysfunctions in general caused by the potentially conflicting interests of structural components, such as strata, organizations and norms; and lays stress on the choice between socially structured alternatives (Merton 1976a: 32–6).

These statements recapitulate the previous discussion: (a) the object of the analysis should be standardized, namely, made typical and recurrent; (b) the actors' subjective dispositions, such as their motives and goals, should be explicitly or implicitly included in the analysis; (c) the latent and the manifest functions, and the dysfunctions, which any relevant social element may have for the social system, or for other units such as individuals or groups, are also included; (d) the notion of functional alternatives for a specific component of the social structure should substitute for the postulate of its indispensability, which has been shown to be untenable; (e) the concept of structural strain points to the interdependence of all the elements constitutive of the social structure.

Merton's distinction between manifest and latent functions may be found in his essay on the functions in the United States' political life of the so-called "machine." This term referred to the consolidated practice of having informal political actors called bosses supplying services, some of which having dubious legal standing, to their customers. The bosses' important function was providing politically powerless groups such as lower-class immigrants with some political and economic power, and with opportunities of social mobility. The boss acted as intermediary between the members of these powerless groups and those of powerful groups, and used his network of social relations to this end. By doing so, the boss fulfilled a social need without undesired interference on the part of the authorities. This function was performed in a pre-given social context of constrained social relations and opportunities; that is, in a social structure, which neither the boss nor his clients could modify. As the instance of the political boss illustrates, in a social structure the various groups and strata have interests and values of their own, in addition to the interests and values they share with others (Merton 1961: 733).

The concept of sociological theory should not be used interchangeably with other related concepts such as: methodology; general sociological orientations on substantive questions; analysis of sociological concepts; post-factum sociological interpretations: and empirical generalizations in sociology. Methodology indicates the rules of the scientific method, and is not specific to sociology or any other discipline. General sociological orientations differ from sociological theory in that they facilitate the formulation of hypotheses, but they are not immediately conducive to this result. The analysis of sociological concepts can make explicit their meaning and significance in any given research area, and provide indicators of social data. Post-factum sociological interpretations are merely plausible insofar as they are congruent with the data; they can accordingly confirm, but not validate, hypotheses. Finally, empirical generalizations, which are theoretically unsupported, may be frequently found in sociology. They are necessary to formulate empirical generalizations, but their theoretical relevance must be demonstrated in every case.

Sociological theory involves employing a procedure, by means of which

a. the scope of the empirical uniformities, which have been detected, is extended: a higher generalization level is thus reached;
b. detecting empirical uniformities may have the important function of cumulating sociological theory with research;
c. alternatively, it may lead to its reformulation;
d. it may also provide logical support to empirical forecasts;
e. finally, sociological theory makes use of statistical data, and is formulated with precision, in order to be empirically verifiable.

Alternative explanations, though possible, become less likely when the theory is empirically supported and consistently formulated. The codification of the findings is instrumental to the purpose of systematizing them, calling attention to problems that would have been otherwise neglected, and contributing to a plurality of theoretical orientations.

Empirical research – as Merton contends – does not merely set to itself the purpose of controlling and verifying hypotheses. It also performs the functions of initiating, reformulating, re-orienting and clarifying theory. As for initiating theory, Merton recalls the not unusual (in his judgment) experience of making accidental discoveries while pursuing a different research objective. The discovery may turn out to be strategic, in the sense of being theoretically very fruitful. So far neglected data, moreover, may re-orient the researcher's theoretical interest when they are reconsidered. They are therefore conducive to the formulation of new variables that become part of some specific theory. This holds true, in particular, in the case of observing "an unanticipated, anomalous and strategic datum" (Merton 1968: 158). Merton calls "serendipity" the discovery of such a datum.[2] This discovery, while accidental, could be scientifically productive. New research methods produce new statistical information, which may lead to a re-orientation of theoretical interest. Empirical research, furthermore, requires the rigorous formulation of concepts. Their clear definition is thus encouraged.

Merton's Studies of the Social and Cultural Structure

The social structure is conceived of as a pre-given social context, which offers but also constrains opportunities for action to individuals. Sociological ambivalence is a property of the social structure, but it affects individual conducts. It occurs when individuals hold incompatible statuses or status-sets. They therefore have conflicting norms and obligations, and perform incompatible social roles. Ambivalence may result when different functions, such as expressive and instrumental, are inherent to the same status of family members, or when performing the same function involves conflicting obligations – for example, the contradictory demands of detachment and compassion, as involved in the role of the physician; of personal attention and impersonal treatment, as requested by members of bureaucratic organizations; of humility and pride for their accomplishments, as requested by members of a scientific community.

Sociological ambivalence can also result from conflicting interests or values which pertain to the same person because of holding different statuses in a status set; or because of performing differing roles associated with one status, as the roles of researcher and teacher associated with the status of academic; or because of conflicting norms and values related to the same institution, as the norms of success and honesty in business conducts; or, finally, because of different cultural values held by the same individuals because of their different group memberships, as occurs for example to immigrants or to the children of racially mixed marriages (Merton and Barber 1976: 6–12).[3] Merton explores in some detail the theme of sociological ambivalence in the particular cases of scientists, medical doctors, and the leaders of voluntary associations. As for leaders, they face a dilemma as to whether they should pursue effectiveness in reaching organizational goals or rather seek democratic participation.

Individuals act in the social structure on the basis of motivations and preferences that originate from their cultural structure. These motivations may be conducive for particular segments of the population to actions that do not conform to – that is, they deviate from – generally accepted norms of conduct, but that nonetheless conform to societal values that are officially upheld. There is, accordingly, a possible strain-producing discrepancy in the cultural structure between norms and values. This occurs when the social system's mechanisms, which should self-regulate themselves, fail to operate properly; when they fail, in other words, to bring into harmony culturally endorsed goals and institutional norms. Merton illustrates the notions of social strain, anomie and deviant behavior, which follow as social-psychological consequences of this failure, with examples for each case of maladjustment.

He does so with the help of a well-known typological schema in which the different modes of individual adaptation to culturally defined and approved goals and institutional norms are specified. According to whether these goals are, or are not, pursued, and to whether these norms are, or are not, complied with,

---

2　On Merton's notion of serendipity, see Maniscalco 1989.

3　On Merton's notion of sociological ambivalence, there is an interesting sociological literature, both exegetical and evaluative. See Donati (1989); Nedelmann (1989).

Merton formulates a five-type schema. The two polar types in this schema are the pursuit of culturally defined goals such as economic success and norm-compliance (conformity); and the detachment from both the goals and the norms (retreatism). The type of conformance is the only non-deviant case in Merton's typology. All the other types involve the rejection of the goals, or of the means, or of both. Let us now consider these five cases in some detail.

Conformity is necessary to the stability and continuity of society. Accordingly, in stable and lasting societies most individuals conform most of the time. Innovation involves the acceptance of the goal of economic success, which is said to be available to everyone willing to make the effort to succeed, no matter what his or her social origins are. Innovators, however, reject the socially approved means such as hard work. Innovation concerns then the means; for when the legitimate means are not available the subjects may resort to crime to pursue this goal. Crime provides an individual solution to problems, which originates in the social and cultural structure, namely the social psychological strain and the consequent frustration that are caused by the incompatibility between the unavailability of legitimate means to obtain economic success, and the acceptance of this dominant goal. Ritualism constitutes a further mode of individual adaptation to the social and cultural structure. Ritualism is indicated by the individuals' emphasis on the socially defined means (hard work), but not on the culturally approved goals (economic success).

Merton illustrates this mode of adaptation with references to civil servants and private employees having a lower-middle class background who have renounced hopes of career advancements, and focus in their work on the rigid observance of rules and regulations, while not caring about their purpose. Retreatism involves withdrawal from both the legitimate goals and the institutionalized means, as mentioned. A variety of social outsiders, such as hobos, beggars, drunkards and drug addicts, fit this mode of individual adaptation to the structure. It is accounted for – according to Merton – by a biographical experience of prolonged failure which has engendered a sense of resignation and personal defeat. Rebellion is the last individual mode of adaptation in Merton's typology. It involves the rejection of the conventional goals and means, and the embracing of new goals and means.

Not to be confused with resentment, which is a sense of rage and hostility that does not set out to change extant values, rebellion recognizes no legitimacy to the social and cultural structure. This structure is completely rejected in favor of an alternative order deemed worthy of active pursuit. Anomie is a societal condition, existing both subjectively and objectively, in which social regulation is weak or absent. It follows from a discrepancy between the goal of economic success and the individual availability of means to reach this goal. This condition affects some social strata, groups and individuals more than others, and some societies like the United States more than other societies, which put less emphasis on the normative goal of economic success. Even in the United States, however, the goal and value of economic success are differently pursued, according to the social class and ethnic group. Anomie is, moreover, strongly affected by socialization as provided by the family. Parents' ambitions regarding their children's accomplishments are especially relevant in this respect.

As Merton himself has acknowledged, his own theory of anomie and deviant behavior is of limited heuristic validity; for it focuses on types of individual adaptation to the cultural and social structure, but it neglects to consider "the socially patterned differentiation of interests and values" as "rooted in the social structure" (Merton 1976a: 38). The individual's mode of adaptation to the social structure, his or her deviant behavior, and degree of anomie as his or her subjective condition, depend then to a great extent on the social class and ethnic group, to which that person belongs. Merton cites in this connection the theoretical and empirical work on juvenile delinquency by Albert K. Cohen (1955). Cohen has emphasized the relevance of deviant subculture in forming the delinquent juvenile's personality, and ultimately, in causing deviant behavior. Innovation, moreover, may also have functional consequences for the social system in that it may determine and institutionalize new conducts, which are better conducive to the attainment of non-deviant goals on the part of a given group.

Furthermore, economic success is not the only culturally conforming goal; and not all deviant behavior constitutes a crime, nor has it necessarily dysfunctional consequences to the social group, in which it occurs. Social deviance and social dysfunction – as Merton is at pains to remark – are not necessarily dysfunctional, and may stabilize (rather than disrupting) the social and cultural system. As for ritualism, Merton recalls some objections that have been formulated to his explanation of this conduct; chiefly, the objection that ritualism is a conduct suggested by a sense of insecurity as to how the person should behave in social relations. What is more, what may be interpreted as a rigid behavior depends on the norms of that person's reference group, rather than on some abstract and a-priori criterion.

Retreatism may be interpreted as a reaction to a subjective condition of pronounced anomie, such as may occur to new widows and widowers, especially if they are socially isolated. Rebellion, finally, results from a conflict between cultural goals and institutional norms rather than from value conflicts. The relative absence of social mobility between members of different ethnic groups, such as blacks and whites, may produce a sense of demoralization as well as ambivalence before processes of upward mobility on the part of members of disadvantaged social strata or ethnic groups. This occurs when ethnic prejudice is found in conjunction with improved opportunities of upward mobility. When there is no marked ethnic prejudice, as in the case of the Italian Americans, and there is a developed welfare state, social barriers to mobility are overcome to some extent.

Bureaucratic organizations require and enforce discipline on the part of their employees. This requirement has become a distinctive value of bureaucratic organization; it is not, however, necessarily compatible with organizational efficiency. Excessive conformance to regulations, whatever their purposes, and solidarity among the employees have become values of their own among the members of bureaucratic structures. Employees tend to promote their own interests, and to ignore those of the public at large. This tendency evidences the dysfunctional character of these values; the relationship between bureaucracy and personality types should be, however, investigated in greater detail. Merton has not himself conducted this investigation, preferring instead to dwell on the social status and roles of the intellectuals, especially insofar as their relations to the public administration and social policies are concerned.

Intellectuals are here defined as those who concern themselves with problems of knowledge, especially social, economic and political knowledge, and contribute to their formulation. Their expertise in any specific domain is dubious and, in fact, frequently questioned by those politicians who consult them for advice. This is so, even when the consulted intellectuals acting as advisers to policy makers think that they are, and in fact are, qualified. Intellectuals active in political and administrative institutions often find their role defined as purely technical, and as a source of frustration. They may have some influence on decisions, and on the solution of problems; this is the case, however, only if these problems have not received a specific formulation, for which they have not been responsible anyway. On the other hand, intellectuals who are external to these institutions have little or no influence on carrying out or defining political decisions; but they are in a better position to avoid making those decisions, which they find ethically objectionable as subservient to private interests.

The following two chapters of Merton's major work (1968) are intended as contributions to reference group theory. According to Merton, this social-psychological theory constitutes a good example of how social theory and applied research can be fruitfully combined. Behavior as influenced by reference groups has been investigated during World War Two by a Research Branch of the US War Department. Merton intends to relate the functional to the reference group theories. Reference group theory impinges on the concept of relative deprivation. This concept has been variously defined. All these definitions have been formulated in an attempt to account for anomalous or inconsistent findings, such as a higher degree of satisfaction among soldiers who had fewer career opportunities. They consider attitudes and judgments of a given group (the in-group) by comparing some of their members' attributes considered in particular relevance, such as social status, length of membership of the group, and combat experience, to similar attributes of others, who constitute a reference term (the out-group).

Merton remarks that the soldiers, whose attitudes had been investigated, had multiple reference groups, and compared their own conditions to those of their fellow soldiers who were similar to themselves in all relevant respects, except that they were involved in overseas active service. The latter condition was considered quite undesirable, and therefore these soldiers did not consider themselves as relatively deprived in respect to this group of soldiers. It is the in-group, in other words, who provides its members with a criterion of reference to compare their own condition to that of the members of out-groups. There can be several out-groups, some of which may have conflicting influences of the attitudes on the part of the members of the in-group, while others may provide reciprocal support in exerting influence on others. Merton points to some theoretical implications of these findings as follows.

First, official, institutional definitions of norms and statuses are relevant to the definition of the reference groups; second, more research is needed to clarify the relative importance for single individuals of their multiple in-groups, such as their colleagues, friends and fellow-bachelors; third, how members of a group perceive the behavioral norms of the other in-group members and of the out-groups; fourth, data should be systematically collected, and compared, on the conducts and attitudes that characterize the in-group and the reference groups; finally, adequate research methods should be used to investigate the unconscious motivations of comparisons with other individuals and groups. A further object of inquiry is whether relative deprivation theory may be applied to a greater number of phenomena than the theory of reference groups.

A few empirical cases – the same ones previously considered – are mentioned to answer this question. According to a hypothesis, which has been derived from the social-psychological literature and in particular from reference group theory, the values and conduct of the would-be members of a group do not conform to their own previously held models of values and conduct; but rather to the values and conduct of the most authoritative and esteemed section of that group. The hypothesis stipulates that an assimilation process has taken place, to the effect that the would-be members of the group and those having a full status there share the same values and conduct. In order to test this hypothesis, Merton has taken a number of steps: he has clarified the concepts used by reference-group theory; he has shown the pertinence of a set of theoretical propositions to reference-group theory; he has thus been enabled to link these concepts to some previously formulated theoretical propositions, which apply to a great variety of social phenomena; finally, the data, which have been systematically gathered, have been conducive to reformulating the concepts.

The investigation on the American Soldier involved a systematic analysis of the attitudes and evaluations of individuals whose status was similar, but their position in the social structure was different. A combination of indexes used in that research measured attributes not only of single individuals, such as their attitudes and evaluations, but also of groups and social structures. A theoretical implication has been that conformity as a variable may be addressed to some out-group, in addition the individuals' in-groups. People, in other words, may conform to different people's norms. Individuals may have been socialized to the norms and values not of their own group but of another group, of which they wish to become members. As a consequence of their anticipated socialization to the norms and values of that group, their adaptation is easier. Their anticipated socialization has therefore been functional to them; this holds true, however, as long as there is a sufficient degree of openness in the social structure to make mobility possible.

On the other hand, anticipated socialization is not functional for the solidarity of the individual's own group or stratum, which does not approve of, nor does it encourage, conformity to the norms of other groups; for this conformity is considered a defection, and the individual him or herself a renegade. His or her distance from the original in-group tends to increase in the course of time with the ever-growing negative image of that person. The legitimacy conferred to a social system is therefore functionally related to norms that conform to the in-group, rather than to reference groups. Conforming to the norms of those groups may point to a legitimacy crisis of the in-group. Referring to an out-group because of anticipated socialization has, accordingly, distinct consequences for the individuals; for their in-groups; and for the social system. As far as the individuals are concerned, their anticipated socialization to the norms of out-groups may lead to over-conformity, and to their consequent rejection on the part of the members of the original in-group.

Leaving an in-group is a frequent source of anxiety, which may be dysfunctional for the individuals; not, however, for the new group they are about to join, depending on specific circumstances that Merton suggests to investigate. Anxiety also comes from permanence, even if only temporary, in centers in which soldiers do not belong to any in-group (in particular, neither to their old, nor to their new in-group), and therefore have no reference groups of their own. Reference group theory is both sociological and social-psychological. Both disciplines contribute to it, each having its own level of analysis. The concept of reference group refers, as already mentioned, to the adherence on the part of some individuals and groups to the values and standards of other individuals and groups. This concept has been anticipated, in one way or another, by several authors, both classical and contemporary. It applies not only to groups, but also to individuals and social categories.

The more general sociological concept of group refers to collectivities, whose members interact with one another according to a pre-established pattern, define themselves as members of that group, and are considered as such by others. The group has contextually defined boundaries; its members belong to it in various degrees and according to particular circumstances. Non-members, by contrast, do not constitute any specific and homogeneous social category; namely, they do not belong to status aggregates, whose members share some social trait (such as sex, age, income, etc.), but do not interact with each other. According to the attitudes on the part of the non-members, the potential new members may aspire to become such, and they are in this sense marginal to the group; or they are indifferent toward their membership; or, finally, they do not want to be members at all, and are therefore antagonist to the group

If the last category of the non-members has all the requisites of membership, but still refuse for whatever motive to become members, their refusal brings into light the group's incompleteness, and hence weakness. Groups may be open or closed, according to their desire to increase or decrease the number of their members. Groups may decide to remain close to preserve to the members the symbolic value of membership, but the very same reason may induce other groups to seek new members. Former members do not, even when their attitude is ambivalent toward their old group, necessarily embrace the values of the new one, which may in fact perceive as a threat their arrival as new members. In any case, the in- and the out-groups often both belong to a larger social organization, which makes them a component of a common structure.

Groups may be referred to in a positive, but also in a negative sense, to the effect that they prompt behavior that is deliberately juxtoposed to that which has been determined to be characteristic of the negative reference group. The individuals that serve as a reference term should not be confused with the social roles they play; furthermore, oftentimes the members of a more prestigious out-group are selected as a reference group. Out-groups in general are selected by the isolated or socially mobile members of a group. The reference groups are often more than one, each with its own norms and values. In this case, individuals tend to be more influenced by those groups of which they themselves are members. Multiple reference groups cannot be easily classified, for identifying the properties that distinguish a particular group may be problematic. A tentative list of these properties is as follows:

1. the extent to which group membership is clearly defined;
2. the extent to which the group regulates and commit the members' sentiments and conducts;
3. the actual and foreseen duration of the group membership;
4. the actual and foreseen duration of the group;
5. the size of the group and of its constitutive parts;
6. the extent to which the group is open or closed;
7. the proportion of actual members to those who would qualify as members, but actually are not so;
8. the extent to which the members are differentiated by social status and roles;
9. the shape and vertical span of the group's stratification;
10. the type and degree of the group's cohesion;
11. the group's tendency to break up in subgroups, or of the subgroups to coalesce into a larger structure;
12. the foreseen and actual amount of the interactions inside of the group;
13. the character of such relations;
14. the degree of the foreseen conformity to the group norms, and of the usually tolerated deviant behavior or norms rejection;
15. the formal or informal way of how normative control is exercised;
16. the extent to which the group members can observe the norms or the conduct, which are related to the role performance of the other group members;
17. the spatial distribution of the group members;
18. the group's degree of the group's autonomy from, or dependence on, groups and institutions that are belong to society at large;
19. the degree of the group's stability and resilience;
20. the degree of stability of the group's social environment;
21. how groups can preserve themselves in a changing environment;
22. the group's position in a status hierarchy.

The foregoing list of the group properties can provide the basis for several distinct classifications; moreover, some of these properties can be derived from others. Each of these properties should be, furthermore, measured by means of a standardized index. Reference groups differ according to their particular norms and values, and to the degree of commitment to them on the part of their members. Future research can answer the question which influence model should be considered preferable; that is, whether it is preferable to assume that relatively few individuals exert influence in several spheres, or rather to assume that relatively numerous individuals exert influence in one sphere only. Research, which was available to Merton when he wrote his major work (1968), suggested to him that the selection of the reference groups, and their performance of social functions for the groups, occurs in keeping with institutional and structural conditions.

These conditions are therefore relevant for the development of sociological theory, and limit the theoretical interest of research on small groups that neglects their structural context. As for the knowledge of norms and values, its relevance for the selection of the reference groups has been brought into light by the social psychological research conducted in the 1950s. Chester Barnard's work on the functions and the authority of the executive is a case in point; as it shows how the necessity to know and keep into due consideration the group norms and values constrain the exercise of this authority. The group not only exerts social control on the authority; it also needs it to survive as a group. The group also needs to be shielded from being completely visible, hence observable, on the part of the authority. Total visibility would be dysfunctional, but the most functional degree of visibility is contingent on the group's culture and social status. A certain amount of nonconformity to norms is necessarily tolerated, though the specific amount is contingent on historical circumstances and the group's culture.

Nonconformity, however, may also result from the authority's inability to enforce norms, because of obstacles in the communication flow that prevent the authority from adapting norms to the contingent situation, or because of the authority's social isolation, or finally because of inadequacies in the leaders' personalities. The authority's visibility depends upon the sentiments, attitudes and expectations of the public opinion, but its relevance for the authority, in turn, depends on the extent to which the public opinion is observed and known by the authority itself. In modern times, the authority is informed by public opinion and mass communication, the skillful use of which may bolster some authority at the expense of others. Nonconformity to norms – i.e., their violation – is not synonymous with criminal deviance, although they are often similarly designated. Criminals pursue their own personal interests, whereas the nonconformists openly and disinterestedly question the legitimacy of the norms which they wish to change, and which are a source of moral indignation for them. Challenging norms calls for courage, and may accordingly elicit sentiments of ambivalent admiration even on the part of those who do not share the nonconformists' norms and values.

Merton conceives of the social structure as a coherent set of statuses and roles. The anthropologist Ralph Linton is here cited for a definition of these concepts. A social status is a set of culturally defined behavioral expectations, while a social role is a set of conducts that conform to these expectations. Linton assumes that every status corresponds to a specific role. Merton argues otherwise; namely, that there is a plurality of interconnected statuses, which he calls a status set, and that a status corresponds to a plurality of interconnected roles, which he calls a role-set. In other words, for any given status, or social position (such as the position of a doctor or a teacher) there are distinct culturally prescribed conducts, which are enacted by different types of social actors. For example, a doctor interacts with the patients, colleagues and possibly others such as medical students, the hospital administration, etc.

The actors who by performing their different roles constitute a role-set are variously situated in the social structure. Accordingly, some of them have values and expectations different from any other actor holding a specific position. Peripheral actors, in particular, often have, if compared to central actors, a lower social status and different values, and are apparently less interested in abiding by the norms of proper role behavior. There is therefore the problem of identifying the mechanisms by means of which the different roles of a role-set are combined and harmonized; for these roles may differ not only because the social actors may be variously interested in performing them, but also because they may be endowed with different power due to their different position in the social structure, by themselves or in a coalition with others. Lack of visibility has the function of facilitating the role performance of the members of those professions, such as priests and doctors, who are obliged to protect the privacy of those who need their services by respecting the professional secret. Complete lack of visibility would, however, prove an obstacle to the indispensable exercise of social control.

Actors who perform different roles that constitute a role-set may find themselves under conflicting obligations. If this is case, it is incumbent upon the peripheral members of the social structure to harmonize their role obligations with those of the other members. Actors having a similar social status, and facing similar problems because their role-set is not well integrated, can avail themselves of the mechanism of social solidarity between themselves to overcome these problems. If this proves impossible, then they may interrupt their relations with some actors, and try to obtain a consensus on the part of the other actors concerning their mutual role expectations. A status set – namely, a set of distinct positions in a social system or between different and interconnected social systems – presents problems similar to those of a role-set; since an excessively articulated status system may interfere, but it does not so necessarily, with the actors' role performances. Functional analysis dwells on the consequences for the social structure, groups and individuals of the processes, which connect any of these elements with the individuals' reference groups.[4]

Models of Social Influence and Mass Communications

Merton has dealt with these two themes – social influence and mass communications – in the following section of his major work (1968). They are related in that the subject of mass communication is studied in its impact on models of interpersonal influence. Merton focuses on two such models, called models of local and cosmopolitan influences. Both models consider influences that are exerted in local communities. The former model concerns itself with individuals who restrain their interests for their most part to their local community, while the latter model concerns individual who are oriented to questions and events that are external to the community, in which they live. A methodological discussion precedes this qualitative study. The discussion underlines the unwelcome consequences, which flow from an excessive delimitation and a premature specification of the initial research question.

In its final reformulation, the research has been articulated in two phases. In a first phase, individuals have been distinguished according to whether they are, or are not, influential. A second phase has focused on the question as to whether the interests of the influential individuals are, or are not, confined to their local communities. As the research has revealed, this typology clearly distinguishes between two sets of influential people, the former called locals, the latter cosmopolitans. More specifically, the typology distinguishes between (a) those who have close ties to their communities, and those who do not; (b) those who are interested in having frequent meeting with as many members as possible of their communities, and those who are not; and (c) those who participate in the local associations primarily because they are interested in the activities of these organizations, and those who rather seek to thereby increase their interpersonal relations, cognitions and abilities.

The locals and the cosmopolitans have followed different paths on their way to achieve influence on their communities. The locals have grown in these communities, and have thus had the opportunity to create a network of good interpersonal relations. The cosmopolitans are newcomers, who can bring along the prestige and abilities they have previously earned and displayed in their profession. The locals' and cosmopolitans' different career paths contribute to account not only for their distinct orientations to their local communities, but also for the different use of their social status. The locals use social status to promote their influence, whereas the cosmopolitans do so to maintain and bolster their reputation and prestige. These two types of influential individuals have their influences shaped and oriented by the specific characteristics of their community, that is, whether it is liberal or conservative, and tolerant or intolerant insofar as the civil liberties are concerned.

Merton goes on to show that the distinction between the locals and the cosmopolitans has a bearing on mass communications theory, as these two types of influential people use the mass media for distinct purposes. Cosmopolitans, in comparison to locals, show a greater interest in newspapers and magazines, which cover and comment upon international events. *Time Magazine* and the *New York Times* would be a case in point, but also *National Geographic*, *Atlantic Monthly*, and other reputed magazines and newspapers. They use these media not only as a source of conversation, but also to exert influence and gain prestige. Locals prefer to read about scandals and so-called human interest stories, as reported by less prestigious media. The media are therefore differently sought and used, in keeping with different social roles. Similar conclusions can be drawn on how locals and cosmopolitans make use of the radio news.

---

4   On Merton's concepts of role-set and status-set, see Coser 1990: 159–74; Hilbert 1990: 177–9.

Irrespective of whether people are locals or cosmopolitans, interpersonal influence on decisions is chiefly exerted by people who are placed at a low or middle level of the social structure. This is so as they are much more numerous than those who are highly placed, even though they might be less influential individually. Influence may be monomorphic or polymorphic, according to whether it is exerted in a restricted area or in a great number of areas, which are not necessarily interrelated. Apparently, most locals are polymorphic, while most cosmopolitans are monomorphic, for their expertise is circumscribed. Interpersonal influence implies an asymmetric relationship between those who exert influence, and those who are subject to it. It is correlated with, but not determined by, the person's position in hierarchies of social class, power and prestige. Influence, finally, rests on a variety of possible sources, such as manipulation, clarification (when there are several courses of action), advice and social exchange.

The theme of the self-fulfilling prophecy is discussed in one of the best known chapters of Merton's main work (1968: ch. 11). Self-fulfilling prophecy starts with a false definition of a situation. This false definition, when made known to others, may produce the undesired consequence of becoming real, in keeping with the so-called Thomas' theorem. Merton provides a few examples of self-fulfilling prophecies: firstly, news concerning a bank's alleged difficulties in honoring contractual obligations with its customers can cause a stampede; customers seek to withdraw their deposits before it is too late. It can also result in the bankruptcy of the institution. Secondly, blacks who were accused by white working class' members of being guilty of conduct detrimental to the interests of the working class because they were strike-breakers and accepting low salaries in order to make a living were refused on these grounds admittance to the trade unions. As a consequence, they were forced to work at any salary, even in periods of labor strikes, thus confirming the white workers' predictions of their conducts.

Merton pays particular attention to a further instance of self-fulfilling prophecy; namely, to predictions on the part of some in-group concerning the behavior of the members of some disreputable racial or religious out-group on the consequence of producing on their part a behavior which is stigmatized whatever its nature. Thus, successful Jewish doctors or business people (the out-group) have become the target of anti-Semitic attack on the part of the members of some in-group of non-Jews. They have interpreted the success of these Jews as evidence not of their capabilities, but of their group's moral inferiority. These attacks have induced representatives of Jewish communities to try to minimize these successes, rather than to be proud of them. It has therefore proved impossible for the members – whether successful or not – of this group to escape negative labeling.

Negative labeling has also targeted the members of the black minority. In this case, however, prejudice on the part of the in-group, which has been sustained by the belief in the intellectual inferiority of this out-group, has prompted representatives of the black community to extol the achievements of some notable black American, disregarding the quantitative or qualitative limitations of these achievements. The efforts of these black representatives have been to no avail. On the contrary, members of the in-group have responded to them with derision and contempt. Concluding that the prejudice against some out-groups cannot be eradicated and that self-fulfilling prophecies are unavoidable would be too hasty, however. Merton recalls instances of successful institutional intervention and controls in the United States to counter these prejudices and prophecies.

The third section of Merton's major work (1968) deals with the sociology of knowledge and mass communications, this last subject having been investigated in conjunction with Paul Lazarsfeld. A rather lengthy introduction precedes the three chapters on the sociology of knowledge. As this introduction states, the sociology of knowledge and mass communications have developed independently from each other, the former in Europe, the latter in the United States. They both belong to a field of studies that deals with the interactions between social structure and communications. Nonetheless, they differ in that the sociology of knowledge inquires into how society shapes knowledge, very broadly defined, whereas mass communication research is interested in finding what the general opinion, attitudes and popular beliefs are with regard to any particular issue. Examples are the effects of mass communication on the public opinion; or how public opinion itself is stratified according to sexual gender, social class, age or other variables.

It is then apparent that these two fields of study are differently oriented in several ways. The sociology of knowledge broaches abstract issues of general import, and relies on scholarly interpretations of these issues. It does not pursue methodological questions such as problems of validity and reliability of the intellectual and cultural problems, which constitute the subject matter, nor does it seek empirical evidence or rigorous data analysis concerning, for example, the effects of the mass media on the audiences. Generally speaking, individual scholars conduct their own investigations, possibly with the support of a few research assistants. By way of contrast, the use of correct methodological procedures and statistical techniques is important for American mass communication research. These procedures and techniques are used to investigate narrow and well-defined questions, whose theoretical import is not ascertained, nor is it considered very relevant.

For the European scholar, differences in interpreting any given question are then considered inevitable, and there are no final interpretations. For the American researcher, different interpretations make the research findings questionable, efforts are made to do away with them, and competition between the mass media and between their owners has promoted the search of financial support from corporations or public institutions. The lone European scholar conversant with the sociology of knowledge and the American member of a team conducting research on mass communication therefore hold different social positions. These different positions correspond to their distinct investigation goals, and may go a long way to account for the divergent European and American tendencies. The following chapters focus first on the sociology of knowledge, and especially on Karl Mannheim's contribution to this field of studies, then on mass communication research.

As for the sociology of knowledge (this term should be interpreted in a broad sense, which includes assertions, modes of thought, world views or ideologies, beliefs), Merton observes that the discipline reflects a current (in Merton's times) societal condition of mutual distrust, a condition, namely, in which statements, beliefs and systems of ideas are no longer accepted at their face value, but rather as evidence of some hidden motive such as personal or collective interests. A correspondence or consistency is assumed to exist between knowledge and society or a societal component, such as groups or classes. This assumption does not apparently escape the pitfall of relativism, for the validity of statements bearing on the sociology of knowledge is – as is the case for all statements – socially conditioned.

Mannheim was apparently aware of this logical fallacy, but his attempts to escape it – especially, by his notions of perspective, total ideology, free-floating intellectuals and relationism – have failed to overcome this problem, according to Merton. A classification of questions and problems, which have proved relevant for the sociology of knowledge, has been formulated in this connection. They are: what are the bases of mental production, whether existential (such as classes, or generations, or social processes), or cultural (such as values or world views)? What kind of mental productions are considered (such as moral beliefs, ideologies, social norms), and what aspects of them (e.g., modes of selection and verification, presuppositions, content)? How are mental productions related to their existential basis (causally, functionally, symbolically, or ambiguously) and why (because they perform manifest or latent functions)? When do these relations obtain (historicist or general analytical theories)? As for the sociology of mass communication, Merton dwells on radio and film propaganda. This term is here defined – in chapter 16 of Merton's major work (1968) – as any set of symbols that influence opinions or actions concerning controversial issues. It is not synonymous of deliberate fraud or deceit, though they may occur.

Radio and film propaganda is considered in its effects on the audience, especially the so-called boomerang effects, that is, the undesired effects due to inadvertent errors. These effects and errors are detected by means of focused interviews with audience samples. There are also boomerang effects which may arise from a variety of sources. They are of different types. In particular, there are erroneous appraisals of the audience's state of mind; appraisals from psychologically differentiated audiences, so that the messages are not effective for particular segments; or from the presence of different and contradictory contents in the propaganda message; or, finally, from unforeseen and undesired responses, such as skepticism and disbelief, on the part of the audiences. Deceitful propaganda of alleged facts, in contrast to propaganda by exhortation, has been used in wartime to mislead the enemy's armed forces or audiences, or even the countries' own audiences. Exhortations may prove counterproductive and cause disbelief when not rooted in the audiences' common sense. Alleged "facts," even if fabricated, may be more effective than exhortations as a source of misguided persuasion.

The last, and perhaps the most frequently referred to, part of Merton's main work (1968) concerns his sociology of science. It consists of five chapters, whose subject matter is the relations between science (the natural rather than the social sciences) and the social structure. This relation is spelled out as follows:

1. the relationship between science and the political order, especially the consequences for science's ethical principles of authoritarian and democratic political orders; building on the example of Nazi Germany, Merton shows the authoritarian orders to be incompatible with science's ethical principles, such as universalism (in the sense of disregarding the scientists' personal and social characteristics); communism (in the sense of prescribed sharing of scientific discoveries); disinterestedness (in the sense of an exclusive commitment to the cause of science); organized skepticism (in the sense of detached scrutiny of what claims to be scientific evidence);
2. the technological byproducts of science, and their consequences on its public image;
3. the relationship between the values and religious orientations of ascetic Protestantism and seventeenth-century capitalism in England, in keeping with Max Weber's hypothesis;
4. Protestant influences on scientific discoveries and developments in seventeenth-century England.

The Reception of Merton's Work

Only partial and incomplete references to the secondary literature on Merton are here possible, since this literature is vast and "the thematic interest of his interests is very wide" (Sztompka 1986: 2). As is the case of all major social theorists, Merton's work has not been in general received with unqualified praise, though always eliciting great interest on the part of the American and the international sociological community. Piotr Sztompka, the authoritative interpreter of Merton, provides a rare instance of unqualified appreciation. Sztompka praises Merton's "coherent system of thought"; his theory of society and structural approach; his conflictual and dynamic image of society; and his "vindication of ... valuable classical heritage," as particularly represented by Marx, Simmel and Durkheim (See Sztompka 1990: 62–3).

The interest, which Merton's oeuvre has elicited, has not been confined to sociological theory; for, as Arthur Stinchcombe has put it, "of all contemporary theorists of social structure, Merton has had the greatest impact on empirical research" (Stinchcombe 1990: 81). This secondary literature has presented and debated the general themes of Merton's work, such as his notions of structural and functional analysis, social structure, and structural constrains and opportunities, on the one hand, and on the other hand, more specific themes, such as his anomie theory, his theses of the self-fulfilling prophecy and the relationship between Puritanism and science, and his sociology of science. General evaluations of Merton's work have been formulated by two of the foremost contemporary social theorists, Giddens and Bourdieu. Both evaluations are ambivalent.

Giddens shows some appreciation for Merton's work, to the extent that it concerns the latter's conception of society in terms of "many overlapping and shifting sets of systematic relationships, often having no clear boundaries from one another" (Giddens 1990: 108). However, Giddens has several times reiterated his objection to functionalism, not only in general, but also insofar as Merton's version of it is concerned. In this connection, Giddens has remarked that "Merton's own distinction between manifest and latent functions ... does not withstand scrutiny"; for it ignores the theoretically important difference between unanticipated and unintended consequences. It also ignores the difference between the unintended consequences of action and the rationality of belief and action. According to Giddens, moreover, Merton has an obscure notion of society and of manifest function. He therefore fails to clarify and seriously consider why actors engage in given practices in keeping with their own intentions, rather than from an external observer's point of view (Giddens 1984: 12–14; see also 1979: 210–16; 1990: 108–10; 1996: 89).

Like Giddens', Bourdieu's evaluation is mainly critical, though criticism is qualified by some appreciation. On the one hand, Bourdieu finds great merit in Merton's attempt to investigate science from a sociological vantage point – a point of view, furthermore, that conjugates an external reading of science, stressing "the social cosmos in which it is embedded," with an internal reading, which considers "the social microcosm in which it is embedded." On the other hand, this attempt by Merton has not been seriously made, Bourdieu argues; as Merton's internal reading of science neglects to consider how the norms of science are embedded in "the social structure of the scientific universe." Merton has accordingly left out of consideration the struggles taking place within the scientific field. This field, like all others, is a world apart, endowed with its own law of functioning and own struggles. These struggles are conducted to "maintain or transform the balance of forces, of strategies, of preservation or subversion, of interests, etc" (See Bourdieu 1990: 297–301).

It may be worth noting that Giddens and Bourdieu have conducted their assessments of Merton, each of them in keeping with his own theoretical presuppositions (see in this connection Alexander 1982). They differ as these presuppositions are different. Peter Blau, a former student of Merton, has provided yet another different assessment, which is in agreement with his Merton-inspired conception of social structure. Blau has interpreted Merton's oeuvre as having a structural rather than a functional orientation. He has therefore focused on Merton's concepts of role-set and status-set as directing attention to different analytical aspects of the social structure, and to the constrains which the structure exerts on individual interactions. Role-sets exert different structural constraints than status-sets. Altering individuals who stand in a specific role relation to egos forms a role-set. A role-set "comprises persons who occupy a different status", while a status-set "directs attention to the various ... dimensions in terms of which social positions are distinguished" (Blau 1975: 119, 126).

Appreciation is given by Blau not only to Merton's notions of status-set and role-set but also to other Merton's notions, such as opportunity structure and unanticipated consequences. Merton uses such notions to conduct the analysis of social structure and structural constrains. These are, Blau maintains, "genuine theoretical terms"; they constitute "a conceptual refinement" which "enables him to raise various theoretical issues." Though Merton's conceptual apparatus are "suited for a general sociological theory," still in Blau's judgment Merton has not formulated such a theory, but only supplied "many tools for it." His concept of middle-range social theories, in particular, expresses "Merton's concern with rigorous theorizing" (Blau 1990). Blau's substantially positive assessment is consistent with Stinchcombe's, who has – like Blau – cultivated for many years an interest in the theory of social structure.

Stinchcombe indicates several strong points in what he calls Merton's "general theory of social action," which focuses on choices between socially structured alternatives. These strong points are, according to Stinchcombe: its "attention to stability and maintenance of social patterns," combined with "attention to disruption of them"; and its structural location of the phenomenon, which is investigated. The generality of Merton's notion of socially structured alternatives is no obstacle to making precise predictions concerning empirical questions, such as the distribution of delinquency rates. These predictions accord with Merton's argument of social structure and anomie. Stinchcombe objects, however, that Merton has "nowhere extracted and systematized" his general theory (Stinchcombe 1990).

Richard Hilbert (1990) has made a different and quite critical assessment of Merton's work from an ethnomethodological viewpoint. Hilbert underscores the theoretical continuity of Merton with Parsons as representative of the functionalist perspective, and remarks that according to Merton norms and rules – which are concepts of great import to these two authors, and this perspective in general – are in fact taken for granted, constantly interpreted, applied and (therefore) re-created at any time when people make use of them. Whenever norms and rules are applied to contingent circumstances in order to explain the social order, they thereby identify it. Merton's notions of status-set and role-set are cases in point; for these notions receive their meaning not by means of abstract definitions, but through their actual use on the part of ordinary actors in everyday life. Abstract definitions such as Merton's are integral components of the social order they purportedly explain.[5]

Merton's critical revision of Parsons' functionalism has elicited several comments, only a few of which will be here touched on. Elster (1990), from the viewpoint of rational choice theory, questions Merton's great reputation among contemporary sociologists. His argumentation recalls to some extent Campbell's (1982) negative assessment of Merton's distinction between manifest and latent functions. It is an ambiguous distinction, according to Campbell and Elster, or "oversimplified," according to others (see Moore 1979: 341). Merton's functional analysis, moreover, as is the case of functional analysis in general, fails "to provide a mechanism by which the consequences uphold or maintain the behavior one wants to explain." Elster shows how this argument is logically untenable and misleading, for "there may be many non-dysfunctional alternatives to a given dysfunctional institution" (Elster 1990: 133).

---

5   We mention here briefly Donati's comment (1989). Donati maintains that Merton has overemphasized society's normative conditioning, which engenders stability. Correspondingly, Merton has underemphasized its symbolic aspect, which produces fluidity and innovation. Donati's comment has been made from a theoretical viewpoint on his own (that of a "relational sociology").

Boudon, writing from the same theoretical viewpoint but in a less critical vein than Elster, brings attention to Merton's unintended consequences paradigm. Its plausibility is uncertain, for it derives, according to Boudon, "from the quality of the psychological statements that the application of the paradigm obligatorily produces" (Boudon 1990: 122).[6] Other evaluations of Merton's sociological theory have been even more favorable. Robert Sampson, the renowned criminologist, has assessed Merton's discussion of middle range theories in positive terms. In Sampson's own words, "that sort of theorizing that Merton pioneered helped elide, or at least diminish, the pernicious distinctions that still rile the field: theory versus research, basic versus applied, positivist versus nonpositivist, and more" (Sampson 2010: 73). Merton's revision of Parsons' functionalism has, furthermore, influenced Luhmann's neo-functionalism. Luhmann has made positive reference to Merton's notion of functional equivalents; this is, according to Luhmann, a principle that could be used by functional analysis instead of social causation, which Luhmann finds methodologically untenable (see Luhmann 1970: 14).

Specific areas of sociological inquiry, to which Merton has contributed, have also elicited scholarly attention. Crothers (1990) is an expert on Merton's sociology of organization, and sociological theory in general. As Crothers has maintained, Merton's model of organizations includes a few different groups such as bureaucrats, leaders and clients. It is not apparent from this model, however, how these groups relate to each other or to the overall organization. Elsewhere, Crothers (1989) has, moreover, qualified the relevance of Merton's theoretical framework by observing that this framework is "unable to apperceive [the] … more exaggerated forms" of phenomena such as "violence, exploitation and power" (Crothers 1989: 220). These criticisms notwithstanding, Crothers maintains that "at least a modest contemporary role for Merton's organizational sociology is justified" because of his "useful insights" he has to offer to this discipline, and of his sophisticated theoretical framework (Crothers 1990: 223–4).

There is also a noteworthy secondary literature on other sociological areas on which Merton has dwelt, such as anomie theory, the sociology of science and the sociology of knowledge (in addition to other areas, such as the sociology of mass media communication, on which it is not possible to linger here for reasons of space). On Merton's notion of anomie there exists an abundant secondary literature (see for instance Orrù 1990). This notion, and the theory on which it is built, have certainly elicited great interest, but also several criticisms. Anomie theory, in particular, has been the object of strictures on the part of the French sociologist Philippe Besnard (1990). This author finds anomie "an unnecessary and uncertain concept" (Besnard 1990: 249). Merton – Besnard contends – does not make it apparent whether the concept refers to "a disjunction between norms and goals," or to "the collapse of the cultural structure as a whole."

Norms, moreover, are "amalgamated with goals" in subsequent editions of "Social Theory and Social Structure"; while, according to qualified commentators of Merton, "norms are assimilated into the social structure." The conceptual confusion has not prevented "a large number of commentators" from seeking "its intellectual antecedents and its ideological connotations." Durkheim cannot, however, be a precursor, according to Besnard. Durkheim, as Besnard points out, has viewed the indeterminacy of goals as "the central characteristic of anomie," whereas Merton views goals as certain from the actors' viewpoint (Besnard 1990: 251–3). What strikes Besnard as an instance of conceptual confusion seems to Lazarsfeld, a renowned methodologist, rather an example of "conceptual ramification"; whereby Merton's "famous anomie paper centers on a cross-classification of cultural goals and institutional means" (Lazarsfeld 1975: 61). Different notions are thus cross-tabulated, leading to other combinatorial results.

Merton's anomie paper has centered on the related notions of reference groups and relative deprivation, and has greatly contributed to make these notions known outside of social psychologists' circles. It has contributed especially to spur debates among sociologists on their precise definitions and theoretical fruitfulness of the concept of relative deprivation. This debate, which has not yet come to a head, has inspired a sizable secondary literature. It has also clarified a number of related questions, such as problems of definition of relative deprivation and reference groups; and the conceptual boundaries, which limit the possibilities of generalizing these notions. According to the secondary literature, which Merton has inspired or influenced, relative deprivation involves comparisons between collectivities that have absolute differences in power and

---

6 We also hint here at Almondo's comment, to the effect that Merton's notion of functional alternative should be considered constitutive of his critique of society.

prestige. These differences may produce discontent, grievances, and possibly also sustained and organized collective action. Collective action tends to occur if the deprived collectivity is large, commands substantial economic and political resources, and is well-linked together; whereas its opponents are perceived as weak, divided and irresolute (Williams 1975).

Furthermore, research on the process of relative deprivation has evidenced the importance of social identities and of unequal distribution of outcomes (Pettigrew 2010). Merton's sociology of science has also commanded considerable attention,[7] and stimulated a sizable secondary literature, which will be only selectively mentioned here.[8] Nico Stehr, a leading student of sociology of science, has distinguished between two periods in Merton's conception of science (Stehr 1990). The first period was characterized by its underscoring the relative openness of the scientific community. The second period has emphasized "the social autonomy of the scientific community," and has investigated its institutionalized process and its claims to have generated valid knowledge (Stehr 1990: 290).

As Stehr argues (1990: 291), Merton's sociology of science is compatible with the conception of science, which the historian of science Thomas Kuhn, and others who have been influenced by him, have formulated. The attempt to bring together Merton's sociology of science with other developments in this field of studies, such as Kuhn's, gains plausibility from Merton's very favorable reception of Kuhn's work on *The Structure of Scientific Revolutions*. Merton received as a complimentary copy before its publication, and "was deeply impressed by the manuscript" (Cole and Zuckerman 1975: 159). A similar attempt to combine Merton's pioneering work with the new tendencies in this field of studies has been recently made by Panowsky (2010).

According to Panofsky, Merton has focused on the links between the manifestations of the scientific ethos[9] and the organization of the scientific communities. These links have been found to be varying and contingent, depending on extra-scientific communities (with particular reference to commercial interests). As Panofsky observes, Merton's critics have argued, however, that the Mertonian tradition has failed to explore the autonomy of the scientific community *vis-à-vis* other communities. The notion itself of a scientific ethos has come under attack on the part of the so-called new sociology of science, which prefers to use a constructivist approach (that is, scientific knowledge is viewed as a social and contingent construction), and maintains that this approach has received greater empirical support as compared to Merton's sociology of science. Panofsky concludes (2010: 158) by advocating "a combination of Mertonian institutionalism and constructivist concern with knowledge production."

Kalleberg has explored the relationship between Merton's essay on science and democracy and the ethos of democracy (Kalleberg 2010). Kalleberg takes Merton to task on several grounds, notably because of his "scientistic conception of the tasks of the social sciences"; for holding normative convictions beyond dispute; and for his "underdeveloped conception of democracy" and of its ethos (Kalleberg 2010: 185). According to Kalleberg (who refers to Habermas in this connection), normative claims as formulated by academics and other public intellectuals are, on the contrary, a legitimate subject of discussion in a public discourse. It is not only an important element in the formation of the democratic ethos, but also an "improvement on the Mertonian structural analysis of the interdependencies between science and society" (Kalleberg 2010: 206).

If the sociology of science may be considered as a part of the sociology of knowledge, as Bernard Barber – a close colleague and pupil of Merton – has said (Barber 1968: 92), Merton's own contribution to the sociology of knowledge has received only scant attention; less attention, in any case, than has been generally the case with Merton's oeuvre in general, and with his sociology of science in particular. Barber's himself has written a rather lengthy essay in this field of studies in an attempt "to recommend a new view of the sociology of knowledge." According to Barber, "in this instance Merton has not had the triumphant success he has had in several other sociological specialties" (Barber 1975: 104). Recently, however, Alan Sica (2010) has

---

7   As Calhoun has written (2010: 12), "Robert Merton was the primary founder of the sociology of science, an enormously influential sociological theorist, and an innovator in empirical research methods." Cole and Zuckerman (1975: 140) have likewise stressed Merton's contribution to the emergence of the sociology of science as a special field of studies.

8   For a brief introduction to Merton's sociology of science, its reception and contraposition to the so-called "new sociology of science" see Statera (1989).

9   On Merton's notion of scientific ethos, see Sztompka 1986: 50–60.

contributed an essay on Merton, Mannheim and the sociology of knowledge, thus remedying what has been so far a flaw in the secondary literature on Merton and the sociology of knowledge.[10]

Sica has dwelt on Merton's early reception of Mannheim. In this connection, he has pointed first to an article Mannheim published in 1937 in the history of science journal *ISIS*, and then to his following contributions to the sociology of knowledge, which were included in *Social Theory and Social Structure*. A comparison between these publications evidences, according to Sica, a sharp change of tone and attitude on Merton's part, from his "refusal to be sucked into the debunking industry invented by Marx and Engels" to "the acerbic critique" that characterized his subsequent works on Mannheim and the sociology of knowledge (Sica 2010: 179). Sica conjectures that Merton wanted to dispose of earlier attempts before producing his own contribution to the sociology of knowledge.

References

Alexander, J.C. 1982. *Positivism, Presuppositions, and Current Controversies*. Berkeley, CA: University of California Press.

Barbano, F. 1968. Introduzione all'edizione italiana. R.K. Merton e le amalisi della sociologia, in R.K. Merton (ed.), *Teoria e struttura sociale*. Bolonia: Il Mulino, vii–lvii.

Barber, B. 1968. The Sociology of Science, in D.S. Sills (ed.), *International Encyclopedia of the Social Sciences*, Volume 13. New York: Macmillan Co & The Free Press, 92–100.

Barber, B. 1975. Toward a New View of the Sociology of Knowledge, in L.A. Coser (ed.), *The Idea of Social Structure: Papers in Honor of Robert K. Merton*. New York: Harcourt Brace Jovanovich, 103–16.

Blau, P. 1975. Structural Constraints of Status Complements, in L.A. Coser (ed.), *The Idea of Social Structure*. New York: Harcourt Brace Jovanovich, 117–38.

Blau, P. 1990. Structural Constraints and Opportunities: Merton Contribution to General Theory, in J. Clark, C. Modgil and S. Modgil (eds), *Robert K. Merton: Consensus and Controversy*. London: Falmer Press, 141–53.

Boudon, R. 1990. The Two Facets of the Unintended Consequences Paradigm, in J. Clark, C. Modgil and S. Modgil (eds), *Robert K. Merton: Consensus and Controversy*. London: Falmer Press, 119–27.

Bourdieu, P. 1990. Animadversiones in Mertonem, in J. Clark, C. Modgil and S. Modgil (eds), *Robert K. Merton: Consensus and Controversy*. London: Falmer Press, 297–301.

Calhoun, C. 2010. Introduction: On Merton's Legacy and Contemporary Sociology, in C. Calhoun (ed.), *Robert K. Merton: Sociology of Science and Sociology as Science*. New York: Columbia University Press, 1–31.

Campbell, C. 1982. "A Dubious Distinction? An Inquiry into the Value and Use of Merton's Concepts of Manifest and latent Functions." *American Sociological Review* 47: 29–44.

Cohen, A.K. 1955. *Delinquent Boys*. New York: The Free Press.

Cole, J.R. and Zuckerman, H. 1975. The Emergence of a Scientific Specialty: The Self-Exemplifying Case of the Sociology of Science, in L.A. Coser (ed.), *The Idea of Social Structure: Papers in Honor of Robert K. Merton*. New York: Harcourt Brace Jovanovich, 139–74.

Cole, S. 1975. The Growth of Scientific Knowledge: Theory of Deviance as a Case Study, in L.A. Coser (ed.), *The Idea of Social Structure: Papers in Honor of Robert K. Merton*. New York: Harcourt Brace Jovanovich, 175–220.

Coleman, J.S. 1975. Legitimate and Illegitimate Use of Power, in L.A. Coser (ed.), *The Idea of Social Structure: Papers in Honor of Robert K. Merton*. New York: Harcourt Brace Jovanovich, 221–36.

Coser, L.A. 1975. Merton's Use of the European Sociological Tradition, in L.A. Coser (ed.), *The Idea of Social Structure*. New York: Harcourt Brace Jovanovich, 85–100.

---

10 It is noteworthy that Coser, in his scholarly essay on Merton and the European sociological tradition (Coser 1975), has given only passing reference to Mannheim. Coser has not mentioned at all, in this or other connections, Merton's discussion of this author in relation to the sociology of knowledge (see Coser 1975: 93–4).

Coser, R.L. 1990. Reflections on Merton's Role-Set Theory, in J. Clark, C. Modgil and S. Modgil (eds), *Robert K. Merton: Consensus and Controversy*. London: Falmer Press, 159–76.

Donati, P. 1989. L'ambivalenza sociologica nel pensiero di R.K. Merton, in C. Mongardini and S. Tabboni (eds), *L'opera di R.K. Merton e la sociologia contemporanea*. Genoa: Ecig, 115–34.

Elster, J. 1990. Merton's Functionalism and the Unintended Consequences of Action, in J. Clark, C. Modgil and S. Modgil (eds), *Robert K. Merton: Consensus and Controversy*. London: Falmer Press, 129–35.

Giddens, A. 1990. R.K. Merton on Structural Analysis, in J. Clark, C. Modgil and S. Modgil (eds), *Robert K. Merton: Consensus and Controversy*. London: Falmer Press, 97–110.

Hilbert, R.A. 1990. Merton's Theory of Role-Sets and Status-Sets, in J. Clark, C. Modgil and S. Modgil (eds), *Robert K. Merton: Consensus and Controversy*. London: Falmer Press, 177–86.

Kalleberg, R. 2010. The Ethos of Science and the Ethos of Democracy, in C. Calhoun (ed.), *Robert K. Merton: Sociology of Science and Sociology as Science*. New York: Columbia University Press. 182–213.

Kendall, P. 1975. Theory and Research: The Case Study of Medical Research, in L.A. Coser (ed.), *The Idea of Social Structure*. New York: Harcourt Brace Jovanovich, 301–21.

Lazarsfeld, P.F. 1975. Working with Merton, in L.A. Coser (ed.), *The Idea of Social Structure*. New York: Harcourt Brace Jovanovich, 35–66.

Luhmann, N. 1970. *Soziologische Aufklärung*, Volume 1. Opladen: Westdeutscher Verlag.

Maniscalco, M.L. 1989. Il concetto di "serendipity" nel'opera di Robert K. Merton, in C. Mongardini and S. Tabboni (eds), *L'opera di R.K. Merton e la sociologia contemporanea*. Genoa: Ecig, 283–93.

Merton, R.K. 1936. "The Unanticipated Consequences of Purposive Social Action." *American Sociological Review* 1: 894–904.

Merton, R.K. 1949. "Discussion of Parsons 'Position of Sociological Theory.'" *American Sociological Review* 13: 164–8.

Merton, R.K. 1961. Social Problems and Sociological Theory, in R.K. Merton and R.A. Nisbet (eds), *Contemporary Social Problems*. New York: Harcourt Brace Jovanovich, 697–737.

Merton, R.K. 1968. *Social Theory and Social Structure*. Glencoe, IL: The Free Press.

Merton, R.K. 1976a. Structural Analysis in Sociology, in P.M. Blau (ed.), *Approaches to the Study of Social Structure*. London: Open Books, 21–52.

Merton, R.K. 1976b. *Sociological Ambivalence and other Essays*. New York: The Free Press.

Merton, R.K. 1981. Foreword: Remarks on Theoretical Pluralism, in P.M. Blau and R.K. Merton (eds), *Continuities in Structural Inquiry*. London: Sage, i–viii.

Merton, R.K. and Barber, E. 1976. Sociological Ambivalence, in R.K. Merton (ed.), *Sociological Ambivalence and other Essays*. New York: The Free Press, 3–31.

Mongardini, C. and Tabboni, S. 1989. *L'opera di R.K. Merton e la sociologia contemporanea*. Genoa: Ecig.

Moore, W.E. 1979. Functionalism, in T. Bottomore and R. Nisbet (eds), *A History of Sociological Analysis*. New York: Basic Books, 321–61.

Nedelmann, B. 1989. Robert K. Merton's Concept of Sociological Ambivalence: The Florentine Case of the 'Man-Ape', in C. Mongardini and S. Tabboni (eds), *L'opera di R.K. Merton e la sociologia contemporanea*. Genoa: Ecig, 135–52.

Orrù, M. 1990. Merton's Instrumental Theory of Anomie, in J. Clark, C. Modgil and S. Modgil (eds), *Robert K. Merton: Consensus and Controversy*. London: Falmer Press, 213–40.

Panowsky, A.L. 2010. A Critical Reconsideration of the Ethos and Autonomy of Science, in C. Calhoun (ed.), *Robert K. Merton: Sociology of Science and Sociology as Science*. New York: Columbia University Press, 140–63.

Parsons, T. 1975. The Present Status of "Structural-Functional" Theory in Sociology, in L.A. Coser (ed.), *The Idea of Social Structure*. New York: Harcourt Brace Jovanovich, 67–83.

Pettigrew, T.F. 2002. Summing Up: Relative Deprivation as a Key Social Psychological Concept, in I. Walker and H.J. Smith (eds), *Relative Deprivation: Specification, Development and Integration*. Cambridge: Cambridge University Press, 351–73.

Selvin, H.C. 1975. On Formalizing Theory, in L.A. Coser (ed.), *The Idea of Social Structure: Papers in Honor of Robert K. Merton*. New York: Harcourt Brace Jovanovich, 339–55.

Sica, A. 2010. Merton, Mannheim, and the Sociology of Knowledge, in C. Calhoun (ed.), *Robert K. Merton: Sociology of Science and Sociology as Science*. New York: Columbia University Press, 164–81.

Statera, G. 1989. Merton e la sociologia della scienza in Europa, in C. Mongardini and S. Tabboni (eds), *L'opera di R.K. Merton e la sociologia contemporanea*. Genoa: Ecig, 77–92.

Stinchcombe, A.L. 1975. Merton's Theory of Social Structure, in L.A. Coser (ed.), *The Idea of Social Structure*. New York: Harcourt Brace Jovanovich, 11–33.

Stinchcombe, A.L. 1990. Social Structure in the Work of Robert Merton, in J. Clark, C. Modgil and S. Modgil (eds), *Robert K. Merton*. London: Falmer Press, 81–95.

Sztompka, P. 1986. *Robert K. Merton: An Intellectual Profile*. New York: St. Martin's Press.

Williams, R.M. 1975. Relative Deprivation, in L.A. Coser (ed.), *The Idea of Social Structure*. New York: Harcourt Brace Jovanovich, 355–78.

Chapter 11
Network and Social Capital Theory

Preliminary Remarks

The two themes, which the title refers to, will be separately dealt with, bearing in mind, however, that the theme of social capital is part of the larger theme concerning the theory of social networks.

Networks

Both in anthropology and in sociology, a network is a set of direct and indirect connections (or ties) among social actors (or nodes), which may be persons, groups, countries or organizations. Within a network, (a) each actor is linked to every other actor through one or more paths; (b) actors are linked two by two by lines; and (c) tie clusters (some actors are linked with one another, rather than with other actors) and shared actors' characteristics (as for example being all corporation managers) may be used to identify the boundaries, in the absence of a clear institutional or cultural delimitation. An actor may belong to several networks at the same time (a single person can be part of a network of co-workers, a family network, and a network of friends). Close are those actors who can reach each other covering a short path (a sequence of nodes and lines). Between actors who reciprocally orient their action, different ties (for example, business and friendship ties) form a single link. All the ties and links among the actors form the analysis unit of "Network Theory." The effects the properties of the ties and links between the actors exert on actors' behaviors are its object of study (for a general introduction, see Piselli 2001b; Wellman 1988. See also, for some of the following points: Aldrich 1982; Berkowitz 1988; Blau 1982; Breiger 1988a; Chiesi 1999; Scott 1997; Wellman and Berkowitz 1988b; White, Boorman and Breiger 1976).

Each actor is situated in link networks, which he/she has not necessarily established, which, however, always condition his/her own and the other actors' behavior. The network can be, in particular, a source of normative and power constraints, and in this case it is relevant as communication flow. Otherwise it can be a source of benefits (often, but not always, deliberately pursued) for some or all participants, and in that case, it is relevant as resource flow. In any case, the network is a relevant social structure to individual behaviors. The study of networks has, therefore, a structural character. The social structure is a set of orderly and stable links established by a plurality of actors: more precisely, it is intended as a network formed, in turn, by the networks the actors establish and maintain.

The Network Theory is a structuralist sociological perspective. A structural investigation abstracts from actors' characteristics, or attributes. Therefore it is not important whether, and to what extent, their behaviors are influenced by variables, such as class positioning, gender, age, political preference, or by ideologies, religious belonging, habits and customs, or by other cultural aspects. A large part of the traditional sociological research has instead focused on the relations between variables, as for example, between class position and political preference. As a consequence, it has neither considered the wider set of relations in which they are situated nor examined the general background in which actors are acting. This tendency involves unfavorable consequences for sociological knowledge, since it does not give information about the properties of ties and networks. On the contrary, the network theory considers:

- The number of nodes and ties (network extent), and the strength of ties, as evidenced by frequency, duration, emotional intensity, customary involvement in exchange relations. Some particular actors, i.e. persons or organizations, establish strong ties with other actors, as well as weak ties with the remaining participants in the network. Strong ties, for example, are established through friendly relations, agreements among producers, and by spending time with colleagues, relatives, or members of the same ethnic group.

- The either hierarchical or egalitarian form of ties, and with one or more centers in the network. According to the network specific form, whether hierarchical or egalitarian, different constraints and opportunities may result for the actors.

- The different types of ties. Ties may be distinguished as follows: (a) simple or multiplex (or multi-stranded) ties; the latter type of ties has two or more different contents; (b) reciprocal or non-reciprocal ties; the former type of ties involves reciprocal orientation between two actors, jointly considered; (c) direct or indirect ties; the latter type of ties is mediated by other actors: for example, when someone relies on other in looking for employment; (d) transitive or intransitive ties; a tie is transitive when, if there are ties between the actors A and B, and between B and C, A and C are also connected; if they are not connected, the ties between A and B, and between B and C are intransitive; (e) ties that are inside of clusters, as are the ties within a group of friends; or ties that bridge two or more clusters, or bridge a cluster with relatively isolated actors.

- The actors' centrality. A large number of direct ties points to a direct centrality in the network (*Degree Centrality*); while there is a *closeness centrality* when the paths to reach indirectly linked actors are short. Actors who are close to most other actors in terms of steps to reach them are autonomous from each of them, as they can indifferently address themselves to any of the other actors. According to still a different measure of centrality (*betweenness centrality*), an actor who holds a central position in a network, acting as a mediator among other actors, controls information flows and available resources, and gains from them power and/or prestige (Aldrich 1982: 288–91; Marsden 1988; Wasserman and Faust 1994: 178–92).

- Bridges. A scarce number of ties in some areas of the network grants to those who are able to establish links (or "bridges") with the remaining areas, the possibility of controlling the available information and resources (Burt 1992), and therefore power and prestige. These advantages are different in a market exchange relation when it is important to reduce the uncertainty of those who participate in the exchanges. Participants can benefit from their exchanges because of the scarce number of their ties, and also because of their personal reputation. A scarce number of ties, that is to say, a scarce number of empty areas or "structural holes" in the network, gives participants an advantage if there are many structural holes in the network. This advantage, in terms of information and resources that flow to each participant in the exchanges, and therefore in terms of reduction of their uncertainty, results from the variety of network segments they are linked with. This variety of network segments results, in turn, from the great number of structural holes existing in their exchange network. Participants in exchanges who have a good reputation draw the highest advantage from it, in terms of uncertainty reduction, if they can exchange with few other participants of their own choice (Podolny 2001).

- The distinction between simple and multiplex ties (which include different contents, as in the case of business and friendly relations). These ties are mutual (in a couple of actors, the tie starts from and is oriented to both of them), symmetrical (in a couple of actors, the tie is mutual and has the same content or form), asymmetrical (in a couple of actors, a tie with a particular content or form originates from one of them and is oriented to the other).

- The distinction between direct and indirect (mediated by other actors) ties; and between transitive and intransitive ties. Ties are transitive if, when there is a tie between actors A and B, and between actors B and C, A and C are linked, too. Ties are intransitive when, given a tie between A and B, and between B and C, A and C are not linked. Different opportunities and constraints for the actors result from direct and indirect ties (for example, if one looks for a new job or advancement). Within the clusters (as ties in a group of friends), or connecting a particular cluster with others, or with relatively isolated particular actors.

- The distinction between so-called Ego-centric networks and networks intended as a structure, i.e. formed by one or more clusters of nodes and ties. In the first case, the analysis unit is provided by the set of ties existing between an actor (Ego) and others, and the constraints the network imposes on Ego's behaviors or the use he/she makes of the network for his purposes. In the second case, the analysis unit is provided by the link structure in which the actors are included. This structure is conceived as a system. The components of the system are in mutual dependence: if a component (either a single actor or a group of actors) changes, the other ones change as well.

- The network density, i.e. the ratio between existing ties and all the possible ones, given a certain number of actors. A network has maximum density if all actors are directly linked two by two. In this case, the network is called a "clique." The clusters (or groups) of nodes (actors) inside the network, as well as the presence of isolated nodes, and hence, empty areas ("holes"), identify the specific configuration, or structure, of a network. Groups and cliques involve the presence inside themselves of transitive ties, and intransitive ties toward the outside. Different consequences may result from it for the actors (such as loyalty and solidarity norms emerging as a consequence of their association), and for the larger networks in which they are included (such as unbalanced power relations in favor of the actors who are more closely linked).

- The possible presence of structurally equivalent relations between actors. These relations take place when two or more actors hold the same social status, that is to say, when they have the same kind and number of ties from and towards all the others. A group of actors characterized in this way, forms – in Network Theory language – a "block." Within a block, actors have equivalent, and therefore similar, links, while their links with external actors are different. The presence of blocks in a network involves clusters of nodes (or actors) and ties in one or more areas. Though absolutely equivalent relations are quite unlikely, nonetheless it is possible to find some good approximations. For example, this happens in countries that economically depend on others almost in the same way, and can be therefore considered as part of a single block. The search for blocks in a network is made by progressively identifying a group of actors who are increasingly similar to one another and dissimilar from others, in terms of number and kind of ties. This procedure either assumes a given network contains blocs, and aims to empirically ascertain their features, or it does not assume that there are blocs, and aims to empirically ascertain where their possible presence.

- The mutual determination of individuals and their groups or another collectivity, to which they belong. The specific nature of a group is determined by the peculiarities of the actors that form it, but the peculiarity of each actor, too, is determined by the specific combination of all groups (family, job-related, friendly groups, etc.) he/she belongs to. In other words, two groups are linked by two or more actors they have in common, but at the same time, the identity of each actor is defined by his/her simultaneous belonging to one or more groups (dualism of the social actor and the group he/she belongs to).

Within network theory, research has highlighted the validity of some generalizations, which can be summarized as follows (Wellman 1988: 40–47):

a. In the majority, ties are mutual, but the resources conveyed through ties are, in most cases, asymmetrical (unequal) in terms of kind and amount.
b. Regardless of other causes, asymmetry – or inequality – results from the presence of positions that connect groups (as the mediator's position), and therefore give centrality and power to those who hold them.
c. In most cases, actors are linked both directly and indirectly, and therefore their behavior is bound by the whole network of links.
d. The clusters that form in a network identify transitive and mutual ties between the actors. Low density ties, which are neither necessarily transitive nor mutual, and create a bridge between clusters, indirectly link all the actors in the network. Therefore they are particularly relevant to the actors and to the configuration of the network.
e. Clusters in one or more areas of the network facilitate the establishment of alliances, coalitions and social movements inside the network, which are aimed at obtaining or keeping power positions, in competition with other closely linked actors.

Within the network theory, some authors have produced contributions that are considered particularly important. We shall briefly dwell now on some works by Harrison C. White (1992, 1998) and Ronald S. Burt

(1982, 1992, and 2001). White was the first author who proposed – with Boorman and Breiger – a model of social structure by blocks, i.e. a structure model which considers clusters of actors as a unit of analysis. According to this model, the structure can be conceived as formed by blocks of actors who have structurally equivalent links, and by other blocks characterized by scarce or no blocks (zero-blocks). Specific links inside each block and between the blocks are thus highlighted (White, Boorman and Breiger 1976). White emphasizes the character of social construction, and therefore arbitrariness and fuzziness, of the network boundaries. For example, medical doctors form several subpopulations, according to their locale, specialty, standing and age (cf. White 1998: 61). His analysis is focused on markets, intended as social structures formed by producers' and buyers' groups or "cliques," which interact and reproduce themselves over time. Both cliques are internally homogeneous. In contrast with economic theory, White insists on the sociological character of his approach, which avoids not only the dubious psychological assumptions of economic theory, but also its individualistic assumption, according to which producers and buyers meet individually. This allows him to tackle problems – such as the presence of unbalanced markets and inequalities between producers – the economic theory has not been able to account for adequately. As White has argued, each producer, in formulating strategies and behaviors, observes and considers both the other producers, and the "cliques" of his or her buyers. In other words, the buyers' and consumers' groups establish and are part of a relation structure. Therefore, the market becomes a social structure.

By observing what the other producers do, and behaving accordingly, each producer seeks a market niche for his products, characterized by an optimal combination or "market schedule" of volumes and production costs, so as to maximize the difference between revenue and cash flow. Higher costs correspond to greater volumes. On the other hand, for any product they may require, buyers look, on the one hand, for an optimal combination of quality (and hence, desirability) and, on the other, of expense. Quality appraisal depends on consumers' taste and therefore cannot be changed, at least in the short run, by producers. For any product, an increase in production volumes does not involve an equivalent increase in the buyers' appraisal, since their tastes are progressively saturated. The prerequisite of the existence of a market is that the optimization of the volume-cost ratio for the producers is compatible with the optimization of the desirability-expense ratio for the buyers. The encounter of these prerequisites implies an increase in volumes and desirability related with an increase in costs and expenses.

Though different kinds of markets meet this condition, not all of them configure a balanced market. A market is balanced when profits grow through a progressive product differentiation. On the contrary, markets are unbalanced – White provides some examples – when the aggregate profit rate grows despite a decrease in the quality-expense ratio, or when this rate grows along with the aggregate production volume, thus causing a consequent explosive and unlimited growth of the market (White 1981, 1988). In keeping with White's development of network theory, this theory has found application not only to investigations on the market, but also to general theoretical issues such as identity and social control. Identity here means social construction rather than a result of values or individual interests. Actors (whether natural persons or organizations), instead, create an identity from actions, which are situated and scattered in different networks and environments and to which they attribute similarity and give consistency. At the same time, an identity is also a source of action that cannot be explained by biological and physical causes, to which the actors attribute a meaning, continuity, and regularity they consider evident. By establishing an organization, identities intertwine and lose flexibility.

However, identities originate in turn from an organization, which has been submitted to uncontrolled external events (called "contingencies"). Improvisation, chaos, and order disruption are their consequences. The attempts to exert social control, whether in advance or after a disruptive event, aim at preserving an identity against the diffusion of others. The control of disruptive events, or contingencies, is necessary in order to establish and keep an identity. Identities form through the conflicts between organizations, and result from a dynamic balance of their actions and reactions. Networks and their identities originate – this is a central thesis for White – for the networks' ongoing efforts to exert control on their social space. When a set of concatenated actions physically and socially decouples from the contingent context of actions in which it was included up to then (through the establishment, for instance, of a priority order), these actions escape the control provided by other identities, and are embedded in a context and action level, which are submitted to the control of a new identity.

The decoupling resulting from conflict between identities makes the creation and existence of new and separate identities possible. These new identities, which are situated in different times and places, can be compared according to some equivalence standard. For example, when a chain of restaurants is well known and has therefore its own identity, buyers are able to compare it with its competitors. All identities create different levels (as families, organizations, towns and cities) in a single complex of links – a single social organization, broadly speaking – which continuously extends itself in time and space. An identity that survives to the competition with others, succeeds in reproducing itself, and thus forms a stable element of social control or, in White's words, a "discipline." A discipline is a set of interconnected actions, which receives recognition over time, has its own identity, and relates with others in a comparison and dominance order. In White's words, disciplines are "self-constituting conveners of social action." They "build around commitments that constrain constituent identities" (White 2008: 8).

White (2008: 9) distinguishes between different species of disciplines: interfaces, arenas, and councils. The meanings of these terms will be presently defined. A discipline may be circumscribed within a given area, in which it has been selected and fits; but it does not so necessarily, and may be compared to other disciplines in this respect. Conflicts between identities and the resulting efforts to control the others' identities produce not only actions and reactions, but also narrations or "stories." By telling stories, we express perceptions of social processes and structures; we plan the control of existing identities and the creation of new ones, with decoupling attempts and concomitant possible failures; we formulate comparative evaluations of the priority or dominance orders. These evaluations – generalized in the form of values – are recurring elements in a plurality of stories. Reminding that the word "discipline" means in this case interconnected actions to which an identity is attributed, in a particular discipline – which is here called "interface" – an evaluation involves an encounter and a comparison with other disciplines, with which it relates in a control dispute.

This occurs, for instance, in the markets among interchangeable (i.e. structurally equivalent) firms, which compete in terms of product quality. While this evaluation process includes not only social, but also biological and physical aspects, another discipline, called "arena" characterizes itself for a merely social comparative evaluation. Actors – for example, producers and buyers, professionals and their clients – choose themselves by means of a mutual selection according to this standard, and therefore are not interchangeable. Finally, in another discipline called "council," actors (political parties and factions) mobilize to create alliances, or to establish new ones in power disputes, making claims adopted by one or the other of the conflicting identities. "Disciplines" (that is, networks of stable interconnections between relations, which have identities), and actors-binding ties, which connect different disciplines and identities, are – in keeping with White – social constructions. Jointly considered, they compose the social space.

The most intensive ties most contribute to the most active to the largest structures, and to the production of best defined identities. When some sets of interconnected actions, that is, of "disciplines," pursue reciprocal control, then those relations that connect them produce their uncoupling from other disciplines. If efforts to create disciplines, and therefore identities and controls, fail, empty areas or "black holes" are formed in the middle of the social space. Within these "black holes" are situated disciplines, identities, and networks of ties, which are perceived as new types of relations. White calls them "catnets," meaning "categories of networks." These are ill-defined connections, which are only partially recognized and, therefore, less subject to control on the part of other and consolidated disciplines and identities such as, for example, a group of friends. These failed attempts to create a new "discipline" produce connections, which tell stories of past conflicts aiming at control (for example, conflicts between ethnic or parental groups).

Stories confer them a stable and taken for granted interpretation. Blocks are sets of networks and values, which correspond to sets of "disciplines," in which the ties and the actors are structurally equivalent. Block models group together networks having a similar form. The social and cultural uncertainty is accordingly reduced, for the rules that set boundaries to the disciplines cause ambiguities and uncertainties both socially (as in power conflicts), and culturally (in the perception and interpretation of these rules). White calls "localities" the networks of relations, which are situated in a physical space disregarding stories that concern them. Institutions are defined here as blocks, which group together species of disciplines that are situated in different networks, or "localities." Institutions simplify the perception and analysis of networks and "disciplines." White provides a few examples of "disciplines," in particular, castes, in which the value of purity gives order to stories and interpretations; the science departments of the American universities, in which the scientific specialties supply this order; the corporations – in the sense of organized representations of interests – where identities are defined, the prerogatives of social action are specified and its boundaries are indicated; and the clients relationships, in which exchange relations between persons differently endowed with power are maintained. By means of institutions, populations of groups and networks, which would be otherwise not connected, become comparable. If these different networks intersect, as do a child's networks of school peers, siblings and parents, distinct identities follow as a consequence. When jointly considered, these identities define a social position. A position is always situated in a larger social context, as in particular the context formed by one or more institutions. Networks of relations, identities, and disciplines intersect all the time in a random and stochastic (probabilistic) way, and cannot be therefore predetermined. In White's own words, "It is identities seeking control that fuels practical activity whatever the context" (White 1992: 9).

If a stochastic process is conducive to stable results, a configuration of networks called "profile" results from the random distribution of its constitutive elements. A "profile" is then an interaction order that contrasts with, and constrains, the disorder or contingency of the interactions, for randomly intersecting networks may evidence some order from the observer's point of view. This is instantiated by those markets, in which producers seek to achieve mutual control by processes of coupling into, and uncoupling from, per-existent networks of relations. The flow of heterogeneous customers through the aisles of a supermarket provides another example on a smaller scale. This flow is perceived as stable and orderly, but a different arrangement of wares on the shelves of the supermarket, or its different location, would change the proportion in which the various components of its heterogeneous customers combined together. Individuals perceive the order which implicitly inheres to any unstable configuration of networks. At the same time they continuously re-create it with their preferences and choices, and with their interpretive frames; in other words, they create this order with their style.

This style derives, generally speaking, from the values, which are embedded in a number of different institutions. Identities and the network of relations in different social spaces are constituted by means of the actors' careers. Actors are not only people, but also social organizations and "disciplines." Actors' careers constitute various identities and networks of relations in different social spaces. Actors thereby produce processes of decoupling and embedding in a new action context. How careers are constructed cannot be established in advance, as their social environment is contingent and stochastic. White employs the term "professionalism" to designate the style, in which careers are constructed. An obsession with the form and symbolic appearances characterizes this style, which presupposes – as it does with careers – a fluid context of social networks and institutions. This fluid context of the careers style makes it necessary to have stories in order to uphold the actors' identities, competences, and aspirations to control other identities.

Social organizations do not just provide control, and therefore consistency, continuity, and boundaries, to an environment subject to chaotic and random contingencies. They also open with disembedding processes a field of action, which overcomes the constraints that originate from previous social obligations. In comparison to routine actions, as produced by disciplines, institutions and styles, the effects of social organizations are more cumulative, on a larger scale, and not foreseeable with an analysis of routine actions. Instances thereof are the sentences of the appellate courts, as compared to sentences of lower courts. A number of consequences flow from social organizations, such as new identities and disciplines; new attempts to control, new processes of disembedding and styles; and possibly also a new social organization, which would involve overhauling the extant relations, and which would produce lesser ambiguity in the boundaries between networks. Thus, the financial, economic, and political crisis of a state or other public administration may bring about a change in some local or national context, as occurred with the *Glasnost* in Soviet Union's last years.

The concepts of social order, system, rationality, and structure belong to the rhetoric of the social sciences, and pay no consideration to the contingent and unforeseeable character of social reality, for actions are subject to the pressure of random and accidental events which originate from their physical and social context. Of much greater use to the study of social organizations are the concepts of meaning, identity, control, and contingency. Identities, in particular, with their projects of control and the meanings, which make their existence possible, originate from contingencies.[1]

---

1 For an introduction to Harrison White's version of network theory, see Jörissen and Könitz 2010.

Insofar as Ronald Burt is concerned, attention will be here paid to his structural theory of action (Burt 1982). More recent works by this author will be presented later, while discussing theories of social capital. Burt's structural theory of action deals with the following three conceptual components: social structure, the actor's interests, and the action. As for social structure, Burt posits that action consist of the following elements: the individuals or groups who act; the peculiar resources that make the action possible; the interests on the part of the individuals, which motivate them to perform the action; the likelihood of performing other actions, in addition to the one that supplies a maximum of utility. Burt's structural theory aims at conducting a selective reception of the atomistic and normative theories of action. The atomistic theory presupposes that actors evaluate alternative courses of action, each actor on his or her own. This is – as Burt observes – a non-realistic presupposition. The normative theory instead assumes that the social system consists of mutually coherent and interdependent role sets. Actors are integrated in the social system by means of the socialization process. They therefore pursue their interests in conformance to the norms – that is, the values and beliefs – they have been taught. Burt objects that there is no empirical support for the presupposition of the social system's consistency, and therefore stability, for the actors' interests, whose position in the social system is distant, cannot be considered interdependent.

Burt accepts the assumption of atomistic theory that actors pursue their interests independently from each other; he also accepts the assumption of normative theory that actors partake of a social context of relations, which originates from the division of social labor, and which is normatively regulated. However, Burt's own structural theory presupposes that actors hold positions in a system or network of relations, which are equivalent and interdependent. Actors, in keeping with Burt, are identified by the position they hold, as defined by the set of their social relations. Other categories of actors, such as those in particular who perform the same role sets (i.e., the consistent sets of roles that define the social positions), are not considered here; for they are ambiguously defined, and therefore the possibility exists that attributes such as stability and indispensability are incorrectly attributed to the system of role sets. The models, which represent the social context by means of network of relations, are called "network models," and provide a scheme that may be of use to describe social differentiation between actors in a system. There are several network models, and their choice depends on what one aims to do by describing social differentiation.

The relational and positional models that are here considered are complementary, therefore not incompatible. The relational model considers Ego-centered relations, which are anchored to particular actors. Its advantage is that the usual methods of research and data analysis may be employed, even when social relations have different contents. The positional model, on the other hand, considers the networks that are constituted by equivalent positions in a context of social relations. This model presents, in keeping with Burt, the following advantages: a) All the relations composing a system or social structure are taken into considerations: not, accordingly, only those that concern a particular actor; b) It is possible to indicate their number, configuration (whether, for instance, there are cliques), and meaning in a social context, which is made of perceptions and actions. The positional model, moreover, is very well suited to formulate a structural theory of action, since it considers all the relations that constitute a social structure.

The positional model may be applied for the purpose of providing a description of how a group of scientists are stratified by means of a system of reciprocal relations, rather than a shared institutional affiliation. In keeping with this description, a group of scientists is the more prominent and prestigious, the denser is the network of the group's inner relations and, therefore, the greater is the group members' ability to coordinate their activities. In turn, the density of this network depends on the similarity of their research interests and of their university education. Another application of the positional model, which has, however, also used the relational model, has as a unit of analysis not persons but firms that are active in different economic sectors. As for the American economic system, each of these sectors occupies a specific position, on which research has been performed. The connections between the corporate boards of directors make it possible to coordinate firms operating in different sectors, thus preventing constrains in obtaining profits, and in their amounts, which are caused by differences in their economic sectors.

Multiplex ties connect firms, which are characterized by their presence in more than one market sector. These firms may have interlocking directorates or ownerships, or may be indirectly connected by means of financial institutions. In any case, their multiplex ties connections make it possible to negotiate better conditions in their market transactions, as compared to the prevalent market conditions.

As for the second component of Burt's structural theory of action, i.e. the actor's interests, Burt maintains that the actors perceive their interests according to their position in the social structure, in keeping with the positional model, rather than to the strength of ties between them, in conformance to the relational model. The actors while evaluating their actions temporarily take the position of others who share their social circumstances; namely, actors occupying structurally equivalent positions reciprocally evaluate the advantages of their actions. This descriptive model of the actors' perception conforms to the findings of important empirical researches, and indeed extends them. Furthermore, the model posits that actors holding structurally equivalent positions have the following characteristics: (a) they share a norm even if they have no direct relations; (b) they experience relative deprivation or feel to be advantaged in relation to others, a resource redistribution or some change in the social system occur; (c) they are more inclined to adopt innovations than other actors.

An example of actors holding structurally equivalent positions is provided by a research, which has concerned the most important journals of sociology and sociological methods. Scientists take into consideration in their work and establish networks of reciprocal influences with those colleagues who concern themselves with similar problems. These reciprocal influences extend to all the scientists holding structurally equivalent positions, in keeping with the positional model; they do not extend only to those scientists with whom a direct relationship has been established, as the relational model would hold. By virtue of these reciprocal influences scientists abide by common norms, which are reflected in the works they publish in specialized journals, for these journals give expression to such common norms which the network of reciprocal influences maintain. The norms, which are thus expressed, are more pronounced among those scientists who are in the board of editors, or who publish with these journals. Within the most important journals, this expression of normative interests may be especially found in the least prestigious ones, but only those interests are expressed which conform to the norms that bind the scholarly communities, which establish which journals should be considered as most relevant.

Authors who are interested in different journals are considered deviants. They do not form a homogeneous category. There are the "rebels," who only publish in non-relevant journals, thereby rejecting the conventional criteria of scientific relevance. There also are the "eccentrics," who publish in non-relevant journals and in others as well. The positional model, as applied to this particular case, considers only the relations between actors who hold structurally equivalent positions in their networks of influence. This model predicts more accurately conformity and deviance (in the aforementioned sense) than the relational model which considers instead all the relations between the actors. Furthermore, authors who belong to a more prestigious group are also those who most agree as to the norms of scientific relevance, by means of which journals are classified. On the other hand, publishing with these journals consolidates the hierarchy of prestige between the different groups of authors.

As for the third component of Burt's structural theory of action, i.e. action, Burt formulates a model which indicates how a role set, which defines a social position in a system of relations, determines the actors' ability to successfully pursue their interests, without being constrained by other actors in the social system. To occupy a social position determines, in other words, the actors' structural autonomy, for they are freed from constrains coming from other actors. This model receives empirical confirmation, but is rudimental; for it does not take into account the following objections: (a) who holds a social position cannot simultaneously be an object and a subject of relations with others; (b) an actor may occupy several positions in a system; (c) formal relations may often be only ambiguous distinguished from informal ones; (d) actors may pursue complementary interests. If they do so, every actor is less constrained in his or her action when the other actors, too, pursue their own interests.

Burt has applied his structural model to a study of the cross-relations between the members of the board of directors of firms, which operate in different economic sectors. This subject has already been considered here, but regarding a different question; that is, whether the connections between firms could be instrumental to obtain greater profits. The question is now rather whether the typical profit margin of a firm, among those which have been considered, depends on its structural autonomy in the particular sector, in which it operates. According to this model, high profit margins accrue to firms, which face low competition with other firms in the same sector, while both suppliers compete fiercely among them and so do buyers. Empirical research has been in line with this model, but has shown that profit margins depend on the competition between suppliers and buyers to a greater extent, than on the absence of competition within that economic sector. The links between the board of directors of firms, which belong to the same economic sector, are the more frequent, the more the firms depend on their suppliers and buyers. Apparently, therefore, these links are then created with the purpose of making profits, rather than of promoting efficiency in transactions and, hence, in the market.

The Reception of Network Theory

This reception has been noteworthy in many ways. The network theory has produced very lively discussions, a great deal of research, but few – if any – undisputed conclusions. This survey of the secondary literature is limited in its scope and exhaustiveness, though hopefully not biased. We shall hint here first at presentations and evaluations that deal with network theory in general, or specifically with the contributions of White and Burt. Then, some attention will be paid to investigations in specific research fields, concerning Ego-centric networks, and networks intended as a structure. As for the literature on network theory in general, Collins' contribution (1988: ch. 12) is distinctive for its ample approach, which includes, in addition to network theory strictly defined, also: exchange theory; Blau's macro-sociological theory; Lin's and Granovetter's theories of individual mobility; White's theory of the market; and networks theories of power.

As Collins observes, network theories set out to describe and explain why networks have a particular structure. Network theories, Collins maintains, has several merits: firstly, they consider the network of relations, rather than the single actors' attributes, such as race, class, age, etc. Secondly, they offer a more realistic vision of how the market works, as compared to economic theory. Thirdly, they may be applied to several different subjects and holds at different levels of analysis. Burt's theory, in particular, may be applied to the sociology of the markets and holds at both the macro and micro levels. According to Collins, however, network theory cannot demonstrate that similar conducts on the part of actors who occupy structurally equivalent positions are due to the influence exerted by their network relations, rather than to specific propertied of their interactions. Emirbayer and Goodwin have also published an evaluation of network theory, which has attracted considerable attention. Their contribution has a more critical character. The authors distinguish, within network analysis, between different "models" of relations between culture, *agency* (what social actors do), and the social structure.

One model is called structural determinism. This model neglects, according to them, the cultural, political, and historical elements that contribute to configure action and structure. An instance of structuralist determinism would be White's early work, in which a "block model" of social structure is formulated, that is, a model in which the relations between actors occupying positions in networks are hypothesized to be structurally equivalent. A second model, structural instrumentalism, pays attention to actors, but it narrowly interprets their action as instrumentally oriented to pursuing a maximum of utility. A third model, finally, called structural constructionism, inadequately deals with the interconnections between culture, actors, and the social structure. According to Emirbayer and Goodwin, only White's later work, and chiefly *Identity and Control*, on which we have dwelt, includes a theory of symbols and cultural discourses. This work, however, is seriously flawed, for it does not explain why actors or identities seek to exert control on each other, nor does it investigate how and to what extent cultural elements matter. These elements shape, and are in turn shaped by, the identities and aspirations of the real social actors. The cultural structures – they argue – constrain social action, but at the same time make it possible (Emirbayer and Goodwin 1994).

Antonio Mutti, in presenting the theoretical and empirical contributions of network analysis (1996), recalls Emirbayer and Goodwin's critique of White, but Mutti extends his critical appraisal to works of economic sociology, such as those produced by White himself, and also those of Burt, Granovetter and Useem. Mutti considers these works not always significantly innovative (with reference to White's and Burt's sociology of the markets), nonetheless remarkable because they re-evaluate particularistic interpersonal relations within the existential horizon of the modern actor (Mutti 1996: 28).

The research areas to which network theory has been applied are numerous. While it is not possible here to supply complete information on these areas, some indication will be provided nonetheless. A distinction will be made between Ego-centric networks, which bring into line personal relations, and networks intended as a structure. The study of former type of networks has an anthropological rather than sociological character.

Among the best-known studies of Ego-centric networks a few will be here recalled as examples. Barnes (2001) has focused on how decisions are made in local associations of fishermen of a small Norwegian community in which everyone is tied to someone else by links of kinship or friendship, and the values of equality and unity are strongly held. Accordingly, in the process of decision-making an effort is made not to bring into light dissent, even if there is one, and to avoid using procedures, such as voting, which would evidence the existence of rivalries and conflicts.

Bott (2001) has investigated conjugal roles in three types of the organization of the family activities:

a. independent organization, in which the family activities are separate and independent;
b. complementary organization, in which these activities are separate but integrated;
c. joint organization, in which they are jointly conducted, or indifferently performed by one or other spouse.

The prevalence of a particular organizational type depends both on the marriage duration, and on the spouses' social class. Spouses' tendency to separate their activities from each other is the more pronounced the lower the spouses' social class, and the more they share networks of relatives, neighbors and friends. Kapferer (2001) has studied how support was mobilized among the members of a network of labor peers, when a dispute erupted. Among the participants, most successful were those who could count on multiplex, instead of simple, relations, and on a large and denser network, which included those who were most influential in that work milieu.

The remaining workers were aware of these differences between the dispute participants, to the effect that the differences favored some contenders at the expenses of the others. They therefore realized that taking sides with the weakest participants may have damaged their relations not only with the strongest participants but also with others who were linked to them. Influential persons stepped in on the behalf of the contenders who had the best social relations because they themselves had closer ties with them, and because a different conduct would have divided the workers among themselves.

Kadushin (1982) has shown that there is a positive correlation between the network density of personal relations, mental health, and one's ability to react to difficulties. Social privilege and stable friendships are here considered as indicators a person's network density. Therefore that person may avail him or herself of resources such as emotional support and normative consistency in social contexts different from those of large cities. These indicators are correlated with the ability to preserve mental health even in situations in which the person experiences strong tensions. A large amount of empirical research has confirmed these conclusions, but it should be kept in mind that dense networks in which strong ties prevail – such as those present in Kadushin's research – are useful to preserve an already existent identity; but networks that are otherwise, which are characterized, namely, by low density and the prevalence of weak ties, are conducive to acquiring new identities (Meo 1999).

Other empirical studies of social networks concern networks intended as a structure of relations, rather than Ego-centric networks. The former type of studies are, like the latter type, numerous and significant. In this case, too, only some researches and research orientations will be considered by way of illustration. We shall start here with a historical investigation, which is very well known, and often cited. This research deals with the ascent to power in Florence of the Medici family in the first decades of the fifteenth century, and shows that Cosimo de' Medici cultivated close relations with two distinct sets of actors. On the one hand, relations were cultivated with some patrician, no-longer dominant families linked to the Medici family through marriage that extended even outside their neighborhood. On the other hand, the Medici had relations with people living in their neighborhood but having lower social status. The Medici were wont to take care of their business and pursue common interests with these people rather than with others who belonged to the other network.

As these two networks were separated, an alliance between all these actors against the Medici family was impossible; on the contrary, the Medici acquired a position of mediation and power. Moreover, the Medici re-established relations that had been turned sour because of political events with some powerful Florentine patrician families. The already existing relations with other families were preserved. The patrician families were linked by multiplex ties, but were nonetheless unable to conduct a common action because of their rivalries. What is more, the Medici took advantage of their position as bankers to finance the municipality of Florence with loans having a high interest rate. By doing so, they obtained public merit and greater wealth. They also endeavored to cultivate the support of other municipalities. Their overall benefit was to strengthen their economic and political position. This conduct was carried out with several distinct actors, in an attempt not to antagonize anybody, and to take prompt advantage of contingent opportunities and of their position of patricians, bankers and rulers of a city neighborhood. The Medici's conduct made it possible that this family presented itself as defenders of the city institutions. Thereby, the Medici consolidated and legitimated their hegemony, and became eventually Florence's rulers (Padgett and Ansell 1993).

As a general conclusion, this investigation has shown how holding a central position of intermediaries in the social structure may be exploited to draw power on other social actors, but also to establish cooperative relations with them. Intermediaries establish a contact between actors who are not directly linked; they do so in exchange for compensation, whether monetary or otherwise. This type of centrality is called "betweenness" in the language of network theory. "Closeness" indicates another type of centrality, namely the actors' dependence on no one else, and their ability to exploit to their advantage their autonomy (Marsden 1982). The Medici's position in their social network was central in two senses. In one sense, they were indispensable intermediaries in marriage or business relations; as everyone else had to address him or herself to them, they did not need anyone in particular. They could, in other words, take advantage of their power to exert exclusion on others by virtue of their wealth and social status, and to prevent others from forming alliances against them because of the power and legitimacy of which they could avail themselves.

Weak actors can ally themselves to redefine to their advantage power relations, but they may be prevented from doing so when at least some of these weak actors consider legitimate the power of strong actors. In the case of the Medici family, considering the configuration of their network, such an alliance between weak actors would have eliminated their central position and therefore their domination. The Medici could, moreover, turn to their advantage the absence of ties between the other actors, and consolidate their legitimacy through frequent marriage or economic exchanges. The Medici could thus modify their potentially competitive relations with other in relations that were stably cooperative (Chiesi 1999: 189–93; Cook 1982, 1990; Lawler and Yoon 1998; Willer et al. 2002). Network theory has found application in some research areas such as, in particular, community studies. Claude S. Fischer's research is especially well known. It applies concepts, which belong to network theory, such as the network density and centrality, and the multiplexity of ties, to verify the effects of urbanization on personal relations.

Kadushin, as it may be recalled, had already investigated on whether there is a relation between urban context, network density and support for individuals. Fisher, however, unlike Kadushin, considers the whole network configuration. His research, moreover, has a broader theoretical interest, since it concerns the validity of some classical theses on urbanization. In keeping with these theses, which originate with Toennies and Wirth, the urbanization process would involve the destruction of the pre-existing communities and the isolation of the individuals. In contrast with them, Fischer finds that these theses hold true only for lower-income people. As for the remaining people, especially those who are better off and more educated, living in a metropolitan context promotes the multiplexity of their networks. Furthermore, networks which have a lower degree of density and centrality, both relative and absolute, do not bring lower psychological well-being for the individuals, contrary to the assumptions of some representatives of classical sociological theory. Fisher, however, recognizes that current research suggests, but does not really confirm, the thesis that urban living promotes the emergence of numerous and different subcultures in a community, as his own theory states (Fischer 1995, 2001).

Among other important community studies, which have made use of network theory, the following one will be here recalled. This research concerned the network of relations between the inhabitants of East York, an English-speaking Toronto suburb (Wellman 1982; Wellman, Carrington and Hall 1988). This research was conducted in two phases, in the 1960s and 1970s. Like Fischer's, this research, too, sets out to verify the thesis put forward by classical sociology regarding the alleged disappearance in urban contexts of communitarian networks. Object of analysis was the frequency, content, and emotional intensity of ties. Its conclusions were mostly negative. Aside from few exceptions, East York inhabitants are members of more than one group, and the networks of these groups were dense, stable, and with strong ties. These networks partly overlap, and are constituted by relatives, friends, neighbors and workmates. Several ties are supportive. This support is not only emotional and moral. It has also the following features: (a) it is practical, as for example, doing small services or providing information: (b) it is reciprocal, with generalized reciprocity (one does not exactly return what has received); (c) it is asymmetrical (non-symmetrical, that is, non-equal) when only one actor has the required resource such as money or information). In all these cases, exchanges may often cause the exclusion of other contacts, which at least one actor may have preferred.

A relevant current of research in network theory has dwelt on the relations between the proximity of social actors, such as people, organizations, cities or states, who partake of a network of social relations, and on the possibility of exerting influence on attitudes and behaviors. The term of proximity means, if restrictively intended, structural equivalence between particular actors or, more broadly, structural equivalence between actors of the same type (as, for example, between members of different administration boards; or between holders of majority shares in different corporations, as discussed in the vast literature on interlocking directorships). In all these cases, it has been assumed that having similar positions in a network promotes contacts between the actors and that, in particular, a relation of influence, control, or reciprocal dependence (cf. for instance Lomi, Corrado and Sandri 1997). Alternatively, the existence of such a relation has been inferred from the network density, to the effect that dense networks would promote relations of influence or of a similar character (see for example Breiger 1990; Laumann and Pappi 2001).

Generally speaking, however, this research current has been affected by methodological inadequacies in their design; as a consequence, it has not been able to demonstrate persuasively that possible influences originate from the actors' positions in a network, rather than from other causes (Marsden and Friedkin 1994). A well-known example of research on structurally equivalent positions in a network, which has used the block modeling procedure, concerns the effects, which the state position in the world system of exchange relations exerts on its economic growth. Every state has different opportunities to control world's economic exchanges, and to exploit them for the purpose of economic growth, according to its position in a system consisting of three blocks of states. The states that belong to the central block are advantaged as compared to those belonging to the semi-peripheral block and even more so, to those of the peripheral block. Disadvantage flows from economic dependence (Snyder and Kick 1979).

This study, which considers structural equivalence between particular states, has been criticized on methodological grounds. Other studies have set out to verify its results. They have preserved the block modeling technique, but have availed themselves of a more accurate methodology (see for example Breiger 1981). In particular, a study has focused on the structural equivalence between types of states, rather than between particular states. Its conclusions, however, have not significantly differed from those of the previous study (Smith and White 1992). According to another investigation, classifying a city in one or the other of these three blocks (central, semi-peripheral and peripheral) depends on the position, which a city occupies in the hierarchies of power and prestige. Except a few large cities such as New York, London, Paris and Tokyo, the city positions do not coincide with those of their states (Alderson and Beckfield 2001).

Still another group of studies has investigated collective movements. These studies very frequently mention themes and theses of network theory, but specific researches in this field of studies are much less frequent. An introductive research on collective movements has shown that the density and multiplexity of ties (whether of cooperation, exchange or identity) in the movements' networks can be a presupposition, but also a consequence, of collective action. Ideological and political affinities jointly that produce a master interpretive frame strengthen the relations within the network. Alliances are accordingly more easily formed, and it becomes easier to mobilize sympathizers to pursue common goals. Which goals are selected depends on the evaluations of the political opportunities. If these opportunities receive favorable evaluations, the goals are specific and open to possible cooperation; otherwise, goals are general and characterized by intransigent contraposition (Diani 1995).

Previous ties with persons and organizations promote collective action, as long as, however, that these ties support identities, which are connected with the social movement, and with which the subjects strongly identify (McAdam and Paulsen 1993). It has been objected, on the other hand, that this research has failed to indicate how cultural and political ties, which pre-exist and are widespread, have been selected and have become relevant to those who have been mobilized. In other words, the relation between the cultural milieu and the political mobilization has not been specified (Emirbayer and Goodwin 1994: 1433).

Within the theory and research on collective movements, their students who are close to a structuralist perspective have paid particular attention to network theory. Their theoretical position does not coincide with Granovetter's emphasis (as we shall see later) on the importance of weak ties in order to produce a collective action. Weak ties are important only if they are centralized, they maintain; for only then it is possible to coordinate a plurality of individuals having sufficient interest and resources to form one or more networks called "cliques." These networks distinguish themselves for being constituted by relatively few people and having a maximum density of ties (relations). These individuals can thus constitute an organization which acts as a critical mass, mobilizes other people and promoted the collective action. The participants' selection, if rationally conducted, should combine the goal to reach a maximum number of people with the one to reach those who are most able to contribute to the movement, considering their resources and the interests that motivate them. There is therefore a critical threshold for the success of the movement; that is, a minimum quantity of persons and a minimum average of interests and resources (Marwell and Oliver 1993).

The literature on the critical mass is related with the more general theme concerning the existence of thresholds for innovation diffusion. Different categories of people have been distinguishes, according to their availability to adopt an innovation, and anticipate the majority of others; or to join those who are ready to social change; or, finally, to lag behind. As research has suggested, it is advisable to distinguish between, on the one hand, those who are more or less ready to accept an innovation concerning society in general, and, on the other hand, concerning their networks of personal acquaintances. These two sets of people do not coincide. They vary, moreover, according to an individual's society and personal network (Valente 1996).

Those investigations should be finally recalled here that regard the effects, which the structure of relation exert on the attitudes and belief systems; investigations, in other words, which concern whether and how some people are influenced by others with whom they are related. In keeping with these investigations, this influence depends on the following conditions: (a) whether it is possible to compare one's attitudes with those of others who are deemed similar regarding aspects, which are significant for the investigation; or with the attitudes of others whom that person would like to meet; (b) the density of ties with others, since density makes comparisons easier; (c) holding structurally equivalent positions, as in this case, too, comparisons become easier. Similar attitudes and belief systems promote relations; vice versa, a network of relations promotes similar attitudes and beliefs. This holds true also for cliques, which are different, but are directly linked by multiplex ties. Indirect ties do not produce this effect, on the other hand, even when there is only one network of relations, of which different cliques partake (Erikson 1982, 1988).

Social Capital

Social capital is a set of permanently available links, or connections, for those who want to benefit from them. Benefits may be material, as money, or non-material, as power, prestige and social approval. In any case, the social capital as a set of available relations is conceptually distinguished from the benefits, which may accrue from them. In other words, social capital is formed by networks of acquaintances that are used for gaining a benefit from them, though this network has not been necessarily established for this purpose (see in this connection Bourdieu 1986; Coleman 1988, 1990. See also Bagnasco 2001: 96–7; Bankston and Zhou 2002: 285–91; Granovetter 1985; Piselli 2001; Portes 1998: 3–6). The links constituting this network may be either direct or indirect, as those established with acquaintances of acquaintances. They may concern relatives, friends, persons having the same territorial origin, or of the same religion – moreover, firms, local communities and national collectivities.

In any case, they are resources that can be permanently used by a plurality of subjects. These subjects correctly assume that they put their trust in others who feel bound to them by moral (and even legal) support, loyalty, and solidarity obligations, and act accordingly. Mutual trust allows the actors to create, preserve, and increase not only the economic, but also the social capital, thus reducing their need to control the action of others with whom they are linked, as well as to cut transaction costs. Moreover, "this applies in particular to long-term non-coercive exchanges," which are characterized by non-consolidated or ineffective procedural rules (Mutti 1998: 50–53). Therefore, mutual trust is a prerequisite of social capital, but not of any link in general. On the other hand, trust may be put in persons, associations, or institutions. A decrease in trust in one of these areas does not necessarily point to a general decrease in trust, and hence, in social capital (Mutti 2000).

The resources connected with social capital are neither physical, nor economic (for these bonds are not redeemed with currency, and payment time is not specified) (La Valle 2000: 2–3; Portes 1998: 7). In addition, the available resources do not belong to a particular individual, whereas on the contrary, the education, or human capital, which this individual has received, belongs to him or her. These resources – namely, stable social links – are rather elements of the social structure, and have the character of public goods available to everyone having stable social links. These links benefit not only from generic trust, as commonly found in the milieu in which actors live, but also from the institutional support, which establishes and enforce their rules of conduct. Therefore, it is possible to appropriate and rationally use them for specific purposes (Bertolini and Bravo 2001: 44–8). Their nature of public assets changes depending on their accessibility, which can be universal or reserved to a particular group (Chiesi 2000: 3–4). The preservation and availability of these resources depend on their temporal stability and continuous use (ephemeral or unused resources cannot become social capital). Furthermore, their preservation is easier when these social links are dense and supported by binding norms.

The goals, which are pursued by means of social capital, are diverse. For example, acquaintance networks can be used to seek a job; to start a business activity; to manage it by availing oneself of reliable suppliers and customers; to receive from one's family encouragement and support for completing studies that later on will prove advantageous; to temporarily entrust one's children to neighbors, or ask them little favors. Research has focused on those who are in possession of social capital, on those who confer it, and on the positive or negative effect of social capital for those who benefit from it and for others. Those who are able to use pre-established networks of links to their benefit, hold social capital. It can occur, in particular, to those who hold a high position in a hierarchy of privilege. In the case of individuals, rather than collectivities, this position means social prestige, which often goes along with privilege in terms of class, culture, and authority (Bourdieu 1986; Lin 2001: 37, 244; Lin, Cook and Burt 2001: 19). Likewise, social capital is available to those who can mobilize in their favor – thanks to stable links characterized by cooperation – available resources. These resources may be in terms of solidarity, loyalty, reciprocity obligations, and shared interests; and also of different kinds of practical, recreational, moral and work-related support, as provided by members of their milieu of acquaintances (Barbieri 1997: 350–51; Fischer 2001a: 142–3).

Boissevain (2001), for example, has considered the role of social brokers in some particular contexts such as Sicily and Ireland. A network of relations is available to the broker, who makes use of it to establish direct or indirect connections with people in order to draw moral credit therefrom. This moral credit, in turn, can be subsequently converted into profit, power or prestige. The brokering service is accordingly supplied without indicating what is requested in return, and when. However, the reciprocity obligation makes it certain that the moral credit thus obtained will be honored. Those who can rely on solidarity not only provided by acquaintances, but also by unknown persons, hold an enlarged social capital. These persons give support since they belong to the same community (ethnic, religious, national, etc.), or because they intend to conform their action to some abstract ideal principles (courtesy, aid to the neighbor, and so on) (Pizzorno 2001: 33–6; Portes 1998: 8–9). They become, consequently, sources of social capital.

If it is granted that those who consider themselves bound to do favors, and in general, to provide utility services to others, give social capital, as for the sources of social capital, many researchers have focused on ethnic communities. Immigrant communities, by making the most of the high density of their links, and hence, the possibility of personal links based on solidarity and mutual control, facilitate the attainment of trust and "solidarity social capital" (Pizzorno 2001: 38) to their members. These members, in turn, greatly promote the acquisition of financial and human capital, as well as entrepreneurial and job opportunities. In some cases, ethnic communities specialize in the production of particular goods or services, or are characterized by the mutual dependence of their business activities (Coleman 1988: S100, S102–S103; 1990: 303–304; 1994: 175–6; Granovetter 1993; Kiong and Kee 1998; Light and Karageorgis 1994). For immigrant communities, as well as for the native population, family and relatives networks represent another important source of social capital. This source of capital can change into economic and human (in terms of received education) capital. However, the support provided by their immigrant community is variable. For, depending on their class position, they offer their members unequal care and attention as well as different opportunities in terms of education, job contacts and practical support. As a consequence, members have opportunities and constraints that keep, in general, their original status in the class structure. This is so both in the course of generations, and in their own generation, among siblings (Ballarino and Bernardi 2000; Bankston and Zhou 2002; Bianco 2001; Degenne, Lebeaux and Lemel 2000: 6; Eve 2000; Sanders and Nee 1996; Wong and Salaff 1998).

The positive or negative effects of social capital on those who make use of it and on others have also considerably drawn scholars' attention. As these scholars have tried to explain, the benefits obtained through social capital – i.e. information, influence, support and recognition (Barbieri 2000: 6) – should not be mistaken for the network of acquaintances that define it (Bankston and Zhou 2002: 289; La Valle 2000: 7–8; Portes 1998: 5). Furthermore, some scholars have underlined that social capital can involve not only benefits, but also negative consequences (positive and negative capital respectively). However, the literature has not always precisely indicated which subjects receive benefits or disadvantages (Mutti 2000: 5). Concerning the negative consequences of social capital, the trust, which inheres to the creation of social capital, may be used to deceive those who have granted it.

Deception, moreover, can result more advantageous if it is perpetrated by a group of wrongdoers, in which each member trusts the others. In both cases, trust and social capital are used for anti-social purposes. Likewise, agreements between firms, while bringing them benefits, may damage competitors and the market. In general, the solidarity and trust that cement a group may be used to exclude others from acceding advantageous economic opportunities. Finally, the density of relatives' or ethnic ties, and the cogency of solidarity norms, may discourage innovative behaviors; hinder the entrepreneurial exploitation of economic opportunities; and keep individuals and collectivities in a state of social and economic inferiority (Coleman 1990: 320; Granovetter 1985: 491–3; Portes 1998: 15–18).

The literature on social capital has also focused on its benefits (for those who directly benefit from it and for others). The importance of benefits has been sometimes highlighted in contrast to the disadvantages which follow from the absence of social capital. Some authors have dwelt, for example, on the consequence for an entire population of the destruction of a pre-existing social organization, without constructing a new one (Sciortino 2000); or, for some individuals, on the causal relation between the lack of a dense network of ties and mental disturbance (Kadushin 1982). One of these benefits would consist in economic development, but in this regard, literature is not unanimous. There is, on the one hand, the thesis that the networks of family businesses have the advantage to easily conform to market contingencies, and to be in a position to avail themselves of the family social capital (Fukuyama 1995. See also Sanders and Nee 1996). Against this thesis, it has been objected, on the other hand, that this can apply to "open families, extended lineages, and family loyalty subject to generalized loyalty," and that "family particularism" may lead or not to economic development depending on the "political and institutional background in which it finds itself to act" (Mutti 1998: 24–5).

As previously mentioned, a further benefit consists in the educational and social support, which individuals receive not only from their relatives' group of origin, but also from acquaintances and friends. This support, stratified by social class, can involve better educational results and, over time, advantages in entering the job market, and subsequently in one's professional career. Research has shown, indeed, how "the available network capital varies depending on the professional position of each person" (Barbieri 2000: 20). In addition, the resources incorporated in the acquaintance network in general, as well as the social prestige of the person with which one has established a connection, prove significant (along with one's educational level) for the socioeconomic status, which has been thereby obtained (Barbieri 1997: 363–4). Less relevant proves, on the other hand, participation in the community life, though some scholars have maintained its importance. Putnam's thesis, that this kind of participation is declining (Putnam 1995), has aroused several objections.

In particular,: (a) the author does not explain which economic and political factors have produced this effect (Mutti 2001: 85–6); (b) the thesis of a decline of social capital is empirically poorly argued, and does not sufficiently consider opposite tendencies (Fischer 2001b; Lin 2001a: chapter 12); (c) even the concept of social capital, in the use made by Putnam, is inadequately defined and can be conveniently replaced by other concepts, such as individualism or retreat in a private world formed by family, relatives, work environment and friends (Fischer 2001b). As a source of social capital and the resulting advantages (achievement of status, alliances and support), the trust placed in other persons is not significant in itself, though it weighs on the quality of life. On the other hand, trust is important not only in the case of ethnic groups, but also within professional groups, and also when it is provided within subgroups, the members of which keep dense and supportive links. The reciprocity norm, on the other hand, regulates their relations that are external to the group (Frank and Yamamoto 1998; Lin 2000; Oliver 1997).

A social capital useful to begin well and continue one's job activity is in general available mainly to persons who have a privilege in terms of status, and/or a prestigious position even before they begin to work (Lin 1999: 471–6, 483; 2001a: 229–32). This applies also in countries ruled by socialist regimes (Voelker and Flap 1999). Concerning those who, instead, do not have such a status, literature has discussed for long time a thesis expounded by Mark Granovetter in the early 1970s. According to this author, weak ties (in terms of quantity of time, emotional intensity, intimacy, mutual services), rather than direct and strong ties, are useful to those who want to find a job or have a successful professional career. For persons of a lower status, the possibilities to improve their social and professional position are entrusted to the unlikely possibility to establish weak links with persons of higher status. Strong ties with persons of a lower status do not give, instead, any mobility opportunity; for the strong links that characterize these relations tend to exclude others, since they are too binding and they do not act as a "bridge" with higher level social cliques. Therefore, they do not allow the transfer of useful information.

Granovetter has considered strong ties between persons who are individually disadvantaged in the job market, but nonetheless able to close in their favor some segments of this market, thanks to their ties with relatives, or ethnic and friendly ties. In this case, strong ties prove advantageous (Granovetter 1998). In summary, strong ties motivate persons to lend support in a working environment, while weak ties convey better information. There is no way, Granovetter argues, to know in advance which factor weighs more, and how much one is able to balance the other (Granovetter 1995: 158; 1998: 273). We shall now briefly dwell on the importance of bridge-ties and social closure. The great deal of literature stimulated by Granovetter's thesis on the relevance of weak ties has yielded some conclusions that are hereafter summarized. The importance of weak ties has been underlined in both cases, while strong ties weigh firstly as sources of influence. It has been also proved that weak ties are essential to promote contacts, and hence the possibilities of mobility between persons of different socioeconomic status (in line with Granovetter's original thesis).

These possibilities are particularly conditioned by one's education level and socioeconomic status. According to an Italian research, weak ties have proved important for the career of privileged (in terms of education and social origin) persons. Strong ties, instead, are important in obtaining a first job: any first job for non-privileged individuals, a good quality job for privileged ones (Barbieri 1997b: 96–100; Lin 1999: 482–3). Furthermore, it has been observed that personal ties (whether weak or strong) provide those who seek and offer a job with better quality information, in terms of completeness and reliability, than other recruitment methods, provided that the number of information transfers is very small (two at most). This kind of information, in turn, proves important in order to protect both parties from the risk of having an unreliable, or for other reasons, unsatisfactory "partner." New personnel can be recruited through recommendations from persons already active in the organization as employees. This procedure seems to allow saving selection and training costs (since the new hire can rely on the person that has recommended him/her).

However, this recruitment method proves advantageous only in the case of recommendations from low-rank employees who are able to propose appropriate candidates. Usually, employers do not make use of recommendations in recruiting the managerial staff. They prefer to use them when employees' unions are present (so, it seems that unions put their stock of personal acquaintances at the company's disposal). From the management's point of view, especially in case of prominent roles, the employees who have, both individually and jointly considered, a diversified network of acquaintances, are particularly appreciated. The social capital is appreciated and remunerated exactly as the human capital (i.e. received education, but its importance can be better appraised considering that it is the result of an encounter of the characteristics of those who seek and those who offer a job. Those who are in possession of social capital and seek employment prefer to make use of informal research methods. In general, this research is carried out through informal methods if there is strong competition with other candidates. Those who offer a job, resort, for their part, to informal methods, since they consider them the most effective way to find the most appropriate persons for the company's requirements, and avoid the damage of a wrong choice (Erikson 2001; Fernandez and Castilla 2001; Flap and Boxman 2001; Follis 1998; Grieco 2001; Marsden 2001).

These studies, and a number of other studies, have examined in depth the relation between social capital and labor market. In addition, there have been some remarkable attempts to critically revise and substantially modify Granovetter's contribution. We shall concisely mention here Burt's and Lin's theories. As for the thesis that weak ties lend themselves better than strong ties to transfer useful information for obtaining the best jobs, Ronald Burt has remarked that the weakness or the strength of ties is of little importance. Redundant ties, which convey the same information, can be either weak or strong. Though the bridges that cross a structural hole in the network and link different "clusters" of actors, bringing them new (non-redundant) information, are formed in general by weak ties (in agreement with Granovetter's thesis), this does not necessarily occur. There is no, in fact, theoretical reason why the strength of ties is related to the information benefits (such as information volume and quality). What matters is the ability of ties to act as a "bridge" by linking actors' clusters divided by structural holes in the network. Without a "bridge" each cluster would be a network. According to Burt, ties can be relevant not only as information sources, but also as sources of control. The structural holes in the network ensure, indeed, benefits in terms of information and control. A social actor can take advantage of a conflict between "clusters" and obtain information from each of them, as well as exert control on both of them ("two dogs strive for a bone, and a third runs away with it," Burt reminds us, quoting Simmel (Burt 1992: 273).

"Redundant" ties link the same actors, and therefore, they do not transfer any further information benefit. In this sense, they are ineffective. Non-redundant ties occur instead between actors belonging to different "clusters" linked by bridges. Each "cluster" of actors is an information source. Non-redundant ties, which involve additional information benefits, assume the presence of structural holes in the network, that is to say, the network is not very dense. There are structural holes in the network when direct or indirect links between actors are few. Indirect links are those in which the actors are connected through the mediation of a common link, which makes the actors structurally equivalent in the network (as happens, for instance, in a competitive market). Each actor is equivalent to all the others from the point of view of the information benefit he/she brings to the network: in the case of indirect contacts, actors are, therefore, structurally equivalent and they all relate with the common link in the same way.

A structural hole in the network – i.e. an almost complete lack of direct or indirect links (through a common link) – occurs under one of the following conditions. First, there is a structural hole when there are no strong direct ties (in terms of frequency and emotional closeness, as between father and child, or between close friends). In this case, the network is characterized by the lack of primary links and cohesion. Secondly, there is a structural hole when there are no indirect ties, which are generally weak. The network, in this case, is characterized by the lack of indirect, or secondary links, and hence, by the absence of structurally equivalent ties. A family and a group of close friends (direct ties), a competitive market (indirect ties), are examples of networks with no empty areas (i.e. without "structural holes"), and therefore devoid of information benefits. The primary structural holes in the network divide direct links, while the secondary ones divide indirect links. Actors' opportunities to obtain information and control benefits, through which they can achieve the maximum social capital, depend not only on the quantity of time and energy invested to relate with other actors provided with resources. These opportunities in turn, also depend on the existence, within their wider network, of the following characteristics:

- Few primary structural holes in his "cluster" of social, job-related, economic and political links, since this circumstance makes the actor (a person, an employee, a company, a nation state) hardly replaceable with others.
- A number of secondary structural holes between the actor's "cluster" and the others, because this condition allows the actor to remain autonomous, and at the same time, to promote and exploit conflicts among the others. In this case, the actor has few constraints and many opportunities, which are the greater, the more the actor succeeds in extending his network and making the most of the secondary structural holes resulting from it.

Each actor has a specific distribution of constraints and opportunities, and hence a structural autonomy, depending on the position of primary and secondary structural holes in his/her network of links. In particular, the position of the structural holes in the network determines: different economic results in the markets;

entrepreneurs' and managers' structural autonomy in a particular market; their ability to obtain information and control benefits to their own or to their company's advantage and to the detriment of competitors. In general, the advantages achieved in this way must be compared with those achieved through the creation of monopolies or oligopolies. In that case, some participants in a network – for example, in a market – exploit the advantages incident to the existence of dense or hierarchical ties between them in order to close the opportunities to the others. Advantages in terms of mutual trust and transaction cost reduction result for the participants who have promoted the closure. These advantages have to be compared with the inconveniences resulting from the difficulty of exploiting direct links and the secondary structural holes in the network (Burt 1992, 2001).

Nan Lin conforms to a conception of social capital, according to which it consists of resources constituted by symbolic and material assets, incorporated in a social structure that provides constraints and opportunities. A plurality of actors, linked with one another, who hold a position in the structure, can avail themselves of social capital if they mobilize in order to keep these resources (expressive actions) or increase them (instrumental actions). This assumes that they have not only access to these resources, but also ability and desire to mobilize. The benefits of expressive and instrumental actions, which often mutually strengthen themselves, can be more easily achieved if the actors have similar available resources, such as authority, prestige or class (Homophily principle). Concerning expressive actions, the benefits – which can be achieved if the actors have strong and homophilic ties – reveal themselves as mental and physical health, and satisfaction regarding their life.

For instrumental actions, the benefits may be economic, political and social (reputation). Inequality is the consequence of whether collective resources (trust, norms) exist or not, and the result of the actors' different possibilities to accede the social capital and mobilize it. The original position of an actor in a link structure or network, as well as the use of weak ties, along with the network extent, influences the resources he/she has available. The resources actors can accede to thanks to their position in a link network, influence in turn the outcome of an instrumental action (in particular, an action aimed at obtaining social status). By reformulating Granovetter's and Burt's theses, Lin argues that in general, it is not a matter of whether weak ties are relevant, as only those that can be used for acceding the social capital are important. A weak tie that creates a bridge between clusters of actors who share a link network is important for this purpose (Lin 1982, 1999, 2001a, 2001b).

There is a considerable amount of literature focused on social capital. We already mentioned Granovetter's thesis, and the discussions aroused by it as regards the relevance of this form of capital in the labor market. We shall now briefly deal with social capital in organizations and collective movements. Concerning organizations (see in general Gabbay and Leenders 2001b), a first important current of study has investigated the way in which persons acting within an organization, make the most of their knowledge of social capital (inside the organization) and organizational structure. The aim consists in obtaining a job, advancement or other benefits. A second current of study focuses on the situations in which firm networks – which, for example conduct research and development projects together – grant single individuals advantages (as new job opportunities) or disadvantages (as new difficulties in carrying out one's job). Advantages and disadvantages may concern not only individuals, but also the firms that form the "nodes" of a network, the activities of which are decided by their respective management. In this case, advantages and disadvantages are expressed in terms of the power these firms exert over other firms, or their impossibility to exert power, according to the position they hold in the network. If firms compete with one another, then the possibilities of success in the competition can be studied within the so-called "ecological theory of organizations" (Baum 1996), rather than within social capital theory. This theory, or better, perspective can be referred to when one or more firms are advantaged compared to the others they are linked with. An advantage position may result – according to one of these explanatory models or to the other – from the central positioning and the multiple ties the financial capital, and especially the banking capital, has at its disposal. It can also result from the control of capital resources and technologies, from a limited number of managers working in big corporations and belonging to the capitalistic class, who are closely linked with each other and with the political elites (Scott 1985; Useem 1979).

A third current of study focuses instead, on how an organization can obtain either favorable or unfavorable consequences (as trust and isolation, respectively) from the presence of link networks between its members. It depends on the context whether or not a specific network (with peculiar characteristics of extent, density, strength of ties, etc.) brings advantages or disadvantages. A network that includes a structural hole can bring control benefits, as predicted by Burt, while a dense network can facilitate links based on trust, as pointed out by Coleman (Johanson 2001). For example, if the tasks of the organizational staff are new, and therefore exploratory, a network of ties between the staff showing structural holes, may bring an organization better results in terms of social capital than a network with weak ties. This configuration, instead, is preferable when tasks involve using already achieved knowledge (Hansen, Podolny and Pfeffer 2001). Furthermore, an organization is advantaged by the presence of work-related and hence instrumental ties between members rather than by emotional ties (because instrumental ties increase the amount of available information and the reciprocal diversity of the members, and consequently the heterogeneity of the organizational structure, and the social capital of the organization) (Harrington 2001).

Finally, some studies have focused on the consequences for an organization resulting from its belonging to an organizational network: if the network is dense, and if it is placed in the center of a larger network of firms, the organization can draw from it social capital and other advantages. For instance, a bank could obtain a reduction in moral risk, which is always inherent in credit granting, by nurturing with its clients informal and personal relations aimed at creating mutual trust, and thus acquire information with no additional costs. When an organizational network is connoted by stable links between its members, it can draw from them a leading position over the companies belonging to a larger network. Bigger and more important corporations are also those that are more closely linked, both economically and legally. These links, marked by the belonging of the same persons to the boards of directors of several companies, establish virtual channels to convey communications, and exert influence and power over the other companies. However, the characteristics of the organizational network (as, for instance, its centrality and composition) and the economic results of the firms are not in clear causal relation (Davis and Greve 1997; Ferrary 1999; Frank and Yamamoto 1998; Meeusen and Cuyvers 1985; Stokman and Wasseur 1985; Ziegler 1985).

In the literature concerning collective movements, there are frequent hints to the themes and theses of the network and social capital theory. Less frequent are, instead specific treatises. In one of them, which is of an introductory nature, it has been underlined that the density and multiplicity of ties (cooperation, exchange and identity) in a network of movements can be a presupposition, but also a result, of collective action. If ideological and political affinities flow into a dominant interpretative pattern, the links inside the network are promoted. As a result, it is easier to form alliances and mobilize sympathizers with a view to the achievement of common goals, which depend on the evaluation of the related political opportunities (in case they are considered favorable, goals are specific and imply potential cooperation, rather than being general and based on intransigent contrast) (Diani 1995). In the field of study of collective movements, the scholars who follow the structuralist approach have particularly directed their attention to the network theory.

Their position departs from Granovetter's thesis on the importance of weak ties in forming a collective action. Weak ties are important only if they are centralized. It is then possible to coordinate several individuals provided with sufficient interests and resources to form together one or more networks dense of links to the utmost, and formed by relatively few persons ("cliques"). On those foundations, these individuals establish an organization that, acting as a critical mass, mobilizes other persons and promotes collective action. If rationally performed, participants' selection should combine the purpose of reaching the highest number of persons with the purpose of reaching those who can better contribute to the movement, considering their resources and the interests that motivate them. Therefore, there is a critical threshold that determines the success of a movement, that is to say, a minimum number of persons and an average minimum of interests and resources (Marwell and Oliver 1993).[2]

---

2   The Actor Network Theory (ANT) is a relatively new interdisciplinary theoretical approach which deserves to be briefly mentioned here. This approach draws from network theory and a number of other sources as well, such as the sociology of science, engineering, semiotics and philosophy. According to ANT, actors can be both humans and non-humans, such as a text, a machine or an organization. The actors' identity is entirely defined by means of their interactions with other actors. ANT investigates the properties and consequences of associations between heterogeneous actors. Actors and networks are considered jointly, insofar as they concur in creating technological change within a sociotechnical world. ANT, in other words, sets out to explore how a given technology has been made available by associated and heterogeneous actors.

References

Alderson, A.S. and Beckfield, J. 2001. "Power and Prestige in the World City System." American Sociological Association Annual Meeting, Anaheim, California, August 18–21.

Aldrich, H. 1982. The Origins and Persistence of Social Networks, in P.V. Marsden and N. Lin (eds), *Social Structure and Network Analysis*. London: Sage, 281–93.

Bagnasco, A. 2001. Teoria del capitale sociale e political economy comparata, in A. Bagnasco, F. Piselli, A. Pizzorno, and C. Trigilia. *Il capitale sociale. Istruzioni per l'uso*. Bologna: Il Mulino, 77–103.

Ballarino, B. 2000. "Uso di dati time-budget per lo studio delle risorse familiari: capitale sociale e culturale dei genitori e disuguaglianza delle opportunità educative." Workshop on Social Capital, University of Trento, October 19–20.

Ballarino, G. and Bernardi, F. 2000. "Uso di dati time-budget per lo studio delle risorse familiari: capitale sociale e culturale dei genitori e disuguaglianza delle opportunità educative." Workshop on Social Capital, University of Trento, October 19–20.

Bankston, C.L. and Zhou, M. 2002. "Social Capital as Process: The Meanings and Problems of a Theoretical Metaphor." *Sociological Inquiry* 72: 285–317.

Barbieri, P. 1997a. "Il tesoro nascosto. La mappa del capitale sociale in un'area metropolitana." *Rassegna Italiana di Sociologia* 38: 343–70.

Barbieri, P. 1997b. "Non c'è rete senza nodi. Il ruolo del capitale sociale nel mercato del lavoro." *Stato e mercato* 49: 67–110.

Barbieri, P. 2000. "Capitale sociale e lavoro autonomo: un esperimento di network analysis e alcune considerazioni." Workshop on Social Capital, University of Trento, October 19–20.

Barnes, B. 2001. The Macro/Micro Problem and the Problem of Structure and Agency, in G. Ritzer and B. Smart (eds), *Handbook of Social Theory*. London: Sage, 339–52.

Berkowitz, S.D. 1988. Afterword: Toward A Formal Structural Sociology, in B. Wellman and S.D Berkowitz (eds), *Social Structures: A Network Approach*. Cambridge: Cambridge University Press, 477–97.

Bertolini, S. and Bravo, G. 2001. "Dimensioni del capitale sociale." *Quaderni di Sociologia* 45(25.1): 37–66.

Bianco, M.L. 2001. Il capitale sociale nello studio delle disuguaglianze: la forza dell'omogeneità occupazionale, in M.L. Bianco (ed.), *L'Italia delle disuguaglianze*. Rome: Carocci.

Blau, P.M. 1982. Structural Sociology and Network Analysis, in P.V. Marsden and N. Lin (eds), *Social Structure and Network Analysis*. London: Sage, 273–9.

Bourdieu, P. 1986. The Forms of Capital, in J.G. Richardson (ed.), *Handbook of Theory and Research for the Sociology of Education*. Westport, CN: Greenwood Press, 241–58.

Breiger, R.L. 1988. The Duality of Persons and Groups, in B. Wellman and S.D Berkowitz (eds), *Social Structures: A Network Approach*. Cambridge: Cambridge University Press, 83–98.

Burt, R.S. 1982. *Towards a Structural Theory of Action*. New York: Academic Press.

Burt, R.S. 1992. *Structural Holes: The Social Structure of Competition*. Cambridge, MA: Harvard University Press.

Burt, R.S. 2001. Structural Holes versus Network Closure as Social Capital, in N. Lin, K. Cook and R. Burt (eds), *Social Capital: Theory and Research*. New York: Aldine De Gruyter, 31–56.

Chiesi, A. 1999. *L'analisi dei reticoli*. Milan: FrancoAngeli.

Chiesi, A. 2000. "Operationalizing the Concept of Social Capital as a Means of Theoretical Clarification." Workshop on Social Capital, University of Trento, October 19–20.

Coleman, J.S. 1988. "Social Capital in the Creation of Human Capital." *American Journal of Sociology* 94: S95–S120.

Coleman, J.S. 1990. *Foundations of Social Theory*. Cambridge, MA: Harvard University Press.

Coleman, J.S. 1994. A Rational Choice Perspective on Economic Sociology, in N.J. Smelser and R. Swedberg (eds), *The Handbook of Economic Sociology*. Princeton, NJ: Princeton University Press, 166–80.

Collins, R. 1988. *Theoretical Sociology*. Orlando, FL: Harcourt Brace Jovanovich.

Cook, K.S. 1982. Network Structures from an Exchange Perspective, in P.V. Marsden and N. Lin (eds), *Social Structure and Network Analysis*. London: Sage, 177–99.

Cressman, D. 2009. *A Brief Overview of Actor-Network Theory: Puctualization, Heterogenous Engineering and Translation*. Burnaby, BC: CPROST, School of Communication, Simon Fraser University.

Davis, G.F. and Greve, H.R. 1997. "Corporate Elite Networks and Governance Changes in the 1980s." *American Journal of Sociology* 103: 1–37.

Degenne, A., Lebeaux, M.O. and Lemel, Y. 2000. *Social Capital in Everyday Life*. Institut National de la Statistique et des Études Économiques, Paris. Working Paper no. 9827.

Diani, M. 1995. "Le reti di movimento: una prospettiva di analisi." *Rassegna Italiana di Sociologia* 36: 341–72.

Emirbayer, M. and Goodwin, J. 1994. "Network Analysis, Culture, and the Problem of Agency." *American Journal of Sociology* 99: 1411–54.

Erickson, B.H. 1982. Networks, Ideologies, and Belief Systems, in P. Marsden and N. Lin (eds), *Social Structure and Network Analysis*. London: Sage, 159–218.

Erikson, B.H. 1988. The Relational Basis of Attitudes, in B. Wellman and S.D Berkowitz (eds), *Social Structures: A Network Approach*. Cambridge: Cambridge University Press, 99–121.

Erikson, B.H. 2001. Good Networks and Good Jobs: The Value of Social Capital to Employers and Employees, in N. Lin, K. Cook and R. Burt (eds), *Social Capital: Theory and Research*. New York: Aldine De Gruyter, 127–58.

Eve, M. 2000. "Integrating into a World of Work. Brothers and Others in Turin." Workshop on Social Capital, University of Trento, October 19–20.

Fernandez, R.M. and Castilla, E.J. 2001. How Much is That Network Worth?, in N. Lin, K. Cook and R. Burt (eds), *Social Capital: Theory and Research*. New York: Aldine De Gruyter, 85–104.

Ferrary, M. 1999. "Confiance et accumulation de capital social dans la régulation des activités de crédit." *Revue française de sociologie* 40: 559–86.

Fischer, C.S. 2001a. La struttura delle relazioni e delle reti, in F. Piselli (ed.), *Reti. L'analisi di network nelle scienze sociali*. Rome: Donzelli, 115–44.

Fischer, C.S. 2001b. "Bowling Alone: What's the Score?" 96th American Sociological Association Meeting, Anaheim, California, August 18–21.

Flap, H. and Boxman, E. 2001. Getting Started: The Influence of Social Capital on the Start of the Occupational Career, in N. Lin, K. Cook and R. Burt (eds), *Social Capital: Theory and Research*. New York: Aldine De Gruyter, 159–81.

Follis, M. 1998. Perché contano i contatti personali nel mercato del lavoro? I microfondamenti della funzione economica dei reticoli sociali e il problema dell'embeddedness, in M. Granovetter (ed.), *La forza dei legami deboli e altri saggi*. Naples: Liguori, 7–114.

Frank, K.A. and Yamamoto, J.Y. 1998. "Linking Action to Social Structure within a System: Social Capital within and between Subgroups." *American Journal of Sociology* 104: 642–86.

Fukuyama, F. 1995. *Trust*. New York: The Free Press.

Gabbay, S.M. and Leenders, R. Th. A.J. (eds). 2001a. *Social Capital of Organizations*. Amsterdam: Elsevier Science.

Gabbay, S.M. and Leenders, R. Th. A.J. 2001b. Social Capital of Organizations: From Social Structure to the Management of Corporate Social Capital, in S.M. Gabbay and R. Lenders (eds), *Social Capital of Organizations*. Amsterdam: Elsevier Science, 1–20.

Granovetter, M. 1985. "Economic Action and Social Structure: The Problem of Embeddedness." *American Journal of Sociology* 91: 481–510.

Granovetter, M. 1993. "Embeddedness and Immigration: Notes on the Social Determinants of Economic Action." *American Journal of Sociology* 99: 1320–50.

Granovetter, M. 1995. *Getting a Job*. Chicago, IL: The University of Chicago Press.

Granovetter, M. (ed.) 1998. *La forza dei legami deboli e altri saggi*. Naples: Liguori.

Gribaudi, M. 1996. "L'analisi di rete: tra struttura e configurazione." *Rassegna Italiana di Sociologia* 37: 31–55.

Grieco, M. 2001. Corby, catene migratorie e catene occupazionali, in F. Piselli (ed.), *L'analisi di network nelle scienze sociali*. Rome: Donzelli, 193–219.

Hansen, M.T., Podolny, J.M. and Pfeffer, J. 2001. So Many Ties, So Little Time: A task Contingency Perspective on Corporate Social Capital in Organizations, in Shaul M. Gabbay and Roger Th. A.J. Leenders (eds),

Social Capital of Organizations (Research in the Sociology of Organizations, Vol. 18). Bingley: Emerald Group Publishing Limited, 21–57.

Harrington, B. 2001. Organizational Performance and Corporate Social Capital: A Contingency Model, in S.M. Gabbay and Roger Th. A.J. Leenders (eds), *Social Capital of Organizations*. Amsterdam: Elsevier Science, 83–106.

Jörissen, B. and Könitz, C. (eds) 2010. *Seeking for Control*. Netzwerk- und Subjectbildung in Relationalenkonstruktivismus. Available at: http://www-e.uni- magdeburg.de/koenitz/Seeking percent20f.or percent20Control.pdf.

Kadushin, C. 1982. Social Density and Mental Health, in P.V. Marsden and N. Lin (eds), *Social Structure and Network Analysis*. London: Sage, 147–58.

Kiong, T.C. and Kee, Y.P. 1998. "Guanxi Bases, Xinyong and Chinese Business Networks." *British Journal of Sociology* 49: 75–96.

La Valle, D. 2000. "Il capitale sociale nella teoria dello scambio." Workshop on Social Capital, University of Trento, October 19–20.

Laumann, E.O. and Pappi, F.U. 2001. Reti di azione collettiva, in F. Piselli (ed.), *Reti. L'analisi di network nelle scienze sociali*. Rome: Donzelli, 255–77.

Lawler, E.J. and Yoon, J. 1998. "Network Structure and Emotion in Exchange Relations." *American Sociological Review* 63: 871–94.

Light, I. and Karageorgis, S. 1994. The Ethnic Economy, in N.J. Smelser and R. Swedberg (eds), *The Handbook of Economic Sociology*. Princeton, NJ: Princeton University Press, 646–71.

Lin, N. 1982. Social Resources and Instrumental Action, in P.V. Marsden and N. Lin (eds), *Social Structure and Network Analysis*. London: Sage, 131–45.

Lin, N. 1999. "Social Networks and Status Attainment." *Annual Review of Sociology* 25: 467–87.

Lin, N. 2000. "Social Capital: Social Networks, Civil Engagement, or Trust?" Workshop on Social Capital, University of Trento, October 19–20.

Lin, N. 2001a. *Social Capital: A Theory of Social Structure and Social Action*. Cambridge: Cambridge University Press.

Lin, N. 2001b. Building a Network Theory of Social Capital, in N. Lin, K. Cook and R. Burt (eds), *Social Capital: Theory and Research*. New York: Aldine De Gruyter, 3–29.

Lin, N., Cook, K. and Burt, R. (eds). 2001. *Social Capital: Theory and Research*. New York: Aldine De Gruyter.

Lomi, A., Corrado, R. and Sandri, S. 1997. La struttura sociale del controllo delle imprese: condivisione dei consiglieri e legami societari, in A. Lomi (ed.), *L'analisi relazionale delle imprese. Riflessioni teoriche ed esperienze empiriche*. Bologna: Il Mulino, 309–45.

McAdam, D. and Paulsen, R. 1993. "Specifying the Relationship between Social Ties and Activism." *American Journal of Sociology* 99: 640–67.

Marsden, P.V. 1988. Brokerage Behavior in Restricted Exchange Networks, in B. Wellman and S.D Berkowitz (eds), *Social Structures: A Network Approach*. Cambridge: Cambridge University Press, 201–18.

Marsden, P.V. 2001. Interpersonal Ties, Social Capital, and Employer Staffing Practices, in N. Lin, K. Cook and R. Burt (eds), *Social Capital: Theory and Research*. New York: Aldine De Gruyter, 105–25.

Marsden, P.V. and Friedkin, N.E. 1994. Network Studies of Social Influence, in S. Wasserman and J. Galaskiewicz (eds), *Advances in Social Network Analysis: Research in the Social and Behavioral sciences*. Thousand Oaks, CA: Sage, 3–25.

Marsden, P.V. and Lin, N. (eds) 1982. *Social Structure and Network Analysis*. London: Sage.

Marwell, G. and Oliver, P. 1993. *The Critical Mass in Collective Action*. Cambridge: Cambridge University Press.

Meeusen, W. and Cuyvers, L. 1985. The Interaction between Interlocking Directorship and the Economic Behavior of Companies, in F.N. Stokman, R. Ziegler and J. Scott (eds), *Networks of Corporate Power*. Cambridge: Polity Press, 45–72.

Meo, A. 1999. "Relazioni, reti e 'social support'." *Rassegna italiana di sociologia* 30:129–58.

Molm, L. 2001. Theories of Social Exchange and Exchange Networks, in G. Ritzer and B. Smart (eds), *Handbook of Social Theory*. London: Sage, 260–72.

Mutti, A. 1996. "Reti sociali: tra metafore e programmi teorici." *Rassegna Italiana di Sociologia* 37: 5–30.

Mutti, A. 1998. *Capitale sociale e sviluppo.* Bologna: Il Mulino.

Mutti, A. 2000. "Social Capital: The Ambiguities of a Debate." Workshop on Social Capital, University of Trento, October 19–20.

Padgett, J.F. and Ansell, C.K. 1993. "Robust Action and the Rise of the Medici, 1400–1434." *American Journal of Sociology* 98(6): 1259–1319.

Piselli, F. (ed.) 2001a. *Reti. L'analisi di network nelle scienze sociali.* Rome: Donzelli.

Piselli, F. (ed.) 2001b. Introduzione, in F. Piselli (ed.), *Reti. L'analisi di network nelle scienze sociali.* Rome: Donzelli, ix–lxxiv.

Pizzorno, A. 2001. Perché si paga il benzinaio. Per una teoria del capitale sociale, in A. Bagnasco, F. Piselli, A. Pizzorno, and C. Trigilia, *Il capitale sociale. Istruzioni per l'uso.* Bologna: Il Mulino, 19–45.

Podolny, J.M. 2001. "Networks as the Pipes and Prisms of the Market." *American Journal of Sociology* 107: 33–60.

Portes, A. 1998. "Social Capital: Its Origins and Applications in Modern Sociology." *Annual Review of Sociology* 24: 1–24.

Putnam, R.D. 1995. "Bowling Alone: America's Declining Social Capital." *Journal of Democracy* 6: 65–78.

Ritzer, G. and Smart, B. (eds) 2001. *Handbook of Social Theory.* London: Sage.

Salvini, A. 2007. *Analisi delle reti sociali. Teorie, metodi, applicazioni.* Milan: Franco Angeli.

Sanders, J.M. and Nee, V. 1996. "Immigrant Self-Employment: The Family as Social Capital and the Value of Human Capital." *American Sociological Review* 61: 231–49.

Sciortino, G. 2000. "How to Destroy Social Capital: Some Lessons from the Cambodian Experience." Workshop on Social Capital, University of Trento, October 19–20.

Scott, J. 1985. Theoretical Framework and Research Design, in F.N. Stokman, R. Ziegler and J. Scott (eds), *Networks of Corporate Power.* Cambridge: Polity Press, 1–19.

Scott, J. 1991. *L'analisi delle reti sociali.* Roma: La Nuova Italia Scientifica.

Smith, D.A. and White, D.R. 1992. "Structure and Dynamics of the Global Economy: Network Analysis of International Trade." *Social Forces* 70: 857–93.

Snyder, D., Snyder, D. and Kick, E.L. 1979. "Structural Position in the World System and Economic Growth, 1955–1970: A Multiple-Network Analysis of Transnational Interactions." *American Journal of Sociology* 84: 1096–1126.

Stokman, F.N. and Wasseur, F.W. 1985. National Networks in 1976: A Structural Comparison, in F.N. Stokman, R. Ziegler and J. Scott (eds), *Networks of Corporate Power.* Cambridge: Polity Press, 20–44.

Stokman, F.N., Ziegler, R. and Scott, J. (eds) 1985. *Networks of Corporate Power.* Cambridge: Polity Press.

Useem, M. 1979. "The Social Organization of the American Business Elite and Participation of Corporation Directors in the Governance of American Institutions." *American Sociological Review* 44: 553–72.

Valente, T.W. 1995. *Network Models of the Diffusion of Innovations.* Cresskill, NJ: Hampton Press.

Voelker, B. and Flap, H. 1999. "Getting Ahead in the GDR: Social Capital and Status Attainment under Communism." *Acta Sociologica* 42: 17–34.

Wasserman, S. and Faust, K. 1994. *Social Network Analysis: Methods and Applications.* Cambridge: Cambridge University Press.

Wellman, B. 1988. Structural Analysis: From Method and Metaphor to Theory and Substance, in B. Wellman and S.D Berkowitz (eds), *Social Structures: A Network Approach.* Cambridge: Cambridge University Press, 19–61.

Wellman, B. and Berkowitz, S.D. (eds) 1988a. *Social Structures: A Network Approach.* Cambridge: Cambridge University Press.

Wellman, B. and Berkowitz, S.D. (eds) 1988b. Introduction: Studying Social Structures, in B. Wellman and S.D Berkowitz (eds), *Social Structures: A Network Approach.* Cambridge: Cambridge University Press, 1–18.

Wellman, B., Carrington, P.J. and Hall, A. 1988. Networks as Personal Communities, in B. Wellman and S.D Berkowitz (eds), *Social Structures: A Network Approach.* Cambridge: Cambridge University Press, 130–84.

White, H.C. 1981. "Where Do Markets Come From?" *American Journal of Sociology* 87: 517–47.

White, H.C. 1998. Varieties of Markets, in B. Wellman and S.D Berkowitz (eds), *Social Structures: A Network Approach*. Cambridge: Cambridge University Press, 226–60.

White, H.C. (1992) 2008. *Identity and Control*. Princeton, NJ: Princeton University Press.

White, H.C., Boorman, S.A. and Breiger, R.L. 1976. "Social Structure from Multiple Networks: I. Blockmodels of Roles and Positions." *American Journal of Sociology* 81: 730–79.

Willer, D., Walker, H.A., Markowsky, B., Willer, R., Lovaglia, M., Thye, Sh, and Simpson, B. 2002. Network Exchange Theory, in J. Berger and M. Zelditch (eds), *New Directions in Contemporary Sociological Theory*. Lanham, MD: Rowman and Littlefield, 109–44.

Wong, S. and Salaff, J.W. 1998. "Network Capital: Emigration from Hong Kong." *British Journal of Sociology* 49: 358–74.

Ziegler, R. 1985. Conclusion, in F.N. Stokman, R. Ziegler and J. Scott (eds), *Networks of Corporate Power*. Cambridge: Polity Press, 45–72.

Chapter 12
Talcott Parsons (1902–1979)

Preliminary Remarks

Talcott Parsons, one of the most influential and well-known twentieth century sociologists, is the author of an enormous body of works, which roused disputes and diverging interpretations. After some discussion of the conceptual aspect of his thought, we shall follow the conventional division of his work into different periods (Alexander 1983b: 46–8, 73–7, 119–20; Hamilton 1989; see also Gerhardt 2002: 58). In support of the decision to adhere to this division, we refer to the differences emerging in epistemological assumptions, theoretical references, and the conceptual patterns in his thought, in particular, the concepts of action and voluntarism, as they are manifest in each period. The argumentation of the thesis of diversity, though adopted by several interpreters of Parsons, has been expounded by the supporters of this thesis in different ways and with argumentative references (see, for instance, Scott 1963 and Alexander's critical remarks in this connection, 1983: 34, and 334–5). Other commentators prefer, instead, to emphasize the continuity of Parsons's work. In their opinion, over the different decades covered by his production, there would have been a progressive theoretical improvement of a single constant conceptual nucleus (Muench 1982).

We limit ourselves to arguing that different themes prevailed depending on Parsons's production periods. A first period, in the 1930s, was characterized by an in-depth study of some European authors – as Durkheim, Pareto and Weber – Parsons greatly contributed to make known also in the United States through the publication of "The Structure of Social Action" (1937); several minor writings anticipate and accompany this major work (Camic 1991: lxv–lxviii). During a central period – until the early 1960s – the author developed some theoretical patterns availing himself of a complex conceptual apparatus he had created. Finally, in the last period, ranging from about the mid-1960s to his death (1979), Parsons focused above all on the theme of social change, for which he developed an explanatory evolutionary pattern.

The first introductory part is devoted to briefly presenting the conceptual apparatus used by the Parsons. We shall then dwell upon each one of these periods, which will be therefore separately considered. As we shall see in the second part of this work, Parsons produced several formulations of concepts and explanatory frameworks, which he often called theories. In this period Parsons also published several studies, which are focused on specific themes (for example, power and influence, social stratification and ethnic groups), and studies in which those concepts and patterns could be applied. These studies refer to research and inquiries carried out by others and are aimed at providing Parsons's theoretical statements with empirical references (Lidz 2000: 420). These inquiries are focused on several subjects: democracy, political power, medical profession and health sociology, education system in Germany and in the United States, family, youth culture, deviance and secularization. Finally, we shall provide some information about the very wide and varied reception of his work. A distinction will be made between contributions published during the author's life (which he could take into account and to which he could reply) (Parsons 1961a) and those published after his death; and between general introductions to his work and particular contributions or production periods.

Parsons's Conceptual Apparatus

This apparatus serves Parsons's purpose of formulating a conceptual framework by means of which to describe and explain the social action. We report hereafter the meanings, such as Parsons indicated them, of some concepts, the use of which – whether frequent or recurrent in the production of this author – will be explained when his works is presented. Their definitions have been directly drawn from Parsons's writings (Parsons 1934, 1949: 43–51, 74–7, 731–48; 1951: 4–5, 11–12, 19–22, 25–36, 48–9, 51–5, 58–67, 79–88, 133–6, 403–405, 480–96, 512–15, 537–41; 1961a, 1961b: 33–49; 1964a: 123–5; 1964b, 1966: 5–29; 1970,

1977, 1978, 2007; Parsons, Bales and Shils 1953: 4–10, 85–109, 163–90; Parsons and Shils 2001; Parsons and Smelser 1957: 101–103). Concerning some specific points, as well as interpretations and analyses of these texts, reference will be made also to other sources. However, we shall not consider in this chapter the shifts in meaning these concepts may have undergone over time or their use in different periods of time (Johnson 1975: 3–4, 26). Some indications of this sort will be provided in the next chapters. At present we wish to focus on the stable elements of his conceptual apparatus.

Theory is understood as a system of laws grounded on empirical generalizations. *Action* indicates a relation with an external object, which is justified and significant for an actor. An *actor* means both s a behavioral system and a personality system. In the second sense, an actor is a subject provided with knowledge he uses for consciously orienting his action in the roles he plays and in the communities of which he is a member. A theory of action aims at identifying, through an analytical abstraction process, the conceptual elements constituting an action. Unit acts, the acts forming the a unit of analysis, are analytical elements considered useful to shed light on the elementary components of each action and on the relations among actions within an "action scheme" or an "action system." The conceptual elements of a theory of action, being of an analytical nature, cannot be found in empirical reality. This pattern acts as a "frame of reference," in the sense that it provides the conceptual apparatus through which any empirically existing action system can be analyzed.

The formulation of a "general theory of action" requires a preliminary formulation of general propositions including interconnected and clearly defined concepts, though these concepts do not form a logical-deductive system. Though a knowledge that allows formulating a "general theory" – in the sense of a system of empirical generalizations – is lacking, it is possible, however, to formulate "paradigms," that is to say, criteria, standards, or "canons," through which one can understand the relations existing among the fundamental variables of a system. Analytically considered, an action is any behavior that can be examined in its constitutive elements, as follows: a behavior assumes there is an actor; it is oriented to a future condition anticipated by the actor; it takes place in a situation an actor does not fully control, which differs from the anticipated one; it involves being able to distinguish the characteristics of an object or of a category of objects (which may also be another individual) and to attribute importance to it; it is regulated by norms, and therefore the actor considers it desirable and compulsory; it requires a motivation or an effort by one or more actors. Parsons calls the attribution of importance and the attachment to an object, and particularly to another actor, "Cathexis," which is a term borrowed from psychoanalysis.

An "actor," whether an individual or a collectivity, can either orient himself to the purpose of obtaining from the outer world a maximum amount of benefits at a minimum cost, or instead can orient himself to a situation defined relevant, conforming to his own interests. An action is "instrumental" when the actor carries it out to obtain a future reward, which otherwise would not be obtained without his intervention. An action is instead "expressive" when it is oriented to the purpose of organizing the reward flow and preventing deprivations in relation to the desired object. A situation can be of a diversified nature, depending on the object to which it is oriented: it can be social (one or more actors are the object of the orientation), cultural (ideas, beliefs, rules, values), or physical. Orienting oneself to a situation implies that the actor has a motivation to address himself to a particular object though it involves an effort on the part of him, and that he does not make it only based on a cost and benefit evaluation, but because he is driven to act so by impulse and motivations ("need dispositions") steadily organized by means of cognitive and evaluative elements that allow the actor not to orient his action only to the present situation.

A "system" is a stable set of interdependent phenomena, provided with analytically established boundaries, which relates to an ever-changing external environment. A "social system" is a system of social interactions between reciprocally oriented actors, and consists of roles, collectivities, norms and values. The social system forms a system of societies, each characterized by relative autonomy, by its own territorial organization, and by its own sense of identity. In a social system, actors relate to one another by jointly orienting themselves to a situation through a language or other shared symbols. A social system comprises several subsystems or collectivities, which are functionally differentiated, interdependent and intertwined, as we shall now explain. Its analysis is focused on the conditions in which interactions form within particular collectivities.

A "cultural system" indicates instead an orderly pattern of meanings. It is socially produced and consists of relatively stable symbolic systems which are passed on through values, norms, beliefs and organized knowledge. A society is a particular collectivity formed by a set of organized relations resulting from interactions between individuals, and is self-sufficient in relation to its environment. Self-sufficiency, in this sense, means that (a) a society is not a subsystem of a more generalized system, and (b) interchanges with the environment are stable and subject to its control. In this way, it is possible to meet the necessary condition that allows a society, and a social system in general, to face problems coming from the external environment. System differentiation into functionally specialized parts is another necessary condition.

Finally, a "personality system" is the action system of a single actor. Being a system, the actor's actions are connected with each other, compatible and integrated. Their organization results from the existence of the actor's needs that have stabilized. They have thus become the actor's own attitudes or need dispositions to consistently act towards other objects, and particularly towards other human beings. The term "need dispositions" defines, in fact, needs that have become stable dispositions of the actor's personality. This term refers to the fact that values and roles, i.e. elements external to the actor, which are learned by him, can integrate, coordinate and change the fulfillment of his needs. Examples of need dispositions, according to Parsons, are not only one's need to be esteemed and obtain approval, responses and love, but also values and roles themselves. Roles, in fact, correspond to an individual's need to stabilize and socially integrate the merely individual needs of the personality system (see Baldwin 1961: 158–62; Joas and Knöbl 2009: 60–67; Prandini 1998: 11–12, 33–4 and note 8).

"Functions" are sets of conditions, within and outside the system, which set limits to the system variations compatible with its integrity and effectiveness. They concern relations based on mutual adaptation or integration among the elements of the social system, and in turn, social system adaptation to its environments. Functions therefore concern the social system's stability or instability, its survival and length in relation to the environments in which it is included. They point out the consequences of processes carried out by actors and communities in the social structure, and distinguish themselves into instrumental and expressive functions. Instrumental functions involve a systemic orientation to the attainment of some purposes, and therefore their prevalence in the system leads to consider them from an instrumental point of view. Expressive functions, instead, involve a systemic "cathectic" orientation, in virtue of which shared feelings of attachment and loyalty to a collectivity are institutionalized among the actors.

A social role is a stable interaction, ruled by norms, which establish the rights and the obligations of the members of a collectivity. Roles are the constitutive units of the social systems. Roles are functionally differentiated from one another. A functional analysis is focused both on social structures and on processes. "Social Structure" designates stable social interaction systems. The stability – or equilibrium – of the social systems depends on the reciprocal orientation and on the consistency of the interests of actors allocated in a system of differentiated roles. System stability does not necessarily involve its immobility, because a system subject to an orderly change is in equilibrium like a static system. A condition of "strain" may be the consequence of an actor's defective integration in an interaction system. Internal conflicts in the actor's personality can be the result of this strain, as well as frustrations in his expectations that other reciprocate his orientation, and even resentment and hostility towards others. A defective integration may, in turn, be the result of conflicts, and in general, of an ineffective integration among the roles forming the social system (Johnson 1975: 36–40). System stability can be empirically identified or assumed, under certain circumstances that from time to time are considered relevant to some particular investigations (Parsons 1951: 36, 490–92; see also Devereux 1961: 51–2, 59–60). "Process" indicates the elements of a system that are important from a theoretical point of view, which change in a time interval judged significant for such investigation.

A "collectivity" is a social system characterized by having both collective purposes shared by several actors who have a common orientation of institutionalized values, and also a single interaction system, the boundaries of which are set by the roles that constitute it. Norms can be either specific for each particular role or function, or can be shared by the participants in a social system, regardless of the peculiar roles they play. In the second case, norms are designated as values. Values indicate an orientation, considered desirable, of one or more actors to an object or a class of objects in a situation. Values, jointly considered, are a constitutive element of the social system. Values, in turn, form a system, and are necessary to make the social system become integrated. A social system is integrated when its constitutive roles, as the norms that govern role behaviors are consistent and coordinated. An "institution" defines in general the conditions of stability of a social system, which result from the need to meet its functional prerequisites. An institution, in other words, can be understood as a set of rules, norms and principles, which establish the performances and the sanctions that are functionally necessary to the system.

This involves regulating social relations and preserving, through laws or other social control mechanisms, the values and the general norms of the system, their consistency, and consequently the social system integration. Like other aspects of the social system, institutions differentiate and functionally specialize in relation to the particular functional requirements of the subsystems. Therefore we can distinguish among relational institutions, which define social status and roles, regulatory institutions, which regulate actors' pursuit of their own interests preventing it occurs in a non-functional way for the social system and, finally, cultural institutions, which concern actors' acceptance of norms and values. Values, norms, collectivity and roles form the structure of the social systems (Williams 1961: 74–6). A "societal community" is a segmented and functionally differentiated system. This system builds up a complex intertwining of communities, which is ruled, notwithstanding its internal differentiation, by shared systems of norms and values. A societal community is connoted by stable and widespread solidarity, and therefore meets the need for integration of a complex society.

If we distinguish among different action orientations – whether instrumental, expressive or moral – the term "pattern-variable" indicates an action orientation, in social systems or individual personalities, which is alternative to another orientation. The overall pattern-variable scheme has the theoretical purpose of analyzing the social, the cultural and the personality systems, and defines a set of dichotomous possibilities, called dilemmas or alternatives, in action orientations, and hence in the relations among social roles. Each alternative corresponds to a particular combination of different and opposed action orientations. According to Parsons, their classification, which intends to be exhaustive, is as follows:

a. the alternative between affectivity and affective neutrality indicates a dilemma between one's choosing a reward or being subject to discipline;
b. self-orientation or collectivity-orientation corresponds to the alternative between considering one's own interest or the collective interest;
c. the dilemma: universalism versus particularism is an alternative between one's conforming to norms of general value and making a "cathectic" attachment orientation towards particular objects (which may also be persons) prevail, and therefore the actor is not neutral towards them;
d. the choice between achievement and ascription, or "quality," shows there is a prevailing consideration of what an actor does or carries out (that is to say, his performances), or of some of his peculiar characteristics or stable attributes, such as age, height, social status, and so on;
e. the choice between an actor's specific instrumental or expressive interest, on the one hand, and an interest characterized by a plurality of indistinct orientations, on the other, corresponds to the alternative between specificity and diffusion (Black 1961: 283–6; Johnson 1975: 26–8; Rocher 1974: 36–40).

As Parsons argues, the first three alternatives point to dilemmas in individual actors' orientations. The fourth and fifth alternatives are instead defined by considering the set of relevant (from the actors' point of view) characteristics of the concerned social objects, which may be other actors with a plurality of orientations of their own. Therefore, reference is no longer made to a single actor, but to the whole set of reciprocal references of all relevant actors. Parsons emphasizes the usefulness of this classification through appropriate examples in studies in which the conceptual apparatus has been, at least partly, applied. The social, the cultural, and the personality systems can be analyzed from a functional point of view considering their internal differentiation, as well as their requisites for surviving and keeping oneself in a relatively stable condition of equilibrium; that is to say, for keeping regular relations within the system notwithstanding environmental changes (Williams 1961: 94–5).

All this implies systemic re-balancing processes if there is a condition of strain depending on a defective integration of the system, which cannot work and develop taking into account the opportunities and the constraints provided by the environment in which it is situated. The four "features" – or dimensions – of a system are, in a "cybernetic" order (using Parsons's words, as we shall explain in the next pages) from a maximum of energy and a minimum of information to the opposite tendency: adaptation, goal-attainment, integration and concealed pattern maintenance. These features are considered by the author "functional imperatives" of every system, that is to say, "problems" every system should be able to successfully cope with in order not to meet with dysfunctional consequences, such as internal strains and/or scarce adaptation to external environments. In Parsons's words, they form, all together, a "four-function paradigm" (Morse 1961: 113–41).

"Adaptation" means that the social system, and any system in general, conforms to requirements imposed by external environments, but at the same time actively transforms them by mobilizing resources so that they can be adapted to the system requirements. "Goal-attainment" designates the system orientation to specific goals that can be functional for it and not subordinated to others. Therefore these goals, in this sense, are "ultimate." "Integration" means that the elements of the social system are reciprocally compatible, and the system is able to keep an internal solidarity and boundaries (analytically intended and not actual borders) in relation to its external environments. "Latent pattern maintenance," or "latency," refers to the problem to preserve, for the social system, actors' motivations, as well as their knowledge, norms and values. All these elements are necessary to allow the system to preserve its own existence and integration (Devereux 1961: 56–9; Fox, Lidz and Bershady 2005: 7–9; Johnson 1974: 40–45; Lidz 2000: 403–404; Morse 1961: 113–27).

Parsons considers that the systemic problems of adaptation and goal-attainment are of an instrumental nature, that is to say, they require performing tasks that concern the system as a whole. On the contrary, the problems of integration and latent pattern maintenance require "expressive" system maintenance activities with the contribution of energies able to solve strains and reconstruct required abilities (Morse 1961: 114–16). Systemic integration in differentiated systems requires appropriate "generalized symbolic media of interchange" between the systems themselves. By generalized symbolic media of interchange," Parsons actually designates some instruments of a symbolic nature, such as money or influence, through which the systems that form a general action system are put in mutual relation according to institutionalized norms prescribing and regulating its use. The use of one or more media of this kind made by an actor does not diminish their availability to the other actors. These media are generalized, in the sense that interchange between systems can take place in a plurality of pre-established circumstances. In particular, concerning the social system, there are specific institutional environments which ensure the development of its integrative and regulatory functions (Prandini 1998: 61–2).

Insufficient systemic integration leads to strains and social changes. Social change takes an "evolutionary" character in differentiated societies. Societies consisting of subsystems distinguished from one another because of their peculiarities and functional importance are characterized in this way. Evolution is a process of social change in which the elements of the social and cultural systems are separated from one another, and therefore can be studied as independent units. "Evolutionary universals" are the evolutionary processes that can be found in several systems, which operate in different conditions. Therefore, evolutionary universals potentially have the greatest relevance in making systems – social systems, in particular – able to conform in the long run to the functional needs of their environments through adaptive upgrading processes.

Adaptation to external environments and subsystem integration assume the use of generalized interchange media, through which "cybernetic mechanisms" automatically adapt themselves to external environments. Thereby, there is a possibility of continuous communication flows and reciprocal equilibrium between, on the one hand, systems providing meanings and information, as for example the cultural system, and, on the other hand, systems providing them with energy. Non-social systems, such as living organisms, are an example of it. In a "cybernetic" control hierarchy (that is to say, of automatic reciprocal adaptation), the systems providing meanings and information, control those providing energy, but are conditioned by them in their ability to adapt themselves to the environments. "Human condition," conceived as a system, includes a structure of four interconnected elements.

In the first place, there is a natural environment, which provides lifeless resources. In the second place, there is a human organic system, which leads to a particular adaptation capacity to the environment. In the third place, there is a general action system provided with peculiar cognitive and symbolic abilities, which is addressed to environment knowledge and normative evaluation. The general system of action comprises four systems placed at a lower analytic level: the cultural system, the social system, the personality system and the organism. Finally, Parsons analytically identifies a system, called "telic system." Through the telic system, the social system and the human beings that form it with their interactions, receive fundamental meanings and value orientations (see, in this connection, among Parsons's interpreters, Hamilton 1989: 159–68; Johnson 1975: 40–45; Rocher 1974: 50–51, 70–73).

The First Period (1928–1937)

Parsons's first period is characterized by the attention placed by the author to economic sociology themes, as the German debate on the definition, the origin and the development of capitalism. Themes related to social science theory and epistemology, with particular reference to the concepts of ideal type, social action and institution, are also relevant here. These themes had previously been dealt with by several representatives of contemporary European social sciences, and Parsons committed himself to studying in depth their works during his extended stays in England and Germany. These studies laid the theoretical foundations of Parsons's entire production of that period, starting from his first essay (late 1920s), "Capitalism in Recent German Literature," which dates back to the late 1920s (Parsons 1928, 1929).

This essay, published by a political economy journal as an evidence of the author's economic education, intends to present, in a condensed form, Sombart's and Weber's thought. It consists of two parts. In the first part, focused on Sombart's production, and particularly on his most famous work, *Modern Capitalism*, Parsons outlines the main purpose of this work – introducing and defining this theoretical subject from both a conceptual and a sociological and historical point of view – and gives an evaluation of it. In this connection, Parsons remarks that Sombart's unit of analysis, capitalism, is arbitrarily formulated without regard for the historical changes it has undergone, and that the scientific quality of Sombart's production is affected by metaphysical determinism: capitalism is taken to be the result of the action of a spirit, whose evolution would follow a law of its own.

The second part of this work is instead focused on Weber, and considers both the epistemological and the historical-sociological works of this author, especially those concerning modern capitalism and the rationality that connotes it. Parsons argues that the Weberian ideal type includes two different concepts, a general one in which the concept of capitalism can be used as a widely applicable instrument for selecting and analyzing some specific historical events, and a concept that instead can be applied only to some particular historical objects, such a modern capitalism. Calling both concepts "ideal types" may give rise to confusion, according to Parsons, because it is not always clear whether Weber is referring to capitalism in general or to modern capitalism in particular. In the following years, Parsons did not exclusively linger on the theme of capitalism any more, but instead turned his attention to the theory and epistemology of the social sciences.

A first result was an essay including notions and introductory remarks to a theory of institutions bearing the title of "Prolegomena to a Theory of Social Institutions." This essay dates back to 1934, but remained unpublished for a long time (Parsons 1990). The author identifies two different ways to study an institution, a subjective and an objective one, depending on whether the point of view of the individual who relates to the institutions, or instead a sociologist's point of view are emphasized. In the first case, the subject pursues his aims while taking the available media into account, but his actions are restrained by the technological, economic and political context. Actions occur in a system of norms and values. As a consequence, the subjective way in which an institution is studied is primarily focused on the relation between an individual, on the one hand, and the social institutions and the leading norms and values of his society, on the other. The latter forms, for this aspect, a moral community that binds the individual, and yet remains external to him. In the second case, a sociologist's point of view is adopted. Accordingly, the fact is taken into account that individuals do not act separately but, rather, in relation with one another, and are bound by common norms in the form of laws and customs. Institutions are then understood as systems of interdependent regulatory norms. Their integration level depends on the degree to which single institutions harmoniously relate to one another. Determining the degree of integration is an empirical matter.

The first book of Parsons, *The Structure of Social Action*, dates back to 1937. This work required a long preparation. Parsons was able to mature it thanks to his stays in England and Germany, and deepen further during the first years in which he was teaching at Harvard (Camic 1991). He once again took up his interest in Weber and in the themes of capitalism and the social institutions. Moreover, for the first time, the author tries to reconstruct, based on some classical authors who belong to the economic and sociological thought, such as

Marshall, Pareto, Durkheim and Weber himself, some fundamental theses concerning social action. Parsons initially remarks that his work is meant to be empirical, as it makes constant reference to the works of these four authors. His analysis starts from the concept of action rationality: any action, in which the means used by the actor conform to the pursued ends with an empirically assessable probability, is rational, given certain conditions that are external to the actor, and consequently are not subject to his control, but can change such action. These conditions are relevant not only to the actor but also to others. In fact, the actor has to take them into account to pursue the ends of the action, and the others to understand its course.

External conditions can exert a merely random influence over action, because they result from factors, such as genetic heritage or environment, which cannot be controlled by the actor. In contrast to this, the influence on action resulting from norms is not random, and therefore represents a source of order for the actor. The positivist theory of action gives importance to external conditions, that is to say, to the objective elements the actor considers random and uncontrollable. This applies also to the utilitarian theory. According to this theory, the actor is driven in his action by what he considers to be his contingent interest. According to Utilitarianism and in the case of positivism as well, ends are random. An idealist theory gives instead importance to normative factors, which have a symbolic and subjective meaning for the actor.

Parsons's "voluntaristic" theory of action distinguishes itself from the the positivist and utilitarian theories of action because it assumes the existence of an independent actor who (1) acts in the absence of determining, external factors, such as genetic heritage or environment; (2) does nonetheless take them into account in pursuing his ends; (3) though driven by norms, he does not limit himself to express them through his action, because he interprets them from his own point of view. His action, considered in its basic elements (actor, media, ends, external conditions, normative orientation), builds the unit act. The actor can combine different actions together, and create complex action systems provided with separate or "emerging properties"; and this in contrast to elementary actions. The actors, the action they carry out, and the media the actors make use of do not concretely exist. Rather, they are abstract concepts formulated for analytical purposes. Action is restrained by objective external factors, such as they appear to the actor, and is guided by the normative order in what concerns the choice of the ends the actor subjectively makes. Ends are chosen willingly: in this sense, Parsons defines his theory of action as "voluntaristic."

He aims at showing how Marshall, Pareto, Durkheim and Weber have contributed to devising, though not deliberately, a voluntaristic theory of action, in the aforementioned sense. To evidence the theoretical convergence existing among these authors, he makes use of a conceptual pattern conforming to the principle of "analytical realism." According to this principle, concepts are used in this theoretical study for the purpose of formulating a theory of action. Therefore they do not correspond to real phenomena, for they do not literally and directly represent reality. Instead, they aim to produce a theoretical pattern to be generally applied, or a "generalized system of action," to be used to understand any really existing phenomenon. This theoretical pattern includes the following separate elements. In the first place, there are external conditions (heritage and environment), intended by the subject as means and pre-established conditions of action, and as a potential source of ignorance and error. In the second place, there is a set of interconnected means and ends. In the third place, there is a consistent set of ultimate values. Finally, there is a factor, which puts in relation the conditional and normative elements of action, consisting in the effort through which norms are turned into practices notwithstanding external conditioning factors.

Parsons recognizes the presence of all these conceptual and theoretical elements, or at least of a part of them, in the works of Marshall, Pareto, Durkheim and Weber, regardless of their terminological and theoretical differences. In his opinion, these differences are of a minor importance compared to the points they have in common. As a matter of fact, all these authors are committed neither to the positivist theory of action nor to the idealist theory. On the contrary, they contribute to produce – each in his own way – an analytical and theoretical pattern which goes beyond this distinction, selects significant elements from reality, and can be used to observe and describe facts that are relevant for empirical research which leads to an integrated and consistent body of knowledge and notions. Among these authors, Parsons dwells in particular upon Durkheim and Weber, whose convergence is, in his opinion, stronger than that of the other two authors, for they both seem to pay greater attention to the relevance of norms in providing an orientation to the action.

The properties emerging from the action systems (in the aforementioned sense) are located at three different abstraction levels, which are the object of study of Economics, Politics and Sociology. Sociology, in particular, has now an analytical and theoretical pattern at its disposal, through which it is possible to progress in the way to sociological knowledge. Weber's contribution in this connection concerns, first and foremost, his having formulated the analytical elements of the "voluntaristic" theory of action. These elements can be whether directly or indirectly inferred from the ideal type conceptual pattern. Weber, however, would not have been able to distinguish – as it would have been advisable, according to Parsons – between two different kinds of motivation understanding, the first one concerning the motivations of actors who act in the real world, the second concerning, instead, the motivations of abstract actors, whose action can be understood as a set of situated meanings not determined in a space-time sense. This second kind of motivations is particularly relevant to an analysis of social action.

The Second Period (1938–1963)

Though Parsons's "empirical" production of this period, which is focused on democracy and related problems in Germany during the years of the Republic of Weimar (1920s and early 1930s), and in the United States during the early 1950s, is quite interesting, we prefer to overlook it, however, and to dwell instead upon his theoretical production. Proceeding in his purpose to formulate a unitary theory of social action (that is to say, a theory that does not conceive action as an effect of heritage and environment), Parsons attempts to explore the theoretical implications of the concepts of action and social norm. An enrichment of the conceptual apparatus is part of this systematically pursued attempt. This is done through a revision of the concepts of norm and institution, and through the formulation of new concepts – function, personality, internalization and social system. These are further developed in his subsequent works. This period is also characterized by the study of the social structure and the social system, an area which had been neglected in the previous period (Hamilton 1989: 110).

The transition between these two periods is marked by a work entitled *Actor, Situation and Normative Pattern*. In this study, which dates back to 1939 but was published only in the 1980s, Parsons continued to focus, as he had previously done, on the concepts of actor, situation and cultural model. However, he began to address himself to the attainment of a purpose he had never previously pursued, namely, the formulation of a structural-functional theory of the social system (Parsons 1986; see also Wenzel 1986). This essay deals first with some themes he had already tackled in *The Structure of Social Action*. These themes include a distinction between the conceptual apparatuses of biology and theory of action, a theoretical frame in which actor and situation are placed in mutual relation, and a typology of the actor's modes of orientation. These are distinguished into cognitive, teleological (that is to say, purposive) and affective orientation. The the cognitive and the teleological modes of orientation refer to objects – such as notions, purposes, norms – and are external to the actor, while the affective orientation is specifically subjective, and consists of two components: on the one hand, positive and negative stimuli; on the other, moral evaluation. A situation resulting from interactive processes among the actors forms the object of their orientations. These orientations may be of a cognitive, teleological, affective (or "cathectic," the term being used here for the first time), and social nature, when several actors participate in a situation.

In the last case, the actor's action can be a condition, a medium or an instrument of exchange, coercion or influence for the other actors, and vice versa. A merely instrumental orientation toward others is countered in general by moral considerations. They make reference to abstract normative patterns, even though moral judgments are usually related to actions and qualities of real persons. These normative models meet the integration requirements of the social system which cannot tolerate an uncontrolled manifestation of individual interests, affections and impulses. Social integration involves an actor knowing clearly and precisely which are the existing normative criteria, and his taking them into account in his actions. Amongst other factors, social system stability depends on the integration of individual personalities. This involves, in turn, a sufficient degree of coordination among actor's different orientation modes, as well as among the different action trends resulting from them. A common normative pattern can meet these requirements as they are expressed by the social system. Individuals' integration in the social system takes place as follows: through the order provided by social stratification, or through an authority that legitimizes positions within the social system, or finally, through the definition of social roles that are able to stabilize individual actions.

The personality system is divided into action subsystems, which have to functionally conform to the specific context of individual acts, and consequently to the actor's situation, to the goals he sets, to the normative and expressive standards guiding his behavior, and to the whole action system. The social system functionally differentiates into roles, though only some of them are necessary to its continuity (not, for example, system differentiation into roles connected to the actors' age). Role performance involves for social actors a division of work, to which corresponds a functional differentiation and specialization within the social system. The differentiation of the social system is distinguished from the functional differentiation of individual activities and roles. To provide a functionally appropriate solution to the problem of order and integration, the social system must divide into institutions, formal organizations and systems of juridical norm. Institutions stabilize and sanction expectations based on norms. Formal organizations place actors in relation with groups with which they interact; they make them depend on an authority, and act in accordance with normative patterns. Juridical norms form a systematic body of laws that constrain the action of groups. This conceptual pattern can be used to provide an explanation of, and a systematic reflection on, actual empirical problems.

The Social System and Toward a General Theory of Action

These two important works, which were both published in 1951, will be jointly considered here. The latter develops some themes dealt with by the former, such as action categories, system, role, personality, value orientations, institution, but does not however introduce any new theme. In these works, Parsons sets some theoretical objectives for himself. In the first place, he aims to develop a conceptual pattern, in order to identify and describe the constitutive elements of the social system. It is intended as a set of actions which are organized through roles and carried out by a plurality of individuals. Roles are interdependent. They maintain their continuous reciprocal orientation and, consequently, their internal pattern. This pattern is put into a changeable relation with the environment because the environment itself is changeable. The second objective consists in analyzing the mechanisms that provide the social actors with the motivations for acting according to the social roles and the norms that govern their behaviors. Finally, these works pursue the aim to study processes of change which are internal to the social system. The author dwells in particular on the first two objectives (social system and actors' motivation), while the theme of change itself is dealt with in the final chapters of these works.

The social system strictly relates to the cultural system (intended as an organized system of norms, values and symbols). There is indeed a dominant system of values, which integrates single individuals into the social system, though this system is subject to modification as a result of the compromises imposed on individuals by contingent situations. Hence, individuals' integration into the social system and their interiorization of the dominant system of values are never lacking (otherwise, the social system would not exist), but always imperfect. In addition, the social system is also strictly related to the personality system (intended as an organized system of need dispositions), since there is a correspondence (albeit also imperfect) between the categories of the social system, such as one's age, one's belonging to a sexual gender or to an ethnic group, and the ways in which the actor classifies him or herself. The social system distinguishes itself from the cultural and the personality systems by the fact that it is formed by roles, which are performed by individuals or communities concerned with this task.

Roles are institutionalized in part: this means that those who act in the system form a collectivity have internalized common values and are subject to obligations and prohibitions. To perform any social role, actors must be in possession of "facilities," whether of a material or symbolic nature, to be used to perform such roles. These facilities can be granted to them either through a decision made by an authority, or through institutionalized rules, or through a competitive process awarding such facilities to the winner. Furthermore, roles can provide a solution to problems concerning an actor's interaction with others, and are of a different nature depending on the kind of interaction involved. Problems may be instrumental, expressive and integrative. Actors impose their particular orientation on the system. This orientation can be either cognitive (when the aspects of a situation that are significant for the actor are defined), or "cathectic" (when it concerns the relevance an actor attributes to the objects he addresses himself to), or evaluative (when an actor selects the aspects he or she considers relevant).

The actors orient themselves towards a future condition of a situation they symbolically anticipates. They may wish to control the situation by acting instrumentally to some end, or by meeting a need dispositions or conforming to a normative orientation. This orientation is put at his disposal by the cultural system. The motivation to act, which results from the personality system, relates through particular mechanisms to the normative and the social systems. An action system is perfectly integrated if the systems that constitute it – namely, the social, the cultural and the personality systems – create an orderly set of interdependent parts, and this set of parts remains separate from its environment. The equilibrium resulting from it can be either static or dynamic. The constitutive elements of the social system, which is intended as a network of interactive relations, are the social act, the statuses held and the roles performed within the social act, and the actor himself, who is a social reference unit for statuses and roles. Each social system should meet some functional prerequisites, or "imperatives," in order to remain an orderly set of elements, and this irrespective of either system stability or change.

These prerequisites include biological imperatives (the satisfaction of which allows for the maintenance and continuation of individual life), psychological-social imperatives (the conditions through which it is possible to achieve a minimum personality stability), and systemic prerequisites (which are the conditions through which a sufficient number of actors are properly motivated to participate in the social system and to refrain from socially destructive deviant behaviors). The order of a system, and consequently its stability, depends on the degree to which actors' motivations are consistent (or "integrated") with the normative standards and the value orientations that prevail in the system. Shared norms and values provide the prerequisite, based on which a group of actors becomes integrated, that is to say, forms a collectivity. Norms and values orient the actors within the institutions they establish, shaping roles and related behavior expectations. The actors orient themselves to the objects that belong to a social system, and in particular, to other actors, in a cognitive, "cathectic" or evaluative way, and provide their actions with an instrumental or expressive orientation. The choice among these modes of orientation is made according to priorities established by the cultural system. If the actors act within the institutions they create, they must internalize their orientation to values. Socially acquired needs which have become actors' need dispositions can be thus determined in a social system. This system, in turn, establishes the values and defines the norms that constitute a particular institution. Cultural institutions, therefore, are always part of a social system, along with other institutions which define actors' reciprocal role expectations, and set the limits within which pursuing private interests is legitimate.

Parsons maintains that for each generalization level there is in the instrumental, expressive or moral orientations of each actor to social roles a limited and established number of alternatives which are institutionally provided for. The social structure changes depending on the alternatives – called "pattern variables" –which the actors show that they prefer in their orientations to roles performed within a social system. This preference results from customary choices, which express culture as the actors have internalized it; and it conforms to the definitions and prescriptions of the social roles and to the value standards. There are, first of all, two pairs of alternatives, which concern expressive and moral orientations. An actor may want to obtain satisfactions or rewards straightaway or instead renounce them in favor of instrumental interests or moral instances (affectivity or affective neutrality). Moreover, the actor can pursue his or her own private interests, or those he or she shares with the other members of their collectivity (orientation to themself or to the collectivity). The choice of one option or another is particularly important for analyzing how much space is left to individuals to pursue their own private interests, and how wide is instead the field of their obligations toward the collectivity. The alternative between universalism and particularism involves choosing which kind of value is enforced in role expectations. A universalistic orientation – in contrast to a particularistic one – leads the actor to disregard his relation with particular actors or other social subjects, not to discriminate therefore in their favor or to their detriment but instead to always orient him or herself to them in the same way.

In particular, the dilemmas of affectivity versus affective neutrality, orientation to oneself versus orientation to the collectivity, universalism versus particularism, make reference to choices actors have to make, and consequently, to their value orientations. Achievement versus ascription (or quality) and specificity versus diffuseness disregard instead the point of view of a particular actor, and make rather reference to objectively existing alternatives in the social system the actor relates to. With achievement versus ascription, reference is made to particular qualities, or attributes, of the object the actor orients himself to, which can be permanently attributed to that social object (ascription or quality). Examples of it are social status, age and degree of kinship. The reference can also concern performances to be attributed to others with whom the actor has established a relation based on roles reciprocity. In that case, all what the actor has done becomes relevant, be it in the area of achievement or performance. With the other pair, specificity versus diffuseness, the alternative is between a specific interest, of an instrumental or expressive nature (for example, in a professional relation), or a general interest, because it is not clearly defined by obligations concerning precise social roles. For example, affective or erotic relations, in which performance reciprocity is not and cannot be calculated, are common.

Pattern variables can systematically relate to one another, if they are considered within the more general context of the theory of action. Lingering first over instrumental orientation, the actor relates to others in a different way, depending on the roles performed from time to time. If the action orientation is expressive, then the actor must turn to others – whether single persons or collectivities – on the right occasions, he must show an appropriate attachment to them and be receptive towards them, and finally, he must correspond to their attitudes in an appropriate manner, considering the terms of the relation. An expressive orientation may not match an instrumental or moral orientation. Likewise, these two orientations may not match one another. Furthermore, a combination of heterogeneous orientations may lead to unstable results. It is however possible to provide some examples of a classification of different kinds of fusion or separation in the elements that form the instrumental and expressive orientation. For example, the fusion of several specific expressive orientation interests can lead to a widespread attachment towards a particular social object (such as a beloved person), and consequently to the pure role type of romantic love, or instead to an abstract cultural object, such as universal love in a religious sense. Specific performances of an instrumental nature are instead separated both from expressive orientation, and also from other instrumental orientation elements.

Actors' motivations and cultural elements, such as norms and values, arrange social relations according to roles. An actor orients himself to a social object, and particularly to another actor, either because the social object belongs to a class of objects considered significant (classification standard) or because it is significant in itself for the actor (relational standard). The alternative between achievement and ascription is relevant for classifying actors among the statuses and roles that form the social system, and to differentiate them within their environment. Systemic solidarity is shown by the actors' common value orientation, and consequently by the prevalence of one of their orientations to the collectivity, provided that system solidarity itself is considered a value. The predominant orientations in a collectivity – universalism versus particularism, achievement versus ascription, and so on – combine together and provide the social system with certain points of reference. Pattern variables are therefore used to analyze the structural elements of the social system.

In particular, the dilemmas affectivity versus affective neutrality, and specificity versus diffuseness, are relevant to providing an orientation to action in the personality system. The dilemmas of universalism versus particularism, and ascription versus achievement are instead relevant as regards the predominant value orientation in the cultural system. Finally, the dilemma orientation to oneself versus orientation to the collectivity is, so to say, internal to the social system, in the sense that it can be useful to its integration. These five dilemmas, jointly considered, have the value orientation of the social system as an object. Their analytical distinction can be also used to classify social structure kinds. Actually existing social structures result, in fact, from combining value orientations with the other elements of the social system. The social system differentiates itself both in terms of roles, and in terms of distribution of statuses and roles in a social structure. Each social system is provided with mechanisms for distributing among the actors all what they need to achieve their purposes, but the actors have limited opportunities due to their limited resources. The presence of material and symbolic rewards can promote relations based on loyalty between an actor and other actors when these rewards are institutionalized.

Institutionalization limits, through norms that are enforced by a legitimate authority, the pursuit of private interests, and consequently, the orientation to oneself; while it promotes the orientation to interests or purposes that concern the collectivity. Institutions are a source of structural differentiation in the social system. Through a classification of the existing institutions it is possible to connect the different parts of the social system and comparatively analyze different social structures. It is possible to formulate a general classification pattern which includes only some clusterings of the pattern variables that can be empirically checked. Parsons dwells upon four kinds of clustering: kinship systems, stratification structures, power system and institutionalized religion. Societies are subject to functional requirements. Therefore, there is a restricted number of empirically existing social structures. These requirements are, on the one hand, the conditions that ensure stability and duration to a social system ("universal imperatives"). On the other hand, there are also compatibility imperatives, which limit the simultaneous presence of different structural elements in the same society. These elements – an example of which is provided by kinship systems and occupational role systems – result from stable patterns of action orientations and from the situation to which they are oriented.

In addition to the social structure, other structures contribute to the institutionalization of the prevailing pattern of values in a society. Ascriptive standards are relevant in this sense, for they allow for the organizion of kinship units into wider structures, such as communities, ethnic groups and social classes. Achievement standards are instead relevant when an actor's universalistic orientation to the collectivity becomes established. Whereas the variable "orientation to oneself or to the collectivity "is important for social integration – which is found only when the second alternative prevails – the other variables become relevant because they designate particular kinds of social structure. The modern kind of social structure that is termed "industrial" – the only one compatible with capitalistic development – is connoted by a universalistic (rather than particularistic), specific (rather than widespread), affective (rather than neutral), and achievement-oriented (rather than ascription-oriented) system of roles. For each of these aspects, this kind of structure is different than others, for instance, than China's "imperial bureaucratic" social structure during the Mandarin age.

Once the complementary role expectations have been established, they can be maintained without any particular mechanism, except for the intervention of two tendencies: in the first place, an actor may not correctly or sufficiently learn the contents of role behaviors, or may not be motivated to put them into effect. Consequently, the actor's socialization process is ineffective. Secondly, an actor may depart from norms prescribing appropriate behaviors, and thereby produce problems and in some cases activate learning and social control mechanisms. The latter keep the system balanced and their defective functioning can generate tensions in the social and the personality systems. The process of internalizing social norm does not only work through rewards and punishments. Accordingly, the interaction with the socialization agent, its imitation, the identification with it, and consequently, the interrnalization of its values the actor permanently orients him or herself to, become relevant.

What we learn through socialization is to become oriented toward values. This value orientation contributes to the formation of the basic structure of the personality, and to a great extent, is also a function of the fundamental structure of roles and of the prevailing system of values. The structure and the functioning process of personality and of the social system cannot be identical, due to the differences existing among individuals, the different outcomes of the secularization process, as well as the existence of possible alternative ways to perform social roles. A deviant orientation is revealed by an actor's motivated tendency, resulting from his socially acquired need dispositions, to infringe one or more normative patterns and thus disturb the equilibrium of the interactive processes. Some compromises arepossible, however, and even quite probable, such as those occurring when the subject has ambivalent reactions toward the ruling systems of norms and values. Deviant tendencies are not such in and of themselves, but are rather to be understood in relation to particular role expectations, which are mutually complementary, and to the situations the actor can encounter.

The kind of deviance that most endangers the social system relates to persons whose relations are incompatible with the systemic and impersonal values of efficiency and performance. As a consequence, there are strains depending on individual difficulties to conform to normative expectations and to correctly interpret them. Strains also follow from institutional difficulties to sanction infringements, and to exert an effective social control in situations in which uncertainty prevails. Conflict of roles generates inner conflicts, which are exasperated in the case of institutional roles. Tramps' social marginalization or sick persons' status are, respectively, deviant and non-deviant individual solutions to the tensions resulting from them. The creation of criminal gangs is instead a collective deviant solution to a socially produced condition of strain. The search for scapegoats, which reveals itself particularly in anti-Semitism, diverges from the previous form of deviance by a claim to legitimacy some actors make for their aggressive actions. This legitimacy claim is accepted by the collectivity to which they belong. The genesis and the consequences of deviance can be therefore studied using the already known conceptual apparatus which is employed in the analysis of social systems. Processes of social control are put into effect in order to prevent and counter deviant tendencies and the conditions that produce them in individuals and collectivities, to put an end to structural strains, and to rebalance interactive processes.

We can then state that:

a. The functional problems of conformity and deviance are inherent in the social systems, given the aforementioned characteristics of the cultural systems.
b. Deviance and social control processes begin with the first socialization process and continue throughout the life of the subject.
c. Any inconsistency between the structure of individual need dispositions and the role system gives rise to systemic strains, which promote a tendency to deviance.
d. This tendency is strengthened by the existing gaps in the social control system, but is countered by some individual psychological mechanisms.
e. When tendencies to deviance resulting from the social structure are not controlled by social control mechanisms, they become one of the major causes of social change.

To summarize, two theoretical problems have been dealt with in *The Social System* so far. First, the development of a conceptual pattern aimed at identifying and describing the major elements that constitute the social system by showing their interrelations. Secondly, an analysis of the motivational processes which originate in the personalities of the individual actors and in the contingent situations in which they act, but have the effect of preserving or changing the social system. The theme of social change is dealt with in the last part of *The Social System* and in *Toward a General Theory of Action*, keeping the concept of system as a key reference. Its discussion, according to Parsons, assumes the one he had previously made. The processes of change within the system, or of the system itself, are relevant here. The social system consists of interactive and reciprocally oriented processes. The equilibrium of the system assumes that the actors have acquired, through the socialization process, the necessary orientations for perfuming their roles, and that social control mechanisms have been activated to balance motivations to deviant behaviors. The theory of systems is intended to analyze the conditions in which a system changes or keeps its stability. The reference to the orientation to values and to their acquisition through the socialization process has allowed formulating the mechanisms by which change is produced. However, though Parsons's position in this connection changed in the following years, he did not formulate in these books a theory of action through which social change could be explained.

The existence of strains resulting from the actors' imperfect integration of need dispositions in the cultural system involves re-balancing processes not only for the actors, but also for the social system. Indeed, actors must interiorize and organize new value patterns, and the system must provide mechanisms able to face the actors' strains. The source of change, as regards the social system, comes from the cultural system, and more precisely, from changes occurring in the subsystems of beliefs, expressive symbols and values. In the final part of his work, Parsons recalls that he has availed himself of the concept of system as a principle to organize and guide his research. The theoretical treatment of this theme has required dwelling upon the institutionalization of the cultural patterns, and particularly upon those referring to the orientation to values, and the interiorized processes through which the actors acquire the motivations to act in the roles that form the social system. The theory of action includes – as the author underlines – theories concerning personality, culture, the social system and the relations among these systems. Sociological theory distinguishes itself from economic theory, from social psychology and from the other social sciences because it considers a variety of organization levels for the rational action, and also because of the specificity of its theoretical-conceptual apparatus.

Other Theoretical Works Belonging to this Period

In this second period, after 1951 (the year in which *The Social System* and *Toward a General Theory of Action* were published), Parsons wrote additional works. Some of them have a general theoretical content, such as *Working Papers in the Theory of Action* (written with Bales and Shils) and *An Outline of the Social System*.

Other works, such as *The Marshall Lectures* and *Economy and Society*, deal with economic sociology themes from a theoretical point of view. In all these works, Parsons introduced some new elements, compared to those published in 1951. He formulated a conceptual pattern, the so-called "AGIL scheme," and introduced the category of generalized media of exchange. Though the pattern-variable frame was not abandoned (see Parsons 1953: 66–7; Parsons, Bales and Shils 1953: 179–90), Parsons judged it appropriate to dwell upon the "AGIL scheme." The connection between the pattern-variable frame and the "AGIL scheme" is mentioned in a contribution (published in 1960, but reprinted some years later) (Parsons 1969a). It was written by Parsons in response to Robert Dubin, who had maintained that the two conceptual patterns differed in content (Dubin 1960).

As Parsons argues in this writing, both schemes can be used to classify action elements and therefore they pursue the same theoretical purpose. However, the pattern-variable frame is considered insufficient, as in fact, it limits itself to defining an action system, and therefore it only analyzes how the actor orients himself in relation to a situation, and how the objects he considers significant (if they are, for instance, characterized by specificity, affectivity, universalism, etc.) present themselves, so that the combination of these objects defines the way in which the actor acts. The pattern variables frame cannot classify kinds of actors and objects. In fact, it does not consider that both the actor and the relevant objects are placed in a stable system of institutionalized norms, characterized by a set of rules and procedures that can be analytically identified and form all together the environment of the action system. The four functional subsystems indicated by the acronym AGIL, which form the system of institutionalized norms, can instead provide this classification of actors and relevant objects, and point, through its use, to the conditions of internal stability of the system and the ways in which the system relates to the environment. Each element of the alternatives mentioned in the pattern-variable frame (for example, specificity versus diffuseness) is included in a single subsystem. This explains how the pattern-variable frame is analytically included in the AGIL pattern; and also how the presence and combinations of these variables in the AGIL system are not random at all, since they incorporate the normative order of this system.

In this second period, Parsons wrote several essays of a theoretical nature. Among these essays, the best known is the monograph *Economy and Society*, written with Neil J. Smelser (Parsons and Smelser 1957). We shall first mention the general theoretical works of the second period (those published after 1951), jointly considered. We shall then dwell upon *Economy and Society*, along with some other works dealing with economic sociology. The continuity of all these works with other works belonging to the same period, and particularly *The Social System*, is both thematic and theoretical, as the theory of action, the personality, the cultural and the social systems, the conceptual relations among these systems, and the equilibrium and change of the social system, continue to remain the main object of the author's interest. This continuity is also partly conceptual. In fact, the themes tackled by the author and the constitutive elements of the social structure – roles, collectivity, values, norms – are indicated and defined in a similar way, while the constitutive elements of personality, retaining the well-known classification made by Freud (Ego, Superego, Id), are now examined more in depth.

Due to their importance throughout the second period of Parsons's production, these constitutive elements are now briefly recalled. Action is intended as a process which takes place within a social system formed by interdependent units, or establishes its boundaries. In other words, the system refers to a set of reciprocally oriented, ordered (not at random) and interdependent interactions among individuals, and to the conditions that make them possible. In addition, the social system has analytically identifiable boundaries with other systems, such as the personality and the cultural ones. A complex social system comprises several subsystems, or segments, each of which is functionally differentiated and connoted by its own norms. Finally, a society is a collectivity and a community which is not included in wider collectivities and communities: it forms a "moral community" responsible for a plurality of functions. Parsons identifies four different essential functions, or "functional imperatives." Each functional imperative corresponds to a particular subsystem of the social system.

Through the "pattern maintenance function," the values and the individual commitment required for conforming to the normative patterns are preserved. Through the "goal-attainment function," the system is able to meet its needs, such as preserving its integrity notwithstanding the changes occurring in the environment. Through the "adaptation function," which aims at obtaining the physical, cultural and economic facilities required by the system itself, the system obtains and distributes inside its structure what is necessary to achieve its goals. Finally, through the "integrative function," the system keeps itself as a unit, notwithstanding its differentiation, by performing the integrative function, namely, by integrating with one another the functional contributions provided by the subsystems. These functional imperatives concern the system, and not single individuals. Therefore, the problem of interactions among individuals requires using different explanatory categories. The AGIL pattern allows conceptually defining even minor changes in a given dimension of action, for example an action provided with a symbolic meaning – rather than a manifest behavior – in pursuing a goal. Moreover, the pattern allows making a distinction among expressive, cognitive and evaluative actions, and may be applied at different levels of generality.

The need for the system to have generalized media of interchange available results from the differentiation of the social structures, which make use of these media as mechanisms of integration. Circulating and interchange media, at a social system level, consist of:

1. Money (as an instrument situated in the economic subsystem, which allows market functioning and development by creating resources/facilities to be mobilized for performing economic functions.
2. Political power (as an instrument situated in the political subsystem, which allows mobilizing and using the resources created in this way).
3. Prestige, or influence (as an instrument situated in the integrative system, which makes it possible to elicit a generalized commitment to enforce solidarity values).
4. Pattern preservation (as an instrument, situated in the L subsystem – pattern maintenance – and assigned to the function of preserving the social system through commitment to enforce norms and values. Norms are binding obligations, while values are conception of what is desirable.

At an action system level, which is more general compared to the social system level, circulation and exchange media consist of:

1. Intelligence (as an instrument situated in the A organism system, through which resources for the solution of cognitive problems can be mobilized.
2. Performance ability (as an instrument situated in the G personality system, aimed at pursuing systemic goals making use of the cognitive, affective and moral means which the subjects have at their disposal.
3. Affection (as an instrument situated in the I system, which is aimed at integrating the action system by permanently binding individuals to other individuals and to the collectivities they belong to, thereby allowing the social system establishing a moral order).
4. Definition of the situation (as an instrument situated in the L system. Its function is to establish the interchanges and the boundaries of the AGIL systems, which in turn form the larger action system). There is a hierarchy of generalities, and consequently, of use possibilities in the control mechanisms included in the social system. Money is placed at the highest generality level (it has therefore the greatest possibilities to circulate within this system), followed by power – especially political power – influence and, finally, commitment to the enforcement of cultural values. The institutions, which are necessary to carry out money transactions, are property rights, job organization and contract.

Power is therefore an element providing legitimation to authority, social solidarity, and integration. Like money, political power can be invested, in the sense of taking legitimate decisions, which have long-term consequences for the power holder and for others. The use of political power is not (borrowing the game theory language that Parsons here employs) "a zero-sum game." The benefit for some persons does not necessarily involve a corresponding disadvantage for others. Power legitimating makes the use of coercion a merely exceptional measure. In the same way, only in exceptional circumstances – that is to say, when there is no longer trust in the credit system – investors ask the banks to have their deposits back. Likewise, money investments involve generalized trust they can be used as symbolic circulation and interchange media, since the gold reserve of a state is not sufficient to guarantee that money performs this function. Therefore, there are considerable analogies between money and power as regards their functions. Influence should not be mistaken for power and wealth. These are all generalized circulation media, but influence – differently from power and wealth – assumes an intention to exert an effect on others' attitudes and opinions through persuasion.

Processes, which maintain a systemic equilibrium in social systems, control by means of a variety of positive and negative sanctions deviant tendencies, whether individual or collective. In contrast with these processes, structural change involves breaking the boundaries of the social system or those of the subsystems. A system moves from a condition, or phase, to another over time. Each phase is defined by a particular combination of alternatives, as indicated by the pattern variables. The transition from a phase to the next one is, to a great extent, regulated and controlled by institutionalized social norms, which show each member how to behave and what sanctions (rewards and punishments) he should expect. Norms are system properties and not individual actors' properties. Their primary function is to keep the systemic phases in harmony with one another and with the system as a whole. These phases – four in all – are defined by the functional activities that take place in each of them and by the kind of orientation and attitude toward the objects (whether things or persons). According to Parsons, systems reveal a general tendency to move from an adaptive phase A, or from an integrative one I, to a phase G, in which the system orients itself to the pursuit of its goals, and to a phase L, in which motivations and personal commitment are preserved or used in the systemic action. The phases G and L designate different directions, which are independent of one another but interdependent, and in which the motivational energy flows in the system.

The Marshall Lectures and Economy and Society

Two other works dealing with the integration of economic and sociological theory belong to this period as well. In the first work – the so-called *Marshall Lectures* published in 1953 – Parsons formulates the analytical categories and outlines a treatment of economy as a social system which includes the non-economic aspects of economy. The second work, written with Neil J. Smelser and entitled *Economy and Society*, dates back to 1956 and deals in particular with the institutional structure and change in the economy. We shall briefly summarize both works here. They are marked by a conceptual and theoretical continuity line with *The Social System* and *Working Papers in the Theory of Action*. The *Marshall Lectures* include some lectures held by Parsons in 1953 at Cambridge before an economists' audience. Parsons, who had received a university education in economics, through this cycle of lectures intended to analyze economy as a particular subsystem of the social system, indicated by the letter A.

Its specific function is making the scarce resources obtained from the outer environment available to the system, in order to provide the other system units and each consumer with the goods and services they need ("adaptive function"). The flow of goods and services supplied by the subsystem to the other subsystems, and to the social system as a whole, occurs in exchange for money. This flow is ruled by:

1. Institutionalized mutual expectations, in particular as regulated through property and contractual rights.
2. The economic values prevailing in the economic system (especially, those relating to production efficiency and property values).
3. Finally, the individual and organizational motivations to correctly and carefully perform their economic roles. Non-economic factors, such as family and work ties, may prevent the usual market re-balancing mechanisms, such as demand and offer, prices and competition, from being effective.

Therefore, economic and sociological theory may find it convenient to the advancement of their sciences to formulate a common conceptual and theoretical scheme. These themes are resumed and further developed first in *Economy and Society*, but even more so in the following works (see in particular, Parsons 1978: 435–40).

Bearing in mind the functional division into four parts designated by the acronym AGIL, the author aims at formulating a widely applicable conceptual scheme, or "paradigm" (Bourricaud 1981: 133–4). This paradigm can point to the constitutive elements, or subsystems, of the general action system, and to the relations among these elements. In *Economy and Society*, Parsons seeks to relate the economic theory to the sociological theory which is identified with the theory of social systems. Economy is considered a subsystem of the social system, functionally separate from other subsystems, and (functionally) differentiated into the sectors, or subsystems, a, g, i, l. Each of the four subsystems belonging to the component A (the economic subsystem) has in fact institutionally regulated contiguity, interchange and integration relations with the four subsystems that form any other component of the social system (G, I, L). For example, the goal-attainment function of the economic system relates to the similar function of the subsystem L (pattern maintenance function), because money exchanges are used not only to obtain goods and services, but also as a symbolic means to achieving prestige (for an in-depth examination of the AGIL pattern in *Economy and Society*, see Holton 1986a: 49–90).

The Third Period (1964–1979)

In the third and last period of his production, the end of which coincided with the end of his life, Parsons continued to keep to the conception of action system. He also continued to use the concept of social system, the AGIL scheme, and the generalized interchange media classification, which belong to the second period. However, for the first time, he began to study in depth the problem of social change, to introduce in this connection the key concepts of evolution, differentiation and adaptive upgrading. In the meantime, he began in the meantime to deal also with the theme of the relations among the three aforementioned systems (the social, the cultural. and the personality systems) and the specific biological processes of the living systems, as well as those related to the physical environment (Parsons 1964b; 1966, 1971; 1977: 279–320). The last part of this period is characterized by the formulation of a complex conceptual quadripartition. Here, the AGIL scheme is taken up once again, but radically revised by considering also other systems in addition to the previously addressed action systems (the social, the cultural, and the personality systems). This new quadripartite pattern conceptually frames the human condition as a "telic" system. That is to say, it is oriented to meeting human beings' search for an ultimate meaning through one which they can provide a foundation and give an order to their own empirical and cognitive world. In a "cybernetic" information and control order, the telic system is assigned the highest rank, because it gives significance and orientation to human action (Parsons 1978: 352–433; 2007: 428–9). We shall first examine the theme of evolutionary change, and then that of the human condition.

Evolution concerns the change of a system, for example the social system, when it is produced by the environments the system relates to. Differentiation indicates a process through which a functionally and structurally well-established unit of a system, or a subsystem, splits up into two or more units. These are distinct by function and structure from each other and from the previous unit. It is then possible to distinguish among different stages, or steps, in the process of evolutionary change of a system. Thi is done through differentiation and adaptive upgrading in relation to the environments, in which the system is placed. Concerning the social and the cultural systems in particular, each stage distinguishes itself from the previous ones by a decisive change in the normative structures. On these grounds, Parsons thinks it is possible to identify a primitive, an intermediate and a modern stage. The transition from the primitive stage to the intermediate one is characterized by the introduction of written language. In fact, this innovation, has allowed for an immense spread, over time and space, of a symbolic culture, which is autonomous in relation to specific social contexts, and has stabilized many social relations. In addition, it has allowed for critical analisis of written documents andmade possible the introduction of innovations in the form of new documents and new interpretations. The cultural systems of the societies of Ancient Greece and Israel have formed the "seedbed societies" for subsequent cultural innovations in several other societies, and have therefore had decisive importance for the evolutionary process. The transition from the intermediate stage to the modern one has, by contrast, been marked by the establishment of a codified normative system, and consequently, of a legal system. Generally speaking, progress in the evolutionary process has depended on a greater social differentiation. In fact, this differentiation process has made it possible for the cultural factors, which are placed on the top of the control and information cybernetic hierarchy, to be freed from the constraints of physical and organic factors, the latter being placed at the bottom of this hierarchy but on the top of a hierarchy of conditioning factors.

From the process of differentiation there results an integration problem, that is to say, one of functional coordination among these units. Adaptive upgrading is the process through which a system – in particular, a social system – receives from the outside, or from its internal components, facilities that make it independent of previous restrictions. These allow it to better conform to its (physical, organic, cultural) environments without being subject to too many strains. Therefore, the system can be better integrated, and consequently, it can better attain its goals and perform its primary functions. These external facilities can be of a different nature. The cultural system, and especially the Catholic and Protestant religions and the Roman law, have yielded new differentiation and legitimation opportunities have historically for the social system, and consequently, new inclusion and integration opportunities. This is the result of a process of value generalization. From the changes that have occurred in a democratic sense in the political system, and from the separation between state and Church, new opportunities of inclusion have resulted in a system of citizenship. The processes of functional and structural differentiation and adaptive upgrading produce a social system that is more complex than the previous one as they include a greater number of goals and functions in their constitutive units.

If differentiation and adaptive upgrading processes evidence themselves, there may be strains between the social, the cultural and the personality systems. To allow for system integration, these strains make a general system of values functionally necessary. This system of values must be able to legitimate this greater variety of goals and functions, and making the formation of a moral community possible. Evolutionary change is also defined by an inclusion process, one which sets itself against differentiation, in the sense that peripheral elements or elements placed outside the system, become included in it and integrated with the other constitutive elements. Inclusion, which can follow or precede a differentiation process, can contribute to the creation of a moral social community. This happens, for example, when different religious groups take an ecumenical cast, and thereby dampen their differences.

A societal community – a complex network of collectivities intertwining with defined loyalties – is the outcome of a successfully completed process of differentiation and evolution, and is connoted by members' widespread and long-lasting solidarity. In a cybernetic control hierarchy, a societal community is placed at the highest level. In fact, it is particularly rich in information that can be transferred to all its members, thanks to communication opportunities among them that cannot be found in lower cultural and social development stages. A written language is also available at less advanced stages, but the the bonds of solidarity that link the members of a societal community, and transcend social and cultural differentiation, can be found only at this stage of evolutionary development. A generalized and institutionalized system of values provides normative order and legitimation to society as a whole, even when it is differentiated into a variety of constitutive elements. Alternative non-ascriptive socialization and loyalty sources in relation to the kinship system, which is ascriptive, as well as legitimation and integration sources in relation to religion, are necessary to processes of differentiation and evolutionary change.

The human condition can be conceptualized in different terms, as compared to the AGIL pattern of the social, cultural and personality systems. The reference to the human condition involves, in fact, the inclusion of new categories, even if they are functionally organized in the quadripartite AGIL scheme. These categories are considered in a growing "cybernetic" order of information and control, and in a decreasing order of "energy" and conditioning factors as follows:

a. The "physical-chemical" system is placed at the sub-organic level. Though being external to the human condition, and thus does not possess symbolic information, it is, however, an ultimate source of "energy," for it provides the necessary facilities for the survival of all living systems.

b. The human "organic system," which is external to the human condition, too, is oriented to goals functional to the organism, considering the conditions of the physical-chemical system and the functional interdependence relations with the action system. The "telic" system establishes the significance of organic life for the human condition.

c. The "action system" is placed within the human condition. It is continuously subject to conditions of interchange with the other systems, and for any human being, it performs an integrative function by integrating human organism and personality. Considered in a time perspective, the "action system" involves "instrumental" processes. It is through these that facilities which are to be used in the future are formed; it also involves "consummatory" processes, through which such facilities are used and destroyed.

d. The "telic" system, which is intrinsic to the human condition, is oriented toward searching for the ultimate meanings of the world and is rich in information about the problems of suffering and evil. It is a "latent" system, and consequently, one which does not directly reveal itself through actions, but goes beyond them and confers on them an "ultimate" meaning (Holton 2001: 156–7; an introduction is included in Bourricaud 1981: 189–231).

Reception of Parsons's Work

Parsons has attracted far more critical attention than most other contemporary sociologists. The literature concerning his work is very extensive, but several introductions to this secondary literature are noteworthy (see Alexander 1983a: 128–35; 1987: 280–85; Bortolini 1998; Holton 1986b, 2001: 159–61; Holmwood 2006a; Lidz 2000: 423–8; Rocher 1974: 152–67; Sciulli and Gerstein 1985; Turner 1986b). Some works, in particular, have attracted specific attention, and we wish briefly to mention the secondary literature that explicitly addresses them. We refer in particular to (1) "Prolegomena to a Theory of Social Institutions," published in 1990, but written in 1934; (2) *The Structure of Social Action*, first published in 1937; (3) *The Social System*, published in 1951; (4) Parsons's economic sociology, with reference not only to the so-called *Marshall Lectures*, but also to *Economy and Society* and to the related exegetic literature; (5) Parsons's production of the 1960s, in which the evolutionary theory of social change was formulated; and (6) his theoretical and applied sociology production of the 1970s, namely, *The Human Condition, The American University*, and *American Society*. However, we do not strictly follow this order in presenting the secondary literature when it jointly deals with different works by Parsons.

Camic's interpretative thesis is noteworthy. According to Camic, Parsons's choice of considering only a few authors in his first work would have based on his intention to protect his own scientific reputation in a university environment. Such an environment was hostile to the school of institutionalist economics, and supportive of an abstract and theoretical approach to the social sciences. This thesis has been disputed by other commentators, who have remarked that the reasons why Parsons did not approach the institutionalist mainstream are not those which Camic has indicated. They may be rather traced to Weber's influence on Parsons, especially insofar as Weber's methodological program was concerned. We then consider the different objections formulated against Parsons's thesis, i.e., that the theories of Weber and Durkheim converge toward a unitary theory of social action. This thesis, according to its critics, would prove groundless, for these authors start from mutually incompatible epistemological assumptions. They also have different conceptual apparatuses, and explain behavioral regularities differently. Parsons replies that their conceptions objectively include a voluntaristic aspect and that a shared conceptual apparatus can be abstracted out of their works. Some commentators have also disputed Parsons's thesis that social order depends on shared norms, that these norms provide goals and rules for behavior, and that they are observed as morally binding obligations. Parsons may have placed too great a value on social integration, and may have overestimated the importance of norms and the extent to which they are internalized, while attributing too limited importance to factors of conflict. The term "social order," and other terms such as equilibrium and integration, have been used, as Parsons observes, only for analytical purposes and do not involve any defense of the existing order.

Parsons's conceptual patterns have stimulated a great deal of debate. Some favorable evaluations have noted that it has introduced greater analytical clearness, and provided for better interpretative and definitional capacity where social events are concerned. They have also observed that it has made possible a unitary and articulated explanation of them, and opened up new opportunities to conduct social research. Negative evaluations maintain that these conceptual patterns are, on the contrary, overly rigid, and so limit their theoretical relevance, and therefore the questions sociological theory is able to address and the answers which is able to provide. In addition, there is the claim that the Parsonian concept of functional equilibrium is inadequately defined, and in general that his conceptual apparatus cannot be used to defend the thesis that the social order has normative grounds. The theoretical relation between the voluntaristic and the normative conceptions of action has been debated as well. Several commentators have argued that Parsons does not make sufficiently clear whether or not these two conceptions are compatible, and whether or not he himself retained the voluntaristic conception of action also in the mid and later periods of his production.

The concept of "societal community," which is particularly relevant in Parsons's latest works, is, according to some interpreters, is not properly defined. The social integration of particular individuals or groups implies the exclusion of others, unless the interpenetration of differentiated and interconnected subsystems with generalized exchange media reconciles the functional need to retain the identities of the constitutive elements as well as to ensure the development of subsystems, and, in general, of the action system. Similarly, numerous commentators have remarked that Parsons's contribution to a theory of social change as an effect of structural differentiation and systemic evolution would be unsatisfactory. No explanation is forthcoming – it has been remarked – in the absence of details about how, by whom, why change has occurred. Change, moreover, can take place in a traumatic way, and the concept of adaptation is too vague to be useful for explanatory purposes and lends itself to ideological use. An analogy between the development of individual personalities and sociocultural development, and between cultural and social change, is hardly tenable. In the social sciences a distinction among different levels of evolution has no empirical foundations. It is possible to shed light on the causes of of historical and social change and to provide other relevant information to describe and explain it, but this can be done only through the empirical analysis of real cases. Finally, the human condition is a metaphysical construction that cannot find legitimate use in the social sciences.

References

Adriaansens, H.P.M. 1979. "The Conceptual Dilemma: Towards a Better Understanding of the Development in Parsonian Action Theory." *British Journal of Sociology* 30: 5–24.

Alexander, J.C. 1978. "Formal and Substantial Rationality in the Work of Talcott Parsons." *American Sociological Review* (43): 177–98.

Alexander, J.C. 1983a. *The Classical Attempt at Theoretical Synthesis: Max Weber*. London: Routledge and Kegan Paul.

Alexander, J.C. 1983b. *The Modern Reconstruction of Classical Thought: Talcott Parsons*. Berkeley, CA: University of California Press.

Alexander, J.C. 1987. *Twenty Lectures: Sociological Theory since World War II*. New York: Columbia University Press.

Alexander, J.C. 1988. *Action and Its Environments*. New York: Columbia University Press.

Alexander. J.C. 1990. "Commentary: Structure, Value, Action." *American Sociological Review* 55: 339–45.

Alexander, J.C. 1992. Durkheim's Problem and Differentiation Theory Today, in H. Haferkamp and N.J. Smelser (eds), *Social Change and Modernity*. Berkeley, CA: University of California Press, 179–204.

Alexander, J.C. 1995. *Fin de Siècle Social Theory*. London: Verso.

Alexander, J.C. 1998. *Neofunctionalism and After*. Oxford: Blackwell.

Alexander, J.C. 2005. Contradictions in the Societal Community: The Promise and Disappointment of Parsons's Concept, in R.C. Fox, V.M. Lidz and H.J. Bershady (eds), *After Parsons*. New York: Russell Sage Foundation, 93–110.

Alexander, J.C. and Colomy, P. 1998. Neofunctionalism Today: Reconstructing a Theoretical Tradition, in J.C. Alexander (ed.), *Neofunctionalism and After*. Oxford: Blackwell, 53–91.

Alexander, J.C. and Sciortino, G. 1998. On Choosing One's Intellectual Predecessors: The Reductionism of Camic's Treatment of Parsons and the Institutionalists, in J.C. Alexander (ed.), *Neofunctionalism and After*. Oxford: Blackwell, 117–46.

Almondo, P. 1998. Le professioni o della razionalizzazione: la tesi parsonsiana, in R. Grandini (ed.), *Talcott Parsons*. Milan: Bruno Mondadori, 152–81.

Archer, M.S. 1985. "The Myth of Cultural Integration." *The British Journal of Sociology* 36: 333–53.

Archer, M.S. 2005. Structure, Culture and Agency, in M.D. Jacobs and Weiss N. Hanrahan (eds), *The Blackwell Companion to the Sociology of Culture*. Oxford: Blackwell, 17–34.

Baert, P. 1998. *Social Theory in the Twentieth Century*. Cambridge: Polity Press. Italian translation: *La teoria sociale contemporanea*, 2002, Bologna: Il Mulino.

Bailey, K. 1984. "Beyond Functionalism: Towards a Nonequilibrium Analysis of Complex Social Systems." *The British Journal of Sociology* 35: 1–15.

Baldwin, A.L. 1961. The Parsonian Theory of Personality, in M. Black (ed.), *The Social Theories of Talcott Parsons*. Englewood Cliffs, NJ: Prentice Hall, 153–90.

Bellah, R.N. 2005. God, Nation, and Self in America: Some Tensions between Parsons, and Bellah, in R.C. Fox, V.M. Lidz and H.J. Bershady (eds), *After Parsons*. New York: Russell Sage Foundation, 237–47.

Black, A. 1961. Some Questions about Parsons' Theories, in A. Black (ed.), *The Social Theories of Talcott Parsons*. Englewood Cliffs, NJ: Prentice Hall, 268–88.

Bershady, H.J. 2005. Affect in Social Life, in R.C. Fox, V.M. Lidz and H.J. Bershady (eds), *After Parsons*. New York: Russell Sage Foundation, 83–90.

Bortolini, M. (ed.) 1998. Elenco dei testi citati e Bibliografia ragionata della letteratura secondaria su Talcott Parsons, in R. Prandini (ed.), *Talcott Parsons*. Milan: Bruno Mondatori, 288–325.

Bourdieu, P. and Wacquant, L.J.D. (eds) 1992. *An Invitation to Reflexive Sociology*. Chicago, IL: The University of Chicago Press.

Bourricaud, F. 1981.*The Sociology of Talcott Parsons*. Chicago, IL: The University of Chicago Press.

Bronfenbrenner, U. 1961. Parsons' Theory of Identification, in M. Black (ed.), *The Social Theories of Talcott Parsons*. Englewood Cliffs, NJ: Prentice Hall, 191–213.

Buckley, W. 1967. *Sociology and Modern System Theory*. Englewood Cliffs, NJ: Prentice Hall,

Burger, T. 1977. "Talcott Parsons, the Problem of Order in Society, and the Program of Analytical Sociology." *American Journal of Sociology* 83: 320–39.

Buxton, W. 1991. "The Marshall Lectures and Social Scientific Practice." *Sociological Inquiry* 61: 81–8.

Camic, C. 1979. "The Utilitarians Revisited." *American Journal of Sociology* 85: 516–50.

Camic, C. 1987. "The Making of a Method: A Historical Reinterpretation of the Early Parsons." *American Sociological Review* 52: 421–39.

Camic, C. 1989. "Structure after 50 Years: The Anatomy of a Charter." *American Journal of Sociology* 95: 38–107.

Camic, C. 1990a. "An Historical Prologue." *American Sociological Review* 55: 313–45.

Camic, C. 1990b. "Interpreting *The Structure of Social Action*: A Note on Tiryakian." *American Journal of Sociology* 96: 455–9.

Camic, C. 1991 (ed.) *Talcott Parsons: The Early Essays*. Chicago, IL: University of Chicago Press.

Camic, C. 1992. "Reputation and Predecessor Selection: Parsons and the Institutionalists." *American Sociological Review* 57: 421–45.

Camic, C. 1997. "The Monist Call to Sociological Theory: A Comment on the Early Parsons." Paper presented at the 92nd Annual Meeting of the American Sociological Association, Toronto.

Camic, C. 2005. From Amherst to Heidelberg: On the Origins of Parsons's Conception of Culture, in R.C. Fox, V.M. Lidz and H.J. Bershady (eds), *After Parsons*. New York: Russell Sage Foundation, 240–63.

Cohen, J. 1975. "Moral Freedom through Understanding: Comment on Pope ASR, August, 1973." *American Sociological Review* 40: 104–106.

Cohen J., Hazelrigg, L.F., and Pope, W. 1975a. "De-Parsonizing Weber: A Critique of Parsons' Interpretation of Weber's Sociology." *American Sociological Review* 40: 229–41.

Cohen J., Hazelrigg, L.F., and Pope, W. 1975b. "Reply to Parsons." *American Sociological Review* 40: 670–74.

Coleman, J.S. 1990. "Commentary: Social Institutions and Social Theory." *American Sociological Review* 55: 333–9.

Collins, R. 2004. *Interaction Ritual Chains*. Princeton, NJ: Princeton University Press,

Colomy, P. 1990. Conclusion, in C. Alexander and P. Colomy (eds), *Differentiation Theory and Social Change*. New York: Columbia University Press, 465–95.

Crespi, F. 1998. Azione e cultura: I limiti della teoria di Talcott Parsons, in R. Prandini (ed.), *Talcott Parsons*. Milan: Bruno Mondatori, 125–51.

Dahrendorf, R. 1958. "Out of Utopia: Toward a Reorientation of Sociological Analysis." *American Journal of Sociology* 64: 115–27.

Dawe, A. 1978. Theories of Social Action, in T. Bottomore and R. Nisbet (eds), *A History of Sociological Analysis*. New York: Basic Books, 362–417.

Devereux, E.C. 1961. Parsons' Sociological Theory, in M. Black (ed.), *The Social Theories of Talcott Parsons*. Englewood Cliffs, NJ: Prentice Hall, 1–63.

DiTomaso, N. 1982. "'Sociological Reductionism' from Parsons to Althusser: Linking Action and Structure in Social Theory." *American Sociological Review* 47: 14–28.

Dubin, R. 1960. "Parsons' Actor: Continuities in Social Theory." *American Sociological Review* 25: 457–66.

Eisenstadt, S.N. 1964a. "Institutionalization and Social Change." *American Sociological Review* 29: 235–47.

Eisenstadt, S.N. 1964b. "Social Change, Differentiation, and Evolution." *American Sociological Review* 29: 375–86.

Emirbayer M. and Mische, A. 1998. "What is Agency?" *American Journal of Sociology* 103: 962–1023.

Etzioni, A. 1991. "Socio-Economics Revisited." *Sociological Inquiry* 61: 68–73.

Fitzhenry, R. 1986. Parsons, Schutz and the Problem of *Verstehen*, in R.J. Holton and B. Turner (eds), *Talcott Parsons on Economy and Society*. London: Routledge, 143–78.

Fox, R.C., Lidz, V.M., and Bershady, H.J. 2005. Introduction, in R.C. Fox, V.M. Lidz and H.J. Bershady (eds), *After Parsons*. New York: Russell Sage Foundation, 1–27.

Garfinkel, H. 2002. *Ethnomethodology's Program: Working out Durkheim's Aphorism*, ed. A.W. Rawls. Lanham, MD: Rowman and Littlefield.

Garfinkel, H. 2008. *Toward a Sociological Theory of Information*, ed. A.W. Rawls. London: Paradigm Publishers.

Gerhardt, U., 2002. *Talcott Parsons: An Intellectual Biography*. Cambridge: Cambridge University Press.

Gerhardt, U. 2005a. "Why Read *The Social System* Today? Three Reasons and a Plea." *Journal of Classical Sociology* 5: 267–301.

Gerhardt, U. 2005b. The Weberian Talcott Parsons: Sociological Theory in Three Decades of American History, in R.C. Fox, V.M. Lidz and H.J. Bershady (eds), *After Parsons*. New York: Russell Sage Foundation, 208–39.

Giddens, A. 1968. "Power in the Recent Writings of Talcott Parsons." *Sociology* 2: 257–72.

Giddens, A. 1979. *Nuove regole del metodo sociologico*. Bologna: Il Mulino.

Giddens, A. 1984. *The Constitution of Society*. Cambridge: Polity Press.

Gould, M. 2005. Looming Catastrophe: How and Why 'Law and Economics' Undermines Fiduciary Duties in Corporate Law, in R.C. Fox, V.M. Lidz and H.J. Bershady (eds), *After Parsons*. New York: Russell Sage Foundation, 44–65.

Gouldner, A. 1959. Reciprocity and Antinomy in Functional Theory, in L.Z. Gross (ed.), *Symposium on Sociological Theory*. Evanston: Harper and Row, 241–70.

Gouldner, A. 1970. *The Coming Crisis of Western Sociology*. New York: Basic Books. Italian translation: *La crisi della sociologia*, 1972, Bologna: Il Mulino.

Granovetter, M. 1979. "The Idea of 'Advancement' in Theories of Social Evolution and Development." *American Journal of Sociology* 85: 489–515.

Granovetter, M. 1982. "Reply to Nolan." *American Journal of Sociology* 88: 947–50.

Habermas, J. 1981. "Talcott Parsons: Problems of Theory Construction." *Sociological Inquiry* 5(1): 173–96.

Habermas, J. 1987. *The Theory of Communicative Action. Lifewold and Systems: A Critique of Functionalist Reason*. Boston, MA: Beacon Press.

Habermas J. 1996b. *Between Facts and Norms*. Cambridge: Polity Press.

Hacker, A. 1961. Sociology and Ideology, in A. Black (ed.), *The Social Theories of Talcott Parsons*. Englewood Cliffs, NJ: Prentice Hall, 289–310.

Hamilton, P. 1989 (1983). *Talcott Parsons*. Bologna: Il Mulino.

Heritage, J.C. 1984. *Garfinkel and Ethnomethodology*, Cambridge: Polity Press,

Holmwood, J. 1996. *Founding Sociology?: Talcott Parsons and the Idea of General Theory*. London: Longman.

Holmwood, J. 2006a. Introduction, in J. Holmwood, *Talcott Parsons*. London: Ashgate, xii–li.

Holmwood, J. 2006b. "Economics, Sociology, and the Professional Complex: Talcott Parsons and the Critique of Orthodox Economics." *The American Journal of Economics and Sociology* 65: 127–60.

Holton, R.J. 1986a. Talcott Parsons and the Theory of Economy and Society, in R.J. Holton and B. Turner (eds), *Talcott Parsons on Economy and Society*. London: Routledge, 25–105.

Holton, R.J. 1986b. Parsons and His Critics: On the Ubiquity of Functionalism, in R.J. Holton and B. Turner (eds), *Talcott Parsons on Economy and Society*. London: Routledge, 179–206.

Holton, R.J. 2001. Talcott Parsons: Conservative Apologist or Irreplaceable Icon?, in G. Ritzer and B. Smart (eds), *Handbook of Social Theory*. London: Sage, 152–62.

Holton, R.J. and Turner, B. 1986a. Reading Talcott Parsons: Introductory Remarks, in R.J. Holton and B. Turner (eds), *Talcott Parsons on Economy and Society*. London: Routledge, 1–24.

Holton, R.J. and Turner, B. 1986b. Against Nostalgia: Talcott Parsons and a Sociology for the Modern World, in R.J. Holton and B. Turner (eds), *Talcott Parsons on Economy and Society*. London: Routledge, 207–34.

Homans, G. 1964. "Bringing Men Back In." *American Sociological Review* 29: 809–18.

Joas, H. and Knöbl, W. 2009. *Social Theory: Twenty Introductory Lectures*. Cambridge: Cambridge University Press.

Johnson, B. 1975. *Functionalism in Modern Sociology: Understanding Talcott Parsons*. Morriston, NJ: General Learning Press.

Lechner, F.J. 1990. Fundamentalism and Sociocultural Revitalization: On the Logic of Dedifferentiation, in J.C. Alexander and P. Colomy (eds), *Differentiation Theory and Social Change*. New York: Columbia University Press, 88–118.

Levine, D.N. 1985. *The Flight from Ambiguity*. Chicago, IL: The University of Chicago Press.

Levine, D.N. 2005. Modernity and Its Endless Discontents, in R.C. Fox, V.M. Lidz and H.J. Bershady (eds), *After Parsons*. New York: Russell Sage Foundation, 148–65.

Lidz, V.M. 2000. Talcott Parsons, in G. Ritzer (ed.), *The Blackwell Companion to Major Social Theorists*. Oxford: Blackwell, 388–431.

Lidz, V.M. 2005. "Social Evolution" in the Light of the Human-Condition Paradigm, in R.C. Fox, V.M. Lidz and H.J. Bershady (eds), *After Parsons*. New York: Russell Sage Foundation, 308–33.

Lockwood, D. 1964. Social Integration and System Integration, in G.K. Zollschan and W. Hirsch (eds), *Explorations in Social Change*. London: Routledge and Kegan Paul, 244–57.

Luhmann, N. 1970a. Reflexive Mechanismen, in *Soziologische Aufklaerung*, Volume 1. Opladen: Weatdeuscher Verlag, 92–112.

Luhmann, N. 1970b. Soziologie als Theorie sozialer Systѐme, in *Soziologische Aufklaerung*, Volume 1. Opladen: Weatdeuscher Verlag, 113–36.

Luhmann, N. 1970c. Soziologie des politischen Systems, in *Soziologische Aufklaerung*, Volume 1. Opladen: Weatdeuscher Verlag, 137–77.

Luhmann, N. 1970d. Evolution und Geschichte, in *Soziologische Aufklaerung*, Volume 2. Opladen: Weatdeuscher Verlag, 150–69.

Luhmann, N. 1987. The Evolutionary Differentiation between Society and Interaction, in J.C. Alexander, B. Giesen, R. Münch and N.J. Smelser (eds), *The Micro-Macro Link*. Berkeley, CA: The University of California Press, 112–31.

Luhmann, N. 1990. The Paradox of System Differentiation and the Evolution of Society, in J.C. Alexander and P. Colomy (eds), *Differentiation Theory and Social Change*. New York: Columbia University Press, 409–40.

Martindale, D. 1960. *The Nature and Types of Sociological Theory*. Boston, MA: Houghton Mifflin. Italian translation: *Tipologia ed storia della teoria sociologica*, 1968, Bologna: Il Mulino.

Martindale, D. 1971. Talcott Parsons' Theoretical Metamorphosis from Social Behaviorism to Macrofunctionalism, in H. Turk and R.L. Simpson (eds), *Institutions and Exchange: The Sociologies of Talcott Parsons and George Caspar Homans*. New York: Bobbs Merril, 165–74.

Mayhew, L. 1984. "In Defense of Modernity: Talcott Parsons and the Utilitarian Tradition." *American Journal of Sociology* 89: 1273–1305.

Mayhew, L. 1990. The Differentiation of the Solidary Public, in J.C. Alexander and P. Colomy (eds), *Differentiation Theory and Social Change*. New York: Columbia University Press, 294–322.

Merton, R.K. 1957. *Social Theory and Social Structure*. New York: The Free Press.

Mills Wright, C. 1956. *The Power Elites*. Oxford: Oxford University Press. Italian translation: *La élite del potere*. Milan: Feltrinelli, 1966.

Mills Wright, C. 1959. *The Sociolgical Imagination*. Oxford: Oxford University Press. Italian translation: *L'immaginazione socologica*, 1968, Milan: Il Saggiatore.

Morse, C. 1961. The Functional Imperatives, in M. Black (ed.), *The Social Theories of Talcott Parsons*. Englewood Cliffs, NJ: Prentice Hall, 100–52.

Muench, R. 1981. "Talcott Parsons and the Theory of Action: I. The Structure of the Kantian Core." *American Journal of Sociology* 86: 709–39.

Muench, R. 1982. "Talcott Parsons and the Theory of Action: II. The Continuity of the Development." *American Journal of Sociology* 87: 771–826.

Muench, R. 1987. Parsonian Theory Today: In Search of a New Synthesis, in A. Giddens and J.H. Turner (eds), *Social Theory Today*. Cambridge: Polity Press, 116–55.

Muench, R. 1990. Differentiation, Rationalization, Interpenetration: The Emergence of Modern Society, in J.C. Alexander and P. Colomy (eds), *Differentiation Theory and Social Change*. New York: Columbia University Press, 441–64.

Nisbet, R.A. 1969. *Social Change and History*. New York: Oxford University Press.

Nisbet, R.A. 1974. *The Sociology of Emile Durkheim*. New York: Oxford University Press.

Parsons, T. 1928. "Capitalism in Recent German Literature: Sombart and Weber, I." *Journal of Political Economy* 36: 641–61.

Parsons, T. 1929. "Capitalism in Recent German Literature: Sombart and Weber, II." *Journal of Political Economy* 37: 31–51.

Parsons, T. 1934. Society, in *Encyclopedia of the Social Sciences*, Volume 14. New York: Macmillan, 225–31.

Parsons, T. 1949 (1937). *The Structure of Social Action*. New York: The Free Press.

Parsons, T. 1951. *The Social System*. New York: The Free Press.

Parsons, T. 1961a. The Point of View of the Author, in M. Black (ed.), *The Social Theories of Talcott Parsons*. Englewood Cliffs, NJ: Prentice Hall, 311–63.

Parsons, T. 1961b. An Outline of the Social System, in T. Parsons, E. Shils, K.D. Naegele and J.R. Pitts (eds), *Theories of Society: Foundations of Modern Sociological Theory*. New York: The Free Press, 30–79.

Parsons, T. 1964a. *Social Structure and Personality*. New York: The Free Press.

Parsons, T. 1964b. "Evolutionary Universals in Society." *American Sociological Review* 29: 339–57.

Parsons, T. 1966. *Societies: Evolutionary and Comparative Perspectives*. London: Prentice Hall.

Parsons, T. 1969a (1960). Pattern Variables Revisited: A Response to Robert Dubin, in W.L. Wallace (ed.), *Sociological Theory: An Introduction*. Chicago, IL: Aldine, 270–89.

Parsons, T. 1969b. *Politics and Social Structure*. New York: The Free Press.

Parsons, T. 1970. "On Building Social System Theory. A Personal History." *Daedalus* 99: 826–81.

Parsons, T. 1971. *The System of Modern Societies*. London: Prentice Hall.

Parsons, T. 1975. "Comment on 'Parsons'Interpretation of Durkheim' and on 'Moral Freedom through Understanding." *American Sociological Review* 40: 106–11.

Parsons, T. 1976. "Reply to Cohen, Hazelrigg and Pope." *American Sociological Review* 41(2): 361–5.

Parsons, T. 1977a. *Social Systems and the Evolution of Action Theory*. New York: The Free Press.

Parsons, T. 1977b. "Comment on Burger's Critique." *American Sociological Review* 83: 335–9.

Parsons, T. 1978. *Action Theory and the Human Condition*. New York: The Free Press.

Parsons, T. 1979 (1967). *Teoria sociologica e società moderna*. Milan: Etas Libri.

Parsons, T. 1986 (1939). *Aktor, Situation und normative Muster*. Frankfurt: Suhrkamp.

Parsons, T. 1990 (1934). "Prolegomena to a Theory of Social Institutions." *American Sociological Review* 55: 319–39.

Parsons, T. 1991 (1953). "The Integration of Economic and Sociological Theory: The Marshall Lectures." *Sociological Inquiry* 61: 10–59.

Parsons, T. 2007 (1979). *American Society: A Theory of the Societal Community*, ed. G. Sciortino. London: Paradigm Publishers.

Parsons, T., Bales, R.F. and Shils, E.A. 1953. *Working Papers in the Theory of Action*. New York: The Free Press.

Parsons, T. and Platt, G. 1973. *The American University*. Cambridge: Harvard University Press.

Parsons, T. and Shils, E.A. 2001 (1951). *Toward a General Theory of Action*. London: Transaction Publishers.

Parsons, T. and Smelser, N.J. 1957. *Economy and Society*. London: Routledge and Kegan Paul.

Peukert, H. 2004. "Max Weber: Precursor of Economic Sociology and Heterodox Economics?" *The American Journal of Economics and Sociology* 63(5): 987–1020.

Pope, W. 1973. "Classic on Classic: Parsons' Interpretation of Durkheim." *American Sociological Review* 38: 399–415.

Pope, W. 1975. "Parsons on Durkheim Revisited: Reply to Cohen and Parsons." *American Sociological Review* 40: 111–15.

Pope, W. and Johnson, B.D. 1983. "Inside Organic Solidarity." *American Sociological Review* 48: 681–92.

Pope, W., Cohen, J. and Hazelrigg, L.F. 1975a. "On the Divergence of Weber and Durkheim: A Critique of Parsons' Convergence Thesis." *American Sociological Review* 40: 417–27.

Pope, W., Cohen, J. and Hazelrigg, L.F. 1975b. "Reply to Parsons." *American Sociological Review* 40: 670–74.

Prandini, R. 1998. Talcott Parsons e la cultura della società, in R. Prandini (ed.), *Talcott Parsons*. Milan: Bruno Mondatori, 1–97.

Rawls, A.W. 2002. Editor's Introduction, in H. Garfinkel, *Ethnomethodology's Program: Working out Durkheim's Aphorism*. Lanham, MD: Rowman and Littlefield, 1–64.

Rawls, A.W. 2008. Editor's Introduction, in H. Garfinkel, *Toward a Sociological Theory of Information*. London: Paradigm Publishers, 1–100.

Rex, J. 1961. *Key Problems of Sociological Theory*. London: Routledge and Kegan Paul.

Ritzer, G. 1991. "Talcott Parsons' Marshall Lectures: Contemporary but Flawed." *Sociological Inquiry* 61: 74–80.

Rocher, G. 1974 (1972). *Talcott Parsons and American Sociology*. London: Nelson.

Sanderson, S.K. 2001. Evolutionary Theorizing, in J.H. Turner (ed.), *Handbook of Sociological Theory*. New York: Springer, 435–55.

Savage, S.P. 1981. *The Theories of Talcott Parsons*. New York: St. Martin's Press.

Schutz, A. 2006 (1940). Parsons' Theory of Social Action, in J. Holmwood (ed.), *Talcott Parsons*. London: Ashgate, 47–92.

Sciortino, G. 1998. Sul concetto di ordine normativo nella teoria dell'azione, in R. Prandini (ed.), *Talcott Parsons*. Milan: Bruno Mondadori, 98–124.

Sciortino, G. 2005. How Different Can We Be? Parsons's Societal Community, Pluralism, and the Multicultural Debate, in R.C. Fox, V.M. Lidz and H.J. Bershady (eds), *After Parsons*. New York: Russell Sage Foundation, 111–36.

Sciortino, G. 2007. Introduction: The Action of Social Structure, in G. Sciortino (ed.), *American Society: A Theory of the Societal Community*. London: Paradigm Publishers, 1–53.

Sciulli, D. 1984. "Talcott Parsons's Analytical Critique of Marxism's Concept of Alienation." *American Journal of Sociology* 90: 514–40.

Sciulli, D. 1986. "Voluntaristic Action as a Distinct Concept: Theoretical Foundations of Societal Constitutionalism." *American Sociological Review* 51: 743–66.

Sciulli, D. 1990. Differentiation and Collegial Formation: Implications of Societal Constitutionalism, in J.C. Alexander and P. Colomy (eds), *Differentiation Theory and Social Change*. New York: Columbia University Press, 367–405.

Sciulli, D. and Gerstein, D. 1985. "Social Theory and Talcott Parsons in the 1980." *Annual Review of Sociology* 11: 369–87. Reprinted, with permission, from the *Annual Review of Sociology*, Volume 11, ©1985 by Annual Reviews www.annualreviews.org.

Schluchter, W. 1979. The Paradox of Rationalization: On the Relations of Ethics and World, in G. Roth and W. Schluchter (eds), *Max Weber's Vision of History: Ethics and Methods*. Berkeley, CA: University of California Press, 11–64.

Scott, J.F. 1963. "The Changing Foundations of the Parsonian Action Scheme." *American Sociological Review* 28: 719–35.

Smelser, N.J. 2001. Introduction to the Transaction Edition, in T. Parsons and E.A. Shils (eds), *Toward a General Theory of Action*. London: Transaction, vii–xix.

Smelser, N.J. 2005a. Parsons' Economic Sociology and the Development of Economic Sociology, in R.C. Fox, V.M. Lidz and H.J. Bershady (eds), *After Parsons*. New York: Russell Sage Foundation, 31–43.

Smelser, N.J. 2005b. "Parsons' Economic Sociology and its Extension to the Global Economy." *Journal of Classical Sociology* 5: 245–66.

Staubmann, H. 2005. Culture as a Subsystem of Action: Autonomous and Heteronomous Functions, in R.C. Fox, V.M. Lidz and H.J. Bershady (eds), *After Parsons*. New York: Russell Sage Foundation, 169–78.

Swedberg, R. 1991. "Thematic Issue: Guest Editor's Introduction." *Sociological Inquiry* 61: 2–9.

Tiryakian, E.A. 1975. "Neither Marx nor Durkheim ... Perhaps Weber." *American Journal of Sociology* 81: 1–33.

Tiryakian, E.A. 1992. Dialectics of Modernity, in H. Haferkamp and N.J. Smelser (eds), *Social Change and Modernity*. Berkeley, CA: University of California Press, 78–94.

Tiryakian, E.A. 2005. Parsons and the Human Condition, in R.C. Fox, V.M. Lidz and H.J. Bershady (eds), *After Parsons*. New York: Russell Sage, 267–88.

Treviño, J. 2005. "Parsons's Action-System Requisite Model and Weber's Elective Affinity: A Convergence of Convenience." *Journal of Classical Sociology* 5: 319–48.

Turner, R.J. 1986a. Sickness and Social Structure: Parsons' Contribution to Medical Sociology, in R.J. Holton and B. Turner (eds), *Talcott Parsons on Economy and Society*. London: Routledge, 107–42.

Turner, R.J. 1986b. Parsons and His Critics: On the Ubiquity of Functionalism, in R.J. Holton and B. Turner (eds), *Talcott Parsons on Economy and Society*. London: Routledge, 179–206.

Turner, R.J. 1998. *The Structure of Sociological Theory*. Belmont, CA: Wadsworth.

Vanderstraeten, R. 2002. "Parsons, Luhmann and the Theorem of Double Contingency." *Journal of Classical Sociology* 2: 77–92.

Warner, R.S. 1981. "Parsons's Last Testament." *American Journal of Sociology* 87: 715–21.

Warner, R.S. 2006 (1978). "Toward a Redefinition of Action Theory: Paying the Cognitive Element Its Due." *American Journal of Sociology* 83: 1317–49.

Wenzel, H. 1986. *Einleitung des Herausgebers: Einige Bemerkungen zu Parsons' Program einer Theorie des Handelns*. Frankfurt: Suhrkamp.

Wenzel, H. 2005. Social Order as Communication: Parsons's Theory on the Move from Moral Consensus to Trust, in R.C. Fox, V.M. Lidz and H.J. Bershady (eds), *After Parsons*. New York: Russell Sage Foundation, 66–82.

White, W.F. 1961. Parsonian Theory Applied to Organizations, in M. Black (ed.), *The Social Theories of Talcott Parsons*. Englewood Cliffs, NJ: Prentice Hall, 250–67.

Williams, R.M. 1961. The Sociological Theory of Talcott Parsons, in M. Black (ed.), *The Social Theories of Talcott Parsons*. Englewood Cliffs, NJ: Prentice Hall, 64–99.

Wrong, D. 1961. "The Oversocialized Conception of Man in Modern Sociology." *The American Sociological Review* 26: 183–93.

Zaret, D. 1980. "From Weber to Parsons and Schutz: The Eclipse of History in Modern Social Theory." *American Journal of Sociology* 85: 1180–1201.

Chapter 13
Rational Choice Theory

Preliminary Remarks

Rational Choice Theory may be defined as a theoretical perspective which aims at explaining either an individual or a collective action as the result of the individual actors' orientation to an efficient attainment of a goal. In other words, action is meant as the effect of desires, and is supposed to be addressed to actors' goals deriving from those desires (intentional, instrumental or purposive action). This perspective is widespread and very influential in sociology, particularly in the area of economic sociology, as well as in the areas of deviance, family, education, religion and social movements. In the course of our exposition, we shall provide some essential information on the major concepts and assumptions of rational choice theory. We shall dwell upon Elster and Coleman, the two authors who have given a particular contribution to this perspective. However, while Elster will be constantly quoted during our exposition, Coleman will be considered separately. In fact, differently from Elster, whose contribution is generally accepted and used by scholars who have dealt with rational choice theory, Coleman's contribution has been much debated, and has produced, along with favorable opinions, also objections and rejections. Finally, we shall briefly mention also the critical comments expressed about rational choice theory in general.

Rational Choice Theory (Generalities)

According to the available literature on this subject (to which reference should be made for an introduction to this theory) (see, in addition to Elster 1986, 1989a: 22–41, also Abell 1992, 2000; Baert 1998: ch. 7; Boudon 1998, 2003; Coleman 1994; Friedman and Hechter 1988: 201–204; Green and Shapiro 1994: ch. 2; Heckathorn 2001; Hedstroem and Swedberg 1996a; Kiser and Hechter 1998; Voss and Abraham 2000), rational choice theory is a theory of social action characterized by the following assumptions:

1. What is to be explained – action – derives understandably from the intentions that may be attributed to individuals, considering their decisions, beliefs, attitudes and previous actions. Intentions are projects aimed at achieving benefits for oneself or for others which one expects as a consequence of the accomplishment of particular behaviors (actor's intentionality) (Elster 1985: 8–10).
2. According to this perspective, intentions explain the behaviors actors actually and deliberately use to follow. Until proved to the contrary, this theory assumes actors behave rationally, according to their beliefs and the information they have at their disposal (methodological individualism) (Elster 1985: 5–7; 2000b: 24–5).
3. The explanation consists in indicating the "causal mechanisms," and the consequent action courses, which – as the author maintains – have been relevant enough in the production of those behaviors. These "mechanisms" are understandable mental processes (such as the desire to obtain a benefit) rational choice theory scholars attribute to the actors in order to infer from them the motivations or the intentions that have guided their choice of action and are consequently in the position to provide "fine-grained explanations" of it. Those who make use of "causal mechanisms" think they sufficiently know the actors' interests, beliefs and action opportunities. The rational choice theory makes use of "causal mechanisms," that is, causal explanations concerning a spatially and temporally restricted action context. This context, in turn, is also specific as it considers actors' norms, beliefs and relationship networks. The lack of indications on what the explanatory and contextual mechanisms of action are characterizes perspectives that differ from this theory, such as functionalisms and structuralism

(Elster 1983: 101–108; 1984: 137–8, 174; 1986: 22–3; 1989a: 3–10; 1989b: 5–7. On the social mechanism concept, see also Bianco 2001: 13; Hedstroem and Swedberg 1996b).

4. A causal statement, as it explicitly indicates the explanatory mechanism considered relevant, may be distinguished in this from an account in which the causes of particular events are instead not explicitly stated. The use of explanatory mechanisms involves that it is impossible to argue the existence of a causal relation among events by simply showing they are related. Of course, it is always possible to plausibly attribute the effect to other causes. Furthermore, the use of explanatory mechanisms makes superfluous the search for necessary causes for producing a particular event. Finally, the use of explanatory mechanisms reduces the general character of an explanation, and hence, the possibility of making predictions (Elster 1989a: 4–9).

5. Actors are able to assess, in terms of costs and benefits, the predictable consequences of their actions (rationality condition). This rationality condition involves actors know (a) the compatibility or incompatibility relations between the ends they pursue in that particular moment and their overall plans of action, and again, between their own ends and those of other actors; (b) the pleasant or unpleasant consequences resulting from their pursuit of ends; (c) the appropriate means to achieve those ends, as well as their availability and possible interference with other means and ends (Garfinkel 1984: 263–8; Schutz 1964: 79–80).

6. An instrumental orientation is attributed to actors in the sense of supposing they pursue their goals using available means in a way they consider effective. Based on the information they have at their disposal, which has been collected according to their desires, actors believe they are in possession of the necessary knowledge on the most appropriate ways to satisfy those desires, and if they are rational, they make the best use, in their opinion, of that knowledge (optimality condition).

7. Beliefs are mutually consistent; desires are mutually consistent; goals are mutually consistent (consistency condition).

8. Actors' knowledge or beliefs result from the information they have at their disposal.

9. Information collection continues up to the point established by the actor's goals and desires.

10. Action is the logical consequence of those desires and information (causal condition).

11. Preferences are reciprocally consistent; that is, if an actor through its choice seems to prefer option "x" to option "y," then the actor cannot choose at the same time "y" instead of "x" (Weak Axiom of Revealed Preferences).

12. The actor exerts its preference among different possible options. If an actor prefers action *a* instead of action *b*, and action *b* instead of action *c*, the actor's preference order results as follows: $a > b > c$ (preference transitivity). It is possible to prove that this axiom derives from the previous one (Sen 1986).

13. Actors have a homogeneous preference order among them; alternatively, there is a mechanism for aggregating their preferences (for example, a mechanism establishing election procedures, when preferences are expressed through a vote) (Friedman and Hechter 1988: 202).

The rationality condition stated at point (5) is particularly important within rational choice theory, since it allows identifying behaviors that do not conform to beliefs, desires, purposes, means availability and actors' expected consequences, and hence are not rational. In this sense, we say that this condition, or assumption, has a "paradigmatic status" for rational choice theory. Whether the rationality condition is considered a useful assumption to explain any action, or only some action classes (such as economic market actions) depends on which particular version of rational choice theory one intends to follow (Hindess 1988: 62–3). The optimality assumption stated at point (6) is considered something that cannot be renounced in this theoretical perspective (Abell 1992: 203–204; 2000: 235; Elster 1986: 16). We meet a further assumption (actors, in pursuing their goals, try to obtain the greatest benefit, or "utility," for themselves) in some versions of rational choice theory which claim to be inspired by the neoclassical economic theory (Becker 1993; Green and Shapiro 1994: 15–16). The last, however, like other versions of rational choice theory, considers the social institutional context of economic action (Zafirovski 2000). In that case, the actor is not only concerned about the consequences of its action, and therefore, rationality is not necessarily instrumental.

Keeping to a narrow meaning of rationality, rational is a behavior complying with a complete, consistent and transitive set of constant preferences (Elster 1983: 1–15; 1984: 147). A broader but weaker notion of rationality includes the actions based on the actor's beliefs and opinions, disregarding their characteristics of truth or falseness, or those aimed at implementing its values, which may be of an altruistic nature. According to this notion of rationality, which is prevailing and judged more realistic, actors pursue their goals inasmuch as they deem it appropriate, considering:

a. Circumstances.
b. The knowledge constraints they have at their disposal to understand them.
c. Desires and preferences. This approach assumes that they have formed without inadequacies in the cognitive processes, or untimely influences from affective drives. Among preferences, particularly relevant are the temporal ones, which guide the evaluation of a future benefit instead of an immediate one.
d. The definitions of a situation, the norms and the rules that regulate those definitions, the interpretative frames applied to a situation and the importance attributed to them. Consequently, depending on provided definitions and used frames, cost and benefit assessment has a different weight (Boudon 1998, 2003; Elster 1983: 15–25; Goldthorpe 1998; Lindenberg 1992: 12–15; 1996: 306–308; Tversky and Kahneman 1986).

Within a broader notion of rationality, different kinds of rationality have been identified:

1. Limited rationality, when it is difficult to anticipate and consider all alternatives and information, and therefore one is satisfied with a set of information deemed sufficient. As we shall see in the following pages, Elster submitted to criticism the concept of limited rationality, thus questioning its utility.
2. Contextual rationality, when a choice involves renouncing to consider other problems and other solutions or options that take place at the same time.
3. "Game" rationality, when the decision-maker must take into account the actions of others with whom the actor relates itself.
4. Process rationality, when the decisional process itself, instead of its outcome, is relevant for the actor.

However, this broad notion of rationality, such as the narrow one, cannot be applied in the following cases: if the subject – instead of orienting its decisions to the goal of attaining a future goal – puts to good use the information learned through its past experiences, or if the subject acts in an institutional context provided with its own rules and procedures. Or, again, if the subject points out to itself its intentions after (and not before) having acted, presenting them to itself "a posteriori" as consistent with its previously pursued goals (March 1986: 147–50).

Quite often, not one individual action, but several actions – a feasible set of actions or available options – satisfy the rationality requirements we previously mentioned. In that case, the choice of an action instead of another becomes indifferent for the rational actor. The actor compares all possible action alternatives two by two, choosing the most convenient action in each couple until it makes a final choice, which, from his or her point of view, is the best one. If there are several optimal options, they can be selected according to habits or customs, or considering social rules prescribing particular behavior obligations. In any case, it is impossible to keep to the optimality assumption by choosing within them either option, since both are indifferent for the rational actor. In the abstract, actions may be studied as though any actor were acting without considering other actors. However, rational choice theory realistically dwells upon the opposite event and considers two distinguished cases.

In a first case, the actor thinks that the social environment in which it acts cannot be changed, if not marginally at the most, by its personal conduct. The actions of the others are then considered as constants, or parameters, to be taken into account, and are therefore called *parametric social actions*. In the case of parametric rationality, the rational (in the narrow sense) actor conforms to the pre-existing environmental constraints, because it thinks the cost it should bear in trying to change the environment would be greater than its resources, or its interest in that direction is not great enough (Kiser and Hechter 1998: 807). In a second case, instead, the actors think they can change their own environment through what they do when pursuing their personal goals, that is, through their *strategic social actions*. If they are rational, the actors must therefore be concerned about how the consequences of their own actions on other persons may involve the latter's reactions, which in turn might interfere with the attainment of the actors' goals. The actors must also be concerned about deciding what action, which they have to take in response to other people's actions is the most appropriate. Rational choice theory has extensively studied strategic social actions (Elster 1986: 23–4; 1989: 3–17). Within these actions, those producing perverse emerging effects prove particularly interesting. Emerging effects are the collective consequences of individual actions, which result from actors' interdependence. These emerging effects may be of different kinds.

A partial list of emerging effects includes:

a. a change in costs and benefits obtained by individuals from the interdependence of their actions;
b. the creation of a social micro-system by actors who make an agreement;
c. the making of a competitive market regulated by a set of exchanges between actors' pairs;
d. the making of collective decisions, which avail themselves of decisional rules, from individual decisions; this happens, for example, in voting;
e. the establishment of formal organizations, with authority hierarchies, from the different power levels of actors who depend on each other;
f. the establishment of collective control rights on individual actions from the development of norms and sanctions.

Emerging effects are called "perverse" when they do not make part of the actors' goals, are not wanted by them – although the actors may have foreseen them – and produce collective consequences judged undesirable. Perverse effects derive from the aggregation or composition of individual actions, each one of which is rational in the narrow sense, since the actors aim at achieving individual utility as much as possible. Consequently, the presence of perverse effects displays a contrast between short-term individual rationality and collective rationality. There are several examples of perverse effects. A well-known example of perverse (that is, neither pursued nor desirable) effect was provided, in 1929, by the financial ruin of most investors produced by a rush to the bank counters in order to withdraw all their savings. The perverse effect of that rush was the bankrupt of the banks and in turn, for most investors, the loss of all their savings, except for those who had withdrawn their money in time. What, individually, was a rational strategy, proved collectively a disaster. Again, the reforms aimed at socially opening access opportunities to university studies have produced the opposite effect, since all students rationally aim at achieving the benefits deriving from having completed the most prestigious educational course, but relatively few students are prepared to win the harsh competition produced by that opening (Boudon 1981a, 1981b; Coleman 1990a: 19–23, 901–903).

An important application of rational choice theory is the "*game theory*." This theory considers the actor as a person engaged in a sequence of moves and countermoves with other actors, in the rationally carried out attempt of obtaining an advantage or a benefit. Furthermore, the actor expects that the other actors, too, have the same purpose and follow it rationally. A "game," or a coordinated sequence of moves between two or more actors with the purpose of achieving a benefit, or a gain/payoff, may be non-cooperative if the actors pursue their own interests even to the detriment of the others and are prepared to cooperate with the others only if they consider it advantageous for themselves. A particular example of non-cooperative "game" is the "zero-sum" game: the gain of one or more participants corresponds to the total loss of all the others (such as it happens in a game of cards where money is at stake). Among participants, such a game produces the highest levels of conflict instead of mutual cooperation.

Cooperative is, instead, a "game" in which participants are able to reciprocally communicate and fully commit themselves in a binding way to achieve a benefit for everyone (Harsanyi 1987: 92). This shared benefit becomes a common or public good for them. A public good is a good from which all the members of a particular community can benefit, and whose production costs are fixed (that is, not depending on the number of those who make use of it). In other words, if only few persons enjoy this good, this does not diminish the benefit amount available to others and this enjoyment cannot be prevented to those who have not contributed to cover the necessary costs for producing that good. Furthermore, the addition of new beneficiaries does not involve any added cost for producing it (Hechter 1987: 34–5; Heckathorn 1996: 253). Public services are an example of it, as the concerned public is formed by the community of either actual or potential beneficiaries. Another example is the services provided free of charge by a religious or political association to a supporters' public. For those who take part in a cooperative game, the common good is the reward they obtain thanks to their cooperation which otherwise would not have been achieved. Every time a community can achieve a common good, the single members are encouraged to benefit from it without taking upon themselves their share of the costs necessary to obtain it: this is the problem of exploiters (or *free riders*).

Based on rational choice theory, we can try to control this problem by imposing costs, or punishments, on free riders. This is much easier in small groups, where these persons can be detected. Otherwise, by giving prizes, or benefits, only to those who prove they have contributed to the costs. The result of these "games" – whether simple or repeated – would have an even more favorable outcome for an individual participant, given the range of available alternatives (that is, given a *feasible set*). Sometimes, this outcome might turn even more profitable for a particular participant if it had other alternatives at its disposal. Since those alternatives are not available, or cannot be put into practice, the participant chooses – so to say – "the lesser evil", the worst consequences of this choice being, in fact, always preferable than the worst consequences of the other options. It is a relative maximum, in this case, or the better action option, considering the constraints put by the choices of the other participants. In the game theory, this strategy is called "maximin" (the maximum of minimums) and is, for rational actors, a "dominant" strategy, because all participants do prefer it to any other option. A dominant strategy leads to a balanced solution among the actors, because of the beneficial results for each one of them, disregarding any other decision the other participants might make. Nonetheless, a balanced solution does not always consist in a dominant strategy.

A social equilibrium solution (called "Nash's equilibrium," after the name of the mathematician who formulated it) is defined as a condition in which no actor is in the position to increase its personal benefit alone, and therefore, nobody is interested in changing its course of action, though it may be unsatisfactory. Often, this solution is different from the "social optimum" theoretical condition, and in that case, socially less preferable. This condition is also-called "Pareto's optimum" (after the name of the famous economist who first investigated it). There is a social, or a Pareto's, optimum when it is not possible to improve the condition of one or several actors without worsening the condition of some other ones. The Pareto's optimum concept establishes a standard in income or property redistribution, which is at the same time economic, social, and ethical, and is therefore important in social policies. In order to achieve a social optimum, actors must renounce – either willingly, or under compulsion –pursuing an immediate maximum individual benefit. They rather must act cooperatively. To this end, they must bear in mind the common good of the community to which they belong. In this way, they produce a particular public good (as they are that public), which consists in the social order. In the game theory language, we say in that case, that actors play a cooperative "game," thus achieving maximum collective rationality, which in the long run becomes also maximum individual benefit.

Whether and how this condition may be achieved or not has been extensively debated (see Elster 1983: 33–42). Elster himself maintains that a cooperative game implies the existence of social norms, along with effective sanctions against those who do not comply with them. Envy imposes action uniformity, and hence action predictability, but does not encourage cooperation, while opportunistic behavior (that is, behavior aimed at one's personal benefit) does not encourage action predictability or actors' cooperation. This double outcome may be achieved by virtue of credible social norms which may prevail thanks to repeated cooperative games among the actors themselves (Elster 1995: 353–401). These norms may be interpreted as rights to act, and are included in the larger category of rules. Among rules, particularly important are those called "metarules," which give importance to keeping and showing a cooperative attitude, and promote consistent behaviors (Lindenberg 1996: 309–10).

In the case of informal norms, the normative control effectiveness is increased by the adhesion to those norms on the part of the actors' group to which the subject belongs. According to Elster, an actor may either follow the norms prescribing cooperation in order to obtain a public good for its group or may take care of his or her own individual benefit, and thus pursue a utilitarian purpose. In the first case, norms may go along with selective incentives. These are incentives particularly addressed to members in order to make cooperation profitable from their point of view, according to Olson's well-known thesis (1965). However, selective incentives are not a necessary or sufficient condition for producing a rational collective action aimed at achieving the public good (Marwell and Oliver 1993: 187). When a non-cooperative game between two or more actors is repeated without pre-established limits, it does not have a dominant strategy, that is, a strategy preferred by all participants (Elster 1995: 67–9). If, however, individuals pursue a utilitarian goal, and the game is non-repeated and non-cooperative, each actor finds it advisable to pursue an individual rationality that is immediate and maximum. Actors, in this case, do not concern themselves with the public good. In the long run, the results of this strategy do not prove profitable for any participant. However, it is possible that participation in a cooperative game may turn profitable for participants both immediately (as in non-cooperative games), and in the long run (as in cooperative games). According to rational choice theory, this only happens if the gain allowed by the public good exceeds participation costs, or in presence of individual (or selective) benefits, as Olson argues (1965).

This happens also if the cooperative behavior of a participant is subordinated to other people's participation. Their minimum number, or "critical mass," for inducing a subject to participate depends on its participation threshold, and is therefore variable. However, the achievement of this critical mass depends on the existence of one or more actors having a sufficient amount of interest and resources for providing their contribution to the attainment of the public good, even though their costs are initially very high. Their initial contribution may, in that case, serve as a "critical mass" inducing further participants, less interested than the previous ones and/or provided with smaller resources, to give their contribution as well. These further participants take upon themselves decreasing and progressively reduced costs, in comparison with those taken by the first participants. However, their contributions in achieving the public good become increasingly less important over time. In that case, also their interest in taking part in the achievement of public good decreases accordingly, as this public good has been already, or almost, achieved. Furthermore, as the number of participants grows, also *free riders*, that is, the actors who have not contributed to the costs, can more easily benefit from that public good (Macy 1991a, 1991b; Marwell and Oliver 1993). Compared to what is needed to attain the public good, contributions may be provided even more than enough if the group rewards the participants who have taken the additional costs upon themselves (as it may occur in groups motivated by strong religious or ideological beliefs) (Coleman 1990a: 273–8, 494; Heckathorn 1993: 342).

In any group, the required collective action for achieving the public good may be voluntary or may be made compulsory by norms created and enforced by the group itself, or may be also the outcome of an equilibrium between actors who want to impose those norms and other actors who are opposed to them. A group may be heterogeneous as regards costs, interests or resources. In other words, the actors may either encounter different costs as regards their contribution to the public good or they may evaluate the public good in a different way or, finally, they may have different resources available, and hence abilities to change other people's behaviors. In heterogeneous groups, resource disparity makes it profitable (other circumstances being equal) for poorer members to do their best to make all members give their contribution, since the members thus submitted to control have greater resources at their disposal. In this way, participation in a collective action is encouraged, on condition that other members are not opposed. In general, heterogeneity promotes collective action if it makes it profitable to participate for members that otherwise would not take part in it. In fact, if the group were homogeneous, some members of the group would not find it profitable to participate because of their lack of interest, high contribution costs or insufficient resources. Heterogeneous groups allow members with scarce power to organize and assert themselves (if necessary, even by breaking the group into opposing factions), whereas homogeneous groups keep the existing power concentration to the detriment of weaker members (Heckathorn 1993).

An adhesion to ethical norms prescribing participation lowers the threshold. However, these norms prevail only when some actors have already taken the initiative to participate, and their participation has proved advantageous. In addition to ethical norms, other factors, too, are relevant in changing, in one sense or another, the participation threshold. Among these factors we wish to point out the assessment of the participation costs (which sometimes rise with a growing number of participants), as well as of the non-participation costs. The latter may be high if there is a social pressure to participate, and/or the subject considers its participation essential. In this sense, relevant factors are the importance the subject attributes to the collective good, and the density of its ties with other prospect beneficiaries (Elster 1995: 55–76, 264–300; Macy 1991a, 1991b). To Elster's attempt to provide his personal explanation to an adhesion to norms that may be complying with rational choice theory, it has been objected that his explanation sheds light neither on how norms have formed nor on how the existence of norms that do not seem to meet the interests of particular communities is possible. Complementary explanations to Elster's, which conform to rational choice theory, call attention on the intervention of two distinct sets of actors: external actors, who are interested in observing and making observe norms, on the one hand; and actors, whose actions are directly regulated by norms (*target actors*), on the other. Target actors benefit from these norms and are in the position to impose sanctions, and hence costs, to those who do not observe them.

When a non-cooperative game – the "Prisoner's Dilemma" is perhaps the best known of them – is repeated several times, it may be the case that cooperation norms prevail by virtue of a conditional cooperative strategy, according to which an actor cooperates only if also the others do the same. Then, the sanction consists in "defecting" (or not cooperating). The threat of defecting is credible when it comes from small groups because only small groups are able to exert relatively low-cost monitoring activities on their members, and impose collective sanctions to defectors (Heckathorn 1990: 374–7; Voss and Abraham 2000: 61–3). In fact, supposing actors are rational in the narrow sense, only groups in which the costs for achieving the public good (a common good shared by all the group members) related to the interest of each member in benefiting from them are limited enough to make its pursuit profitable, as it occurs in small groups (Olson 1965). However, public good may be also achieved in larger groups, on condition that one of the following circumstances occurs: when the group succeeds in increasing the public good value, or when some group members do not contribute individually, but act so that other ones who have not given their contribution are punished (hypocritical cooperation). In that case, the success of a collective action depends on the ability of all members interested in its success (even those who have not contributed to it) to start the collective action before others, who are opposed to it, may succeed in nipping it in the bud (Heckathorn 1996: 275–6).

Though the achievement of public good in small groups ultimately derives from an evaluation of its benefits and costs made by members, it is the direct result of its solidarity, that is, of the group ability to induce its members to follow its rules even without a payment. The more a group is united, the more it is able to reserve exclusively to members the enjoyment of the provided good, since the group is exclusively formed by members. In turn, this ability depends on the degree to which this public is socially isolated, as there are few or no possibilities to belong to other groups and thus have access to alternative benefits (Hechter 1987: 30–58; Marwell and Oliver 1993: 187–90). This development of rational choice theory avails itself of the contribution of another theoretical current, the *Network Exchange Theory*. This theory assumes that actors try to maximize their power, meant as control on others, and hence as a benefit, while they try to resist to a relation of subordination to others, meant as a cost (for an introduction to the *Network Exchange Theory*, see Molm 2001; Willer et al. 2002). In this regard, particular relevance has one of its versions, called "elementary theory," whose full compatibility with rational choice theory has been indicated (Willer 1992).

The theme of individual costs and benefits referred to participation in cooperative and non-cooperative games, as well as the associated theme of the dilemmas encountered by participants, has been extensively studied within the framework of rational choice theory. It can be assumed that rational actors are either completely or incompletely informed according to their stock of knowledge and beliefs on their personal preferences and available options and those of all the others, also on the information the others have at their disposal, and therefore, on the consequences of their own action. It should be remarked that information – whether complete or incomplete – is possessed before the actors enter in a mutual relationship, that is, before the game begins (as soon as the game begins, information –whether perfect or imperfect – concerns the moves, or the actions, which participants have already carried out). If information is incomplete, actors must make choices that may involve unknown consequences for them. If the actors are able to precisely evaluate that these consequences may occur, these consequences are designated by the term of "risks." By definition, risks can therefore be always calculated. Instead, if actors can only imprecisely evaluate those probabilities, their condition is designated as uncertainty. We assume that risks and uncertainty are shared by all actors (Elster 1989b: 10–13; Voss and Abraham 2000: 58. For an in-depth examination of these issues, cf. Harsanyi 1987).

A great deal of literature on game theory assumes that actors completely know the consequences of their choices. Based on the assumption of complete information, which does not foresee any risk or uncertainty, we are able to identify separate and alternative action courses (called "dilemmas" in the game theory language), namely whether each actor only cares for its personal advantage or payoff, or the actors care for their common advantage, thus establishing cooperative relations. Among these dilemmas, the most famous one is the so-called "Prisoner's Dilemma," upon which we wish to dwell now before mentioning other kinds of "dilemmas." If two actors are engaged in a non-repeated non-cooperative game, we can imagine a situation in which both of them might achieve a benefit in the long term if they cooperated. Instead, in the "Prisoner's Dilemma" there is no cooperation, because each actor (there are at least two of them) pursues his or her own immediate advantage, and since there is no mutual trust, each of them thinks that the other actors act likewise. The achieved result implies an equilibrium situation that is not optimal for any participant.

This is the well-known and extensively studied case of the "Prisoner's Dilemma." This game, which is the prototype of non-cooperative games, assumes there are two prisoners only. Each prisoner has no possibility of communicating with the other one, and receives from the authority the promise to be released from prison if he or she confesses to the crime of which he is charged, provided the other prisoner has refused to confess. In that case, the latter would be punished with lifelong imprisonment, which is the maximum punishment. A reciprocally disloyal behavior is thus encouraged, because cooperation with the authority is rewarded, whereas the loyalty to the prison mate is instead punished. In fact, bearing in mind that the actors do only take care of their own advantage (as it happens in any non-cooperative game), each actor fears receiving the maximum damage if he or she decides to be loyal or cooperative towards the prison mate by not confessing. Meanwhile, the prison mate has instead a disloyal, non-cooperative behavior towards the other prisoner as he or she cooperates with the authority. It is also assumed that the authority decides to inflict, in the form of a given number of years of imprisonment:

- a smaller, but in any case considerable, punishment, in comparison with lifelong imprisonment (many years of imprisonment), to both prisoners if they decided to defect from one another (that is, if each one were disloyal to his prison mate by confessing, and hence, cooperating with the authority), since they would have confessed a serious crime;
- an even smaller damage, though not any punishment at all (few years of prison), if each actor decided to loyally cooperate with the other, and both refused to confess. In fact, in the lack of a confession, the authority cannot inflict a severe punishment and must limit itself to condemn both prisoners for some minor crime.

In the light of these assumptions on the authority behavior, each prisoner would have the advantage of being condemned to a few years in prison if he or she refused to confess, instead of lifelong imprisonment (if only one of them confesses), or many years in prison (if both of them confess). However, each prisoner – since he or she does not trust in the prison mate's cooperation – prefers to confess, risking a long imprisonment (which is, however, shorter than lifelong imprisonment), but hoping to be released if the prison mate –mistakenly placing his confidence in the other prisoner's loyalty – had decided not to confess. If both prisoners think in this perfectly rational way, then they would face in any case long imprisonment. If both of them had trusted in the other's loyalty, they would have been sentenced only few years of prison. Long imprisonment is a Nash's equilibrium condition that is suboptimal for the actors. In fact, neither prisoner has any interest in behaving differently for the fear of lifelong prison, but both prisoners would have preferred short imprisonment, which they would have attained only if they had trusted in each other.

Short imprisonment duration constitutes the public good for the public of the prison mates, which is not attained in this non-cooperative game. A situation similar to the "Prisoner's Dilemma" occurs when one or more individuals take an advantage from other people's cooperation, while they do not concur in covering the costs that are necessary for achieving a benefit, of which they take an advantage as well. The achieved benefit is a public good for those who enjoy it and, such as any other public benefit, may incur the problem of possible profiteers, who choose an opportunistic conduct. Tests aimed at checking the paradoxical conclusion of this "game" (with punishments and rewards that are of course different from the years of imprisonment and reduction of sentence) have indicated that this game leads to different results if it is repeated an unspecified number of times. In that case, in fact, each participant makes an idea of his or her own about the other's loyalty based on the past behaviors of the latter, and acts accordingly.

A lack of mutual loyalty, once it is evidenced by experience, leads participants to non-cooperative behaviors, whereas cooperative behaviors are encouraged by the loyalty, which the prison mate has previously shown. To be or not to be in possession of a reputation of correctness and loyalty allows then overcoming the "Prisoner's Dilemma," and provides information on the other participants' reliability. Nonetheless, if participants know how many times the game has been repeated, in the last turn they stop being mutually loyal, because they cannot any longer have the possibility of rewarding or punishing the other participant, who in turn is no more interested in behaving loyally. In the last and no longer cooperative turn, the game takes the shape of a "Prisoner's Dilemma." Lacking participants' reputation, this dilemma may be overcome only if participants are reciprocally identifiable, for they are in this case in the position to give prizes and inflict sanctions to each other. In that case, each one of them can induce the others to show cooperative behaviors. However, this is only possible in small groups, the only ones – as we previously wrote – in which the costs of mutual control are not too high as to make it advantageous for the single members to exert it (Hechter 1987: 73–5).

Another well-known game is the "Chicken Game" ("chicken" meaning in American jargon a coward person). Such as the previous game, this game encourages non-cooperative behavior in participants. However, the worst result does not occur to the actor who defects while the other one does it unilaterally, as in the "Prisoner's Dilemma." The model of this game is provided by a popular challenge among the American teenagers. Participants point one against the other in their cars at high speed. The winner is the one who has the courage not to swerve even at the very last moment, obviously on condition that the other participant has instead swerved, thus proving a coward. If both of them swerve, nobody wins, but nobody loses, either. This is the optimal solution for both participants, though individually, it is less preferable than the solution in which only the other cooperates to the participants' common good (that is, only the other swerves, thus saving his or her and the other's life), while the former benefits from it without paying its costs (without proving a coward).

The worst solution for both of them occurs when neither participant cooperates in achieving the common good for both of them (saving lives) in the hope of obtaining the highest individual benefit (winning the challenge). Therefore, participants crash into each other. This solution is certainly less preferable, compared to the unilateral cooperation of the "chicken" that loses the challenge, but saves his or her life. Readers surely remember that in the "Prisoner's Dilemma," unilateral cooperation (being loyal, thus contributing to the public good, and consequently to the other's good, whereas the other is disloyal) is the worst solution, though the choice of mutual disloyalty (or defection) is in any case unsatisfactory, and hardly preferable to unilateral cooperation. In this game, too, as in the previous one, the choice of not cooperating, when made by both participants, leads the game to a Nash's equilibrium unfavorable for both of them. Similar situations to the "Chicken Game" occur any time the actors have a common interest, for there is a common interest of not crashing one into the other in this game. Likewise, there may be in a social movement an interest of all followers to achieve common goals. Actors, however, are competing in some other respect: for example, on the best ways (which may be uncompromising or ready to compromise) to attaining those goals.

We would like to briefly mention two further "games." In the first game, participants – such as in the previous cases – have partly common and partly opposite interests, while in the second game, there are only common interests. The first "game," called in a playful way "The Battle of the Sexes," assumes that a couple would like to spend the night together going to a cinema or a restaurant. The woman prefers the cinema, the man prefers the restaurant. The worst solution for both of them is to carry out one of these activities, or the other, alone. The two equilibrium solutions foresee that they go out together either to the cinema or to the restaurant, which involves a greater advantage for one member of the couple than for the other. Both solutions are in any case preferable to an "individualist" choice, in which everyone does what he or she likes independently. Outside family relations, this game can be applied, for example, in the case of an agreement on sales prices among oil producers (called "cartel"), when one or more oil producers have different production costs in comparison with other producers. All oil producers, in fact, are interested in keeping high price levels and in not entering in mutual competition in this area, but those who have lower costs are also interested in diminishing the prices established by the cartel, hoping to increase in this way their product sales. It is understood that, if this decision were made, it would damage producers who have higher production costs and cannot therefore decrease their prices without running into losses.

In the "Assurance Game," all participants have a common interest that leads them to keep a cooperative behavior, without any contrasting individual interest. It is therefore a different game, compared to all the other "games" considered up to now. In this case, the public good can be fully achieved only if everyone cooperates. As the name of this "game" tells, an example is participation in a collective action depending on the assurance that all the others, too, take part in it. Another example is the choice of a restaurant. Each participant is prepared to choose a particular restaurant, on condition that also the others choose it. In this case, there is no assumption that there are opposite preferences (such as in "The Battle of the Sexes"), but rather that participants succeed in coordinating their choices. The public good, which is achieved through the collective action goal, goes along, in this case (in contrast with the "Prisoner's Dilemma" game), with the value attributed to the participation in the game. Universal participation represents therefore a solution of equilibrium that becomes a dominant strategy. Opportunistic behaviors – such as leaving to others the task of participating in the choice, and enjoying then the public good achieved in this way (for example, a dinner all together) – are not advantageous, because participation (in this case, the choice of a restaurant) receives by itself a positive value. However, opportunistic behaviors are in any case preferable for the single persons compared to non-achievement of a public good due to participants' disagreement (for example, there is no agreement on the choice of the restaurant) or to other people's opportunistic behaviors (Baert 1998: 157–63; Heckathorn 1996: 256–60).

James S. Coleman (1926–1995)

James S. Coleman is one of the most outstanding and controversial representatives of rational choice theory. We shall particularly consider in this case his most famous and influential work, *Foundations of Social Theory* (1990. See also Coleman 1988, 1992, 1994; Coleman and Fararo 1992. Introductions to this work can be found in Frank 1992: 147–62; Lindenberg 2000: 531–9; Ritzer 2000: 296–305). The subject of his explanations is the social system behavior "emerging" from the aggregation of behaviors and orientations in actors who aim at attaining particular purposes (*purposive action*). This action may be carried out to maximize the interests (or utility, or benefit) actors would obtain through the attainment of their purposes. Actors do not always understand or foresee the systemic effects of their actions. There are different ways in which micro-actions combine, thus producing macro-effects. For example, individual actors' actions may involve consequences, or externalities, for others. Or it is possible to proceed from the "macro" (aggregated) explanatory level of the social system to the actors' "micro" level, as their behaviors and orientations are not affected by constraints and systemic opportunities. Or again, only micro-sociological explanations are considered, through which, for example, individual actors' values are related to their behaviors. Finally, it is possible to formulate explanations from a "macro" to a "micro" level and from a "micro" level to a "macro" one.

In the *first part* of his work, Coleman deals with basic (or "elementary") actions and relations. The care of one's interests involves actors making agreements, or transactions, for a rational exchange of resources, which in this case are considered as bundles of rights of control on particular events. Resources may consist of divisible goods (such as economic goods) or indivisible goods (such as, for example, norms), whose fruition cannot be reserved to particular actors (unlike divisible goods). If goods exchanged are of a social nature, the utility actors draw from that exchange cannot be compared. In fact, in that case, there is not a common measurement unit, such as money in economic exchanges. As regards social goods, a maximum satisfaction level may be only established if at the beginning there is among them a distribution of the control on resources and a common system of shared values before the exchange. This condition is here called the "constitution of a system", a social system being actually determined by actors, resources and a constitution.

Given a distribution of resources, a condition of equilibrium is achieved when no participant is damaged by social exchanges, or – if that occurs – when coercive norms safeguard the rights of some participants to control the actions of the others. Those who exert authority, in the sense of the right to control other people's actions, should have freely received it from their subordinates in exchange for expected benefits. A joint authority relation implies that subordinates deem that they share common interests with those who hold that authority (such as the members of a union towards an organization). They may entrust the pursuit of their interests to those who hold that authority, taking no further interest in them: this is the problem of the so-called "profiteers," or "free riders" ("free riders" being those who travel by public transport without paying the ticket). In a disjoint authority relation, such as between superiors and subordinates in a bureaucratic organization, subordinates accept their subordination in exchange for a wage or another reward, and may be not interested in cooperating with the authority. Several constraints limit in any case the authority. When transactions involve a cost – even a non-economic one – duration, and consequently, a risk, their accomplishment demands trust. Trust allows non-profitable actions – in terms of potential gains and losses – for those who give trust.

In the *second part*, Coleman deals with action structures. The necessary elements to determine a social system are actors, resources or events, and the initial distribution of resource control among actors dictates the system constitution. The power of an actor lies in its control on events provided with a value. The value of an event consists in the interests powerful actors have in that event. However, interests are an actors' property and derive from the utility they draw from a good, while value is a property of the system. It consists in the non-monetary gain obtained by exchanging a resource. If resources or events may be assimilated to private goods divisible among actors in competition, a social system is balanced – and therefore, the final distribution of resource control is known – when the actors' interests, their power, and initial distribution are known. If, instead, resources or events cannot be divided among the actors, then it is only possible to determine the influence of each actor on the final control distribution.

In an authority relation, subordinates transfer to others – those who hold that authority – the control on their own actions. If this relation is disjointed, superiors can avail themselves not only of the right to control subordinates' actions (simple authority), but also of the right to transfer this control to their deputies (complex authority). If aggregated, the actions by which some actors grant their trust to others change the social system behavior. In turn, the system by assuming a particular configuration changes individual decisions on whether providing trust, or deserving it. In the systemic phenomena called "collective behavior," everyone unilaterally transfers to others the control of its actions, without, however, necessarily providing the social system they form with equilibrium. Examples of an unbalanced system are the attempts to fly away from a shared danger (for example, a fire).

The question of how and why a norm develops may be treated within rational choice theory. A social norm (which is different from a legal norm) is the right to exert one's control on a particular action when that right is socially established and acknowledged in an informal manner, and is not held by the actor, but by others. The efficiency of a norm depends on its ability to produce benefits rather than costs. If norms are disjointed, the actors who draw from peculiar actions costs exceeding benefits make collectively use of power – in the case they have power at their disposal – in order to form and impose the observance of norms that are in favor of them. The observance of joint norms, too, depends on the existence of powerful and reciprocally organized actors. However, in that case the benefit is granted to all involved actors, and becomes then a public good for those actors. The existence of a public good not only demands that its enjoyment is forbidden to those who have not borne its costs for their share of competence. It also demands that actors are prepared to bear the necessary costs to reward cooperative behaviors, and punish through sanctions non-cooperative behaviors. The larger is the community in which those behaviors occur, the harder it is to punish them. By social capital is meant a set of resources concerning a network of social relationships available to individuals so that they may draw a benefit from them. These resources are systemic, non-individual properties, and reveal themselves in mutual obligations and expectations, whose assumption is being considered trustworthy. Social capital is a public good for all those who draw some benefit from it.

In the *third part*, Coleman deals with the action of corporate actors, such as organizations. These actors are in a position to impose on other actors, who accept them as lawful norms, joint and disjoint norms (depending on who is imposing them and on who is bound by them, whether they coincide or not). Two different groups of interests characterize each corporate actor: those of the single individuals, and those of the corporate actor itself. The corporate actor's action is the result of the interests of each individual actor and its power. Which are the conditions for an optimal constitution, in the sense of maximizing the actors' cost and benefit ratio by reconciling at the same time their opposite interests? With reference to rational choice theory, we can say that the public interest choice made by voters whose sum of weighed interests and power is greater will prevail. This power may even be potential. The outcome of a public interest choice may change if at the beginning, the choice is made among several courses of action, instead of between two alternatives only.

If we consider corporate actors, such as organizations, as action systems, we can make within them a distinction between principals and their salaried agents, at different authority levels, ranging from managers to workers. Individual actors' costs and benefits should be proportioned to the organization ones. Differently from what happens in a market context, actors' rights and obligations, and hence their relations, are in fact submitted to constraints concerning the positions they formally hold in the organization structure. Bearing in mind that an organization is in the position to balance possible imbalances in the relations among individual participants, it needs to find its own global viability between the benefits granted to participants and the contributions requested to them. The difficulty in precisely measuring the benefits and marginal contributions the organization is asked to provide to and request from each participant makes it difficult for it to achieve a global viability.

New constitutions (in the sense of new stipulations of actors' rights and obligations) – such as the co-partnership of employees' representatives in corporate decisions provided for by the law in Germany – aim at harmonizing the organization's collective goals with those of the individual components. If events relevant for persons who have an interest in an organization – because, for example, they are working in it – are subtracted from their control to a large extent, these persons decrease their level of satisfaction and trust in the organization, which in turn may suffer damage. Holding to a micro-level explanation, trust in an authority depends on its actual power, evidenced by its ability to reward and punish. We assume, in that case, the actor rationally pursues its personal interests despite the environment complexity. The more an actor takes into account how other actors' interests may change, hamper or encourage its personal interests, the more it is rational.

In an organization, the corporate actor can always achieve an optimal control on individual actors, when their respective interests coincide. If this does not happen, then control is achieved if the corporate actor's interests – such as they can be deduced from its behavior – derive from those of more powerful individual actors, or if a particular set of interests (for example, religious interests) links both the actors one to another, and the corporate actor (to the community). The single actor's interests form the motivations of its action and, in this sense, its inner world. Actor's identification with others changes its relations with the outer world, with which the actor relates in a variety of ways.

In the *fourth part*, Coleman applies his theory to modern society, and particularly refers to organizations, considered as impersonal and corporate actors. These actors control most rights and existing resources, and hence, sovereignty and power, though their rights find their origin in persons' consent. The legal conception of a corporate subject (corporation) distinguishes the rights of that subject from those of natural persons. The latter, if acting within and on behalf of a corporate subject, such as an organization, have two different kinds of resources at their disposal: their own ones and those that belong to that subject. The relations between organizations and natural persons, which are increasingly frequent in modern societies, often involve a power asymmetry in favor of organizations. Relations among organizations are increasingly numerous as well. The interests an organization must take into account are consequently various and different, either inside the organization, or outside the company, but represented or institutionally safeguarded in it. A single economic system, including interdependent companies, has partly taken the place of a number of domestic economies, mostly not depending on each other. Domestic economy, in turn, has split as a consumption unit as soon as the number of generations and members has decreased. This new social structure has negative consequences on the making of the social capital.

The erosion of the previously existing social capital, which used to ensure obligation observance and personal reliability, and allowed individuals to cover their social and economic needs, has made a new social science necessary. This new social science has the task of showing how power is socially spread and accumulated, and how persons can better satisfy their interests in a social system where large-size corporate actors, which can only partly replace families and local communities, use to prevail. As regards bureaucratic organizations, an efficient right allocation should be in the position to overcome the problem of non-disinterested and opportunistic behaviors kept by those who operate within the organization itself. Similarly, the problem of conflicting interests in multinational corporations, which have no territorial borders and do control the economic power, with those of the nations that exert their sovereignty on established territories and keep some properties of the pre-modern corporate actors, must be solved. These properties do not originate from their being composed by social positions, but by natural persons. A new social science should be appropriate to the new social structure. It should create theoretical knowledge and apply it, in order to put opportunities to good use and avoid any associated problem.

The *fifth part* aims at better explaining the different passages – from a micro-analytical level to a macro one, and vice versa – occurring within the social system. As we previously mentioned, actors are interested in controlling resources, or events, and in the consequences of those resources for the actors themselves. To simplify, the author first assumes that:

• these resources may be compared with divisible economic goods;
• the greater is the good utility for the actors, the more they are interested in it;
• the greater is the quantity of goods actors have available, the smaller is the good utility;
• actors who do not have at their disposal a sufficient quantity of goods, are interested in using them in a rational way, and if possible, to obtain these goods in the desired quantities through exchanges with other actors. This exchange is of a social nature. For example, personal favors may be exchanged, but not using money.

In the light of these assumptions, given an initial distribution of goods among actors and their preferences about desired quantities, in a perfect social system (that is, without relations with the outside, and with rational and reciprocally reachable actors), two actors engaged in exchanging a good reach an equilibrium if an increase or a decrease in exchanged quantities reduces the utility for either actor. If there are different points of equilibrium, actors have the possibility of mutually exchanging goods in different quantities and always maximize the utility they draw from exchange. The proportions in which goods are exchanged and the final distribution of goods between the two actors are properties of the exchange system resulting ("emerging") from exchange. The starting properties of this system are the norms, or institutional rules, that control exchange and the initial distribution of each actor's preferences.

The presence of more than two actors creates a situation of competition among them. In perfect competition conditions, there is equilibrium between demand and offer of goods in all actors, and the power of each actor is given by the sum of all the values it possesses. The total amount of value in a social system is provided by the sum of both the powers of all actors and the value of all goods: both sums are identical. The actors' interests in particular resources or events, and resources themselves are of a micro-sociological kind. In turn, the value of a resource and the power of an actor are properties of the social system. The actors – who at the beginning have all the same power at their disposal – may at the end of the exchanges have a different amount of power at their disposal, and hence a different control over resources and interests in comparison with the initial situation. Stronger actors do not care about norms and associated sanctions, because these actors know that norms and sanctions would not affect them. On the other hand, weaker actors observe the norms, because they know that otherwise they would become indictable. Sanctions are therefore virtual, that is, they are never applied. In a perfect social system, the social capital is complete and resources are perfectly transferable. Actors' interests, jointly considered, may be divided into two components. The active component shows actors' psychological investments in other actors. The passive component considers actors as receptors of events placed under other people's control.

The simplified or basic theory assumes that individuals considered as receptors of events have the same importance as if they were considered active subjects. Events (or resources) depend on other events through actors' mediation. In the so-called "expanded" theory, instead, there is no actors' mediation, and events directly depend on other events. A structure of reciprocally dependent events, in which actors are interested, has consequences (or "externalities") on the actors, although they have power at their disposal. A perfect social system may be divided into two sets, or groups, of actors (for example a group of students and their teachers), or resources (for example, economic and political resources). The interdependence of the two groups amplifies the number of transactions. In a non-perfect social system, transactions between an actor and any other controlling resources the actor may consider interesting, involve losses in the value of what has been exchanged. This happens because these transactions are subject to constraints, whether legal ones or of a different nature, outside the system, and hence its costs are not inexistent. The condition of equilibrium in a generalized economic exchange therefore is absent.

Non-perfect social systems are closer to reality, but it is not clear how a rational actor should behave in those systems. In a social exchange, rational actors try to assess whether and how much their potential partners deserve trust, and act accordingly. To achieve a condition of equilibrium among participants, mutual trust is more relevant than the interest in what the other actor controls. If an actor does not enjoy the trust of all the others, then it has a reduced power at its disposal in comparison with the others, and less control on their actions. Finally, if one or more actors mistrust the others, they have – compared to the others – a greater power and a lesser interest in their actions. In a social system, individual interests are evaluated, or weighted, starting from an initial resource (for example, richness or power) allocation, based on the quantity of resources the individual actors control, and consequently, the associated impact of their interests on the distribution in the social system of interests, rights and resources.

Different resources are evaluated by the social system in terms of power. However, the existence of social norms, along with sanctions, appears as a constraint in the use of those resources, and changes power distribution accordingly. This is particularly important as regards the norm of not causing damage to the others. The sanctions that go along with this norm may be ineffective, either because they are too slight, or because some actors do not have wealth or power enough at their disposal to make the safeguard of their rights profitable. If for any actor the weighted interest to implement a norm individually is lower than the weighted interests of others who set themselves against the actor's implementation of that norm, then everybody is interested in handing over the implemental rights to the community. This is a pure case of a prohibition norm characterized by a general acknowledgement of public utility. In real social systems, the accomplishment of such norms (joint norms) is made easier by transferring the implemental rights from the person who carries out an action to the person who suffers its consequences, and also by an utmost extension of the social capital and reduced transaction costs.

In the case of disjoint norms, instead, the persons whose behaviors are the object of norms (for example, children) are different from those who are interested in their observance and benefit from it (for example, adults). Only the latter are obliged to consider those norms lawful. A difference in interests and a power inequality in favor of the beneficiaries are necessary in order to implement those norms and inflict sanctions in case of non-observance. Furthermore, norm compliance grows if an infringement involves definite costs. Norms take shape, or 'emerge,' when there are interests in this direction, along with sufficient power. If the social capital is lacking, application chances in rational actors grow proportionally to the control on the others an actor has at its disposal. Infringing a binding norm may not turn advantageous even to powerful actors in the position to avoid sanctions, if observing a norm that is beneficial to everybody would help consolidating it. When several actors unite in order to carry out a project of common advantage, its realization involves observing the norm according to which each actor must contribute to the project if it does not want to incur the other actors' sanctions. Both the project and the sanction become a public good for them (that is, for all of them together, but not for an individual actor in particular).

The control of indivisible resources involves two different stages. In the first stage, called "constitutional" stage, norms are formulated that establish which actors (for example, those who have the right to vote) and through which procedures (for example, electoral ones) the rights of control on particular kinds of resources have to be allocated. In the second stage, called "post-constitutional" stage, the control over resources for which the rights have been allocated is acquired. The post-constitutional stage assumes there are actors provided with authority, and therefore legitimated to make decisions in the name and on behalf of the community. Control of events or resources, such as it was in the authority original intentions, changes in favor of concentrated interests and to the detriment of dispersed ones, which have difficulties in finding representation.

In real social systems, which are not perfect, decision-making rules are important as regards achieved results. The consent rule assumes a general agreement, after a discussion, and does not explicitly provide for vote procedures. By this rule, one implicitly takes into account, such as in the majority rule, that there are different interests supported by different powers. Only the unanimity rule does not consider different interests; each negative vote corresponds, in this case, to a right of veto. The results of a decision-making process are unstable when interests are not weighted up according to their power (this is actually the case of the unanimity rule), and the interests outside the system have no relevance. Any decision-making rule grants power to the person who expresses a negative vote, but this becomes particularly important in the unanimity rule. The majority rule may produce instability in decisions made. This outcome is further emphasized if external interests are represented in the decision-making process.

In a social exchange system, we can distinguish two different processes. In the first place, an adjustment of the values of the resource quantities some actors are prepared to hand over to the values of other resource quantities, which other actors are prepared to provide in exchange in order to get those goods. In conditions of equilibrium between demand and offer, the demand and offer values coincide. In the second place, adjustments of the resource quantities are exchanged by the actors to the values that are established in conditions of equilibrium. After that adjustment, both the distribution of the resources owned by an actor, and the group of actors who are in possession of a given resource may change. In exchanges among actors (in conditions of equilibrium), the interests of an actor in a resource are weighed up through the power, or control, the actor exerts on that resource. In the case of several actors, both exchanged quantities, and the values to which they have been exchanged are interdependent. Being a social exchange (without the use of money), since several exchange means are used, there are barriers that reduce the actors' interest in making transactions. In addition, the equilibrium values between demand and offer can be reached more slowly under those circumstances, or cannot be reached at all. Finally, we should consider that there may be new events or resources; or new actors provided with their own resources; or, to conclude, some of the already present actors may leave the system and take away the resources which they control.

If the social system is not balanced, the effects may sometimes become disruptive on the system, as some collective behaviors evidence. In a first case (*single-contingency collective behavior*), everybody – trying to maximize his or her personal utility without being concerned about that of the others – carries out an individual action that, aggregated with the others' action, produces general damage (such as in the case of behaviors, produced by panic, on the part of investors who withdraw all together their savings). In a second case (*double-contingency collective behavior*), everybody carries out a set of actions which, combining with other actors' sets, brings disadvantage to some actors (as it happens in the case of sacking and lynching) or to all of them (as it happens when all the spectators try to reach the exit of a closed place in which a fire has burst out, with the result of blocking one another). Knowing other actors' relevant characteristics makes it easier to predict whether the others will follow cooperative behaviors, that is, cooperation for the common good. Panic behaviors, which are disruptive for the social system, may be prevented in different ways, particularly through the development of norms against such behaviors. The observance of those norms becomes more probable if it is due to the one who benefits from them to inflict sanctions rather than to the one who contributes to their costs, and if the actors have at their disposal the social capital that may reduce those costs.

The natural actors' action systems do not coincide with those of the corporate actors. The latter, such as the former, have interests, control resources, set goals, and pursue them trying to maximize their utility, but differently from the former actors, they can neither interiorize norms, nor become socialized. If two corporate actors are interested in achieving reciprocally incompatible outcomes, the actor prevails whose interest in a result, weighed up with its degree of control on it, is greater. The overall system interest in a resource is given by the sum of actors' interests, weighed up with the power they have at their disposal on that resource. The subordinate actors' weighted interests go to make up the corporate actor's interest. The corporate actor, in turn, is included in a wider system that forms its environment. The corporate actor's interest (for example, an organization) does not necessarily conform to what the environment (for example, the market) offers and demands, thus compromising its own viability opportunities. Actors – being natural persons – may develop an internal constitution, that is, norms that are valid for themselves and in the position to assign right and resource allocation. The internal constitution rationality consists in the ability to produce actions, which allow a person to achieve the highest possibilities of survival.

The Reception of Coleman's Works

This reception, particularly as regards *Foundations of Social Theory*, has been conspicuous in quantitative terms, but not unanimous. It has emphasized the proximity of Coleman's conception of rationality with that widespread among economists. It has also emphasized the fact that Coleman's theory shares the assumptions characterizing rational choice theory. We refer, in particular, to the following assumptions:

a. methodological individualism;
b. pursuit of a maximum benefit (or, in the economic language, a maximum utility) on the part of properly informed actors;

c. and consequently, making optimal choices within a range of possible options;
d. existence of constraints in making those choices, due to scarce resources and existing institutional bonds;
e. existence of individual choice aggregation mechanisms. We can – however with some inaccuracy – maintain that some important scholars, whose theoretical orientation coincides with that of rational choice theory, or is close to it, have expressed themselves positively, although with some important reservations. On the other hand, Coleman's reception among scholars close to different sociological approaches has been mostly negative, and in some case even totally negative.

We shall jointly consider in this paragraph the comments of these two groups of scholars. Among the positive evaluations, some commentators have appreciated Coleman's attempt to provide a clear formulation and a convincing argumentation to his sociological theory. This theory has been deemed to be, at once, unitary, comprehensive and suited to conduct empirical research. As a unitary theory, it starts from considering individual actors who, by pursuing their personal interests, stipulate agreements with others; this theory, however, is at loggerheads with the current tendency to fragmentation of this discipline. As a comprehensive theory, Coleman's theory dwells upon the connections between micro and macro levels in the social system, specifies the procedures or mechanisms through which those connections are operating, and points to a wide-ranging application sphere in some particular theoretical and research fields. These fields are, for example, the development of social norms, the concept of social capital, and the occurrence of collective actions, such as behaviors prompted by panic. As a scientifically fruitful theory, it can explain in terms of costs and benefits, interests and available resources, power legitimacy and uneven distribution, many interactions occurring in everyday life, such as the development of a relationship based on trust or subordination (see, in particular, Favell 1996; Frank 1992: 147–8, 152; Lindenberg 2000: 540; Zablocki 1996).

Critical remarks have particularly concerned a plurality of theses discussed in *Foundations of Social Theory*. Some of these critical comments may be extended to rational choice theory in general, but they mostly refer to this work by Coleman in particular. Among these comments, we wish to mention the following ones (see Ahrne 1991; Alexander 1992; Dahlbaeck 1991; Frank 1992; Hannan 1992; Lindenberg 1996, 2000: 540–41; Rambo 1995; Rawls 1992; Sica 1992; Stinchcombe 1992; Tilly 1997):

a. For an individual, the utility of a kind of good usually also depends on the utility, and hence, the quantities, of the other kinds of good, whilst the utility function assumed by Coleman does only consider a particular kind of good.
b. More in general, Coleman's theory does not sufficiently consider the consequences and interdependences of individual rational decisions: for example, on the effects mediated by the environment, as in the case of economic or demographic change. Its consideration would involve a parametric, instead of an instrumental, rationality.
c. Coleman's theory has produced a number of more specific theories, which have not been verified so far. Moreover, Coleman's theory lends itself, by focusing on exchanges between rational actors who transfer rights of control, to be one-sided in its description and explanation of social events and processes.
d. The connection between the actors' "macro" and "micro" analytical level has not been sufficiently investigated.
e. This theory does not explain how norms may be developed without the actors' conscious intention in this direction. More in general, this theory neglects the meaning of action, which constitutes its humanly and theoretically significant aspect. It cannot therefore explain how shared meanings and collective actions are formed.
f. Coleman's theory of action, which assumes independent and rational individuals, is so simplistic that it cannot even account for the statements and theses supported by the author himself. The explanations, which Coleman each time provides, are not linked to and consistent with his theory of action.
g. Whether the relation between organizations and the outer social and political system, which is a source of opportunities (and particularly, rights) and constraints (and particularly, norms), has been examined or not, considering organizations as rational actors leads to a different evaluation of the power asymmetry between organizations and natural persons.

h. The allocation of the rights of control on resources (the "constitution," in Coleman's language) and the consequent institutionalization of norms and values cannot only result from actors' different interests in the resources to be distributed. This distribution is also determined by the power, which a shared culture exerts on actors, by establishing what the most appropriate allocation principles are.

i. Coleman does not consider the set of meanings and feelings to which actors refer when they act, since actors are conceived as rational and separate units. Consequently, social order is explained implausibly as a result of transactions taking place among actors. By pursuing their interests, those actors transfer to others – whether private or public organizations – the right of control on a part of their resources. After this transfer, actors, meant as natural persons, lose their independence in favor of those organizations, which hold rights, responsibilities, purposes and constraints. Therefore, the assumption of an actor who, as a natural person, rationally and freely pursues its personal goals loses its meaning.

j. External, or monetary, costs and benefits are not always important in developing and keeping social norms, while the consideration of internal, or psychological, costs and benefits is incompatible with the assumption of an actor who rationally pursues its own ends.

k. Likewise the development of a trust relationship is not necessarily the consequence of considerations foreshadowing an advantage, as is proved by numberless examples of cooperation among unknown persons.

l. Individuals' choices are rarely independent from some forms of legal authority. Therefore, setting these choices as a theoretical assumption makes this theory non-realistic.

m. There are many cases of disjoint authority in an organization (where subordinates hand over the control on their own actions to others in exchange for a reward) in which norms assert themselves, such as those of a particular organizational culture, which have nothing to do with the existence of material rewards.

n. The dominating power of organizations on those who work within them does not depend on the organizations' size. Rather, they depend on employees' competition for achieving privileged positions.

o. Actors evaluate the rationality of an action according to the interpretation they give to the context of meaning, in which the action itself is placed. In rational choice theory, not taking into account individuals' moral feelings or solidarity ties leads to wrong prediction of their behaviors, and of the overall power distribution.

To a part of this criticism, Coleman answered arguing that:

1. A set of beliefs and actions creates, maintains or destroys the rights that are transferred. Actions, on one side, and beliefs, on the other side, are in turn changed through external incentives, but also through norm and value interiorization, as Coleman himself points out (cf. points a, g, i).

2. The control on resources is partly held collectively, and – in the case of democratic governments – the exercise of the rights of control takes place under the electorate control. Furthermore, organizations do not only impose new constraints to natural persons, but do also provide them with new opportunities (cf. points b, c, d).

Evaluations of the Rational Choice Theory

The rational choice theory has been, and still is, a matter of contrasting opinions, which may be classified into different groups:

a. Positive evaluations without reservations, such as those made by Becker (1993) and Coleman (1986, 1990); or,

b. Cautiously positive evaluations, in which space is given to a consideration of the limits of this theoretical current of thought. Elster (cf. 1983, 1984, 1989a, 1989b, 2000a) is the author to whom reference will be mostly made in this regard; or again,

c. Balanced evaluations, in which the cognitive contribution of rational choice theory is acknowledged, along with the need to amend its gaps and integrate it with different perspectives. Among other scholars, Collins formulates this kind of evaluation; or, finally,

d. Absolutely negative evaluations, which come from commentators close to theoretical currents of thought, which underline the need to consider the sense of actions non-schematically. Denzin (1990) and Sica (1992) are examples of this current, while other scholars, such as Baert (1998) and Green and Shapiro (1994), prefer instead to remark its methodological and empirical deficiencies.

Positive Evaluations

The most definite support to rational choice theory has been provided by a well-known economist, Gary Becker. Becker is aware that it is not possible to explain all human behaviors as the result of actors' intention to maximize their benefits (or utilities, in the economic language), given their preferences, or after having achieved an optimal amount of information. However, he argues that following this assumption provides an explanatory pattern that can be extensively applied (Becker 1986, 1993). This evaluation is fully shared by Coleman. In Coleman's opinion, the most appropriate theoretical strategy in sociology is to consider the action of actors who, acting interdependently, establish a social system as if it were oriented to a purpose (*purposive action*). In fact, this strategy has the double advantage – according to Coleman – of allowing precise predictions about actors' future behavior, and of being simple; for a goal-rational action rationally is actually simple. These qualities make it possible to rigorously ascertain whether, and to what extent, this theory holds in a variety of application areas. Coleman maintains (Coleman 1986: 1312; 1990: 13–19) that often actors do not actually act rationally, but rather according to their interpretation of problems and of the available options. Therefore, this cannot be considered an objection to its use (Tversky and Kahneman 1986). Coleman's thesis about the theoretical opportunity of not giving importance to the doubtful empirical assumptions of rational choice theory has been found objectionable, as we shall see in the following paragraph.

Positive Evaluations with Some Reservations and Restrictions

Elster shares with the previously mentioned authors and with some other commentators (Abell 1992: 203) the opinion that rational choice theory, by virtue of its assumption that actors are "by and large rational" (Elster 1990b: 26), is "without much doubt the best available model" for explaining human behavior (Elster 1984: 112). This is so because this assumption makes mutual understanding, and hence communication, possible and not depending on other assumptions, and also because other assumptions have proved highly inadequate. Elster himself, however, points to the limits of the explanatory ability of this assumption when reference is made to a narrow meaning of rationality. An optimality assumption is not maintained because information collection stops as soon as the actors consider it "satisficing," and hence enough for their purposes. Therefore, a social action researcher does not have an available theoretical apparatus, by means of which it is possible to know when this information may be actually considered "satisficing." Accordingly, information collection continues as long as individual preferences demand it, but this point cannot be foreseen or established a priori (Elster 1989a: 35–6; 1989b: 29–30).

Since different elements involve uncertainty about the choice of the best course of action, and consequently limit the explanatory and predicting ability of rational choice theory, it is impossible to make a single optimal choice. Alternatively, there are no optimal choices. In the first place, given a set of beliefs and a given quantity of empirical evidence, there may be either several optimal actions or none at all. In particular, there is no optimal action when the actor is not in the position to evaluate and compare two by two all the options (the feasible set) it has available, as it is the case when the actor has to compare the utilities of different actors, or when the temporal horizon considered in this comparison is infinite. On the other hand, it would be irrational to compare the entire feasible set of options due to the high costs involved in terms of time, engaged energies, and even money. The problem, which Elster points out, is particularly relevant. In fact, we should bear in mind that many non-cooperative games (such as, for example, the "Prisoner's Dilemma") have several points of equilibrium, and hence, several suboptimal actions (Harsanyi 1987: 102).

The elements of uncertainty that will be considered now do not derive from the presence of several optimal actions, but rather from their non-existence, and therefore from the impossibility of making a rational choice. In the second place, given an established amount of empirical evidence, it might not be rational for an individual to have well-grounded beliefs. It is in fact possible that the actor may get benefits or avoid damages even if it is in possession of false information (for example, an overconfidence in its individual abilities may lead an actor to persist in a course of action which, thanks also to other circumstances, turns at the end into a success). Furthermore, well-grounded beliefs may not turn into consistent actions, because of one's weakness of will, as it happens to persons who, though being fully aware of the benefits of a regular physical activity, always postpone the moment of beginning it. Weakness of will may be the consequence of passions that dim one's judgment on the consequences of actions, or derive from desires that have something that cannot be achieved as a goal. Therefore, due to a psychological mechanism of adaptation, that goal is perceived as less desirable than before, or less preferred than other goals. Again, well-grounded beliefs may remain without any effect because of errors about the correct way of putting these beliefs into practice.

In the third place, an individual may not be in the position to make an opinion on the behavior of others who are equally involved in a non-cooperative game; because each participant has the opportunity to make its choice among several optimal actions, and the other participants do not know which option will be chosen. We must remember that the previously described game called "The Battle of the Sexes" provides for two different solutions of equilibrium equally preferable, compared to other solutions not welcomed by both participants (whether not going to a cinema or a restaurant, or going there alone). In the fourth place, given a set of pre-existing desires and beliefs, the amount of empirical evidence one can rationally achieve may be undetermined, because the marginal costs the search for further information would involve, as well as the marginal benefits that would derive from them, are neither known nor assessable (Elster 1983: 123–4, 143–57; 1986: 17–22; 1989a: 30–41; 1989b: 1–35; Elster 2000a: 8–11).

Further objections concern the cases in which rational choice theory does not show any explanatory or predicting ability. This theory does not explain how preferences form, and is not compatible with the preference inconsistency and instability empirical inquiries have highlighted when persons must choose among several options. Again, the revealed preference thesis is untenable. According to this thesis – frequently adopted by some representatives of this theory – a choice reveals, without any need to make reference to the actor's motivations, its preference (revealed preference). In fact, a choice should be interpreted with reference to sensible psychological assumptions. Finally, a choice does not indicate the actors' preferences when their choices are interdependent. This process is well described by the "Prisoner's Dilemma," in which actors rationally make choices that are scarcely advantageous (or suboptimal, in rational choice theory language) for them (Baert 1998: 168–9; Sen 1986; Tversky and Kahneman 1986).

Balanced Evaluations

Some further evaluations of this perspective have equally acknowledged its explanatory abilities, but have also emphasized the theoretical and methodological problems its use may involve. We shall mention here only a few comments expressed by some famous scholars who, though being not close to rational choice theory, are however not hostile to it. As regards theoretical problems, Goldthorpe (1998) upholds the opportunity of making use of a "subjective" conception of rationality that systematically dwells upon the conditions that lead an actor to act rationally from its point of view, and upon the criteria through which it is possible to distinguish from the outside (particularly, as regards sociologists) a subjectively rational action from another one that is not so. Instead of saying that this perspective has a general explanatory ability, it is preferable to show which are the bases, or assumptions, of non-rationality. Collins (1988, 1996) argues that rational choice theory – on condition it provides a non-restricted conception of rationality – may contribute in bringing greater unity among the different theoretical currents, though a complete theoretical unification is not possible. Though being prepared to acknowledge the merits of this perspective, Collins reminds us that individuals seldom engage themselves in cost and benefit estimates, since they rather take for granted the definition of situation and social reality that prevails in a contingent circumstance. Therefore, rational choice theory must be integrated by a micro-social process model that may consider emotions as an incentive to action.

Friedman and Hechter (1988) underline that rational choice theory is concerned about relating the micro- and macro-analysis levels, and remark that this theory is in the position to explain a variety of empirical phenomena. However, they also call attention to the doubtful empirical foundation of some assumptions of this theory, such as the actors' tendency to maximize the expected utility (that is, the benefits actors expect from their actions) and the stability of their preferences. These authors, and some other commentators as well (for example, Abell 2000: 233–5; Mooney Marini 1992), do not share Coleman's position, according to which these empirical deficiencies would not have any theoretical importance. On the contrary, in their opinion, within this theoretical current there is no empirically validated explanation on how preferences are formed. Bohman (1992; see also Mooney Marini 1992: 33–42) expresses some critical remarks that are not basically different. He does not deny the ability of rational choice theory (considered in the narrow sense) to explain social action, when it is the consequence of individuals' desires formed according to their beliefs. This author, however, maintains that this cannot be a globally applicable explanatory theory, considering the limits of its assumptions. Its intentionality and optimality assumptions cannot be applied except for some actions, conventions, and norms. As regards the latter, in particular, an irrational coercion deriving from their socio-institutional environment is often in the position to better explain these behavioral regularities.

There are several methodological problems pointed out by literature:

a. A tendency to provide explanations, compatible with rational choice theory, about any detected empirical regularity. It is always possible to find a posteriori some good reason for it, that is, a plausible explanatory mechanism, without worrying about formulating different explanations incompatible with this theory.

b. A tendency to formulate theoretical propositions in such a way as to make it impossible to actually verify them. Empirical data (such as tastes, preferences, decisional rules) cannot in fact be directly observed, and therefore have to be interpreted as confirmations, or non-denials, of theoretical predictions.

c. Finally, a tendency to dwell upon empirical cases that confirm this theory, instead of dwelling upon discordant cases (Baert 1998: 166–7; Green and Shapiro 1994: 33–46).

Negative Evaluations

Some evaluations are mostly, or totally, critical, because of a claimed incompatibility of rational choice theory with a sufficiently profound understanding of action, due to the methodological deficiencies it has been charged of, and finally, because its assumptions are empirically untenable. We shall now briefly refer to these critical comments, and group them into two different types. The first kind of criticism, which is also shared by symbolic interactionism and ethnomethodology, is focused on the different and contrasting ways in which lived experience is interpreted, depending on whether prevails a typical everyday-life attitude, or instead, a typically scientific inquiry attitude carried out with the purpose of formulating theories. These two attitudes differ in the strictness by which one aims at achieving consistency between aims and means; by which clearness and specificity in concept meaning is sought, these purposes being pursued in themselves when the scientific attitude is prevailing; by which, finally, the definition of a situation (for example, a course of action) is compatible with the scientific knowledge on that matter.

The difference between these two attitudes is such that rational choice theory is not in a position to provide a description and an account of the conduct usually followed in everyday life. Emotions and feelings, such as solidarity among the members of a group, therefore remain outside its explanatory range (Denzin 1990; Garfinkel 1984: 262–83). To this objection, formulated by Denzin and particularly addressed to Hechter (1987), Elster replies – perhaps unwittingly – showing how a rational actor can and must protect itself against the undesirable consequences produced by a deployment of emotions and passions (Elster 2000a: 7–24).

A second kind of criticism concerns the social actor model adopted by rational choice theory, and hence, methodological individualism and intentionality assumption. Beliefs and desires of an actor do not satisfy both the consistency condition and the causal condition, which are indicated in the assumptions of rational choice theory. In fact, beliefs and desires are not necessarily stable and consistent, and do not necessarily reflect in the actors' intentions, or in the behaviors that may derive from them. Again, the identification of beliefs, desires and intentions, and in general the actors' mental states and the meanings they want to give to what they do, may be deduced only in an uncertain way from their behaviors. Uncertainty grows particularly when actors belong to different cultures from that of the researcher. Attributing to them intentions conforming to rational choice theory (for example, obtaining, whether for oneself or for others, benefits that are expected because some behaviors have been accomplished) exempts from carrying out a potentially illuminating inquiry on the motivations specific actors had to perform those particular actions in some circumstances.

In addition, this theory does not consider that often actions are not a direct consequence of beliefs, desires and intentions, but there is instead, prior to action, a deliberation, which can avail itself of a variety of considerations, techniques and procedures the actor deems adequate, and an external observer may not know or imagine. Finally, social actors may not be natural persons, but corporate actors, such as companies, parties, governments. In that case, the methodological individualism assumption can be hardly maintained (Baert 1998: 167–8; Hindess 1988).

References

Abell, P. 1992. Is Rational Choice Theory a Rational Choice of Theory?, in J.S. Coleman andT.J. Fararo (eds), *Rational Choice Theory: Advocacy and Critique*. Newbury Park, CA: Sage, 183–206.

Abell, P. 2000. Sociological Theory and Rational Choice Theory, in B.S. Turner (ed.), *The Blackwell Companion to Social Theory*. Oxford: Blackwell, 223–44.

Ahrne, G. 1991. "Book Review." *Acta Sociologica* 34: 140–41.

Alexander, J.C. 1992. "Shaky Foundations: The Presuppositions and Internal Contradictions of James Coleman's Foundations of Social Theory." *Theory and Society* 21: 203–17.

Baert, P. 1998. *Social Theory in the Twentieth Century*. Cambridge: Polity Press. Italian translation: *La teoria sociale contemporanea*, 2002, Bologna: Il Mulino.

Becker, G.S. 1986. The Economic Approach to Human Behavior, in J. Elster (ed.), *Rational Choice*. Oxford: Blackwell, 108–22.

Becker, G.S. 1993. "Nobel Lecture: The Economic Way of Looking at Behavior." *Journal of Political Economy* 101: 385–409.

Bianco, M.L. 2001. Prefazione, in M.L. Bianco (ed.), *L'Italia delle diseguaglianze*. Rome: Carocci, 11–21.

Bohman, J. 1992. The Limits of Rational Choice Explanation, in J. Clark (ed.), *James S. Coleman*. London: The Falmer Press, 207–28.

Boudon, R. 1981a. Undesirable Consequences and Types of Structures of Systems of Interdependence, in P.M. Blau and R. Merton (eds), *Continuities in Structural Inquiry*. London: Sage, 255–84.

Boudon, R. 1981b. *Effetti perversi dell'azione sociale*. Milan: Feltrinelli.

Boudon, R. 1998. "Limitations of Rational Choice Theory." *American Journal of Sociology* 104: 817–28.

Boudon, R. 2003. "Beyond Rational Choice Theory." *Annual Review of Sociology* 29: 1–21.

Coleman, J.S. 1986. "Social Theory, Social Research, and a Theory of Action." *American Journal of Sociology* 91: 1309–35.

Coleman, J.S. 1988. "Social Capital in the Creation of Human Capital." *American Journal of Sociology* 94: S95–S120.

Coleman, J.S. 1990a. *Foundations of Social Theory*. Cambridge, MA: Harvard University Press.

Coleman, J.S. 1990b. Rational Action, Social Networks, and the Emergence of Norms, in C. Calhoun, M.W. Meyer and W.R. Scott (eds), *Structures of Power and Constraint*. Cambridge: Cambridge University Press, 91–112.

Coleman, J.S. 1992. "The Problematics of Social Theory." *Theory and Society* 21: 261–83.

Coleman, J.S. 1994. A Rational Choice Perspective on Economic Sociology, in N.J. Smelser and R. Swedberg (eds), *The Handbook of Economic Sociology*. London: Sage, 166–80.

Coleman, J.S. 1996. A Vision for Sociology, in J. Clark (ed.), *James S. Coleman*. London: Falmer Press, 343–9.

Coleman, J.S. and Fararo, T.J. 1992. Introduction, in J.S. Coleman and T.J. Fararo (eds), *Rational Choice Theory: Advocacy and Critique*. London: Sage.

Collins, R. 1988. *Theoretical Sociology*. Orlando, FL: Harcourt Brace Jovanovich. Italian translation: *Teorie sociologiche*, 1992, Bologna: Il Mulino.

Collins, R. 1996. Can Rational Action Theory Unify Future Social Science?, in J. Clark (ed.), *James S. Coleman*. London: The Falmer Press.

Dahlbaeck, O. 1991. "Book Review." *Acta Sociologica* 34: 139–40.

Denzin, N. 1990. "Reading Rational Choice Theory." *Rationality and Society* 2: 172–89.

Elster, J. 1983. *Sour Grapes*. Cambridge: Cambridge University Press.

Elster, J. 1984. *Ulysses and the Sirens: Studies in Rationality and Irrationality*. Cambridge: Cambridge University Press.

Elster, J. 1985. *Making Sense of Marx*. Cambridge: Cambridge University Press.

Elster, J. 1986. Introduction, in J. Elster (ed.), *Rational Choice*. Oxford: Blackwell, 1–33.

Elster, J. 1989a. *Nuts and Bolts for the Social Sciences*. Cambridge: Cambridge University Press.

Elster, J. 1989b. *Solomonic Judgements*. Cambridge: Cambridge University Press.

Elster, J. 1995. *The Cement of Society*. Cambridge: Cambridge University Press. Italian translation: *Il cemento della società*, 1995, Bologna: Il Mulino.

Elster, J. 2000a. *Ulysses Unbound: Studies in Rationality, Precommitment, and Constraints*. Cambridge: Cambridge University Press.

Elster, J. 2000b. Rationality, Economy, and Society, in S. Turner (ed.), *The Cambridge Companion to Weber*. Cambridge: Cambridge University Press, 21–41.

Favell, A. 1996. Rational Choice as Grand Theory: James Coleman's Normative Contribution to Social Theory, in J.S. Coleman and T.J. Fararo (eds), *Rational Choice Theory: Advocacy and Critique*. London: Sage, 285–98.

Friedman, M. and Hechter, M. 1988. "The Contribution of Rational Choice Theory to Macrosociological Research." *Sociological Theory* 6: 201–18.

Frank, R.H. 1992. "Melding Sociology and Economics: James Coleman's *Foundations of Social Theory*." *Journal of Economic Literature* 30: 147–70.

Garfinkel, H. 1984. *Studies in Ethnomethodology*. Cambridge, Polity Press.

Goldthorpe, J.H. 1998. "Rational Action Theory for Sociology." *British Journal of Sociology* 49: 167–92.

Green, D. and Shapiro, I. 1994. *Pathologies of Rational Choice Theory*. New Haven, CT: Yale University Press.

Hannan, M.T. 1992. Rationality and Robustness in Multilevel Systems, in J.S. Coleman and T.J. Fararo (eds), *Rational Choice Theory: Advocacy and Critique*. London: Sage, 120–36.

Harsanyi, J.C. 1987. Advances in Understanding Rational Behavior, in J. Elster (ed.), *Rational Choice*. Oxford: Blackwell, 82–107.

Heckathorn, D.D. 1990. "Collective Sanctions and Compliance Norms: A Formal-Theory of Group-Mediated Social Control." *American Sociological Review* 55: 336–84.

Heckathorn, D.D. 1993. "Collective Action and Group Heterogeneity: Voluntary Provisions versus Selective Incentives." *American Sociological Review* 58: 329–50.

Heckathorn, D.D. 1996. "The Dynamics and Dilemmas of Collective Action." *American Sociological Review* 61: 250–77.

Heckathorn, D.D. 2001. Sociological Rational Choice, in G. Ritzer and B. Smart (eds), *Handbook of Social Theory*. London: Sage, 273–84.

Hechter, M. 1987. *Principles of Group Solidarity*. Berkeley, CA: University of California Press.

Hedstroem, P. and Swedberg, R. 1996a. "Rational Choice, Empirical Research, and the Sociological Tradition." *European Sociological Review* 12: 127–46.

Hedstroem, P. and Swedberg, R. 1996b. "Social Mechanisms." *Acta Sociologica* 39: 281–308.

Hindess, B. 1988. *Choice, Rationality, and Social Theory*. London: Unwin Hyman.

Homans, G.C. 1990. Rational-Choice Theory and Behavioral Psychology, in N.J. Smelser and R. Swedberg (eds), *The Handbook of Economic Sociology*. London: Sage, 77–89.

Kiser, E. and Hechter, M. 1998. "The Debate on Historical Sociology: Rational Choice Theory and Its Critics." *American Journal of Sociology* 104(3): 785–816.

Lindenberg, S. 1992. The Method of Decreasing Abstraction, in J.S. Coleman and T.J. Fararo (eds), *Rational Choice Theory: Advocacy and Critique*. London: Sage, 3–20.

Lindenberg, S. 1996. Constitutionalism versus Relationalism: Two Versions of Rational Choice Sociology, in J. Clark (ed.), *James S. Coleman*. London: Falmer Press, 299–311.

Lindenberg, S. 2000. James Coleman, in G. Ritzer (ed.), *The Blackwell Companion to Major Social Theorists*. Oxford: Blackwell, 513–44.

Macy, M.W. 1991a. "Chains of Cooperation: Threshold Effects in Collective Action." *American Sociological Review* 56: 730–47.

Macy, M.W. 1991b. "Learning to Cooperate: Stochastic and Tacit Collusion in Social Exchange." *American Journal of Sociology* 97: 808–43.

Macy, M.W and Skvoretz, J. 1998. "The Evolution of Trust and Cooperation between Strangers: A Computational Model." *American Sociological Review* 63: 638–60.

March, J.G. 1986. Bounded Rationality, Ambiguity, and the Engineering of Choice, in J. Elster (ed.), *Rational Choice*. Oxford: Blackwell, 142–70.

Marwell, G. and Orwell, G. 1993. *The Critical Mass in Collective Action*. Cambridge: Cambridge University Press.

Molm, L.D. 2001. Theories of Social Exchange and Exchange Networks, in G. Ritzer and B. Smart (eds), *Handbook of Social Theory*. London: Sage, 260–72.

Mooney Marini, M. 1992. The Role of Models of Purposive Action in Sociology, in J.S. Coleman and T.J. Fararo (eds), *Rational Choice Theory: Advocacy and Critique*. London: Sage, 21–48.

Olson, M. 1965. *The Logic of Collective Action*. Cambridge, MA: Harvard University Press.

Rawls, A.W. 1992. "Can Rational Choice be a Foundation for Social Theory?" *Theory and Society* 21: 219–41.

Ritzer, G. 2000. Modern *Sociological Theory*. Boston, MA: McGraw-Hill.

Schutz, A. 1964. *Collected Papers II: Studies in Social Theory*, ed. A. Brodersen. The Hague: Martinus Nijhoff,

Sen, A. 1986. Behavior and the Concept of Preference, in J. Elster (ed.), *Rational Choice*. Oxford: Blackwell, 60–81.

Sica, A. 1992. "The Social World as a Countinghouse: Coleman's Irrational Worldview." *Theory and Society* 21: 243–62.

Stinchcombe, A. 1992. "Simmel Systematized: James S. Coleman and the Social Forms of Purposive Action in His Foundations of Social Theory." *Theory and Society* 21: 183–202.

Tilly, C. 1997. "James S. Coleman as a Guide to Social Research." *The American Sociologist* 28(2): 82–7.

Tversky, A. and Kahneman, D. 1986. The Framing of Decision and the Psychology of Choice, in J. Elster (ed.), *Rational Choice*. Oxford: Blackwell, 123–41.

Voss, T. and Abraham, M. 2000. Rational Choice Theory in Sociology: A Survey, in S.R. Quah and A. Sales (eds), *The International Handbook of Sociology*. London: Sage, 50–83.

Willer, D. 1992. The Principle of Rational Choice and the Problem of a Satisfactory Theory, in J.S. Coleman and T.J. Fararo (eds), *Rational Choice Theory: Advocacy and Critique*. London: Sage, 49–78.

Willer, D. et al. 2002. Network Exchange Theory, in J. Berger and M. Zelditch (eds), *New Directions in Contemporary Sociological Theory*. Lanham, MD: Rowman & Littlefield, 109–44.

Zablocki, B. 1996. Methodological Individualism and Collective Behavior, in J. Clark (ed.), *James S. Coleman*. London: Falmer Press, 147–60,

Zafirovski M, 2000. "The Rational Choice Generalization of Neoclassical Economics Reconsidered: Any Theoretical Generalization for Economic Imperialism?" *Sociological Theory* 18(3): 448–71.

Chapter 14
The Phenomenological Perspective of Alfred Schutz (1899–1959)

Preliminary Remarks

This chapter dwells upon the founder and the best-known representative of the phenomenological approach in sociology, Alfred Schutz. It will not be possible to consider also other representatives of this approach, and in this regard reference should be made to already existing introductions (Ferguson 2001; Vaitkus 2000; Wolff 1978). We shall briefly outline:

1. The object of Schutz's sociology.
2. Its relation with the phenomenology of the German philosopher Husserl, with whom Schutz was associated during the 1930s before his emigration to the United States, and by whose works he was deeply influenced.
3. His relation with Weber's interpretive sociology, which Schutz studied carefully, and of which he intended to become the follower.
4. His relationships with some representative authors of pragmatism, such as James, Dewey and Mead. In fact, in the two decades of his stay in America, which cover the last 20 years of his life, Schutz partly opened on the influence of these authors (Luckmann 1973: xviii–xx; Wagner 1981: 382, 385).
5. The directions and contents of Schutz's research, which form the central and most extensive part of this chapter.
6. The reception of his thought by other phenomenology scholars with whom he directly related himself, and by Schutz's contemporary scholars. Concerning the latter, reception is divided into two parts, depending on whether it deals with general introductions or with contributions on particular themes of Schutz's works.

The Object of Schutz's Sociology

Husserl's phenomenological teachings led Schutz to study the constitution of the meaning of action in subjects who act in the everyday life world, and interpret it by intentional acts of consciousness. Weber's sociological teachings suggested him, instead, to consider *social action* (that is, action provided with a meaning and conducted by a subject towards other subjects); how other subjects understand that meaning; and the possibility of forming and keeping a world having a meaning shared by all those who take part in it. Bearing in mind both teachings, Schutz's research has a double object: on the one hand, social action and what we mean by sense of action; on the other hand, the world in which everyday action takes place, or life world. Schutz does not only investigate the assumptions and procedures by which those who take part in it understand this world, but also the way in which social science researchers interpret it. The contents of Schutz's research correspond to this double object of study. The intersubjective structures of sense and the constitution of the social world, as a socially constructed life world, are therefore the peculiar research field of this sociological perspective.

The Relation with Husserl's Phenomenology

In keeping with Husserl, Schutz investigates on how subjects, starting from their lived experiences of consciousness, constitute a world provided with a meaning, and take it for granted during their everyday life, considering it as an undisputed or paramount reality. In general, this requires that subjects do not call into question either the assumptions and meaning of this world, or its reality both for themselves and for the others ("natural attitude," in the phenomenological language). In conformance to Husserl's phenomenology, Schutz's sociology dwells upon the everyday life world in which the "natural" attitude prevails. However, the validity of knowledge subjects have at their disposal (typical previous experiences, basic rules of conduct, intuitions) may not be adequate, and so consequently may also be their ability to act in the world, considering their purposes and interests. In that case, the world becomes problematic in some of its aspects: for example, in a period of famine, understanding whether a mushroom is edible or not becomes a relevant matter if a subject who is not a mushroom expert sees it during a walk, and recognizes it as a mushroom.

Husserl and Schutz wonder how it is possible that subjects are able to communicate and understand each other, thus constituting a world provided with an objective sense (the problem of transcendental intersubjectivity). First of all, both authors maintain that this mutual understanding actually exists, since these subjects keep a non-problematic ("natural") attitude face to face with their experience of the world. In addition, they maintain that a "natural" or pre-phenomenological attitude, that is, not disjointed from the investigators' assumptions, is kept by any scientific study, including those carried out in the area of social sciences, with the "numerous and complex problems" (Husserl 1976c: 902) of how an objective knowledge may be achieved through intersubjective experiences (Husserl 1976a: 61; Husserl 1976b: 766–82; 1976c: 899–903; 1997: 310–27).

However, these two scholars provide different answers to the problem of transcendental intersubjectivity (the problem of how it is possible to understand each other and communicate), and to the problem of the possibility of a scientific knowledge. According to Husserl, there are cultural communities that – considering their common lived experiences – allow even subjects who are distant in space and time to achieve intersubjective experiences, and based on those experiences, also natural and social sciences (Husserl 1976b: 766–82; 1976c: 899–903). Schutz objects that this theory does not explain how any subject or an external observer – a philosopher or a social science researcher – may succeed in making other people's lived experience something of his or her own and, together with those others, take part in community based on shared, and in this sense objective, meaning. Furthermore, according to Schutz, Husserl does make a distinction between, on the one hand, the understanding of other people's experiences by subjects who are present and share with them a context of spatial-temporal experiences; and, on the other hand, the understanding by subjects who, instead, are distant in space and/or time, and therefore have not their same field of perception and their same horizon of lived experiences. Again, Husserl does not consider how an experience lived by other people may be interpreted through collectively constructed and maintained categories (typifications, in Schutz's terminology).

From these critical remarks, Schutz concludes that Husserl has not solved the problem of transcendental intersubjectivity, and that in addition, there is no solution to this problem, unless by keeping a "natural," or pre-phenomenological, attitude towards the world of lived experience. Accordingly, social science, and particularly phenomenological sociology, keeps a "natural" attitude towards the world of lived experience, since it aims at shedding light on its intersubjective structures of sense and its character of social construction.

The Relation with Weber's Interpretive Sociology

Following Weber's footsteps, Schutz focuses his investigation on social action. Weber considers social action as a way of acting – that is, a behavior provided with a sense – oriented to the others. While social action understanding takes place in everyday life, its understanding and explanation are pursued by interpretive sociology through the construction of ideal types (Weber 1956: 1–12). Much more in depth than Weber, but placing himself in continuity with him, Schutz studies:

a. What is meant by behavior, meaning, sense-giving, action (particularly, rational action), action orientation, social relationship.
b. How particular others are significant for an actor.
c. How the understanding of those others, whose behavior the actor tries to understand, and of the others in general, takes place.

d. How subjective understanding of an action can be distinguished from objective understanding.
e. How the attitudes of those who take part in a social action, which both authors call social relationship, can be distinguished, when two or more individuals reciprocally orient their actions.

While we shall dwell upon these issues at a later stage, we would like to mention in this section Schutz's critical remarks to Weber. All these remarks are linked to a basic criticism, according to which Weber would have left implicit the meaning of the most relevant concepts for an interpretive sociology.

These critical remarks may be summarized as follows. In the first place, the actors' sharing of other people's interpretative frames, which is usually taken for granted in everyday life, is taken for granted by Weber, too, as regards both the actors and the observers who study their action. Therefore Weber is not concerned with the problem of an intersubjective consistency of those frames. In the second place, according to Schutz, Weber's distinction between "actual," or direct, understanding of an action and understanding of the reasons of this action, or explanatory understanding, is not acceptable. According to Schutz, any direct understanding of the meaning of other people's action is possible if the actors' motivations have been already understood. For example, chopping wood refers to the subjective meaning of this action, and consequently to the actors' motivations: does the person who is chopping the wood carry out this action as a job, or is this action a part of another action (this is not its real job, but now it has to chop the wood in order to carry this job out), or are there any other reasons (for example, does it do it for a hobby?). Again, according to Schutz, the distinction between a typical-ideal construction adequate as regards the sense and causally adequate, and Weber's formulations concerning the construction of an ideal type do not always allow applying the ideal type to theoretical and abstract fields of study, such as economics and law.

Finally, Weber does not sufficiently, or does not at all, make certain distinctions. In particular, distinctions between:

- action and behavior;
- sense of action in progress and sense of action after it has been carried out, and hence the product of that action;
- "in order to" motives (the purposes for which one is acting, that is, the project of a not already carried out action) and "because" motives (when an already carried out action is justified by foregone lived experiences of the consciousness of the person who is acting, such as its desire to avenge suffered offences);
- actor's understanding of its own action and lived experience, as well as others' actions and lived experiences;
- motives of others with whom one interacts and others with whom this is not possible; concerning the latter, motives of contemporaries, predecessors and successors;
- again, understanding of another person's action devoid of any communicative intention (notifying action);
- understanding of the action of some known, or unknown, others;
- understanding of a social action by the actors themselves, or by scholars (respectively, subjective and objective understanding).

In addition, within a social relationship, Weber does not distinguish between the possibility that participants limit themselves to reciprocally orient their attitudes, which may refer for example to liking and disliking (social relationship of attitudes, in Schutz's language), and, instead, the possibility that one or more participants try to influence the action of the other participants (social relationship of effectiveness). Finally, Weber does not make any distinction between different ideal types of behavior: on the one hand, particular ways of acting corresponding to ideal types of persons (for example, the ideal type of a post office employee); on the other hand, different courses of action that correspond to particular results or products.

The Relation with James's, Dewey's and Mead's Pragmatism

As we previously mentioned, Schutz's interest in pragmatism fully revealed itself in the last part of his life during his stay in America. In his scanty evaluation of pragmatist philosophy in general (that is, without considering any particular author), Schutz seems to share the thesis, according to which we pursue the knowledge we consider valuable and useful in solving practical problems; and only within these limits we try to achieve its clearness and precision. However, he objects that the pursuit of knowledge does not always depend on its relevance of the moment, and that it is not always correct to interpret an action as if it were dictated by the satisfaction of biological needs. Finally, the author objects that towards world experience, pragmatist philosophy keeps a common-sense, "natural," or pre-phenomenological attitude, that is, an attitude not free from assumptions as regards the attributes, or predicates, of what is experienced. Furthermore, Schutz rejects the pragmatist theory of instrumental truth, according to which the truth of an idea depends on its ability to make a society or a community relate themselves with other parts of the experience they have collectively available (Murphy 1990: 51–2; 1997: 79–80). Though Schutz occasionally refers to Peirce and Royce, his references to the works by James, Dewey and Mead are much more frequent. Therefore, we shall briefly mention Schutz's reception of these three representatives of pragmatism. We shall neglect, instead, the references to Cooley, who is occasionally mentioned for his theory of the social making of the Self and for his "face-to-face relationships" and "primary group" concepts.

Schutz's reception of *James* regards some parts of *The Principles of Psychology* (James [1890] 1950), perhaps the most famous work of this American thinker. We refer to excerpts concerning, respectively:

- The method of introspective observation of the states of consciousness (in chapter 7 of the first volume of the work by James, which deals with methods and traps in psychology). Schutz remarks that this method shares with Husserl's phenomenological investigation the assumption that there is a unitary consciousness about which the subjects do not doubt (see the following point), though James kept a "natural," or pre-phenomenological, attitude towards the phenomena perceived by consciousness.
- The concept of *stream of thought, stream of consciousness* (in chapter 9 of the first volume, entitled *The Stream of Thought*). According to James and Schutz, subjects perceive consciousness as a stream with a subjective time, or duration, a sense of temporal continuity. Schutz remarks that according to James, and to Husserl as well, the stream of consciousness indicates the essence of personal intimate life, and consequently, James's investigation anticipates Husserl's phenomenology.
- The associated distinction James makes between two kinds of knowledge: on the one hand, superficial, indistinct and inconsistent knowledge (*knowledge of acquaintance*), which includes the "fringes" of the stream of consciousness; on the other hand, in-depth, clear and consistent knowledge (*knowledge-about*) (at the end of chapter 8 of the first volume entitled "The relation of mind with other things"). Referring to James, Schutz argues that a word, an image, or a thought have a halo, or "fringe" This "fringe" is an undefined aspect, which allows the mind to introduce this element in a relation pattern within the stream of consciousness, thus providing it with a meaning. In any interaction, the core of what participants wish to communicate is associated to "fringes" of different kinds.
- The "specious present," concerning the perception of duration in the stream of consciousness (in chapter 15 of the first volume, where James analyzes time perception). Schutz recalls this concept within his treatment of multiple realities, which is dealt with in the following point.
- The different orders, or worlds, or sub-universes of reality. According to James, these worlds are selected by the mind as relevant, that is, they are perceived as the reality that each time mostly deserves attention (in chapter 21 of the second volume, entitled by James "The perception of reality"). Schutz dwells several times upon this issue, and develops it even much more extensively than James. However, he remarks that the term "worlds of reality" suggests the existence of an objective reality, disregarding its subjective meaning. Therefore, he prefers to designate these "worlds" as "finite provinces of meaning." Furthermore, according to Schutz, paramount reality is not the same as James's one, in which perception goes along with the feeling of what is perceived; it is instead the taken-for-granted reality of everyday life.

• The concepts of "Self," "I," and "Me" (in chapter 10 of the first volume). Schutz treats these concepts introduced by James mostly in the formulation given by Mead (upon which we shall later dwell), sometimes quoting both authors together.

Schutz's reception of *Dewey* is almost exclusively limited to the theme – developed in his work: *Human Nature and Conduct* (1922) – concerning the choice of a course of action among different alternatives: between acting and non-acting, among several courses of action. According to Dewey and Schutz, a definite choice among several alternatives is demanded when in everyday life a rising problem prevents us from continuing our previous activities, and obliges us to deliberate and plan our future conduct. If we plan an action, we do not consider it while it is progressing (since it would be impossible), but through our imagination we anticipate its result, as if it had already taken place. It is an "empty" anticipation, Schutz adds, which may be "filled" in the future by an accomplished action. This theme concerns phenomenological sociology, because it states the difference between the inner time of a subject and the outer time of the objective world. This choice depends on the subject's prevailing interest system, and finally, on its overall life experience. However, Schutz's adhesion to Dewey's thesis is not extended to the author's interpretation of human conduct as something determined by habits and stimuli. In addition, Schutz does not share the continuance in Dewey of a "natural" attitude, which takes social reality for granted. Dewey does not consequently question the assumptions of experience and the related intersubjectivity problem, as he mistakenly thinks that a reflection on action alternatives may take place outside the stream of consciousness. Finally, Schutz concurs with Dewey in maintaining that there are no problems in human conducts as long as there is no system of interests determining what the problematic issues are. Rather, problems arise when something, which at first was not problematic, becomes so later. However, Schutz objects to Dewey that the solution does not consist in a purely rational – that is, neither emotional nor affective – choice for the most appropriate action, as that would be a non-realistic description of how decisions are made; but in re-establishing the non-problematic, opaque and unclear character of everyday life.

Schutz's reception of *Mead* is selective as well, and his evaluation is not completely favorable. This reception is focused on themes, examined in separate parts of Mead's works, which refer to the social and temporal nature of reality (Mead [1934] 1967; [1956] 1977), and are discussed by Schutz within the issue of everyday life stratification. Though with some reservations, he accepts, first of all, Mead's thesis that the core of reality is formed by an "operative" (Schutz), or "subject to manipulation" (Mead) zone. This zone spatially consists of what is actually and physically (and not only potentially) in the range of subjects, that is, of the things on which subjects can act either through parts of their bodies (hands, feet, etc.) or through a tool. The individuals with whom the subjects have a face-to-face relationship are part of this "zone of operation," too. In terms of time, this "zone of operation" is formed by the present, either it is real or it may be restored through the memory of the past, or achieved through future expectations. However, Schutz argues that a phenomenological sociology, and hence, a sociology studying "natural" attitudes and the world of lived experience, consider relevant also what is not actually but only potentially in our range, since it can be perceived by hearing and seeing. Several individuals, whether they share or not the same "operative zone," may share together a spatial-temporal reality, which is lived in the "vivid present," and therefore as an evident everyday reality.

In the second place, Schutz only partly accepts and newly formulates Mead's distinction between the two components of the Self, namely the "I" and the "Me." In accordance with Schutz's new formulation, by placing itself as an active subject operating in the "vivid present," the individual experiences itself as a unitary subject. In that case, the "I" includes the whole undifferentiated body of the acting Selves. When an individual turns its eyes to actions carried out in the past, then it perceives itself and the other individuals with whom it had previously shared the same present time flow, as partial Selves, which have carried out particular actions within a related action system. These particular actions are social roles and the different partial Selves which have carried them out are – in James' and Mead's language, also shared by Schutz – "Mes," in which the impersonal, anonymous, "generalized" other is objectified. In the constitution of what Mead calls "generalized other" both the situation and what is socially relevant are objectively defined. Though action, Self, memory, time and reality are mutually related, as Schutz remarks in agreement with Mead, the latter maintains, in Schutz's opinion, a fallacious epistemological position. Mead formulates a theory on the origin of the Self and social reality, which preserves, despite some changes and in contrast to James, some features of behavioral psychology; namely, its insistence on the theoretical relevance of stimuli and answers, and on the exclusive relevance of directly observable behaviors. Interpretable behaviors, if carried out by subjects who cannot have a face-to-face relationship, would no longer therefore be a matter of study.

Directions and Contents of Schutz's Research

Bearing in mind the double object of study in Schutz's sociology – on the one hand, social action and what is meant as action sense; on the other hand, the world in which everyday action, or life world, is carried out – we can understand the selective and critical character of Husserl's, Weber's and the other American pragmatists' reception. As regards Husserl, Schutz underlines his non-solution of the problem of intersubjectivity, and hence his non-analysis of the common sense world. Concerning Weber, Schutz points to his insufficient formulation of interpretive sociology categories, particularly the category of understanding the social action sense. As regards the pragmatist philosophers, Schutz emphasizes their uncritical maintenance of a natural attitude. Accordingly, it is not clear how experience and the possibility of intersubjective communication may be formed. Particularly in the case of Dewey and Mead, Schutz points to their partial adhesion to behavioral psychology as regards the matter of study and the factors determining social behavior. The directions in which Schutz's sociology develops are, however, strongly influenced, despite these critical remarks, by Husserl, Weber and – among the American pragmatists – particularly by James.

Each direction corresponds to particular research themes. *A first direction* in Schutz's research concerns the themes of social action and individual and intersubjective understanding of its meaning. These themes are dealt with from different points of view: substantive (answering the questions: What is action? What is social action?), theoretical (How can subjects acting in everyday life understand and explain social action?), methodological (How can social science researchers understand and explain social action?). *A second direction* concerns the intersubjective structures of sense, that is, the social world or life world structures, assuming that the results of the first direction have been achieved. *A third direction* concerns the sense boundaries that mark the limits of the different contexts, or "provinces," of the life world and the procedures through which the passage from one "province" of meaning to other ones is indicated (*boundary crossing*): these are marks, indications, signs and symbols. To this research direction belongs the study of language, meant as a structure of signs that allows constructing common interpretative frames, and hence, a common social world. The construction of shared interpretative frames – according to Schutz – occurs, in fact, despite the different individual lived experiences and the different "provinces" of meaning in the social world. This third research direction assumes that the results of the first two ones have been achieved.

First Research Direction: (a) Action, Social Action and Understanding of Its Meaning

Schutz defines these concepts following Husserl's and Weber's teachings. By meaning, or sense, Schutz intends to define a lived experience context to which the subject – by adopting the point of view of a new experience – retrospectively addresses its attention. Therefore not the single experiences but rather their contexts have a meaning. The subject establishes this context in its consciousness considering single experiences as a unitary body and distinguishing them from all other experiences. In other words, lived experiences ("lived experiences of consciousness") have a sense when they become an object of reflection after their completion, in terms of a new lived experience. Therefore, there is no meaning if particular lived experiences are not temporally distinguished from other ones within the stream of consciousness. A set of lived experiences, in their flowing, form a spontaneous consciousness activity, which becomes a behavior only if the subject provides it later on with a sense. All lived experiences – whether external ones, such as natural and social world experiences, or internal ones, such as judgment contents, volitions and fancies – are given to the subject in a synthetic order, or frame, or meaning context. Nonetheless, the subject is not in the position to identify how this order is formed.

Motives are sets of meanings the actor interprets and connects to his or her own actions. An *action* is a spontaneous consciousness activity (a conduct, in Schutz's language) carried out in view of a project – of an "in order to motive" – whose future achievement is imagined as if it had already occurred. If there is a project, consciousness anticipates it as a carried out action, since the subject has already acted in the past in circumstances similar to the present ones. A kind of conduct, and particularly, an action, may be either carried out or not carried out deliberately (*overt* and *covert action*). In addition, they may be oriented to other subjects: in phenomenological terms, they are in this case lived experiences of consciousness that intentionally refer to other ones. After having carried out an action and completed a project, a consideration at a later stage may change their original sense. In particular, the subject may think over the project in the light of past and jointly investigated lived experiences, that is, in the light of "because motives" to which the subject later attributes its action. The meaning a subject links to its action is *subjective*, as the subject interprets it as a unitary body of lived experiences. The meaning a subject attributes to other people's lived experiences (to "extraneous lived experiences") is instead *objective*, as the subject does not consider how its own consciousness or other people's consciousnesses have produced those lived experiences. Therefore, an objective meaning concerns the products of consciousness and belongs to the sphere of the social world. The social world is anonymous, impersonal, but in any case always comprehensible, and hence, interpretable.

Action is called *social* not only when it is intentionally referred to others (as with Weber), but when it also has the purpose (the "in order to motive") to effectively act on those others, thus producing particular lived experiences in their consciousness. Two subjects may reciprocally orient their action ("social relationship"). Based on indexes of their lived experiences, this reciprocal orientation may be deduced – with different certainty levels – by an observer who wants to understand their social action, being, however, extraneous to it. Not any social action is reciprocally oriented, that is, not any social action establishes a social relationship and, particularly, an effective social relationship (*Wirkensbeziehung*). In the last case, the "in order to" motives of a participant are anticipated by it as "because" motives of the behavior it expects from the other participant.

First Research Direction: (b) Understanding and Explaining Action and Social Action in Everyday Life

Those who take part in a social action share the common-sense assumption that they have the possibility of communicating with one another, or in other words, to understand the world in a similar way, and transfer their experience to the others, though this process occurs in a different way for anyone of them. Understanding means interpreting both one's own and extraneous (not one's own) lived experiences. In particular, understanding an action still in progress or which has already been carried out means interpreting the "in order to" and "because" motives of lived experiences intentionally referred to others. The interpreter includes these lived experiences in its own experience context, and attributes to them a meaning. In the case of extraneous lived experiences, since the subject is not in the position to experience the streams of consciousness of other subjects, it interprets its own lived experiences as if they were evidences of theirs. Any interpretation of extraneous lived experiences assumes a basic similarity between the interpreter's lived experiences and those of the others. This similarity is taken for granted in everyday life. In fact, those who take part in the social world usually do not question the possibility of understanding other subjects' lived experiences of consciousness, or whether theirs may be understood or not. They conform to common sense and expect that the others do the same. To conform to common sense (to keep a natural attitude, in Husserl's and Schutz's language) means that the possibility of reciprocally understanding one another, and consequently, the possibility of a social world is not questioned.

Common sense attributes to the world, such as it is experienced in everyday life, and particularly to the social world, the character of a fundamental, unquestionable reality. Real is the world that is not only an object of thought, but also offers resistance to the efforts of a person, and that is actually or potentially in its range (here, Schutz refers to Mead). Therefore, a world in which a person can physically take part with its body and on which it can directly or indirectly act in that moment together with others, or on which it could act in the past and, based on its experience, would be able to act again; or, finally, a world the person expects may be in its range sooner or later in the future. Therefore, real is the world that can be socially changed by persons who understand it in a similar way, and consequently are able to reciprocally communicate.

Though reality is socially built and shared, each subject provides its own particular order to the reality it experiences. This occurs through reference patterns, by which things that are not known are brought back through generalizations, or "typifications," to a familiar reality, that is, a reality belonging to the subject's own experience. Formulating these generalizations involves selecting the aspects of known reality, which become objects of attention in a particular moment. Selection is not only made on the base of the relevance system according to which some objects of attention are more important than others, and which, at the same time, is both individual and socially learned. This selection is also carried out on the basis of how different types of relevance combine. In fact, we can distinguish among a *thematic relevance*, an *interpretative relevance* and a *motivational relevance*. These three kinds of relevance are interdependent.

Thematic relevance concerns a particular object. This object may attract attention insofar as it is unusual and attention-calling (imposed relevance), for example a poisonous snake, or because it is considered interesting and deserves attention (voluntary relevance), or because the object meaning is hypothetical, as it is not immediately clear (hypothetical relevance). *Interpretative* relevance assumes that attention has already been addressed to an object, which consequently is thematically relevant, and that, in order to understand it, it is necessary to relate that object with different experiences. The stock of knowledge the subject has at its disposal is, in this case, necessary for understanding it, whether that object is recognized as a familiar, non-problematic one, or instead not as such, and it is then necessary to explain its nature (is this object a rolled up rope or a poisonous snake?). When an object is not sufficiently determined despite a first explanation attempt, its interpretation requires using further elements from one's stock of knowledge that may prove relevant in explaining its nature (Does this object move? Can I see something looking like the skin of a snake? If it is a snake, is it a poisonous or a harmless snake?). *Motivational* relevance concerns the most appropriate conduct to be kept in a particular circumstance, bearing in mind the thematic and interpretative relevance of an object. Since snakes may be dangerous (thematic relevance), and a person, based on his own stock of knowledge, cannot exclude that this object is a snake (interpretative relevance), a problem rises (there is here an object that might be a snake). How does this problem change its previous conduct and how its conduct should be now? In answering these questions both kinds of motivations are relevant: the "in order to" ones (the subject reacts, for example, flying away, in order to avoid this danger), and the "because" ones (the subject tries to avoid snakes because is frightened by them).

Common-sense concepts, which are not well defined, are formulated by means of already existing and available generalizations, or "typifications," the subject considers complying with its own experience and sufficient to understand other people's actions, and be consequently in the position to act in the social world. A person who uses common sense, either as a participant in a social action or as an observer of other people's actions, knows that everybody has a set of objects within the reach of its senses and its range of action. In addition, everybody has their own life experience, and hence their own point of view and relevance system (due to which a person considers some aspects of its own world more important than others). However, this person also knows – as common-sense knowledge – that the objects within the reach of senses and in the range of action of the others would be within its own reach as well, if it were in their place, and vice versa (interchangeability of points of view). In addition, this person knows that the things it takes for granted are also taken for granted by the others, because, until one has proof of the contrary, their relevance systems are reciprocally compatible (consistency of relevance systems). Therefore, common sense assumes reciprocity in individual approaches.

Individual relevance systems have their origin in the basic anxiety produced in a person by being aware of their future death: its anticipation causes the feelings and drives to formulate projects and try to carry them out, in the attempt to become the master of the world they experiences. Relevance systems guide a person both in building their own world of meaning, and in building a common social world with other persons. The individual's world of meaning is structured into multiple realities, that is, into several separate experience and knowledge contexts ("finite provinces of meaning"). Each "finite province of meaning":

a. receives from the individual a particular accent of reality;
b. is internally consistent;

c. is characterized by a peculiar cognitive way, or style;
d. demands from consciousness a certain attention level, which may be ranging from a maximum degree as regards the reality context submitted to the direct control of a person, and particularly the world of sense of work, to a minimum degree as regards the "province of meaning" of dreams.

Examples of finite provinces of meaning are the world of dreams, imagination (which may lead to an action project), fancies (whose realization is impossible), arts, theatre, religious experience, scientific contemplation, games, insanity, etc. For an individual, absolutely real is the world subject to its actual or potential action, that is, within his or her own range, and therefore is experienced as if it were of the utmost relevance. This world receives the subject's utmost attention. It is characterized by a particular form of sociality (the common action for carrying out a project) and temporal perspective in which the objective social time and the subjective individual time do meet. In the natural attitude of those who do not question the existence of reality, the passage from one "province" to another means passing from one reality to another, for example, from the reality of everyday life to that of religious experience, or the reality of a theatre performance that one attends. According to Schutz, this passage produces a shock, that is, becomes traumatic for the person.

In the construction of a common social world, the more immediately a subject learns the processes of consciousness of the others, the more it shares with them, in addition to space and meeting place, also their social biographical experience backgrounds. These experiences may consist of general knowledge concerning motives, purposes, behavioral models, expressive and interpretative patterns, languages, etc., or instead, of specific knowledge concerning particular categories or groups of persons. In both cases, this knowledge may be divided either into common notions, which are necessary in guiding one's conduct in everyday life, or specialized competences covering a limited part of reality (this distinction is derived from James). In "face-to-face" relationships, we use this either general or specific knowledge and change it in the light of our new experience of the other. We are then able to learn from the other with different immediacy degrees, from a maximum level, such as in a love relationship or in a friendly relationship, to a minimum level, such as in the superficial relationship between persons who are indifferent one another. In other words, from the highest intimacy level to the highest anonymity one. The evidences of extraneous lived experiences may be gestures, judgments, results of other persons' actions, or even objects produced in the outer world, such as appliances or monuments. These evidences are not necessarily meant as to transfer a meaning to others, since they do not always have a significant function.

The person who interprets the evidences of others' lived experiences may believe that those evidences even have a subjective meaning, that is, those who left them meant to transfer a meaning to others. In that case, in order to reconstruct their meaning at a later stage, the interpreter has not only to resort to their own knowledge as regards their objective meaning, but also to their own entire experience about the patterns and expressive habits of those who left those evidences. Understanding other people's lived experiences involves, therefore, learning both their objective meaning (for example, the meaning of words said by the other, as it results from a dictionary), and subjective meaning (the meaning meant by the other and communicated during that particular occasion, and by means of it). Their causal explanation involves evaluating the suitability of the means used by others in view of achieving particular purposes. Explanation, such as understanding, of which it is a particular case, must conform to the objective and subjective sense of other people's action.

First Research Direction: (c) Social Science Researcher's Understanding and Explaining Action and Social Action

An observer does not understand extraneous lived experiences, and hence a social action, as soon as they are produced, but rather as soon as they are carried out. Therefore, it has only an indirect access to the observed persons' motivations. This observer may be either an ordinary person or a social science researcher. In case it is an ordinary person, the observer refers to its own biographical situation and the stock of knowledge derived from it, and assumes that, by using common-sense concepts, it is in the position to understand the fragments of other people's action courses, to which it could have access. If, instead, the observer is not an ordinary person but a researcher, then it refers not only to the stock of common-sense knowledge, but also to the stock of available knowledge in its own specific field of study, which it takes for granted or, on the contrary, rejects with arguments. Availing himself of this theoretical knowledge and throughout his investigation activity, the researcher employs typical-ideal concepts. If these concepts are correctly formulated they derive from the stock of common-sense concepts but are constructed in a non-contradictory way, and are not only compatible with the researcher's experience of the intersubjective world of everyday life (adequacy based on sense), but also with the existing scientific knowledge. Unlike common-sense concepts, ideal types are clear and distinct concepts, that is, devoid as much as possible of connections with other elements of that universe of discourse and with other emotional and irrational aspects (referring to James, Schutz calls these connections "fringes"). Furthermore, the researcher marks the limit of what is relevant, thus stating the problem about which it intends to bring knowledge. In his or her investigation, typical-ideal concepts are considered as tools for understanding and explaining the subjective meanings with which the subjects have provided their action. By formulating these concepts, the researcher sheds light on the objective meanings of the social world. These meanings are connected to typical action courses.

By interpreting his or her own lived experiences, the researcher aims at acknowledging a-posteriori the "in order to" and "because" motives of actors to whom it attributes typical lived experiences of consciousness, to which it makes correspond a typical action. Consequently, the typifications of both action and the corresponding lived experiences of consciousness are possible only when an action has already taken place. Typical-ideal understanding concerns therefore an accomplished action and not an action in progress. In this way, a political economy researcher attributes to an abstract economic actor, for example a financial operator wishing to make an investment, particular and typical lived experiences, to which it makes to correspond an action in keeping with the principle of marginal utility. In this case, action is rational, compared to the financial operator's "in order to" motive to maximize the investment utility. For those who act, action rationality involves having available and using appropriate knowledge, which concerns what they want to achieve, compatibility of this end with other ones, desired or perverse effects, existence of alternative means, as well as their availability and consequences of their use. Starting from concrete actions – for example, the actions of real financial operators – the researcher constructs:

a. A personal ideal type ("the typical financial operator"). It is an artificially created character ("a puppet") to which the researcher fictitiously attributes a lived experience provided with subjective sense, and hence, with "in order to" and "because" motives based on the stock of knowledge owned by the researcher itself;
b. A type of its action course, which instead is provided with an objective meaning, because it has led to a certain impersonal result or product.

The researcher formulates ideal types based on a particular theoretical problem, and hence, on a particular point of view: therefore, the ideal type must be relevant according to the researcher's relevance system and to the reference patterns the problem involves. In addition, this ideal type of a fictitious person (for example, a financial operator) must be formulated so that its mind and its thoughts have a comprehensible relation with its activities. Again, the construction of the ideal type must conform to the sense; that is, to any action carried out by actually existing person, which conforms to what the ideal type shows must be understandable to both those who carry it out, and to the others. Finally, a typical-ideal action must be rational, that is, provided with the appropriate means to achieve the actor's purposes. It is attributed to the actor a clear and distinct knowledge of any information relevant in the choice of his or her conduct.

Second Research Direction: The Structures of Social World, or Life World

Up to now, we haveconsidered the concepts of action and social action, and how extraneous (other people's) lived experiences are understood by those who are directly involved in an action, or by external observers (either ordinary persons, or social science scholars). A further research direction assumes that all these results are achieved and refers to intersubjective structures of sense, that is, the structures of social world, or life world. We should bear in mind that, according to Schutz, the experience of the other may be learned in the most immediate way in face-to-face relationships, and hence in Thou- or We-relationships, although with different intimacy levels (or "lived closeness"). Failing face-to-face relationships, the other may be only experienced in an indirect or mediated way, and the social world becomes stratified, or structured, into growing anonymity degrees and decreasing immediacy degrees and indications for learning the consciousness processes of the other.

Since reference patterns and relevance systems are socially shared, reality – and particularly, the paramount reality of everyday life – has an order formed and taken for granted by those who take part in any social action. Among the constitutive elements of the social world, Schutz identifies the "world environment" (*Umwelt*, the domain of directly experienced social reality), the world of contemporaries, and finally the world of predecessors and successors. When there is a direct, "face-to-face" relationship, those who take part in it share both the space and the time in which their streams of consciousness are placed. Anyone of them, by taking part – although temporarily – in the life of the other, shares with it the same "world environment." The participant orients himself to the other as a person either unilaterally ("Thou-relationship," in Schutz's words) or reciprocally. In the second case, participants orient their attention to one another ("We-relationship"). Consequently, they coordinate their experiences, which reciprocally determine and relate themselves.

These relationships, respectively the Thou- and the We-relationships, may be studied from a formal point of view, disregarding the particular persons who constitute them. In that case, they are called "pure," or abstract, relationships. Pure relationships, instead of actual ones, are at the heart of Schutz's interest. Each participant – the author argues – is provided with its own inner time and specific stock of experience. However, each is aware of the existence of the others, and – if necessary – also of their peculiar characteristics. In fact, in a relationship we start communicating with another person. Therefore, experiences may be interpreted and projects may be experienced whether they are carried out or not. In particular, each participant has the opportunity to understand how he or she is experienced by the other participants in a relationship. The similarity between its own lived experiences and those of the others may be then caught in the most immediate and profound way.

This can only happen if, by observing and interpreting communication, the participant gets information (such as words, expressions, movements, gestures, and tones) enough to learn the consciousness processes of the other. These processes remain obviously extraneous to its own consciousness, but a "face-to-face" relationship allows the participant to check whether its own interpretation is correct or not. We have an example of "We-relationship," which assumes non-linguistic communication, when two or more persons play a piece of music together. There is, in that case, synchronization and coordination between the performers' streams of consciousness and also between their streams of consciousness and those of the audience, and finally the composer's (though the composer does not belong to the "vivid present" of that particular music performance). A "pure We-relationship" can become an object of reflection not during its development, but once it is accomplished and participants do not coordinate their streams of consciousness any longer.

From spatial, temporal and – to some extent – sociobiographical experience sharing, which characterizes face-to-face relationships between more or less intimate persons, we pass to the relationships with contemporaries. Towards them, or better, towards their streams of consciousness, we orient ourselves in a more or less impersonal manner ("They-relationships") by asserting our own social world knowledge. The passage from a Thou-relationship and a We-relationship to a They-relationship involves a loss in concreteness, and in turn, an increase in generalities, in typifications, and hence in the stock of knowledge we use to understand the lived experiences of other subjects. This loss in concreteness is smaller if contemporaries are persons we know, though they are not present in that particular moment, especially if we think we may establish with them (for the first time, or again) a face-to-face relationship in the future. On the contrary, the loss in concreteness is greater if contemporaries are unknown persons. In that case, what we seek to know is achieved through generalizations, or typifications, of characters, functions, social roles (such as the role of a post office employee), or communities (such as a state, a nation, or an institution). In the making of all these common-sense typifications, and of the ideal types the researcher derives from them, the direct experience of the other does not concur, since there is no communication with it.

The world of contemporaries is different from the predecessors' and successors' worlds. The world of predecessors does not take part in the life world, does not have any future, and is definitively concluded. Therefore, living persons do not directly experience it, because they cannot establish reciprocal relationships with any predecessor. However, this world may indirectly influence their world in different ways. In the first place, it is possible to establish a Thou- or We-relationship with persons who communicate their past lived experiences. In the second place, the world of predecessors has left sources and documents, and in general evidences of their lived experiences, which can be understood by contemporaries through typifications. In both cases, the interpretative frames have changed, and consequently, what contemporaries can understand is not the same experience lived by the other persons at the time – already past – in which they experienced it.

The historian, being a person who studies the predecessors' world, necessarily examines already carried out actions, and not action courses. It investigates objective sense connections in the light of the evidence it has available; and, if necessary, also investigates the subjective sense connections of those who have left those evidences of their lived experiences. The worlds of predecessors and successors share the impossibility of a reciprocal – even though only potential – relationship among subjects who are present at the same time, and also of a relationship with contemporaries. However, the world of the past is completely determined; whereas the world of the future is absolutely undetermined, that is, open to any event. Furthermore, only the world of the past can be understood through typifications, while the cognitive validity of typifications concerning the future world is the more doubtful the more this future is distant. In fact, these typifications do not refer any longer to experience, apart from that connected to generation turnover.

Third Research Direction: The Construction a Common World of Sense among Different Provinces of Meaning

The construction of a common world of sense is a consequence of the belief of those who take part in a social action in the interchangeability of their own points of view with the points of view of the other participants. The knowledge the other participants have produced thus becomes a part of their own actual or potential knowledge. This means that the whole knowledge is produced socially. This may occur in one of the following ways: by learning from others their experience during a talk; or through an account of events, whose meaning is extraneous to one's relevance context, and hence would become inaccessible to those who share that context without this account; Or, again, by having access to the opinion of others who have the same relevance context as the subject, but who, compared with him or her, have a more in-depth knowledge of the facts on which they base their opinion; or, finally, by having access to the opinion of others who know the pertaining facts such as the subject does, but introduce them into a different relevance context.

The different "provinces" of meaning are limited by boundaries marked by the passage from the cognitive style of a particular "province" to another. For those who experience a meaning within a particular "province," the references that go beyond "here and now" experience relate this particular experience to other experiences they make in different "provinces." The passage from one "province" to another is marked by indications, marks, signs, and symbols. In particular, indications are facts, objects or events that can be perceived by an individual and by the same are connected with its belief in the existence of other facts, objects or events, though the nature of that connection is not quite clear to it. Marks are mnemonic devices used as personal references (and hence, not addressed to others). Indications and marks neither assume the existence of others nor the possibility of communicating with them. They thus distinguish themselves from signs and symbols, which instead assume a common communication milieu. Consequently, reciprocity in perspectives and a consistency in relevance systems are assumed, which are taken for granted by common sense until proved otherwise.

Signs – in which some aspects of indications and marks combine within a communication context – are facts, objects or events that may be learned and interpreted by others, disregarding whether this is wished for, and whether or not those others are known by the individual (in this sense, smile and blushing, but also handwriting, if examined by a graphologist, are signs). In communication, though a sign is addressed to either known or unknown others, it is not necessarily addressed to the person who interprets it. Communication is successful when the person who sends a sign and the person who receives and interprets it share common interpretative patterns. The person who wants to communicate successfully should know how, within the group to which it turns, reality is interpreted, and how the knowledge of this reality is socially distributed. In fact, according to Schutz, the social distribution of knowledge is not homogeneous. This makes it possible, according to Schutz, to identify three ideal types of knowledge-bearing subjects:

- the ordinary person ("the man in the street"), whose knowledge, although vague, is sufficient for his or her own practical purposes;
- the expert, who has a clear and distinguished knowledge in a limited field;
- and the well-informed citizen, who has at their disposal information enough to make a reasonably grounded opinion in fields that have no practical relevance for it, and tries to reduce what is irrelevant, being aware, as a citizen, that in the "province of meaning" of what seems to be absolutely irrelevant a potential danger might be concealed.

Only the expert and the well-informed citizen contribute to the making of public opinion.

Communication availing itself of non-linguistic signs, such as expressive (waving, clapping, etc.) or imitative gestures, in which a certain object is represented in a figurative way, may be successful. If instead there are only linguistic signs, the success of communication is ensured not only by the existence of dictionaries and syntactic rules, which allow catching the meaning of a sequence of words and sentences, but also by the existence of a "We-relationship" among those who take part in that communication. Indeed, when we begin learning a language, it becomes imperative to establish a face-to-face relationship through which we can directly observe and experience the expressions of the face, the gestures, and the typical conduct of our counterpart. Through a "We-relationship" we do not learn a language in the abstract, but rather the peculiar version of that language employed in a particular social and territorial context, bearing in mind its social structure and the distribution of the social stock of knowledge. Without a face-to-face relationship, there is neither a direct experience of the other within a particular time and place setting, such as during a meeting, nor a direct experience of particular "finite provinces of meanings." Nonetheless, language allows to indirectly experiencing them.

Learning the semantic-syntactic structure of language by shaping the pre-linguistic frames of experience and the pre-linguistic typifications of reality, actually allows receiving the social stock of knowledge that has become, through language, an objective stock of knowledge; that is, an impersonal resource of the social structure, which is available to, and binding for, everyone. Thanks to language, we are able to formulate common interpretative patterns, and we are consequently prepared to take part in a common social world. On the other hand, both the "We-relationship" and the language weigh also on the subjective relevance systems, and on the individual typifications processes. Especially the subjective interpretative relevance systems concerning motives are socially learned; so are also the ways in which indications, marks, signs and sign systems, such as language, are placed and interpreted. Sign systems, in turn, allow incorporating a subjective set of knowledge into an objective stock, in order to create and maintain a common meaning structure.

Symbols can be distinguished from indications, marks and signs because they go beyond the "finite province of meaning" of everyday life, and more in general, the sense boundaries that limit the different "provinces" of the life world. Thus, a meaningful relationship can be established between two or more of these provinces, each one with its own cognitive style (for example, the reality of everyday life and religious experience). There are different symbols acting as meaning vehicles in the passage from one "province" to another. These symbols may be, for instance, either elements of the surrounding physical world, such as planets, the sun, or mountains, or animals, or parts of the body, such as the sexual organs, or movements of the body, or historical events, such as the Olympic Games or social events, such as weddings or funerals. In any case, while the natural attitude and meanings are transferred from the "province" to which a symbol originally belongs to another one, the belief in a non-problematic reality is suspended, and therefore, roles and social distribution of knowledge are temporarily abandoned. The passage from one "province" of meaning to another is therefore traumatic. Symbolic is the We-relationship (for example, a friendly relationship), as it goes beyond the existence of each component, and hence, beyond their individual reality of everyday life. For the same reason, and even more clearly, symbolic is the experience made – by the common person, as well as by the researcher – of social and political organizations, and in particular celebration circumstances, even of society itself (Schutz, 1962, 1964, 1970, 1974, 1975, 1996; Schutz and Luckmann 1973, 1989).

Schutz's Reception by Other Phenomenology Scholars

Schutz's reception has produced a great deal of literature, often written by scholars who were close to Husserl's phenomenology, or in any case knew it very well. Schutz's sociological thought has directly impacted on a limited number of scholars and followers, who often belong to Garfinkel's ethnomethodological school (Fele 2001). His indirect influence is, instead, widespread, thanks to the works written by some outstanding contemporary sociologists. We refer particularly to the works by:

* Berger and Luckmann (1967), on reality considered as a social construction;
* Habermas (1986: ch. 6; 1987: ch.6), concerning the relation between communicative action and life world;
* Goffman (1974), on the analysis of frames, or reality interpretative patterns;
* Giddens (Giddens 1984: 4, 6–7, 44), as regards the concept of "practical consciousness," that is, actors' reflexive monitoring of their own conduct (cf. De Biasi 2001; Fine 1990: 139; Kaspersen 2000: 37–8; Protti 2001: 21; Rogers 2000: 385).

While Berger and Luckmann seem to fully adhere to Schutz's epistemology and sociological theory, Habermas, Goffman and Giddens raise, instead, several objections, upon which, however, we shall not dwell in this work (Goffman 1974: 5–6; Giddens 1979: 28–41, 230; Habermas 1986: 744–8; 1987: 148–52).

We shall instead devote some space to Schutz's reception by authors who kept a personal relationship with him, such as friends, acquaintances, and collaborators, and by more recent commentators. Concerning the latter, we shall compare a few general introductions and briefly mention a limited number of comments on Schutz's thought. Some non-recent introductions prove particularly interesting because the authors, such as Gurwitsch, Luckmann, Natanson, Wagner and Wolff, had established a personal relationship with Alfred Schutz and his wife Ilse. In fact, after the death of her husband, Ilse Schutz cooperated with Luckmann, Wagner and other researchers (cf. Brodersen 1964: xv; Van Breda 1962: XII; Zaner and Parent 1973a: xii), to the publication of many unpublished Schutz's papers. We shall then consider also some more recent introductions published as from the early 1980s. The first group and the second group of introductions will be compared with the purpose of pointing to some differences in Schutz's themes with which they deal. Finally, we shall briefly mention the critical literature concerning Schutz's works, whose reception, distinguished from general introductions, has taken uncontrollable proportions (Grathoff 1989: 12). About this literature, we can only give a partial and concise report. For any other issue, reference should be made to introductions and bibliographies dealing particularly with Schutz's work reception (see, for example, Endress 1999: 346–9; Grathoff 1989: 444–70; Muzzetto 1997: 119–97, 329–41; Protti 1995: 251–78; 2001).

Introductions to Schutz by Authors Close to Him

Among Schutz's closest collaborators, Aron Gurwitsch was a pupil and follower of Husserl. As a phenomenologist, he developed an original conception of consciousness (Gurwitsch 1966). With Schutz, Gurwitsch did not only keep a continuous friendly relationship, but also an intellectual exchange (Rogers 2000: 368–9; Wagner 1981: 387–8). In his introduction to Schutz's thought, Gurwitsch particularly underlines the typification process through which subjects orient themselves in their natural and social world according to their interests and relevance systems, whose existence and sense they take for granted. He also emphasizes the stock of knowledge subjects draw from this process for both the single persons and the communities, to which they belong. Hence, the intersubjective character of knowledge and the world of experience, which originate in face-to-face relationships. These relationships are in turn the premises of social scientists' concepts and interpretations (Gurwitsch 1975).

Thomas Luckmann, an outstanding sociologist follower of the phenomenological approach, was one of Schutz's pupils and the editor of the numerous notes and comments left by his teacher. He was also one of the co-authors of the two volumes, published after Schutz's death, concerning the life world structures (Schutz and Luckmann 1973, 1989). Luckmann's contribution to these unpublished papers by Schutz is so important that this posthumous work should be actually attributed to both authors, although it shows an absolute continuity with the other already known works by Schutz (Luckmann 1973: xxii–xxiii; see also Protti 1995: 222–4; Zaner and Engelhardt 1973: xxviii; Zaner and Parent 1989b: xii–xiii). In the preface to the first volume, after having remarked that Schutz was an original follower of Weber and Husserl, Luckmann upholds a thesis worthy of note. Though the study of James, Mead and the other pragmatists during his stay in the United States had brought him an enrichment, Schutz would have shown nonetheless a thematic continuity with the previous period, his central theme being a systematic description of common-sense world as a social reality. Schutz's research, after having considered face-to-face relationships, would have emphasized the other layers of the elementary structures of everyday life upon which social experience, language, social action and hence, the complex historical world of human life are based (Luckmann 1973: xx-xxi).

Like Luckmann, Maurice Natanson was one of Schutz's pupils and commentators. He shared Schutz's phenomenological approach and edited his posthumous works. In his comprehensive introduction to the thought of his teacher, upon which we now wish to dwell (Natanson 1962), Natanson identifies as guiding thread of his intellectual life a particular concern for the meaning structure of the everyday life world, whose existence is taken for granted and whose components and reciprocal relations Schutz would aim at exploring (Natanson 1962: xxv). His introduction considers first the world of common sense and the issue of intersubjectivity. Individuals take part in the world of common sense through typifications, each individual in a different way depending on one's biographical situation, stock of knowledge and space-time placement within a network of relationships. This participation assumes the possibility of taking the point of view of others upon oneself. It is then possible to communicate with those who are present in a place at the same moment, though the single individuals may be influenced also by other contemporaries or predecessors towards whom they orient their action, and may turn to successors. The theme of action takes up the central part of Natanson's introduction, which dwells upon the concepts of subjective and objective meaning interpretation, definition of a situation, spatial-temporal horizons of action, "in order to" and "because" motives, individual's fragmentation into an "I" and a "Me," which changes depending on the social roles performed, and relevance of an undertaken course of action. Finally, Natanson outlines the theme of multiple realities, natural attitude and basic anxiety, mentioning the methodological indications provided by Schutz.

We owe to Helmut Wagner a well-known intellectual biography of Schutz, of whom he was a pupil in the 1950s at the New School for Social Research (Wagner 1981). Wagner agrees with other interpreters in considering that the analysis of the basic processes that take place in life world is the focus of Schutz's attention. After having illustrated Schutz's reception of Husserl's phenomenology, particularly as regards individual life world experience and knowledge, and their social origin, Wagner deals with the theme of relevance, such as it had been treated by Schutz, and with the associated theme of typification. In fact, in order to orient themselves in the everyday life world, individuals select and group into homogeneous classes, or types, what is relevant using socially approved classification and relevance systems. Wagner considers action in view of an "in order to" motive – distinguished from a "because" motive, which can be only retrospectively caught – and a project that may guide its course chosen among other possible ones in consequence of a deliberation. He also investigates Schutz's treatment of the problem of intersubjectivity, and hence, of the possibility of mutual understanding (reciprocity of motivations and perspectives). In this regard, he briefly mentions the social world stratification into layers of growing anonymity in non-face-to-face relationships, the theme of finite provinces of meaning, the methodological theme concerning ideal types, the epistemological theme concerning the object of study in sociology, as well as Schutz's intellectual relationships with other European and American scholars (Wagner 1970).

Kurt H. Wolff, an eminent phenomenologist and sociologist, kept a personal and epistolary relationship with Schutz (Wolff, personal communication; cf. also Wagner 1981: 386). Besides other contributions concerning the works by Schutz and their reception, Wolff is also the author of an introduction to phenomenological sociology, which becomes in its central part an introduction to Schutz's thought, too. In this introduction, Wolff particularly underlines Schutz's relation with Weber and Husserl. As regards Weber, the author refers to Schutz's critical treatment of the basic categories of interpretive sociology, particularly the distinction between subjective and objective meaning, and the associated typification issue. Concerning Husserl, the author refers to the concept of judgment suspension, in the particular use Schutz made of it in his analysis of the natural attitude. Finally, Wolff outlines Schutz's epistemology of social science and particularly, the opportunity for those who study these sciences, as well as for those who directly interact with others, to approach the subjective sense of other individuals only through typifications (Wolff 1978: 515–20).

We have considered so far the interpretative contributions of scholars who had not only the opportunity to have access to Schutz's papers and works, but also kept a direct or indirect relationship with him. A joint consideration of these contributions may point out similarities or differences in the outlined themes and in their connections. Among the issues discussed and considered central in Schutz's sociology, reference is constantly made to:

- the world of common sense and the distinction between subjective and objective sense;
- its multiple reality structure and its stratification in the contemporary, the predecessors,' and the successors' world environment;
- relevance as a guidance instrument in the world, and the associated themes of typification and intersubjectivity;
- the theme of social action and the difference between "in order to" and "because" motives;
- the distinction between common-sense knowledge and knowledge brought by social sciences.

The usually followed introduction order is similar to the above one. However, the single interpreters have sometimes dealt more with one issue than with another, or have also outlined other issues (for example, Wagner, more than other scholars, particularly dwelt upon the themes of relevance and reality stratification, Gurwitsch upon the theme of intersubjectivity, whereas Natanson mentioned the individual's fragmentation possibility between an "I" and a "Me" that change depending on the social roles one performs). Some contemporary Schutz's commentators, too, have published summaries and formulated introductory comments.

Introductions to Schutz by Contemporary Scholars

In this section, reference is made to some contributions published as from the 1980s. Many of these essays/ comments were published in books and journals dealing with contemporary sociological thought. In fact, after the translation into English of Schutz's complete works on social world phenomenology (1967), it has become by now customary to include a chapter especially dedicated to Schutz and, in general, to phenomenological sociology (to which ethnomethodology is reconducted), as an evidence of the considerable impact of this approach on contemporary sociological theory (Ritzer 2000: 73). The introductions to Schutz's thought published in the last two decades include all the issues with which the earlier introductions had dealt, and the order of exposition does not change significantly. Instead of pointing out the discussed topics and identified interconnections, as in the previous section, we now prefer to briefly mention how a few peculiar interpreters have developed some themes. The order of exposition is double, as it is both chronological and based on interpreters' nationality.

Among the Italian commentators, Izzo, in his introduction, particularly emphasizes Schutz's criticism to Weber and its validity (Izzo 1991: 330–34, 340–41). Protti (1995) and Muzzetto (1997, 2006), authors of two monographic essays concerning Schutz's works and reception, also dwell upon Husserl's influence on his thought. In addition, however, Protti considers Schutz's intellectual relationship with Bergson and Parsons, as well as the themes of common knowledge in life world, relevance and typification, subjectivity and intersubjectivity. Crespi, Jedlowski and Rauti, in their concise introduction to Schutz's thought, mainly consider the concepts and theses included in his early work on social world phenomenology, particularly as regards the formulation of a theory of action, which is both phenomenological and Weberian at the same time. The authors also briefly mention the themes of typifications and relevance attributions, as well as the social scientist's function. Muzzetto examines in more depth a number of themes present in Schutz: "methodological constructivism" (in the sense that common sense and scientific knowledge is constructed through typifications); the stock of knowledge, which is available to the subject in order to construct and preserve his or her own life world of meaning; the typifications, namely, those processes by means of which the subject refers to this stock of knowledge for the purpose of selecting the particular portion of data flowing to consciousness, which has relevance to any contingent experience; and the "We-relationship" as the foundations of intersubjectivity. A comparison between Husserl and Schutz has been made insofar as such processes are concerned.

Among the American commentators, Jonathan H. Turner sets Schutz's thought against the background of interactionism meant as a perspective moving from the assumption that the structure of society is created and maintained by individual actions and interactions. To this perspective would also belong, among other scholars, Weber, Simmel and Mead. In Turner's interpretation, Schutz's phenomenological interactionism is characterized by a thesis, according to which persons use to act tacitly assuming that their world is formed in virtue of a stock of shared and socially learned knowledge, and hence, is common with other ones. This thesis would be the outcome of an encounter between Husserl's and Mead's influences (Turner 1998: 343, 354–7). Mary Rogers points out the phenomenological and epistemological assumptions of Schutz's sociology. From a phenomenological point of view, Rogers dwells then upon the description of the social relationship the subjects who communicate one another establish and keep within the boundaries of finite provinces of meaning. From an epistemological and methodological point of view, this commentator dwells upon the distinction between the role of a person who lives in the life world interacting with others, and the role of a social science researcher, and likewise, between common-sense concepts and ideal types (Rogers 2000: 369–83).

Vaitkus and Ferguson are the authors of two recent introductions to phenomenological sociology, which include a concise presentation of Schutz's works. Vaitkus makes a distinction among three different levels in the common-sense world, or life world: the first level consisting of knowledge of the other considered as a spatially, temporally and socially distinguished being. In the second level, the other is introduced – based on common-sense knowledge – into a social group. Finally, in the third level, the actor is able to understand the actual, "in order to" and "because" motives of other people's action. These three levels are subject to typifications through which it is possible to carry out practical projects and social actions, and may be related to the person by articulating life world into finite provinces of meaning, which are symbolically limited and distinguished according to their relevance (Vaitkus 2000). In contrast with other interpreters, Ferguson insists on the elements of Schutz's thought that distinguish it from Husserl's approach:

- The immanent and worldly, instead of transcendental, character of Schutz's phenomenological approach to social reality;
- Schutz's eclecticism, which would approach him to Bergson, James and Weber, rather than to Husserl, whose analysis of consciousness Schutz would have simplified and distorted;
- His conception of society, which is close to the theories expressed by the preceding and contemporary American sociology (Ferguson 2001).

Among the German sociologists, we briefly mention in this section only the exegetic contributions of Grathoff and Endress. Grathoff, a well-known phenomenologist and editor of the book on the letter exchange between Schutz and Gurwitsch, is also the author of an introductory essay to Schutz's works, which is considered very authoritative (1989). In his essay, the author points out a central question for Schutz, whether there may be or not "a methodology and theory of social action providing a foundation to social sciences and to their theories," and which it may be. The answer would be given through "three basic lines, which determine and limit his concept of science" (1989: 27): in the first place, the rational organization of everyday life demands, for being understood, appropriate theories and methods. In the second place, sociology is meant as a scientific analysis of the sense constitutive processes in everyday life world. In the third place, sociology is meant as an analysis of everyday life complying with the peculiar styles by which world understanding is socially constructed.

Bearing in mind Schutz's concept of science and the field of study of sociology, such as they have been determined so far, according to Grathoff, Schutz's works would comprise three theoretical areas:

a. Social action theory, according to which action (but not action in progress) has a sense shared with others. Its explanation provided by social sciences involves a revision of the common-sense explanations social actors use in everyday life.
b. Everyday life sociology, according to which different finite provinces of meaning may be identified. These provinces are characterized by peculiar cognitive styles, relevance patterns and attention levels.

In this regard, according to Grathoff, Schutz seems to abandon the previous distinction between subjective and objective sense.

c. Typification and relevance as structures of life world, according to which any typification – including the ideal types formulated by social sciences – ultimately derives from either thematic, motivational, or interpretative relevance structures. These relevance structures establish what the problematic situations among those experienced in everyday life, and what the effective solutions, are.

Endress is the editor of Schutz's complete works, published in Germany from 1999. He is also the author of a comprehensive biography, published in the first two volumes of this work. The themes, on which Endress chiefly focuses in his introduction to Schutz (1999), are those with which also other introductory works usually deal; the expositive order is the usual one as well. Preceded by biographical notes and followed by outlines on Schutz's reception, Endress' statements move from the thesis that Schutz's sociology builds a theory of life world whose task is to "reconstruct the meaning structure of the social reality produced by the reciprocal action of human beings" (Endress 1999: 334). The author first considers the phenomenological premises of interpretive sociology (the subject, we remember, of Schutz's early book); then Schutz's life world theory; and finally, his directions concerning social science methodology.

Outlines on Schutz's Critical Reception

We outline in this section a limited number of contributions published as from the early 1970s, ordered on the base of some particular features of Schutz's work that have become an object of study. We shall therefore consider (a) some essays focused on epistemological or methodological issues; (b) studies concerning Schutz's relations with Husserl and Weber; finally, (c) some in-depth studies on specific themes in Schutz's sociology.

a. Gorman's thesis (1975), according to which Schutz would have conceived the image of a social actor who is unable to escape the thought and action frames suggested by common sense, has become the object of several critical comments (Izzo 1991: 340; Muzzetto 1997: 102, 134; Protti 1995: 227–8). Carroll (1982), dwelling upon Schutz's postulate of adequacy, according to which the concepts social sciences employ should be compatible with common-sense concepts, maintains that this postulate involves a few methodological problems, and indicates how they can be faced. Eberle (2001), too, dwells upon the same assumption resuming Husserl's and Schutz's thesis of a "basic distance between scientific models and life world reality" (Eberle 2001: 99) in order to uphold the opportunity – in epistemological terms – to reduce that distance. To that end, Eberle suggests constantly recalling the formulation of scientific concepts, "the actors' approach towards the life world," and avoiding any opposition between qualitative and quantitative social research.

b. We wish to briefly mention now some contributions that examine Schutz's attempt to merge – in an epistemological, methodological and theoretical sense – Husserl's phenomenology with Weber's interpretive sociology. Sociology researchers know very well, in particular, the dense essay by Robert Williame (1973). While the fourth and last chapter of this essay includes a phenomenological interpretation of Max Weber's works, the first three chapters may be read as a critical introduction to Schutz. His project would have been "making a kind of phenomenology constitutive of the natural attitude" (Williame 1973: 115). However, Schutz's phenomenology seems to be hovering between an analysis of the natural attitude we use in everyday life and an analysis of the constitutive structures of the social world, which, as regards everyday life, are instead pre-established and taken for granted. In addition, it would be only in the position to describe the ways in which action is theoretically understood, but not to justify this description from a phenomenological point of view (Williame 1973: 116–21; cf. also Muzzetto 1997: 119–21).

In the same years, the critical introduction by Heap and Roth (1973) to some writings dealing with "phenomenological sociology" has contributed to a wider circulation of Schutz's thought in the United States. Heap and Roth aimed at explaining in which sense sociology may be defined as phenomenologically oriented; what have been the sociological contributions of Husserl's and Schutz's phenomenology; and what is the relation between phenomenology and ethnometodology. In more recent years, Isambert (1989), after having introduced and discussed a partial translation of Schutz's works into French, examines the way in which Schutz's conception of typicality (*typicité*) is related both to Weber's methodology and to Husserl's phenomenology. This interpreter also maintains that the need to employ this conception to achieve a scientific knowledge of everyday life would impoverish the sense subjects attribute to their lived experiences.

    a. Among the numerous contributions debating Schutz's relation with Weber's theory and methodology, we wish to mention here only the most outstanding ones. Izzo and Zaret argue that Schutz's ideal type concept does not take into account the problem of historical-social knowledge, which would be instead relevant, from a Weberian point of view, for assessing the actors' "because" and "in order to" motives (Izzo 1991: 340–41; Zaret 1980: 1192–93). Prendergast (1986) recalls the influence of the Austrian economic school on Schutz's ideal type concept. From this school, and namely from Menger, Schutz would have learned the assumptions of the marginal-utility law, that is, the subjective theory of value and the use of abstract and formal concepts in social sciences, though he remarks that the Austrian school does not possess an acceptable theory on intersubjective understanding and concept-making. The ideal type instrument, as devised by Weber would have been used by Schutz because it is compatible with the marginalist theory, while exempt from its epistemological inconveniences. Some commentators object that Izzo's, Zaret's and Prendergast's remarks are the consequence of twisting or misunderstanding Schutz's thought and works (Muzzetto 1997: 147–50).

    b. Finally, some other essays deal with particular substantive themes of Schutz's sociology. Several themes treated by Schutz have become the object of attention, in-depth examinations and even exegesis. Leaving aside some essays that formulate interpretations, which are considered textually untenable (see for example Perinbanayagam 1975, and his criticism in Malhotra, Deegan 1978; Muzzetto 1997: 230–31, 238–40), we wish to raise the following points, as dealt with by the secondary literature: firstly, the concepts of common sense and perspective reciprocity; and among the associated themes, the aspects that connote the common-sense character of an event; the procedures through which common sense may be interpreted by different kinds of social actors (Garfinkel 1963: 212–17; Jedlowski 1994); the concepts of action, project and routine (Nicotera 2001); and equality as the result of a social construction process (Longo 2001).

References

Berger, P. and Luckmann, T. 1967. *The Social Construction of Reality*. New York: Doubleday.

Brodersen, A. 1964. Editor's Note, in A. Schutz, *Collected Papers II: Studies in Social Theory*, ed. A. Brodersen. The Hague: Martinus Nijhoff, viii–xv.

Carroll, R. 1982. "Adequacy in Interpretative Sociology: A Discussion of Some of the Issues and Implications of Alfred Schutz's Postulate of Adequacy." *Sociological Review* 30: 392–406.

Crespi, F., Jedlowski, P. and Rauti, R. 2000. *La sociologia. Contesti storici e modelli culturali*. Rome: Bari.

De Biasi, R. 2001. Dalle provincie di significato ai "frames." Note su Schutz e Goffman, in M. Protti (ed.), *QuotidianaMente. Studi sull'intorno teorico di Alfred Schutz*. Lecce: Pensa Multimedia, 277–301.

Eberle, T. 2001. La fondazione metodologica della ricerca sociale interpretativa tramite l'analisi del mondo della vita di Alfred Schutz, in M. Protti (ed.), *QuotidianaMente. Studi sull'intorno teorico di Alfred Schutz*, Lecce: Pensa Multimedia, 89–124.

Endress, M. 1999. Alfred Schutz (1899–1959), in D. Kaesler (ed.), *Klassiker der Soziologie*. Munich: Beck, 354–2.

Fele, G. 2001. Alfred Schutz e lo studio delle relazioni sociali: considerazioni dal punto di vista dell'etnometodologia, in M. Protti (ed.), *QuotidianaMente. Studi sull'intorno teorico di Alfred Schutz*. Lecce: Pensa Multimedia, 223–59.

Ferguson, H. 2001. Phenomenology and Social Theory, in G. Ritzer and B. Smart (ed.), *Handbook of Social Theory*. London: Sage, 232–48.

Fine, G.A. 1990. Symbolic Interactionism in the Post-Blumerian Age, in G. Ritzer (ed.), _Frontiers of Social Theory: The New Synthesis_. New York: Columbia University Press, 117–57.

Garfinkel, H. 1963. A Conception of, and Experiments with, "Trust" as a Condition of Stabled Concerted Actions, in O.J. Harvey (ed.), _Motivation and Social Interaction: Cognitive Determinants_. New York: The Ronald Press Company, 187–238.

Giddens, A. 1979. _Nuove regole del metodo sociologico_. Bologna: Il Mulino.

Giddens, A. 1984. _The Constitution of Society_. Cambridge: Polity Press.

Goffman, E. 1974. _Frame Analysis_. New York: Harper & Row.

Gorman, R.A. 1975. "Alfred Schutz: An Exposition and Critique." _The British Journal of Sociology_ 26(1): 1–19.

Grathoff, R. 1989. _Milieu und Lebenswelt_. Frankfurt am Main: Suhrkamp.

Gurwitsch, A. 1975. Introduction, in A. Schutz, _Collected Papers III: Studies in Phenomenological Philosophy_, ed. I. Schutz. The Hague: Martinus Nijhoff, xi–xxxi.

Gurwitsch, A. 1966. A Non-Egological Conception of Consciousness, in _Studies in Phenomenology and Psychology_. Evanston, IL: Northwestern University Press, 287–300.

Habermas, J. 1986. _Teoria dell'agire comunicativo_. Bologna: Il Mulino,

Habermas, J. 1987. _The Theory of Communicative Action_. Boston, MA: Beacon Press.

Heap, J.L. and Roth, P.A. 1973. "On Phenomenological Sociology." _American Sociological Review_ 38: 354–67.

Husserl, E. 1976a. _Idee per una fenomenologia pura e per una filosofia fenomenologica, Libro primo. Introduzione generale alla fenomenologia pura_. Turin: Einaudi.

Husserl, E. 1976b. _Idee per una fenomenologia pura e per una filosofia fenomenologica, Libro secondo. Ricerche fenomenologiche sopra la costituzione_. Turin: Einaudi.

Husserl, E. 1976c. _Idee per una fenomenologia pura e per una filosofia fenomenologica, Libro terzo. La fenomenologia e i fondamenti delle scienze_. Turin: Einaudi.

Husserl, E. 1997. _La crisi delle scienze europee e la fenomenologia trascendentale_. Milan: EST.

Isambert, F.A. 1989. "Alfred Schutz entre Weber et Husserl." _Revue Française de Sociologie_ 30: 299–319.

Izzo, A. 1991. _Storia del pensiero sociologico_. Bologna: Il Mulino,

James, W. 1950 (1890). _The Principles of Psychology_. New York: Dover,

Jedlowski, P. 1994. "'Quello che tutti sanno.' Per una discussione sul concetto di senso comune." _Rassegna Italiana di Sociologia_ 35(1): 49–77.

Joas, H. 1997. _G.H. Mead: A Contemporary Re-examination of His Thought_. Cambridge, MA: The MIT Press.

Kaspersen, L.B. 2000. _Anthony Giddens: An Introduction to a Social Theorist_. Oxford: Blackwell.

Lalli, P. 2001. Le arene del senso comune, ovvero "il cittadino metainformato," in M. Protti (ed.), _QuotidianaMente. Studi sull'intorno teorico di Alfred Schutz_. Lecce: Pensa Multimedia, 189–222.

Longo, M. 2001. La dimensione relazionale dell'uguaglianza: un commento ad Alfred Schutz, in M. Protti (ed.), _QuotidianaMente. Studi sull'intorno teorico di Alfred Schutz_. Lecce: Pensa Multimedia, 151–87.

Luckmann, T. 1973. Preface, in A. Schutz, and T. Luckmann (eds), _The Structures of the Life-World_, Volume I. Evanston, IL: Northwestern University Press, xvii–xxvi.

Malhotra, V. and Deegan, M.J. 1978. "Comment on Perinbanayagam's 'The Significance of Others in the Thought of Alfred Schutz, G.H. Mead and C.H. Cooley.'" _The Sociological Quarterly_ 19(1): 141–5.

Mead, G.H. (1934) 1967. _Mind, Self, & Society_, ed. C.W. Morris. Chicago, IL: The University of Chicago Press.

Mead, G.H. (1956) 1977. _On Social Psychology_, ed. A. Strauss. Chicago, IL: The University of Chicago Press.

Murphy, J.P. 1990. _Pragmatism: From Peirce to Davidson_. Boulder, CO: Westview Press.

Murphy, J.P. 1997. _Il pragmatism_. Bologna: Il Mulino.

Muzzetto, L. 1997. _Fenomenologia, etnometodologia_. Milan: FrancoAngeli.

Muzzetto, L. 2006. _Il soggetto e il sociale_. Milan: FrancoAngeli.

Natanson, M. 1962. Introduction, in A. Schutz, _Collected Papers I: The Problem of Social Reality_, ed. M. Natanson. The Hague: Martinus Nijhoff, xxv–xlvii.

Nicotera, F. 2001. Azione e routine nel pensiero di Alfred Schutz, in M. Protti (ed.), _QuotidianaMente. Studi sull'intorno teorico di Alfred Schutz_. Lecce: Pensa Multimedia, 125–50.

Perinbanayagam, R.S. 1975. "The Significance of Others in the Thought of Alfred Schutz, G.H. Mead and C H. Cooley." _The Sociological Quarterly_ 16: 500–21.

Prendergast, C. 1986. "Alfred Schutz and the Austrian School of Economics." *American Journal of Sociology* 92(1): 1–26.

Protti, M. 1995. *Alfred Schutz. Fondamenti di una sociologia fenomenologica.* Milan: Unicopli.

Protti, M. 2001. Lo stato dell'arte su Alfred Schutz. Premessa a questi studi, in M. Protti (ed.), *QuotidianaMente. Studi sull'intorno teorico di Alfred Schutz.* Lecce: Pensa Multimedia, 7–35.

Ritzer, G. 2000. *Modern Sociological Theory.* Boston, MA: McGraw-Hill.

Rogers, M. 2000. Alfred Schutz, in G. Ritzer (ed.), *The Blackwell Companion to Major Social Theorists.* Oxford: Blackwell, 367–87.

Schutz, A. 1962. *Collected Papers I: The Problem of Social Reality,* ed. M. Natanson. The Hague: Martinus Nijhoff.

Schutz, A. 1964. *Collected Papers II: Studies in Social Theory,* ed. A. Brodersen. The Hague: Martinus Nijhoff.

Schutz, A. 1967. *The Phenomenology of the Social World.* Evanston, IL: Northwestern University Press.

Schutz, A. 1970. *On Phenomenology and Social Relations,* ed. H.R. Wagner. Chicago, IL: The University of Chicago Press.

Schutz, A. 1974. *La fenomenologia del mondo sociale.* Bologna: Il Mulino,

Schutz, A. 1975. *Collected Papers III: Studies in Phenomenological Philosophy,* ed. I. Schutz. The Hague: Martinus Nijhoff.

Schutz, A. 1996. *Collected Papers IV,* ed. H. Wagner, G. Psathas and F. Kersten. Dordrecht: Kluwer Academic Publishers.

Schutz, A. and Luckmann, T. 1973. *The Structures of the Life-World,* Volume I. Evanston, IL: University Press.

Schutz, A. and Luckmann, T. 1989. *The Structures of the Life-World,* Volume II. Evanston, IL: Northwestern University Press. Turner, J.H. 1998. *The Structure of Sociological Theory.* Belmont, CA: Wadsworth.

Vaitkus, S. 2000. Phenomenology and Sociology, in B.S. Turner (ed.), *The Blackwell Companion to Social Theory.* Oxford: Blackwell, 232–48.

Van Breda, H.L. 1962. Preface, in A. Schutz, *Collected Papers I: The Problem of Social Reality,* ed. M. Natanson. The Hague: Martinus Nijhoff, vi–xiii.

Wagner, H.R. 1970. Introduction: The Phenomenological Approach to Sociology, in A. Schutz, *On Phenomenology and Social Relations,* ed. H.R. Wagner. Chicago, IL: The University of Chicago Press, 1–50.

Wagner, H.R. 1981. Die Soziologie der Lebenswelt: Umriss einer intellektuellen Biographie von Alfred Schutz, in R.M. Lepsius (ed.), *Soziologie in Deutschland und Oesterreich: 1918–1945.* Opladen: Westdeutscher Verlag, 379–94.

Weber, M. 1956. *Wirtschaft und Gesellschaft.* Tübingen: Mohr.

Williame, R. 1973. *Les fondaments phénoménologique de la sociologie compréhensive: Alfred Schutz et Max Weber.* La Haye: Martinus Nijhoff.

Wolff, K.H. 1978. Phenomenology and Sociology, in T. Bottomore and R. Nisbet (eds), *A History of Sociological Analysis.* New York: Basic Books, 499–556. Italian translation: *Fenomenologia e sociologia,* 1984, Rome: La Goliardica.

Zaner, R.M. and Engelhardt, H.T. 1973a. Translators' Introduction, in A. Schutz and T. Luckmann, *The Structures of the Life-World,* Volume 1. Evanston, IL: Northwestern University Press, xxvii–xxxiii.

Zaner, R.M. and Parent, D.J. 1973b. Translators' Preface, in A. Schutz and T. Luckmann, *The Structures of the Life-World,* Volume 2. Evanston, IL: Northwestern University Press, xi–xiv.

Zaret, D. 1980. "From Weber to Parsons and Schutz: The Eclipse of Reason in Modern Social Theory." *American Journal of Sociology* 85(5): 1180–1201.

Chapter 15
Structuralism in Sociology and Other Social Sciences

Preliminary Remarks

We aim at illustrating here the meaning and use of the notions of structure and structuralism as referred, in particular, to sociology. Though there is no universally shared definition of structuralism and structure, we want nonetheless to give some indication on how these terms have been intended, keeping to a distinction between two different definitions of structure. This distinction was formulated by Boudon (1970) and – in different terms – also by other authors (see, for instance, Blau 1981: 18–19; Rossi 1981). Both definitions intend the term of "structure" as the relations existing among the parts of a system provided with an order, or pattern, that can be ascertained in any particular moment, or over time. These relations form the investigation object of structuralism (Boudon 1970: 9, 14; see also Bates and Peacock 1989; Bottomore and Nisbet 1978: 556, 558–9; Peacock 1991; Remotti 1998: 420; Runciman 1969).

These two definitions of structure are basically different, despite these concordances. The first definition of this word, called "intentional" by Boudon, clarifies the notion of this term by specifying that it refers to a system of interdependent elements, which are explicitly specified by the definition itself, and are opposed to other elements outside the system. In this case, structuralism is a perspective meant for the study of structures, the empirical existence of which is evident. The second definition, called "effective" by this author, seeks instead to formulate a theory (meant as a set of axiomatic, or evident, propositions), the implicit (non-evident) notion of structure or system results from. In this case, structuralism is a method aimed at making this notion explicit. Though accepted with reservations by some scholars (Homans 1976: 63–5), the "intentional" and "effective" definitions proposed by Boudon represent a useful criterion to organize the definitions and concepts of structure and structuralism we are going to consider. The distinction made by Boudon between these alternative conceptions shall be used as a leading thread to present and compare the sociological meanings of structure, and the different research directions that refer to one of these meanings or to the other.

Focusing on the "intentional" definitions, in this chapter we shall briefly mention only the concepts of structure formulated by Blau, Homans, Coleman, Merton and Parsons. While we shall dwell on Blau's contribution to structuralism, the contribution of the other mentioned authors will be dealt with in separate chapters. Homans' contribution will be presented within the sphere of the exchange theory; Coleman's contribution within the rational choice theory; finally, Merton and Parsons, whose thought is presented in different and separate chapters, will be considered as representatives of the structural-functionalist perspective. The Rational Choice Theory, the Network Theory, the Exchange Theory, the Network Exchange Theory, and Structural Functionalism, are sociological perspectives oriented to structuralism, but they move from the assumption that the presence of constraints and opportunities is evident in individuals' action.

As regards, instead, the "effective" definitions of structure (according to which the structure is implicit, and can be observed only by researchers who have appropriate investigation means at their disposal), we shall briefly mention in this chapter the developments of structuralism towards non-sociological branches of knowledge, such as linguistics (with reference to Saussure), psychology (Lacan), analysis of literary texts, anthropology (Lévi-Strauss), and philosophy (Althusser and other representatives of the Marxist structuralism). The limited space available does not allow us dwelling on other authors – unrelated to sociology, too – who have contributed to linguistics and to a structuralist analysis of myths and literary texts, as Jacobson, Barthes and Chomsky. In separate chapters, we shall deal with Bourdieu and Foucault. Whether these authors are structuralist is contentious, even though they are usually considered within the sphere of sociology, and keep to this implicit notion of structure.

"Intentional" Definition of Structure

If we keep to the "intentional" definition of the notion of structure, in Piaget's extremely rigorous version (1968: 5–16), this notion implies the following three characteristics: totality, transformations and self-regulation. Totality, in the sense that the constitutive elements are submitted to laws concerning the whole set, or system, of these elements; transformations, in the sense that the constitutive elements are subject to changes – whether immediate or occurring over time – the totality of the whole set results from; self-regulation, in the sense that changes concern only the constitutive elements of the system, which consequently preserves itself, or changes according to its own laws. Other versions refer to at least one of the characteristics mentioned by Piaget.

Smelser has proposed a broader notion of structure, and argued its relevance for sociological theory. This version includes the following constitutive elements:

a. The relations between individuals or communities (i.e. groups or classes) as the unit of analysis.
b. When there are several units of analysis, they relate non-randomly.
c. The relations within the analysis units, and between them, are stable, that is to say, non-contingent.
d. Internal relations are divided from external relations.
e. To a different extent, a structure is open to external environmental influences.
f. Within the sociological theory, a variety of explanations have been proposed about the causes of the structure cohesion and its differentiation from the environment.

Focusing on this notion of structure, different conceptions of social structure are considered compatible with it. Among the different macro-sociological conceptions, the structure can be considered the effect of a variety of causes, such as the need to survive and operate in the outer environment, consensus on norms and values, or domination and coercion. Among the different micro-sociological conceptions, the structure can be considered the aggregated effect of interactions, or emerging from interactions provided with sense, reconstructed through the formulation of ideal types (Smelser 1988).

This definition complies with the definition proposed by Piaget: all the constitutive elements form the units of analysis, and are subject to overall changes according to their own principles. We shall mention now some further developments of the concept of social structure compatible with its "intentional" definition. Some of them suggest the criteria for making a distinction among different ways to formulate this concept. In particular, Warriner (1981; see also Paci 1998: 427–8) proposes to distinguish among different conceptions that concern the social structure: a first conception considers the relations between persons as a unit of analysis; a second conception, the relations between social positions or roles; and finally, a third conception, the relations between organizations or institutions. This distinction can be taken into account to classify the definitions, or conceptions, of social structure that will be illustrated in keeping with an intentional definition of this term. If interpersonal relations form the unit of analysis, the interpersonal relations between individuals become relevant. These relations can be formulated in terms of exchange (as, for instance, with Homans), or communication, or establishment or preservation of identities. Keeping to the third conception, we have focused on the meanings which these structures – intended as networks of relations – have for the actors who establish and keep them, and on the similarities and differences between perspectives that share this interest. In sociology and anthropology, they are, respectively, the perspectives of the British School of Cultural Studies and those of Symbolic Interactionism (Fine and Kleinman 1983; Musolf 1992). Some commentators, however, have argued that the second perspective, in Herbert Blumer's version, is incompatible with the notion of social structure, even in the sense of a structure of meanings (Smelser 1988: 122).

Alternatively, the relations between social positions or roles, rather than those between individuals, can form the unit of analysis of the social structure. The influential definition and conceptions of social structure, as formulated by Radcliffe-Brown, Parsons, Merton, and Blau, conform to this assumption. Radcliffe-Brown (1952: 10–11, 180, 188–204) defines the social structure as a network of mutual relations between individuals, organized by roles: through their functional activities, individuals give continuity to these relations and thus keep the structure itself into existence (see, in this regard, also Paci 1998: 432–3; Smelser 1988: 108–109). Parsons intends the structure in several ways (Paci 1998: 433). In particular, he conceives the structure as a system of actions, which are organized through roles (the elementary unity of the social system, as Parsons argues), and institutionalized through shared values that provide the roles with an orientation (Parsons and Shils et al. 2001a: 23–7; 2001b: 47–9, 190–97). According to Merton (1976), the structure is formed by a set of social positions, stratified in terms of advantages or disadvantages they involve for those who hold them.[1] In sociology, structural analysis, at a micro-analytical level, is focused on the choice between alternatives that are institutionalized, and hence, imposed on individuals. At a macro-analytical level, structural analysis is focused on the unequal, and historically contingent, social distribution of power, authority, influence and prestige. It is also focused on the social and individual consequences of this distributive inequality.

Blau, in formulating his personal definition of structure (1976b: 221; 1981: 9–16; 1990), has underscored his continuity with Merton and Parsons. Like these authors, he understands the social reality described by the term "structure" as the effect of external constraints, which limit actors' choices and behaviors. As a consequence, in defining the concept of social structure, our attention should focus – according to Blau – on the presence of objectively existing social constraints, rather than on their consequences. This conception of structure integrates another conception formulated by Blau, and is complementary to it. This author argues that the social structure consists not only of its constitutive elements – i.e. roles or social positions – but also of the direct and indirect relations between these elements. As Blau remarks, in agreement with a number of other authors, such as the students of Network Theory (see Marsden and Lin 1982: 8), the consequences of the existence of constraints are the relatively stable aspects of the relations between actors, and between social positions.

Homans considers these consequences, rather than the constraints, while Coleman lingers on how the actors' purposes and power shape social relations (Blau 1976a: 3–15). We shall consider now these authors individually. Homans (1976) refers in general to the considered elements as definers of a social structure. They are the aspects of the social behavior that are considered persistent, fundamental and interconnected as parts of a system. In addition, Homans remarks that the system is considered by sociologists – in some unspecified way – greater than the sum of its constitutive elements. Homans' conception mentions all these elements, except the last one: structures are the relatively permanent "features" of societies and groups, the characteristics of which are subject to descriptions, analyses and explanations (Homans 1976: 63–4).

In outlining his conception of structure, Coleman focuses, instead, on the notion of social system. This system is formed by relations between actors (whether persons or organizations) who rationally act in order to maximize the usefulness of those relations by controlling their own resources, since they are interested in obtaining resources controlled by others with whom they are in competition, and have established interdependent relations at the same time. For each actor, the environment, as formed by the system, can be assumed as either directly relevant, since it is binding for the actor, who is not able to change it, or as indirectly relevant, since the changes an actor brings to the system may involve direct or indirect consequences for him. Interdependent relations between the actors can change themselves over time, due to the changes occurring in the social system as a consequence of their actions. These changes, however, do not necessarily involve a balanced condition in the system (Coleman 1976, 1990: 28–31, 546–52, 899–900).

Warriner (1981: 186–7) dwells only briefly on the third and more abstract conception of social structure, which has the relations between organizations – intended as public or private institutions – as its unit of analysis. The text he refers to in this connection considers organizations as elements of the wider social system (Presthus 1962: 11–12). However, Parsons, through his conception of "Symbolic Media of Interchange" has provided a more extensive and elaborated contribution to this conception of structure. In Parsons' treatment, the symbolic media of interchange – money and power are the most outstanding examples – have the following characteristics: they are institutionalized; they can be used only in a particular kind of interchanges (there are, for instance, some interchange relations that cannot be mediated by money); they circulate among different subsystems; finally, their increase within an interchange sphere (as in the case of an interchange of political power) does not involve an equivalent decrease in its availability in other spheres (Parsons 1976). The integration among the elements of the social systems, and especially among subsystems, is a consequence of their common orientation in terms of values, and hence, actions (Parsons 2001a, 2001b: 202–204, 221–3, 275).

---

1 On Parsons and Merton's notions of structure, and on their thought in general, more information is provided in separate chapters.

Despite their dissimilarity, Homans,' Coleman's, Blau's, Radcliffe-Brown's, Merton's, and Parsons' contributions are compatible with an "intentional" definition of social structure. This not only results from the treatment of the theories of these authors in separate monographic chapters, but also from their explicit definitions, since they refer to the notion of social system as a whole, the constitutive elements of which are explicitly pointed out. Several other contributions are compatible with this definition of structure. We wish to briefly mention some of them. Bates and Peacock have formulated a concept of social structure which provides for different levels of complexity in the relation system. Starting from elemental structures formed by links between norms, the investigation extends itself to more and more complex structures. The units of analysis, which are abstract concepts used for classification purposes, and not empirically observable phenomena, change as complexity grows. Complexes of norms create roles, complexes of roles create social positions, and complexes of positions create groups (Bates and Peacock 1989; Peacock 1991). Wallace (1981) outlines a structure of social phenomena, in which the constitutive behaviors of the structure (that is to say, links between organisms, which can be whether human or non-human) can aggregate at different hierarchical levels. Each hierarchical level – for instance, individual actors, or the groups and the communities they form – highlights regularity in behaviors. A structural investigation can concern a collectivity at any aggregation level, or also the behavioral links between members of a collectivity, or finally, the degree to which their relations are regular, that is, orderly and constant.

Sewell (1992) adds that to conceive the structure in terms of pre-established constraints and models, which shape social actions, leaves their ability to influence other structures (their "depth") unspecified, as well as the power resources they have available, and individual or collective actors' ability to control these resources. Finally, Boudon (1981), formulates a notion of structure as an interdependence system between actors (whether individuals or organizations) and dwells on the emerging, or aggregated effects resulting from them. From the actors' point of view, these effects have not been pursued, and may be desirable or undesirable; furthermore, they may completely, partly, or not at all, conform to their objectives, but in any case, they impose themselves on actors. Thus, an interdependent structure between actors produces consequences that get out of their control.

Peter Blau's Structural Theory

As from the 1970s, the sociologist Peter M. Blau (1918–2002), who had previously distinguished himself for his contribution to exchange theory, aimed at formulating an exclusively macro-sociological theory of the social structure. Bearing in mind that every individual holds a number of social positions, the social structure is intended as a multidimensional space of differentiated and interrelated social positions. Social positions, in turn, are defined as the standards that are implicit in the distinctions individuals make in their associative life. Blau's theory intends to deductively explain social relation models only by availing itself of concepts pertaining to the social structure, rather than explain individual behaviors by means of psychological or cultural categories. This theory is deductive, as all the theorems that form it derive from some original suppositions and definitions.

Blau argues that to formulate a macro-sociological theory it is necessary to meet two conditions. First of all, to identify some structural parameters which provide the social structure with a specific configuration. Examples of these parameters are the degree of wealth concentration in a society and its ethnic composition. In the second place, to identify the characteristics, or "emerging properties," that do not belong to the constitutive elements of the structure. Structural parameters determine individuals' distribution in the different social positions, and hence, constraints and opportunities to establish and keep social relations. According to Blau, the most important parameters are heterogeneity, inequality and the intertwining of social differences. Heterogeneity is the differentiation degree of a collectivity into nominal groups, such as, for instance, linguistic groups. The more a collectivity is heterogeneous, the more unlikely is that two individuals chosen at random belong to the same group. Inequality is the differentiation degree of a collectivity into separate groups according to a gradation standard, such as wealth concentration degree and education level. The intertwining of social differences indicates the correlation degree between social differences of a different nature, as for example, education, ethnic belonging and income.

According to Blau, the emerging properties of a social structure are (1) the size or the number of constitutive elements of a social aggregate; (2) the relations between those who hold the social positions; (3) the aggregate characteristics that are reflected in the differences between its constitutive elements; and (4) the abstractions concerning the aggregate, which can result from properties of its constitutive elements. Blau's macro-structural theory contains (1) a basic assumption, in virtue of which social relationships are influenced by the constraints and the opportunities created by the social structure; (2) a limited number of original suppositions, as for example that individuals who hold similar social positions tend to associate themselves, and that these associations are the larger, the greater the number of contact opportunities; and (3) a list of theorems deduced from these suppositions. An example is the following theorem: both heterogeneity and the intertwining of social differences promote relations between groups, while inequality facilitates relationships between individuals of different social prestige (Blau 1977. Concise formulations of this theory can be found in Blau 1976a, 1981, 1990, 1994: 1–52; Turner 1998: 531–41).

The reception of Blau's macro-sociological theory has not been unanimous. Its impulse to empirical research concerning the relation between social heterogeneity and chance of contacts between different groups is considerable (Blum 1985). Favorable appraisals have appreciated the capability of this theory to be applied to relevant sociological issues, such as the ways in which different levels of the social structure interpenetrate (Haveman 1995: 224), as well as to the study of concrete interpersonal relationships, without any reference to actors' values and orientations (Calhoun and Scott 1990: 23). On the other hand, Calhoun and Scott, as well as Giddens and Turner, have called into question Blau's claim that his theory seeks to remain within a strictly sociological sphere while avoiding any reference to actors' culture and motivations. These references, which should not be mistaken for psychological references, are, however, unavoidable. As a matter of fact, the concepts of social position and structural parameters, involve a reference to actors' ability to make a distinction between different conducts and identities. To a great extent, these abilities are culturally determined. Furthermore, there are standards which are employed by a population to attach importance to specific structural parameters, such as inequality and heterogeneity. The very existence of such standards assumes sociologists' ability (Blau included) to discern and investigate them. Therefore, there is an implicit reference to an interpretative sociological perspective.

We should add to these objections further remarks concerning sociologists' comprehension or interpretation of the motives attributable to actors. Sociologists can come to the formulation of causal propositions (for instance, concerning the effects of emerging properties) only by investigating the motives ascribable to actors who put a particular conduct into effect, which is being studies, and by considering that actors interpret and modify their conduct bearing in mind the consequences resulting from it. The existence of relations between structural variables does not point to a causal relation between them, but only that actors have followed, whether intentionally or not, specific practices, which have shown to be linked with one another. Therefore, there is no theoretical justification for macro-sociological explanations, i.e. explanations that disregard the sense actors attribute to what they do (Calhoun and Scott 1990: 23–5; Giddens 1984: 210–13; Turner 1977b).

"Effective" or "Relational" Conception of Structure

All versions of the notion of structure we mentioned refer to its "intentional" conception, in the meaning Piaget attributes to this term. External constraints and stable aspects in relationships, from which the transformations and self-regulation of the social structure result, are indeed empirically observable. This conception of social structure is opposed to another, called by Piaget "effective definition" of a structure, and "relational structuralism" by Ino Rossi (1981, 1982), since formal relationships, in terms of differences and oppositions between elements, are the subject of research (Remotti 1998: 421). Anticipated by Radcliffe-Brown, who has distinguished between a really existing and directly observable structure, and a structural form that can be only described by scholars (1952: 192–3), this conception assumes the existence of a deep structure – and consequently, not immediately observable – of constitutive relations of the social system.

Keeping to this conception, the structure does not result from a definition, but rather from the theory itself – which can be assessed or not – through a sequence of pre-established operations (i.e. through a calculation process), on condition that the analyzed subject is considered a system. A system can be defined in the characteristics and number of its elements, as in the case of a set of matrimonial rules, or be undefined, as for instance, a social system is. If we keep to the effective definition of structure, in the aforementioned sense, the possibility of reconstructing all the apparent characteristics of the relation system results from theory. This possibility is directly assessable because such characteristics are perceived or experienced. In this case, structuralism can be conceived as an analytical method to highlight all that escapes a superficial investigation; that is to say, an observed object has fundamental properties in virtue of which the constitutive elements of the object form a system because they are reciprocally related (Ehrmann 1966a: i–x; Lane 1970: 30–32; Lévi-Strauss 1966a: 39–40). Intended in this way, structuralism has found application above all outside of sociology, in linguistics, anthropology, and in a particular school of Marxist thought. Sociologically relevant are considered the structuralist contributions provided by Bourdieu and Foucault. We shall separately deal with both authors more in depth. However, we shall first consider some non-sociological contributions. After having mentioned Saussure's linguistic structuralism and Lacan's psychoanalytic approach, we shall briefly outline Lévi-Strauss' thought in anthropology, and Althusser's, Balibar's, Godelier's and Poulantzas' thought within the sphere of Marxist structuralism.

Saussure's Linguistic Structuralism (1857–1913) (Outlines)

Linguistic structuralism studies the relations between the signs, provided with meaning, that form a language. We shall avoid to use here technical terms (as phoneme, morpheme, syntagm, etc.) introduced by Saussure, which, although currently used in linguistics, are not necessary in the case of a concise introduction. We can distinguish in a language words, phrases, and systems of signs (as well as other constitutive elements of the language). Each constitutive element can be identified by its specific properties (Pettit 1975: 110–12). The work by Ferdinand de Saussure, *Cours de Linguistique général*, which collects the lectures the author gave between 1907 and 1911 at the University of Geneva, has laid the foundations of structural linguistics. Saussure formulated in this work some theses that have had an enormous direct and indirect influence (Barber 1966: 239; Benveniste 1966). We report here some of these theses, or principles:

a. The linguistic sign connects a concept with an image or a sound the senses can perceive, as in particular, a word.
b. An image or a sound is called a signifier, while what they designate – namely, the meaning – is called the signified.
c. The linguistic sign, i.e. the link between signifier and signified, is arbitrary. In fact, different languages make use of different words, and consequently, different signs, to indicate the same concept.
d. When these signs are sounds, they are perceived in temporal succession. This does not necessarily apply for signs perceivable through the sight.
e. In a discourse, it is possible to distinguish between "language" (*langue*) and "word" (*parole*). "Language" indicates the set of linguistic conventions that make communication possible. "Word" designates, instead, an individual use of linguistic conventions: everybody has his or her own way to speak.
f. Language has a relative stability within a linguistic community (*masse parlante*). As language changes, the relation between signifier (which is an image or a sound) and associated meaning changes, too.
g. The study of a language can be made in a synchronic way, i.e. by considering it a system of signifying signs, regardless of its change over time (static linguistics), or in a diachronic way, considering its change (diachronic linguistics) (De Saussure 1970; see also Wells 1970).

Some commentators consider linguistic structuralism the only one for which it is possible to give answers to structuralist questions. Indeed, only in the case of language, reality constructed through the structuralist method (language as a system of signs) corresponds to an objective reality, given its concrete nature (the actual reality of the language spoken in a linguistic community). Therefore, the structure to be investigated is well defined, and can be systematically investigated. Language concreteness does not prevent it from being studied, regardless of particular forms of language or linguistic elements. Furthermore, structuralist questions, which concern the constitutive elements of language and their relations, owe their scientific interest to a conceptual apparatus that cannot be found in common language. There are, however, some objections. First, there is disconnection between conceptual pattern and results of structuralist investigations, since the latter do not change the pattern. Secondly, a distinction between synchronic and diachronic linguistics can be hardly applied to the study of real cases. Finally, some key terms are badly defined: in what sense is language of a concrete nature? Which of its elements, as words or phrases, can be called concrete, and why? Furthermore, does the term "system" applied to language, mean that it is stable, at least in the short run, or that a balance condition prevails in language, in the sense that any linguistic change immediately influences the language as a whole? (Lane 1970: 27–8; Pettit 1975: 113, 116–23; Remotti 1998: 420–21).

Lacan's Psychoanalytical Structuralism (1901–81) (Outlines)

Jacques Lacan's thought focuses on the structure of the unconscious he has put in relation with the structure of language, arguing that the unconscious –as well as the subject – exist in virtue of language. Following Saussure, Lacan intends language as systems of signs consisting of signifiers and meanings. The value of each sign depends on its relations of association and replacement with all the other linguistic signs. As a consequence, linguistic analysis is the best method to highlight the structure of the unconscious. The unconscious expresses itself through an archaic and forgotten language, especially in dreams, but also in other circumstances, such as jokes, fancies, and psychoanalytic sessions, and leaks out in every discourse that aims to be objective. Analysis is focused on the linguistic material used by the unconscious: this material is characterized not only by the use of metaphors but also by the distortion of the relation between signifier (the sound of words) and meaning, which is established in ordinary language.

In pre-verbal childhood, a flow of words comes from the mother figure. Their sense has to be discovered both by interacting with the mother figure an infant wants to please and by organizing sounds into systems of meanings, through which the baby's needs, wishes and emotions find expression. The mother figure is, for the infant, the other, the object of desire, the source of pleasure and, at the beginning, the source of visual and verbal identification, until the infant learns to distinguish his or her individuality from the mother's one, in the "mirror stage," according to Freud's terminology. The mother figure is also bearer of a symbolic order passed on through the language, which is a system of significant signs. For a baby, the relationship with his or her mother is a fundamental experience, which is always sought after its interruption, in which being and meaning are melted together.

The maternal order is countered by the paternal order, which forces the babies to detach themselves forever from their emotional identity with their mother, to repress their desire for her and, in general, their own desires and emotional satisfactions, to take a male or female gender identity, and to channel the experience of pleasure into socially accepted forms. Thus, the paternal order is the source of socialization. Through the paternal order, the subject re-orients his desire towards a new symbolic order focused on the paternal figure, which – representing the social order – is an alternative source of meanings to the maternal order. Language – an expression of the paternal order – allows us to communicate, and hence, to live in society – but cannot recreate the fundamental experience of the original union with our mother. Therefore, linguistic communication is devoid of emotional truth, is perceived as inauthentic, and creates a barrier. Only in the imaginary does the subject imaginatively establish an authentic and significant relationship with the other. The psychoanalytic session, which suppresses ordinary language, aims at bringing to light this original relationship with the maternal order, which has been channeled and distorted by the relationship with the other imposed by the paternal order. The original relationship is unconscious, non-biased (non-alienated), and expresses itself though a peculiar and mysterious language the patient recovers with the help of the analyst (Lacan 1970; see also Miel 1970; Resch 2005a).

Lacan's thought reception has been extensive, but substantially confined within the sphere of psychoanalysis, philosophy, linguistics, and literary criticism (Clark 1993). Concerning social sciences as sociology or anthropology, Lacan's work has been interpreted as a method for a critique of ideologies, as other schools of thought, and in particular, Althusser's structuralism (Resch 2005b: 433). Several commentators have appreciated its ability to overcome the dichotomy between objective and subjective, present in the Marxist thought thanks to the syntactical (and hence, structural) order given by language to the construction the subject makes of his or her symbolic representations (Rossi 1982: 13).

Structuralism in the Analysis of Literary Texts (Outlines)

Structuralist analysis has been applied to some texts, such as Bible stories, myths, poems and tragedies. Concerning Bible stories and myths, reference should be made to some examples (Leach 1970; Robinson 1970), which underline the relations (of incompatibility, mutual opposition and brokerage) between the roles the biblical or mythological text refers to. We shall then provide some concise indications concerning Lévi-Strauss' structuralist investigations of myths. We now wish to illustrate how structuralism has analyzed some literary texts, focusing on two works by Baudelaire and Corneille. Jacobson and Lévi-Strauss (1970) produced an analysis of a poem by Baudelaire, "Les chats" ("The Cats"). The authors find out several standards, based on which it is possible to distinguish in the poem phonetic, grammatical, metrical, as well as other elements related to the meaning of words, their either masculine or feminine gender, the order in which the strophes follow one another, their contents, and the number of lines that compose them. Elements of the same nature – for instance, phonetic elements – are put in relation, showing their continuity or opposition. In particular, as regards conveyed meanings, strophe analysis highlights a plurality of relations, which may be of equivalence or contiguity, closure or opening.

The analysis made by Ehrmann (1966b) of the tragedy by Corneille, "Cinna," is another well-known example of the application of structuralism to the study of a literary text. Considering some details of this analysis, it focuses on the relationships of the main characters of this tragedy: the Roman emperor Augustus; Emilia, who aims at avenging the death of her father, decided by Augustus, and at putting an end to his tyranny; Cinna and Maximus, Augustus' counsellors and love rivals for Emilia. Ehrmann highlights the existence of two systems of symmetrical exchanges between which Cinna is not able to decide, since he is uncertain whether he should prefer Augustus' favors to the detriment of Emilia (who cannot rely on him to avenge herself on Augustus), or prefer instead the favors of Emilia to the detriment of Augustus. Augustus' decision to give Cinna both the empire and Emilia, does not solve Cinna's dilemmas, since Emilia keeps her intention to assassinate Augustus at the hand of Cinna, who nonetheless has taken out a debt of gratitude with Augustus.

Emilia, who offers herself to him in exchange for his committing the murder of Augustus, is therefore, at the same time, Augustus' present to Cinna, and the prize Emilia intends to offer him if he accepts to carry out this action against the emperor. When Maximus decides to reveal to Augustus Emilia's and Cinna's intention to assassinate him, and declares his love for Emilia, the emperor finds himself in a condition of imbalance in the structure of his relationships, since after this disclosure, Augustus can neither rely on Emilia, nor on Cinna, nor finally on Maximus. However, the emperor succeeds in escaping this painful condition by acting in a manner so to oblige each of them to take out a moral debt with him, thereby rebalancing his relationships with all the other characters. Indeed, he forgives Emilia and Cinna, agrees with their marriage, and invites Maximus to recover his role as counselor.

The structuralist analysis of these two examples of texts has been subject to criticism, which has underlined the arbitrary nature of the procedures through which the elements of opposition are constructed. According to these critical remarks, by ignoring the meanings that words, or other textual elements, take in these texts and in other writings by the same authors, structuralist scholars build analogies, equivalences and oppositions in an a-priori way and to their liking. An example of this harsh criticism has concerned the structuralist analysis of the poem "Les chats." This analysis considers the poem within the sphere of Baudelaire's overall poetic production, and identifies its symbolic meaning by countering really existing cats, which symbolize contemplative life, with a supernatural cat, a symbol of concealed truth and an object of contemplation. According to this criticism, this symbolic meaning cannot be caught through Jacobson's and Lévi-Strauss' structuralist analysis, but rather through a traditional literary analysis (Riffaterre 1970). The critique that structuralism does not catch, or that constrains, the meanings of the texts, can be formulated more in detail, by pointing out that (a) structuralism has no standards by means of which to argue the choice of the subject of study, (b) the inner consistency of a system or a structure is never perfect, and (c) the investigation categories of structuralism are not universal, but culturally determined (Remotti 1998: 426).

Lévi-Strauss' Structuralism

Claude Lévi-Strauss (1908–2009), a French anthropologist and ethnologist, is one of the most famous and influential representatives of the structuralist thought. He applied structuralism to the study of the typical cultural elements (such as myths and habits) and parental and kinship relationships of populations in possession of a culture relatively preserved from contacts with modern culture. He calls this culture "primitive" (*sauvage*) without any intention to diminish its interest and complexity. As a matter of fact, primitive thought is as logical as the modern one, in particular scientific thought. Primitive thought distinguishes itself from modern thought, due to its absolute concreteness, which reveals itself in a meticulous attention paid to the observable properties of the animal and vegetable kingdom. On the other hand, this difference is stressed by the tendency – extreme, as well – to make use of analogies, distinctions and oppositions, in order to provide the reality of their physical, social and mental world with a metaphoric meaning (Lévi-Strauss 1962: 18–321). Ethnography is assigned to abstract from the peculiarities of a society, or a civilization, in order to achieve a sufficiently detached point of view on what is human in general (Lévi-Strauss 1955: 46–7).

We shall now illustrate his conception of culture, structure and structuralism. In general, according to this author, a culture is any ethnographic set that shows, from an investigation point of view, significant deviations in relation to other sets. It consists not only of peculiar communication forms as language but also of rules to be applied to every particular kind (or "strategic level") of communication. Indeed, the author makes a distinction between communication made by exchanging females, goods and services, and messages, and communication based on kinship or marriage rules. To the latter kind of exchange, the rules drawn from information theory – which is a systemic theory – apply (Lévi-Strauss 1974: 351–8, 384).

There are no objectively important deviations, or differences, among cultural elements, but they become important if researchers want to focus their attention on the elements of discontinuity that divide systems, which internally are sufficiently homogeneous. A structure should be intended as a system of oppositions and correlations, that reveals itself only to external observers (i.e., that is not evident to the social actors). It includes all the elements of an overall situation, formed – as well as by the social actors, jointly considered – also by their representations and procedures. Using an equivalent expression, a structure is a system (or network) of mutual links amongst a limited number of elements. These links can be assessed in different times (as a kinship system). A structure allows its constitutive units to play an essential role they would not be able to perform by themselves: to ensure the permanence of the social group.

The focus of Lévi-Strauss' attention is the construction of an image of the world, such as, for instance, a myth, through the primitive thought. This construction reflects, although not literally, the social relationships existing in a population, and is logically consistent. It takes place through analogies, oppositions, and distinctions with which aspects of reality – whether physical, mental or social – are related to one another and take a symbolic and metaphoric meaning. For example, the sun and the moon – nothing else but celestial bodies, according to the Western thought – in the primitive thought, when they are not indicated by the same term or verbal root, are distinguished by a set of characteristics attributed to the sun (heat, a specific masculine or feminine gender, a position in a mythical kinship system as brother or sister, a specific character, or a physical strength or influence degree), by opposite characteristics attributed to the moon. Myths, rituals and religious beliefs, provide with a meaning these sets of characteristics, which are considered permanent or changeable in an imaginary temporal course.

Classification systems, as in particular the totemic ones, are countered by those based on sacrifice; even though both systems reveal and incorporate a certain image of the world. Indeed, classification systems establish a stable homology relation between natural species (plants, animals) and human groups. On the contrary, systems based on sacrifice establish a temporary relation (up to the destruction of the victim) of metaphoric contiguity among sacrificer, victim and divinity. Furthermore, classification systems have a sense for those who develop them, and make use of a linguistic code, while those base on sacrifice are only procedures aimed at obtaining specific results (as the divinity's benevolence) and have, therefore, neither a meaningful nor a linguistically elaborated sense. Structuralist investigation – on which we shall dwell in the next paragraphs – is assigned to discover the mechanisms, in virtue of which a structure can play this role (Lévi-Strauss 1955: 305–306, 328, 336, 356; 1962: 35–6, 49, 130–33, 144 -147, 174, 268–73, 318–21; 1966a: 42; 1970, 1974: 208, 242, 351–2, 369, 376; 1976: 137; 2002: 8, 45, 82–3, 113, 121).

A society includes a variety of structures (in the aforementioned sense) of mutual relation systems. Systems of cultural elements or kinship relationships provided with their typical inner specificity and homogeneity; a social organization in which a particular order principle or conceptual pattern asserts itself (such as a reciprocity, dual opposition or hierarchy principle); social (for instance, castes) and economic stratifications, are as many examples of structure. A structure can have objective reality, but this does not necessarily occur. A culture carves out a sphere of reality depending on the problems it poses to itself. The categories, through which it organizes reality, show the ways – which vary depending on historical circumstances and place – through which individuals and populations relate with their environment. A primitive culture (in the neutral and non-depreciating sense in which Lévi-Strauss makes use of the term "primitive") builds an image of the world in a synchronic and diachronic way (i.e., regardless of its change, or on the contrary, taking it into account).

The construction of an image of the world is logically consistent and takes place through analogies, oppositions and distinctions, in which the physical, mental and social aspects of reality take a symbolic and metaphoric meaning. Classification systems, and in particular totemic ones, are opposed to those focused on sacrifice, although both systems disclose and incorporate an image of the world. The classification systems used by primitive populations break up reality according to different levels of generality, up to an ultimate level. Social reality is broken into individuals and roles, while the animal and vegetal reality into parts (as the mouth of a fish, or the unfolded flower of a particular plant) and attitudes (attributed also to plants). Each part, at any generality level, is characterized by a name. The animal and vegetal entity is broken up in this way, and then recomposed as an individual (as a particular plant or an animal).

Classification establishes a stable relation of homology and metaphoric identification between natural species (plants, animals) and human groups. Therefore the messages concerning one of these spheres receive a meaning, through a transformation process, also in the other sphere. By identifying himself or herself as an integral part of a clan, and his or her clan with no matter what plant or animal, a person shows at the same time to himself or herself, and to the others, what he or she is not. Systems based on sacrifice, instead, establish a temporary relationship (up to the destruction of the victim) of metaphoric contiguity among sacrificer, victim and divinity. Furthermore, classification systems have as sense for those who develop them, and make use of a linguistic code, while the systems based on sacrifice are merely procedures aimed at obtaining specific results (such as a divinity's benevolence), and therefore have neither a meaningful nor a linguistically elaborated sense.

From a synchronic point of view, a society consists of reciprocally communicating individuals and groups. In primitive populations, communication occurs through exchanges, according to a reciprocity principle. Items of exchange may be women, who are natural goods, or products and services, which are cultural goods. Exchanges may be limited to the same groups, or extended to new groups. From a diachronic point of view, both an historical-geographic perspective, and a structural perspective become relevant. The latter outlines an institutional pattern by means of which it is possible to explain analogies among societies that are distant in time and space. This may be done by disregarding the peculiarities of a society or a civilization in order to show in them the action of the same, or opposed, order principles. These principles, which are present in primitive thought, are constitutive of the social order of a population, even if its members are unconscious of them.

The structure results from an investigation able to highlight the constant elements of the investigated reality, which form these specific and internally homogeneous systems. So, for example, from the apparent diversity and inconsistency of matrimonial rules, from a complex set of habits and customs which are governed by these rules, from combinations in a myth of narrative elements, which at first sight may seem odd or absurd, the structuralist investigation draws a limited number of simple principles or properties that can be found without any changes several times in different environments, although differently combined. These principles create an objective (even if not directly observable) reality, which abstracts from the subjects. The structuralist analysis of myths, rituals, or other manifestations of social life highlights, as well as their interrelations, also their own code, or internal order, the subjects are not conscious of, which is kept and re-established by them even when life circumstances change. This code – as second rank codes – adds itself to the linguistic code, or to a code of a different kind (for instance, a pictorial or spatial code) through which these manifestations can be expressed.

This code, furthermore, is an inborn characteristic of the human mind. It often expresses itself by juxtapositions, through which a social reality is not represented as it actually is (since it is considered unsatisfactory), but rather as it could be, or as we would like it to be. The transformation from a condition to another is expressed by a set of equivalences, through which every element of the first condition is countered by another; in other words, it is its equivalent of the opposite sign. Therefore, there is balance between symmetry and asymmetry, correlation and juxtaposition, unity and diversity. For example, an analysis of the events narrated in a myth of a Canadian population living in British Columbia, highlights a juxtaposition pattern concerning an opening condition (characterized by female characters, horizontal displacements, famine, large spatial movements), and a final condition (characterized, instead, by male characters, upwards or downwards displacements, abundance, gradual cessation of movements).

Other specific functions in a particular structure and population can be brought back to the main function of a structure. For example, in the light of a structural analysis, a practice of ethnographic interest can prove functional to the (unconsciously pursued) purpose of solving or dissimulating an inconsistency in the social structure of that population. To keep the prestige and endogamy (inbreeding, marriage closure) of the upper caste would have damaged social cohesion, if there had not existed the opposite practice, exogamy, by means of which every person was allowed to marry only outside his or her group. As a matter of fact, the individuals who belonged to that population were divided into separate and reciprocally autonomous groups ("moieties," or halves), regardless of their position in a caste. Likewise, different solutions – as polyandry and male homosexuality – solve, in different populations, the problem posed by the habit to reserve the privilege to have several women to the chief, leaving the other men an insufficient number of women with whom to legitimately mate (Lévi-Strauss 1955: 201–203, 228–9, 255–6, 383; 1962: 68–71, 89, 112–13, 117–18, 148–53, 156–8, 189, 191–3, 211, 220, 247–51, 256–7, 268–9, 272–3, 318–19; 1966a, 1966b: 43–7; 1974: 46–7, 73, 124, 208, 242, 248, 254–5, 351–2; 1976: 79, 83, 110–11, 137, 164–5, 172–3, 181, 204, 268; 2002: 42–5, 54–5, 58, 65–6, 120–21, 130–31, 143).

Lévi-Strauss' structuralism has enjoyed a wide reception and a number of accurate interpretations, which have underlined its scientific interest. It has been remarked, in particular, that (1) his anthropology is characterized by the aim to identify "the rules that allow a transition from a system to another," considering the existence of systems (of kinship, marriage or mythical-cosmological) localized in a particular territory and historical period) (Remotti 1998: 424); (2) the invariant principles, which are constitutive of the code highlighted by structuralist analysis, are actually present in the unconscious of the individuals belonging to the populations the research is focused on (Bonomi 1968: 26); and (3) structuralist analysis – such as it was conducted and formalized by Lévi-Strauss – does not close itself to the study of historical change or the local and cultural context. On the contrary, just from this study, it inductively obtains the constitutive principles of the structure, which results from the combination of the elements that remain constant in the relations among the investigated cultural aspects. Abstract form and empirical contents, deep and surface structures, are therefore equally relevant in structuralist analysis, which necessarily avails itself of the study of the cultural products existing in any particular social organization (Bottomore and Nisbet 1978: 583–4; Rossi 1981: 61–2, 71–5; 1982: 8).

Lévi-Strauss structuralism, as well as a large amount of exegetic literature has produced some criticism, however:

1. Not all cultural forms can be reduced into binary juxtapositions.
2. The ethnographic, and in general, empirical material the author mentions to support his interpretations does not conform to other empirical materials, and has been chosen without taking them into account.
3. The empirical results that seem compliant are made such by means of appropriate expedients, such as the use of inversions and permutations.
4. The author does not mention how he has succeeded in formulating the fundamental dichotomies he attributes to primitive thought.

5. The inborn properties of the human mind are, at the same time, subject and instrument of his research.
6. The identification of elementary and mutually related constitutive properties in the subject of study is a methodological objective structuralism shares with any scientific investigation. Similarly, it is not a statement that characterizes only structuralism to affirm that the value of an investigation consists in specifying, based on empirical results, which relations can be found in these elementary properties.
7. The question of how deep, or unconscious, structures change is ignored (Baert 1998: 27–8; Leach 1981: 31–47; Runciman 1969: 257–8).

Marxist Structuralism

The concept of structure is considered relevant by Marxist scholars. Its use results from the intention to argue Marxist theses; as, for instance, the thesis of the structural change brought by falling rate of profit (Appelbaum 1978). Marx himself made use several times of this concept. An accurate analysis of these passages, some of which are famous, has highlighted its fundamental meaning: structure as a socially produced form of social, or production, relations, which sets itself against superstructure (Lefebvre 1966). Within the area of Marxist thought, French Marxist structuralism is characterized by the following theses:

a. The capitalist system is a structure consisting of relations between capital and labor, and therefore any internal or external event in it able to change one of these events changes the structure too.
b. The structure is real, but it is not an empirically observable phenomenon. On the contrary, the relations that form it are invisible, though they can be highlighted through an investigation that avails itself of the structuralist method.
c. Marx's dialectics has nothing in common with Hegel's dialectics.
d. The study of the structure in itself has priority over the study of its origin and evolution.
e. Structural events (which concern the relations between capital and labor) ultimately determine superstructural – i.e. political and ideological – events.
f. There is epistemological discontinuity between Marx's early works, as until the first half of nineteenth century he had not yet developed his conception of dialectics, and the later works belonging to the period of his maturity, with particular reference to *Capital*.
g. In the works of his maturity, the greatest theoretical importance is attributed neither to individual actors' practices, nor to their historical positioning, but rather to the general and abstract relationships among collective actors as capital and labor stakeholders (concerning the theses of structuralist Marxism, see Althusser 1996a; Althusser et al. 1996; Balibar 1996b; Godelier 1970; Poulantzas 1969, 1973, 1975a, 1975b).

With reference to these mentioned representatives of structuralist Marxism, and trying to highlight the specific contribution of each of them, we shall begin our presentation with Louis Althusser (1918–90), who is the most famous representative, also on a global scale, of French Marxist structuralism, and perhaps more than others contributed to the elaboration of the previously presented structuralist theses. We shall therefore dwell on his thought, which is focused on Marx's reflection on his own work, on the scientific purpose it pursued, on its innovation and difference compared to the classical and modern economic doctrine. Concerning the thesis of an epistemological break between Marx's early works and those of his maturity, Althusser has argued that the former, still written under Hegel's influence, have theoretical importance only insofar as they anticipate the works of Marx's maturity, showing their inner unity of thought. The theme of human nature, or man's essence, belongs to his early period (until 1845).

This theme – young Marx's theoretical humanism – is considered apart, regardless of production forces and relations, as well as the relations between structure and superstructure. Therefore it is an ideology, in the sense of a rigorous set of representations that play a historical role in a specific society, since they make all (even the ruling class) accept the relations between exploitation and domination as natural and justified. Dealing with the field of ideologies as a unitary field, young Marx foreshadows, but does not yet develop, the central issue ("the scientific problem"), which instead became the subject of his reflection in the period of his maturity. This issue can be inferred through a "symptomatic" reading of the writings belonging to that period, able to highlight the essential – invisible at first reading because it is covered by non-essential elements. Not ideology, but instead, the actual reality of contradiction and class conflict has formed what is essential, the central problem in Marx's maturity.

Marx did not merely overturn in a materialistic sense Hegel's dialectics (as in his early writings), but changed its terms and transformed its structure. The contradiction between capital and labor (which is also the contradiction between production forces and production relations) is now intended as the essential one. This contradiction produces a revolutionary change only if the specific and heterogeneous individual wills and the historical, national, and international circumstances that express the fundamental contradiction from time to time condense or blend into a single real unit, thus producing a revolutionary situation. If this fusion takes place, the fundamental contradiction between capital and labor is re-established, and – using Althusser's words – "overdetermined" (*surdéterminée*) by these specific circumstances. Though the ideological superstructure is relevant in producing a revolutionary situation, the basic structure is ultimately decisive in the long run. Change in a revolutionary sense takes place through a social transformation work: through social practices, in Althusser's language. Social practices are political, ideological and theoretical.

Theoretical practices consist in Marxist, and hence, scientific knowledge, which in the form of a structured system of scientific concepts, guides political and ideological practices in order to complete the revolutionary transformation. Thanks to them, Marxism distinguishes itself from forms of conflict that are spontaneous or led by non-Marxist ("opportunist") organizations. Scientific knowledge does not only assume an abstraction process from reality (as in Hegel), but also a scientific generalization process that leads to a new kind of generality, in any case of an ideological nature (as in the case of empiricist thinkers). Finally, through an epistemological breaking and a process called of "theoretical practice," it leads to a further generalization process, able to produce useful knowledge to understand the basic contradiction between capital and labor, and to prepare the social process of revolutionary transformation. Scientific knowledge, in this sense, involves real abstraction, and not only from reality. The political and theoretical practice of Marxism excludes, along with Hegel's dialectics, the use of his concepts, as those of alienation, overcoming, denial of denial, etc. The fundamental contradiction rules over the other contradictions of the capitalist mode of production. Each of these other contradictions is the condition of existence of the fundamental structure, the one referring to the capitalist mode of production, which represents the main contradiction. All contradictions, jointly considered, form a structured unit, in virtue of which the contradiction between capital and labor is fundamental and supra-ordinate compared to the others.

The scientific subject of the work *Capital* can be detected only through a theoretical critical reading able to highlight its philosophical principles, its basic concepts, and its departure from Marx's earlier works and from the classical and modern economic doctrine. This critical reading reveals Marx's discoveries, as the genesis of money, the organic composition of capital (constant and variable capital), the general rule of capitalist accumulation, the tendency of the rate of profit to fall, the land rent theory, the distinction between use and exchange value, as well as that in connection with concrete and abstract labor. The merits of classical economic theory – in particular, Smith and Ricardo – consist in having isolated and analyzed, though using an imprecise language, some important concepts as value and surplus value, and in having highlighted through these abstract concepts, the essential and real character of economic phenomena, looking beyond their outward appearances. On the other hand, classical economic theory conceives the economic categories of capitalism in a fixed, non-historical manner, which prevents us from interpreting capitalism as a structure situated in a specific historical time.

Every kind of history – economic, political, religious, of ideologies, of philosophy, etc. – has its own and autonomous historical time, marked by its peculiar problems, and characterized by theoretical and epistemological discontinuities, compared to other historical periods. It is not immediately evident and must be built in its structure, essence and specificity. Considering capital, the investigation must move from its theoretical subject (the capitalistic mode of production), and aim at highlighting its individual and specific historical form. The investigation should disregard the timing of events over the course of a historical time, but consider the determinations of the concept produced by history. Capital is a merely conceptual theoretical investigation subject, regardless of its concrete history.

This investigation, moreover, is the only one in a position to bring knowledge of it. Therefore Marxism sets itself against historicism, and consequently against the interpretations – in particular Gramsci's interpretation – that have intended Marxism as humanism and absolute historicism. Absolute historicism assumes there is no valid knowledge apart from real history. In this case, there would be no reason for being, for a Marxist philosophy – dialectic materialism – provided with its own subject of study, distinct from historical materialism, and its own theoretical problems. Only a "symptomatic" reading can highlight the theoretical and epistemological elements of Marx's text, which are not visible at a superficial reading, and its profound continuity and coherence.

The subject of capital is different from that of political economy (in the sense of economic doctrine). For the latter, the concept of *homo oeconomicus* is relevant insofar as it is a subject that is carrier of needs, producer and consumer of use values and committed to exchanging goods (commodities). This subject is invested with anthropological properties and in particular with rationality, and is abstract compared to real subjects. According to Marx, in the period of his maturity (the period of *Capital*), instead, consumption is not separately considered, but refers to the production modes, forces, and relations. Distribution is considered an economic phenomenon determined by production relations. Finally, production is examined as characterized by the same relations, given the material and technical conditions in which the production process takes place. Groups of agents (workers and capitalists) tied by juridical and functional relationships, act within this process. Production agents are not real individuals, but are defined by their social relationships (connected to production, but also political and ideological). Production relations are therefore relations based on domination and form a structure a theoretical, non-empirical investigation is focused on (as, on the contrary, political economy has tried to do).

The theoretical questions posed by an investigation of this kind, are as follows: what concept, or set of concepts, can be helpful to determine the elements of a structure? What are the structural relations among these elements? What are the causal effects of these relations on the elements of the structure? To establish what these causal effects are, it is necessary to define a concept of causality, which is able to express the determination of the structural elements by means of the structure itself. The previously formulated concept of "supra-determination" meets this requirement. In this sense, the structural elements are internally determined. Therefore, it is possible to say that the existence of the structure consists only in the effects it produces. The study of the structure (i.e. the capitalistic mode of production) is hampered by the presence of remains of different modes of production, and consequently, of other structures. However, Marx has not provided a theory concerning the transition from a mode of production to another (for a concise introductory text to Althusser, see Lechte 2005a).

Étienne Balibar (1942–) was a close collaborator of Althusser, and is perhaps the greatest expert of his work (Balibar 1996a). However, we shall examine here, in particular, his writings on Marxism, which join those written by Althusser, in the attempt to give Marxism a rigorously structuralist interpretation. We shall examine an important essay by Balibar concerning the fundamental concepts of historical materialism (Balibar 1996b). This essay includes also a theory of transition, which was not fully formulated by Marx, but outlined in some of his works, starting from "The German Ideology" (1845/6). Among Marx's concepts, the one concerning the mode of production – which is the theoretical subject of *Capital* – and the concepts in connection with it are considered central, given their function of epistemological breaking with the traditional philosophy of history. According to Marx, the antagonism – housed in the economic structure of each mode of production – between production forces and relations determines the transition from a mode of production to another, and consequently, from a structure to another. This antagonism is not an evident historical element, but was produced by Marx himself, as a creator of a science of history. For this purpose, Marx availed himself of two principles. There is, firstly, a synchronic articulation principle of practices at three levels: economic base, juridical and political superstructures, and finally, forms of social consciousness. There is, furthermore, a diachronic principle of periodization into separate ages, which follow one another without any continuity between them.

The economic structure, that is to say, the mode of production, is the distinctive standard. The economic structure has its relative autonomy, which allows establishing it as an independent research field. Research concerns, then, the distinct modes in which the economic structure is modified in the course of history by virtue of human actions that are, at the same time, of a practical and theoretical nature. Labor is organized in every historical age according to specific forms, which are functional to the work process. Technical and social elements flow into the work process. "Mode of production" should be intended as a "system of forms, which represents a state of the variation [i.e., a configuration] of the sets of elements that necessarily get into the considered [work] process" (Balibar 1996b: 435). By what standards can modes of production, or systems of forms, be distinguished? In other words, which are the elements of these systems? Marx identifies three of them: (a) workers, (b) means of production (object and working means), and (c) non-workers, who appropriate the surplus value in virtue of property relations.

The third element should be distinguished from producers' appropriation of natural resources, which can be found in every mode of production. There is therefore, in general, a production process, and in particular, in the case of capitalism, a process of increase in the capital value. Within the capitalist world, producers cannot perceive production relations, since they consider them natural rather than determined by social, political and ideological factors. The previously divided elements of the capitalist mode of production form the structure of the production process. Their combination, which is not casual, explains its operating way. In property relations there is a juridical, i.e. superstructural, component and, in particular, property and contractual rights, and within them, the rights concerning the labor contract. Juridical forms express and codify, but at the same time, disguise the capitalist production relations. As a matter of fact, juridical forms universally and abstractly express the mercantile exchange, which instead is not of a juridical nature, and is achieved only on a historically determined basis of capitalistic relations. Within these relations, the typical unity of craftmanship breaks into labor force and labor means, while in its stead, a unity between labor means and labor object is formed.

Through the succession from a form of material existence of the work process to another, the transition from an economic structure to another takes place. This change is not partial, since it includes all the three elements that create a mode of production. In historical materialism, the analysis of production forces is not limited to considering the technical conditions in which production occurs, but it is an integral part of the analysis of the social structure of a mode of production. History, as a science, is the history of the succession of modes of production, or structures. It is a theoretical, and hence scientific, history, with no human subjects. The relations between production forces involve, for each mode of production, different forms of individuality. Individuals are only an expression of the social relations the social structure involves.

When is the concept of mode of production applied? To use this concept, indeed, it is not sufficient to limit ourselves to consider the structural effects of each mode of production. It is also necessary to make of history discontinuity – marked by epistemological breaking – a property of this concept. Thus, it is necessary to combine an analysis of the formation of the capitalistic mode of production with an analysis of its dissolution. A theory of the reproduction of a mode of production can play – as the concept of mode of production – a relevant scientific role, in many respects. It allows us, in fact, to study the intertwining of individual capitals, to connect the different levels of the structure, to express the change and the new structure of the general production conditions. Simple reproduction – in which there is no capital accumulation, since the surplus value obtained from time to time is not reinvested –is not conducive to highlight social production as a whole; for the analysis of simple reproduction involves a consideration of the individual capital cycles. The result is an apparent and fictitious concurrence in the movements of the capital cycles that characterize the individual production sectors.

On the contrary, enlarged reproduction involves considering this whole, and consequently, the circulation, distribution, and consumption unit within a mode of production. Thus, the mode of production is a unitary structure, or system, the elements of which are the functions of the social production process. An analysis of a mode of production, and in particular the capitalistic mode, highlights its constitutive social relations and its operating way. The dissolution movement of capitalism, as in general, of a mode of production, cannot be explained by the conditions that preside over its operation. It is therefore necessary to resort to a different conceptual apparatus. With reference to the first volume of *Capital* concerning the origin of the capitalistic production mode (the so-called primitive accumulation), the transition from private property based on personal labor to the one based on other people's labor exploitation is argued. Workers are therefore deprived of control over their own work force, much as through the dissolution of capitalism capitalists are deprived of the property of the production means.

Primitive accumulation analysis concerns the original formation of the two constitutive elements of the capitalistic structure, that is to say, free labor and capital. These elements are of different and independent origin. Therefore, the structure resulting from their combination cannot be found in them. The outer and accidental circumstances of capitalistic development can delay it, at worst, or promote it within limits determined by intrinsic and structural causes. These causes – in particular, the combination of the tendency of the rate of profit to fall with the tendency of the rate of the surplus value to rise – work in the long term. The effect inside this structure (for instance, economic crises) cannot change the intrinsic limits of the production structure, but can contribute to produce external effects, such as for example, the particular form of class struggle. The succession of the modes of production does not obey to a temporal and historical principle. A diachronic analysis of a production mode (i.e. that takes into account the passing of historical time) has no autonomous theoretical relevance, compared to a synchronic analysis, in which the determinants of a production mode (i.e., of a structure), as well as the development within it, are shown.

This internal development conforms to the time of social labor, which in turn, depends on labor productivity and by the ratio in which social work – divided into work required for the reproduction of the labor force, and unnecessary work, which produces surplus value and hence, capital accumulation – is distributed among the different production sectors. The social work time – which is not the empirically ascertainable time in which a worker works – has the function of preserving a production mode, as in particular, the capitalistic mode, which changes as production relations change. It is a change inside the structure, which takes place according to a pace determined by the structure itself. In this sense, the proportion of constant capital (which does not produce surplus value) on overall capital is important, since its tendency to rise indicates the development stage of capitalism, up to its final crisis. The particular form in which production relations and forces, in which scientific knowledge is incorporated, correspond to each other, depends on the ways in which political practices – which present themselves as class struggle, law and state – intervene in the economic practices, and change them. The different forms in which political practices present themselves can be delayed in relation to the economic structure, as happens in transition periods from a mode of production to another.

Balibar seems to adopt Althusser's conceptual apparatus, in particular the key concept of structure, by which a central Marxist category is identified as a mode of production, and the concept of practices. Likewise, he adopts Althusser's thesis, according to which *Capital* is Marx's central work, and its accurate analysis can highlight its concealed structure. Only this kind of analysis, according to Althusser and Balibar, is of a scientific nature, differently from other historical-empirical scientific studies that do not go beyond the appearances of phenomena. Furthermore, according to both authors, the economic structure determines, though ultimately, political and ideological practices. Balibar seem instead to depart from Althusser not only by making lesser use of other concepts formulated by Althusser, as the concept of "overdetermination" one; but also as regards his greater reflection effort on the theoretical issue of the transition from a mode of production to another, and on the problem in connection with a concept of time compatible with a Marxist-structuralist investigation.

Maurice Godelier (1934–) has examined the relation between capital and labor as a constant element of the economic structure of capitalism, and hence, the element from which the study of its origin and evolution has to be prompted. On the other hand, non-economic structures concur with the economic structure to determine events, and have their own content, their own operating way, and their own evolution. Therefore, they are autonomous and the study of them is an integral part of any structuralist investigation. At the same time, this investigation considers the form and the existence conditions of the capitalist mode of production as a unitary structure, provided with objectively existing properties (Godelier 1970, 1982). Godelier seems to stress, more than Althusser, the causal weight of non-economic structures, while for the rest, he puts himself in continuity with Althusser's structuralist interpretation of Marx (Sayer 1987: 9–10, 70).

Nicos Poulantzas (1936–79) resumed Althusser's distinctions among economic, political and ideological power (political and ideological power sanctions and legitimizes economic power inequalities resulting from production relations), and between mode of production and social formation (a mode of production as the capitalistic one, reproduces itself within a particular and historically determined social formation). On the other hand, these distinctions are used by Poulantzas in order to focus, more than Althusser, on the concept of social class. This concept assumes the action of class struggle in social formations. Class is determined, in general, by the production relations that characterize a particular mode of production. The capitalist mode of production produces only two basic classes, bourgeoisie and proletariat. The former is the ruling class, while the latter is the ruled class, both in economic terms, and consequently, in political and ideological terms. However, every particular social formation includes different fractions of the two basic classes, such as commercial bourgeoisie and labor aristocracy. Further classes are identified, such as the traditional petty bourgeoisie and the new petty bourgeoisie. All these classes and class fractions can form alliances, resulting in ruling and ruled historical blocks. Class struggle determines the operating way of the state bodies, and therefore how they maintain the economic, political and ideological power of the ruling block.

Production relations, as well as political and ideological relations (in particular, family and state bodies, as school and army) that intervene in reproducing the economic structure, determine the continuity of power positions, regardless of the individuals who hold them. The role of the capitalist state consists of economically, politically and ideologically organizing the ruling block, and in disorganizing (in all these senses) the ruled block. The exercise of these functions involves the possibility for the state to protect the interests of some of the ruled classes, and impair, in the short term, the interests of the ruling classes, if this is necessary to preserve the interests of the ruling block in the long term. In this sense, the capitalist state benefits from a certain autonomy in the class struggle, though it is never neutral. To keep the cohesion of the existing class structure despite the presence of conflicts of interest within the ruling block, to preserve economic exploitation and political domination to the detriment of the ruled classes, to legitimize the violence of the state over them: these are the functions of bourgeois ideology (Poulantzas 1969, 1973, 1975a; 1975b).

Poulantzas' thought diverges from Althusser's and Balibar's structuralism because of its openness to empirical investigations and to the contribution (even if critically received) of some "bourgeois" sociologists as Weber (Turner 1977a). His reception has occurred, nonetheless, within the wider context of the French Marxist structuralism As a consequence, his reception has been affected by widespread negative appraisals of this approach. These appraisals are barely mitigated by the recognition that, thanks to it, some "serious and fundamental questions" have been raised about the nature of scientific and intellectual work in political regimes that would be expected to be liberal and democratic (Lechte 2005b: 811). The following critical remarks have been addressed to Althusser and Balibar, as well as Poulantzas.

It has been remarked, first of all, that their version of Marxism does not leave any theoretical space to investigate on the possibility of a historical change in capitalism through a spontaneous collective action. The consequences are pessimism and political apathy (Heydebrand 1981):

a. In addition, due to its non-empirical (and hence, hostile to sociology) orientation, structuralist Marxism is compelled to accept, as "useful" information, the results of surveys and investigations conducted by "bourgeois" sociologists, although this empirical material is considered ideological. The use Poulantzas made of Weber's sociology, illustrates this orientation (Turner 1977a).

b. Structuralist Marxism departs from Marx's and Engels' teaching in its attempt to provide a closed and abstract version of the Marxist key concepts – as, for instance, the concept of production relations – since it aims at pursuing consistency in theoretical formulations, and moves from the wrong assumption that the discourse spheres concerning facts and theories are completely divided, and that ideology always forms, regardless of how social relations reveal themselves (Sayer 1987).

c. Althusser's structuralism deliberately omits to investigate on the meaning real actors attribute to their actions, and consequently, on the relation between structure and collective action, which indeed depends on what they intend to do, and hence, on how they interpret their interests (Kaviraj 1989; Paci 1998: 436).

d. A theoretical reflection about the relation between structure and superstructure is insufficient. As a matter of fact, the conditions in which this relation can produce the transition to socialism are not specified. In addition, it is not specified why the contradictions of capitalism pave sometimes the way to socialism, and sometimes, instead, to fascism. Finally, no theoretical attention is paid to the questions of whether different levels of exploitation and class domination within capitalistic production relations are possible, or how is it possible to conceptualize and ascertain this diversity, considering French structuralists' disdain for concepts that may prove useful to conduct empirical investigations (Parkin 1979).

e. The distinction in Marx's writings between his early period and the period of his maturity, which would be marked by an epistemological breaking, is hardly tenable by comparing the styles and the topics that characterize these two periods (Bottomore 1978: 121–2).

f. Based on Marx's writings, it is possible to reconstruct several structures, in the sense of sets of necessary conditions, according to the adopted points of view: the set of conditions that produce the capital does not coincide with the set of conditions that produces workers' alienation. Therefore, there is not a single structure, as Althusser maintains (Ollman 1976: 285–6).

Nonetheless, these critical remarks, even if prevailing and formulated also within the Marxist theoretical production, should not overshadow several positive appraisals. Some Marxist authors, who have not shared these critical remarks, have in particular appreciated Althusser's (a) determination, in the last analysis – which is therefore invisible through merely descriptive methods – of the political and ideological relations established by production relations; (b) his alleged ability to balance theory and research by formulating concepts that can be applied to different modes of production, though they can suit also particular social formations; and (c) finally, his maintained ability to highlight exploitation and the ideology that legitimizes it (Resch 1992a: 22–9).

References

Althusser, L. 1996a. *Pour Marx*. Paris: La Découverte.

Althusser, L. 1996b. *Du "Capital" à la philosophie de Marx*, in L. Althusser et al. (eds), *Lire "le Capital."* Paris: PUF, 1–79.

Althusser, L. 1996c. L'objet du "Capital," in L. Althusser et al. (eds), *Lire "le Capital."* Paris: PUF, 245–418.

Appelbaum, R.P. 1978. "Marx's Theory of the Falling Rate of Profit: Toward a Dialectical Analysis of Structural Social Change." *American Sociological Review* 43: 67–80.

Baert, P. 1998. *Social Theory in the Twentieth Century*. Cambridge: Polity Press.

Balibar, E. 1996a. Avant-propos pour la réédition de 1996, in L. Althusser (ed.), *Pour Marx*. Paris: La Découverte, i–xiv.

Balibar, E. 1996b. Sur les concepts fondamentaux du matérialisme historique, in Althusser, L. et al. (eds), *Lire "le Capital."* Paris: PUF, 419–568.

Barber, E. 1966. Linguistics, in J. Ehrmann (ed.), *Structuralism*. Garden City, NY: Doubleday, 239–44.

Bates, F.L. 1989. "Conceptualizing Social Structure: The Misuse of Classification in Structural Modeling." *American Sociological Review* 54: 565–77.

Benveniste, 1966. *Problèmes de linguistique générale*, vol. 1. Paris: Gallimard.

Bierstedt, R. 1982. Comment on Lenski's Evolutionary Perspective, in P.M. Blau (ed.), *Approaches to the Study of Social Structure*. London: Open Books, 154–8.

Blau, P.M. 1976a. Introduction: Parallels and Contrasts in Structural Inquiries, in P.M. Blau (ed.), *Approaches to the Study of Social Structure*. London: Open Books, 1–20.

Blau, P.M. 1976b. Parameters of Social Structure, in P.M. Blau (ed.), *Approaches to the Study of Social Structure*. London: Open Books, 220–53.

Blau, P.M. (ed.) 1976c. *Approaches to the Study of Social Structure*. London: Open Books.

Blau, P.M. 1977. *Inequality and Heterogeneity: A Primitive Theory of Social Structure*. New York: The Free Press.

Blau, P.M. 1981. Diverse Views of Social Structure and Their Common Denominator, in P.M. Blau and R.K. Merton (eds), *Continuities in Structural Inquiry*. London: Sage, 1–23.

Blau, P.M. 1990. Structural Constraints and Opportunities: Merton's Contribution to General Theory, in J. Clark, C. Modgil and S. Modgil (eds), *Robert K. Merton: Consensus and Controversy*. London: Falmer Press, 141–55.

Blau, P.M. 1994. *Structural Contexts of Opportunities*. Chicago, IL, and London: The University of Chicago Press.

Blum, T.C. 1985. "Structural Constraints on Interpersonal Relations: A Test of Blau's Macrociological Theory." *American Journal of Sociology* 9(3): 511–21.

Bonomi, A. 1968. Introduzione, in J. Piaget, *Lo strutturalismo*. Milan: Il Saggiatore.

Boudon, R. 1970. *Strutturalismo e scienze umane*. Turin: Einaudi, 9–34.

Bottomore, T. 1976. Structure and History, in P.M. Blau (ed.), *Approaches to the Study of Social Structure*. London: Open Books, 159–71.

Bottomore, T. 1978. Marxism and Sociology, in T. Bottomore and R. Nisbet (eds), *A History of Sociological Analysis*. New York: Basic Books, 118–48.

Bottomore, T. and Nisbet, R. 1978. Structuralism, in T. Bottomore and R. Nisbet (eds), *A History of Sociological Analysis*. New York: Basic Books, 557–98.

Boudon, R. 1981. Undesired Consequences and Types of Structures of Systems of Interdependence, in P.M. Blau and R.K. Merton (eds), *Continuities in Structural Inquiry*. London: Sage, 255–84.

Calhoun, C. and Scott, W.R. 1990. Introduction: Peter Blau's Sociological Structuralism, in C. Calhoun, M.W. Meyer and W.R. Scott (eds), *Structures of Power and Constraint: Papers in Honor of Peter M. Blau*. Cambridge: Cambridge University Press, 1–36.

Clark, H. 1993. "Lacan's Return: Reading and Paranoia." *Semiotic Review of Books* 4(2): 8–10.

Clark, P.P. and Clark, T.N. 1982. The Structural Sources of French Structuralism, in I. Rossi (ed.), *Structural Sociology*. New York: Columbia University Press, 22–46.

Coleman, J.S. 1976. Social Structure and a Theory of Action, in P.M. Blau (ed.), *Approaches to the Study of Social Structure*. London: Open Books.

Coleman, J.S. 1990. *Foundations of Social Theory*. Cambridge, MA: Harvard University Press, 76–93.

Ehrmann, J. 1966a. Introduction, in J. Ehrmann (ed.), *Structuralism*. Garden City, NY: Doubleday, vii–xi.

Ehrmann, J. 1966b. Structures of Exchange in Cinna, in J. Ehrmann (ed.), *Structuralism*. Garden City, NY: Doubleday, 158–88.

Eisenstadt, S.N. 1981. Some Observations on Structuralism in Sociology, with Special, and Paradoxical, Reference to Max Weber, in P.M. Blau and R.K. Merton (eds), *Continuities in Structural Inquiry*. London: Sage, 165–76.

Eisenstadt, S.N. 1982. Symbolic Structuralism and Social Dynamics with Special Reference to Studies of Modernization, in I. Rossi (ed.), *Structural Sociology*. New York: Columbia University Press, 149–79.

Fine, G.A. and Kleinman, S. 1983. "Network and Meaning: An Interactionist Approach to Structure." *Symbolic Interaction* 6(1): 97–110.

Giddens, A. 1984. *The Constitution of Society*. Cambridge: Polity Press.

Godelier, M. 1970. System, Structure and Contradiction in *Das Kapital*, in M. Lane (ed.), *Introduction to Structuralism*. New York: Basic Books, 340–58.

Godelier, M. 1982. The Problem of the "Reproduction" of Socioeconomic Systems, in I. Rossi (ed.), *Structural Sociology*. New York: Columbia University Press, 259–91.

Goode, W.J. 1976. Homans' and Merton's Structural Approach, in P.M. Blau (ed.), *Approaches to the Study of Social Structure*. London: Open Books, 66–75.

Hartmann, G. 1970. Structuralism: The Anglo-American Adventure, in J. Ehrmann (ed.), *Structuralism*. Garden City, NY: Doubleday, 137–58.

Haveman, H. 1995. "Review of Structural Contexts of Opportunities by P.M. Blau." *American Journal of Sociology* 101: 222–4.

Heydebrand, W.V. 1981. Marxist Structuralism, in P.M. Blau (ed.), *Approaches to the Study of Social Structure*. London: Open Books, 81–119.

Homans, G.C. 1976. What Do We Mean by Social Structure?, in P.M. Blau (ed.), *Approaches to the Study of Social Structure*. London: Open Books, 53–65.

Jacobson, R. 1970. On Russian Fairy Tales, in M. Lane (ed.), *Introduction to Structuralism*. New York: Basic Books, 184–201.

Jacobson, R. and Lévi-Strauss, C. 1970. Charles Baudelaire's "Les Chats," in M. Lane (ed.), *Introduction to Structuralism*. New York: Basic Books, 202–21.

Katz, F.E. 1982. Structural Autonomy and the Dynamics of Social Systems, in I. Rossi (ed.), *Structural Sociology*. New York: Columbia University Press, 99–121.

Kaviraj, S. 1989. On Political Explanation in Marxism, in K. Bharadwaj and S. Kaviraj (eds), *Perspectives on Capitalism*. New Delhi, London: Sage, 132–74.

Lacan, J. 1970. The Insistence of the Letter in the Unconscious, in J. Ehrmann (ed.), *Structuralism*. Garden City, NY: Doubleday, 101–37.

Lane, M. 1970. Introduction, in M. Lane (ed.), *Introduction to Structuralism*. New York: Basic Books, 11–39.

Leach, E.R. 1970. The Legitimacy of Solomon, in M. Lane (ed.), *Introduction to Structuralism*. New York: Basic Books, 248–92.

Leach, E.R. 1981. British Social Anthropology and Lévi-Strauss Structuralism, in P.M. Blau and R.K. Merton (eds), *Continuities in Structural Inquiry*. London: Sage, 27–49.

Lechte, J. 2005a. Althusser, Louis, in G. Ritzer (ed.), *Encyclopedia of Social Theory*. London: Sage, 10–12.

Lechte, J. 2005b. Structuralist Marxism, in G. Ritzer (ed.), *Encyclopedia of Social Theory*. London: Sage, 804–11.

Lefebvre, H. 1966. Il concetto di struttura in Marx, in R. Bastide (ed.), *Usi e significati del termine "struttura."* Milan: Bompiani, 107–31.

Lenski, G. 1982. Social Structure in Evolutionary Perspective, in I. Rossi (ed.), *Structural Sociology*. New York: Columbia University Press, 135–53.

Lévi-Strauss, C. 1955. *Tristes Tropiques*. Paris: Plon.

Lévi-Strauss, C. 1962. *La pensée sauvage*. Paris: Plon.

Lévi-Strauss, C. 1966a. I limiti del concetto di struttura in etnologia, in R. Bastide (ed.), *Usi e significati del termine "struttura."* Milan: Bompiani, 37–43.

Lévi-Strauss, C. 1966b. Overture to *le Cru et le cuit*, in J. Ehrmann (ed.), *Structuralism*. Garden City, NY: Doubleday, 31–55.

Lévi-Strauss, C. 1970. The Sex of the Heavenly Bodies, in M. Lane (ed.), *Introduction to Structuralism*. New York: Basic Books, 330–39.

Lévi-Strauss, C. 1974. *Anthropologie structurale*. Paris: Plon.

Lévi-Strauss, C. 1976. *Structural Anthropology*, Volume 2. New York: Penguin Books.

Lévi-Strauss, C. 2002. *Le totémisme aujourd'hui*. Paris: Presses Universitaire de France.

Lidz, C.W. 1982. Toward A Deep Structural Analysis of Moral Action, in I. Rossi (ed.), *Structural Sociology*. New York: Columbia University Press, 229–56.

Martinet, A. 1966. Structure and Language, in J. Ehrmann (ed.), *Structuralism*. Garden City, NY: Doubleday, 1–9.

Marsden, P.V. and Lin, N. 1982. Introduction, in P.V. Marsden and N. Lin (eds), *Social Structure and Network Analysis*. London: Sage, 9–11.

Merton, R.K. 1976. Structural Analysis in Sociology, in P.M. Blau (ed.), *Approaches to the Study of Social Structure*. London: Open Books, 21–52.

Miel, J. 1970. Jacques Lacan and the Structure of the Unconscious, in J. Ehrmann (ed.), *Structuralism*. Garden City, NY: Doubleday, 94–101.

Musolf, G.R. 1992. "Structure, Institutions, Power, and Ideology: New Directions within Symbolic Interactionism." *The Sociological Quarterly* 33(2): 171–89.

Ollman, B. 1976. *Alienation*. Cambridge: Cambridge University Press.

Paci, M. 1998. Struttura sociale, in *Enciclopedia delle Scienze Sociali*, Volume 8. Rome: Istituto della Enciclopedia Italiana, 427–45.

Parkin, F. 1979. *Marxism and Class Theory: A Bourgeois Critique*. London: Tavistock.

Parsons, T. 1976. Social Structure and the Symbolic Media of Interchange, in P.M. Blau (ed.), *Approaches to the Study of Social Structure*. London: Open Books, 94–120.

Parsons, T. 1982. Action, Symbols, and Cybernetic Control, in I. Rossi (ed.), *Structural Sociology*. New York: Columbia University Press, 49–65.

Parsons, T. and Shils, E.A. 2001. *Toward A General Theory of Action*. London: Transaction.

Parsons, T., Shils, E.A. et al. 2001a. Some Fundamental Categories of the Theory of Action: A General Statement, in T. Parsons and E.A. Shils (eds), *Toward A General Theory of Action*. London: Transaction, 3–27.

Parsons, T. and Shils, E.A. et al. 2001b. Values, Motives, and Systems of Action, in T. Parsons and E.A. Shils (eds), *Toward A General Theory of Action*. London: Transaction, 45–275.

Peacock, W.G. 1991. "In Search of Social Structure." *Sociological Inquiry* 61: 281–98.

Pettit, P. 1975. *The Concept of Structuralism: A Critical Analysis*. Berkeley, CA: University of California Press.

Presthus, R. 1962. *The Organizational Society*. New York: Vintage Books.

Piaget, J. 1968. *Le structuralisme*. Paris: Presses Universitaires de France.

Poulantzas, N. 1969. "The Problem of the Capitalist State." *New Left Review* 58: 67–78.

Poulantzas, N. 1973. "On Social Classes." *New Left Review* 78: 27–54.

Poulantzas, N. 1975a. *Potere politico e classi sociali*. Rome: Editori Riuniti.

Poulantzas, N. 1975b. *Classi sociali e capitalismo oggi*. Milan: Etas Libri.

Radcliffe-Brown, A.R. 1952. *Structure and Function in Primitive Society*. London: Cohen & West.

Remotti, F. 1998. Strutturalismo, in *Enciclopedia delle Scienze Sociali*, Volume 8. Rome: Istituto della Enciclopedia Italiana, 419–27.

Resch, R.P. 2005a. *Althusser and the Renewal of Marxist Social Theory*. Berkeley, CA: University of California Press, 1992.

Resch, R.P. 2005b. Lacan, Jacques, in G. Ritzer (ed.), *Encyclopedia of Social Theory*, Volume 1. London: Sage, 428–33.

Riffaterre, M. 1970. Describing Poetic Structures: Two Approaches to Baudelaire's *les Chats*, in J. Ehrmann (ed.), *Structuralism*. Garden City, NY: Doubleday, 188–230.

Robinson, M.S. 1970. "The House of the Mighty Hero" or "The House of Enogh Paddy"? Some Implications of a Sinhalese Myth, in M. Lane (ed.), *Introduction to Structuralism*. New York: Basic Books, 293–329.

Rossi, I. 1981. Transformational Structuralism: Lévi-Strauss Definition of Social Structure, in P.M. Blau and R.K. Merton (eds), *Continuities in Structural Inquiry*. London: Sage, 51–80.

Rossi, I. 1982. Relational Structuralism as an Alternative to the Structural and Interpretive Paradigms of Empiricist Orientation, in I. Rossi (ed.), *Structural Sociology*. New York: Columbia University Press, 3–21.

Runciman, W.G. 1969. "What is Structuralism?" *British Journal of Sociology* 20(3): 253–65.

Saussure, F. de 1970. Introduction, in M. Lane (ed.), *Introduction to Structuralism*. New York: Basic Books, 11–56.

Sayer, D. 1987. *The Violence of Abstraction*. Oxford: Basil Blackwell.

Scheffer, H.W. 1970. Structuralism in Anthropology, in J. Ehrmann (ed.), *Structuralism*. Garden City, NY: Doubleday, 56–79.

Sewell, W.H. 1992. "A Theory of Structure: Duality, Agency, and Transformation." *American Journal of Sociology* 98(1): 1–29.

Smelser, N.J. 1988. Social Structure, in N.J. Smelser (ed.), *Handbook of Sociology*. London: Sage, 103–31.

Stinchcombe, A.L. 1982. The Deep Structure of Moral Categories, in I. Rossi (ed.), *Structural Sociology*. New York: Columbia University Press, 66–95.

Turner, B.S. 1977a. "The Structuralist Critique of Weber's Sociology." *British Journal of Sociology* 28(1): 1–16.

Turner, B.S. 1977b. "Blau's Theory of Differentiation: Is It Explanatory." *The Sociological Quarterly* 18: 17–32.

Turner, J. 1998. *The Structure of Sociological Theory*. Belmont, CA: Wadsworth.

Wallace, C.K. 1981. Hierarchic Structure in Social Phenomena, in P.M. Blau and R.K. Merton (eds), *Continuities in Structural Inquiry*. London: Sage, 191–234.

Warriner, C.K. 1981. Levels in the Study of Social Structure, in P.M. Blau and R.K. Merton (eds), *Continuities in Structural Inquiry*. London: Sage, 179–90.

Wells, R.S. 1970. De Saussure's System of Linguistics, in M. Lane (ed.), *Introduction to Structuralism*. New York, 85–123.

Chapter 16
Symbolic Interactionism

Preliminary Remarks

In this chapter, an introduction to this perspective to indicate its defining elements and, consequently, its field of study will be provided. Some authors who are considered among its most outstanding representatives, such as Cooley, Thomas, Mead and Blumer, will be then dealt with, and their thought synthetically outlined. The conceptual and theoretical relations among these authors, some recent interpretations of their thought, and finally the current developments of this perspective, will also be mentioned.

Symbolic Interactionism: Defining Elements and Field of Study

It is a difficult and debatable task of outlining the defining elements, and hence the field of study, of the symbolic interactionism perspective. Nevertheless, on this matter we shall here report some indications we prefer to other ones, as they take into account the classic formulations, particularly those by Mead and Blumer, and the latest developments. These indications summarize the defining elements of symbolic interactionism, specify their basic premises, and consequently outline their field of study, as follows:

1. Human beings have relevant symbolic abilities in their interactions, among which are, particularly, the Mind and the Self; therefore, unlike animals, their behavior does not automatically respond to a stimulus.
2. Individuals were not born as human beings, but become human beings by virtue of these symbolic abilities and social interactions.
3. Individuals use their Mind and their Self to actively and consciously interact with the world, dialoguing with themselves and to the others, and shaping their behavior, though within the limits of environmental conditionings.
4. During these interactions, definitions of the situation take shape, and individuals contribute to them and take them into account for their own purposes. To define a situation involves carrying out some activities within it: to establish aims, apply the point of view of other significant individuals or reference groups to a particular situation, point out to oneself what is relevant for that situation (persons, things, ideas, etc.), take upon oneself the role of other individuals or groups, define oneself within a situation (what an individual does, what happens and what concerns it, how an individual judges itself, what identity it attributes to itself, how it emotionally interprets what it is experiencing), imagine the future effects of one's action, and apply knowledge and memories of the past to a situation.
5. Society does not exist independently of the interactions and the meanings that are attributed to them. On the contrary, it is formed – in a non-rigidly structured way – by those interactions and the associated meanings.
6. The study of those interactions and meanings involves using methods suitable to obtain a sympathetic comprehension of the individuals or groups that are the object of inquiry (Sandstrom et al. 2001: 218–19; see also Charon 2001: 203–205; Plummer 1991a: x–xi).

Individual and Society in the Thought of Charles H. Cooley (1864–1929)

In his pioneering version of the interactionist approach, Cooley set himself the objective to convey into a unitary conceptual and theoretical pattern some categories. Some of them were derived from other thinkers, such as the "Self" (from William James) and "Society"; the author himself introduced other categories, such as "primary group" and "social organization." We shall dwell upon these categories and try to show their interconnections.

The Individual and Social "Self"

According to Cooley, "Self," or "I," indicate any idea or object that can stir in the individual a sense of power, possession and specificity towards the natural and social world surrounding it. Its body, objects like its house, persons like the members of its family, and also opinions, aims and desires considered as something of its own, constitute this world. The assertion of one's "I" is opportune and proper when the individual gives with its work and its person an effective contribution to society. A "Social Self" is a system of ideas, which, although recognized by individuals as something of their own, are socially generated. This "Social Self" goes along with a sense of identification with other individuals with whom they share cooperative activities. Therefore, the existence of an individual and social "Self" assumes that there are persons or communities to which reference is made and in comparison with which the individual wants to distinguish him or herself. This involves, in turn, a communication – however performed – with others, which may allow an individual or a community to not only assert and make its own way of thinking understood, but also have a personal idea on those others. Therefore, social and moral reality symbolically exists in the mind of people or groups that communicate one to another. The method of sympathetic penetration, which Cooley recommended, enables researchers to grasp this existence.

Quite often, the reference to persons or communities takes the shape of the image of how one's "Self" appears to the mind of particular others: the "Self" is a mirror of how a subject – either an individual or a group – imagines being seen by those others. When, more or less consciously, a subject associates with that image an opinion concerning its own "Self" or some of its features (such as aspect, character, behavior), depending on circumstances, it gets feelings of pride or mortification as a result. In this sense, the "Self" has a social origin, though a subject may seek to change it by changing its own image in others people's eyes. The making of the "Self," conforming to one's image of other people's opinions, already occurs in early childhood, but it is a better-defined and more complex process in adults.

Individual, Primary Group, Social Organization and Society

By the words "individual" and "society" are meant, respectively, the particular and general aspect of human life. If society is a community of individuals, these individuals do not and cannot exist independently of the society in which they functionally act. Likewise, individual and social consciousness are two different but connected aspects of moral life. Accordingly, it may be easily comprehended how discontent and social problems originate from the impossibility of the single individual to find in society a satisfaction of needs that are deeply rooted in human nature, such as the need for self-expression, appreciation and sufficient safeness. The primary groups, such as the family, children's groups of playmates, neighbors and adult community groups, are characterized by social organization, that is, by the intimate association and cooperation of their members, providing them with a first complete experience of social life. Primary groups are also a necessary condition to establish, along with a social consciousness or awareness of society, social rules or ideals, above all the universally shared ideal of group moral unity. Therefore morality assumes the existence of primary groups and, in general, of society meant as a system. Public opinion, or public spirit, must know morality in order to pursue rational aims. Consequently it must also know the social system that girds it, as well as the social organization or structure in which this public spirit is expressed.

Society is composed of several aggregates of different sizes, from primary groups to institutions, considered as organized attitudes of the public spirit (such as the family, Church, economic and political institutions), up to and including the whole of human kind. In addition, traditions and social processes also compose it. There are imitation, differentiation and adaptation processes, but also processes aimed at encouraging the sense of participation to a common social and spiritual comprehensive group. These processes can be either cooperative or non-cooperative. The forming of society as a moral body depends on cooperative communication and mutual influence processes. Non-cooperative or conflict processes, self- or group- achievement processes in contrast or in competition with others, promote contacts among individuals, classes, institutions, drive the parties to pursue their ideals, and encourage changes and social progress. When conflict is controlled and regulated, as it may happen in modern life, hostile feelings are restrained in favor of the awareness of a common morality. This occurs because universally valid rules involve the obligation to relate to others without mutual destruction. Emulation is conveyed into a common benefit, provided that the search for one's benefit – particularly in the economic and social areas – does not hamper the feeling of belonging to a larger unity, and hence the making and maintenance of a "Social Self." A lack of it creates resentment and hostility, as unregulated class conflicts evidence.

Society is a single organic system, though differentiated structurally, in the sense of being articulated in social parties or types, such as family, other primary groups and institutions, social classes and processes, and functionally, to the effect that individuals perform special functions, according to their occupation. The structural and functional differentiation of society is also the condition for achieving, along with a widening of social organization, a development the public spirit, and therefore in the way of thinking and in the sense of moral unity among persons, nations, races and classes. In the political area, communication, and the modern technologies that are instrumental to it, allow the organizing of public opinion and, thereby, democracy. Democracy is the consequence and expression of public opinion, for it promotes an enlargement of the spirit of service and, in the political field, training in judgment and self-control (Cooley 1909, 1922).

The Reception of Cooley's Thought (an outline)

Researchers usually underline a continuity of Cooley thought with the philosopher William James and some of Cooley's own contemporary thinkers, particularly Mead, as both social thinkers were close to pragmatism and symbolic interactionism. In this regard, reference may be made to several items. They are (a) the analytic categories of "I" and "Social Self"; (b) the thesis, according to which the "Self" is a mirror of how a subject imagines to be seen by particular others; (c) the relation between the individual and society; the related theme of communication, considered as a presupposition to the formation of individual and collective abilities; and (d) the social and moral reality. While Cooley openly recognized his intellectual debt with James (Cooley 1922: 170), the continuity between Cooley and Mead was recognized by Mead himself (1930: xxxviii). After a reconsideration of Cooley's thought, some researchers have questioned the validity of Mead's critical appraisals, as will be later considered more in detail. According to these appraisals, Cooley would have neglected, with his thesis about the mental or psychical nature of the "Self," its social and objective origin in the communication process (Mead 1930: xxxi–xxxviii; 1967: 173, 224; cf., however, Joas 1997: xiv; Visalberghi 1963: xxvii–xxviii). Moreover, researchers have sought to specify the lasting contributions of Cooley's thought to the sociological theory. These contributions can be mostly identified in his concept of primary group. Also relevant, however, is Cooley's stress on social interaction in the forming of personality, on social organization in the rise and consolidation of institutions, and on the sympathetic introspection method to understand and describe the activities to be studied. One may add to these still relevant elements of interest the attention Cooley paid to social disorganization processes, considered as factors of change in the institutional structure.[1] However, the study of these processes made a few years later by Thomas is better known.

The Psychologically Oriented Sociology of William I. Thomas (1863–1947)

William I. Thomas was the author of works that had a lasting conceptual, theoretical and methodological influence on the later developments of symbolic interactionism, particularly through his monumental

---

1 See Farbeman 1991a: 60–64; Izzo 1994: 262–4; Jonas 1991: 440; Martindale 1972: 549–54; Timasheff and Theodorson 1976: 162–8; Visalberghi 1963.

study – written in cooperation with Floran Znaniecki – concerning Polish farmers in Europe and in America (1918–21). A number of factors provided Thomas with an extraordinarily wide range of experiences and cultural horizons he was able to use in an original and creative way. It is worth mentioning in this connection his early interests in literature, ancient and modern languages and natural sciences. Further, his studies of ethnology in Germany, in which he sojourned at a young age, and the subsequent sociological training at the newly established Department of Sociology of Chicago University. Later on, his collaboration with this Department (until 1918) and his relations with some of the most outstanding representatives at Chicago University of the pragmatist philosophy, such as Dewey and Mead. Finally, there was his deep knowledge of Spencer's sociology and Boas' anthropology (Janowitz 1966). Thomas' contribution to the interactionist approach will be first considered from an epistemological and methodological point of view, and then from a conceptual and theoretical one.

Epistemology and Methodology

Thomas mostly focused on matters concerning epistemology and methodology. He sought to outline the fields of study of psychology, social psychology and sociology, and indicate the research methods mostly suited to the sociological discipline. As regards the specific fields of study, the author attributed to psychology the study of the most elementary phenomena that are produced in an essentially identical way in the consciousness of all individuals. Social psychology focuses instead on attitudes, particularly the most general and fundamental cultural attitudes, while sociology – being the theory of social organization – investigates the existing relations between social rules (that are considered as particular values) and individual attitudes. Social psychology and sociology, jointly considered, constitute social theory, which aims at analyzing the necessary and sufficient causes of the totality of social processes. The method based on life histories, which Thomas constantly analyzed and used, is one of the relevant methodological contributions he gave to the interactionist approach. This inductive method takes into account that any individual has its own life history, different from any other one, but shares social conditions, and hence attitudes and values, with other individuals.

Any individual and any social attitude or value can be only understood as a combination of social and individual phenomena, and therefore in conjunction with the whole social life of which it is a part. A joint examination of several stories of life allows achieving, through an inductive method, a comprehensive systematic knowledge of the complex social life of a particular community. In this case, researchers apply a research method, or approach, called "situational," of which the method of life stories is an important application. The study of actual situations an individual encounters or creates by relating itself with the others, highlights the overall environmental influence produced by the existing institutions and groups of the local community, and the consequent change in its attitudes, values and hence behavior.

Concepts and Theories: Social Organization, Disorganization and Reorganization, Attitudes and Values, Character and Social Personality

Some of these concepts – particularly those concerning social disorganization, social situation and definition of a situation – introduced or spread by Thomas, have contributed to permanently enrich the sociological vocabulary (Timasheff and Theodorson 1976: 177). By social organization, the author means to indicate all the institutions, that is, all the socially harmonized behavioral patterns that are imposed to individuals as rules. Social disorganization means a loss of influence of behavioral rules on the single members of a group. Previous behavioral rules lose their influence in consequence of the achievement of new attitudes, and particularly new personal needs and desires, such the individualistic search for pleasures, new experiences, personal achievement, and economic security. Social disorganization is opposed to social reorganization, by which reference is made to the production process of new behavioral patterns and new institutions that better conform to the changing requirements of a group. To control its own social reality, and therefore to pursue its aims, the individual has to develop some general patterns of situations – such as, for example, moral principles, social habits, economic forms – into which it can convey the changing social situation with which it comes across. Stability and organization to its life are the result. Values are cultural elements of any kind, either with a material or a symbolic character, which have an objective life for a group and a meaning for its single members. To these members, values appear like impulses, aims and desires. Wishes can be included in four general classes: wishes for new experiences, security, response (that is, to be reciprocated in one's feelings and love manifestations) and social recognition.

Attitudes (such as words, intentions, desires and emotions) are processes that take place in the individual consciousness, and determine real or possible individual activities in the social world. A consistent set of attitudes, and wishes in particular, forms the character of an individual, whereas a specific combination of values and attitudes constitutes a social personality. In a given environment, it is possible to formulate an ideal-typical classification of social personalities. Social personalities are not simply behaviors produced by external stimuli. The attitudes of the individual, considered as a social personality, have a meaning that an observer must interpret. Characters, and therefore social personalities, may be classified in different types according to how new situations are defined and faced by the subjects. A general classification includes three types. The first type completely conforms its activities to the prevailing rules and definitions of a situation, and prefers security to new experiences and to the achievement of its individuality. The second type sets differs from the first one in that it is looking for new situations and rejecting the prevailing patterns of behavior and thought. Finally, the third type tries to provide rules and principles by means of which it can create a new social organization.

The primary group is the immediate environment of an individual, comprising family and community. The primary group provides the individual with guidance to help it to face the current changing situations. However, this guidance is lacking as soon as a process of social disorganization not effectively contrasted by the group sets in, and individuals and groups of individuals introduce new contrasting definitions of situations. Consequently, attitudes and values, and hence individual and collective behaviors, change as well. This change is mediated by the definitions the individual and the groups to which it belongs bring to these situations. In fact, whatever their foundation, such definitions have real consequences. If, because of rapid social change, neither the state community nor the local one is able to control the single behaviors of individuals, these individuals lose their bearings within the social world and display individualistic conducts, as they pursue the satisfaction of their desire for new consumer goods and new experiences. On the other hand, some individuals who set themselves as innovative leaders within the local community may succeed in carrying out a social reorganization and reconstruction process, and succeed in harmonizing the values and attitudes of their community with those of the wider national community.

Among those who have left their national community and have emigrated, different kinds of attitudes may be found. There are those who by entering a new community deliberately adopt it as if it were their own. Some people remain instead in their country of origin, being convinced of its superiority. There are still those who keep values of opposition towards the existing order even in a new country. Also, those who become assimilated in the new culture, or who nourish the hope to go back to their country of origin as soon as their economic resources are sufficient. Finally, those who do not succeed in putting the high cultural capital achieved in their country of origin to good use. Immigrant integration in a new country can be successful only on certain conditions. Attitudes and values of the emigration and immigration countries should be similar, and the institutions of the new country should endeavor to meet their requirements and foster in them attitudes of cooperation, as expressed particularly through associations and economic activities promoted by the immigrants themselves. Breaking off the traditional normative system may promote rebellious attitudes. Satisfying desires that could not be previously satisfied, or even revolutionary attitudes, which can be exploited for a fruitful social reconstruction action, can check these attitudes (Thomas 1966).

The reception of Thomas's thought on the part of the Chicago sociological school has underlined the relevance of the concept of "definition of a situation" for symbolic interactionism. Thomas, however, made use of this concept in a way that is neither sufficiently clear nor consistent. Most importantly, they have emphasized the significance of his work as the founder of that school (together with Albion Small) and his relation with Robert E. Park, who during the 1920s and 1930s was its most influent representative. Researchers have highlighted their common interests in the themes of social changes and reforms, and therefore in the issue of which actors and ways are the most suitable to encourage and guide the process of towards desirable goals. On the other hand, they have underlined some differences between the two authors, and particularly the greater importance Thomas gave to the reform activity of progressive, enlightened and cultivated élites, as well as the greater attention he paid to matters concerning research methods and institutional changes.[2]

The Social Psychology of George Herbert Mead (1863–1931)

George Herbert Mead was at the same time a thinker in the wake of the pragmatist philosophical tradition, and an author who contributed decisively to the theory and conceptual apparatus of social psychology. This discipline was beginning to take shape in the first decades of twentieth century. His social psychology focused on some particular themes. Among them, we mention the definition of social psychology; the relations between individual, social group and environment; the difficulties encountered by traditional behavioral psychology in explaining consciousness and the world of experience; the forming of Mind, Self and Society. These subjects will be separately examined.

Object of Study and Basic Concepts of Social Psychology

According to Mead, psychology deals with the study of the individual's experience and the general conditions to which it is related. *Social psychology* is focused on social conditions. Behavioral social psychology is particularly addressed to the study of the individual's experience through its conduct, especially the conduct the others are able to observe. In other words, it studies the activity and conduct, or behavior, of an individual based on the organized conduct of the group to which it belongs. Any act is an impulse produced by stimuli. By *social act*, Mead means all the acts involving cooperation of several individuals and having their conduct, considered as a whole, as an object. Hence, the social act becomes an object of study in social psychology. Mead makes a distinction between a physical experience, which belongs to the individual meant as an organism, and a mental or internal experience of the surrounding world, or environment, which actually concerns psychology. The internal experience, upon which he dwells, is the behavior that is accessible only to the individual him or herself, though it is set up by socially learned meanings. Therefore, the experience a person has of the world is both individual and social at the same time.

Consciousness identifies itself with the experience of the world. Considered as an individual experience, consciousness is the environment of individuals' experience insofar as they form, one by one, that environment. In that sense, consciousness distinguishes an individual from the other individuals in a particular moment and from itself in some other moments. If it is instead considered as a social experience, consciousness is the environment of group experience insofar as a group collectively forms that environment. In that sense, consciousness indicates a cooperative activity situated in the natural and social world, and rationally addressed to form and control it. In both cases – either as an individual or a social experience – consciousness involves a constructive selection towards the world, or environment. The world, or environment, has an objective existence. Therefore, consciousness is not situated in the brain but in the world, which is formed by it through significant gestures. This involves giving a meaning to environmental stimuli and selecting them according to the meaning they receive. Consequently, environment is provided with a meaning from the point of view of both the individual and the social group. Through *self-consciousness*, the individual understands the attitude of the others towards him or herself, and in turn acts towards the world in a conscious manner. By doing so, he or she sets himself as a different individual compared to the environment to which he or she belongs.

Attitudes are impulses of the organism, characterized as follows: (1) they express themselves through an act, or behavior; (2) they give organization to its different stages; (3) they allow an organism to actively respond to a complex environment. *Gestures* are stimuli, or acts, addressed to the others. Therefore they produce responses; they represent, in other words, the stage of the social act in which an individual – either a human being or an animal – by addressing itself to other individuals stimulates their responses. In the social act, gestures are used for adjusting the attitudes of each individual to the attitudes and actions of any other one, and hence for making it takes the roles of the others with which it has to cooperate. Gestures can be found not

---

2 See Fisher and Strauss 1991a; Joas 1987: 96–9; Janowitz 1966: viii, liii–liv; Stryker 1980: 32–3.

only in the human kind but also in some species of superior animals, such as dogs. In a dogfight, for example, a dog – whether it attacks or defends itself – takes in consideration the attitudes of its antagonists. Among these dogs, there is in fact a primitive, non-linguistic communication through reciprocally addressed stimuli or – as Mead states – a conversation of gestures. In some species of animals, and sometimes also in persons, a communication may occur in the strict sense of direct, thoughtless responses to environmental stimuli. This is what in fact happens in a dogfight, or when an audience is under the influence of a speaker. However, these gestures are not meaningful, and therefore there is no language.

On the contrary, it is an exclusively human feature, and not an animal one, that a social act involves conscious role-taking of the others. A person consciously reflects upon his experience and, in the light of this reflection, is able to change its response to the gestures of the others. To do it, it is necessary that the objects of experience – or the objects with which persons come across and which they contribute to construct in their social environment – have a symbolic character. In fact, the objects of experience are created by complying with the meanings that are attributed to them within the social process of experience and behavior. Any communication, and particularly linguistic communication, assumes the use of symbols in the position to stir up the same stimulus in all participants. All those who belong to the same social group, namely, all those who take part to a common social process of experience and behavior, can understand the meaning of symbols. In this sense, this meaning is universal. Objects, and environment as a whole, have a meaning for an individual because it relates to them with highly organized attitudes. These attitudes guide its response to environmental stimuli allowing it to consciously act, and hence control, its social and natural environment. Individuals who are involved in a social process of experience and behavior reciprocally adjust their responses (actions, gestures) through communication (by gestures, during the first evolution stages, and later by language). Meaning has an objective and not an individual existence. It is generated, situated and develops in an environment in which stimuli, or gestures, are reciprocally related.

Any gesture, or any stimulus addressed to the others, represents a stage in a social act. Gestures evidence the single stages of this process in a mix of reciprocal responses. Some gestures start a social act, and produce adjustment responses from other organisms, within a social act provided with a meaning. In particular, language is a human prerogative that includes a range of significant gestures or symbols, by which an individual consciously recalls in him or herself the response has elicited in the other. Recalling that gestures are stimuli addressed to others, thinking may be defined an inner conversation of gestures. Since any social act, or behavior, is provided with a meaning and is a condition of consciousness, meaning precedes the consciousness, or awareness of it. When individuals are aware of both their own and the other people's behaviors, gestures turn into symbols. Symbols are not interpreted through a mental process. Rather, the interpretation of symbols is a process taking place outside the individuals, in a real field of social experience, and has therefore an objective character. This social process is mostly formed by communication, and makes it possible.

Mind is the ability to convey meanings to ourselves and others. It is a socially acquired mechanism, peculiar to the human kind (not then to animals), by which individuals are able to solve their problems of adaptation to the environment. Mind is made of thoughts. Thinking is, in fact, a conversation process with ourselves through words, that is, through vocal gestures having a meaning. Therefore, thinking involves knowing and using a language. By thinking, an individual takes the attitude of the other, and is thereby able to represent the other's world and environment to itself in view of its own future conduct. By a process of thought abstraction, an individual can take an attitude that does not belong to any particular individual but is shared by its entire group: the attitude of the *generalized other*. Through the individual's introjection of this attitude, the group can guide and control its behavior. The more a thought is abstract, the wider is the group, up to the whole of humankind. Taking – or adopting – the attitude of the generalized other leads a person to place the attitudes of the others in its field of experience and thought. This holds not only for the attitudes towards oneself or the reciprocal ones, but also for those towards the different aspects of their common social activity considered as a whole. A systematic role-taking of the others provides the material for the making of self-consciousness. Through it, the different attitudes in response to other people's attitudes can be recalled. Thus, the individual has an objective field (that is existing objectively, not individually) at his disposal, by which a cooperative social act can take place in such a way as to give an expression to all the roles it involves. Within a fully developed and organized society or community, common interests mingle with other ones that are in conflict with either individuals, or small groups, or different parts of personalities, or selves. *Institutions* are organized sets of common responses to the others (though in their individual specificity) within a community. Therefore, institutions are the responses an individual receives from its group, and namely, from the generalized other. A community becomes an institution when its members share the same attitudes towards all the individuals who find themselves in the same circumstances.

Thanks to their mind, this specifically human ability that avails itself of language and thought, persons:

1. Are able to control their natural and social environment, by selecting in a constructive way the stimuli (or gestures) coming from that environment, and consequently organizing their responses to them.
2. Are consequently able to form their consciousness.
3. Can therefore consciously and deliberately control their conduct.
4. Can finally start a dialogue with themselves, consciously guide their conduct, create their own personality and distinguish themselves from the environment.

The mind – this ability to guide one's conduct and to control the environment by it – organizes its own *Self* through experience and the conscious introjection of the organized social structure. Through its mind, the individual is able to examine this social structure and change it according to the contingent requirements of social evolution, on the base of common social interests.

Therefore, the Self is the part of an individual (a part with a cognitive character and consequently separated from the biological part) to which it can turn with its thoughts, and hence with its mind. In other words, the Self is the part of an individual that can become an object of reflection for the individual itself. In reflection, individuals particularly use their imagination to determine the course of action they have to take in a given temporal setting, and present the results of the different courses to themselves. In reflective experience, the Self does not appear during an act, but only at the completion of it, when we grasp it in our memory. By the memory of experience, individuals do not only retain their Self in any moment, but also the environment in which it has been formed. This is a selective memory: the Self cuts out a certain part of non-essential contents of experience. By organizing their Self, individuals organize their conduct, that is, all the attitudes towards their own social environment. As a consequence, the Self involves being able to take the attitude of those with whom individuals play a role, being so engaged in a cooperative action.

The Self includes two components, the "Me" and the "I." In its organization, the "*Me*" is formed by the individual's response to the others, insofar as it takes their attitudes. In other words, the "Me" is formed by roles, namely by all the other people's attitudes adopted by an individual. Therefore, the "Me" represents social roles, which are at the same time the customary and organized ways of conduct of the community to which an individual belongs, but also the role an individual plays in a cooperative social action. In contrast, the "*I*" is the response of an individual to the attitudes of the others, and consequently to the social situation that becomes a part of his own experience. This response is not predetermined. Therefore, it is the "I" that gives an individual a sense of freedom and initiative, and it is with the "I" that an individual identifies itself. The "I" does not exist outside a social situation. On the contrary, it just expresses itself in a social situation, or in the "Me." Together, the "I" and the "Me" form the personality and are both engaged in thoughts and conversation, as thinking is a conversation between the "I" and the "Me."

The Difficulties of Traditional Behavioral Psychology in Explaining Consciousness and the World of Experience

According to Mead, the making and the existence of the mind cannot be explained as a result of mechanisms of conditioned stimuli, for we would then deny its distinction from the environment, and hence its existence. Traditional behavioral psychology, particularly represented by John B. Watson, exclusively dwelt on human or animal conducts to be observed within the artificial environment of a laboratory. The explanation he had proposed, according to which conducts are responses to environmental constraints through stimuli, would exclude consciousness as an explanatory factor. There are, however, some complex conducts, which do not occur in concomitance with particular stimuli (in fact, there is not necessarily a correspondence between particular stimuli and particular responses in human behavior), but rather with thoughts. Thinking, which is necessarily a symbolic, and hence, a universal process, involves interpreting those stimuli. Individual responses to stimuli are elaborated in virtue of this interpretation process, and therefore do not have an automatic and immediate character. In the case of a verbal stimulus, the person consciously learns the meaning of that stimulus, making it become a part of its experience.

On the contrary, animals and very young children are not able to formulate ideas, and consequently thoughts. They are to be sure able to react to particular stimuli, by learning for example particular behaviors or words, but cannot voluntarily use a stimulus by recalling their response within themselves. Consequently, they cannot either consciously condition that response, or start and keep a communication with themselves ("a conversation of gestures," in Mead's language). In other words, only human beings who have passed early childhood are able to relate other people's attitudes to themselves, use these attitudes to control their conduct, and achieve mental processes that, unlike those of animals, include an anticipation of future significant events, mentally isolated from other occurrences. These events have their own life and sense, which may be communicated to the others through symbolically significant gestures, and may be also mentally represented, in order to select the best course of action among all the possible ones. Therefore, reciprocal communication between individuals assumes that any individual may dialogue with itself, and thus possess a consciousness. Only in human societies, we are able to find reciprocal communication and influence, since only in them an individual can recall the role of the others in itself, and consciously guide its response to the others, and ultimately, its conduct.

The Making of Consciousness, Mind, Self, Self-Consciousness and Society

As we previously outlined, consciousness is the individual and social experience of the world involving a selection of the stimuli that derive from it, while self-consciousness consists in adopting the attitude of the generalized other. In individuals, the development of Consciousness, Mind, Self and consequently Self-consciousness, depends on a continuous social process of experience and behavior. In particular, the making and existence of the mind can be explained in behavioral terms. In fact, persons and animals understand the meaning of a conversation of gestures, in which any gesture recalls or stimulates another one. The making of the Self involves the presence of a Mind in the individual, intended as an ability to organize responses to environmental stimuli. For, the Self can only exist insofar as the Selves of the others, with whom an individual establishes a relationship, become a part of its own experience. Accordingly, the Self takes shape through a social process in which the individual influences itself while it is influencing the others. The individual communicates, identifies itself, and participates with them in creating and keeping a shared universe of discourse. To do so, it mentally takes the role of all its counterparts. With a reflexive conduct, the individual is in the position to elicit in itself their attitude, and hence the attitude of the generalized other. This entirely social ability is learned in childhood. The making of the Self is a presupposition to the development of society.

Little children address the experience of the forming process of their mind to themselves, thus becoming aware of the existence of other individuals, different from themselves, with whom they interact and whose roles they take. There is no clear distinction between physical and social objects during the first development stage of the Mind, and consequently of the Self. The physical environment is considered as if it were formed by animated beings to which children have the possibility of relating. The social environment is formed by imaginary companions – such as, for example, their puppets – or by real persons, such as their mothers, nursery-school teachers, and so on. Children take their roles for fun, producing in themselves the answers the particular role they have taken involves. In this first stage, we can still talk about individual *play*. At a later stage, children create their Self by learning to take the roles of all the other persons in the course or by means of interactions organized with them, until they are able to form in themselves *the attitude of the generalized other*. These roles are pre-established and interconnected in order to pursue a common purpose. In this way, children are able to build their self, and hence their personality. This does not simply happen by taking a role now and then, but because they succeed in organizing within an organic unit all the attitudes of their group, and consequently learn to become members of a wider society. Team games are an early example of a cooperative activity consciously performed with the others. Within a *game*, each player takes, or is prepared to take, the role of any other player, and knows what it and all the others have to do for carrying out that game.

In any cooperative activity, the individual elicits in the others an answer to which it may reply, so as to engage both components of its Self (the "Me" and the "I"). The meaning of a symbol, or a range of symbols, is as universal as the community is. The widest community is the one formed by rational individuals. The organization of a community, aware of what it does and prepared to act as a generalized other, depends on communication and mutual influence among its members. An individual who asserts him or herself within an organized community, while drawing its attitudes from a group, is also able to give them new characteristics, though it still remains a member of that community. It can open a dialogue with its community and try to reform it. Institutions are necessary for the development of personalities, and particularly educational institutions prove essential, as they carry out the process of gathering all organized responses. They are therefore a constituent element of a community.

Mind and Self are social products assuming individual experience and behavior. If it is able to thoughtfully, consciously and rationally organize its conduct towards the physical and social environment, the individual succeeds in submitting it both to his own control and to the control of those to which it cooperatively relates. Individual and group rationality involves that individuals take other people's attitudes, control their own actions through these attitudes, and their actions through their own attitudes. The achievement of the Self in the particular situation in which it begins to develop, involves the making of the "Me" by means of relations established with a plurality of groups, the broadest of which is the world society of rational beings, the community of rational language. At the same time, the achievement of the Self assumes that individuals reflect the social process of experience and behavior, and the complete structure of the organized social behavior of that society or community, from their own peculiar point of view. Important differences and variations among the individual Selves are therefore not precluded. Through their mind, which is a socially acquired mechanism for solving environmental problems, individuals are able to rationally modify the social structure, depending on the contingent requirements of social evolution, on the base of common social interests. Change occurs both in personalities and in the social order at the same time. Though a differentiation among individuals may generate conflicts at the beginning, by an evolutionary progress, it produces a functional specialization in persons, who become able to assimilate and take the attitudes of the others, thus actively taking part to the complex organization of society.

In the light of these theses, we can understand Mead's ambivalent evaluation of Cooley's ideas. According to Mead, his contribution is many-sided. Cooley studied society as the result of association and cooperation of the primary group in its face-to-face organization. In addition, he pointed to a mutual relation between individual and group in the making of the Self. However, his assumptions did not highlight the process of the making of the Self. Cooley assumed that the Self is a product of the imagination of how a subject thinks to be seen by the others, and that society does not exist but in the mind of individuals. According to Mead, this process demands, on the contrary, mentally adopting the attitudes of the others with whom an inner conversation takes place. Therefore, it is of a cognitive and objective – instead of an affective and subjective – nature. Consequently, Cooley's assumptions do not allow understanding that world experience is not a mental event that takes place in individual consciousness but, on the contrary, something external to them. By the same token, and as a consequence, society and the origin of the Self are also external to the individual (Mead 1967, 1977).

The Symbolic Interactionism of Herbert Blumer (1900–87)

Herbert Blumer, Mead's follower and pupil, supplied an influent version of the symbolic interactionism perspective, which he was the first to name in this way in 1937. In giving an outline of his thought, reference will be made here mostly to his work *Symbolic Interactionism* (1969), which includes some articles dealing with this perspective, and particularly with its specific methodology. Except for a long and very relevant introduction, all the other chapters of this work had already been published previously and separately. In this connection, the premises that, according to Blumer, characterize this perspective will be dwelt upon, his concepts of social action, attitude, self and concept examined, and his evaluations of the theories of his contemporaries considered. Finally, we shall dwell upon the methodological directions he provided.

The Premises of Symbolic Interactionism

Blumer defined symbolic interactionism as a reality-oriented approach to scientific study of the natural world of group life and human behavior. Blumer outlined the premises of this approach in some texts that are not perfectly coinciding. His first and most popular formulation includes three assumptions, called premises by the author: (1) human beings act towards physical and symbolic things on the basis of the meaning they have for them; (2) this meaning is formed in the course and by means of social interactions; (3) meanings are used and modified through an interpretative process. As a consequence of these premises, pre-established meanings do not exist, as they are formed through an interpretative process by which the actor first indicates to himself the physical or symbolic things towards which it is acting. Then, by virtue of this self-communication process, the actor treats these meanings (namely, it selects, combines, transforms them, etc.), bearing in mind its own situation and the direction of his or her action.

Blumer's second formulation is based on four assumptions, called central conceptions (rather than premises):

1. Either separately or collectively, persons are prepared to act on the basis of the meaning of the objects that form their world.
2. The association of people is necessarily in the form of a process, in which they mutually give indications to themselves and interpret the indications of the others; external factors, such as rules, roles, values, etc., are relevant insofar as they enter in the definition and interpretation of other people's acts.
3. Social acts, whether individual or collective, are constructed through a process in which the actors note, interpret and assess the situations that confront them. Analytic categories (role, institution, process) have a sense only if they are seen and formulated in terms of social action, and therefore, referred to single or collective actors.
4. The complex interconnections of acts forming organizations and institutions, and also, division of labor and interdependence among activities, and hence among persons, in an organization have a dynamic character, and should be considered as arrangements of those who take part to the organization. These arrangements are characterized by the ways in which participants define, interpret and face situations from their respective positions within the organization. Thus, an organization does not exist in itself, but is formed by those individual arrangements (1969: 2–6, 16–20, 47, 50–60, 87–9).

Both formulations concerning the premises of symbolic interactionism place the origin and interpretation of meanings in interaction, and establish that interpreting these meanings is the necessary condition for any social action. The second formulation integrates the first one by stating that:

a. A social action may be performed either by single individuals or collectively.
b. The attribution of a meaning involves observing, interpreting and evaluating the situations individuals encounter, create and sustain in their associative life.
c. An interpretation process is also carried out towards elements that are external and pre-existing to the social action, such as organizations and institutions. This process allows understanding some of their sociologically relevant aspects, such as, for example, personnel morale, communication system performance, actual power distribution within the organization hierarchy.
d. Joint actions can be carried out by a harmonization of the interpretations of other people's actions. Consequently, they can be studied only considering what participants do, the meaning they give to the type of situation in which these actions are produced, the definition of their own and the other people's approach, and the connection with previous joint actions.
e. Social institutions and organizations form a large range of interconnected and diversified actions, and are therefore particular cases of joint actions. Finally,

f. Research categories can be legitimately applied only bearing in mind the point of view of the social actors.

Self, Act, Social Interaction

Blumer's conception of symbolic interactionism considers the human being as an organism, which – unlike non-human organisms – is provided with symbolic abilities. The Self makes these symbolic abilities possible. In other words, a human being may become an object of its own action. It can provide indications both to itself, by giving a meaning and evaluation to what it remarks concerning the way of interpreting the world before acting in its own environment, and also to the others by interpreting their indications. Whatever an individual may indicate to itself, the object is provided with a meaning that enables the individual to make rational judgments and decisions among alternative courses of action. The formation of the Self is the result of an interactive process, in which a person is able to see himself from the outside by placing himself in the position of the others. In turn, the Self makes possible performing the act, as the individual can set objectives, interpret other people's actions, evaluate a situation, decide a course of action, etc., by behaving as an active organism. This also makes the interactive process of mutual indication and interpretation possible. For any actor, the actions of the others are relevant in forming its own conduct, as social interaction has a symbolic character. Consequently, it must be continuously interpreted and (re)defined to the others, so that the lines of conduct may be coordinated with them and the interaction performed. The actors understand each other when a gesture has the same meaning for all of them. The meaning associated to an object is a social product, guides actions towards that object, and may be modified.

Social interaction occurs among actors, or persons, and not among roles or other factors that may be attributed them. Society consists of joint actions and not of a steady structure of relations. Any action has its own career or history. Individuals set up and guide these actions within a social framework, that is, by interpreting other people's acts. The harmonization of these interpretations allows carrying out collective actions. A gesture indicates a common action, which is a consequence of the coordination of those who have made it with those to whom it is destined, when each part takes the role of the other one. In general, a joint action indicates a collective form of action deriving from a harmonization of the lines of conduct of different persons (a transaction, a ceremony, a robbery, etc.). A joint action may include one or more orientation of participants, one or more definitions. Structural elements, such as cultural rules, social positions, social roles and systems, social stratification, only set the conditions for an action but do not determine it. These elements define a formal conduct, but generally, social life is not rigidly formal. These concepts are important only if they can help the interpretation and definition process through which joint actions are formed. Therefore, any macro-sociological explanation should indicate how the actors define their situations. It should dwell upon the ways in which participants in interactions reciprocally consider, perceive, define, judge, identify themselves and consequently provide themselves with indications. It should further consider how actors organize, guide, and submit to restrictions their own actions throughout the course of an interaction (1969: 8–9, 13–16, 76, 80–82, 87–9, 106–11).

Sociological Theory, Variables and "Sensitizing" Concepts

According to Blumer, for a social theory that intends being scientific, and therefore intends developing analytical schemes of the empiric world, it is necessary to indicate the nature of the classes of objects and their relations. By doing so, it is possible to guide research and receive indications from it. Currently, – as he stated in the 1950s – apart from few exceptions, there is a divorce between theory and research. Theory is confined within some isolated groups of researchers, and it neither guides research nor keeps it in consideration. Again, according to Blumer, the current habit of using concepts without checking their usefulness in the study of particular empirical cases has contributed to this absence. An improper use of concepts depends on a separation from the world of experience, which leads to conceptual constructions of no use for research. It is also the consequence of a tendency to conceptual elaboration without making sure whether these concepts are necessary or not; of labeling the object of study without translating labels into concepts; of using scientific concepts as though they were common sense.

In fact, the current tendency to reduce social life to variables does not consider the interpretation or definition process carried out by individuals while, either individually or collectively, they confront themselves with objects and transform their experiences into activities. Attitudes, for example, reveal themselves and are contingently influenced in the course of interactions, and therefore, they are not permanent attributes of individuals. Consequently, it is not advisable to translate attitudes into variables with the purpose of measuring some of their constituent aspects. Any scheme by which we want to analyze human actions should conform to this interpretation process. The connection between theory and research demands the formulation of "sensitizing" concepts – which are neither well established nor conclusive – to be applied to the study of the world of everyday life. In this world, each element has unique characteristics and is linked to a context, which is unique as well. "Sensitizing" concepts are useful for providing references, suggestions and guidance when we have to face empiric cases. Examples of these concepts are culture, institutions, social structure, habits, personality, attitude, self, socialization and social control. We can test and refine these concepts through empiric studies illustrating their references and having a sense according to our personal experience. In this way, we have the opportunity to better formulate an initially imprecise concept (1969: 127–82).

Methodological Principles of Empirical Science

The methodological position of symbolic interactionism favors a direct examination of the social empirical world. It does not take care of translating into operational terms any particular concepts, such as "Self" and "generalized other." Among these principles, it has to be noted that attention is focused on the empiric world, which though existing only in human experience, is provided with resistance and ability to react to individual actions. This does not mean that a particular world is unchangeable. For research purposes, it should be portrayed by images, whose correctness has to be checked. In methodological terms, three are the principles to be followed:

1. All research should conform to a methodology. This involves possessing and using a previous frame of the empirical world object of study, in the light of which patterns, problems, data, connections, concepts and interpretations should be constructed.
2. A validation can only be made through a direct examination of the empirical social world, in order to ascertain whether the empirical area corresponds to the image we have of it, and whether problems, concepts and data are relevant compared to empirical reality. An operational procedure, namely a procedure standardized by a test, a scale, or a particular research method (such as intelligence tests), cannot be considered as a validation of what has been the object of this procedure.
3. Researchers should be familiar with the world they have chosen for their study and should have a first-hand knowledge of it that cannot be replaced by theoretical activities or by compliance with a scientific protocol. One's preconceived images of this world, unavoidable in themselves, should be tested and reviewed. When there is not the consent of observers and observations are weak and uncertain, it is advisable to develop a rich and intimate familiarity with a studied conduct, using one's imagination.

Valid and reliable research includes two different stages: exploration and inspection. In contrast with the pre-established procedure of a scientific protocol, by exploration we aim at providing a wide and intimate knowledge of a sphere of social life, and at developing and refining research, in order to keep it anchored to the empiric world. The object of research, which is not well identified at the beginning, is then established in the course of the investigation. In addition, it is also advisable to avail ourselves of privileged witnesses; to raise any kind of questions on what we are studying, and to record the observations that do not conform to our approach. An accurate description of what was previously a problematic matter may often dispense with theories and analytic schemes. Inspection is a later stage of research, with an analytic character, by which we aim at highlighting existing relations, determining the empirical referents of concepts, and formulating theoretical propositions. This analysis is the core purpose of empirical science. Inspection is an intense examination of both the empirical contents of any employed analytic element (for example, integration, social mobility, assimilation, etc.), and also the empirical nature of the relations among those elements. Inspection consists of a close examination, through a non-standardized procedure, of those elements from different points of view, but always bearing in mind the empirical world. Exploration and inspection represent what we use to call naturalistic research, which is necessary for scientifically studying human social life (1969: 27, 31–2, 40, 43, 46–7; 1980: 412–13).

Conceptual and Theoretical Relations between Mead and Blumer

As previously indicated, Blumer gave a personal definition of the research object characterizing the interactionist approach, the object being to highlight the interpretations of the meanings actors give to what they do, which take shape in the course and by means of interactive processes. According to Blumer, this object of research indicates a line of continuity between himself and Mead in defining the point of view and the field of study of the interactionist perspective. According to this perspective, which Blumer says to share with Mead, social behavior is not confined to an interaction based on stimuli and responses between two organisms, but considers the reciprocal view and definition of the persons engaged in that interaction. Social behavior should not be necessarily open, but should also include the individual's communication with himself, and should not be reduced to quantitative units in order to measure it (1980: 416–19).

Blumer's definition of symbolic interactionism has continued to exert its influence, in conjunction with his methodological indications and studies on racial relations, collective behavior and the formation of public opinion.[3] However, the continuity between Mead and Blumer has been questioned by means of several arguments. First of all, some commentators have remarked that Blumer did not make any reference to Mead's social psychology in dealing with empirical sociological matters, such as industrial or ethnic relations or public opinion. Furthermore, some researchers who have referred to Mead's teachings – as from the 1950s and 1960s with the "Iowa School" and, more recently, with the "Illinois School" – have laid stress on the structural, or macro-sociological (and particularly normative) bonds to which interactions, and consequently also definitions of the situations, are submitted. They have also emphasized the stability of the individual Selves. In this regard, those researchers have sought to ascertain what are the constituting elements of the Self (such as occupation, sex gender, religious belief, quality of the character a person attributes to itself). In addition, they have intended to establish a place in a hierarchy of importance (salience) for each one of these elements from the point of view of any single person who has taken part to this investigation. The more important or salient is one of these constituting elements, the more a person takes it into account in its behavior.[4]

In consonance with the Iowa and Illinois schools, but in open contrast with Blumer, some commentators have also formulated an interpretation of Mead that would approach him to social behaviorism. They have also emphasized that social actors show a convergence in responding to a significant symbol, and that shared meanings are possible for them. This interpretation consequently proposes the research methods used in behaviorist social psychology (McPhail and Rexroat 1979, 1980). Also in contrast with Blumer, some researchers have maintained that he would have misinterpreted his teacher Mead. Blumer's alleged underlining the subjective or mental aspect of interactions to the detriment of their objective or behavioral aspect, and adopting a nominalist theoretical position instead of a realist one, have been mentioned as instances of his misinterpretation (Lewis 1976; Warshay and Warshay 1991a; Wood and Wardell 1983).

Still, Blumer defended his interpretation arguing his theoretical, epistemological and methodological continuity with Mead (and also with Thomas). Moreover, he maintained that the theses of his critics are groundless, particularly as regards their interpretation of Mead's epistemology and key concepts

---

3   See Becker 1988; Charon 2001: 149–52, 170–71; Fine 1990: 118; 1993: 64; Meltzer, Petras and Reynolds 1980: 9; Shibutani 1988.

4   Kuhn and McPartland: 1954. See also Fine 1993: 63–4; Fisher and Strauss 1991a: 195; Meltzer, Petras and Reynolds 1980: 59–67; Turner 1998: 360–73.

(such as society, social interaction, self, mind, act), and his own reception of Mead's thought (Blumer 1969: 61–77; 1980, 1991a: 318–23; 1999: 199). Some other scholars concerned with pragmatism and symbolic interactionism are, at least partially, aligned with Blumer (Johnson and Shifflet 1981; Rochberg-Halton 1987: 345–7). The relation of continuity between Mead and Blumer still remains controversial. So, it would perhaps be better to give up any intention to either support or demolish a given interpretation line of Mead's thought – such as the one argued by Blumer or his opponents – and decide, on the contrary, to use these interpretations to achieve theoretical progresses within the interactionist perspective or other approaches (Fine and Kleinman 1986: 137).

An Outline of Some Recent Interpretations of Mead's and Blumer's Thought, and Current Developments of Symbolic Interactionism

How the contribution of the classics of symbolic interactionism have been *currently* received may be briefly presented as follows:[5]

1. Some researchers have examined the relations, within the theoretical framework of the Chicago School, between Mead's social psychology and Thomas and Park's sociology. In this regard, they have remarked that, according to these authors, progress derives from the joint efforts of the members of a community to solve their objectively existing problems. Accordingly, the achievement of this goal entails forming a democratic audience that includes learned citizens able to sustain mutual communication. Yet, it was only Mead who dealt with the theme of psychological and social conditions enabling the whole human kind to achieve (to the extent that it is possible) a common language. In addition, he dealt with the theme of cultural, economic and political conditions that are conducive (as much as possible) to the establishment of a universal community. Different economic and social values and interests constitute, however, an obstacle.

2. Some commentators have sought to obtain a better grasp of Mead from a sociological and philosophical point of view, without achieving, however, univocal results. Mention should be made here of the opposed theses of Natanson and Joas, authors of two in-depth monographic studies on Mead's work. Natanson has aimed at formulating an epistemological criticism of this work. Joas has set out instead to evidence its unity despite the plurality of themes Mead dealt with, such as theoretical philosophy, social philosophy, and social psychology. According to Natanson, Mead did not succeed in solving the dualism between the individual and the external natural and social world. In his thought, the individual and the world assume themselves one another, because the basic epistemological question (which on the contrary is raised by Husserl's phenomenology) of how an individual may achieve the knowledge of the external world, is not tackled (Natanson 1973: 56–87). Joas has a quite different opinion. Mead's central thesis is that this knowledge – and even the entire knowledge – is practically formed by means of interactions in the world of life. This thesis, Joas contends, proves convincing both in epistemological and empirical terms, unlike the phenomenological thesis of the constitution of the world through the action of a single subject (Joas 1997: 6–7, 208–209).

3. Bearing in mind a frequently expressed criticism towards Mead for not having clearly and consistently defined his basic concepts (Fine and Kleinman 1986: 133–5; Meltzer, Petras and Reynolds 1980: 81–90), some scholars have tried to clarify the meaning of his major concepts. "Social act" should be considered as the impulse – selective of environmental stimuli – of an actor addressing itself in a significant manner to other actors. "Attitude" would mean the initial predisposition to an

---

5   For an introduction to the reception of Mead's work, see Joas 1997: vii–xxvii. For the subsequent points see in general, except for specific references, Baert 1998: 73–5; Berger 1963: 93–121; Charon 2001: 23–5, 77–90, 132–3; Denzin 1983b; Fallding 1982; Fine 1990: 119–20; 1991, 1993: 68–9, 78–9; Fine and Kleinman 1983, 1986; Fisher and Strass 1978: 485; 1991a: 194–204; Helle 1999: 170–77; Joas 1997: 5–9, 167–98; 1987: 83; 2001: 96–8; McKinney 1955; Miller 1991a; Natanson 1973: 6–20; Plummer 2000: 197–8, 206; Sandstrom et al. 2001: 220, 227; Strauss 1977: xiv–xvii; Turner 1998: 346–9.

act. "Self" should be understood as the ability of individuals to imagine themselves as objects of an evaluation while they interact with the others. Alternatively, it means an activity generated by the social act, by which individuals communicate with themselves, and perceive themselves while relating to the environment according to shared meanings. Consequently and particularly, the "Self" may be either meant as an identity defined by social positions or roles, and as self-control. The "Me" should be intended in the first place as an expression of the generalized other and hence as the controlled part of the Social Self, and as an action consciously oriented towards the social situation. It should also mean the presence and awareness in individuals of the human experience of past actions and thoughts. The "I" should be considered as a non-social and non-controlled part of the Self, and consequently an individual and impulsive action of which the subject is not aware, but with which it keeps a dialogue with the "Me" through its thoughts. Therefore, with its own "I," the individual responds in a creative way to the attitudes of the others producing innovation in its social environment. The "generalized other" should be considered as the constitution within the individual's Self of the social organization, which has an objective existence. "Mind" should be meant as a socially constituted ability to use symbols to identify the objects (in a broad sense) located in our environment. But, also, to imagine alternative lines of action towards those objects, provide ourselves with indications, and choose a particular course of action instead of other ones. And therefore, as an ability to consciously act towards the world, instead of automatically responding to environmental stimuli, and – relating to the world – to face and solve problems. "Reflectivity" should be considered as the individual's reflection on its own experience, but also as the reflection made collectively and rationally by the members of a community on their collective experience, in order to control the environment and thus achieve social progress. "Situation" is a concept that may be understood as a social construction, internal as well as external to the individual. As a social construction, the situation is constraining the individual actor, but the individual itself may also interpret and modify it. "Society" should be considered as an organization of interactions among individuals.

4. Mead's theses on the making of the Self have been further examined, showing the importance of the interactive context to which a number of children take jointly part (Denzin 1978), and the excessive rigidity of Mead's functionalist interpretations. In this regard, it is worth mentioning the influential contribution of Shibutani (1955), who refined the Meadian concepts of "significant other" and "generalized other" by arguing that the perspectives provided by the reference groups are relevant for individual's socialization and the construction of social worlds.

5. Mead's thought has been developed in different directions. As regards the image individuals have of themselves in contemporary culture, and the situations with which they come across and which they have contribute to create, interpreters have emphasized either their stability (Iowa School, Stryker) or lack of it (Berger, Blumer, post-modern interactionists). Some critics have contended that the attention symbolic interactionism pays to contingent situations would involve analytic deficiencies in the study of social structures (Gonos 1977. See also Meltzer, Petras and Reynolds 1980: 84, 100–103). However, the growing number of interactionist investigations on organizations and institutions, and the formulation, within the interactionist approach, of concepts and theories that have proved relevant in macro-sociological analyses are not compatible with this criticism (Fine 1991; Maines 1977: 247–53; Musolf 1992).

6. New areas of research have been explored, particularly with reference to Mead's thesis, according to which the experience of the flow of time is socially (that is, interactively) formed (Joas 1997: 167–98; Maines et al. 1983; Natanson 1973: 74–9).

7. As for Blumer, researchers currently underline his contribution to the study of macro-sociological research themes, such as social movements and industrial or racial relations, in contrast with previous interpretations maintaining that Blumerian interactionism is exclusively micro-sociological (Gusfield 1994: 60, 66–7).

8. Finally, the difference between sociologically oriented symbolic interactionism and social psychology has been specified (Thoits 1995).

Contemporary social interactionism in general may be considered apart from its relations of continuity with Cooley, Thomas, Mead and Blumer. In this case, the attempt is worth mentioning to convey this perspective into the wider theoretical stream of everyday life sociology, and highlight the micro- and macro-sociological foundations of this approach. Furthermore, commentators have called attention to the absence so far of a univocal definition of its field of study. Though, during the 1970s, the interactionist perspective was considered in decline (Mullins and Mullins 1991a: 412), recently its fields of research have been enlarged and studied in greater depth. New research objects have been added to traditional but still current themes, such as self and identity, social movements, deviance and labeling, construction of social problems and social worlds (Adler, Adler and Fontana 1987; Fine 1990, 1991, 1993; Plummer 1991b; Stryker 1991a). Considering first of all *the in-depth study* of the traditional objects of study, we note that:

1. The constitutive dimensions of self-definition, or identity, compared to the actual perception of oneself and to an ideal identity, have been precisely stated. The contributions of Paul Burke, Morris Rosenberg, Sheldon Stryker, and Ralph Turner have been particularly useful to this effect. Among the constitutive dimensions of identity, we mention the esteem the individual has of self (self-esteem), and individual self-definitions concerning some of its characteristics. They are, for example, being a person who is open- or narrow-minded, individualist or oriented to the others, responsible or irresponsible, mature or immature (identity meaning). Other individual characteristics include the identification of an individual with one or more social categories (locative dimension of identity), and the consistency in different situations and times among the different conceptions an individual has of himself or herself. Consistency is particularly relevant if and when the normal process of identity maintenance breaks down (integrative dimension of identity). Distinct aspects, or dimensions, of identity are also the importance of identity for individuals, depending on the situations they have to face (identity salience), and the persons encountered (commitment to an identity).[6]
2. Roles have been studied in-depth from a sociological viewpoint, particularly as regards the concept of role-taking, and the conditions that determine people's attitudes to the roles they play (Turner). The reformulation of some themes of the "Iowa School" has led a group of researchers to dwell on the premises of social coordination among members of small groups, and on the conditions in which role identities are formed. Instances of such conditions are the cohesion among those identities, and their salience or relevance in comparison with other identities (McCall and Simmons).[7]
3. The connection between the interpretation the members of social groups give to their own actions, and the construction of their individual and collective identities was studied.[8]
4. Finally, attention has been paid to the processes by means of which collective identities (Cerulo 1997: 387–91), and in general, social reality are constructed. Social constructionism is considered "the dominant contemporary interactionist orientation within social problems theory" (Sandstrom et al. 2001: 223). This approach is related to symbolic interactionism to the extent that it lays emphasis on the definition of a situation, as a social problem created by persons who interact with different roles, and on the consequences of that definition. Those who report complaints, those who start opinion movements, organizations that make themselves responsible for meeting people's requests, provide examples of these roles (Rubington and Weinberg 1995: 292). If applied to themes concerning deviance and social problems, the constructionist approach can be interpreted in a narrow sense. An interactionist and ethnomethodological point of view may be thus emphasized. According to this approach so defined, there are neither deviant behaviors in themselves, nor objective social problems (namely, those existing apart from the commonsense practices and procedures by which they are constructed). Otherwise, this approach can be interpreted in a broad sense. It is assumed, in this case, that social conditions have a contextual and objective character, the existence of which is

6 Brennan et al. 2000; Burke 1991; Charon 2001: 86–8; Owens and Aronson 2000; Rosenberg and Owens 2000; Sciolla 1994: 501–503; Stryker 1980: 59–62, 81–4, 129–34; 2000: 21–8; Turner 1976; Turner 1998: 374–7.

7 Turner 1956, 1968, 1978, 1998: 377–81.

8 Cerulo 1997; Hunt, Benfors and Snow 1994; Laraña, Johnston and Gusfield 1994; Pichardo 1997: 414–15; Sciolla 1994: 503–505; Stryker, Owens and White 2000.

recognized and highlighted, and that they encourage, along with deviant behavior, the construction of social problems.[9]

As regards *the extension* of the object of study in symbolic interactionism, new fields of research may be mentioned. Micro-sociological objects of inquiry have been the study of emotions (with the contributions of Hochschild, Kemper and others), personal problems (Emerson and Messinger), and political activities performed for the purpose of achieving and maintaining power. Instances are control of the information stream, and symbolic mobilization of political support (Hall). In macro-sociological terms, the interactionist approach intends social structure as a combination of regular thoughts and actions lying in the consciousness of individuals, and in the interactions to which they take part. Within this approach, post-Blumerian sociology has dwelt on the study of social movements and particular elements of the social structure, such as organizations (Maines and others), racial and sexual inequalities, and the mass media. Finally, in cultural terms, interactionist sociology of the post-modern age, characterized by social "worlds" considered segmented and fluid, has emerged (Denzin).[10]

From a methodological point of view, the widening and deepening of research fields was encouraged by a frequent use of "sensitizing" concepts. As previously reported, these concepts should provide, according to Blumer who used this term for the first time, "a general sense of reference and guidance in approaching empirical instances" (Blumer 1969: 148). In contemporary applications, they have proved useful not only to the study of the post-modern age, whose features are changeable and scarcely defined, but also and more in general, to the study of the meanings of experiences and activities from the point of view of actors. The actors through their definitions and interpretations of contingent situations provide these meanings. Actors do not act and interpret separately. Rather, they do so within informal groups or formal organizations that they establish, keep or change, while establishing, keeping or changing their personal and collective identities.

The most commonly used research methods in the interactionist approach – life histories, participating observation, non-structured interviews, text analyses, such as letters, recordings, movies or further "human documents" – are aimed at encouraging in scholars a direct knowledge of the temporal and social world experienced by the actors, in compliance with Blumer's methodological indications. These methods conform to the analytic induction procedure, aimed at inductively achieving generalization, giving deliberately up statistical methods and tools. It involves accurately examining a large number of empiric cases (such as events or life histories), paying selective attention to relevant cases, especially those that are different from other ones for aspects considered significant, and consequently selecting theoretical, instead of random, samples. The interactionist perspective also selects as many representative samples as possible of the population on which the investigation focuses, and makes use of reliable and valid indicators of the conducts object of inquiry. It formulates causal explanations of those behaviors, and strives to achieve reliable results for a generality of cases, of which those examined in the inquiry are considered typical. The selection of random samples, and in general resorting to statistical procedures, serve as integration and complement to the analytic induction procedure.[11]

References

Adler, P.A., Adler, P. and Fontana, A. 1987. "Everyday Life Sociology." *Annual Review of Sociology* 13: 217–35.
Baert, P. 1998. *Social Theory in the Twentieth Century*. Cambridge: Polity Press.
Becker, H.S. 1988. "Herbert Blumer's Conceptual Impact." *Symbolic Interaction* 11(1): 13–21.

---

9 Best 1995: 343–7; Denzin 1977; Fine 1993: 75–6; Hester and Eglin 1992: 269–71; Rock 1991a: 236–40; Sandstrom et al. 2001: 224.

10 Cerulo 1997: 391–3; Charon 2001: 80–90; Ciacci 1996: 27–8; Denzin 1983b: 135–43; 1988; Emerson and Messinger 1977; Fine 1990, 1993: 71–8; Hall 1972; Hochschild 1979; Maines 1977, 2001: 229–33; Mills and Kleinman 1988; Musolf 1992; Plummer 2000: 202–12; Sandstrom et al. 2001: 219–28; Sciolla 1995; Sheff 1988; Shott 1979; Strauss 1991b; Stryker 1980; Turner 1998: 435–7.

11 See Denzin 1970: 194–9; Manning 1991b; Prus 1991b.

Berger, P. 1963. *Invitation to Sociology*. New York: Anchor Books.

Best, J. 1995. Debates about Constructionism, in E. Rubington and M.S. Weinberg (eds), *The Study of Social Problems*. New York: Oxford University Press, 341–51.

Blumer, H. 1969. *Symbolic Interactionism*. Berkeley, CA: University of California Press.

Blumer, H. 1980. "Mead and Blumer: The Convergent Methodological Perspectives of Social Behaviorism and Symbolic Interactionism." *American Sociological Review* 45: 409–19.

Blumer, H. 1991a. Going Astray with a Logical Scheme, in K. Plummer (ed.), *Symbolic Interactionism. Volume 1: Foundations and History*. Aldershot: E. Elgar 313–23.

Blumer, H. 1999. Ein Interview mit Herbert Blumer (1900–1987), in H.J. Helle, *Verstehende Soziologie*. Munich: Oldenbourg, 192–204.

Brennan, K.M., Ritter, C., Salupo, M.M. and Benson, D. 2000. "Measuring Identity Processes: A Reinterpretation and Application of Stryker's and Burke's Identity Theories." Paper submitted to the American Sociological Association Annual Meeting, Washington, D.C., August.

Burke, P.J. 1991. "Identity Processes and Social Stress." *American Sociological Review* 56: 836–49.

Charon, J.M. 2001. *Symbolic Interactionism: An Introduction, an Interpretation, an Integration*. Upper Saddle River, NJ: Prentice Hall.

Cerulo, K.A. 1997. "Identity Construction: New Issues, New Directions." *Annual Review of Sociology* 23: 385–409.

Ciacci, M. 1983. Significato e interazione: dal behaviorismo sociale all'interazionismo simbolico, in M. Ciacci (ed), *Interazionismo simbolico*. Bologna: Il Mulino, 9–52.

Ciacci, M. 1996. Interazionismo simbolico, *in Enciclopedia della Scienze Sociali*, Volume 5. Rome: Istituto della Enciclopedia Italiana, 22–9.

Collins, R. 1992. *Teorie sociologiche*. Bologna: Il Mulino.

Cooley, C. 1909. *Social Organization*. New York: Charles Scribner's Sons.

Cooley, C. 1983 (1922). *Human Nature and The Social Order*. New Brunswick, NJ, and London: Transaction Books.

Denzin, N. 1970. *The Research Act*. Chicago, IL: Aldine.

Denzin, N. 1971. "The Logic of Naturalistic Inquiry." *Social Forces* 50: 166–82.

Denzin, N. 1977. "Notes on the Criminogenic Hypothesis: A Case Study of the American Liquor Industry." *American Sociological Review* 42: 905–20.

Denzin, N. 1978. *Childhood Socialization*. San Francisco, CA: Jossey-Bass.

Denzin, N. 1983a. Interazionismo simbolico e etnometodologia, in M. Ciacci (ed.), *Interazionismo simbolico*. Bologna: Il Mulino, 221–53.

Denzin, N. 1983b. Interpretative Interactionism, in G. Morgan (ed), *Beyond Method*. London: Sage, 129–46.

Denzin, N. 1988. "Blue Velvet: Post Modern Contradictions." *Theory, Culture and Society* 5: 461–73.

Emerson, R.M. and Messinger, S.L. 1977. "The Micro-politics of Trouble." *Social Problems* 25(2): 121–34.

Fallding, H. 1982. "G.H. Mead's Orthodoxy." *Social Forces* 60: 723–37.

Farbeman, H.A. 1991a. The Foundations of Symbolic Interaction: James, Cooley, and Mead, in K. Plummer (ed.), *Symbolic Interactionism. Volume I: Foundations and History*. Aldershot: E. Elgar, 58–72.

Fine, G.A. 1990. Symbolic Interactionism in the Post-Blumerian Age, in G. Ritzer (ed.), *Frontiers of Social Theory: The New Synthesis*. New York: Columbia University Press, 117–57.

Fine, G.A. 1991. "On the Macrofoundations of Microsociology." *The Sociological Quarterly* 32: 161–77.

Fine, G.A. 1993. "The Sad Demise, Mysterious Disappearance, and Glorious Triumph of Symbolic Interactionism." *Annual Review of Sociology* 19: 61–87.

Fine, G.A. and Kleinman, S. 1983. "Network and Meaning: An Interactionist Approach to Structure." *Symbolic Interaction* 6(1): 97–110.

Fine, G.A. and Kleinman, S. 1986. "Interpreting The Sociological Classics: Can There Be A "True" Meaning of Mead?" *Symbolic Interaction* 9(1):129–46.

Fisher, B. and Strauss, A.L. 1978. Interactionism, in T. Bottomore and R. Nisbet (eds), *A History of Sociological Analysis*. New York: Basic Books, 457–98.

Fisher, B. and Strauss, A.L. 1991a. The Chicago Tradition and Social Change: Thomas, Park and Their Successors, in K. Plummer (ed.), *Symbolic Interactionism. Volume 1: Foundations and History*. Aldershot: E. Elgar 73–91.

Fisher, B. and Strauss, A.L. 1991a. George Herbert Mead and the Chicago Tradition of Sociology, in K. Plummer (ed.), *Symbolic Interactionism. Volume 1: Foundations and History*. Aldershot: E. Elgar 177–205.

Gonos, G. 1977. "'Situation' Versus 'Frame': The 'Interactionist' and the 'Structuralist' Analyses of Everyday Life." *American Sociological Review* 42: 854–67.

Gusfield, J.R. 1994. The Reflexivity of Social Movements: Collective Behavior and Mass Society Theory Revisited, in E. Laraña, H. Johnston and, J.R. Gusfield (eds), *New Social Movements*. Philadelphia, PA: Temple University Press, 58–78.

Hall, P.M. 1972. "A Symbolic Interactionist Analysis of Politics." *Sociological Inquiry* 42 (3–4): 35–75.

Hall, P.M. 1987. "Interactionism and the Study of Social Organization." *Sociological Quarterly* 28: 1–22.

Helle, H.J. 1999. *Verstehende Soziologie*. Monaco: Oldenbourg.

Heritage, J.C. 1987. Ethnomethodology, in A. Giddens and J. Turner (eds), *Social Theory Today*. Oxford: Polity Press, 224–72.

Hester, S. and Eglin, P. 1992. *A Sociology of Crime*. London: Routledge.

Hochschild, A. 1979. "Emotion Work, Feeling Rules, and Social Structure." *American Journal of Sociology* 85(3): 551–75.

Hunt, S.A., Benford, R.D. and Snow, D.A. 1994. Identity Fields: Framing Processes and the Social Construction of Movement Identities, in E. Laraña, H. Johnston and, J.R. Gusfield (eds), *New Social Movements*. Philadelphia, PA: Temple University Press, 185–208.

Izzo, A. 1994. *Storia del pensiero sociologico*. Bologna: Il Mulino.

Janowitz, M. 1966. Introduction, in *W.I. Thomas on Social Organizations and Social Personality*, ed. M. Janowitz. Chicago, IL: The University of Chicago Press.

Johnson, G.D. and Shifflet, P.A. 1981. "George Herbert Who? A Critique of the Objectivist Reading of Mead." *Symbolic Interaction* 4(2): 143–55.

Jonas, F. 1991. *Histoire de la sociologie*. Paris: Larousse.

Joas, H. 1987. Symbolic Interactionism, in A. Giddens and J. Turner (eds), *Social Theory Today*. Oxford: Polity Press, 82–115.

Joas, H. 1997. *G.H. Mead: A Contemporary Re-examination of His Thought*. Cambridge, MA: The MIT Press.

Joas, H. 2001. The Emergence of the New: Mead's Theory and Its Contemporary Potential, in G. Ritzer and B. Smart (eds), *Handbook of Social Theory*. London: Sage, 89–99.

Kuhn, M. and McPartland, T.S. 1954. "An Empirical Investigation of Self-Attitudes." *American Sociological Review* 19: 68–76.

Laraña, E., Johnston, H. and Gusfield, J.R. 1994. Identities, Grievances, and New Social Movements, in E. Laraña, H. Johnston and J.R. Gusfield (eds), *New Social Movements*. Philadelphia, PA: Temple University Press, 3–35.

Lewis, J.D. 1976. "The Classic American Pragmatists as Forerunners to Symbolic Interactionism." *The Sociological Quarterly* 17: 347–59.

McKinney, J.C. 1955. "The Contribution of George H. Mead to the Sociology of Knowledge." *Social Forces* 34: 144–9.

McPhail, C. and Rexroat, C. 1979. "Mead vs. Blumer: The Divergent Methodological Perspectives of Social Behaviorism and Symbolic Interactionism." *American Sociological Review* 44: 449–67.

McPhail, C. and Rexroat, C. 1980. "Ex Cathedra Blumer or Ex Libris Mead?." *American Sociological Review* 45: 420–30.

Maines, D.R. 1977. "Social Organization and Social Structure in Symbolic Interactionist Thought." *Annual Review of Sociology* 3: 235–59.

Maines, D.R. 2001. *The Faultline of Consciousness*. New York: Aldine De Gruyter.

Maines, D., Sugrue, N. and Katovich, M. 1983. "The Sociological Import of G.H. Mead's Theory of the Past." *American Sociological Review* 48: 161–73.

Manning, P.K. 1991b. Analytic Induction, in K. Plummer (ed.), *Symbolic Interactionism*, Volume 2. Aldershot: E. Elgar 401–30.

Martindale, D. 1972. *Tipologia e storia del pensiero sociologico*. Bologna: Il Mulino.

Mead, G.H., 1967 (1934). *Mind, Self, & Society*. Chicago, IL: The University of Chicago Press.

Mead, G.H. 1977. *On Social Psychology*, ed. A. Strauss. Chicago, IL: The University of Chicago Press.

Mead, G.H. 1983 (1932). Foreword: Cooley's Contribution to American Social Thought (1930), in C.H. Cooley, *Human Nature and the Social Order*. New York: Schocken Books, xxi–xxxviii.

Mead, G.H. 1999. Meads Verstaendnis von I und Me, in Helle, H.J. (ed), *Verstehende Soziologie*. Munich: Oldenbourg, 183–90.

Meltzer, B.N., Petras, J.W. and Reynolds, L.T. 1980. *L'interazionismo simbolico*. Milan: Franco Angeli.

Miller, D.L. 1991a. George Herbert Mead: Symbolic Interaction and Social Change, in K. Plummer (ed.), *Symbolic Interactionism. Volume 1: Foundations and History*. Aldershot: E. Elgar 119–29.

Mills, T. and Kleinman, S. 1988. "Emotion, Reflexivity, and Action: An Interactionist Analysis." *Social Forces* 66(4): 1009–1027.

Morris, C.W. (1934) 1967. Introduction, in G.H. Mead, *Mind, Self, & Society*. Chicago, IL: The University of Chicago, IL: ix–xxxviii.

Musolf, G.R. 1992. "Structure, Institutions, Power, and Ideology: New Directions within Symbolic Interactionism." *The Sociological Quarterly* 33: 171–89.

Mullins, N.C. and Mullins, C.J. 1991a. Symbolic Interactionism: The Loyal Opposition, in K. Plummer (ed.), *Symbolic Interactionism. Volume 1: Foundations and History*. Aldershot: E. Elgar 389–418.

Natanson, M. 1973. *The Social Dynamics of George H. Mead*. The Hague: Martinus Nijhoff.

Owens, T.J. and Aronson, P.J. 2000. Self-Concept as a Force in Social Movement Involvement, in S. Stryker, T.J. Owens and R.H. White (eds), *Self, Identity, and Social Movements*. Minneapolis, MN: University of Minnesota Press, 191–214.

Pichardo, N.A. 1997. "New Social Movements: A Critical Review." *Annual Review of Sociology* 23: 411–30.

Plummer, K. 1991a. Introduction: The Foundations of Interactionist Sociologies, in K. Plummer (ed.), *Symbolic Interactionism. Volume 1: Foundations and History*. Aldershot: E. Elgar, x–xx.

Plummer, K. 1991b. Introduction: The Future of Interactionist Sociologies, in K. Plummer (ed.), *Symbolic Interactionism*, Volume 2. Aldershot: E. Elgar, ix–xix.

Plummer, K. 2000. Symbolic Interactionism in the Twentieth Century, in B.S. Turner (ed.), *The Blackwell Companion to Social Theory*. Oxford: Blackwell, 193–222.

Prus, R. 1991b. Generic Social Processes: Maximizing Conceptual Development in Ethnographic Research, in K. Plummer (ed.), *Symbolic Interactionism*, Volume 2. Aldershot: E. Elgar, 450–93.

Rock, P.S. 1991a. *Symbolic Interaction and Labelling Theory*, in K. Plummer (ed.), *Symbolic Interactionism. Volume 1: Foundations and History*. Aldershot: E. Elgar 227–45.

Rochberg-Halton, E. 1987. "Situation, Structure and the Context of Meaning." *Sociological Quarterly* 23: 455–76.

Rosenberg, M. and Owens, T.J. 2000. "Low Self-Esteem People: A Collective Portrait." Paper submitted to the American Sociological Association Annual Meeting, Washington, D.C., August.

Rubington, E. and Weinberg, M.S. 1995. Social Constructionism, in E. Rubington and M.S. Weinberg (eds), *The Study of Social Problems*. New York and Oxford: Oxford University Press, 287–93.

Sandstrom, K.L., Martin, D.D. and Fine, G.A. 2001. Symbolic Interactionism at the End of the Century, in G. Ritzer and B. Smart (eds), *Handbook of Social Theory*. London: Sage, 217–31.

Sciolla, L. 1994. Identità personale e collettiva, in *Enciclopedia delle Scienze Sociali*, Volume 4. Rome: Istituto della Enciclopedia Italiana, 496–506.

Sciolla, L. 1995. "La dimensione dimenticata dell'identità." *Rassegna Italiana di Sociologia* 36(1): 41–52.

Sheff, T.J. 1988. "Shame and Conformity: The Deference–Emotion System." *American Sociological Review* 53 (3): 395–406.

Shibutani, T. 1955. "Reference Groups as Perspectives." *American Journal of Sociology* 60: 562–9.

Shibutani, T. 1988. "Herbert Blumer's Contributions to Twentieth-Century Sociology." *Symbolic Interaction* 11(1): 23–31.

Shott, S. 1979. "Emotion and Social Life: A Symbolic Interactionist Analysis." *American Journal of Sociology* 84(6): 1317–1334.

Strauss, A. 1977. Introduction, in *G.H. Mead on Social Psychology*, ed. A. Strauss. Chicago, IL: The University of Chicago Press, VII-XXXI.

Strauss, A. 1991b. Interorganizational Negotiation, in K. Plummer (ed.), *Symbolic Interactionism*, Volume 2. Aldershot: E. Elgar 134–51.

Stryker, S. 1980. *Symbolic Interactionism: A Social Structural Version*. Menlo Park, CA: The Benjamin/ Cummings Publishing Company.

Stryker, S. 1991a. The Vitalization of Symbolic Interactionism, in K. Plummer (ed.), *Symbolic Interactionism. Volume 1: Foundations and History*. Aldershot: E. Elgar 419–35.

Stryker, S. 2000. Identity Competition: Key to Differential Social Movement Participation?, in S. Stryker, T.J. Owens and R.H. White (eds), *Self, Identity, and Social Movements*. Minneapolis, MN: University of Minnesota Press, 21–40.

Thoits, P.A. 1995. "Social Psychology: The Interplay between Sociology and Psychology." *Social Forces* 73(4): 1231–43.

Thomas, W.I. 1966. *On Social Organizations and Social Personality*, ed. M. Janowitz. Chicago, IL: The University of Chicago Press.

Timasheff, N.S. and Theodorson, G.A. 1976. *Sociological Theory: Its Nature and Growth*. New York: Random House.

Turner, J.H. 1998. *The Structure of Sociological Theory*. Homewood, IL: The Dorsey Press.

Turner, R.H. 1956. "Role-Taking, Role Standpoint, and Reference Group Behavior." *American Journal of Sociology* 61: 316–28.

Turner, R.H. 1968. *Role: Sociological Aspects*, in D.L. Sills (ed.), *International Encyclopedia of the Social Sciences*, Volume 13. New York: Macmillan & Free Press, 552–7.

Turner, R.H. 1976. "The Real Self: From Institution to Impulse." *American Journal of Sociology* 81: 989–1016.

Turner, R.H. 1978. "The Role and the Person." *American Journal of Sociology* 84: 1–23.

Visalberghi, A. 1963. Introduzione, in C.H. Cooley, *L'organizzazione sociale*. Milan: Comunità, xv–xxviii.

Warshay, L.H. and Warshay, D.W. 1991a. The Individualizing and Subjectivizing of George Herbert Mead: A Sociology of Knowledge Interpretation, in K. Plummer (ed.), *Symbolic Interactionism. Volume 1: Foundations and History*. Aldershot: E. Elgar 276–87.

Wood, M. and Wardell, M.L. 1983. "G.H. Mead's Social Behaviorism vs. the Astructural Bias of Symbolic Interactionism." *Symbolic Interaction* 6(1): 85–96.

Index of Names

General Index